Holidays, Festivals, and Celebrations

of the World Dictionary

Holidays, Festivals, and Celebrations of the World Dictionary

Detailing More Than 1,400 Observances from All 50 States and More Than 100 Nations

A Compendious Reference Guide to Popular, Ethnic, Religious, National, and Ancient Holidays, Festivals, Celebrations, Commemorations, Holy Days, Feasts, and Fasts, Supplemented by a Special Section on Calendar Systems, Tables of State and National Public Holidays, Special Indexes of Chronological, Cultural and Ethnic, Geographic, Historical, Religious, and Sports Holidays, and a General and Key-Word Index

Compiled by
Sue Ellen Thompson
and
Barbara W. Carlson

Omnigraphics, Inc.

Penobscot Building
Detroit, MI 48226

Editorial Staff

Sue Ellen Thompson and Barbara W. Carlson, *Editors*
Frank R. Abate, *Editorial Director*
Jacquelyn S. Goodwin, *Associate Editor*
Daniel Partner, *Contributing Editor*

Marion Darling, Kathleen Mallory, Donna Rhein, *Researchers*
Jennifer Feola, Terri Finkeldey, *Editorial Assistants*

Data Processing and Typesetting: Weimer Graphics, Inc., Indianapolis, Ind.

Omnigraphics, Inc.

Eric Berger, *Vice President, Production*
Laurie Lanzen Harris, *Editorial Director*
Peter E. Ruffner, *Vice President, Administration*
James A. Sellgren, *Vice President, Operations & Finance*

Frederick G. Ruffner, Jr., *Publisher*

Copyright © 1994 Omnigraphics, Inc.

Library of Congress Cataloging-in-Publication Data

Thompson, Sue Ellen.
   Holidays, festivals, and celebrations of the world dictionary : detailing more than 1,400 observances from all 50 states and more than 100 nations. A compendium reference guide to popular, ethnic, religious, national, and ancient holidays, festivals, celebrations, commemorations, holy days, feasts, and fasts, supplemented by a special section on calendar systems, tables of state and national public holidays, special indexes of chronological, cultural and ethnic geographic, historical, religious, and sports holidays, and general and key-word index / compiled by Sue Ellen Thompson and Barbara W. Carlson.

      p.   cm.
   Includes index.
   ISBN 1-55888-768-7 (lib. bdg. : alk. paper)
      1. Holidays—Dictionaries.   2. Festivals—
Dictionaries.   I. Carlson, Barbara W.   II. Title.
GT3925.T46   1993   93-6220
394.2′6—dc20   CIP

The information in this publication was compiled from sources considered reliable. While every possible effort has been made to ensure reliability, the publisher will not assume liability for damages caused by inaccuracies in the data, and makes no warranty, express or implied, on the accuracy of the information contained herein.

This book is printed on acid-free paper meeting the ANSI Z38.48 Standard. The infinity symbol that appears above indicates that the paper in this book meets that standard.

Printed in the United States of America

Contents

Holidays, Festivals, and Celebrations of the World Dictionary 1-379

Foreword

All countries have their festivals and many also have secular holidays to mark the achievements of famous individuals or celebrate historical events.

From primitive times onwards, festivals have celebrated the religious mysteries of existence—the enigma of birth, death, and rebirth in the environment and the pattern of human experience. Such festivals filled a deep-seated need in the human psyche, evoking profound emotions associated with the changing pattern of the year—the promise of spring, the joys of summer, the harvest, the decline of the year through fall to the rigors of winter, and the promise of a new spring. The divine origin of this mystery was to be acknowledged, honored, and propitiated, so that human prosperity and fertility flourished in the struggle for existence through the progress of the seasons and the passing of time.

Inevitably such festivals required a measurement of time, so that seasonal festivals could be celebrated at regular dates in the cycle of the year. But for thousands of years, primitive and pantheistic concepts of the universe inhibited the exact timing of festivals. In the natural division of time, the solar day is the daily revolution of the earth and alternation of light and darkness; the solar year is the circle of seasons in the earth's revolution around the sun. Months are divisions resulting from the lunar cycle of phases of the moon. But division of time into hours, days, or a regular month is more arbitrary, and it was not until early Roman times that the calendar as such was formalized for civil convenience; the word "calendar" itself derives from the Latin *Kalendae*. By the time of Julius Caesar, the Roman civil year had become three months out of phase with the true astronomical year. The Julian calendar reform in the first century B.C., which became the standard in Western countries, corrected the discrepancy and regularized a calendar based on the solar cycle. But the Julian calendar, too, had mathematical discrepancies, since a calendar year of 365.25 days with an extra leap year day every three years became progressively out of step with the real lunar year of 365.242199 days.

In a papal bull of February 24, 1582, Pope Gregory inaugurated the Gregorian calendar, which required the deletion of ten days from the calendar at that time, and the occasional adjustment whereby three out of every four round figure "century" years are not leap years. This rearrangement of the calendar was bewildering to many people, who clamored "Give us back our ten days!" But the Gregorian calendar was eventually adopted, at least for civil purposes, throughout the West, and remains a worldwide standard to this day. Meanwhile, of course, other ancient calendars such as the Jewish and Islamic have continued to exist side by side with the Gregorian calendar. The *Holidays, Festivals, and Celebrations of the World Dictionary* includes a discussion of the history of ancient and modern calendars, and clarifies such complexities.

Different religions have continued to find common ground in the concept of special days to mark the supreme mysteries of life. Three of the great world religions—Judaism, Christianity, and Islam—have all recognized a holy rest day from the week of toil. The Sabbath of Judaism was moved by Christians from Saturday to Sunday, and for Muslims the rest day became Friday, the birth day of the prophet Muhammad.

Many different religions meet in their interpretations of festival times of the year. With the rise of

Christianity in Europe, some of the old pagan festivals were retained by the new Church, although given different religious interpretations. Yet behind the feasting and merrymaking of Christmas, one might still hear dim echoes of the Roman Saturnalia, the Druidic rites with mistletoe, and the strange gods of Saxon mythology.

In addition to religious festivals, the ancient Romans made a distinction between religious and secular events, and the institution of secular holidays has since proliferated in the countries of the world. Even so, holidays still have their roots in the concept of some special significance of certain days, necessitating a break in the daily toil of normal life. The very word "holiday" is derived from "holy day."

Secular holidays excite special emotions. We love to celebrate the birthdays of family members and friends with greetings and presents. So, too, we feel a special sense of belonging to a social group or nation in the observance of our secular holidays, which unite us in common ties of special interest, ethnicity, or national pride.

The range of religious festivals and secular holidays is now a vast one in the various countries of the world. In modern times, the proliferation of national and local holiday events has also resulted in scores of special group days, and even whimsical and bizarre observances, ranging from Buzzard Day in Hinckley, Ohio, to the Rat's Wedding Day in China.

In the past, the great festivals and holidays were kept alive by folk memory, or by the many almanacs sold by peddlers, giving the dates of fairs and other events and anniversaries, together with lunar information, tides, eclipses, and even prophecies, spiced with quaint aphorisms and proverbs.

In nineteenth-century Britain, antiquarians published various volumes of discursive lore, listing the significance of days of the calendar, festivals, and holidays, and their history. The best of these was the delightful work, *The Book of Days: A Miscellany of Popular Antiquities in Connection with the Calendar: Including Anecdote, Biography & History, Curiosities of Literature, and Oddities of Human Life and Character*, by Robert Chambers (1862-64), reissued by Omnigraphics in 1990.

Such books are fascinating to browse through for their out-of-the-way information and bygone lore of the calendar, but although many of the festivals and holidays discussed are still celebrated, there have been scores of newer holidays in the U.S. and elsewhere in the present century.

Until the ***Holidays Dictionary*** there has never been a truly comprehensive annotated dictionary of national and international festivals and holidays. The present work is the most complete of its kind, including over 1,400 descriptive entries covering religious, cultural, ethnic, historical, popular, and sports celebrations from all over the world. In addition to a General Index of people, places, institutions, and other keywords, there are also three other sets of indexes to facilitate easy reference: Chronological; Religious; and Special Subject. The latter includes Ancient/Pagan, Calendar, Folkloric, Historic, Promotional, and Sporting indexes. The style of the entries is such that they will be equally accessible for scholars, students, and the general public.

This is a key reference work for schools and public libraries, but it is also a multi-purpose dictionary. Ministers of different denominations will find it valuable for its broad coverage of the festivals not only of Christianity but also of other world religions. Business people planning promotional journeys will find its information of special value when visiting foreign countries and different states in the U.S. School children can learn about the significance of individual holidays and the observances of different religious and ethnic groups, as well as the popular, fun festivals of various states.

All kinds of travelers will value the listing of public holidays in the U.S. and other countries, and it will also add special interest to the planning of personal vacations at home and abroad. In addition to the often spectacular religious festivals of the world, there are now scores of light-hearted and tongue-in-cheek popular holiday events, such as the Great American Duck Race in Deming, New Mexico, or the Horn Dance at Abbots Bromley, England. From state to state, and country to country, there are humorous, quaint, and diverting events which have become great tourist attractions. Journalists will find this an indispensable desk book for news stories on the significance of days.

This is also a book that can enhance understanding of ethnic groups and different nationalities, through knowledge of the manifold celebrations of life, and the emotions of reverence, joy, and laughter which we share in our individual festivals and holidays.

Leslie Shepard

County Dublin, Ireland
December 1993

Introduction and How to Use This Book

Holidays, Festivals, and Celebrations of the World Dictionary (*HFCWD*) contains up-to-date information about more than 1,400 holidays, festivals, celebrations, commemorations, holy days, feasts and fasts, and other observances from all parts of the world. Entries include events for which people come together for a day or periods of up to a few days or (rarely) weeks for special activities or rituals. A further criterion was that the event had a story to tell, by which we mean that it is significant, unusual, or somehow remarkable. Holidays and festivals for more than 100 countries, as well as events specifically observed in every state of the United States, are included.

The entries cover holidays and festivals that are popular, secular, religious, or a combination thereof. The great bulk of the entries are events still celebrated or observed, but a few ancient and discontinued events are included because allusions to them still appear in literature or art.

Birth or death anniversaries of famous individuals generally are not included, nor simple anniversaries of historical events. But those few such events that are regularly observed with significant celebrations or special activities, or that have particular cultural significance, such as **Martin Luther King's Birthday** or **Anzac Day**, are included.

Most entries in *HFCWD* have national or wide regional significance, but some local events that are offbeat, colorful, distinctive, or bizarre, such as the **Gilroy Garlic Festival**, have also been included. Entries for the well-known days of religious significance, such as **Christmas, Rosh ha-Shanah,** and **Ramadan**, contain information seldom found in current reference sources.

Main Entries and Alternate Forms

Main entries appear in **boldface**. Well-known alternate forms of the main entry appear in parentheses immediately after the main entry, e.g., **Hanukkah (Chanukah)**. Such alternate forms also appear as cross-references in their proper alphabetical position. Less common alternate forms appear in **boldface** within the text of the entry, and cross references to other entries appear in CAPITAL letters.

Alphabetic Order of Main Entries

Since most people looking for information on a given subject will not know its official title, main entries have been written with the key words first. Thus, words such as *birthday of, death of, feast, festa, festival, fête, fiesta, national,* and *international* have usually been transposed to the end of the main entry, e.g.: **Bab, Birth of the; Bastille, Festival de la; Old-Time Fiddlers' Contest, National,** etc.

Spelling and Forms Used for Main Entries

HFCWD deals with events that relate to many cultures, the original names of which involve a number of alphabets and non-Roman writing systems. As much as possible, spellings and forms for main entries were standardized for ease of access. The following were used as guides on spelling standardization:

for Islamic events: *Concise Encyclopedia of Islam*, Cyril Glassé, Harper and Row, 1989.

for Jewish events: *Encyclopedia of Judaism*, Geoffrey Wigoder, Macmillan, 1989.

For Asian holidays and events no single standard was used. The form used is that appearing most often in sources consulted.

Dates

On the line below the main entry, the date of celebration or observance is given in italics. For those entries whose date is based on a lunar calendar, we have first shown the approximate date in the Gregorian calendar followed by the exact lunar date. The exception is for events based on the strictly lunar Islamic calendar, where only the Islamic month and day are given (see the section on **Calendars** for a detailed explanation of the Islamic calendar).

Religious Holidays

For the most part, entries for religious holidays are spelled and described in terms of the major religion that observes them. If only some followers of a major religion observe a holiday, or if different branches or sects commemorate something different (or nothing at all) on a given holiday, the entry specifies the practice of the particular group. **St. John the Baptist's Day**, for instance, is recognized by most Christians, and so is described (and indexed) as "Christian," despite the fact that some Christians do not venerate saints. The holy day of **Ashura** is observed quite differently by Sunni and Shi'ite Muslims, and so both practices are described.

Christian Denominations

For Christianity, references to the West or Western church generally include the Roman Catholic Church, the churches of the Anglican Communion, and major Protestant denominations. References to the East or Eastern church include Orthodox Christians, such as Greek and Russian Orthodox, and all those Christians acknowledging the primacy of the Patriarch of Constantinople.

Special Indexes

Several different Special Indexes provide reference to entries (as appropriate) for each of the following categories.

Chronological Indexes

> Fixed Days and Events—Indexes events that are celebrated on a specific date.
> Movable Days—Indexes events whose date of celebration is not fixed, particularly those that are observed according to non-Gregorian calendars and those that depend on the date of Easter.

Major Religious Groups Index

> Indexes events with a significant religious element.

Special Subject Indexes

> Ancient/Pagan—Indexes holidays rooted in ancient times.
> Calendar—Indexes festivals that deal specifically with the calendar.
> Folkloric—Indexes events rooted in folklore and tradition.

Historic—Indexes festivals commemorating specific events from history.

Promotional—Indexes festivals that promote something, be it a location or activity.

Sporting—Indexes festivals that are based on or revolve around sporting events.

General and Key-Word Index

The General and Key-Word Index lists all people, places, institutions, and other items of significance appearing within the text of the entries, with reference to the entry or entries in which they appear. For example, foods or activities closely associated with an event are indexed, either those that are the subject of or very significant in a festival (but perhaps not part of its name), or those specific to a given celebration or observance.

Acknowledgements

Holidays, Festivals, and Celebrations of the World Dictionary would not have been possible without the assistance, inspiration, and diligence of many people. Our thanks go to Donna Rhein, Kathleen Mallory, and Marian J. Darling for the exhaustive research they did to unearth new information for even the most written-about holidays, and to reveal additional details about those less well-known.

We also wish to recognize the assistance provided by a number of clergymen, especially Rabbi Carl Astor of Congregation Beth-El; the Rev. Ralph W. Merrill, St. James Episcopal Church, and the Rev. Constantine J. Simones, St. Sophia Hellenic Orthodox Church, all in New London, Conn.; and the Rev. Paul E. Lutz, St. Paul Lutheran Church, Old Saybrook, Conn. Their prompt responses to our many questions and their willingness to look up arcane information were indispensable.

Chuck Lacy of Weimer Graphics, Inc. handled data processing and typesetting with superb skill. The demands imposed by editorial and publishing specifications never compromised the quality and efficiency of his work.

Even with all the essential contributions of the individuals mentioned above and others, we must add that the responsibility for any errors or omissions in *HFCWD* rests solely with the editors.

Legal Holidays by State

The "standard six" holidays observed throughout the United States are:

New Year's Day	January 1
Memorial Day	last Monday in May (not celebrated in Alabama)
Independence Day	July 4
Labor Day	first Monday in September
Thanksgiving	fourth Thursday in November
Christmas	December 25

In addition, state offices throughout the United States are usually closed on Election Day, the first Tuesday after the first Monday in November. Veterans' Day, November 11, is observed in some manner by all the states.

The following list is of other legal holidays observed by the various states, Washington, D.C., and Puerto Rico. Under each the arrangement is by Gregorian calendar order.

Alabama

Martin Luther King, Jr. and Robert E. Lee birthdays	January, third Monday
Washington's Birthday	February, third Monday
Confederate Memorial Day	April, fourth Monday
Jefferson Davis' Birthday	June, first Monday
Columbus Day	October, second Monday
Fraternal Day	October, second Monday

Alaska

Martin Luther King, Jr. Day	January 19
Presidents' Day	February, third Monday
Seward's Day	March, last Monday
Alaska Day	October 18

Arizona

Martin Luther King, Jr. Day/Civil Rights Day	January, third Monday
Lincoln's Birthday	February, second Monday
Washington's Birthday	February, third Monday
Mother's Day	May, second Sunday
Father's Day	June, third Sunday
American Family Day	August, first Sunday
Constitution Day	September 17
Columbus Day	October, second Monday

Arkansas

Martin Luther King, Jr. and Robert E. Lee birthdays	January, third Monday

Washington's Birthday	February, third Monday
Christmas Eve	December 24

California

Martin Luther King, Jr. Day	January, third Monday
Lincoln's Birthday	February 12
Washington's Birthday	February, third Monday
Good Friday	Friday before Easter
Admission Day	September 9
Columbus Day	October, second Monday

Colorado

Martin Luther King, Jr.'s Birthday	January, third Monday
Washington-Lincoln Day	February, third Monday
Columbus Day	October, second Monday

Connecticut

Martin Luther King, Jr. Day	January, first Monday on or after January 15
Lincoln's Birthday	February 12
Washington's Birthday	February, third Monday
Columbus Day	October, second Monday

Delaware

Martin Luther King, Jr. Day	January, third Monday
Presidents' Day	February, third Monday
Columbus Day	October, second Monday

District of Columbia

Martin Luther King, Jr.'s Birthday	January, third Monday
Washington's Birthday	February, third Monday
Columbus Day	October, second Monday

Florida

Martin Luther King, Jr.'s Birthday	January 15
Robert E. Lee's Birthday	January 19
Lincoln's Birthday	February 12
Susan B. Anthony's Birthday	February 15
Washington's Birthday	February, third Monday
Good Friday	Friday before Easter
Pascua Florida Day	April 2
Confederate Memorial Day	April 26
Jefferson Davis' Birthday	June 3
Flag Day	June 14
Columbus Day and Farmers' Day	October, second Monday

Georgia

Robert E. Lee's Birthday	January 19
Martin Luther King, Jr.'s Birthday	January, third Monday

Washington's Birthday	February, third Monday
Confederate Memorial Day	April 26
Jefferson Davis' Birthday	June 3
Columbus Day	October, second Monday

Hawaii
Martin Luther King, Jr.'s Birthday	January, third Monday
Presidents' Day	February, third Monday
Jonah Kuhio Kalanianaole Day	March 26
Good Friday	Friday before Easter
King Kamehameha I Day	June 11
Admission Day	August, third Friday

Idaho
Martin Luther King, Jr.–Idaho Human Rights Day	January, third Monday
Washington's Birthday	February, third Monday
Columbus Day	October, second Monday

Illinois
Martin Luther King, Jr's Birthday	January, third Monday
Lincoln's Birthday	February 12
Washington's Birthday	February, third Monday
Casimir Pulaski's Birthday	March, first Monday
Good Friday	Friday before Easter
Columbus Day	October, second Monday

Indiana
Martin Luther King, Jr.'s Birthday	January, third Monday
Lincoln's Birthday	February 12
Washington's Birthday	February, third Monday
Good Friday	Friday before Easter
Columbus Day	October, second Monday

Iowa
Martin Luther King, Jr.'s Birthday	January, third Monday
Washington's Birthday	February, third Monday

Kansas
Martin Luther King Day	date set by governor
Lincoln's Birthday	February 12
Washington's Birthday	February, third Monday
Columbus Day	October, second Monday

Kentucky
Robert E. Lee's Birthday	January 19
Franklin D. Roosevelt Day	January 30
Martin Luther King, Jr. Day	January, third Monday
Lincoln's Birthday	February 12

Washington's Birthday	February, third Monday
Confederate Memorial Day & Jefferson Davis Day	June 3
Columbus Day	October, second Monday

Louisiana

Battle of New Orleans	January 8
Robert E. Lee's Birthday	January 19
Martin Luther King, Jr.'s Birthday	January, third Monday
Washington's Birthday	February, third Monday
Good Friday	Friday before Easter
Confederate Memorial Day	June 3
Huey P. Long Day	August 30
Columbus Day	October, second Monday
All Saints' Day	November 1

Maine

Martin Luther King, Jr. Day	January, third Monday
Patriot's Day	February, third Monday
Washington's Birthday	February, third Monday
Columbus Day	October, second Monday

Maryland

Martin Luther King, Jr.'s Birthday	January 15
Lincoln's Birthday	February 12
Washington's Birthday	February, third Monday
Maryland Day	March 25
Good Friday	Friday before Easter
Defenders' Day	September 12
Columbus Day	October 12

Massachusetts

Martin Luther King, Jr. Day	January, third Monday
Washington's Birthday	February, third Monday
Patriot's Day	April, third Monday
Columbus Day	October, second Monday

Michigan

Martin Luther King, Jr. Day	January, third Monday
Lincoln's Birthday	February 12
Washington's Birthday	February, third Monday
Columbus Day	October, second Monday

Minnesota

Martin Luther King, Jr.'s Birthday	January, third Monday
Washington-Lincoln Day	February, third Monday
Columbus Day	October, second Monday

Mississippi

Robert E. Lee & Martin Luther King, Jr. birthdays	January, third Monday
Washington's Birthday	February, third Monday
Confederate Memorial Day	April, last Monday
National Memorial Day and Jefferson Davis' Birthday	May, last Monday

Missouri

Martin Luther King, Jr. Day	January, third Monday
Lincoln's Birthday	February 12
Washington's Birthday	February, third Monday
Columbus Day	October, second Monday

Montana

Martin Luther King, Jr. Day	January, third Monday
Washington's and Lincoln's birthdays	February, third Monday
Columbus Day	October, second Monday

Nebraska

Martin Luther King, Jr. Day	January, third Monday
Presidents' Day	February, third Monday
Arbor Day	April, last Friday
Columbus Day	October, second Monday

Nevada

Martin Luther King, Jr.'s Birthday	January, third Monday
Washington's Birthday	February, third Monday
Columbus Day	October 12
Nevada Day	October 31
Family Day	November, Friday after fourth Thursday

New Hampshire

Civil Rights Day	January, third Monday
Washington's Birthday	February, third Monday
Columbus Day	October, second Monday

New Jersey

Martin Luther King's Birthday	January, third Monday
Lincoln's Birthday	February 12
Washington's Birthday	February, third Monday
Good Friday	Friday before Easter
Columbus Day	October, second Monday

New Mexico

Martin Luther King, Jr.'s Birthday	January, third Monday
Washington-Lincoln Day	January, third Monday
Presidents' Day	February, third Monday
Columbus Day	October, second Monday

New York
Martin Luther King, Jr. Day	January, third Monday
Lincoln's Birthday	February 12
Washington's Birthday	February, third Monday
Flag Day	June, second Sunday
Columbus Day	October, second Monday

North Carolina
Robert E. Lee's Birthday	January 19
Martin Luther King, Jr.'s Birthday	January, third Monday
Washington's Birthday	February, third Monday
Greek Independence Day	March 25
Good Friday	Friday before Easter
Halifax Resolves, Anniversary of signing of	April 12
Confederate Memorial Day	May 10
Mecklenburg Declaration of Independence, Anniversary of	May 20
Columbus Day	October, second Monday
Yom Kippur	September/October

North Dakota
Martin Luther King, Jr.'s Birthday	January, third Monday
Washington's Birthday	February, third Monday
Good Friday	Friday before Easter

Ohio
Martin Luther King, Jr. Day	January, third Monday
Washington-Lincoln Day	February, third Monday
Columbus Day	October, second Monday

Oklahoma
Martin Luther King, Jr.'s Birthday	January, third Monday
Washington's Birthday	February, third Monday
Jefferson Day	April 13
Oklahoma Day	April 22
Mothers' Day	May, second Sunday
Senior Citizens' Day	June 9
Cherokee Strip Day	September 16
Indian Day	September, first Saturday after full moon
Oklahoma Historical Day	October 10
Will Rogers' Day	November 4
Youth Day	Spring, first day

Oregon
Martin Luther King, Jr.'s Birthday	January, third Monday
Presidents' Day	February, third Monday

Pennsylvania
Martin Luther King, Jr. Day   January, third Monday
Presidents' Day   February, third Monday
Good Friday   Friday before Easter
Flag Day   June 14
Columbus Day   October, second Monday

Puerto Rico
Eugenio Maria de Hostos' Birthday   January 11
Good Friday   Friday before Easter
Jose de Diego Day   April 16
Antonio R. Barcelo Day   April, second Sunday
Luis Munoz Rivera Day   July 17
Constitution, Day of the   July 25
Jose Celso Barbosa's Birthday   July 27
Santiago Iglesias Pantin Day   September, first Monday
Columbus Day and Discovery Day   October 12

Rhode Island
Martin Luther King, Jr.'s Birthday   January, third Monday
Washington's Birthday   February, third Monday
Rhode Island Independence Day   May 4
Victory Day   August, second Monday
Columbus Day   October, second Monday

South Carolina
Martin Luther King, Jr.'s Birthday   January 15
Robert E. Lee's Birthday   January 19
Washington's Birthday   February, third Monday
Confederate Memorial Day   May 10
Jefferson Davis' Birthday   June 3

South Dakota
Martin Luther King, Jr.'s Birthday   January, third Monday
Native Americans' Day   October, second Monday

Tennessee
Martin Luther King, Jr. Day   January, third Monday
Washington's Birthday   February, third Monday
Good Friday   Friday before Easter
Columbus Day   October, second Monday

Texas
Confederate Heroes Day   January 19
Martin Luther King, Jr. Day   January, third Monday
Washington's Birthday   February, third Monday
Texas Independence Day   March 2
San Jacinto Day   April 21
Emancipation Day   June 19

Lyndon Baines Johnson's Birthday	August 27

Utah

Martin Luther King, Jr.'s Birthday and Human Rights Day	January, third Monday
Presidents' Day	February, third Monday
Pioneer Day	July 24
Columbus Day	October, second Monday

Vermont

Martin Luther King, Jr.'s Birthday	January, third Monday
Lincoln's Birthday	February 12
Washington's Birthday	February, third Monday
Town Meeting Day	March, first Tuesday
Bennington Battle Day	August 16
Columbus Day	October, second Monday

Virginia

Lee-Jackson-King Day	January, third Monday
Washington's Birthday	February, third Monday
Columbus Day and Yorktown Day	October, second Monday

Washington

Martin Luther King, Jr.'s Birthday	January, third Monday
Presidents' Day	February, third Monday
Columbus Day	October 12

West Virginia

Martin Luther King, Jr.'s Birthday	January, third Monday
Lincoln's Birthday	February 12
Washington's Birthday	February, third Monday
West Virginia Day	June 20
Columbus Day	October, second Monday

Wisconsin

Martin Luther King Jr. Day	January 15
Washington-Lincoln Day	February, third Monday
Columbus Day	October, second Monday

Wyoming

Martin Luther King, Jr.'s Birthday and Wyoming Equality Day	January, third Monday
Washington-Lincoln Day	February, third Monday

Legal Holidays by Country

The following list of legal holidays celebrated by the various countries of the world is arranged by Gregorian calendar order. The holidays for the former USSR, Czechoslovakia, and Yugoslavia have been included because many of them are still observed by the people, and because they are often referred to in literature.

For Jewish holidays and those Christian holidays based on the Julian calendar (Easter, Pentecost, etc.), we have given the range of months during which the day may fall. The more precise dates and the dates on the Jewish calendar may be found at the main entry in the text of **HFCWD.** Some Christians still use the Julian calendar to determine all holy days, and therefore their dates for major feasts will be different.

The dates given for both Muslim holy days and holidays in Islamic countries are approximate since the exact date is only determined a few days before the actual event.

Asian festival dates fluctuate from country to country and may even be different in various parts of the same country because of the variety of traditions observed and calendars used. The dates given here are approximate. (See the section on **Calendars** for a detailed explanation of calendar systems.)

Albania:
    Anniversary Day   January 11

Algeria:
    New Year   January 1
    Labor Day   May 1
    Independence Day   July 5
    Revolution Day   November 1

Antigua and Barbuda:
    New Year   January 1
    Good Friday   Friday before Easter: March–April
    Easter Monday   Monday after Easter
    Labor Day   May 6
    Whit Monday   Monday after Whitsunday: May–June
    Queen's Birthday   June 8
    Carnival   August 5-6
    Merchant Holiday   October 7
    Independence Day   November 1
    Christmas   December 25–26

Argentina:
    New Year   January 1
    Maundy Thursday   Thursday before Easter: March–April
    Good Friday   Friday before Easter

Malvinas Day	April 2
Labor Day	May 1
National Day	May 25
Flag Day	June 20
Independence Day	July 9
Death of San Martin	August 17
Discovery of America	October 12
Immaculate Conception	December 8
Christmas	December 25

Australia:

New Year	January 1
Australia Day	January 26; January 29
Good Friday	Friday before Easter: March–April
Easter Monday	Monday after Easter
Anzac Day	April 25
Christmas	December 25–26

Austria:

New Year	January 1
Epiphany	January 6
Easter Monday	Monday after Easter: March–April
Labor Day	May 1
Ascension Day	May 9
Whit Monday	Monday after Whitsunday: May–June
Corpus Christi	May 30
Assumption Day	August 15
National Day	October 26
All Saints Day	November 1
Immaculate Conception	December 8
Christmas	December 25–26

Bahamas:

New Year	January 1
Good Friday	Friday before Easter: March–April
Easter Monday	Monday after Easter
Whit Monday	Monday after Whitsunday: May–June
Labor Day	June 7
Independence Day	July 10
Emancipation Day	August 5
Discovery Day	October 12
Christmas	December 25–26

Bahrain:

New Year	January 1
National Day	December 16

Bangladesh:

Shaheed Day	February 21
Independence Day	March 26
New Year	April 15
May Day	May 1
Jumatul Bida	May 5
Dashami	October 10
National Revolution Day	November 7
Victory Day	December 16
Christmas	December 25

Barbados:

New Year	January 1
Errol Barrow Day	January 21
Good Friday	Friday before Easter: March–April
Easter Monday	Monday after Easter
Labor Day	May 1
Whit Monday	Monday after Whitsunday: May–June
Kadooment Day	August 5
United Nations Day	October 1
Independence Day	November 30
Christmas	December 25–26

Belgium:

New Year	January 1
Easter Monday	Monday after Easter: March–April
May Day	May 1
Ascension Day	April–June
Whit Monday	Monday after Whitsunday: May–June
National Holiday	July 21
Assumption Day	August 15
All Saints Day	November 1
Armistice Day	November 11
King's Birthday	November 15
Christmas	December 25–26

Belize:

New Year	January 1
Baron Bliss Day	March 9
Good Friday	Friday before Easter: March–April
Holy Saturday	Saturday before Easter
Easter Monday	Monday after Easter
Labor Day	May 1
Commonwealth Day	May 25
St. George's Caye Day	September 10
Independence Day	September 21
Colombus Day	October 12
Garifuna Settlement Day	November 19

Legal Holidays by Country

Christmas	December 25–26

Bermuda:

New Year	January 1
Good Friday	Friday before Easter: March–April
Bermuda Day	May 24
Queen's Birthday	June 17
Cup Match	August 1
Somers Day	August 2
Labour Day	September 2
Remembrance Day	November 11
Christmas	December 25–26

Bolivia:

New Year	January 1
Good Friday	Friday before Easter: March–April
Labor Day	May 1
Corpus Christi	May 30
Independence Day	August 6
All Saints Day	November 1
Christmas	December 25

Botswana:

New Year	January 1–2
Good Friday	Friday before Easter: March–April
Easter Saturday	Saturday before Easter
Easter Monday	Monday after Easter
Ascension Day	April–June
President's Day	July 15–16
National Day	October 1
Christmas	December 25–26

Brazil:

New Year	January 1
Good Friday	Friday before Easter: March–April
Easter Monday	Monday after Easter
Tiradentes Day	April 21
Labor Day	May 1
Corpus Christi	May–June
Independence Day	September 7
Nossa Senhora de Aparecida	October 12
All Saints Day	November 1
Proclamation of the Republic	November 15
Christmas	December 25–26

Bulgaria:

New Year	January 1
Liberation Day	March 3

Labor Day	May 1–2
Day of Bulgarian Culture	May 24
Days of Liberation	September 9–10
October Revolution Day	November 7

Burma (Myanmar):

Independence Day	January 4
Union Day	February 12
Peasants' Day	March 2
Armed Forces Day	March 27
Thingyan (Water Festival)	April 14–16
Myanmar New Year	April 17
Workers' Day	May 1
Martyrs' Day	July 19
Christmas	December 25

Cameroon Republic:

New Year	January 1
Youth Day	February 12
Good Friday	Friday before Easter: March–April
Easter Monday	Monday after Easter
Ascension Day	April–June
Labor Day	May 1
National Day	May 20
Assumption Day	August 15
Christmas	December 25

Canada:

New Year	January 1
Good Friday	Friday before Easter: March–April
Easter Monday	Monday after Easter
Victoria Day	May 20
Canada Day	July 1
Labour Day	September 2
Thanksgiving Day	October, second Monday
Remembrance Day	November 11
Christmas	December 25–26

Chile:

New Year	January 1
Good Friday	Friday before Easter: March–April
Easter Saturday	Saturday before Easter
Labor Day	May 1
Navy Day	May 21
Corpus Christi	May–June
St. Peter's and St. Paul's Day	June 29
Assumption Day	August 15
National Liberation Day	September 11

Independence Day	September 18
Army Day	September 19
Columbus Day	October 12
All Saints Day	November 1
Immaculate Conception	December 8
Christmas	December 25

China, People's Republic of:

Spring Festival (Lunar New Year)	February 15
Women's Day	March 8
Labor Day	May 1
Founding of the Communist Party of China	July 1
Birthday of the People's Liberation Army	August 1
National Day	October 1

Colombia:

New Year	January 1
Epiphany	January 6
St. Joseph's Day	March 14
Holy Thursday	Thursday before Easter: March–April
Good Friday	Friday before Easter
Labor Day	May 1
Ascension Day	April–June
St. Mary's Day	May 13
Corpus Christi	May–June
St. Peter's and St. Paul's Day	July 1
Battle of Boyaca	August 7
Assumption Day	August 19
Columbus Day	October 12
All Saints Day	November 1
Independence of Cartagena	November 11
Immaculate Conception	December 8
Christmas	December 25

Congo:

New Year	January 1
President's Day	February 5
Youth Day	February 8
Congolese Women's Day	March 8
Death of President Marien Ngouabi	March 18
Labor Day	May 1
Foundation of the National People's Army	June 22
Upswing of the Revolution	July 31
"Three Glorious Days" (Anniv. of the Revolution of August 1963)	August 13–15

Independence Day	August 15
Children's Day	December 25
Foundation of the Congolese Labor Party	December 31

Côte d'Ivoire (*see* Ivory Coast)

Cuba:

National Liberation Day	January 1
International Workers Day	May 1
National Rebellion Day	July 26
Beginning of War of Independence	October 10

Cyprus:

New Year	January 1
Epiphany	January 6
Green Monday	February 18
Greek Independence Day	March 25
Good Friday	Friday before Easter: March–April
Easter Monday	Monday after Easter
Greek Cypriot Independence Day	April 1
May Day	May 1
Kataklysmos	May 27
Assumption Day	August 15
Independence Day	October 1
Greek National Day	October 28
Christmas	December 25–26

Czechoslovakia (former):

New Year	January 1
Easter Monday	Monday after Easter: March–April
May Day	May 1
Liberation Day	May 9
Independence Day	October 28
Christmas	December 25–26

Denmark:

New Year	January 1
Maundy Thursday	Thursday before Easter
Good Friday	Friday before Easter
Easter Day	March–April
Easter Monday	Monday after Easter
Great Prayer Day	April 26
Ascension Day	April–June
Whitsunday	May–June
Whit Monday	Monday after Whitsunday
Constitution Day	June 5
Christmas	December 25–26

Ecuador:

New Year	January 1
Carnival	February–March
Good Friday	Friday before Easter: March–April
Labor Day	May 1
Pichincha Day	May 24
Simon Bolivar Day	July 24
Independence Day	August 10
Independence of Guayaquil Day	October 9
Columbus Day	October 12
Memorial Day	November 2
Independence of Cuenca Day	November 3
Christmas	December 25

Egypt:

Union Day	February 22
Sham-El-Nassim	April 11
Sinai Liberation Day	April 11
Labor Day	May 1
Bairam Holiday	May 6
Revolution Day	July 23
Armed Forces	October 6
National Liberation Day	October 23
Victory Day	December 23

Ethiopia:

Christmas	January 7
Epiphany	January 19
Adwa Day	March 2
Victory Day	March 6
Patriots Victory Day	April 6
Good Friday	Friday before Easter
Easter Day	April–May
Labor Day	May 1
Revolution Day	September 12

Finland:

New Year	January 1
Epiphany	January 19
Good Friday	Friday before Easter
Easter Day	March–April
Easter Monday	Monday after Easter
May Day Eve	April 30
Labor Day	May 1
Ascension Day	April–June
Whitsunday	May–June
Midsummer Eve	June 21
Midsummer Day	June 22

All Saints Day	November 1
Independence Day	December 6
Christmas	December 24–26

France:

New Year	January 1
Easter Day	March–April
Easter Monday	Monday after Easter
Labor Day	May 1
VE Day	May 8
Ascension Day	April–June
Whitsunday	May–June
Whit Monday	Monday after Whitsunday
Bastille Day	July 14
Assumption Day	August 15
All Saints Day	November 1
Armistice Day	November 11
Christmas	December 25

French Polynesia:

New Year	January 1
Good Friday	Friday before Easter: March–April
Easter Monday	Monday after Easter
Labor Day	May 1
Ascension Day	April–June
Whit Monday	Monday after Whitsunday: May–June
Bastille Day	July 14
Assumption Day	August 15
All Saints Day	November 1
Armistice Day	November 11
Christmas	December 25

Gabon:

New Year	January 1
Renovation Day	March 12
Easter Day	March–April
Easter Monday	Monday after Easter
Labor Day	May 1
Ascension Day	April–June
Whit Monday	Monday after Whitsunday: May–June
Liberation of African Continent Day	May 25
Assumption Day	August 15
Independence Day	August 16–18
All Saints Day	November 1

Gambia:

New Year	January 1
Independence Day	February 18

Good Friday	Friday before Easter: March–April
Labor Day	May 1
Assumption Day	August 15
Christmas	December 25–26

Germany:

New Year	January 1
Epiphany	January 6
Good Friday	Friday before Easter: March–April
Easter Monday	Monday after Easter
Labor Day	May 1
Ascension Day	April–June
Whit Monday	Monday after Whitsunday: May–June
Corpus Christi	May–June
Day of Unity	June 17
Assumption Day	August 15
All Saints Day	November 1
Day of Prayer and Repentance	November 20
Christmas	December 25–26

Ghana:

New Year	January 1
Independence Day	March 6
Good Friday	Friday before Easter
Easter Sunday	March–April
Easter Monday	Monday after Easter
May Day	May 1
Revolution Day	June 4
Republic Day	July 1
Christmas	December 25–26

Gibraltar:

New Year	January 1
Commonwealth Day	March 12
Good Friday	Friday before Easter: March–April
Easter Monday	Monday after Easter
May Day	May 1
Spring Bank Holiday	May 28
Queen's Birthday	June 17
Late Summer Bank Holiday	August 27
Christmas	December 25–26

Greece:

New Year	January 1
Epiphany	January 6
Shrove Monday	February–March
Independence Day	March 25
Good Friday	Friday before Easter

Easter Sunday	April–May
Easter Monday	Monday after Easter
Labor Day	May 1
Day of the Holy Spirit	May 26
Assumption Day	August 15
National Holiday	October 28
Christmas	December 25–26

Hong Kong:

New Year	January 1
Lunar New Year	February 14-16
Good Friday	Friday before Easter
Easter Day	March–April
Easter Monday	Monday after Easter
Queen's Birthday	June 15–17
Liberation Day	August 26
Christmas	December 25–26

Hungary:

New Year	January 1
Anniversary of Hungarian Revolution	March 15
Liberation Day	April 4
Easter Monday	Monday after Easter: March–April
Labor Day	May 1
Constitution Day	August 20
Christmas	December 24–26

Iceland:

New Year	January 1
Maundy Thursday	Thursday before Easter
Good Friday	Friday before Easter
Easter Day	March–April
Easter Monday	Monday after Easter
First Day of Summer	April 25
Labor Day	May 1
Ascension Day	April–June
Whitsunday	May–June
Whit Monday	Monday after Whitsunday
Republic Day	June 17
Shop & Office Workers Holiday	August 5
Christmas	December 25–26

India:

New Year	January 1
Republic Day	January 26
Good Friday	Friday before Easter: March–April
Labor Day	May 1
Independence Day	August 15

Mahatma Gandhi's Birthday	October 2
Christmas	December 25

Indonesia:

New Year	January 1
Prophet's Birthday	February 12
Nyepi Day	March 17
Good Friday	Friday before Easter: March–April
Ascension Day	April–June
Waisak Day	May 28
Independence Day	August 17
Christmas	December 25

Iran:

Revolution Day	mid-February
Iranian New Year	March

Iraq:

New Year	January 1
Army Day	January 6
Anniversary of the 1963 Revolution	February 8
First Day of Spring Festival	March 21
Day of FAO	April 17
Labor Day	May 1
National Day	July 14–17
Revolution Day	July 17
Day of Peace	August 8

Ireland, Republic of:

New Year	January 1
St. Patrick's Day	March 17
Easter Monday	Monday after Easter: March–April
June Holiday	June 3
August Holiday	August 5
October Holiday	October 28
Christmas	December 25–26

Israel:

Purim	February–March
Passover	March–April
Independence Day	April 30
Shavout	May–June
Jewish New Year	September–October
Yom Kippur	September–October
Sukkot	September–October
Simchat Torah	September–October
Hanukkah	November–December

Italy:

New Year	January 1
Epiphany	January 6
Easter Monday	Monday after Easter: March–April
Liberation Day	April 25
Labor Day	May 1
Assumption Day	August 15
All Saints Day	November 1
Immaculate Conception	December 8
Christmas	December 25–26

Ivory Coast (Côte d'Ivoire):

New Year	January 1
Good Friday	Friday before Easter: March–April
Easter Monday	Monday after Easter
Labor Day	May 1
Ascension Day	April–June
Whit Monday	Monday after Whitsunday: May–June
Assumption Day	August 15
All Saints Day	November 1
Peace Day	November 15
National Day	December 7
Christmas	December 25

Jamaica:

New Year	January 1
Ash Wednesday	February–March
Good Friday	Friday before Easter: March–April
Easter Monday	Monday after Easter
Labor Day	May 23
Independence Day	August 5
National Heroes Day	October 21
Christmas	December 25–26

Japan:

New Year	January 1
Traditional Bank Holiday	January 2–3
Adults' Day	January 15
Foundation Day	February 11
Vernal Equinox Day	March 21
Greenery Day	April 29
Constitution Day	May 3
National Holiday	May 4
Children's Day	May 5
Respect for Aged Day	September 15
Autumnal Equinox Day	September 24
Health and Sports Day	October 10
Culture Day	November 3

Labor Thanksgiving Day	November 23
Emperor's Birthday	December 23

Jordan:

New Year	January 1
Labor Day	May 1
Independence Day	May 25
Army Day	June 10
Accession of King Hussein	August 11
King Hussein's Birthday	November 14
Christmas	December 25

Kenya:

New Year	January 1
Good Friday	Friday before Easter: March–April
Easter Monday	Monday after Easter
Labor Day	May 1
Madaraka Day	June 1
Moi Day	October 10
Kenyatta Day	October 20
Independence Day	December 12
Christmas	December 25–26

Korea, South:

New Year	January 1–3
Folklore Day	February 15
Independence Movement Day	March 1
Arbor Day	April 5
Children's Day	May 5
Buddha's Day	May 21
Memorial Day	June 6
Constitution Day	July 17
Liberation Day	August 15
Thanksgiving Day	September 22
Armed Forces Day	October 1
National Foundation Day	October 3
Korean Alphabet Day	October 9
Christmas	December 25

Kuwait:

New Year	January 1
National Day	February 25

Lebanon:

New Year	January 1
Feast of St. Maron	February 9
Good Friday (Western)	Friday before Easter
Easter Day (Western)	March–April

Good Friday (Eastern)	Friday before Easter
Easter Day (Eastern)	April–May
Labor Day	May 1
Assumption Day	August 15
All Saints Day	November 1
National Day	November 22
Christmas	December 25

Lesotho:

New Year	January 1
Army Day	January 21
Moshoeshoe's Day	March 12
National Tree Planting Day	March 21
Good Friday	Friday before Easter: March–April
Easter Monday	Monday after Easter
King's Birthday	May 2
Ascension Day	April–June
Family Day	July 1
Independence Day	October 4
National Sports Day	October 7
Christmas	December 25–26

Liberia:

New Year	January 1
Armed Forces Day	February 11
Decoration Day	March 8
J.J. Robert's Birthday	March 15
National Redemption Day	April 12
Fast and Prayer Day	April 14
President Samuel K. Doe's Birthday	May 6
National Unification Day	May 14
African Liberation Day	May 25
Independence Day	July 26
National Flag Day	August 24
National Youth Day	October 29
Thanksgiving Day	November 2
W.V.S. Tubman's Birthday	November 29
Christmas	December 25

Libya:

British Evacuation Day	March 2; 8; 28
National Day	June 11
Italian Evacuation Day	July 23; September 1; October 7

Luxembourg:

New Year	January 1
Carnival Monday	February–March
Easter Monday	Monday after Easter: March–April

Labor Day	May 1
Ascension Day	April–June
Whitsunday	May–June
Whit Monday	Monday after Whitsunday
National Day	June 24
Assumption Day	August 15
All Saints Day	November 1
All Souls Day	November 2
Christmas	December 25–26

Malawi:

New Year	January 1
Martyrs Day	March 3
Good Friday	Friday before Easter: March–April
Easter Monday	Monday after Easter
Kamuzu Day	May 14
Republic Day	July 6
Mother's Day	October 17
National Tree Planting Day	December 21
Christmas	December 25–26

Malaysia:

Chinese New Year	February 15–16
Labor Day	May 1
National Day	August 31
Christmas	December 25

Malta:

New Year	January 1
Feast of St. Paul's Shipwreck	February 10
Feast of St. Joseph	March 19
Good Friday	Friday before Easter: March–April
Freedom Day	March 31
Labor Day	May 1
Commemoration of 7 June 1919	June 7
Feast of St. Peter and St. Paul	June 29
Assumption Day	August 15
Feast of Our Lady of Victories	September 8
Independence Day	September 21
Immaculate Conception	December 8
Republic Day	December 13
Christmas	December 25

Mauritius:

New Year	January 1–2
Thaipoosam Cavadee	February
Chinese Spring Festival	February 15
Maha Shivaratree	February

Independence Day	March 12
Ougadi	April 6
Labor Day	May 1
Ganesh Chaturthi	September 5
Divali	October
All Saints Day	November 1
Christmas	December 25

Mexico:

New Year	January 1
Epiphany	January 6
Constitution Day	February 5
Benito Juarez's Birthday	March 21
Maundy Thursday	Thursday before Easter
Good Friday	Friday before Easter
Easter Day	March–April
Labor Day	May 1
Anniversary of the Battle of Puebla	May 5
Independence Day	September 15–16
Columbus Day	October 12
Anniversary of the Revolution	November 20
Christmas	December 25

Morocco:

New Year	January 1
National Day	March 3
Labor Day	May 1
Green March Day	November 6
Independence Day	November 18

Mozambique:

New Year	January 1
Heroes Day	February 3
Women's Day	April 7
Labor Day	May 1
National Day	June 25
Victory Day	September 7
Armed Forces Day	September 25
Family Day	December 25

Myanmar (*see* Burma)

Namibia:

New Year	January 1
Good Friday	Friday before Easter: March–April
Workers Day	May 1
Ascension Day	April–June
Day of Goodwill	October 1

Human Rights Day	December 10
Christmas	December 25–26

Netherlands:

New Year	January 1
Good Friday	Friday before Easter: March–April
Easter Monday	Monday after Easter
Queen's Birthday	April 30
Liberation Day	May 5
Ascension Day	April–June
Whit Monday	Monday after Whitsunday: May–June
Christmas	December 25–26

New Zealand:

New Year	January 1–2
New Zealand Day	February 6
Good Friday	Friday before Easter: March–April
Easter Monday	Monday after Easter
Anzac Day	April 25
Queen's Birthday	June 3
Labor Day	October 28
Christmas	December 25–26

Nigeria:

New Year	January 1
Good Friday	Friday before Easter: March–April
Easter Monday	Monday after Easter
Labor Day	May 1
National Day	October 1
Christmas	December 25–26

Norway:

New Year	January 1
Maundy Thursday	Thursday before Easter: March–April
Good Friday	Friday before Easter
Easter Monday	Monday after Easter
Labor Day	May 1
Ascension Day	April–June
Constitution Day	May 17
Whit Monday	Monday after Whitsunday: May–June
Christmas	December 25–26

Oman:

Eid-Al-Fitr	1st Shawwal
Eid-Al-Adha	10th Dhu-l-Hijjah

Pakistan:

Pakistan Day	March 23

May Day	May 1
Independence Day	August 14
Defence Day	September 6
Anniversary of the death of Quaid-e-Azam	September 11
Iqbal Day	November 9
Birthday of Quaid-e-Azam	December 25

Panama:

New Year	January 1
Martyr Day	January 9
Carnival	February–March
Good Friday	Friday before Easter: March–April
Independence Day	November 3
Cry of Independence	November 10
Separation from Spain	November 28
Mother's Day	December 8
Christmas	December 25

Paraguay:

New Year	January 1
San Blas	February 3
Heroes' Day	March 1
Maundy Thursday	Thursday before Easter: March–April
Good Friday	Friday before Easter
Labor Day	May 1
Independence Day	May 15
Chaco Peace	June 12
Foundation of Asunción	August 15
Immaculate Conception	December 8
Christmas	December 25

Peru:

New Year	January 1
Good Friday	Friday before Easter: March–April
Labor Day	May 1
Independence Day	June 28–29
St. Peter & St. Paul	June 29
All Saints Day	November 1
Immaculate Conception	December 8
Christmas	December 25

Philippines:

New Year	January 1
People Power Day	February 25
Holy Thursday	Thursday before Easter: March–April
Good Friday	Friday before Easter
Labor Day	May 1

Day of Valor	May 6
Independence Day	June 12
All Saints Day	November 1
National Heroes Day	November 30
Christmas	December 25
Rizal Day	December 30

Poland:

New Year	January 1
Easter Monday	Monday after Easter: March–April
Labor Day	May 1
Constitution Day	May 3
Corpus Christi	May–June
Assumption Day	August 15
All Saints Day	November 1
National Day	November 29
Christmas	December 25–26

Portugal:

New Year	January 1
Shrove Tuesday	February–March
Good Friday	Friday before Easter
Easter Day	March–April
Liberation Day	April 25
Labor Day	May 1
Corpus Christi	May–June
National Day	June 10
Assumption Day	August 15
Republic Day	October 5
All Saints Day	November 1
Independence Day	December 1
Immaculate Conception	December 8
Christmas	December 25–26

Qatar:

Independence Day	September 3

Romania:

New Year	January 1–2
Workers Holiday	May 1–2
National Day	August 23–24

Saudi Arabia:

Eid-Al-Fitr	1st Shawwal
Eid-Al-Adha	10th Dhu-l-Hijjah

Senegal:

New Year	January 1

Confederal Agreement Day	February 1
Good Friday	Friday before Easter: March–April
Easter Monday	Monday after Easter
Labor Day	May 1
Ascension Day	April–June
Whit Sunday	May–June
Assumption Day	August 15
All Saints Day	November 1
Christmas	December 25–26

Seychelles:

New Year	January 1–2
Good Friday	Friday before Easter
Easter Sunday	March–April
Labor Day	May 1
Corpus Christi	May–June
Liberation Day	June 5
Independence Day	June 29
Assumption Day	August 15
All Saints Day	November 1
Immaculate Conception	December 8
Christmas	December 25

Singapore:

New Year	January 1
Chinese New Year	February 15–16
Good Friday	Friday before Easter: March–April
Hari Raya Puasa	April 16
Labor Day	May 1
Vesak Day	April–May
Hari Raya Haji	June 23
National Day	August 9
Deepavali	November
Christmas	December 25

South Africa:

New Year	January 1
Good Friday	Friday before Easter: March–April
Family Day	April 1
Founders Day	April 6
Workers Day	May 6
Ascension Day	April–June
Republic Day	May 31
Kruger Day	October 10
Day of the Vow	December 16
Christmas	December 25
Day of Goodwill	December 26

Spain:

New Year	January 1
Epiphany	January 6
St. Joseph's Day	March 19
Good Friday	Friday before Easter: March–April
Easter Monday (Barcelona and Mallorca only)	Monday after Easter
Labor Day	May 1
Corpus Christi	May–June
St. James's Day	July 25
Assumption Day	August 15
All Saints Day	November 1
Immaculate Conception	December 8
Christmas	December 25

Sri Lanka:

Tamil Thai Pongal Day	January 14
National Day	February 4
Good Friday	Friday before Easter: March–April
May Day	May 1
Special Bank Holiday	May 20–22; June 30
Christmas	October 14; December 12; December 25

Sudan:

Independence Day–New Year	January 1
National Unity Day	March 3
Christmas	April 4–6; December 25–26

Swaziland:

New Year	January 1
Good Friday	Friday before Easter: March–April
Easter Monday	Monday after Easter
King's Birthday	April 19
National Flag Day	April 25
Ascension Day	April–June
Public Holiday	July 22
Independence Day	September 6
Christmas	December 25–26

Sweden:

New Year	January 1
Epiphany	January 6
Good Friday	Friday before Easter
Easter Sunday	March–April
Easter Monday	Monday after Easter
Labor Day	May 1
Ascension Day	April–June
Whitsunday	May–June

Whit Monday	Monday after Whitsunday
Midsummer Day	June 21
All Saints Day	November 2
Christmas	December 24–26
New Years Eve	December 31

Switzerland:

New Year	January 1
Good Friday	Friday before Easter: March–April
Easter Monday	Monday after Easter
Ascension Day	April–June
Whit Monday	Monday after Whitsunday: May–June
Swiss National Day	August 1
Christmas	December 25–26

Syria:

New Year	January 1
Revolution Day	March 8
National Day	April 17
Labor Day	May 1
Martyrs Day	May 6
Christmas	December 25

Taiwan:

January 1	Founding Day of Republic of China
Youth Day	March 29
Tomb Sweeping Day	April 5
Dragon Boat Festival	May 28
Confucius' Birthday	September 28
National Day	October 10
Taiwan Retrocession Day	October 25
President Chiang Kai-shek's Birthday	October 31
Dr. Sun Yat-sen's Birthday	November 12
Constitution Day	December 25

Tanzania:

New Year	January 1
Zanzibar Revolution Day	January 12
CCM Day	February 5
Good Friday	Friday before Easter: March–April
Easter Monday	Monday after Easter
Union Day	April 26
International Workers Day	May 1
Peasants' Day	July 7
Independence Day	December 9
Christmas	December 25

Thailand:

New Year	January 1
Magha Puja	January–February
Chakri Day	April 6
Songkran Day	April 13
Visakha Puja	April–May
Coronation Day	May 5
Asalha Puja	June 26
Khal Phansa	June 27
Queen's Birthday	August 12
Chulalongkorn Day	October 23
King's Birthday	December 5
Constitution Day	December 10
New Years Eve	December 31

Trinidad and Tobago:

New Year	January 1
Good Friday	Friday before Easter: March–April
Easter Monday	Monday after Easter
Whit Monday	Monday after Whitsunday: May–June
Corpus Christi	May–June
Labor Day	June 19
Emancipation Day	August 1
Independence Day	August 31
Republic Day	September 24
Christmas	December 25–26

Tunisia:

New Year	January 1
Independence Day	March 20
Youth Day	March 21
Martyr's Day	April 9
Labor Day	May 1
Republic Day	July 25
Women's Day	August 13

Turkey:

New Year	January 1
National Sovereignty and Children's Day	April 23
Commemoration of Atatürk and Youth Day	May 19
Victory Day	August 30
National Day	October 29

Uganda:

New Year	January 1
Liberation Day	January 26

Good Friday	Friday before Easter: March–April
Easter Monday	Monday after Easter
Labor Day	May 1
Independence Day	October 9
Christmas	December 25–26

Union of Soviet Socialist Republics (U.S.S.R.) (former):

New Year	January 1
International Women's Day	March 8
Labor Day	May 1
Victory Day	May 9
Constitution Day	October 7
October Revolution	November 7

United Arab Emirates:

New Year	January 1
National Day	December 2
Christmas	December 25

United Kingdom:

New Year	January 1
Bank Holiday (Scotland)	January 2
St. Patrick's Day (N. Ireland)	March 17
Good Friday	Friday before Easter: March–April
Easter Monday	Monday following Easter
May Day Holiday	May 6
Spring Bank Holiday	May 27
Holiday (N. Ireland)	July 12
Bank Holiday (Scotland)	August 5
Late Summer Holiday (not Scotland)	August 26
Christmas	December 25–26

United States of America:

New Year	January 1
Martin Luther King's Birthday	January, third Monday
Washington's Birthday	February, third Monday
Memorial Day	May, last Monday
Independence Day	July 4
Labor Day	September, first Monday
Columbus Day	October, second Monday
Veterans Day	November 11
Thanksgiving Day	November, fourth Thursday
Christmas	December 25

Uruguay:

New Year	January 1
Epiphany	January 6

Holy Week	week before Easter: March–April
Labor Day	May 1
Battle of Las Piedras	May 18
General Artigas Birthday	June 19
Constitution Day	July 18
Independence Day	August 25
Columbus Day	October 12
All Souls Day	November 2
Christmas	December 25

Venezuela:

New Year	January 1
Epiphany	January 6
Holy Thursday	Thursday before Easter: March–April
Good Friday	Friday before Easter
Independence Day	April 19
Labor Day	May 1
Ascension Day	April–June
Corpus Christi	May–June
Carabobo Day	June 24
St. Peter and St. Paul	June 29
Independence Day	July 5
Simon Bolivar's Birthday	July 24
Assumption Day	August 15
Columbus Day	October 12
All Saints Day	November 1
Immaculate Conception	December 8
Christmas	December 25

Yemen Republic:

Labor Day	May 1
National Day	September 26

Yugoslavia (former):

New Year	January 1–2
Labor Day	May 1–2
Combatant's Day	July 4
Republic Day	November 29–30

Zaire:

New Year	January 1
Martyrs of Independence Day	January 4
Labor Day	May 1
Party Day	May 20
Fishermen's Day	June 24
Independence Day	June 30
Parents' Day	August 1
Youth Day	October 14

Three-Z Day	October 27
Army Day	November 17
Anniversary of New Regime	November 24
Christmas	December 25

Zambia:

New Year	January 1
Youth Day	March 12
Good Friday	Friday before Easter: March–April
Holy Saturday	Saturday before Easter
Labor Day	May 1
Africa Freedom Day	May 25
Heroes' Day	July 1
Unity Day	July 2
Farmer's Day	August 5
Independence Day	October 24
Christmas	December 25

Zimbabwe:

New Year	January 1
Good Friday	Friday before Easter: March–April
Easter Saturday	Saturday before Easter
Easter Monday	Monday after Easter
Independence Day	April 18
Workers' Day	May 1
Africa Day	May 25
Heroes' Day	August 11
Armed Forces Day	August 12
Christmas	December 24–25

Words Relating to Periods of Time

A descriptive listing of words related to periods of time is included below. Many of the words are adjectives in form, but also are commonly used as nouns, e.g., *the bicentennial of the U.S. Constitution.* All terms are defined in two separate lists: first by number referred to, then alphabetically.

Listed by number:

diurnal, per diem, quotidian   daily; of a day.

nocturnal   nightly; of a night.

nichthemeron   a period of 24 hours.

semidiurnal   twice a day.

hebdomadal   weekly; a period of 7 days.

semiweekly   twice a week.

biweekly   **1.** every 2 weeks. **2.** twice a week.

fortnightly   once every 2 weeks.

triweekly   **1.** every 3 weeks. **2.** 3 times a week.

novendial   a period of 9 days.

monthly, tricenary   **1.** relating to a period of one month. **2.** 30 days.

bimonthly   **1.** every 2 months. **2.** twice a month.

semimonthly   twice a month.

bimester   relating to a period of 2 months.

trimester   relating to a period of 3 months.

trimonthly   **1.** every 3 months. **2.** 3 times a month.

biquarterly   twice every 3 months.

biannual   twice a year (not necessarily at equally spaced intervals).

triannual   3 times a year.

semiannual, semiyearly, semestral   every half year or six-month period.

annual, solennial, quotennial, per annum   yearly; once a year.

biennial, biennium, biyearly, diennial   relating to a period of 2 years.

triennial, triennium   relating to a period of 3 years.

quadrennial, quadrennium, quadriennial   relating to a period of 4 years.

quinquennial, quintennial, quinquennium   relating to a period of 5 years.

sexennial, sextennial   relating to a period of 6 years.

septennial, septenary, septennium   relating to a period of 7 years.

octennial   relating to a period of 8 years.

novennial   relating to a period of 9 years.

decennial, decennium, decennary   relating to a period of 10 years.

undecennial   relating to a period of 11 years.

duodecennial   relating to a period of 12 years.

quindecennial   relating to a period of 15 years.

septendecennial   relating to a period of 17 years.

vicennial, vigintennial   relating to a period of 20 years.

tricennial, trigintennial   relating to a period of 30 years.

quinquagenary, semicentennial, semicentenary   relating to a period of 50 years.

centennial, centenary, centennium, centurial   relating to a period of 100 years.

quasquicentennial   relating to a period of 125 years.
sesquicentennial, sesquicentenary   relating to a period of 150 years.
bicentennial, bicentenary, bicentennium   relating to a period of 200 years.
tricentennial, tercentennial, tercentenary   relating to a period of 300 years.
quadricentennial, quatercentennial   relating to a period of 400 years.
quincentennial, quincentenary   relating to a period of 500 years.
sexcentenary   relating to a period of 600 years.
septicentennial   relating to a period of 700 years.
antemillenial, premillenial   relating to the period before the millenium.
millennial, millennium   relating to a period of 1,000 years; 10 centuries.
postmillenial   relating to the period after the millenium.
sesquimillennium   relating to a period of 1,500 years; 15 centuries.
bimillennial, bimillenary, bimillennium   relating to a period of 2,000 years; 20 centuries.
perennial   occurring year after year.
plurennial   lasting for many years.
aeonial   everlasting.

Listed alphabetically:
aeonial   everlasting.
annual   yearly; once a year.
antemillenial   relating to the period before the millenium.
biannual   twice a year (not necessarily at equally spaced intervals).
bicentenary, bicentennial, bicentennium   relating to a period of 200 years.
biennial, biennium   relating to a period of 2 years.
bimester   relating to a period of 2 months.
bimillenary, bimillennial, bimillennium   relating to a period of 2,000 years; 20 centuries.
bimonthly   **1.** every 2 months. **2.** twice a month.
biquarterly   twice every 3 months.
biweekly   **1.** every 2 weeks. **2.** twice a week.
biyearly   relating to a period of 2 years.
centenary, centennial, centennium, centurial   relating to a period of 100 years.
decennary, decennial, decennium   relating to a period of 10 years.
diennial   relating to a period of 2 years.
diurnal   daily; of a day.
duodecennial   relating to a period of 12 years.
fortnightly   once every 2 weeks.
hebdomadal   weekly; a period of 7 days.
millennial, millennium   relating to a period of 1,000 years; 10 centuries.
monthly   **1.** relating to a period of one month. **2.** 30 days.
nichthemeron   a period of 24 hours.
nocturnal   nightly; of a night.
novendial   a period of 9 days.
novennial   relating to a period of 9 years.
octennial   relating to a period of 8 years.
per annum   yearly; once a year.
per diem   daily; of a day.
perennial   occurring year after year.
plurennial   lasting for many years.

postmillenial   relating to the period after the millenium.
premillenial   relating to the period before the millenium.
quadrennial, quadrennium, quadriennial   relating to a period of 4 years.
quadricentennial   relating to a period of 400 years.
quasquicentennial   relating to a period of 125 years.
quatercentennial   relating to a period of 400 years.
quincentenary, quincentennial   relating to a period of 500 years.
quindecennial   relating to a period of 15 years.
quinquagenary   relating to a period of 50 years.
quinquennial, quinquennium, quintennial   relating to a period of 5 years.
quotennial   yearly; once a year.
quotidian   daily; of a day.
semestral, semiannual   every half year or six-month period.
semicentenary, semicentennial   relating to a period of 50 years.
semidiurnal   twice a day.
semimonthly   twice a month.
semiweekly   twice a week.
semiyearly   every half year or six-month period.
septendecennial   relating to a period of 17 years.
septenary, septennial, septennium   relating to a period of 7 years.
septicentennial   relating to a period of 700 years.
sesquicentenary, sesquicentennial   relating to a period of 150 years.
sesquimillennium   relating to a period of 1,500 years; 15 centuries.
sexcentenary   relating to a period of 600 years.
sexennial, sextennial   relating to a period of 6 years.
solennial   yearly; once a year.
tercentenary; tercentennial   relating to a period of 300 years.
triannual   3 times a year.
tricenary   1. relating to a period of one month. 2. 30 days.
tricennial   relating to a period of 30 years.
tricentennial   relating to a period of 300 years.
triennial, triennium   relating to a period of 3 years.
trigintennial   relating to a period of 30 years.
trimester   relating to a period of 3 months.
trimonthly   1. every 3 months. 2. 3 times a month.
triweekly   1. every 3 weeks. 2. 3 times a week.
undecennial   relating to a period of 11 years.
vicennial, vigintennial   relating to a period of 20 years.

Calendar Systems Around the World: Gregorian, Julian, Jewish, Islamic, Hindu, and Buddhist

A calendar is a means of reckoning time through the application of divisions—days, weeks, months, and years. Some of these divisions, such as months, originate in observations of phenomena in nature. Others, such as weeks, are quite arbitrary. Primitive people had reckoned by cycles of the moon (months), but when a more convenient, shorter period was needed days were grouped, e.g., intervals between market days probably led to the use of the seven-day week. The originally Jewish seven-day week became a standard throughout Western civilization starting from the third century B.C.E.

The Day

The day is a fairly natural division, despite the variation in the length of sunlight through the year. The Babylonians introduced divisions of the day into twenty-four hours, but the length of hours varied through the year. Only with the development of accurate clocks, the demand for which was a byproduct of the interest in maritime navigation that came with the Renaissance, was the day given scientific regularity.

The Month

A lunar month, the period of a complete cycle of the phases of the moon, lasts approximately 29.5 days, is easy for all to recognize, short enough to be counted without using large numbers, matches closely with the female menstrual cycle and, given its relation to the tidal cycle, with the duration of cyclic behavior in some marine creatures. Its simplicity and minimal ease of observation (if one discounts cloudy skies) led to its great significance, and it was widely used as the basis for calendars in many cultures. The length of each month varied according to the culture, e.g., the Babylonians alternated between twenty-nine- and thirty-day months, the Egyptians fixed them at thirty days, etc.

The Seasons

But the problem inherent in the use of a lunar calendar is that the cycles of the sun, not the moon, determine the seasons, the predictability of which is essential to the success of agriculture. The seasons could be determined by solar observation, either by measuring the cycle of the midday shadow cast by a stick placed vertically in the ground, or by sophisticated astronomical calculations. Either system resulted in a solar year of approximately 365 days, incompatible with the twelve 29.5-day lunar months that resulted in a 354-day year.

Civilizations attempted to reconcile lunar months with the solar year in varied ways. The most influential ancient effort was that of the Egyptian astronomers, working from precise mathematical observations and borrowing from Babylonian astronomy, who drew up the Roman calendar that Julius Caesar introduced.

Julian Calendar

Julius Caesar ordered the change of the reformed Roman lunar calendar to a solar-based one in 46

B.C.E. The intercalation of ninety days corrected a discrepancy that had been growing between the seasons and the months in which they had traditionally fallen. Prior to this intercalation, the Roman civic year had come to be about three months "ahead" of the seasons, so spring began in June. The year 46 B.C.E. was assigned 445 days to make the adjustment; it was called *ultimus annus confusionis*, 'the last year of the muddled reckoning.' The new calendar, based on the Egyptian solar calendar, provided for a year of 365 days with an additional day in February every fourth year. The addition of this leap year and day gives the Julian year an average length of 365.25 days—very close to the actual solar cycle. The Julian calendar remained in civic use in the West for more than 1600 years, is still the basis of the "Old Calendarist" Orthodox Christian liturgical calendar, and is used by all Orthodox Christian churches to determine the date of Easter.

Gregorian Calendar

By the late sixteenth century, the difference between the Julian calendar and the seasons had grown to ten days because the Julian year, averaging 365.25 days, was slightly longer than the actual length of a solar year, which, by modern calculation, is known to be 365.242199 days long. Fixed holy days began to occur in the "wrong" season, both for the church and for farmers, who used certain holy days to determine planting and harvesting. Pope Gregory XIII ordered the reform that deleted ten days from the year 1582; in that year, October 15 was the day after October 5. This change, coupled with the elimination of leap days in "century" years unless evenly divisible by 400 (e.g., 1600, 2000), corrected the calendar so that today only occasional "leap seconds" are needed to keep months and seasons synchronized. At first adopted only in Roman Catholic countries, the Gregorian calendar gradually came to be accepted throughout the West, and today has become the calendar used by most of the world, at least for business and government.

Islamic Calendar

The Islamic calendar, called *hijri* or Hegirian, is still strictly lunar-based. Moreover, the *actual* beginning of a month depends on the sighting of the new moon. Traditionally, if the sky is overcast and the new moon is not visible, the previous month runs another thirty days before the new month begins. However, the *practical* beginning of a month is according to astronomical calculations of lunar cycles. The Islamic era begins July 16, 622, the date of the hegira or flight into exile of the Prophet Muhammad from Mecca to Medina.

There are twelve Islamic lunar months, some of twenty-nine, others of thirty days; these yield 354 days in the Islamic year. The fixed holidays set in the Islamic calendar thus move "backward" about ten days each year in relation to the Gregorian calendar. In roughly thirty-six years, Ramadan, the Islamic holy month of fasting, moves back through the entire solar year. The Islamic day runs from sundown to sundown.

Other calendars were developed in Islamic countries for the sake of agriculture, which depends on a solar calendar. The Coptic calendar, a variation of the Julian, was used until recently, but is now limited primarily to Egypt and the Sudan, countries with large Coptic populations. The Turkish fiscal calendar, also Julian-based, was used in the Ottoman Empire. Nowadays, the Gregorian calendar is followed nearly everywhere for civic purposes, and the Islamic calendar determines only the days of religious observance. Saudi Arabia is the one exception, and, at least officially, uses the Islamic calendar as the calendar of reference.

The names of the Islamic months are an ancient reflection of the seasons of the solar year:

Muharram: the sacred month
Safar: the month which is void
Rabi al-Awwal: the first spring
Rabi ath-Thani: the second spring
Jumada-l-Ula: the first month of dryness
Jumada-th-Thaniyyah: the second month of dryness
Rajab: the revered month
Shaban: the month of division
Ramadan: the month of great heat
Shawwal: the month of hunting
Dhu l-Qadah: the month of rest
Dhu-l-Hijjah: the month of pilgrimage

Jewish Calendar

In 358, Hillel II introduced a permanent calendar based on mathematical and astronomical calculations, eliminating the need for eyewitness sightings of the new moon with which the new month begins. Due to doubts as to when the new moon appeared, Biblical law stated that those living outside of Israel would observe two days rather than one for each festival, except for Yom Kippur, the Day of Atonement. The Talmud required that this custom continue even after the calendar was formulated. The Jewish era begins with the date of Creation, traditionally set in 3761 B.C.E.

Only slight modifications were made to Hillel's calendar and it has remained unchanged since the tenth century. A day is reckoned from sundown to sundown, a week contains seven days, a month is either twenty-nine or thirty days long, and a year has twelve lunar months plus about eleven days, or 353, 354, or 355 days. To reconcile the calendar with the annual solar cycle, a thirteenth month of thirty days is intercalated in the third, sixth, eighth, eleventh, fourteenth, seventeenth, and nineteenth years of a nineteen-year cycle; a leap year may contain from 383 to 385 days. The civil calendar begins with the month of Tishri, the first day of which is Rosh ha-Shonah, the New Year. The cycle of the religious calendar begins on Nisan 15, Passover (Pesah).

The names of the months in the Jewish calendar were borrowed from the Babylonians. The pre-exilic books of the Bible usually refer to the months according to their numerical order, beginning with Tishri, but there are four months mentioned with different names: Nisan/Abib, Iyyar/Ziv, Tishri/Ethanim, and Heshvan/Bul:

Nisan: mid-March to mid-April
Iyyar: mid-April to mid-May
Sivan: mid-May to mid-June
Tammuz: mid June to mid-July
Av: mid-July to mid-August
Elul: mid-August to mid-September
Tishri: mid-September to mid-October
Heshvan: Marheshvan mid-October to mid-November
Kislev: mid-November to mid-December
Tevet: mid-December to mid-January

Shevat: mid-January to mid-February
Adar: mid-February to mid-March

The intercalary month of Adar II is inserted before Adar as needed.

Hindu Calendar

Of the multitudinous regional Hindu calendars, used only for religious holidays, the majority divide an approximate solar year of 360 days into twelve months. Each day is 1/30th of a month, with the intercalation of a leap month every sixty months. Time measurements based on observations of the constellations are used along with the calendar. Each month, counted from full moon to full moon, is divided into two fortnights: *krsna* (waning *or* dark half) and *sukla* (waxing *or* bright half) of the moon. Many references to the Hindu calendar (depending on the source) are given as follows: month, fortnight (either S=waxing or K=waning), and number of the day in that fortnight, e.g., Ramanavami: Caitra S. 9.

The names of the Hindu months are given below, with the Burmese name for the month in brackets:

Caitra [Tagu]: March-April
Vaisakha [Kasone]: April-May
Jyaistha [Nayhone]: May-June
Asadha [Waso]: June-July
Sravana [Wagaung]: July-August
Bhadrapada [Tawthalin]: August-September
Asvina [Thadingyut]: September-October
Karttika [Tazaungmone]: October-November
Margasirsa [Nadaw]: November-December
Pausa [Pyatho]: December-January
Magha [Tabodwei]: January-February
Phalguna [Tabaung]: February-March

Buddhist Calendar

Theravada Buddhists (those primarily in Sri Lanka, Laos, Burma, Thailand, and Cambodia), using a Hindu calendar as their basis, calculate the months by the moon and the new year by the sun's position in relation to the twelve segments of the heavens, each named for a sign of the zodiac. The solar new year begins when the sun enters Aries, usually between April 13th and 18th. The lunar months alternate between twenty-nine and thirty days in length. The first lunar month is usually sometime in December, except for the Burmese Buddhist calendar, which begins in April (see Hindu Calendar for the Burmese names). Periodically, the seventh month has an intercalary day, and an intercalary month is added every few years. Cambodia, Laos, and Thailand refer to the months by number.

Mahayana Buddhists (those primarily in Tibet, Mongolia, China, Korea, and Japan) base their holidays on Buddhist, Chinese, or Gregorian calendars.

Comparative Table of Calendar Systems

GREGORIAN CALENDAR	JEWISH CALENDAR	HINDU, JAIN, BUDDHIST, & SIKH CALENDAR	BURMESE CALENDAR
SEPTEMBER			
	TISHRI	ASVINĀ	THADINGYUT
OCTOBER			
	HESHVAN	KARTTIKA	TAZAUNGMONE
NOVEMBER			
	KISLEV	MARGASIRSA	NADAW
DECEMBER			
	TEVET	PAUSA	PYATHO
JANUARY			
	SHEVAT	MAGHA	TABODWEI
FEBRUARY			
	ADAR	PHALGUNA	TABAUNG
MARCH			
	NISAN	CAITRA	TAGU
APRIL			
	IYYAR	VAISAKHA	KASONE
MAY			
	SIVAN	JYAISTHA	NAYHONE
JUNE			
	TAMMUZ	ASADHA	WASO
JULY			
	AV	SRAVANA	WAGAUNG
AUGUST			
	ELUL	BHADRAPADA	TAWTHALIN

Bibliography

Holidays, Festivals, and Celebrations of the World Dictionary was compiled with information received from cities, states, international tourism and marketing offices; chambers of commerce, resorts and vacation areas, convention and visitors bureaus, state fair headquarters; associations, museums, and cultural centers; periodicals, travel and tour books by the Automobile Association of America, Baedeker, Birnbaum, Fielding, Fodor, Frommer, Lonely Planet, Passport, and Sunset Travel; and through phone calls and letters. In addition, the reference books listed below were also frequently consulted.

The American Book of Days, 3rd ed., Jane M. Hatch, ed.; xxiv + 1214 pp.; New York, NY: H.W. Wilson, 1978. 0-8242-0593-6.

American Holidays and Special Days, George and Virginia Schaun; xix + 194 pp.; Lanham, MD: Maryland Historical Press, 1986. 0-917882-19-9.

Anniversaries and Holidays, 4th ed., Ruth W. Gregory; xiii + 262 pp.; Chicago, IL: American Library Association, 1983. 0-8389-0389-4.

The Book of Days, a Miscellany of Popular Antiquities, 2 vols., R. Chambers, ed.; 1672 pp.; London (Eng.): W.R. Chambers, 1862–1864. Republished by Omnigraphics Inc., 1990. 1-55888-848-9.

The Book of Festivals, Dorothy Gladys Spicer; xiv + 429 pp.; New York, NY: The Womans Press, 1937. Reprinted by Omnigraphics 1990. 1-55888-841-1.

The Book of Holidays Around the World, Alice van Straalen; 192 pp.; New York, NY: E.P. Dutton, 1986. 0-525-44270-7.

California Festivals (paper), 3rd ed., Carl and Katie Landau with Kathy Kincade; 269 pp.; San Francisco, CA: Landau Communications, 1992. 0-929881-13-3.

Chase's Annual Events 1992; xvi + 526 pp.; Chicago, IL: Contemporary Books, 1991. 0-8092-3978-7.

The Christian Year, J.C.J. Metford; 144 pp.; United Kingdom: Thames and Hudson, 1991. No ISBN.

The Concise Encyclopedia of Islam, Cyril Glassé; 472 pp.; San Francisco, CA: Harper & Row, 1989. 0-06-063123-6.

Days and Customs of All Faiths, the Rev. Howard V. Harper; xiv + 399 pp.; New York, NY: Fleet Publishing, 1957. Republished by Omnigraphics, 1990. 1-55888-850-0.

A Dictionary of Days, Leslie Dunkling; xiii + 156 pp.; New York, NY: Facts On File, 1988. 0-8160-1916-9.

Bibliography

Dictionary of Mythology, Folklore, and Symbols, 3 vols., Gertrude Jobes; 1759 pp. (vv. 1 & 2) + 482 pp. (Index); New York, NY: Scarecrow Press, 1962. No ISBN.

The Encyclopedia of Judaism, Geoffrey Wigoder; ed.; 768 pp.; New York, NY: Macmillan, 1989. 0-02-628410-3.

The Festival Hopper's Guide to California and Nevada, 3rd ed. (paper), Darrin and Julie Craig; 519 pp.; San Jose, CA: Creative Chaos, 1991. 0-9624538-2-X.

The Folklore of American Holidays, 2nd ed., Hennig Cohen and Tristram Potter Coffin, eds.; xxxi + 508 pp.; Detroit, MI: Gale Research Inc., 1991. 0-8103-7602-4.

The Folklore of World Holidays, Margaret Read MacDonald, ed.; xxix + 739 pp.; Detroit, MI: Gale Research Inc., 1992. 0-8103-7577-X.

Funk & Wagnalls Standard Dictionary of Folklore, Mythology, and Legend, (paper), Maria Leach, ed.; 1236 pp.; New York, NY: Harper & Row, 1972. 0-06-250511-4.

A Guide to Fairs and Festivals in the United States, Frances Shemanski; viii + 339 pp.; Westport, CT: Greenwood Press, 1985. 0-313-21437-9.

A Guide to World Fairs and Festivals, Frances Shemanski; vii + 309 pp.; Westport, CT: Greenwood Press, 1985. 0-313-20786-0.

Indian America, A Traveler's Companion, 2nd ed., Eagle/Walking Turtle; 434 pp.; Santa Fe, NM: John Muir, 1989. 0-945465-91-2.

Music Festivals in America, 4th ed., (paper), Carol Price Rabin; 271 pp.; Great Barrington, MA: Berkshire Traveller Press, 1979. 0-930145-01-1.

The Perennial Dictionary of World Religions, Keith Crim, ed.; 830 pp.; New York, NY: Harper & Row, 1981. 0-687-00409-5.

Saints and Festivals of the Christian Church, H. Pomeroy Brewster; xiv + 558 pp.; New York, NY: Frederick A. Stokes, 1904. Republished by Omnigraphics, 1990. 1-55888-878-0.

Holidays, Festivals, and Celebrations of the World Dictionary

A

Abbey Fair
Early August

The Abbey Fair in Bethlehem, Connecticut is a two-day monastic fair sponsored by the Benedictine sisters of the Abbey of Regina Laudis. Since it was first held in 1952, the fair has expanded considerably. It offers a wide variety of unusual events and activities, including performances of Gregorian chant; a sale of food, flowers, and crafts produced by the abbey; blacksmithing demonstrations; and a world-famous Neapolitan crêche in the horse stable formerly owned by an eighteenth century Congregational minister. The sisters are responsible for much of the food that is served, and there is a raffle for one of the Abbey's Cheviot lambs and a baby calf. Even the hamburger and hotdog stand uses only Abbey-grown beef. In contrast to the many traditional attractions that are associated with life at the Abbey, there is also a fashion show, a basketball clinic, and sales of used furniture and clothing.

According to the nuns who run the annual fair, its purpose is to celebrate the "true values of life, of friendships that endure, and those happy moments that remain constant in memory."

'Abdu'l-Baha, Ascension of
November 28

A holy day in the Baha'i religion, commemorating the death of Abbas Effendi, known as Abdu'l-Baha, in 1921 in Haifa, Palestine (now Israel). The eldest son of Mirza Husayn Ali, known as Baha'u'llah, the prophet-founder of the Baha'i faith, he was named the leader of the Baha'i community in his father's will, which also appointed him to interpret Baha'i writings. In turn, Abdu'l-Baha appointed his eldest grandson, Shoghi Effendi (1896–1957) as his successor and Guardian of the Cause. Today the affairs of the worldwide Baha'i community are administered by the Universal House of Justice, a body that meets in Haifa and is elected every five years.

Aboakyer Festival
April–May

The Effutu people of Ghana celebrate the **Deer Hunting Festival** by making an offering to the god Panche Otu. Two groups known as the Asafo companies, each consisting of about 150 people ranging in age from young boys to grandfathers, compete in a deer hunt that begins at dawn with the pounding of drums and the ringing of bells. When the first deer is caught, the victorious company brings it back alive and presents it proudly to their chief. Then the deer is taken back to the village, where dancing and drumming continue in an effort to placate Panche Otu so that he will bring them a bountiful year.

Abu Simbel Festival
February 22 and October 22

This festival celebrates the two days of the year on which the light of the rising sun can reach the 180-feet-deep innermost chambers of Abu Simbel, the great temple of Ramses II, in Egypt. The temple was designed so that only on these two days in February and October does the sun shine on the four gods in the sanctuary, Ptah, Amen-Re, Ramses, and Re-Horakhty. This temple, the most colossal in Egypt, was built by Ramses II between 1300 and 1233 B.C., and is famous for its four sixty-five-foot statues of the seated Ramses.

It is actually two temples—one for Ramses and one for queen Nefertari and is extraordinary for its grandeur, beauty, and history. It was unknown to the European world until Swiss explorer Johann Burckhardt found it in 1812. The Italian Giovanni Belzoni excavated the entrance and explored the temple in 1816. In 1964, when the new Aswan Dam was to be built, creating a lake that would have drowned the temple, it was cut into 2,000 pieces and reassembled at a site about 180 feet higher. It is not as perfect as it was at the foot of the cliff—but it was saved.

It is thought that there must have been ritual celebrations in ancient times on the days when the sun penetrated the sanctuary. Today, television covers the event, and people gather to see the sunrise and to meditate. The sun now shines on the sanctuary a day earlier than it did before the temple was moved.

Acadian Day
August

The original Acadians were the seventeenth century French colonists who settled in the area known as Acadia, which covered what is now Nova Scotia as well as Prince Edward Island, and parts of northern Maine and Quebec. Their French-speaking descendants in the Maritime Provinces continue to honor their heritage by holding many local Acadian Day celebrations, usually during the summer months.

Fifty thousand people attend the **Acadian Festival** in Caraquet, New Brunswick, the largest of these celebrations. The festival takes place for ten days in August each year and includes Acadian dance performances, cabaret, and concerts as well as sporting contests. The highlight of the festival is "L' Acadie en Fête," a huge celebration involving Acadian musicians, singers, artists, and actors.

Acadian Festival
Length varies, usually 3–4 days at the end of June

The Madawaska Territory, which at one time ran along the Canadian border between Maine and New Brunswick, was settled by a small group of farmers who were chased out of Acadia by the English in the late eighteenth century. As the settlements grew, they were separated into Canadian and American communities, with Edmundston on the Canadian side and Madawaska and St. David on the American side of the St. John River.

In 1978 the local historical society in Madawaska proclaimed June 28 as Acadian Day in the state of Maine, and since that time it has been the site of an Acadian (or French-Canadian) festival lasting anywhere from one day to a week. Regular events include French music and dancing, an Acadian Supper featuring *pot en pot* and *fougère*, a parade with bands and marching units from both Maine and Canada, and an Acadian Mass followed by a procession to the white marble cross that marks the site of the original Acadian settlement. The festival usually coincides with a reunion of the original thirteen families who settled here.

Acadiens, Festivals
Third weekend in September

A combination of several festivals (food, music, crafts, and more) to celebrate the Cajun culture in Lafayette, La., known as the capital of French Louisiana. When they were expelled from Nova Scotia by the British in the 1770s, the French Acadian farmers settled in the area around Lafayette in a region of twenty-two parishes that came to be known as Acadiana. Cajun comes from Acadian.

One part of the celebration is the Bayou Food Festival, which offers a range of Cajun cooking from crawfish gumbo to alligator sausage to corn maque-chou. The Louisiana Native Crafts Festival features handmade Cajun crafts and demonstrations by blacksmiths, decoy carvers, alligator skinners, and story tellers. The Festival de Musique Acadienne features centuries-old music sung in French. Modern crafts are also on exhibit, and lectures and workshops on the Acadian language and history are part of the weekend.

Adelaide Cup Day *See* **Hobart Cup Day**

Adelaide Festival of the Arts
February–March in even-numbered years

The city of Adelaide, South Australia was geographically isolated and a cultural wasteland until a group of businessmen got together in 1960 and decided that what their city needed was a festival of the arts. The resulting event, which has been held biennially since that time, put Adelaide on the map and made it one of the world's top performing arts centers. In addition to the events held in the Adelaide Festival Centre, the Festival Theatre, and four other theaters built especially to accommodate the more than three hundred festival performances, other programs are held across the city in smaller theaters, town halls, clubs, parks, and in the streets. There is chamber music, classical ballet, symphony concerts, modern jazz, and rock music in addition to experimental plays, poetry readings, mime, and workshops where literary ideas, directions, and styles are discussed.

Admission Day
Varies from state to state

Many American states celebrate the anniversary of their admission to the Union by observing a public holiday on or near the actual day. Sometimes the day is referred to by the name of the state—as in **Colorado Day, Indiana Day, Nevada Day**, or West Virginia Day—and is marked by special celebrations. Other states let the anniversary of their admission pass unnoticed. In Vermont, admission day coincides with VERMONT TOWN MEETING DAY.

Adults Day *See* Seijin-no-hi

Advent
Sunday closest to November 30 through December 24 in West; November 15 through December 24 in East

The Advent season marks the beginning of the Christian year in Western Christianity. Its length varies from twenty-two to twenty-eight days, beginning on the Sunday nearest to St. Andrew's Day and encompassing the next three Sundays, ending on CHRISTMAS EVE.

In the Roman Catholic Church and those of the Anglican Communion the third Sunday is called Gaudete Sunday, from the first word of the introit, "Rejoice." Rose-colored vestments may replace the purple, and flowers may be on the altar. Originally a period of reflection and penitence in preparation for CHRISTMAS—in much the same way that LENT is in preparation for EASTER—Advent has sometimes been referred to as the **Winter Lent.** But over time the restrictions of Advent have become greatly relaxed. Today it is usually associated with the Advent calendars that parents give their children to help them count the days until Christmas.

In Orthodox (Eastern) Christianity, the church year begins on September 1, and Advent begins on November 15. The Advent fast is called the **Little Lent**, because it's shorter than the **Great Lent** preceding Easter.

Afghan Independence Day *See* Jeshn

African Methodist Quarterly Meeting Day
Last Saturday in August

The **Big August Quarterly** of the African Union Methodist Protestant Church, which takes place annually in Wilmington, Delaware, celebrates the founding of the A.U.M.P. Church in 1813 as the "Mother Church" for African-Americans. The first independent black congregation in Wilmington was started by an influential black religious leader named Peter Spencer, who led a group of forty-one followers out of Wilmington's Asbury Methodist Church in 1805 because white members of the congregation refused to let them participate fully in the services. Before the Civil War, slaves in the surrounding areas were given time off to attend this special weekend of revival

preaching, gospel singing, and reunions with family and friends.

Modeled on the Quakers' quarterly meetings, it was originally a rousing religious festival that drew tens of thousands of African-Americans from Delaware and the surrounding states. Although it no longer draws the crowds it used to, the Big August Quarterly has undergone a resurgence in recent years. It features soul food, musical entertainment, and an opportunity for people to reminisce about the Big August Quarterlies of the past.

Ages, Festival of the *See* Jidai Matsuri

Agricultural Field Days *See* National Fieldays

Agriculture Fair at Santarém, National
Second week in June

The most important agricultural fair in Portugal is held during the second week in June each year at Santarém, capital of the rich agricultural province of Ribatejo. Although the focus of the **Ribatejo Fair** is on farming and livestock breeding, there is also a colorful program of bullfighting, folk singing, and dancing, as well as a procession of *campinos* or bull-herders. Many other European countries exhibit farm animals and machinery at the **Feira Nacional de Agricultura**. Santarém is also the site of an annual gastronomy festival in October, which focuses on traditional cooking from all over the country.

Agua, La Fiesta de
First Sunday in October

A ritual cleansing festival held in San Pedro de Casta, Peru, the **Water Festival** pays homage to Pariapunko, the god of the Water. The town mayor goes to the cave where Pariapunko is believed to reside and implores him to flood the community with fresh water. Then La Toma, the gate that holds back the Carhuayumac River, is opened and the water is allowed to course through the irrigation ditches that have just been cleaned and repaired. A procession of horsemen accompanies the water as it makes its way to the gorge of Carhuayumac.

Agwunsi Festival
August–September

Agwunsi is the god of healing and divination among the Igbo people of Nigeria. He is also the patron of doctors, because he gives herbs and other medicines their power to cure. On the

Agwunsi feast day, patients who have been healed send animals as a token of gratitude to the doctors who cured them.

Airing the Classics
Sixth day of sixth lunar month

In China the **Double Sixth** is the day when the Buddhist monasteries examine the books in their library collections to make sure that they haven't been damaged. It commemorates the time when the boat carrying the Buddhist scriptures from India was upset at a river crossing, and all the books had to be spread out to dry. Setting aside a special day for "Airing the Classics" is especially important in tropical climates, where books are more susceptible to mold and insects. It is also the day when women shampoo their hair and bathe their pets.

Air Races, National Championship
Four days ending on second weekend after Labor Day

A four-day nostalgia trip for air buffs, held since 1964 in Reno, Nev. About 95 to 100 aircraft are generally registered for the races, providing some 150,000 spectators with the sight and sound of piston-engine planes flying around closed-pylon race courses. The planes entered include such World War II planes as the powerful P-51 Mustang and the bent-wing Chance-Vought F2G Corsair; the eerie sound the Corsair made was called "whistling death" by the Japanese of WWII. The race is the only one in the world that covers all four classes: Unlimited (vintage and modified warbirds and homebuilt racers), AT-6 (WWII pilot trainers), Formula One (super-midget planes), and Biplane (double-winged barn stormers). Air shows of military demonstrations, parachuting exhibits, and military fly-bys are also part of the events.

Ak-Sar-Ben Livestock Exposition and Rodeo
September/October

Billed as the "World's Largest 4-H Livestock Show," the Ak-Sar-Ben (Nebraska spelled backwards) Livestock Exposition and Rodeo in Omaha dates back to 1928, when its purpose was to get the state's young people interested in livestock breeding. It was originally a full-scale national breed show, but when parimutuel racing (when run by nonprofit agricultural organizations) was legalized by the state in the mid-1930s, thoroughbred racing became an important part of the event. A significant percentage of the profits is contributed to agricultural research.

The exposition lasts five days and features a World Championship Rodeo, a Catch-a-Calf contest, and entertainment by well-known country and western stars. But the show's main purpose is to showcase 4-H activities.

Alabama Blueberry Festival
Third Saturday in June

A one-day celebration of the blueberry in Brewton, Ala., the only area of Alabama still shipping blueberries commercially. The celebration, dedicated to Dr. W. T. Brightwell, whose improved varieties of Rabbiteye blueberry were introduced here in 1961, features tours of the local blueberry farms. Events include live entertainment, children's rides, arts and crafts, a food contest, and food booths selling all kinds of locally prepared blueberry dishes, among them cobbler, waffles, ice cream and cakes. Attendance is about 28,000.

Alacitas Fair
January 24

For hundreds of years the Aymara Indians of Bolivia have held an annual celebration at La Paz in honor of their god of prosperity named Ekeko, a little man with a big belly, an open mouth, outstretched arms, and wearing a backpack. Miniature replicas of Ekeko are sold, as well as miniature items of food, clothing, and other goods that the Aymaras would like to have. They believe that if they fill one of Ekeko's packs with these miniature objects, he will bring them the real things they represent. The children cry "Alacitas!", which means "Buy me!"

Alamo Day
March 6

The cry "Remember the Alamo!" has particular significance for the natives of Texas, which was once part of Mexico. In 1836 a garrison of Texans took a stand against the Mexican army at a Franciscan mission in San Antonio named after the grove of cottonwood trees (*alamo* in Spanish) that surrounded it. Lead by Lieutenant William Barret Travis, the band of 187 volunteers, including border heros Davy Crockett and James Bowie, was besieged for thirteen days by nearly 3,000–5,000 Mexicans under the leadership of General Antonio López de Santa Anna. Travis refused to surrender and the Alamo was overrun by the opposing army on the morning of March 6. Only women and children among the defenders survived. The heroic action at the Alamo gave the Texans time to organize the forces necessary to save their independence movement. Six weeks after the Alamo's fall, General Sam Houston defeated and captured

Santa Anna at the battle of San Jacinto (see SAN JACINTO DAY), forcing him to sign a treaty recognizing Texas's independence. Since 1897, this day has been celebrated as **Texas Heroes' Day.**

Alaska Day
October 18

An official holiday in America's forty-ninth and largest state, Alaska Day commemorates the formal transfer of Alaska from Russia to the United States on October 18, 1867. The event, which took place at Sitka, was a sad one for the Russian colonists who had already made Alaska their home, and it must have seemed that Mother Nature was conspiring against them. A strong wind caught the Russian flag during the transfer ceremony, tangling it in the halyards. The seaman who was finally hoisted up to free it dropped the flag by mistake, and another gust swept it into a group of Russian bayonets. The tattered remains were presented to the weeping wife of Prince Dmitri Maksoutsoff, the last Russian governor. Today the lowering of the Russian flag and the raising of the Stars and Stripes is reenacted every year as part of this three-day festival in Sitka.

After the transfer, Alaska was eventually organized as a territory and maintained this status until it became a state on January 3, 1959.

Alaska Festival of Music
June

A major cultural event in Alaska, held since 1956 in Anchorage. The festival, held on five evenings in June, emphasizes chamber music, although a full orchestral/choral work has become the traditional finale each year. Both international and Alaskan musicians perform. There are pre-concert lectures and midnight-sun receptions after the performances, giving patrons a chance to meet the artists.

Albuquerque International Balloon Fiesta
Early October

The world's largest gathering of hot-air balloonists. More than 500 balloons, some more than six stories high, present dizzying colors and designs in the skies of New Mexico for a nine-day fiesta that attracts about a million spectators. Besides the daytime ascensions, illuminated balloons light up the night skies. The fiesta also boasts skydivers, marching bands, and food of all sorts.

See also HOT AIR BALLOON CHAMPIONSHIP, NATIONAL.

Alexandra Rose Day
A Saturday in June

Sometimes called **Alexandra Day** or simply **Rose Day**, this day commemorates the arrival of Queen Alexandra, wife of King Edward VII, in England on June 26, 1912. The Danish-born queen died thirteen years later, but the day is still celebrated by selling rose emblems to raise money for hospitals. See HOSPITAL DAY.

Alholland Eve *See* Halloween.

All American Championships Sled Dog Races
Third weekend in January

Originally known as the **Minnesota Arrowhead Championship**, this annual racing event is held in Ely, Minnesota on the third weekend in January, when the snow is at its deepest. Contestants come from all over Canada, Alaska, and as far east as New Hampshire to compete in the two-day event, sometimes referred to as the **Ely All-American**. Both sprints and endurance racing—which requires larger teams of dogs and much longer courses—are included in the championships. Spectators gather at crossings, checkpoints, and rest stops to watch the mushers and their teams pass. The races are run against the clock, and the fastest time for two days wins.

Ely is home to Will Steger, the man who led sled-dog-powered expeditions to the North and South Poles and who is largely responsible for the increased attention being paid to the sport. Other important sled dog races in the state include the Cannon Valley Classic, also in January, and the Beargrease Dog Sled Marathon, which runs over five hundred miles from Duluth to Grand Portage and back. The latter commemorates John Beargrease, a Chippewa Indian who carried the mail by dog sled.

All American Indian Days
Last weekend in July or first weekend in August

This three-day celebration, held annually in Sheridan, Wyoming, was established in 1953 as a means of promoting understanding and respect for the area's American Indians. Sheridan has a long history of conflict between the Indians and the United States Army; its founder, General Philip Sheridan, was known for his statement that "the only good Indian is a dead Indian." But after Lucy Yellowmule, a member of the Crow tribe, was chosen queen of the Sheridan-Wyo Rodeo in 1951, it became obvious that the old resentments had faded and that it was time to make a real effort to raise the local population's consciousness. Two years later the first All American Indian Days festival was held.

Today the event attracts thousands of American Indians from thirty tribes throughout the Southwest, the West Coast, and the Plains states. Participants in the Indian dances, athletic contests, and ceremonial events live in a tepee village which is also open to visitors. The tribes—primarily Crows, Cheyennes, and Sioux—compete in such activities as a tepee construction race, a war dance contest, and a special Crow version of football played by couples holding hands or linked by handkerchiefs. The celebration includes the crowning of Miss Indian America and the presentation of an award for the Outstanding Indian of the Year.

See also AMERICAN INDIAN DAY.

All-American Soap Box Derby
Second Saturday in August
The Soap Box Derby is a youth racing program that has been run nationally since 1934. The idea came from an Ohio journalist named Myron Scott, who was assigned to cover a race of gravity-propelled cars built by young boys in his home town of Dayton and was so impressed by the event that he began to develop a similar program on a nationwide scale. In 1935 the race was moved to Akron because of its hilly terrain, and the following year a permanent track was constructed through the efforts of the Works Progress Administration (WPA).

The World Championship finals held at Derby Downs in Akron consist of three racing divisions: the Stock Division for girls and boys ages nine through sixteen competing in simplified cars built from kits; the Kit Car Division for youngsters competing in more advanced models, although still using standardized kits and shells; and the Masters Division for girls and boys ages eleven through sixteen who want to test their creativity and design skills. They can build a car from scratch or purchase and assemble a Masters Kit and shell.

Competitors arrive on the Monday before the race and spend the week working on their cars, participating in trial runs, and relaxing before the big race on Saturday. The home-built cars used in the derby today bear little resemblance to derby cars in the 1930s, many of which were actually built out of soap boxes.

All Fools' Day *See* **April Fools' Day**

All Hallows' Day *See* **All Saints' Day**

All Saints' Day
November 1 in West; first Sunday after Pentecost in East
In the Roman Catholic, Anglican, and many Protestant churches, the first day of November is a celebration of all the Christian saints—particularly those who have no special feast days of their own. Also known as **All-Hallomas** or **All Hallow's Day**, the idea for this holy day goes back to the fourth century, when the Greek Christians kept a festival on the first Sunday after PENTECOST (in late May or early June) in honor of all martyrs and saints. When the Pantheon at Rome was converted into a Christian place of worship in the seventh century, Pope Boniface IV dedicated it to the Virgin and all the martyrs, and the anniversary of this event was celebrated on May 1.

Moving the day to November 1 may have been an attempt to supplant the pagan Festival of the Dead (also known as SAMHAIN or the feast of Saman, Lord of death), which had long been celebrated on November 1.

All Souls' Day
November 2 in West; 3 Saturdays prior to Lent and the day before Pentecost in East
Long before Christianity, the pagans had their **Festival of the Dead.** It was St. Odilo, the abbot of Cluny in France, who in the tenth century proposed that the day after ALL SAINTS' DAY be set aside in honor of the departed—particularly those whose souls were still in purgatory. Today, the souls of all the faithful departed are commemorated. Although All Souls' Day is observed informally by some Protestants, it is primarily a Roman Catholic, Anglican, and Orthodox holy day.

In many Catholic countries, people attend churches, which are appropriately draped in black, and visit family graves on this day to honor their ancestors. In Shropshire and Cheshire, England, children still go out "souling" from house to house, although they are no longer given the traditional "soul cakes" that were supposed to rescue souls from purgatory. The evening of November 1 is often called All Souls' Eve and is a time to decorate graveyards and light candles in memory of the dead.

Orthodox Christians commemorate the dead on the three Saturdays prior to Lent and on the day before Pentecost.

In Mexico, it is a national holiday called the **Día de los Muertos 'Day of the Dead'**. The Spanish-Indians believe that the spirits of the dead return to enjoy a visit with their friends and relatives on this day. Long before sunrise, people stream into the cemeteries laden with candles, flowers, and food that is often shaped and decorated to resemble the symbols of death. Children eat tiny chocolate hearses, sugar funeral wreaths, and candy skulls and coffins. But the atmosphere is festive.

In many homes the Indians set up *ofrendas*, or altars to the departed. These are decked with lighted candles, special foods, and whatever the dead enjoyed when they were alive. The Day of the Dead is also a popular time to see performances of the ancient Spanish drama *Don Juan Tenorio*, about a reckless lover who kills the father of a woman he has tried to seduce and then erects a statue of his victim. The statue eventually comes alive and drags Don Juan down to hell to account for his crimes.

In Portugal, November 2 is known as **Día dos Finados** (All Souls' Day) and is observed with special Masses and processions to cemeteries. Similar celebrations are held for All Souls' Day in Ecuador, El Salvador, the French West Indies, Macao, and Uruguay. In the United States, **el Día de Los Muertos** is celebrated in areas such as Los Angeles, Calif. where there is a large Mexican-American population.

In Italy **Il Giorno dei Morti** or All Souls' Day begins at dawn with a solemn Requiem for the dead. Church bells toll and people decorate the graves of their family members with flowers and candles. But Il Giorno dei Morti is not entirely a somber occasion. In Sicily the children who have prayed for the *morti* or souls of the departed leave their shoes outside doors and windows, where they are filled with gifts. In Rome, it is customary for young people to announce their engagements on the Day of the Dead. The man sends the engagement ring to his fiancée in a small white box, which in turn is packed in an oval container filled with *fave dei morti* or 'beans of the dead'—little bean-shaped cakes made of ground almonds and sugar combined with eggs, butter, and flour.

Almabtrieb
September

The **Return from the Mountain Pasture** is an autumn festival that takes place in the German Alps on the day that the cattle are driven down from the mountain pastures to their winter shelter. The cattle are decorated with flowers and the *Sennerinnen* 'herd-girls' who lead them wear traditional costumes that vary from place to place. Sometimes the cattle are brought to their final destination on flower-decked boats that ferry them across the mountain lakes. Once the cattle are safely in for the winter, the farmers hold welcome home feasts which are followed by music, dancing, and singing.

See also ALPAUFZUG.

Alma Highland Festival and Games
Memorial Day weekend

Like other American cities and towns founded or settled primarily by Scots, Alma, Michigan celebrates its Scottish heritage by holding a traditional Highland Festival for three days in late May each year. The festival was originated by a local resident who attended the Scottish games in Boston in 1962 and decided that a similar event should be held in Alma, a city founded by Scots and with a Scottish name. Activities include Scottish athletic events, border collie demonstrations, fiddling contests, an arts and crafts show, piping, drumming, and highland dancing. Participants come from all over the United States and Canada, and some even come from Scotland. The food served at the festival includes meat pies, haggis (a traditional Scottish dish made from the heart, liver, etc. of a sheep or calf, minced with suet and oatmeal, seasoned, and boiled in the stomach of the animal), bridies (hot sausage or meat rolls), and shortbread.

Aloha Week Festivals
September–October

A celebration of Hawaiian culture that was once a week long. Now it's a two-month affair that starts in Honolulu in early September and runs through the end of October, with a week of festivities on every island of Hawaii. The celebrations include canoe races between the islands of Molokai and Oahu, coronations of royal courts as commemorations of the former Hawaiian monarchy, street parties, and parades and pageantry.

Alpaufzug
May or June

An old custom in Switzerland is this springtime 'ascent to the mountains,' when goats and cows are driven to higher pasture. In the canton of Appenzell in eastern Switzerland and also in the Alpine canton of Valais, there are picturesque festivals, with herders and their families dressing in traditional costume (the Appenzell men wear red vests and yellow knicker-type pants) and everyone enjoying the cow fights that establish the leader of the herd. In September and October, bringing the herds back down to the valleys, known as *Alpabfahrten*, also prompts festivals, and the cow that has been the greatest milk producer is feted and decked with flowers.

Alpenfest
Third week in July

At an altitude of 1,348 feet, Gaylord is one of the highest incorporated communities in Michigan. Five rivers rise nearby and flow in different directions. Gaylord receives nearly 150 inches of snow each year and the town's main streets are lined with Swiss-style architecture. The annual Alpenfest is basically a celebration of summer.

A highlight of the festival is the "Burning of the Boog." People write their troubles on slips of paper and place them in the "Boog"—a three-hundred-pound, ten-foot-high monster—which is then burned, giving spectators a chance to watch their troubles literally go up in smoke. The festival also boasts a number of outdoor cafes which host "the World's Largest Coffee Break."

Amarnath Yatra
July–August; full moon of Sravana

A pilgrimage to the Amarnath Cave, high in the Kashmir Himalayas, near Pahalgam, in northern India. This cave holds a natural ice lingam, the Hindu phallic symbol of Lord Shiva. The trek to the cave, at an altitude of about 12,700 feet, is along narrow, winding mountain trails. The thousands of pilgrims who make this trip include everyone from *sadhus* (holy men) walking barefoot over the stones and snow to wealthy people being carried by coolies.

American Birkebeiner
Three days in late February

The Birkie started in 1973 as a fifty-five kilometer cross-country ski race from Hayward, Wisconsin to Telemark Lodge in the neighboring town of Cable, with only thirty-five skiers competing. Now it is the largest and most prestigious cross-country ski race in North America, an event that attracts top cross-country skiers from all over the world. In addition to the fifty-five kilometer Birkie, there is also the Kortelopet or "short race" of twenty-nine kilometers, which is open to competitors ages thirteen and up. Other races held during the three-day festival include the Barnebirkie (for children), the Jack Rabbit 10K Classic, telemark race (cross-country skiing on a downhill slalom course), and a biathlon competition combining cross-country ski racing and target shooting. The American Birkebeiner is part of the Worldloppet, an international series of twelve marathon races held in Japan, Switzerland, Sweden, Norway, France, Germany, Austria, Finland, Italy, Canada, Australia, and the United States.

The American race was patterned after the Birkebeiner Rennet in Lillehammer, Norway. During the thirteenth century, a foreign invader was about to capture Norway's infant prince and heir to the throne. He was saved by two Viking warriors-called "Birkebeiners" for the birch-bark leggings they wore. These men took the child and skied fifty-five kilometers to safety. The baby eventually became the great Norwegian king, Haakon Haakonson.

American Folklife, Festival of
Last weekend in June, first weekend in July

Since 1967 the Festival of American Folklife has been held on the National Mall in Washington, D.C. to celebrate the richness and diversity of American and world cultures. Since that time the Festival has presented more than fifteen thousand musicians, craftspeople, storytellers, cooks, workers, performers, and other cultural specialists from every region of the United States and from more than forty-five other nations. Recent festival programs have included musicians from the former Soviet Union, demonstrations of African-American coil basketry and Italian-American stone-carving, the performance of a Japanese rice-planting ritual, and exhibits illustrating the occupational cultures of working people—taxicab drivers, firefighters, waiters, and railway workers.

The Festival is designed to expose visitors to people and cultures who would not ordinarily be heard in a national setting. It emphasizes folk, tribal, ethnic, and regional traditions in communities throughout the U. S. and abroad. Each year the festival features a particular state (or region) and country. One year, for example, the featured region was "Family Farming in the Heartland." More than a hundred farmers from twelve Midwestern states came to the nation's capital to talk to visitors about changes in farming methods and farm life, and to demonstrate both modern and traditional farming skills. The featured country was Indonesia, and there were demonstrations of Buginese boat-building and traditional mask carving, in addition to an all-night Indonesian shadow-puppet show.

American Indian Day
Various

In 1914 Red Fox James of the Blackfeet tribe

rode a pony 4,000 miles to present his request—endorsed by the governors of twenty-four states—that a day be set aside in honor of American Indians, or Native Americans, a name many prefer. The first general American Indian Day was observed on the second Saturday in May 1916, but now the observance and its date are left to the individual states and they vary widely. A number of states—including Illinois, Arizona, California, and Connecticut—observe it on the fourth Friday in September. Massachusetts, New York State, Oklahoma, and Maine have chosen different dates, or vary the date from year to year. In South Dakota it is called **Native Americans' Day**, and is celebrated on the second Monday in October.

Although the holiday has not yet gained nationwide recognition, few would argue that the plight of American Indians today is a grim one, with unemployment, illiteracy, and high school drop-out rates among the highest in the country. Although the largest Indian populations can be found in Oklahoma, Arizona, California, New Mexico, and North Carolina, many other states have come up with ways to draw attention to their unique contribution to American culture and to the need for improving their condition. Most celebrations focus on educational and promotional events, displays of Native American art and dance, and agricultural fairs.

See also ALL AMERICAN INDIAN DAYS.

American Royal Livestock, Horse Show and Rodeo

Two weeks in November

Also known as the **American Royal** or simply **The Royal**, this is the oldest and one of the largest livestock shows and rodeos in the United States. It dates back to the period just after the Civil War, when Texans returning from the battlefield discovered that their cattle herds had multiplied unchecked. They were forced to conduct massive roundups that reached as far west as Kansas City, Missouri, which soon became a center for the consignment of cattle. Meat packers started building plants there to accommodate the supply, and breeders began to show their stock. The National Hereford Show, held in the Kansas City Stockyards in 1899, is now considered the first American Royal. Over the years the Hereford breeders were joined by breeders of other cattle as well as sheep, swine, and poultry. Draft and carriage horses were first shown at the Royal in 1903.

Although the Royal has suffered some setbacks over the years-including a fire that nearly destroyed the American Royal Building in 1922 and a serious flood in 1951—it has continued to expand and now draws more than 300,000 visitors. There are special tours and instruction for school children, 20,000 of whom come to the show to learn more about agribusiness. The **American Royal Rodeo** is the first rodeo of the season on the professional circuit, featuring over seven hundred professional riders and offering over $100,000 in prize money. There are also livestock auctions, barbecue competitions, and a parade through downtown Kansas City that has been called America's largest hometown parade.

America's Cup, The

Held whenever The Cup is challenged, usually every 3–4 years

Named for the trophy, originally called the Hundred Guinea Cup by the Royal Yacht Squadron of Great Britain, that was won by the 100-foot schooner *America* in a race around the Isle of Wight in 1851. The America's Cup races are the world's longest-running international sporting event. The Cup was given by *America*'s owner, J.C. Stevens, to the New York Yacht Club, who successfully defended it against international challenges for 130 years. In 1984, the challenger *Australia II* defeated the American defender *Courageous* in races off Newport, Rhode Island, marking the end of the longest winning streak in international sports. In 1987, the American challenger *Stars & Stripes*, sailing for the San Diego Yacht Club, regained the Cup in races off Perth, Australia. *Stars & Stripes* succesfully defended the cup in 1988 against New Zealand, and in 1992 *America³* retained the Cup for the United States by defeating the Italian boat four races to one.

The race is usually held every three to four years, with challengers coming from England, Canada, France, Sweden, Italy, New Zealand, Australia, Japan, and other countries. The rules require that the defenders and challengers sail in closely matched boats built to the same general specifications, but designs have varied over the years as sailing technology has grown more sophisticated. A new class of boats, the America's Cup class, was introduced in 1991.

America's Discovery Day *See* Columbus Day

Anastenaria

May 21–23

A fire-walking ceremony in Greece, in the communes of Agia Eleni near Serres and of Langada near Thessalonike. Men and women, some holding red kerchiefs and some carrying icons of St. Constantine and St. Helen—in whose honor the ceremonies are held—dance barefooted on red-hot coals while folk musicians play. The custom is supposed to have originated in an ancient form of worship that was brought by travelers from Kosti in Eastern Thrace and adapted to Christian beliefs.

Fire walking has been practiced in many parts of the world and has been thought at times to ensure a good harvest and at other times to purify the participants.

Anchorage Fur Rendezvous
Mid–February (February 14–23 in 1992)
A ten-day city-wide celebration, also called the Rondy and sometimes the Mardi Gras of the North, held in Anchorage, Alaska. The Rondy had its origins in the days when fur trappers, joined by miners, capped off a season of trapping by carousing in Anchorage; this annual rendezvous was formalized as a winter carnival in 1936.

Highlighting the celebration is the World Championship Sled Dog Race, a seventy-five-mile race run in three twenty-five-mile legs on three successive days, starting and ending in Anchorage. Contestants come from throughout the United States. Other contests include one for Mr. Fur Face, obviously the man with the most luxuriant beard. Among the scores of other events and exhibits are parades, the Miners and Trappers Ball, Eskimo blanket tossing, Eskimo dances, a snowshoe baseball game, wrestling matches, and performances of an old-time melodrama. Special Alaskan foods sold include sourdough pancakes.

See also IDITAROD TRAIL SLED DOG RACE.

Andorra National Day
September 8
The Principality of Andorra, located in the Pyrenees Mountains between France and Spain, was founded by the Emperor Charlemagne, who recovered the region from the Muslims in 803. His son later granted part of his empire to the Spanish bishop of Urgel, and by the late thirteenth century the citizens of Andorra were ruled by two princes, one in Spain and one in France. Ever since that time, the principality has been been governed jointly by the bishop of Urgel and the president of France. On September 8, 1278, Andorra's first constitutional document, known as the "Pareatges," was signed. Among other things, it

stated that each of the co-rulers would receive a token tribute each year known as the Questia. The president receives $2 biennially; the bishop $8, plus six hams, six cheeses, and twelve hens in alternate years.

The people of Andorra celebrate their **National Day** by honoring Our Lady of Meritxell, their patron saint. Pilgrims climb to her hilltop sanctuary near the villages of Encamp and Canillo, where her statue was found by a shepherd under an almond tree (some say rose bush) blooming out of season. The pilgrims stop to refresh themselves with drinks that have been cooled in the nearby springs, and after the sermon, they celebrate by dancing and eating lamb grilled on slabs of slate.

Andrew Jackson's Birthday
March 15
Andrew Jackson (1767–1845), the seventh president of the United States (1829–1837), became a national hero during the War of 1812 when he successfully fought the British at New Orleans, despite the fact that he was so sick he could barely stand without assistance, and no one knew that a peace treaty had been signed two weeks earlier. His soldiers thought he was as "tough as hickory," resulting in his nickname, "Old Hickory." The anniversary of his birth is a legal holiday in Tennessee, and the President of the United States usually brings or sends a wreath to be placed on Jackson's grave in the garden at his home The Hermitage, near Nashville.

Other tributes paid to Jackson during this week include radio speeches and newspaper editorials, school essay contests, and Jackson Day dinners sponsored by the Democratic party, of which he is considered one of the founders. Sometimes these celebrations are held on January 8, BATTLE OF NEW ORLEANS DAY. In Virginia, Jackson's birthday is celebrated in January along with those of Martin Luther King, Jr. and Robert E. Lee (see LEE-JACKSON-KING DAY).

Angelitos, Los
October 30
For the Mayan Indians of the Yucatán Peninsula in southeastern Mexico, October 30 was a day devoted to children who had died—the *angelitos* 'little angels.' It was customary for families to decorate their doors with flowers and to prepare special foods for the *angelitos* who would visit them that night. Los Angelitos marked the beginning of the period during which all the dead were commemorated.

Today, Mexican Indians celebrate the DAY OF THE DEAD, or Día de los Muertos, on November 2.

Annie Oakley Festival
Last full week in July

The legendary markswoman known as Annie Oakley was born Phoebe Ann Moses near Willow Dell, Ohio on August 13, 1860. Her father died when she was very young, and Annie learned to shoot game for her family with her father's rifle. At the age of fifteen she was invited to participate in a shooting match in Cincinnati with Frank Butler, a champion marksman. She won the match and married Butler a year later. Together they toured the country with their shooting act, "Butler and Oakley," and in 1884 they joined Buffalo Bill's Wild West Show. They performed with the show throughout Europe and the United States for seventeen years, including a command performance for Queen Victoria during her Jubilee year (1887). Annie and Frank returned to Ohio in the 1920s to be near their family and friends. She died in Greenville on November 3, 1926 and he died eighteen days later.

The Annie Oakley Festival in Greenville commemorates "Little Miss Sure Shot" (as she was dubbed by the great Sioux Indian Chief, Sitting Bull) with eight days of shooting and sports competitions and demonstrations of hide tanning, knife throwing, bead working, and other activities associated with the Old West. There is a tour of Annie Oakley's gravesite and a Miss Annie Oakley Shooting Contest for young girls. A highlight of the festival is the Annie Oakley Days Parade on the last day.

Anniversary Day *See* Australia Day

Annual Patriots' Weekend
Last weekend in September

Initiated in 1975, the Annual Patriots' Weekend held in the Bethel/Redding area of Connecticut honors all American patriots, from the Revolutionary War to the Persian Gulf War. Held at the Putnam Memorial State Park, activities include encampments of both British and American soldiers, artillery demonstrations, infantry drills, and crafts of the Revolutionary period. In the late afternoon, there is a parade to the park's Revolutionary War battlefield. This is followed by a battle reenactment that is unusual in that it does not attempt to replay the historic events. Instead both sides fight to win using the same military tactics that were used during the Revolution (but without live ammunition, of course). Spectators are kept a safe distance away, but they are encouraged to observe and ask questions. In some years, depending upon the availability of horses, there are cavalry demonstrations as well.

Annunciation of the Blessed Virgin Mary, Feast of the
March 25

This day celebrates the appearance of the Archangel Gabriel to the Virgin Mary announcing that she was to become the mother of Jesus. The date for this feast couldn't have been fixed until the date of CHRISTMAS was established, and obviously the two dates had to be nine months apart. In England, the feast of the Annunciation is commonly called LADY DAY.

Annunciation usually falls during LENT, and is kept as a feast day in the midst of the Lenten fast. If it should happen to fall on MAUNDY THURSDAY or GOOD FRIDAY, it is transferred to a date following EASTER. According to medieval superstition, it was a bad omen when Easter and the Annunciation fell on the same day.

In Sweden it was called *Varfrudagen* 'our Lady's Day.' Common pronunciation turned it into *Vaffeldagen* 'waffle day.' This is the source of heart-shaped waffle irons: the waffles commemorate the heart of the Virgin Mary.

Anthesteria
February–March

A spring festival held for three days annually in ancient Athens during the month of Anthesterion (February-March). Its purpose was to celebrate the beginning of spring and the maturing of the wine stored during the previous year. The first day was celebrated by tasting the new wine from the previous vintage. This was known as the Pithoigia 'opening of the casks'. The second day, the Choes or 'pitcher feast', was a merry celebration of the marriage of the chief archon's (magistrate's) wife to the god Bacchus. A festival of the dead was held on the third day. This was called the Chutroi or 'feast of pots.' This was a time of mourning to honor the dead, and to placate or expel ghosts. The three days of the Anthesteria incorporated the theme of birth-growth-death.

Antique and Classic Boat Rendezvous
Last weekend in July

Every July since 1975, classic wooden yachts of pre-1952 vintage have gathered for the annual Antique and Classic Boat Rendezvous at Mystic Seaport Museum in Mystic, Connecticut. Although some boats built as early as 1890 have participated, most date from the 1920s to the 1940s. Many are one-of-a-kind and have been kept in mint condition by their owners. More than fifty boats from throughout the Northeast participate each year, making it one of the largest gatherings of its kind.

The boats can be viewed at dockside on Friday evening and early on Saturday. Saturday afternoon the vessels begin their colorful parade down the Mystic River to Noank, led by the museum's eighty-four-year-old steamboat *Sabino* with a Dixieland jazz band on board. The boats are "dressed" with brightly-colored signal flags, and many carry crews in period costumes as they compete for awards in various categories.

Antrosht (Mother's Day)
October–November

There is no fixed date for this holiday in Ethiopia because it occurs whenever the rainy season ends. Girls and boys come from all over to visit their parents, the girls bringing the necessary ingredients for a vegetable hash and the boys bringing with them a bull or a lamb which they slaughter the next day so their mothers can prepare a meat hash. The mother and the girls anoint themselves with butter, and songs celebrating family and tribal heroes are sung. The entire festival lasts two or three days, and each time the children arrive and leave, they kiss their parents and receive their blessings.

Anzac Day
April 25

A national holiday in Australia and New Zealand, this day takes its name from the initial letters of "Australia and New Zealand Army Corps." It commemorates the landing of the Anzac troops on the Gallipoli Peninsula in European Turkey on April 25, 1915 during World War I. Like MEMORIAL DAY in the U.S., this day is celebrated with veterans' parades and church services. Observed as a holiday since 1920, Anzac Day now honors those who have died in both world wars as well as in Korea and Vietnam.

Aoi Matsuri (Hollyhock Festival)
May 15

One of the three major festivals of Kyoto, Japan, believed to date from the sixth century. The festival's name derives from the hollyhock leaves adorning the headdresses of the participants; legend says hollyhocks help prevent storms and earthquakes. The festival owes its present form to the time in the Heian Period (792–1099) when

imperial messengers were sent to the Kyoto shrines of Shimogamo and Kamigamo after a plague (or a flood) that came about because the shrines were neglected. Today the festival, which was revived in 1884, consists of a recreation of the original imperial procession. Some 500 people in ancient costume parade with horses and large lacquered oxcarts carrying the "imperial messengers" from the Kyoto Imperial Palace to the shrines.

Also see JIDAI MATSURI and GION MATSURI.

Apache Maidens' Puberty Rites
July 4

A celebration of the coming-of-age of girls of the Mescalero Apache Tribe, held for four days and four nights around the Fourth of July in Mescalero, N.M. Besides the puberty rites, there are other events: a rodeo, a powwow with cash prizes for dancers, a parade on July 4, and the nighttime Dance of the Mountain Gods.

The rites are related to the belief that soon after the creation of the world, White Painted Woman appeared in the east as a beautiful young woman, moved to the west, and disappeared when she was old. On the first and last days of the ceremonial, the girls must run around a basket four times, symbolically going through the four stages of life (infancy, childhood, adulthood, and old age). On the last day, their faces are painted with white clay and they enact the role of White Painted Woman, taking on her qualities and preparing for a rewarding adult life. On each of the four nights, the girls dance in the Holy Lodge, which was set up on the first day, while singers sing of the creation and beat time with deer-hoof rattles. The celebrations also involve feasting and elaborate ceremonial dresses.

In the 1800s, the U.S. government forbade the Apaches to congregate, but in 1911 decreed that they could congregate on July 4 to celebrate the nation's birthday. The Apaches then chose that date for their most important cultural ritual as an insult to their conquerors.

Apple and Candle Night
October 31

Another name for HALLOWEEN among the children in the Swansea, area of Wales. The traditional game of "Apple and Candle" is played by suspending a stick from the ceiling with an apple fastened to one end and a lit candle to the other. The object is to eat the apple without using hands and without getting burned by the swinging candle. To make the game more challenging, players are sometimes blindfolded and the stick is twirled around before the game begins.

See also MISCHIEF NIGHT.

Appomattox Day
April 9
The Civil War ended on April 9, 1865, in the village of Appomattox Court House, Virginia, when Lieutenant General Ulysses S. Grant of the Union army accepted the surrender of General Robert E. Lee of the Confederacy. The Confederate soldiers were allowed to keep their horses and return to their homes; the officers were allowed to retain their side arms and swords as well. Thus ended the bloody four-year conflict that had cost more than half a million lives.

The most widespread celebration of Appomattox Day took place in 1965 during the Civil War Centennial year. Thousands of people attended the ceremonies at the Appomattox Court House National Historical Park. Participants included the Union leader's grandson, Ulysses S. Grant III, as well as Robert E. Lee IV, great-grandson of the Confederate leader. The day was noted across the country—but particularly in the South—with costumed pageants, books and articles reflecting on the war, and concerts of martial music. Although the anniversary is not observed on a yearly basis, re-enactments of the historic surrender are held about once every five years.

April Fools' Day
April 1
There are many names for this day-including **All Fools' Day, April Noddy Day, Gowkie Day, Huntigowk Day,** and **St. All-Fools' Morn**—just as there are many practical jokes to play on the unsuspecting. One theory about its origin points to Noah as the first "April Fool." It is said that on that day he mistakenly sent the dove out to find dry land after the flood. Another points to the adoption of the Gregorian calendar in 1582, when NEW YEAR'S DAY was officially moved from March 25 to January 1. People who forgot about the change were often mocked by their friends, as they continued to make New Year visits just after the old March date.

The simplest pranks usually involve children who, for example, tell each other that their shoelaces are undone and then cry "April Fool!" when the victims glance at their feet. Sometimes the media get into the act, broadcasting fictitious news items designed to amuse or alarm the public.

British television, for example, once showed Italian farmers "harvesting" spaghetti from trees. The French call it **Fooling the April Fish Day** (the fool being the *poisson d'avril*) and try to pin a paper fish on someone's back without getting caught.

In Mexico, April Fools' Day is celebrated on December 28, HOLY INNOCENTS' DAY.

Araw ng Kagitingan *See* Bataan Day

Arbor Day
Last Friday in April; April 22 in Nebraska
Julius Sterling Morton, one of the earliest conservationists, settled on the treeless plains of Nebraska in 1855, where he edited the Nebraska City *News* and developed a lifelong interest in new agricultural methods. Believing that the prairie needed more trees to serve as windbreaks, to hold moisture in the soil, and to provide lumber for housing, Morgan began planting trees and urged his neighbors to do the same. On April 10, 1872, when he first proposed that a specific day be set aside for the planting of trees, the response was overwhelming: a million trees were planted in Nebraska on that day alone.

All fifty states now observe Arbor Day—usually on the last Friday in April—and the idea has spread to other countries as well. Most observances take place in the public schools, where the value of trees is discussed and trees and shrubs are planted. At the White House, the President, First Lady, or a presidential designate plants a special tree on the grounds each year on Arbor Day. But it is in Nebraska City, Nebraska that Morton is best remembered as the originator of Arbor Day, with celebrations taking place on his birthday, April 22. A special ceremony is held at Arbor Lodge, Morton's homestead and one of the earliest known attempts at conservation and beautification in America.

Some states call this day **Bird and Arbor Day**, emphasizing the planting of trees that are attractive to birds.

Argentine Independence Day
May 25
Argentina was originally one of a number of Spanish colonies controlled by the Spanish viceroy in Lima, Peru. When the colonies became too large to be controlled from one site, a separate viceroyalty was formed in 1776, with its headquarters in Buenos Aires.

On May 25, 1810, Buenos Aires declared its independence from the viceroyalty but continued to pledge loyalty to the Spanish crown. Although May 25 is observed throughout the country as Independence Day or **Argentine National Day**, independence from Spain wasn't declared until July 9, 1816—an event that provoked a long series of civil wars in which rival political leaders fought for national control. Both days are national holidays and are observed with religious services at the cathedral and special performances at the Colón Theatre in Buenos Aires. The city's *Plaza de Mayo* (May Square) was named for the month in which independence was declared.

Argungu Fishing Festival
February

A fishing and NEW YEAR festival held along a sacred mile of the Sokoto River, a tributary of the Niger River, near Argungu in northwestern Nigeria. About 5,000 men from throughout Nigeria take part in the approximately forty-five minutes of the frenzied fishing period. Using nets with calabashes (gourds) as floats, they can catch perch of up to 140 pounds. The largest perch are presented to the emirs (rulers) who hold the festival.

Armed Forces Day (Egypt)
October 6

An important national holiday in Egypt marking the surprise attack on Israel that began the October War of 1973 (also known as the Yom Kippur War). Egypt's ally in the war was Syria. The war ended with a cease-fire secured by the United States, and was declared a victory by Egyptian President Anwar el-Sadat. It strengthened his position and enabled him to seek an honorable peace with Israel. In 1974 and 1975, agreements were signed that paved the way for the return of the Sinai to Egypt in April, 1982; Israel had occupied the peninsula since the Six-Day War of 1967, in which Egypt had been crushed. In 1977, Sadat made his dramatic trip to Jerusalem to address the Israeli Knesset (Parliament); a year later, Sadat, Israeli Prime Minister Menachem Begin and United States President Jimmy Carter held talks at Camp David, Md., that led to the Israeli-Egyptian peace treaty of 1979.

The holiday is celebrated with grand parades, speeches by government officials, and fireworks. It was while reviewing a military parade on this day in 1981 that Anwar Sadat was assassinated by opponents of peace with Israel.

Armed Forces Day (U.S.)
Third Saturday in May

Before President Harry S Truman proclaimed the third Saturday in May as Armed Forces Day in 1949, the three major branches of the United States armed forces—the Army, the Navy, and the Air Force—held elaborate celebrations on three different days during the year. Although the service units continue to celebrate their own days on April 6 (Army), October 27 (Navy), the second Saturday in September (Air Force), and Nov 10 (Marine Corps, part of the Navy), the purpose of Armed Forces Day is to promote the unification of the three branches under the Department of Defense (which took place in 1947) and to pay tribute to those serving in all the armed forces.

While commemorations of the individual service units are usually confined to military bases, the celebration of Armed Forces Day entails much broader participation. In addition to the huge parade held on this day each year in New York City, the armed forces often hold "open house" to acquaint the public with their facilities and to demonstrate some of the latest technological advances.

Armenian Grape Festival *See* Blessing of the Grapes

Armenian Martyrs' Day
April 24

The day of rememberance for the one million Armenians who died in the Turkish massacre of 1915–16. On April 24, 1915, Turks arrested the Armenian political and intellectual leaders in Istanbul, killing 250 of them. That was the start of deportations, forced marches in the desert, rapes, and imprisonments that killed half the Armenian population in Turkey.

Armenian communities throughout the world observe this day. In the United States, many state governors issue proclamations of remembrance, and special programs, with speeches and prayers, are held in state capitols. There are also special services in Armenian churches.

Armistice Day *See* Veterans Day

Arrival of the Tooth Relic *See* Esala (Asadha) Perahera

Arts and Pageant of the Masters, Festival of
Mid–July–August

A display of art works in arty Laguna Beach,

Calif., along with breathtaking *tableaux vivants*—living pictures that recreate master art works. Since the 1940s, artists have created the tableaux to reproduce paintings by such varied masters as Leonardo da Vinci, Henri Matisse, and Winslow Homer. They don't stop there; they also transform delicate pieces of jewelry, sculptures, antique artifacts, and even scenes from postage stamps into life-size works of art. The tableaux, presented for two hours each evening at the Irvine Bowl, are created by some 300 models who have used 1,000 yards of fabric and 100 gallons of makeup. Example of a tableau: three gilded men and two gilded styrofoam horses appear in a setting that reproduces a five-inch Scythian gold comb.

Asarah be-Tevet (Tenth of Tevet)
Between December 13 and January 10; 10 Tevet
Asarah be-Tevet is a Jewish fast day commemorating the beginning of the siege of Jerusalem by the Babylonians under King Nebuchadnezzar in 586 B.C. that was a prelude to the destruction of the First Temple. The fast begins at first morning light on the tenth day of the month of Tevet.

In Israel it is a day to remember the victims of the Holocaust. However, Jews outside Israel observe YOM HA-SHOAH as the Holocaust Memorial Day.

Ascension Day
Between April 30 and June 3; forty days after Easter
Ascension Day is one of the earliest Christian festivals, dating back to the year 68. According to the New Testament, Jesus met several times with his disciples during the forty days after his Resurrection to instruct them in how to carry out his teachings. Then on the fortieth day he took them to the Mount of Olives, where they watched as he ascended to heaven.

Reflecting both Christian and pagan custom, Ascension Day celebrations include processions symbolizing Christ's entry into heaven and, in some countries, chasing a "devil" through the streets and ducking him in a pond or burning him in effigy—symbolic of the Messiah's triumph over the devil when he opened the kingdom of heaven to all believers.

Other customs attached to this day include "beating the bounds"—switching young boys with willow branches as they are driven along parish boundaries, not only to purify them of evil but to teach them the limits of their parish. This gave rise to the name **Bounds Thursday** in England,

where it is also sometimes called **Holy Thursday**, though in the rest of the world that applies to MAUNDY THURSDAY.

In Germany it is sometimes called Father's Day because Protestant men have *herrenpartien* 'outings' on this day. In Sweden many people go out to the woods at three or four o'clock to hear the birds at sunrise. It is good luck if a cuckoo is heard from the east or west. These jaunts are called *gök-otta* 'early cuckoo morning'.

See also BANNTAG.

Asheville Mountain Dance and Folk Festival
First Thursday, Friday and Saturday in August
The oldest folk and dance festival in the country, held since 1928 in Asheville, N.C. Dedicated to ancient southern Appalachian music, it draws more than 400 performers: dulcimer sweepers, tune bow and mouth harp players, mountain fiddlers, and dancers who compete in smooth and clog dancing. Bluegrass and old-time bands also are on hand. ("Bluegrass" is not named for the Kentucky grass, but for the Blue Grass Boys, a band formed in 1938 by Bill Monroe whose style of country popular music is still widely imitated. See BLUEGRASS FAN FEST.

Other events of the weekend include a quilt show and the Gee Haw Whimmy Diddle World Competition at the Folk Art Center, which usually draws about 50 contestants. The whimmy diddle, an Appalachian whittled folk toy, is a notched wooden gadget with a propeller on one end; when a stick is rubbed across the notches, the propeller spins. The idea of the contest is to control the spin, to make the propeller gee (turn to the right) and haw (turn to the left). The winners of cash prizes are those who get their whimmy diddle to change the direction of rotation the most times. There is also a cash prize for the Most Unusual and World's Largest Whimmy Diddle.

Ashura (Husain Day)
First ten days of Muharram
On the tenth of Muharram in the year 680, Muhammad's grandson Hussein was killed in a skirmish between Sunnis and the small group of Shi'ite supporters with whom he was travelling to Iraq. They had been cut off from water and had suffered for ten days before the men were killed and the women and children taken to Damascus, Syria, along with the heads of the men. His battlefield grave in Kerbela, about sixty miles southwest of Baghdad, became a pilgrimage site almost im-

mediately, and to this day it remains a devotional center for Shi'ite Muslims around the world. Many aging Shi'ites settle in Kerbela or ask in their will to have their bodies carried to the holy city. So many dead have been sent to Kerbela that the town has been transformed into one vast burial ground.

This Islamic holy day, celebrated in the first month of the Islamic year, was derived by Muhammad from the Jewish fast of Yom Kippur; he later changed it to an optional fast day and it is so observed by modern-day Sunni Muslims. But for Shi'ites throughout Asia, the festival is dedicated to Hussein and begins on the first day of Muharram, when people put on their mourning clothes and refrain from shaving or bathing. The story of Hussein's martyrdom is recited in Muslim halls, with as much elaboration as possible. The celebration culminates on the tenth day of Muharram, in a large procession designed as a reenactment of Hussein's funeral, with many men whipping themselves bloody with whips and knives to take on the pain of Hussein. Since the early nineteenth century, the Tenth of Muharram celebration has culminated in the performance of a *ta'ziyah* or Passion play in which Hussein's life, death, and burial are recreated in a loose sequence of forty to fifty scenes.

The Fatimid dynasty (969–1171) transferred Hussein's head to Cairo and built the Mosque of the Hasanain ('the two Hasans': Hasan and his brother, Hussein) over the relic. It is an especially holy place and is venerated also by Sunnis.

In India non-Shi'ites frequently take part in the processions, whereas in Iraq they would not be tolerated. Small replicas of Hussein's tomb, called *Ta ziyehs* (from the Arabic *aza*, meaning 'mourning'), are carried and buried in the local "Kerbela" grounds: India is so far from Kerbela, Iraq, that Indian Shi'ites consecrate local lands so they, too, may be buried in "Kerbela" grounds.

In Jamaica and Trinidad the festival is called **Hosay** and is celebrated by Muslims and Hindus as a symbol of East Indian unity. In Guyana, it is called **Tadja** and is now celebrated by Afro- and Indo-Guyanese, after having been outlawed in the 1930s because of clashes between Muslims and Hindus when it coincided with DURGA PUJA or Dussehra.

In West Africa the holy day is combined with African beliefs, and ensuring prosperity is of uppermost importance: everyone eats as much as possible, inviting poor people to join them, be-

cause a full belly ensures prosperity. The *Hausa* give a fowl or goat's head to each member of the household, which they eat with their backs to each other. In Senegal, Guinea, and Sierra Leone, the dried head and feet of the ram killed at ID AL-ADHA are cooked and eaten. Symbolic bathing in rivers and purification by leaping over small fires are followed by torchlight parades and contests.

In Turkey, the tenth Muharram is called **Yevmi Ashurer** 'day of sweet soup or porridge' and commemorates Noah's departure from the Ark onto Mount Ararat. They must share Allah's gifts with others, so everyone makes *ashurer*, which is a sweet soup or porridge made of boiled wheat, dried currants, grain, and nuts, similar to that supposedly made by Noah and stored in the bins of the Ark. Each person is assigned a day to invite his neighbors to come and share it.

Ash Wednesday
Between February 4 and March 10

The first day of LENT in the West. For fourteen centuries the season of Lent has been a time for self-examination and penitence in preparation for EASTER. The name comes from the Saxon *lengtentide*, referring to the lengthening of the days and the coming of spring. This forty-day period of abstinence recalls the fasts of Moses, Elijah, and Jesus, all of which lasted forty days. It was originally begun in the Western Church on a Sunday. But since Sundays were feast days, in the latter part of the sixth century Pope Gregory I moved the beginning of Lent ahead four days.

Gregory is also credited with having introduced the ceremony that gives this day its name. When public penitents came to the church for forgiveness, the priest would take some ash (made by burning the palms used on PALM SUNDAY of the previous year) and mark their foreheads with the sign of the cross as a reminder that they were but ashes and dust. Eventually the practice was extended to include all who wished to receive ashes.

In the East, ashes are not used, and Lent begins on the Monday before Ash Wednesday.

On this day in Iceland, children try to hook small bags of ashes or stones to the back of people's clothing.

See also SHROVE TUESDAY.

Aspen Music Festival
Late June to late August

One of the finest and most important musical events in the United States, this event was founded in 1949 in Aspen in the Colorado Rocky Mountains. Symphonic orchestra and chamber-music concerts are staged in the white-tented amphitheater designed by Finnish-born architect Eero Saarinen, and smaller presentations in a renovated opera house and a church. Programs range from baroque to modern. Each season new compositions are introduced by "composers in residence"; Virgil Thomson and Aaron Copland have been among them. A school of music operates along with the festival and has an enrollment of more than 900 students.

Aspen was a wealthy silver-mining town in the 1880s, but lost its glitter when silver prices collapsed in the 1890s. Its rebirth began in the late 1930s, largely because of the enterprise of Chicago industrialist Walter Paepcke, who thought Aspen would be suitable for a Platonic community. It is now a popular though pricey skiing resort.

Ass, Feast of the
January 14

This festival commemorating the flight of Joseph, Mary, and Jesus into Egypt to escape King Herod reached its peak during the Middle Ages in France. It was customary to have a girl carrying a baby and riding an elaborately decorated ass led through the streets to the church, where a Mass was said. But the celebration gradually took on comic overtones, with the priest and congregation imitating the braying of an ass at appropriate times during the service and the ass itself being led into the church and given food and drink. By the fifteenth century the feast had obviously degenerated into a farce, and it was suppressed thereafter by the Church , although it didn't disappear entirely until much later.

Assumption of the Blessed Virgin Mary, Feast of the
August 15

Assumption Day, called the Dormition of the Most Holy Mother of God in the East, commemorates the belief that when Mary, the mother of Jesus, died, her body was not subjected to the usual process of physical decay but was "assumed" into heaven and reunited there with her soul. Like the IMMACULATE CONCEPTION, the Assumption wasn't always an official dogma of the Roman Catholic Church—not until Pope Pius XII ruled it so in 1950. It is, however, a pious belief held by most Orthodox and some Anglicans. It is regarded as the principal feast day of the Virgin Mother.

This festival may be a Christianization of an earlier Artemis harvest feast, and in some parts of Europe it is still called the **Feast of Our Lady of the Harvest.** The people of Queven, France, actually re-enact the Assumption by lowering a wooden angel from the tower of the church and then making her rise again toward "heaven." In Elche, Spain a two-day enactment of the apocryphal gospels is performed each year. It is the national holiday of the Acadians in the Maritime Provinces of Canada, called *tinta marre* 'a racket.' At 6 p.m. on the fifteenth, pots and pans are banged, whistles blown, and drums beaten. On the nearest Sunday, all boats are decorated and sail past the dock where the priest blesses the fleet. Messina, Sicily celebrates with a two-week festival including a human tableau of the Assumption, and giant figures believed to symbolize the mythical founders of the city, Zancleo and his wife. The girl who portrays the Madonna is allowed to pardon one criminal.

In Sao Paulo, Brazil and other parts of southern Brazil, the feast is called **Nosa Senhora dos Navegantes** 'Our Lady of the Navigators'. Pageants are held on decorated canoes, each holding a captain, a purser, three musicians, and two rowers. They travel to small villages and settlements to entertain and be feasted. Towns may have a church procession with musicians portraying the Three Wise Men.

See also BLESSING OF THE GRAPES.

Ati-Atihan Festival
Third weekend in January

One of the most colorful festivals in the Philippines, held in Kalibo, the capital city of the province of Aklan. Originally falling on the Feast Day of Santo Nino (the infant Jesus), the celebration combines Christian and pagan elements.

Its origins are in the thirteenth century, when ten families fled Borneo and landed on the Philippine island of Panay. There the resident Ati people gave them land. The Ati (also called Negritos or Pygmies) were small dark people, and after receiving the land, the story goes, the Malayan people blackened their faces to look like the Ati. Years later, the Spanish Christians, having converted much of the country, persuaded the inhabitants to darken their skin, wear warlike clothing, and pretend they were Ati to frighten away the Muslims. They were victorious over the Muslims, and attributed their victory to Santo Niño. At that time, religion came into the festival.

Ati-Atihan means 'to make like Atis.' During

the present-day festival, revelers cover their skin with soot and wear Ati costumes that are patchworks of coconut shells, feathers, and fronds. They converge on the main streets and around the town plaza and, to the beat of drums, shout, "Hala Bira," ('Go on and fight!'), pound their spears, and repeatedly dance a two-step dance. From a distance, the celebrants look like a solid mass of people lurching and swinging in a frenzied rhythm.

See also DINAGYANG, SINULOG.

Atomic Bomb Day *See* Hiroshima Peace Ceremony

August Bank Holiday *See* Bank Holiday

Australia Day
January 26 or following Monday

The anniversary of the first British settlement in Australia on January 26, 1788 was formerly known as **Foundation Day** or **Anniversary Day**. Captain Arthur Phillip and his company of British convicts arrived first at Botany Bay, and when that proved to be an unsuitable location they moved on to Port Jackson, where the city of Sydney was eventually established. They built a penal colony there to help relieve overcrowding in the British prisons.

First celebrated in Sydney in 1817, Australia Day has been a public holiday since 1838. It is usually observed on January 26 or the first Monday thereafter.

Australian Open (tennis)
January

The year's first event in the Grand Slam of tennis, the Australian, French, and U.S. OPENS, and WIMBLEDON. It is played on synthetic hard courts at Sydney, Australia and Melbourne, Australia, and known officially as the Australian Championships. Tennis took root in Australia in 1880 at the Melbourne Cricket Club. The championship for men began in 1905, and the women's championship in 1922. The matches became an open (to both amateurs and professionals) in 1969.

Margaret Smith Court, an Australian known for her powerful serve and volley, is the all-time champion in the women's division of the open; she won the title eleven times between 1960 and 1973. In 1970, she was the second woman to win the Grand Slam; Maureen Connolly had swept the four tournaments in 1953, and Steffi Graf won all four in 1988.

Top multiple winners in the men's division of the Australian Open have been Roy Emerson, who took six titles (1961 and 1962–67); Jack Crawford, Ken Rosewall, and Pat Wood, who each won four; and Rod Laver, Adrian Quist, and Mats Wilander, who each won three.

In 1990, for the first time in Open Grand Slam history, the eight singles titles for men and women were won by eight different players.

Autumnal Equinox
September 22–23

The sun crosses the plane of the earth's equator twice a year: on or about March 21 (see VERNAL EQUINOX) and then again six months later, on or about September 23. On these two occasions, night and day are of equal length all over the world. In the Northern hemisphere, September 22 is the first day of autumn.

Autumnal Equinox Day is a holiday in Japan, observed on either September 23 or 24 to celebrate the arrival of autumn and to honor family ancestors.

Aviation Day
August 19

National Aviation Day honors the birthday of the American inventor and early manufacturer of airplanes, Orville Wright, as well as the progress that has been made in manned flight since the Wright Brothers made their historic 120-foot flight at Kitty Hawk, North Carolina in 1903 (see WRIGHT BROTHERS' DAY). President Franklin D. Roosevelt proclaimed August 19 as Aviation Day in 1939, and since that time celebrations have been sponsored in a number of states by organizations involved in aviation. Parachute jumping, glider demonstrations, films, airplane rides, and displays of new and antique aircraft are popular events on this day, and open house celebrations are often held at local airports. One of the more impressive observations of Aviation Day occurs when military aircraft fly in formation, often at lower-than-usual altitudes, over airports or other locations where celebrations are being held.

Awa Odori *See* Obon Festival (Festival of the Dead)

Awoojoh
Various

A thanksgiving feast in the West African nation of Sierra Leone, the Awoojoh honors the spirits of the dead, who are believed to have influence over the fortunes of the living. It may be held at any time of year, and the guests include not only friends and relatives but, in a small community, the entire village. The day begins with a family visit to the cemetary, where a libation is poured over the relatives' graves and the dead are invited to join in the thanksgiving celebration. Two kola nuts, one red and one white, are split in half and thrown upon the grave, and the pattern in which they fall is believed to carry a message from the ancestors. It is essential for all family quarrels to be settled before the feast begins.

Many popular African dishes—such as fried bean cakes, fried plantains, rice bread, and "Awoojoh beans"—are served, but the highlight of the meal is an elaborate stew, a portion of which is set out for the dead ancestors or thrown to the vultures, who are believed to embody the souls of the departed. Although the practice of holding a thanksgiving feast originated with the Yoruba, who came to Sierra Leone from Nigeria, Christians and Muslims give them as well.

Awuru Odo Festival
Biannually in April
Among the Igbo people of Nigeria, the Odo are the spirits of the dead, who return to the earth to visit their families every two years. They arrive sometime between September and November and depart in April. Before they leave, there is a big theatrical performance known as the Awuru Odo in which masked players, representing the Odo spirits, reenact the story of their visit to the living and the agony of their departure. The performance takes place on a ritual stage in the market square.

Because the Odo festival occurs only once every two years, elaborate preparations are made to welcome the returning spirits. The masks used in the performance are refurbished or new ones are made. Fences are put up around the shrines where the Odo will worship. Many of these preparations are carried out in secrecy by the men, while the women, who are totally excluded from and can have no knowledge of the activities, are responsible for providing enough food for the celebration.

Ayyam-i-Ha
February 25–March 1
These are intercalary days (that is, extra days inserted in a calendar) in the Baha'i calendar. The calendar is made up of nineteen months of nineteen days each (361 days), plus the period of four days (five in leap years) of Ayyam-i-Ha added between the eighteenth and nineteenth months, which allows for the year to be adjusted to the solar cycle. The days are set aside for rejoicing, hospitality, gift-giving, special acts of charity, and preparing for the Baha'i fast, from March 2–20. March 21 is NEW YEAR'S DAY (NAW-RUZ), and the first day of the Baha'i calendar.

The new calendar was inaugurated by Mirza Ali Muhammad, known as the Bab, founder of the Babi religion from which the Baha'i faith emerged. Baha'is believe that the new age of unity they foresee should have a new calendar free of the associations of the older calendars.

The Baha'i observe nine days on which work connected with trade, commerce, industry, and agriculture should be suspended. These days are the first, ninth, and twelfth days of the FEAST OF RIDVAN, NAW-RUZ, and the anniversaries of the BIRTH OF THE BAB, DECLARATION OF THE BAB, MARTYRDOM OF THE BAB, BIRTH OF BAHA'U'LLAH, and ASCENSION OF BAHA'U'LLAH.

B

Bab, Birth of the
October 20

A holy day in the Baha'i religion to celebrate the birthday in 1819 or 1820 of Mirza Ali Mohammad in Shiraz, Persia (now Iran). In 1844, Mirza Ali declared himself the Bab (meaning 'Gate') and foretold the coming of one greater than he. The day, on which work is suspended, is a happy social occasion for Baha'is.

See also BAB, DECLARATION OF THE.

Bab, Declaration of the
May 23

A joyous Baha'i festival to celebrate the Bab's announcement in 1844 in Shiraz, Persia (now Iran) that he was the "gate" (which is the meaning of *Bab*) to the coming of the promised one of all religions. This proclamation is considered the beginning of the Baha'i faith, although the religion was founded after the Bab's death.

The Bab, who was born Mirza Ali Muhammad, founded an independent religion known as the Babi faith which grew out of Shi'a Islam. At the time of this proclamation, the Bab also announced that it was his mission to herald a prophet who would be greater than he (paralleling St. John the Baptist as the forerunner of Jesus). After his proclamation, the Bab assembled eighteen disciples.

This day is holy to Baha'is and a day on which work is suspended. Its observation begins at about two hours after sunset.

Bab, Martyrdom of the
July 9

A solemn commemoration of the day in 1850 when the Bab, the first prophet of the Baha'i faith, was executed in Tabriz, Persia (now Iran). Prayers and readings mark the Baha'i holy day, and work is suspended.

After founding the Babi, a new religion growing out of Shi'a Islam, in 1844, the Bab was repeat-edly exiled and imprisoned by Muslim rulers and priests who opposed the idea that the Bab would provide another avenue to the truth. They saw the Babis as revolutionaries and heterodox despoilers. A committee of priests demanded the Bab's execution, and he was led to the town square and tied to a post in front of 750 riflemen. The Baha'i's say that shots were fired, but they only severed the ropes binding him. When the smoke cleared, the Bab was found in his cell completing the work he had been doing before the volley of shots—dictating holy words to a scribe. He was taken before a second regiment of riflemen, and this time he was killed. His body was disposed of in a ditch, but was retrieved by his followers and eventually placed in a mausoleum on Mt. Carmel in Haifa, Israel, where the Baha'i headquarters is today.

Babin Den
January 20

In Bulgaria the old women who helped deliver babies—much like the modern midwife—were called *baba*, or grandmother. It was widely believed that the baby received some of the *baba's* wisdom, and it was customary for the baby's parents to bring the *baba* flowers on a particular day each year, called **Grandmother's Day**. Eventually the children grew up, but they would continue to visit their *baba* each year.

Most babies in Bulgaria today are born in hospitals, so the children bring flowers to the doctors and nurses who assisted at their birth. Another traditional activity on this day involves boys ducking girls in the icy waters of rivers and lakes, supposedly to bring them good health in the coming year.

See also GRANDPARENT'S DAY.

Baby Parade
Second Thursday in August

Started in 1901 by Leo Bamberger, founder of New Jersey's Bamberger's Department Store chain, the Baby Parade that takes place along the boardwalk at the seaside resort of Ocean City on the second Thursday in August each year allows children up to the age of ten to participate and compete for prizes. There are four different divisions: Division A is for children in decorated strollers, go-carts, wagons, etc., and is further divided into three sections according to the age of the child; Division B features children in comically decorated vehicles, as well as walkers; Division C is for floats; and Division D is for larger commercial and noncommercial floats. The children are reviewed by the judges as they walk or wheel along the boardwalk from Sixth Street to Twelfth Street, and every child who enters receives a sterling silver identification bracelet. Cash prizes are given to the best entry in each division. More than fifty thousand spectators are drawn to the **Ocean City Baby Parade** each year. Similar baby parades are held in August in Avalon, Sea Isle City, and Wildwood.

Bacchanalia *See* Dionysia

Bachelors' Day *See* Leap Year Day

Bach Festival, International
June

Started in 1979 as an event that would draw tourists to Madeira Island in the Azores during its off-season, the International Bach Festival at Funchal now attracts world-class performers, conductors, ensembles, and soloists as well as thousands of visitors. The concerts are held in the town's fifteenth century Se Cathedral and in its Municipal Theater. Although past festivals have focused primarily on the works of Johann Sebastian Bach, it has since expanded to include pieces by Mozart, Telemann, Vivaldi, Haydn, and other composers.

Bad Durkheim Wurstmarkt (Sausage Fair)
Saturday to Tuesday on second weekend of September; Friday to Monday on third weekend of September

Germany's biggest wine festival, held in Bad Durkheim. The name is said to have originated about 150 years ago because of the immense amounts of sausage consumed. Today there are about forty wheelbarrow stands selling sausage and also chicken and shish-kebab. The religious origins of the feast are traced to 1417, when the villagers sold sausages, wine, and bread from wheelbarrows to pilgrims going to Michelsberg

(St. Michael's hill) on MICHAELMAS, (ST. MICHAEL'S DAY).

The opening day of the festival features a concert and a procession of bands, vineyard proprietors, and tapsters of the tavern stalls with decorated wine floats. The official **opening** is conducted by the mayor of Bad Durkheim and the German Wine Queen, and is followed by the tapping of the first cask. The following days are a medley of fireworks, band playing, dancing, and singing through the night. At the three dozen or so tavern stalls, wine is served in glasses called *Schoppen* that hold about a pint. Before the festival is over, some half a million people will have drunk more than 400,000 *Schoppen*.

From July through late October, there are numerous other wine festivals, mainly in the villages of the Rhine and Moselle valleys. Among them are Rudesheim, Bernkastel-Kues, St. Goarshausen, Boppard, and Neustadt.

Baha'u'llah, Ascension of
May 29

The anniversary of the death in 1892 of Mirza Husayn Ali, known as Baha'u'llah, founder of the Baha'i religion. "Ascension" is not meant literally, but is considered the ascension of the spirit. The day is one of nine Baha'i holy days on which work is suspended. It is observed by gathering together at 3:00 A.M., the time of Baha'u'llah's death in Acre, Palestine (now Israel), for prayers and sometimes readings from Baha'i historical works.

Baha'u'llah, Birth of
November 12

The anniversary of the birth in 1817 of the founder of the Baha'i religion and a holy day on which work is suspended. Mirza Husayn-Ali, later known as Baha'u'llah ('Glory of God'), was born in Tehran, Persia (now Iran). He was an adherent of Islam, and later a follower of the Bab, who founded Babi faith, an independent messianic religion. Thirteen years after the Bab's execution in 1850, Husayn-Ali declared himself the messenger of God, foretold by the Bab.

See also FEAST OF RIDVAN.

Bahia Independence Day
July 2

The consolidation of Brazilian independence in the state of Bahia is remembered each year with a procession following the path that the Brazilians took when they defeated Portuguese troops there in 1823. Folkloric characters like the *caboclo*, who symbolizes the superiority of native strength over the colonizers, have worked their way into this primarily civic celebration.

Baisak(hi) *See* Vaisakh

Bal du Rat Mort (Dead Rat's Ball)
Between end of January and beginning of March; usually the weekend before Lent

A huge carnival and ball, concentrated in the casino of Ostend, Belgium, but also spreading out all over the town. The carnival began at the end of the nineteenth century, launched by members of the Ostend Art and Philanthropic Circle who named the affair for a café on Montmartre (a hilly part of northern Paris home to many artists) where they had whiled away pleasant hours. People are masked at the ball, and there's a competition for the best costume.

Balfour Declaration Day
November 2

Jews, particularly those in Israel, observe Balfour Declaration Day in memory of a turning point in modern Jewish history. On November 2, 1917, Arthur J. Balfour, British Secretary of State for Foreign Affairs, sent a letter to Lord Rothschild indicating that the British government was in favor of establishing a national home for the Jewish people in Palestine. Although this may not seem to be as significant an event as ISRAELI INDEPENDENCE DAY, the Jewish people felt that the British government's commitment to their cause was very important. The day on which it was made has been kept as a semi-holiday ever since.

Baltic Song Festivals
Summer, every five years

Massive festivals of song and dance, emphasizing folk music and national culture, held every five years in the Baltic countries of Estonia, Latvia, and Lithuania. These festivals came to symbolize nationhood, especially after the countries came under Soviet domination.

The first all-Estonian song festival, called the **Laulupidu**, was held in Tartu in 1869 with 845 performers singing to 15,000 people. Nationalist leaders, led by J. V. Jannsen, publisher of the first Estonian-language newspaper, had organized the festival to demonstrate that their culture had survived its conquerors.

In 1975 the festival drew 30,000 on stage and 200,000 spectators, and when it ended, the people rose and sang their unofficial anthem, "My Fa-therland Is My Love," as tears streamed down their cheeks. The anthem was written in World War II by Lydia Koidula, the daughter of Song Festival originator Jannsen, and put to music by Gustav Ernesaks. In 1988, as political activities heightened, there were spontaneous song fests throughout Estonia. In 1990, the festival was at the Song Festival Amphitheater outside Tallinn.

In Latvia, the first Song Festival was held in 1873 at the Keizardarzs (the Czar's Garden), a park created in 1721 and named for Czar Peter I. Janis Cimze began collecting the melodies of folk songs in 1869, and these songs, some more than 1,000 years old, were performed by thousands of singers in huge choirs at the first and later festivals. The festival in Riga in 1990 attracted Latvians from around the world.

In Lithuania, each region has its own distinct musical style. Northeastern Aukstaitija, for example, is known for a kind of polyphonic round not found in any other region or in neighboring countries. The rhythms are syncopated, and the rounds sound very dissonant. The most recent of the massive Song Festivals was in 1989 in Vilnius at a concert stage that can accommodate 20,000 singers.

The old town of Vilnius is the site each May of "Skamba kankliai," performances by vocalists, instrumentalists, and dancers.

Banana Festival, International
Mid–September

A glorification of the banana, culminating with the serving of a one-ton banana pudding, in the twin cities of Fulton, Ky., and South Fulton, Tenn. The festival began in 1963 when most bananas were still shipped by rail after being unloaded at Gulf of Mexico ports. The twin cities were the distribution point for 70 percent of all bananas brought to the U.S., and also a checkpoint where the bananas were refreshed with ice or heated, as the weather directed.

Bananas and the Fultons became associated more than a century ago. This was an important railroad switching point, tying New Orleans to Canada. The Illinois Central Railroad, with major facilities in the cities, was the first railroad to develop refrigerated cars, and it began shipping bananas out of New Orleans in 1880. Suddenly people in the hinterlands could have this exotic fruit that had been enjoyed only by those in port cities. The emphasis on the banana trade in the twin cities won the communities the title " Banana Crossroads of the United States," and, more chauvinistically, "Banana Capital of the World."

It doesn't matter to the citizens of the twin cities that carloads of bananas no longer arrive here. Festival events sprawl over a period of two weeks, beginning with a Banana Princess Pageant in the Fulton City High School. Other events include a Banana Bake-off, a Banana Bonnet Contest, a no-hands Banana Split Eating Contest, a model railroad show, a flea market, an antique car show, an arts and crafts exhibit, and on the final day, a grand parade. The parade ends with the serving of the "World's Largest Banana Pudding." It's made each year by about sixteen people following a recipe that calls for 3,000 bananas, 250 pounds of vanilla wafers, and 950 packages of cream pudding, all prepared in a bowl three feet tall and five feet across. Servings: 10,000.

Bank Holiday
Various

In England there are typically six "bank holidays"—weekdays when the banks are closed for business: NEW YEAR'S DAY, GOOD FRIDAY, EASTER MONDAY, August (or Summer) Bank Holiday, CHRISTMAS DAY, and BOXING DAY. These official public holidays were established by law in 1871 and are traditionally spent at the local fairgrounds.

In the United States, the Great Depression of 1929 had caused many people to withdraw their savings and the banks had trouble meeting the demand. In February 1933 the Detroit banks failed and this caused a country-wide panic. President Franklin D. Roosevelt proclaimed his first full day in office (March 6, 1933) a national "Bank Holiday" to help save the country's banking system. The "holiday" actually lasted ten days, during which "scrip" (paper currency in denominations of less than a dollar) temporarily replaced real money in many American households.

Banntag
Between April 30 and June 3; Ascension Day

In the canton of Basel in Switzerland, this is a day when village citizens walk the village boundaries. *Banntag* means community—or town—boundary day.

Until the Reformation, Ascension Day was a time for the blessing of the fields and checking of boundary markers. The religious aspect of the day declined, and now Ascension Day, which is a national holiday, is seen as a community festival. Citizens of Basel canton, accompanied by a local

offical, flag bearers, and musicians, walk along the boundaries to a certain spot where the president of the town council greets them and discusses town topics. In some communities, the walk is followed by a church service and community meal.

Baptism of the Lord, Feast of the
Sunday following Epiphany

Jesus' baptism by John the Baptist in the River Jordan has always been considered a significant manifestation of Jesus' divinity, and has been celebrated on EPIPHANY by the Orthodox church since the end of the second century. However, in 1961 the Roman Catholic church began to celebrate it as a separate feast in its own right. Their original date for the feast was January 13, but when their church calendar was reorganized in 1969, the Feast of the Baptism of the Lord was moved to the Sunday following the EPIPHANY. They omit the observance in years when it coincides with the Epiphany, especially in places like the United States, where celebration of the Epiphany has been shifted from the traditional January 6 observance to the Sunday between January 2 and 8.

See also TIMKAT.

Barbados/Caribbean Jazz Festival
Late May

Established in 1985 to promote jazz that is distinctly Caribbean in imagery and rhythm, the Barbados-Caribbean Jazz Festival has featured musicians from Antigua, Barbados, Colombia, Cuba, Curaçao, Guadeloupe, Guyana, Jamaica, Martinique, Panama, Puerto Rico, St. Lucia, St. Vincent, Trinidad and Tobago, and Venezuela. But jazz groups and musicians from the United States and Europe have participated in the festival as well—including Ellis Marsalis (father of the jazz trumpeter Wynton and saxophonist Branford), the Dirty Dozen Dixieland Jazz Band from New Orleans, and Donald Byrd. Indoor performances are held at The Frank Collymore Hall, the island's largest musical auditorium, and at The After Dark, Barbados' top jazz club. There are also open-air concerts in Bridgetown, the island's capital. The festival is held from Thursday to Sunday in late May.

Bar-B-Q Festival, International
Mid–May

A two-day mouth-watering event in Owensboro, Ky., which calls itself the Bar-B-Q Capital of the World. In the course of the weekend, ten tons of mutton, 3,000 chickens, and 1,500 gallons of burgoo are cooked and served. Kentucky burgoo is a thick soup made of chicken, mutton, beef, tomatoes, cabbage, potatoes, onions, and corn.

The festival had its beginnings at the turn of the century when the many Roman Catholic churches in the area had summertime picnics in their parishes. Each church had a cooking team to vie with the others in cooking the best barbecue. Eventually, the idea struck someone that there could be a city-wide barbecue if all the church barbecues were combined. Out of that grew the present festival, which now attracts more than 40,000 people. The barbecue-pit fires are lit on Friday afternoon on the banks of the Ohio River, and the chicken and meat—always mutton, not beef—is barbecued the next day when the coals are red. The Roman Catholic parish chefs still compete, but the cooking contest has expanded to be open to anyone. Events besides cooking and eating include arts and crafts exhibits, bluegrass and country music, street dancing, and contests of pie eating, keg throwing and horseshoe throwing. There are also likely to be political speeches.

Barcelona Festival
October

The month-long **International Music Festival** that takes place in Barcelona, Spain each year began in 1963 as a showcase for young Catalan composers and performers. But since then the festival has taken on a more international flavor, with musicians and composers from other countries participating as well. The commitment of the festival's organizers to Catalan artists remains strong however, and each year the festival premieres the work of about 180 local composers.

The Barcelona Festival is always held in October as part of the Fiestas de la Merced, or the festival honoring Barcelona's patron saint, Our Lady of Mercy.

Barnum Festival
June–July

Bridgeport, Connecticut was the home of Phineas Taylor Barnum and the birthplace of Charles Sherwood Stratton, known by his circus name of "General" Tom Thumb a twenty-eight-inch tall man who was the main attraction of Barnum's nineteenth century circus, the Greatest Show on Earth. Barnum was also Bridgeport's mayor in 1875, and his contributions to the city included bringing in new industrial jobs and building a number of parks. Since 1949 he has been honored with a seventeen-day festival, beginning in late June and extending through the FOURTH OF JULY. Occasionally it continues through July 5, which is Barnum's birthday. The idea behind the festival, which is sponsored by the P.T. Barnum Foundation, Inc., is to get away from Bridgeport's industrial image and to promote the city's circus heritage.

One of the highlights of the festival is the Saturday evening event known as "Champions on Parade," the largest senior drum corps competition in the Northeast. On Sunday there is a Barnum Memorial Ceremony at the cemetery where he is buried. Many of the events focus on Barnum's circus background, including entertainment by clowns and a visit to the Barnum Museum, where there is a miniature replica of his circus. The festival is preceded by the selection of an honorary Tom Thumb. There is also an honorary Jenny Lind (the Swedish-born soprano who toured the United States under Barnum's sponsorship). Other figures associated with Barnum and his circus are recognized in this way as well.

Bartholomew Fair
August 24

Although **St. Bartholomew's Day** isn't really celebrated any more, for over seven hundred years (1133–1855) it was the day on which the Bartholomew Fair was held at Smithfield on the outskirts of London. What began as an opportunity for buying and selling cloth eventually turned into a major national event. Almost every type of commodity could be purchased there, and a number of sideshows and other crude sources of entertainment were available as well-earning the Fair its present-day reputation as "the Coney Island of medieval England."

Eventually the entertainment aspects of the Fair outweighed its commercial purposes, and although it was very much a part of English life there was a movement to close it down. In 1822, thousands of people rioted in protest against the threat of closing the Fair. But finally, in 1855, it was permanently abolished.

St. Bartholomew's Day is also known for the massacre of the Huguenots (Protestants) in France, which began at the instigation of Catherine de' Medici, in Paris on the night of August 23–24, 1572 and spread throughout the country for two more days until between 5,000 and 10,000 had been killed.

Basant Panchami *See* **Vasant Panchami**

Basket Dances

Late October through November

Ceremonial dances by Hopi Indian women held in the plaza of their mesa villages in northeastern Arizona. The dances celebrate the time when all the men were gone from the villages, and the women were the keepers of the spiritual life of the people. The women are costumed to represent various spirits, and while they dance they throw small gifts from baskets to the "little people" (spirits) who will then ensure good hunting, fishing, or gathering.

Basque Festival, National

First weekend in July

A sports-music-dance-barbecue celebration of the Basque heritage, held annually since 1962 in Elko, Nev. The Basque people settled in the west, largely in Nevada and Idaho, in the late 1800s, many becoming shepherds and sheep ranchers.

Participants in the festival wear the traditional red, white, and green of the Basque provinces of Spain. The men also wear the traditional Basque beret.

The festival begins on Friday with social and exhibition dancing. On Saturday there's a parade of more than fifty floats, and major contests of weight lifting, sheep hooking (sheep are hooked with a crook, dragged to a designated spot, and tied by one leg), sheepdog-working, yelling, and dancing the native *jota*. Each year, there is also a three-event contest of log chopping, weightlifting, and a strength-and-endurance event in which contestants race to pluck each of thirty beer cans (they were ears of corn in the old country) from a line and deposit them in a trash can. Some years, when contestants from Spain are present, there are pentathlons—five-event contests that largely involve lifting, dragging, and walking with enormous weights (for example, a 1,200-pound granite slab is dragged). On Sunday, the events wind up with a big barbecue of steak, marinated lamb, and spicy sausages called *chorizo*. Music and dancing are important parts of the festival, and *bertsolaris*, 'troubadours' entertain with song improvisations in the Basque language.

Other Nevada Basque festivals are held in Winnemucca on the second weekend in June and in Reno in August. Another major event is the Basque Association Picnic in Gooding, Idaho, in late July.

Bastille Day (Fête Nationale)

July 14

The Bastille was a fourteenth-century fortress that became a notorious state prison in Paris. An angry mob assaulted the Bastille—which had come to symbolize the oppression of the French monarchy—on July 14, 1789, freeing the political prisoners held there and launching the French Revolution.

Although the building itself was razed a year after the attack, the Bastille became a symbol of French independence, and July 14 has been celebrated since that time in France as well as in her territories in the Pacific with parades, fireworks, and dancing in the streets. This period in French history is familiar to many through Charles Dickens' portrayal of it in *A Tale of Two Cities*.

In Tahiti and the rest of French Polynesia it is called **Tiurai** or **Heiva**, and is celebrated for most of the month. The festival includes European type celebrations plus Polynesian competitions, including for men and women, and a **play** about the enthronement of a Tahitian high **chief**. The highlight is the nightly folklore spectacle—a competition of music and dance among groups from throughout French Polynesia who have practiced all year for the event.

Bastille, Festival de la

Weekend closest to July 14

Because the storming of the Bastille on July 14, 1789 (see BASTILLE DAY) marked an important turning point in the history of France, members of the Club Calumet in Augusta, Maine chose this day (or the nearest Friday, Saturday, and Sunday) to celebrate the state's French-Canadian (or "Acadian") heritage. Events include entertainment by Cajun bands, French folk dancers and Maine cloggers, a huge fireworks display, and a parade through downtown Augusta.

In 1991 the festival honored eighty-five visitors from Paris—all members of the Sarthois Club who were in this country as part of an exchange with its sister club, Le Club Calumet. But the festival is not limited to the French or descendants of the original Acadian settlers. More than 13,000 visitors come to Augusta each year to participate in the festival. About one-fourth of Maine's current population is of Acadian French descent (see ACADIAN FESTIVAL).

Bataan Day (Araw ng Kagitingan)

April 9

A national holiday in the Philippines in commemoration of the disastrous World War II Battle of Bataan on this date in 1942, in which the Philippines fell to the Japanese. Also remembered on this date are the 37,000 U.S. and Filipino soldiers who were captured and the thousands who died during the infamous seventy-mile "death march" from Mariveles to a Japanese concentration camp inland at San Fernando. Ceremonies are held at Mt. Samat Shrine, the site of side-by-side fighting by Filipino and American troops.

Bat Flight Breakfast
Second Thursday in August

Carlsbad Caverns in southern New Mexico was proclaimed a national monument in 1923 not only for its geologic formations but for its teeming bat population. Carlsbad's summer colony of Mexican free-tailed bats, whose numbers vary from one hundred thousand to a million, migrates to the cave each spring. They eat, sleep, digest, communicate, mate, and raise their young while hanging upside-down. The accumulation of guano—a valuable source of fertilizer—can reach depths of up to forty feet.

Although many visitors to the park witness the bats' spectacular outbound flight at sunset, when they leave the cave in a dense black cloud for their night's feeding in the Pecos River Valley, far fewer are there to witness their return—except those who attend the annual Bat Flight Breakfast. Started in the late 1950s by a group of park employees who wanted to encourage people to witness this natural phenomenon, the breakfast soon became an annual tradition. About four hundred people arrive at the cave before sunrise on the second Thursday in August and eat sausages and scrambled eggs in their official yellow "bat breakfast hats" while they wait for the bats to return to their roosts. It is said that the bats generate an eerie sound as they rocket downward with folded wings.

When a television crew was there to film the event in 1989, the bats failed to return as expected. No one is sure how or when they got back into the cave, but thirteen hours later, at sunset, they left in droves as usual.

Battle of Britain Day
September 15

In England, September 15, 1940, is remembered as the day of the biggest daylight bombing raid of Britain by the German Luftwaffe. The German air attacks had begun in June 1940, and beginning September 7 bombs rained on London for fifty-seven consecutive nights. The Royal Air Force (RAF), while greatly outnumbered, had a secret advantage—radar—and the early-warning chain gave RAF pilots a half-hour's notice of German planes taking off from France. The Luftwaffe was finally defeated in April 1941, ending the first extended battle ever fought for control of the air. Winston Churchill, in a speech in August 1940, was referring to the RAF pilots when he said, "Never in the field of human conflict was so much owed by so many to so few."

Battle of Flowers, Vienna
Summer

The Battle of Flowers is the culmination of a huge flower festival in the capital city of Vienna, Austria. Hundreds of floats are elaborately decorated with flowers, often to symbolize a particular aspect of Austrian history or culture. Sometimes they re-create entire scenes from Austrian operettas or ballets. The people of Vienna dress up in their best clothes and hats—similar to what Americans do on EASTER—to watch the parade, which is reviewed by government officials and the leaders of various cultural organizations.

Similar "Battles of Flowers" are held in other Austrian cities, such as Linz, Salzburg, and Innsbruck. A particularly famous one is held on a lake in south Upper Austria known as the Traun See, where barges and boats, rather than floats, are decorated with flowers.

Battle of Germantown, Reenactment of
First Saturday in October

In October of 1777, George Washington's battle strategy to recapture Philadelphia from the British called for an assault on the little community of Germantown to the northwest of the city. The British soldiers took refuge in a new stone house, Cliveden, that had just been built by Benjamin Chew. Although the house was pounded by cannon balls, the stone walls withstood the assault and Washington's men were eventually forced to retreat. The thick fog proved to be a decisive factor, hindering the movements of Washington's soldiers at a point where they appeared to be on the verge of winning. Although the Americans were defeated, the Battle of Germantown was considered a moral victory, especially when it was followed two weeks later by the victory of General Horatio Gates at Saratoga.

Since the early 1970s, there has been a reenactment of Washington's defeat by the British in Germantown, now a suburb of Philadelphia, on the first Saturday in October. British and American troops stage a mock battle from house to house.

At Cliveden, which now belongs to the National Trust for Historic Preservation, visitors can still see the scars left by American bullets.

Battle of New Orleans Day
January 8

When eight thousand British soliders attacked New Orleans on January 8, 1815, they were met by a ragtag army of militiamen, sailors, and pirates fighting from behind barricades. The defending U. S. troops were led by General Andrew Jackson, whose stunning victory—the British suffered some two thousand casualties, while the Americans lost only eight men—made him a national hero.

This day is no longer as widely celebrated as it was before the Civil War, but it remains a legal holiday in Louisiana, where it is also known as **Jackson Day** or, in honor of Jackson's nickname, as **Old Hickory's Day.**

Battles of the Flowers
Between March 10 and April 13; during Carnival

Flowers play an important role in CARNIVAL celebrations in Nice, for it is in the south of France that the flowers for French perfume are grown. During the twelve days of Carnival festivities, there are several afternoons devoted to Battles of the Flowers, where people bring their own "ammunition" and, at a predetermined signal, start throwing flowers at each other. The city streets are often knee-deep in flowers by the time these fragrant mock-battles are over.

Bawming the Thorn Day
Late June

This is the day on which the people of Appleton in Cheshire, England celebrate the centuries-old tradition of bawming the thorn, or decorating the hawthorn tree that stands in the center of their town. Children dance around the tree after draping its branches with flowers, flags, and ribbons. The original hawthorn tree was planted there in 1125, but the custom may date back even farther to the ancient custom of worshiping trees as guardians.

Bayreuth Festival
Late July through end of August

An internationally famous month-long festival in Bayreuth, (pronounced buy-ROIT) Germany celebrating the music of Richard Wagner. It features six to eight Wagner operas, and is usually sold out a year in advance. Performances are in the Festspielhaus ('Festival Theatre') designed by

Wagner himself specifically for the presentation of his works. The festival was launched with the first complete performance of the four-opera *Der Ring des Nibelungen* ('The Ring of the Nibelung'), triumphantly presented in the new Festspielhaus on Aug. 13, 14, 16, and 17, 1876. Except for wartime interruptions, the festival has been staged every year since then. Wagner had moved to Bayreuth in 1874, and lived in the house he called *Wahnfried* ('Peace from Delusion') until his death in 1883. During those years, he composed his last work, the sacred festival drama *Parsifal*, and it was produced at Bayreuth in 1882. The festival was directed after Wagner's death by his wife Cosima; their son Seigfried took over as director in 1930, and grandsons Wieland and Wolfgang Wagner revived it in 1951, after World War II.

Bean-Throwing Festival *See* Setsubun

Bear Festival
Early December

Among the Ainu people of the northernmost islands of Japan, the baiting and killing of a young bear was not considered a brutal act but a ceremonial send-off to the spirit world. The "divine" cub was ceremoniously killed and arranged with fetishes. Then some of his own cooked meat and a dish of his own blood, along with cakes and dried fish were laid before him. He was supposed to bring these gifts to his parents when he arrived in heaven. After a time he would be reincarnated and return to earth as another cub.

Befana Festival
January 5

Sometimes referred to simply as **La Befana**, this is the TWELFTH NIGHT festival in Italy where the *Befana*, a kindly witch, plays much the same role that Santa Claus plays in the United States on CHRISTMAS EVE—giving toys and candy to the children who have been good and a lump of coal or a pebble to those who haven't. According to legend, the Befana was sweeping her house when the Magi, or three Wise Men, stopped by on their way to Bethlehem. But when they asked her to accompany them, she said she was too busy. She later changed her mind and set out to find the Christ Child, but she got lost. Every year *la Befana* passes through Italy in her continuing search for the *Gésu Bambino*, leaving gifts for the children.

The festival begins on EPIPHANY EVE, when the Befana is supposed to come down the chimney on her broom to leave gifts in the children's stockings. In Rome, the Piazza Navona is thronged with children and their parents, who shop for toys and exchange greetings. Bands of young people march around, blowing on cardboard trumpets, and the noise level in the square can be deafening. In the countryside, bonfires are often lit on Epiphany Eve, and people try to predict the weather by watching the direction in which the smoke blows.

See also DÍA DE LOS TRES REYES.

Beggar's Day *See* **St. Martin's Day**

Beheading, feast of the *See* **Martyrdom of St. John the Baptist**

Belgian-American Days
August
Ghent, Minnesota, named after the famous city in Belgium, is the state's only predominantly Belgian community. The annual Belgian-American Days celebration gives the descendants of Ghent's original Belgian settlers an opportunity to compete in the traditional Belgian sport of *rolle bolle*, which is similar to lawn bowling or Italian bocci. The game is played on bare ground or grass, with stakes set thirty feet apart. The eight-pound disc called a *bolle* is rolled from one stake to the other. The bolle that lands closest to the stake scores. Teams usually consist of three players, and the first team to score eight points wins the game. As many as three hundred bollers participate in the championship round, which is held on the third day of the four-day event.

Although rolle bolle is the biggest attraction, the festival also features a softball tournament, parades, a firemen's dinner, and a dance.

Belmont Stakes
June; fifth Saturday after Kentucky Derby
The final race of the Triple Crown of horse-racing, the Belmont Stakes is traditionally run on the fifth Saturday after the KENTUCKY DERBY (or the third Saturday after the PREAKNESS STAKES). Founded in 1867, it takes place at the Belmont Park Race Track in western Nassau County on Long Island, named for August Belmont, a well-to-do German who played an important role in establishing horseracing in New York.

The horse that sweeps the Triple Crown receives a one million dollar bonus in addition to the winner's share of the purses, but in years when no horse wins the Triple Crown, the bonus goes to the horse competing in all three races and scoring the highest on a 5-3-1 point system for finishing first,

second, or third. The chances of a single horse winning all three races are relatively slim: in 114 years only eleven horses have managed to do it.

Many breeders pay more attention to the Belmont than they do to the other races when it comes to selecting stud prospects because they believe that in the long run, Belmont winners make better sires.

Beltane
April 30
Beltane (also **Beltine**) is the Celtic name for the first day of May (see MAY DAY), which divided the ancient Celtic year in half. It was believed that each day began with the setting of the sun the night before, so Beltane was celebrated by lighting bonfires to honor the sun god. Cattle were driven through the "Beltane fire"—or between two fires—to protect them from disease before putting them out to pasture for the new season. Sometimes people followed the same ritual to forestall bad luck and to cure barrenness. Contact with the fire was symbolic of contact with the life-giving sun. See also MIDSUMMER DAY.

Along with LAMMAS (August 1), HALLOWMAS (November 1), and CANDLEMAS (February 2), Beltane was one of the British QUARTER-DAYS or term days when rents were due and debts were settled. The day is still observed in parts of Ireland, the Scottish Highlands, Wales, Brittany, and the Isle of Man, with most of the celebrations revolving around fire and reflecting ancient fertility rites.

Benjamin Franklin's Birthday
January 17
The commemoration of the birth of Benjamin Franklin—printer, scientist, inventor, statesman, diplomat, writer, editor, wit, and aphorist. Born in Boston on this day in 1706, Franklin helped write and was a signer of the Declaration of Independence, and was a framer of the Constitution. The common-sense moralities of his *Poor Richard's Almanac* became catch-phrases in his time and are still quoted today. For example: "Make haste slowly"; "Fish and visitors smell in three days"; "He that goes a-borrowing, goes a-sorrowing." He invented bifocals, proposed Daylight Saving Time in 1786, and unsuccessfully recommended the wild turkey rather than the bald eagle as the national bird. When he died in 1790 in Philadelphia, he was given the most impressive funeral that city had ever seen: 20,000 people attended.

Since 1991, the Bower Award and Prize in Science—a cash prize of more than $300,000—has been presented on Jan. 17 by the Franklin Institute in Philadelphia to a person who has made a scientific contribution of a practical nature in the manner of Franklin. Also in Philadelphia, the Franklin Institute Science Museum holds a two-day "birthday bash" that often involves people dressing as Franklin. The celebration takes place on the weekend preceding MARTIN LUTHER KING JR. DAY, which is the Monday after Jan. 15.

Bennington Battle Day
August 16

During the Revolutionary War, Colonel Seth Warner and 350 of his Green Mountain Boys, a group of soldiers from Vermont, played a vital role in defeating the British forces who had come to capture the American supply depot at Bennington, a town in southern Vermont near the New York border. The anniversary of the fighting that took place along the Walloomsac River on August 16, 1777 is a legal holiday in Vermont, and a 306-foot tower has been erected in the town of Old Bennington, two miles west of Bennington proper. A statue of Seth Warner stands nearby. Across the state border in New York's Rensselaer County, the Bennington Battlefield State Park includes the site where the heaviest fighting took place.

Berchtold's Day
January 2

In Switzerland, the day after NEW YEAR'S DAY is known as **Berchtold's Tag** and is celebrated primarily by children who hold neighborhood parties that feature nut eating and nut games followed by singing and folk dancing. A favorite game is the building of "hocks" composed of four nuts placed close together with a fifth balanced on top. The children begin gathering and hoarding nuts for the Berchtold's Day festivities in early autumn.

Bergen International Festival
May–June

The Bergen International Festival is the major cultural event in Norway, and features more than a hundred events in music, drama, folklore, opera, ballet, and the visual arts. Most of the musical events are held in Bergen's Viking Castle, Haakon's Hall (built in 1250), at the Grieg Concert Hall, at Edvard Grieg's home (known as "Troldhaugen"), and at Lysoen, the island home of composer and violinist Ole Bull. It was, in fact, Edvard Grieg—the composer and founder of the Norwegian nationalist school of music—who originated the idea for a musical festival and who first sponsored such a festival back in 1898. But the Bergen International Festival as it exists today

didn't really get started until 1952. Although the primary attraction is music—ranging from classical to jazz, organ concerts, military band performances, and folklore opera—sometimes films and art exhibits are featured as well.

Bering Sea Ice Golf Classic
Mid–March

This golfing challenge, played on a six-hole course with bright orange golf balls, takes place on the frozen Bering Sea off Nome, Alaska at a time when the winds can be gale-strength. Par is forty-one, but winners have claimed scores as low as twenty-three. Entry fees benefit the Lions Club. The tournament, not a wholly serious affair, coincides with the final days of the IDITAROD TRAIL SLED DOG RACE that starts about the first of March and ends in Nome about two weeks later.

Berkshire Music Festival
July–August

The 210-acre estate, donated in 1937 by Mrs. Gorham Brooks, in the Berkshire Mountains of western Massachusetts and known as Tanglewood, is the summer home of the Boston Symphony Orchestra. What is popularly known as the Berkshire or **Tanglewood Festival** originated in 1934 and in 1940 became part of the Berkshire Music Center, where advanced American and foreign musicians come to study and perform for nine weeks each summer. The festival includes concerts by the Boston Symphony and the Berkshire Music Center Orchestra as well as chamber music, jazz, choral and vocal concerts, and music theater productions. In early August there is a Festival of Contemporary Music that focuses on new works, some of which have been specially commissioned for the festival.

The grounds at Tanglewood open about two hours prior to the concerts so people can picnic on the lawns. More than 350,000 people come to Tanglewood over the course of the festival each summer.

Bermuda College Weeks
March–mid-April

College Weeks began as **Rugby Weeks** in the 1950s, when Ivy League rugby teams came to the island of Bermuda to spend their spring holidays and compete against Bermudian and British teams. But parties and socializing soon took precedence over the rugby competition, and College Weeks became a time for young people from colleges and universities all over the United States to meet in Bermuda and get an early start on the summer season.

The Bermuda government organizes and pays for all of the activities that are scheduled during this period, issuing courtesy cards that entitle college students free admission to everything from a "Get Acquainted" dance at one of the major hotels to beach parties, boat cruises, and steel band concerts. Scores of moped-riding college students take advantage of the island's hospitality, making Bermuda one of the most popular spring break destinations.

Bermuda Race *See* **Newport to Bermuda Race**

Bermuda Rendezvous Time
December–mid-March

The winter season (December through mid-March) on the island of Bermuda is known as **Rendezvous Time**, a period during which the local Department of Tourism plans a number of special events for visitors. One of the most popular is the **Skirling Ceremony** held Mondays at noon at Fort Hamilton, which is a ceremonial performance by bagpipers in kilts, drummers, and dancers. Other regularly scheduled events include exhibitions of local crafts, walking tours of the seventeenth-century town of St. George, and visits by motorbike or ferry to the rustic village of Somerset. Bermuda also hosts an annual Festival for the Performing Arts during this period (early January to mid-February) which includes theater, dance, opera, classical, and modern music performances.

Bianou
First new moon of February

A celebration of the end of the winter season in the market town of Agadés (or Agadéz. The festivities are held for three days, and start with the sound of distant drumming and chanting of the *muzzein* calling people to prayer. As people assemble, the drummers appear. Behind them come the Tuareg nomads, wearing long blue robes and spinning around in their special dance, the guedra. The Tuareg turbans are folded in a way that suggests a cock's comb, since the cock is the symbol of the new season. Agadés is in northern Niger in the Sahara Desert. It was the seat of a Tuareg sultanate in the fifteenth century, and has been a crossroads for Fulani cattle herders, Tuareg traders, and Haussa merchants. The nomadic peoples also hold an annual gathering in Ingal town in Au-

gust to take a census, at which time medical care is given by the national government.

See also CAMEL MARKET.

Big Iron Farm Show and Exhibition
September

The upper midwest's largest agricultural exposition, the **Big Iron** is held at the Red River Valley Fairgrounds in West Fargo, North Dakota. Established in 1981 so that farmers would have a place where they could come to view the latest innovations in farming and agricultural equipment, the Big Iron prides itself on being a business event rather than a carnival. In the words of one organizer, "We don't distract people with music, pots and pans, and dog and pony acts." The three-day show regularly attracts more than 60,000 visitors, who come to see not only the farm equipment that is on exhibit but field demonstrations of tillage, crop-spraying, irrigation, and other equipment.

A special program for women takes place on "Ladies' Day." Seminars on such subjects as "Heirloom Art" and "The Changing Role of the Rural Woman" are offered, as well as other activities designed to inform and entertain the women who participate in the running of a family farm.

Bike Week *See* **Motorcycle Week**

Bill of Rights Day
December 15

The first ten amendments to the U.S. Constitution of 1787—referred to collectively as the Bill of Rights—were ratified on December 15, 1791. This landmark document protected American citizens from specific abuses by their government and guaranteed such basic rights as the freedom of religion, freedom of speech, and freedom of the press. In 1941 President Franklin D. Roosevelt designated December 15 as Bill of Rights Day and called upon Americans to observe it with appropriate patriotic ceremonies.

On December 10, 1948 the United Nations General Assembly unanimously adopted the Universal Declaration of Human Rights, and member countries of the U.N. began to observe December 10 as Human Rights Day. In the United States, the observance extended from December 10 to December 17 and was referred to as Human Rights Week. Since it encompasses December 15, the two events are now observed in conjunction and are typically celebrated with essay contests on the importance of freedom and democracy, special radio and television shows, and speeches on the themes of personal freedom and human rights.

In Massachusetts, the week of December 8-15 has been celebrated as Civil Rights Week since 1952. It honors not only the ratification of the Bill of Rights but the adoption of the state's first code of laws, the Body of Liberties, on December 10, 1641.

Billy Bowlegs Festival
First full weekend in June

The oldest and one of the biggest festivals in northwest Florida, held in Fort Walton Beach to commemorate the pirate William Augustus Bowles, also known as Capt. Billy Bowlegs. Bowles arrived in what's now known as the Florida panhandle in 1778 when the Spanish, English, and Americans were maneuvering for control of the Gulf shores. He put together a force of Indians and "White Banditti," created his own throne, and formed the State of Muskogee. To support it, he ran raids on the Gulf of Mexico and on the mainland. He was finally seized and imprisoned in Morro Castle in Cuba, where he starved himself to death in 1803.

This is not a particularly joyous saga, but the festive affair of the Billy Bowlegs days goes on for a week. The festival began in 1954 and today attracts about 40,000 spectators. Activities begin with a simulated naval gun battle on Friday night. The following day, the pirate captain and his red-kerchiefed "krewe" members storm the city from the pirate ship "Blackhawk." As events move on there are spectacular fireworks displays, a treasure hunt, a boat parade with about 300 boats, arts and crafts, numerous food vendors, concerts, and sports events that include a midnight run. More than 100 floats take part in a torchlight parade, and parade participants rain gold doubloons and assorted trinkets on the clamoring crowds.

Billy Moore Days
Second weekend in October

A celebration of the pioneer who established a stage stop, general store, and saloon in what became Avondale, Ariz. Avondale and the other Tri-City towns of Goodyear and Litchfield Park commemorate Billy Moore with a carnival, arts and crafts fair, golf and softball tournaments, A nighttime five-kilometer run, a street dance, and a 100-unit parade in which assorted politicans and the Arizona Maid of Cotton take part. The celebration has been held since 1954.

Billy Moore's story is surrounded by legend. He

is supposed to have belonged to the gang of guerrillas led by William Clarke Quantrill, but historians think he was a young blacksmith with the gang, not one of the pillagers. Whatever he was, he was exiled by the governor of Missouri for his part in the Quantrill gang, and he headed out for Arizona Territory in 1867. Before setting up business, he either had a run-in with an outlaw or was attacked by Apaches; in any event, he was seriously injured, and a Yaqui Indian woman who later became his wife nursed him back to health. In the late 1880s Moore bought 280 acres of land at the stage stop known as Coldwater for twenty-five cents an acre under the Desert Lands Act of 1877. He became a justice of the peace and was postmaster at the Coldwater station until 1905, when the post office was moved to a different location because liquor and the mail were being distributed from the same station in violation of the law. Billy Moore died in 1934 at the age of ninety-two.

Birchat Hahamah *See* **Blessing the Sun**

Birmingham Festival of the Arts
Third week in April

This display of performing and visual arts honors a different nation each year, and has been held since 1951 in Birmingham, Ala. A ten-day affair, the festival celebrates the chosen country's theater, literature, history, music, customs, and food with films, lectures, exhibits, and book-and-author luncheons. Traditional dance and folk music ensembles from the honored country perform, and the Alabama Symphony Orchestra presents concerts. There are also parades and street dances. Great Britain was spotlighted in 1991, Spain in 1992.

Bi-Shevat (B'Shevat; Tu Bishvat; Hamishah Assar Bi-Shevat)
Between January 16 and February 13; 15 Shevat

Hamishah Assar Bi-Shevat, also known as **New Year for Trees**, is a minor Jewish festival equivalent to ARBOR DAY. It is first referred to in the late Second Temple period, when it was the cut-off date for levying the tithe on the produce of fruit trees. When Jewish colonists returned to Palestine about fifty years ago, they reclaimed the barren land by planting trees wherever they could. It became customary to plant a tree for every newborn child: a cedar for a boy and a cypress or pine for a girl.

Today the children of Israel celebrate Bi-Shevat with tree planting and outdoor games. In other countries, Jews observe the festival by eating fruit that grows in the Jewish homeland—such as oranges, figs, dates, raisins, pomegranates, and especially, almonds, the first tree to bloom in Israel's spring.

Bisket Jatra
April 13 or 14; First day of Vaisakha

The festival of the new year in Bhaktapur, Nepal. **Nava Varsa**, the new year, is celebrated in Nepal with exchanges of greetings and, in some areas with ritual bathing. The most important celebration is Bisket Jatra, which means the 'festival after the death of the serpent.' In Bhaktapur, the new year is celebrated by parading images of gods in chariots. The main attraction of the festival is the erection of a ceremonial pole—a lingam or phallic symbol. This is a peeled tree trunk as much as eighty feet in length that is erected using bamboo and heavy ropes while crowds watch. On New Year's Day, the pole is torn down.

There is a legend behind this ceremonial pole. The daughter of the king of Bhaktapur was insatiable and demanded a new lover every night, but she left her lovers dead by morning. Then a brave prince appeared to try his luck. He managed to stay awake through the night, and saw two thread-like wisps emerging from the princess's nostrils. These wisps turned into poisonous snakes, so the prince drew his sword and killed them. Of course the prince and princess lived happily ever after. This story is recalled with the raising of the pole of Bisket Jarta.

Most holidays in Nepal are set by the lunar calendar, but New Year's Day is an exception and always falls in the middle of April.

See also BAISAKHI.

Bix Beiderbecke Memorial Jazz Festival
Last weekend in July

Leon Bismarck "Bix" Beiderbecke (1903–1931) was an American jazz cornetist and composer whose recordings of "Singin' the Blues" and "A Good Man Is Hard to Find" remain jazz classics. Since 1972 he has been commemorated in his home town of Davenport, Iowa with an annual jazz festival, popularly known as **Bix Fest**, featuring concerts by many of the world's top traditional jazz bands. The festival is held at LeClaire Park on the banks of the Mississippi River, where musicians perform in a bandshell. The Bix Fest is staffed by volunteers and sponsored by the Bix Beiderbecke Memorial Society.

Beiderbecke's playing inspired a generation of jazz musicians. His life has been depicted in films and novels, such as Dorothy Baker's *Young Man with a Horn*. His compositions include "In a Mist," a piano piece inspired by the French Impressionist composers.

Black Christ, Festival of the
October 21

There are two legends associated with the observance of the **Black Christ Festival** in Portobelo, Panama. One says that during a cholera epidemic on the Isthmus, the people found a crate floating on the water near the beach. When they brought it ashore and opened it, they discovered a statue of a black Christ. They brought it into the church and, within a few days, the cholera had completely disappeared from Portobelo, even though it continued to rage elsewhere.

The other legend concerns a ship carrying the black Christ statue from Spain to Cartagena, Colombia. The ship stopped for supplies in Portobelo, but when it attempted to leave, it was turned back five times by sudden storms. The crew finally threw the crate containing the statue overboard, but local residents rescued it and put it in a place of honor in their church. The image of the black Christ, which is made of dark brown coco-bolo wood, has been credited with everything from miraculous cures to helping the city win the national lottery.

The people of Portobelo honor their patron saint, El Jesús Nazarene, by carrying the statue in procession on a decorated platform through the city streets. Pilgrims come from all over Panama, as they have for more than three hundred years, to celebrate with folk dancing, music, and songs. (See also BLACK NAZARENE FIESTA)

Black Cowboys Parade
First Saturday in October

A salute to the black cowboys who helped settle the West, held since 1975 in Oakland, Calif. Hundreds of mounted cowboys and marching bands participate in the parade, the only one of its kind in the nation. There are also arts and crafts exhibits and food booths.

Black Friday
Various

Black Friday usually refers either to the infamous Wall Street Panic of September 24, 1869 when Jay Gould and James Fisk tried to "corner" the gold market, or to September 19, 1873 when stock failures caused the Panic of 1873. In England, it is often used by workers to describe May

12, 1926, the day on which the General Strike was ended. It is occasionally used to refer to GOOD FRIDAY.

Shoppers and retailers in the United States sometimes refer to the day after THANKSGIVING as Black Friday because it marks the beginning of the CHRISTMAS commercial season and is traditionally a frenetic day of shopping.

Black Hills Motor Classic
First Monday of August through following Sunday

A mammoth yearly rally of 250,000 or so motorcyclists in small Sturgis, S.D. (population 7,000). There are races, merrymaking, band music, and usually some misbehavior: in 1990, there were 203 arrests for drunken driving, 78 accidents with injuries, and 11 fatalities (one caused by shooting). Motorcycle drag racing runs eight days, and other official events include bike shows, a swap meet, monster truck races, Tough Man and Tough Woman Contests (the titles determined by fights in which biting and kicking but not much else are forbidden), and a fireworks show. Unofficial events are weddings; bikers find it romantic to get married during the rally, and in 1990, the fiftieth anniversary rally, 176 motorcyling couples exchanged vows.

The rally began in 1938 when Clarence (Pappy) Hoel, a local motorcycle dealer, invited some fellow bikers to a get-together. His wife, Pearl, made hot dogs, potato salad, and iced tea for the crew. The rally has been held ever since, except for two years during World War II, and has become part of biker lore.

Black Hills Passion Play
June–August

One of Europe's oldest productions, the Passion Play—which recreates events during the last seven days of the life of Christ—was first presented on the American stage in 1932. It was brought to the United States from Germany by Joseph Meier, who continues to produce and direct the drama three nights a week from early June through the end of August in an outdoor amphitheatre in Spearfish, South Dakota. Known as the Black Hills Passion Play since 1939, when the company settled in Spearfish, the huge outdoor production features Roman soldiers on horseback, a camel caravan, and pigeons escaping from cages as merchants and moneylenders are driven from the Temple. The amphitheatre, which seats six thousand, was built specifically for the Passion Play and claims to have the world's largest stage.

A series of permanent sets are used to portray Bethany , the home of Mary and Martha; the palace of Pontius Pilate, the Roman governor; the Temple; the Garden of Gethsemane; the Tomb; and Mount Calvary.

Black History Month
February

Black History Month grew out of **Negro History Week,** which was established in February 1926 by the African-American historian Carter G. Woodson. Expanded in 1976 to a month-long observance, this celebration of the contributions and achievements of African-Americans was initially designed to encompass the birthday of the abolitionist orator and journalist Frederick Douglass on February 14 as well as Abraham Lincoln's birthday (see LINCOLN'S BIRTHDAY). The event is widely observed by schools, churches, libraries, clubs, and organizations wishing to draw attention to the contributions of African-Americans.

Douglass was a fugitive slave who assumed this name when, by posing as a sailor, he escaped to New Bedford, Massachusetts. His former master's wife had secretly taught him to read and write, and after his escape Douglass became a skilled orator who lectured widely in favor of abolition. He settled for a while in Rochester, New York, where he founded an anti-slavery newspaper, and eventually ended up in Washington, D.C., where he held a number of government positions. One of his former residences there now houses the Museum of African Art and the Frederick Douglass Institute.

Black Madonna of Jasna Gora, Feast of the
August 15

The most famous icon in Eastern Europe can be found at the monastery on Jasna Gora, in the city of Czestochowa, Poland. The *Czarna Madonna* or Black Madonna is so called because of the dark complexion in the portrait of the Virgin Mary that, according to legend, was painted by St. Luke on a linden wood tabletop built by the apprentice carpenter, Jesus of Nazareth. Each year on August 15, the feast of the ASSUMPTION, hundreds of thousands of pilgrims attend the **Feast of Our Lady of Czestochowa** to seek forgiveness for their sins, recovery from injury or illness, or to offer gratitude for a favor granted. With their rosaries in hand, the pilgrims—some on their knees—climb Jasna Gora, which means the 'Hill of Light,' to attend Mass at the monastery, celebrated above them, on the high monastery walls, by priests in golden chasubles.

More than eighty miracles have been documented at the shrine, which is only one of many dedicated to the Virgin Mary throughout the country. King Jan Kazimierz proclaimed the Virgin Mary to be the Queen of Poland in 1656 after an unlikely victory over the Swedes at Jasna Gora prevented the latter from overrunning the monastery and looting its treasures. Mary is the patron saint of Poland.

Black Nazarene Fiesta
January 1–9
The **Fiesta of Quiapo District** is the largest festival in Manila. It is held each year in honor of the Quiapo District's patron saint—the Black Nazarene, a life-size statue of Jesus carved from blackwood, whose shrine is located in Quiapo's baroque church. The traditional nine-day fiesta features nightly cultural events, band concerts, and fireworks. On the last day of the festival there is a procession of barefoot men pulling a carriage that holds the 200-year-old statue of Christ on the way to Calvary. Those members of the procession who are not pulling the carriage carry candles and circle throughout the district.

Black Poetry Day
October 17
Jupiter Hammon, the first African-American poet to publish his own verse, was born on this day in 1711 and lived most of his life in the Lloyd Neck area of Huntington, Long Island. Hammon was a slave—first to the merchant Henry Lloyd, lord of the Manor of Queen's Village (now Lloyd Neck), and later to Joseph Lloyd, an American patriot who moved to Hartford, Connecticut during the Revolution. Hammon eventually returned to Lloyd Neck as slave to Joseph's grandson, John Lloyd. Hammon learned how to read and was allowed to use his master's library. On Christmas Day, 1760, he published his first poem, "An Evening Thought," at the age of forty-nine. He went on to publish other poems and a number of prose pieces as well.

Black Poetry Day was first proposed in 1970 by Stanley A. Ransom of Huntington, who was concerned that there were no existing celebrations to honor the contributions African-Americans have made to American life and culture. When Ransom relocated to Plattsburgh, New York, he brought Black Poetry Day with him. Although it is celebrated all over the state, it has yet to be formally proclaimed a state holiday. Oregon has already proclaimed October 17 as Black Poetry Day, and schools elsewhere have taken advantage of the opportunity to encourage African-American students to express their thoughts and feelings through poetry. Other celebrations include essay contests and poetry readings. In 1985, the African-American poet Gwendolyn Brooks spoke at SUNY-Plattsburgh in honor of Jupiter Hammon's contribution to American culture. In 1993 Rita Dove, an African-American, was named poet laureate of the United States.

Black Ships Festival
May 16 and 17 in Shimoda, Japan; last weekend in July in Rhode Island
"Black ships" or *Kurofune*, is what the Japanese called the black ships that Commodore Matthew C. Perry anchored off Shimoda, Japan on July 8, 1853. He forcefully negotiated the Treaty of Kanagawa—the first treaty between the United States and Japan—in 1854. The treaty opened trade between the two countries and ended two centuries of self-imposed isolation for Japan.

In 1934, Shimoda began commemorating the arrival of Commodore Perry and his black ships. It is the site of the first American consulate in Japan, placed there by the Japanese to keep the (American) "barbarians" from the capital, then called Edo. The first consul-general, Townsend Harris, arrived in August 1856. Twenty years later, Shimoda became the sister city to Newport, Rhode Island, where Perry was born. In 1984, Newport celebrated a reciprocal Black Ships Festival emphasizing Japanese art, culture, and education. Events include Japanese tea ceremonies, ikebana (flower arranging), origami (paper folding), kendo (martial arts), Sumo wrestling, Japanese kite flying, and traditional Japanese performing arts. In 1986 the Black Ships Festival was expanded to form the Japan-America Society of Rhode Island, which now sponsors the festival and works to develop cooperation and understanding between the citizens of Rhode Island and Japan.

Blajini, Feast of the (Sarbatoarea Blajinilor)
Second Monday after Easter
Among the peasants in Romania there is a widespread belief in the existence of the *Blajini*, 'meek' or 'Kindly Ones'—a lost race who keep to themselves, know nothing of the world of men, and live in a fairy-land "by the Sunday-water." They are beloved by God because of their purity and innocence. On the Monday after EASTER MONDAY, Romanian women throw red Easter egg

shells on running streams, since they believe that the *Blajini* live on the banks of the river fed by all the streams of the world. Their hope is that the *Blajini* will find the shells and know it is time to celebrate the EASTER feast.

Blessed Sacrament, Feast of the
First weekend in August

The **Festival of the Blessed Sacrament** held annually in New Bedford, Massachusetts coincides with a similar festival on the Portuguese island of Madeira. The American festival, which was first held in 1914, celebrates the safe arrival of the Portuguese immigrants who came to New Bedford in the early nineteenth century after braving rough seas and stormy weather en route. The descendants of these immigrants, many of whom served aboard American whaleships, give thanks each year by holding what they would like to think of as the largest Portuguese feast in the world on the first weekend in August. Preparations for the festivities go on throughout the year, and the events include a parade, Portuguese folkloric dancers and singers, Portuguese specialties such as *cabra* (goat) and *bacalhau* (codfish), and a colorful procession to the Immaculate Conception Church. The festival is held at Madeira Field, although the events extend throughout the city. New Bedford, once a thriving New England whaling port, remains home to a large Portuguese-American community.

Blessing of the Grapes (Haghoghy Ortnootyoon)
Sunday nearest August 15

In ancient times the people of Armenia dedicated their grape harvest to Astrik, the goddess of the hearth, in a New Year celebration called *Navasard*. Nowadays the festival is associated with the FEAST OF THE ASSUMPTION, and is celebrated on the Sunday nearest to August 15, which is the feast day. No one is supposed to eat grapes until this day, when a tray filled with them is blessed in the church. Each member of the congregation is given a bunch of grapes as he or she leaves, and parties are held after the church ceremony in homes and in the vineyards. It is also traditional for women named Mary to entertain their friends on this, their name day.

Blessing of the Shrimp Fleet
Last weekend in June

In the coastal town of Bayou La Batre, the "Seafood Capital of Alabama," the two-day event has been celebrated since 1950. The "main street" of the town, founded in 1786, is actually the bayou, where trawlers are often tied up three- or four-deep. Shrimp is the mainstay of commercial fishing here, and more than 350 shrimp boats work out of the town, while several hundred other vessels operate in the waters off the port harvesting oysters, crab, and finfish. Seafood products landed in the port have a dockside value of $33 million annually, but the total seafood industry, including processors, is thought to produce $300 million for the local economy. Boat building and repair are also major industries.

The fleet blessing began simply: a priest went up and down the bayou blessing the boats tied to the docks. From the start, a wreath has been lowered into the bayou to honor fishermen lost at sea. Now some 25,000 people come for the highlight and final event of the weekend: the blessing ceremony by the priest of St. Margaret Roman Catholic Church and a parade of between fifty and one hundred boats decorated with pennants, bunting, and papier mâché figures. Other events include contests in oyster shucking, shrimp heading, and crab picking; seafood and gumbo dinners; a land parade; a fiddler-crab race for children; and the crowning of the Fleet Queen. The affair is sponsored by St. Margaret Church.

In the port city of Biloxi, Mississippi, **Blessing of the Fleet** is a celebration of the start of the fishing season, where seafood is the major industry. The blessing began in 1924 when sailing craft made up most of the fleet. Today up to eighty boats parade past the Blessing Boat, where the pastor of St. Michael's Roman Catholic Church (known as the Church of the Fisherman) stands and bestows the blessings. The boats are decorated with flags and elaborate three-dimensional plywood constructions of such figures as mermaids, shrimp, paddlewheels, and fishnets. The blessing is the culmination of the weekend; before that, there are net throwing and oyster-shucking contests, the crowning of a king and queen, and street dances known as *fais-do-do*. Supposedly "fais-do-do" was the song sung to children to tell them to go to sleep, and the dance got its name because adults danced when the children slept. The weekend also offers lots of local food—mullet, boiled shrimp, and Biloxi bacon.

Blessing of the Waters Day *See* Orthodox Epiphany

Blessing of Throats *See* St. Blaise's Day

36

Blessing the Sun (Birchat Hahamah)
Every 28 years on a Wednesday

According to Jewish tradition, God made the sun, the moon, and the stars on the fourth day of Creation—a Wednesday, according to ancient reckoning—and once every twenty-eight years the sun returns to the same astronomical position that it held on that day. The Talmud says that the turning point of this twenty-eight year sun cycle occurs at the VERNAL EQUINOX on a Tuesday evening (the first in the month of Nisan) at 6:00 p.m. in Jerusalem. But since the sun is not visible at that time in all parts of the world, the blessing isn't recited until the following morning at sunrise. The blessing is said while standing, and the sun must be visible.

The last blessing of the sun occurred on April 8, 1981, with about 50,000 Jews gathered at the Wailing Wall in Jerusalem, Judaism's holiest shrine. Similar celebrations took place on top of Israel's highest building in Tel Aviv and at the Empire State Building in New York City. The next **Blessing of the Sun** will take place in 2009.

Blowing the Midwinter Horn
December–January; beginning of Advent through Sunday after Epiphany

The custom of **Midwinterhoorn Blazen** in the province of Overijssel, the Netherlands is believed to have originated over two thousands years ago. The local farmers make their winter horns out of fitted sections of curving birchwood. The horns are about forty-five inches long and when soaked in water, they give out a shrill, plaintive sound that carries for great distances over the frozen countryside. Although in pagan times the blowing of the horns was thought to rid the earth of evil spirits, today the horns announce the coming of Christ.

In Oldenzaal, a special melody composed by the area's champion hornblower is played from the four corners of the local church tower, beginning at dawn on ADVENT EVE and continuing until THREE KINGS' DAY.

Bluegrass Fan Fest
Third weekend in September

A festival for fans that follows a week-long trade show of the International Bluegrass Music Association, held the third week in September in Owensboro, Ky. Owensboro was the choice for the fest because Bill Monroe, the founder of the seminal bluegrass group The Blue Grass Boys and father of bluegrass music, was born in Ohio County, thirty miles from the city. Between thirty and forty bluegrass groups perform, and proceeds from admission sales go to a trust fund for IBMA members.

Boat Race Day
March–April

This is traditionally the day on which the annual rowing race between the Oxford and Cambridge University "eights" (as the crews of the eight-oared rowing shells are called) is held on the Thames River in England. Beginning in Putney and ending four-and-a-quarter miles downriver at Mortlake, the race attracts large crowds of spectators-many of whom are hoping for the drama of an unexpected capsizing.

Boat Race Day in Okinawa
Fourteenth day of the fifth lunar month

On Okinawa, the largest of the Ryukyu Islands southwest of Japan, the fourteenth day of the fifth month is both a religious festival and a sporting event. In Minatogawa, for example, this is the **Festival of the Gods of the Sea.** The villagers first go to the religious sites to make offerings and pray, and then they attend the boat races held in the estuary of the river. In Taira, it is the day on which fishing canoes from Taira race against competitors from the neighboring village of Kawata.

Boggy Bayou Mullet Festival
Third full weekend in October

A festival of seafood, folk culture, sports, and pageants held since 1976 in Niceville, Fla. It celebrates the unappreciated mullet, the underdog of seafood, and serves up ten tons of fried and smoked mullet, plus vast quantities of "mullet dogs," mullet filets on buns. Estimated attendance was 270,000 in 1991.

Niceville is a small town about fifty miles east of Pensacola on the Florida panhandle. But people kept calling Niceville "Nashville", so to publicize the town, and to promote mullet the Boggy Bayou Festival was begun. Mullet, abundant in the local Gulf waters, is a cheap source of high-quality protein but has had a bad reputation among seafood fanciers because of its feeding habits. Mullet are bottom-feeding vegetarians, and they taste like what they eat. The people of Niceville know that only mullet caught from waters with clean bottoms—like those on Florida's Gulf Coast—are worth eating.

This sleepy bayou town's festival has exploded into a fully-rounded affair. It has beauty pageants to name not only the Queen of the Mullet Festival but also Miss Teen Mullet Festival, Junior Miss

Mullet Festival, and Little Miss Mullet Festival. Sports events include golf, rugby, and racquet-ball tournaments, and a canoe race; the U.S. Army Rangers bring their reptile exhibit of a six-foot alligator and rattlesnakes; free entertainment is on stage all weekend. Then there is the food. Beyond the mullet, these are samplings from the food booths: CaJune specialties like crawfish pie, gumbo, and gator sausage; American Indian staples of fried bread and *pasole*, which is like pizza; barbecued rabbit, stingray and barracuda on a stick, fried oysters, boiled shrimp, apple dumplings, strawberry pie, and Mexican fried ice cream.

Bok Kai Festival

Usually March or April; second day of second month of Chinese lunar year

A two-day event in Marysville, Calif., that began as a Chinese religious event to honor Bok Eye (or Bok I), the god who has the power to control flooding and the waters of irrigation and the rains. The festival, held since the 1880s, is now more of a cultural tribute to the Bok Kai legend.

Chinese immigrants came to northern California in the 1850s to find work in the gold fields or on the railroads being built through the Sierra Nevada mountains. When the railroads were completed, they settled in Marysville, which became the third largest Chinese community in the country, after San Francisco and Sacramento.

Between 1825 and 1862, three floods caused hundreds of fatalities in the Marysville area. In 1865, the Chinese first built a temple on the Yuba River, naming it Bok Kai Mui, meaning temple (Mui) on the north (Bok) side of the stream (Kai). (The temple was destroyed by fire and rebuilt in 1880.) Several gods were placed in the temple, but Bok Eye, meaning Northern or Dark North God, was the central deity. By building the temple in his honor, the Chinese people hoped to protect the city from future flooding.

The celebration of Bomb Day—Bok Eye's birthday—began in the 1880s. Today the celebration of Bomb Day/Bok Kai Festival is a community-wide affair, drawing thousands of vistors from as far as Hong Kong. A parade is the highlight of the festival, and a 150-foot dragon is the highlight of the parade. It winds its way along the parade route on the legs of 100 volunteers, accompanied by floats and marching bands, Clydesdale horses and a Wells Fargo stagecoach—more than 100 entries in all. The current dragon is the second one to be used in the parade. The first,

brought to the United States before 1900, was retired in 1937 and now rests in the temple.

Besides the parade, there are vendors' markets for foods and crafts, demonstrations of martial arts, lion dancing, art displays, and performances by celebrated Chinese artists; these have included a master of Chinese brush painting, a pianist from China, and a composer and poet.

The Bok Kai Temple in Marysville is the only religious shrine to Bok Eye outside of Asia and is a designated historical landmark.

Bologna Festival
July

In 1906 a bologna maker named T. J. Minnie set up his shop in Yale, Michigan. Over the next several decades, a number of other bologna makers settled in Yale, but today only one remains: C. Roy Inc., which produces Yale Bologna. The annual Bologna Festival, established in 1989, is designed to attract true bologna lovers with its booths serving bologna rings, bologna hot dogs, bologna and sauerkraut, and fried bologna sandwiches. A King and Queen Bologna are crowned, and they ride through town on the C. Roy float in the Big Bologna Parade wearing crowns made out of bologna rings.

Bom Jesus dos Navegantes
January 1

In Salvador, Brazil, the festival known as Bom Jesus dos Navegantes is celebrated on NEW YEAR'S DAY. A procession of small boats decorated with flags and streamers carries a statue of the **Lord Jesus of Seafarers** from the main harbor to the outlying beach of Boa Viagem. Thousands of spectators line Salvador's beaches to catch a glimpse of the spectacle. According to legend, sailors participating in the event will never die by drowning.

A similar procession takes place on the same day in Angra dos Reis, ninety miles south of Rio de Janeiro.

Bonfim Festival (Festa do Bonfim)
January

There is a church in Salvador, Bahia, Brazil, known as Our Lord of the Happy Ending (*bonfim*). It was built by the captain of a ship, wrecked off the coast of Bahia in 1875, who promised God that if his men survived, he would build him a church in gratitude. Today during the Bonfim Festival, hundreds of Brazilian women dress in the traditional white dresses of colonial Bahia and form a procession to the church. The *bahianas* carry pots of water on their heads, perfumed with white flowers. The washing of the steps at Bonfim Basilica on the final Sunday is the highlight of this week-long festival.

Bonfire Night
Various

There are a number of holidays that are referred to by this name. GUY FAWKES DAY (November 5) in England is sometimes called Bonfire Night, and in Scotland the name is applied to the Monday nearest May 24th, the former EMPIRE DAY. The original bonfires were actually "bone-fires" in which human or animal bones were burned to appease the gods. But nowadays bonfires are lit primarily for amusement. Other traditional bonfire nights include the eve of MIDSUMMER DAY (June 23), when fires were lit to cure disease and ward off evil spirits, and the WINTER SOLSTICE, when bonfires heralded the return of the sun.

Bonneville Speed Week
Third week in August

A competition to set speed records on the Bonneville Salt Flats near Wendover, Utah. The salt flats were once under Lake Bonneville which was formed about two million years ago and covered 19,000 square miles in what are now Utah, Nevada, and Idaho. The Great Salt Lake to the east of the flats is all that remains of that prehistoric lake. Bonneville is so flat that it is the only place in the United States where the curvature of the earth can be seen. Its salt surface is as hard as concrete by summer's end, and the many miles of unobstructed space create an anomaly of nature found nowhere else in the world. These conditions are ideal for land speed racing.

Speed Week has been held since 1949. About 300 cars and motorcycles come here from all over the world to try to break land speed records. The one-mile automobile speed record was set in 1983 by Britain's Richard Noble who zipped over the flats in the Thrust 2 at 633.6 mph. The first person to set a speed record on the Bonneville Salt Flats was Teddy Tetzlaff who drove a Blitzen Benz 141 mph in 1914.

Boomerang Festival
Usually October (October 12 in 1991)

A national roundup in Hampton, Va., of throwers of boomerangs, the curved sticks that after being thrown return to the thrower. Top performers compete in a series of throwing events for speed, maximum time aloft, accuracy, consecutive catches, and other categories. The competition, which began in 1985, is topped off by an awards banquet.

The boomerang has been used in Australia for about 20,000 years as a weapon and for felling game animals. It is also believed to have been used by ancient Egyptians and American Indians. As a sport, boomeranging has grown more popular in this country during the last twenty years. World championship meets are held in various countries at irregular times; in April 1991, the World Boomerang Cup Tournament was held in Perth, Australia, and American teams took the two top prizes.

Booths, Feast of *See* Sukkot

Borrowed Days
March 29, 30, 31

According to an old Scottish rhyme, the last three days in March were "borrowed" from April, in return for which March promised to destroy three young sheep. But the weather proved to be an obstacle, and the promise was never fulfilled. Other references to the **Borrowing Days** go back even farther. Both an ancient calendar of the Church of Rome and a 1548 book known as the *Complaynt of Scotland* allude to the days at the end of March as being more like winter than spring. Whatever their origin, it seems likely that the wet, windy weather that so often comes at the end of March gave rise to the notion that this month had to "borrow" some additional time.

In the Scottish Highlands, there is an ancient belief that February 12, 13, and 14 were "borrowed" from January, and that it was a good omen for the rest of the year if the weather was as stormy as possible on these days. But if they were fair, no further good weather could be expected through the spring.

Boston Marathon
April 19 or nearest Monday

The oldest footrace in the United States was first held on PATRIOTS' DAY, April 19, 1897. Organized by members of the Boston Athletic Association (BAA), the race involved only fifteen runners. Nowadays the Boston Marathon draws anywhere from seven to more than nine thousand official starters, who must meet established qualifying times. Several thousand additional runners participate on an unofficial basis. In 1972, it became the first marathon to officially admit women runners.

The 26.2 mile course begins exactly at noon in Hopkinton, Massachusetts, includes the infamous "Heartbreak Hill" (a section of Commonwealth Avenue in Newton Centre, Massachusetts that marks the race's twenty-first mile), and ends in front of the Prudential Center in downtown Boston. Well-known American winners of the Boston Marathon include the "old" John Kelley, who won twice and continues, in his eighties, to complete the race; the "young" John J. Kelley (no relation), who was the first American victor in the post-World War II era; "Tarzan" Brown, who in 1938 took a break at the nine-mile mark for a quick swim in Lake Cochichuate; and, among the more recent winners, Bill Rodgers. Among the women, Rosa Mota of Portugal was the first to win three official Boston Marathon titles. And few people will forget the infamous Rosie Ruiz in 1980, who many believed tried to defraud the BAA by showing up at the end of the race to capture the women's laurel wreath, the traditional symbol of victory, without having actually run the full distance; this was substantiated by television coverage of certain checkpoints. Jackie Gareau of Canada was later declared the women's winner, although Ruiz continued to insist that she'd run the race fairly.

Boston Massacre Day
March 5

Celebrated in New Jersey as **Crispus Attucks Day**, March 5 marks the anniversary of the 1770 street fight between a group of colonial American protesters and a squad of British troops quartered in Boston—an event that reflected the unpopularity of the British regime in colonial America and set the stage for the American Revolution. A British sentry was pelted with stones and snowballs by a mob of about fifty people. He called for help and Captain Thomas Preston sent several soldiers. The soldiers fired and five of the protesters were killed. One of them was Crispus Attucks, a runaway slave who'd spent twenty years as a whaleman. It was Attucks who led the crowd from Dock Square to King Street (now State Street), where the confrontation occurred, and who later became known as the first martyr of the American Revolution.

The name "Boston Massacre" was invented by the colonists and used as propaganda to force the removal of the British troops.

In Massachusetts, the anniversary of the "Boston Massacre" is observed annually with patriotic songs and speeches recalling Attucks' sacrifice.

On the 200th anniversary of the massacre in 1970, and again five years later on the 200th anniversary of the outbreak of the Revolutionary War, the Charlestown Militia Company staged a reenactment of the event. In New Jersey, Crispus Attucks is often honored in conjunction with Martin Luther King, Jr. (see MARTIN LUTHER KING, JR.'S BIRTHDAY).

Bottle Kicking and Hare Pie Scramble, Annual
Between March 23 and April 26; Easter Monday

This seven-hundred-year-old event is the high-point of the local calendar in the small village of Hallaton in Leicestershire, England. Opposing teams from Hallaton and the neighboring town of Medbourne scramble to maneuver two out of three small wooden beer kegs across a goal line in a game that has been described as being "unsurpassed for sheer animal ferocity." The chaos on the field may have something to do with the fact that players drop out of the game from time to time and have "a pint."

The event begins when the local rector blesses the Hare Pie—originally made of hare but now of beef. After handing out slices to some of the villagers, he scatters the remainder on the rectory lawn, where people scramble for it. Then comes the contest for the beer-filled kegs.

Where did these activites originate? According to legend, a village woman was crossing a field when she was attacked by a bull. A running hare diverted the bull's attention and she escaped. She bequeathed a field to the town in gratitude. The connection between the legend and the modern festivities is vague.

Boun Phan Vet
October–November; Month 12

In the Laotian capital of Vientiane, national rites commemorating Lao origins and historical events are held on this day in That Luang, the temple where the Buddha's relics have traditionally been housed. Outside the capital, Boun Phan Vet is celebrated at different times in different communities to honor Prince Vessantara, an earlier incarnation of the Buddha. There are dramatic performances, lovesong contests, cockfights, banquets, and other social gatherings at which the villagers entertain their neighbors from other villages. This is also a time for young men to be ordained into the *sangha* or Buddhist monkhood.

Boxing Day
December 26

The term 'Boxing Day' comes from the little earthenware boxes that servants, tradespeople, and others who rendered services to the public used to carry around on the day after CHRISTMAS to collect tips and year-end bonuses. Although the custom of distributing gifts (usually money) to public servants and employees has continued, it often takes place before Christmas rather than after, and boxes have nothing to do with it. But the name has remained, and Boxing Day is still observed in England, Canada, Australia, and many other nations. In South Africa, it is known as the **Day of Good Will**. If December 26 falls on a Saturday or Sunday, the following Monday or Tuesday is usually observed as a bank or public holiday.

See also JUNKANOO FESTIVAL.

Boy Scouts' Day
February 8

The Boy Scout movement was started by a British cavalry officer, Robert S. S. Baden-Powell, who was well-known not only for his heroic defense of Mafeking in southern Africa during the Boer War, but also for his publication of a military pamphlet, "Aids to Scouting," which emphasized the need for a strong character and outdoor survival skills among British soldiers. King George V ordered Baden-Powell to retire from the military so that he could help British boys learn about camping, hiking, signaling, plant identification, swimming, and other such activities. Baden-Powell's 1908 book, *Scouting for Boys*, was an immediate success, and he devoted the rest of his life to the task of promoting the scouting movement.

The Boy Scouts of America, the nation's largest youth organization, was founded on February 8, 1910. A Chicago publisher, William D. Boyce, who had experienced the courtesy and helpfulness of a young scout firsthand while staying in London, decided that young American boys needed the same kind of training. Two existing organizations—Dan C. Beard's Sons of Daniel Boone and Ernest Thompson Seton's "Woodcraft Indians"—had already introduced boys to the same idea, and the Sons of Daniel Boone eventually merged with the Boy Scouts of America. Cub Scout "Blue and Gold" dinners, flag ceremonies, parents' nights, shopping center demonstrations, and the presentation of advancement awards are popular ways of celebrating this day, which is part of **Boy Scout Month**, an annual anniversary celebration extending throughout February.

Boys' Dodo Masquerade
Full moon of Ramadan

A children's entertainment introduced by Hausa traders during the mid-nineteenth century, the **Dodo Masquerade** performed in Burkina Faso, (formerly called Upper Volta) has changed considerably over the years, and now reflects the local Mossi culture. As the RAMADAN season approaches, boys between the ages of twelve and sixteen form groups consisting of a principal singer, a chorus, five or more dancers, a drummer, a few costumed wild animals based on local folklore, and a leader who dresses in military style. The boys decide on their roles and dance steps, which are usually variations on a dozen well-known patterns. Each dancer wears knee bells made from tin can tops and carries two sticks decorated by painting or peeling the bark away in special patterns.

On the night of the full moon during the Islamic month of Ramadan, the boys in their masks and costumes perform their dance for each household or compound while the chorus sings. Younger boys (seven to twelve years of age) started forming their own "Petit Dodo" groups and by the mid 1950s, little boys were dancing Dodo in many of the Mossi villages.

Boys' Rifle Match *See* Knabenschiessen

Braemar Highland Gathering
September

In the eleventh century, King Malcolm held a gathering of the Scottish clans in Braemar to test their strength and to choose the hardiest soldiers. Competitors were asked to toss the caber—a pole sixteen to twenty feet long and weighing 120 pounds—in such a way that it landed on its other end, much the way loggers used to toss logs across a river. The Braemar Gathering is still an annual event in the village of Braemar in Scotland, and the participants are still required to wear kilts and toss the caber. But the event has been expanded to include traditional Highland dancing, bagpipe music, games, and other athletic competitions as well.

See also HIGHLAND GAMES.

Brauteln
Between February 3 and March 9; Shrove Tuesday

The **Wooing a Bride Ceremony** in Sigmaringen, Germany is part of a CARNIVAL custom that dates back to 1648. After the Thirty Years' War was over, hunger and disease were widespread in Sigmaringen. This discouraged young men from marrying and starting families. The population dropped so rapidly that the mayor offered to reward the first young man brave enough to become engaged with the *Brauteln* or bride-wooing ceremony during which the lucky bachelor was carried at the head of a colorful procession around the town square.

Today the custom continues. On SHROVE TUESDAY any man who has married within the last twelve months, who has just moved into town with his wife, or who has celebrated his twenty-fifth or fiftieth wedding anniversary is invited to be *brautelt*. Heralds dressed in traditional costumes carry the eligible men around the town pump to the accompaniment of drummers and pipers.

Bregenz Festival
July–August

The Bregenz Festival held each summer in Bregenz, Austria is perhaps best known for its floating stage, built on Lake Constance. Started in 1946 to give people some enjoyment after the end of World War II, the festival has since added a new indoor Festival House on the shore of the lake and regularly attracts as many as 100,000 visitors. It is famous for its performance of opera, operetta, plays, ballet, and symphonic concerts.

Bridge Day
Third Saturday in October

A celebration of the New River Gorge Bridge in Fayetteville, W. Va., and a day of bliss for daredevils. The bridge, completed in 1977, is the world's longest steel-arch span and is one of the highest bridges in the nation. Its span is 1,700 feet, with a rise of 360 feet, putting it 876 feet above the New River Gorne National River. On Bridge Day, celebrated since 1980, parachutists jump from the bridge onto the river's banks below. The less bold walk over the bridge. About 200 vendors offer food, crafts, and souvenirs for sale. Attendance is about 150,000.

British Open
Summer (usually July at present)

The oldest and one of the most prestigious international golf championship tournaments in the world. It is officially the **Open Championship of the British Isles** but in Great Britain is known simply as **The Open**. It began in 1860 at the then twelve-hole Prestwick course in Scotland and is now rotated among select golf courses in England and Scotland. Scot Willie Park won the

first tournament, which is memorable for the tourney's highest single-hole stroke total—twenty-one.

Other notable years in the Open:

In 1901, Scot James Braid, who became one of Scotland's greatest golf heroes, won the first of five Open championships.

In 1907, Arnaud Massy of France was the first player from outside Great Britain to win.

In 1910, the Open's fiftieth anniversary was celebrated at St. Andrews (considered by many to be the premier golf course of the world) in a tempest of a rainstorm that put some of the greens under water.

In 1914, at Prestwick, the great triumvirate of golf, Braid and Englishmen John Henry Taylor and Harry Vardon, entered the match with each having five Open titles behind them. Vardon won with a final total round of seventy-eight.

In 1921, Bobby Jones (Robert Tyre Jones Jr.), the legendary golfer and lawyer from Atlanta, Ga., lost his temper at the par-three eleventh hole at St. Andrews and shredded his scorecard while the gallery gaped.

In 1926, that same Bobby Jones won the cup; it was the first time in twenty-nine years that an amateur had won.

In 1930, Jones won and went on to sweep the United States Open and the British Amateur and U.S. Amateur for golfing's Grand Slam, after which he retired. The feat hasn't been equaled. (Later, in 1958, Jones became the first American since Benjamin Franklin to receive the freedom of the burgh of St. Andrews.)

In 1973, Gene Sarazen, celebrating his fiftieth anniversary of play, shot a first-round hole-in-one on the par-three, 126-yard eighth hole (known as the Postage Stamp) at Royal Troon. In the second round, he deuced the hole.

In 1975, American Tom Watson won the first of five championships.

In 1977, Watson and fellow American Jack Nicklaus left the field behind them and dueled to a dramatic final round; Watson won by a stroke with a seventy-two-hole total score of 268.

The Open has a special cachet for golfers since Scotland is considered, if not the birthplace of golf, the place where it developed into its present form played with ball, club, and hole. (At one time, pub doors were the target). The game may actually have originated in Holland, where they called it *kolven*, but golf in Scotland goes back before 1457. That year, Scottish King James II banned "fute-ball and golfe" because they interfered with his subjects' archery practice. The ban didn't take. Golf was confined pretty much to Scotland until 1603 when King James VI of Scotland also assumed the throne of England and brought golf there, even though many English sportsman sniffily derided it as "Scottish croquet."

Broken Needles, Festival of *See* **Hari-Kuyo**

Brother and Sister Day *See* **Raksha Bandhan**

Brotherhood Sunday
Sunday nearest Washington's Birthday (February 22)
Every year since 1934 Brotherhood Week has been proclaimed by the President of the United States, sponsored by the National Conference of Christians and Jews, and observed by the country as a whole. The original idea was to set aside a week each year when people of all faiths would get together, discuss their differences, and reaffirm the human brotherhood that underlies the differences in their religious beliefs. Schools, churches, synagogues, civic groups, and other organizations across America celebrate this week—and, in particular, Brotherhood Sunday—by bringing together people of different faiths and backgrounds.

The decision to celebrate Brotherhood Week at the same time as WASHINGTON'S BIRTHDAY called attention to George Washington as a symbol of America's commitment to freedom from racial and religious prejudice. When Washington was president he wrote a letter to the Hebrew congregation in Newport, Rhode Island, in which he assured them that in this country there would be "to bigotry no sanction, to persecution no assistance." This quotation has become practically a slogan for the National Conference of Christians and Jews, which in addition to organizing Brotherhood Week is engaged in a continuing effort to promote interfaith relations.

Buccaneer Days
Last weekend in April through first weekend in May
A time when the city of Corpus Christi, Tex., by proclamation of the mayor, is under pirate rule,

similar to GASPARILLA DAY in Tampa, Fla. Buccaneer Days began in 1940 to honor the discovery of Corpus Christi Bay by Spanish explorer Alonzo Alvarez Pineda in 1519. It has become a ten-day carnival, calling to mind the days of the early nineteenth century when the settlement was a hideaway for pirates, who did a brisk trade in contraband. Events of the festival include sailboat regattas, parades, sports events, concerts, a coronation and ball, and fireworks on the bayfront.

Buchmesse *See* **Frankfurt Book Fair**

Bud Billiken Day
Second Saturday in August
Bud Billiken is the "patron saint" of Chicago's African-American children. Created in 1923 by Robert S. Abbott, the founder of the *Chicago Daily Defender* newspaper, Bud Billiken is a symbol of things as they should be—not necessarily as they are—and his day is primarily a children's event. There is a parade held on a Saturday in August each year that goes on for four hours, complete with marching bands, baton twirlers, floats holding celebrities and politicians, and units from the Navy, Air Force, and National Guard. The formalities end when the parade reaches Washington Park in the Grand Boulevard area of Chicago, where families have picnics and cookouts and the children can watch swimming shows in the park's three Olympic-sized pools.

Buddha's Birthday *See* **Vesak**

Buddhist Rains Retreat *See* **Waso**

Buena Vista Logging Days
Last Saturday in February
In the 1800s the logging of Minnesota's pine forests near Bemidji was in full swing. During the winter timber harvest, lumberjacks guided teams of Percheron horses, who hauled logs along ice-covered roads. Although the timber industry still works the woods around Bemidji, the golden days of the Minnesota logging boom only lasted fifty years. But the area continues to remember, recreate, and celebrate the skills of the old time lumberjack by holding a festival at Buena Vista village and logging camp located north of Bemidji. Each year participants dressed in red plaid wool shirts demonstrate log scaling and compete in axe chopping and crosscut sawing contests. They also guide teams of Percheron, Belgian, and Clydesdale draft horses in log loading and hauling demonstrations.

Visitors are transported to the logging camp aboard horse-powered sleighs and are served lumberjack camp meals all day long. Buena Vista village is also the home of the Lumberjack Hall of Fame, where up to 100 of the old lumberjacks are honored and inducted during the festival. Many of those fabled laborers of the northwoods, some of whom are nearly 100 years old, attend the festival each year.

Buffalo's Big Board Surfing Classic
February

Two days of surfing contests at Makaha Beach, Oahu, Hawaii, where the surf is sometimes twenty feet high. The classic is a tribute to "Buffalo" Keaulana, one of the state's premiere watermen. Old-timers ride the waves on the huge wooden surfboards that were used in Hawaii's early days; other events include canoe surfing, team bodyboarding, and tandem surfing. There are also food booths and Hawaiian entertainment

Bumba-meu-Boi Folk Drama
June 13–29

The Bumba-meu-Boi is a Brazilian folk drama that is typically performed in small towns and villages. The characters in the play include a sea captain riding a wicker hobby-horse, the Ox, the cowboys Mateus and Birico, Catarina (the pregnant mistress of Mateus), the Doctor, and the Chorus. A colorful procession announces the arrival of the players, who sometimes stage playful attacks on the spectators lining the streets. Performances usually take place in a room of the house belonging to the most important family in town, or else in front of a church or in the town's main square.

Bumbershoot
Four days over Labor Day weekend

The premier festival of Seattle, Wash., held since 1971 and now a wide-ranging round-up of many arts. It started as Festival '71, but became Bumbershoot in 1973: Bumbershoot is English slang for umbrella, and the festival is supposed to be an umbrella for the arts; the word also calls to mind Seattle's rainy climate.

In recent years, Bumbershoot attractions have included Japanese Kabuki theater, Russian rock, robot art, flamenco dance, and readings by contemporary writers. In 1991, performers included: Foday Musa Suso, a Mandingo *griot*, or hereditary musician and oral historian of the Mandingo people of West Africa; Roger Ferguson, the former National Flat-Pick Guitar Champion, presenting

bluegrass music; and the Mazeltones, singing Jewish music in Yiddish, Hebrew, and English. The food offerings yield Cajun-style salmon, Pennsylvania Dutch funnel cake, Italian calzone, Lebanese falafels, Thai beef sticks, strawberry shortcake, etc. In other words, Bumbershoot is a gallimaufry of music, dance, theater, visual and literary arts, children's activities, food, and crafts. It's held at the Seattle Center, the site of the 1962 World's Fair, and attracts about 250,000 people.

Bun Bang Fai (Boun Bang Fay; Rocket Festival)
April–May; Full moon day of Vaisakha

A rain ceremony celebrated in Laos and northeastern Thailand during Buddhist VESAK or Vaisakha Puja, observed on the full moon day of the sixth lunar month (Vaisakha). The Bun Bang Fai (*bun* means 'festival' in Lao) pre-dates Buddhism, and is intended to insure good crops.

In Laos, this is one of the country's wildest celebrations, with music and irreverent dances, processions, and merrymaking. The celebration ends with the firing of bamboo rockets into the sky, supposedly prompting the heavens to commence the rainy season and bring water to the rice fields. Prizes go to the fastest, highest, and brightest rockets.

In Thailand, the celebration is usually on the second weekend in May and is especially festive in Yasothon, with villagers shooting off huge rockets. Before the shooting, there are beauty parades, folk dances, and ribald entertainment.

Bunka-no-hi (Culture Day)
November 3

A Japanese national holiday on which medals are awarded by the government to those who have made special contributions in the fields of arts and sciences. The day was formerly celebrated as the birthday of Emperor Meiji, the great-grandfather of the present Emperor Akihito, who ruled from 1868 until his death in 1912. The years of his reign were a time of turning away from feudalism and toward Western rationalism and science, and were known as the age of *bummei-kaika* 'civilization and enlightenment.'

Bunker Hill Day
June 17

Observed primarily in Boston, Massachusetts, Bunker Hill Day commemorates the Revolutionary War battle of June 1775 between 3,000 British troops under the leadership of General William Howe and half that number of Americans under

Colonel William Prescott. In fact, Breed's Hill was fortified, not nearby Bunker Hill, and that is where the British attacked the rebels three times, eventually driving them out of their hastily constructed barricade, but only after losing over a thousand men. The American revolutionaries, who had exhausted their small store of ammunition, ended up fighting the British bayonets with the butts of their muskets.

Although the Americans were driven from their fortification and lost some 450 men, the battle boosted their confidence and has always been looked upon as one of the great heroic battles of the American Revolution. A 220-foot granite obelisk in Charlestown, just north of Boston, marks the site of the battle on Breed's hill, which itself is only eighty-seven feet high. This day is sometimes referred to as **Boston's Fourth of July**.

Burgsonndeg
February–March

On this day, which falls between February and March, young people in Luxembourg build bonfires to celebrate the sun and to signify the end of winter.

Burning of Judas, the
Between March 22 and April 25; Easter

La Quema de Judas takes place throughout Venezuela on the evening of EASTER. In contrast to the many solemn rituals organized by the Roman Catholic church during HOLY WEEK, JUDAS BURNING takes place at the village or urban neighborhood level. The preparations go on all week, beginning with the selection of an appropriate Judas—usually a public figure in the community, but sometimes an individual of state or national prominence—against whom the group has decided to stage a protest. The women construct a life-size effigy of this person, making sure to include elements of dress or appearance that leave no mistake about its identity. The men build a wooden stand in a central location where the Judas figure will be placed.

On Easter morning, the people proceed to the house where the effigy has been stored for safekeeping and demand that Judas Iscariot, the disciple who betrayed Jesus, be turned over for punishment. The Judas effigy is placed on the stand, where everyone gets a chance to slap, punch, or kick it. At dusk the leader of the group recites the list of grievances that the people have against this individual—a document known as "The Testament of Judas," which is often written in verse and quite humorous. Then the Judas is doused

with gasoline or kerosene and set on fire. The drinking, dancing, and fireworks continue late into the evening.

Although no one seems to know exactly how the custom originated, accounts of it have been traced back as far as thirteenth-century Spain.

Burning the Devil
December 7

La Quema del Diablo takes place in Guatemala. Men dressed as devils chase children through the streets from the start of ADVENT until December 7. On this day, trash fires are lit in the streets of Guatemala City and other towns, and the devils' reign of terror comes to an end. CHRISTMAS is preceded by nine days of POSADAS, during which people reenact Mary and Joseph's search for shelter in preparation for the birth of the infant Jesus.

Burning the Moon House
Fifteenth day of the first lunar month

The festival known as **Dal-jip-tae-u-gee** in the Kyungsang Province of Korea pays tribute to the moon by watching it rise through a moon house or moon gate—a carefully constructed pile of pine twigs which are set on fire. The moon gate is usually built on the top of a hill or at the seashore, where it is easier to see the moon rise through the flames. Jumping over the flames is believed to ward off evil, and the direction in which the moon gate collapses is an indication of whether the coming year will bring good luck or bad.

In other parts of Korea, a similar moon festival known as **Dal-ma-ji** is celebrated on the eve of the First Full Moon. People climb hills and build bonfires (without the "gate" aspect) to welcome the moon. Various folkloric beliefs concerning the harvest and the weather are associated with the color and brightness of the moon on this night.

Burns Night
January 25

The anniversary of the birthday of Scottish poet Robert Burns, who was born in 1759 in a clay cottage that blew down a week later, and died in 1796. The day is celebrated not only in Scotland but Newfoundland, where there is a sizeable settlement of Scots, and wherever there are devotees of this lusty poet. The celebrations generally take the form of recitations of Burns's poetry (Tam O'Shanter is a standard), the imbibing of quantities of single-malt Scotch whisky, and the serving of a haggis, a Scottish dish made of a sheep's or calf's innards (liver, heart, etc.) cut up with suet and oatmeal, seasoned, and boiled in the stomach of the animal. At the point of the carving of the haggis, it is traditional to recite "To a Haggis," with its line, "Great chieftain o' the pudding race!"

In the course of things, the Selkirk grace is also read:

"Some hae meat, and canna eat,
And some wad eat that want it;
But we hae meat and we can eat,
And sae the Lord be thanket."

And other favorite lines will be heard—for example, "O, my luve's like a red, red rose," and "O wad some Pow'r the giftie gie us/ To see oursels as others see us!" The evening always ends, of course, with "Auld Lang Syne."

Butter and Egg Days
First weekend after last Wednesday in April

A promotional event in Petaluma, Calif., that recalls the historic days when Petaluma was the "World's Egg Basket," producing millions of eggs that were shipped all over the world. The first Butter and Egg Days was a modest affair in 1983; it now draws about 25,000 for a parade with floats, bands, bagpipers, and children dressed as such things as butter pats and fried eggs. There are also street fairs, an antiques show, an egg toss, a butter-churning contest, and the presentation of the Good Egg award to a Petaluma booster.

The seed of this event was laid in 1918 when the first Egg Day parade was held. With the food shortages of World War I, people were being urged to eat less meat, and Petalumans decided to promote the idea of eating more eggs. Petaluma had the eggs; there were more hatcheries here than anywhere else. In 1878, the incubator developer L. C. Byce had established the Petaluma Incubator Co., which allowed great numbers of baby chicks to be artificially hatched. The town became a thriving poultry center, and boasted the world's only chicken pharmacy. The Egg Days, which ran from 1918 to 1926, brought the town national attention. These were huge celebrations, with nighttime illuminations, balls, chicken rodeos, and pa-

rades with gigantic Humpty Dumptys and white leghorn chickens. The chicken-and-egg industry waned in the 1950s, and the dairy industry moved in, and is now honored along with eggs.

Butter Sculpture Festival
Fifteenth day of first lunar month

The celebration of the Buddhist New Year (LOSAR) in Tibet is followed by MONLAM, a two-week prayer festival. On the fifteenth day, everyone goes to a monastery to view the butter sculptures. The most famous are at Jokhang Monastery in Lhasa, Tibet's capital. Completed over a period of months, the huge sculptures are made out of yak butter pigmented with dyes. They are fastened to thirty-foot high frames for display purposes and illuminated by special butter lamps. Each monastery maintains a workshop where its own artists shape the cold-hardened butter into depictions of legends, or other themes, different each year. The government awards a prize to the best sculpture.

Buzzard Day
March 15

About seventy-five turkey vultures, also known as turkey buzzards, return to Hinckley, Ohio, each March 15 to spend the summer. While these carrion-eating birds may lack the charm of the swallows of Capistrano, thousands of people celebrate them at the Hinckley Buzzard Day Festival, held since 1958 on the first Sunday after March 15. It features a pancake breakfast, an arts and crafts display, souvenir sales, and talks by naturalists at Metro Park, where the buzzards roost.

The vultures' return was first documented by a park patrolman who logged their arrival date for twenty-three years. Why the birds return, however, isn't known. One theory recalls the Great Hinckley Varmint Hunt on Dec. 24, 1818, when 475 men and boys lined up along Hinckley's borders and moved inward, slaughtering predators that were killing farm animals. The tons of carrion, of course, provided fine repasts for vulturine tastes.

See also BAT FLIGHT BREAKFAST.

C

Cabrillo Day
September 28

Juan Rodriguez Cabrillo was the Portuguese explorer who discovered California on September 28, 1542, when he sailed into the bay that would eventually be called San Diego. He went on to explore the upper California coast, naming both Catalina and San Clemente islands after his ships, but he failed to discover San Francisco Bay before being driven south again by a severe storm.

In the San Diego area, Cabrillo Day celebrations were relatively modest until the early 1960s, when the week-long Cabrillo Festival became a yearly event. Activities include Portuguese-American music and dancing, the placing of a wreath at the base of Cabrillo's statue on Point Loma, and a costumed renactment of the discovery of San Diego Bay.

Cactus Jack Festival
Second weekend of October

A celebration honoring the outspoken vice president of the United States, John Nance Garner, in Uvalde, Tex., where he made his home. Garner, born in 1868, was a member of the House of Representatives from 1903 until being chosen as vice president under Franklin Delano Roosevelt. He served two terms, from 1933 to 1941, but never quite let the position go to his head: he supposedly told a reporter that the vice presidency "isn't worth a bucket of warm spit." (It has since been revealed that Garner didn't use the word spit, and that the reporter cleaned up the quote.) On another occasion, he said the vice president was "a spare tire on the automobile of government." And furthermore, he said, "Becoming vice president was the only demotion I ever had."

So much for the vice presidency.

Cactus Jack earned his nickname in 1901 when the Texas legislature was deciding on a state flower. Garner led the faction that wanted the prickly-pear cactus, but the bluebonnet won by one vote. The name Cactus Jack stuck because he was a prickly kind of person who told people what he thought.

The Ettie R. Garner Museum here is the house where Garner and his wife, the former Mariette Rheiner, lived for thirty-seven years. She was his secretary and advisor until her death in 1948; Garner donated the home in her memory to the town. He died in 1967, just short of his ninety-ninth year.

The celebration features a parade, dance, horseshoe and washer pitching, sports events, arts and crafts, and a typical south Texas barbecue of *fajitas* (small strips of marinated beef) and tacos.

Calaveras County Fair and Frog Jumping Jubilee
Third weekend in May

A four-day county fair, established in 1928, in Angels Camp, Calif. It includes the official, original frog-jumping contest based on Mark Twain's story, "The Celebrated Jumping Frog of Calaveras County," as well as a children's parade, livestock competitions, a professional rodeo, a demolition derby, fireworks, and art exhibits. About 3,500 frogs are jumped in daily contests leading up to the Grand Finals on Sunday, in which there are 75 to 100 frog contestants. Jumps are measured from starting point to the landing point of the third hop. The world's record is 21'–5¾", set in 1986 by Rosie the Ribiter. There are cash prizes for winners in various divisions, and anyone breaking Rose's world record will win $5,000.

Mark Twain wrote the story of the jumping frog in 1865 and claimed it was told to him as the true story of an episode in Angel's Camp in 1849. In his story, the original frog, named Dan'l Webster, was owned by one Jim Smiley, who educated it to be a fine jumper. When a stranger came along, Smiley bet him $40 Dan'l Webster could out-jump any frog in Calaveras County. The time arrived for the contest, but the stranger had secretly filled

Dan'l Webster with quail shot, and the frog couldn't move. The stranger took the money and left, saying (according to Twain), "Well, *I* don't see no p'ints about that frog that's any better'n any other frog."

Calends *See* Ides

Calgary Exhibition and Stampede
July

The ten-day Calgary Exhibition and Stampede, originally called the **Calgary Stampede**, is Canada's largest rodeo event, similar to the CHEYENNE FRONTIER DAYS in the United States. The stampede offers a world-class rodeo competition in saddle bronc and bareback riding, steer wrestling, calf roping, and bull riding as well as a chuck wagon race that carries a $175,000 prize. Most of the rodeo events are held in the 130-acre Stampede Park in downtown Calgary, but there's also a Wild West town called Weadickville (named for Guy Weadick from Cheyenne, Wyoming, who founded the event in 1912), an Indian Village populated by representatives of five Indian tribes from the nearby Plains, a Frontier Casino with blackjack tables and roulette wheels, and agricultural and livestock exhibits.

Calico Pitchin', Cookin', and Spittin' Hullabaloo
Palm Sunday weekend

A celebration highlighting a tobacco-spitting contest and recalling the nineteenth-century heyday of Calico, a silver-mining ghost town in Southern California about ten miles north of Barstow. The contest for World Tobacco Spitting Champion began in 1977 and has led to two mentions in the Guinness Book of Records for distance in juice-spitting: Randy Ober of Arkansas spat a record 44'-6" in 1980 and then topped that record the next year with 47'-10". Other contest categories are accuracy in juice-spitting and distance in wad-spitting (wads are required to be at least half an inch in diameter). Contestants have come not only from the United States but also from Great Britain, Germany, and Japan.

The hullabaloo also features a stew cook-off and flapjack racing, plus more standard fare such as horseshoe pitching contest, egg-tossing, greased-pole climbing, and bluegrass music.

The date of the event recalls the time of year in 1881 when the miners arrived and named the town Calico because they thought the reds, greens, and yellows of the rock formations looked like a calico skirt. It was the location of one of the largest silver strikes in California, producing about $86 million in silver during the twenty years it flourished. When silver prices sank, so did Calico. In San Bernardino County, Calico is visited by tourists year-round.

Calvin Coolidge Birthday Celebration
July 4

The village of Plymouth Notch, Vermont contains what many consider to be the best preserved and most authentic of all presidential homesites. It was here that Calvin Coolidge (1872–1933), thirtieth president of the United States, spent his boyhood and was sworn in as president by his father following the death of Warren Harding in 1923. The Coolidge Homestead was donated to the State of Vermont by John Coolidge, the President's son, in 1956. The state eventually acquired his birthplace, the general store and post office owned by his father, the homes of his mother and stepmother, his paternal grandparents' farmhouse, the family church, and the cemetery where the President and six generations of Coolidges are buried.

On the FOURTH OF JULY each year, the anniversary of Coolidge's birth, there is a noontime march from the green near the Plymouth Post Office to the Notch Cemetery, lead by a Vermont National Guard colorguard with a bugler and a chaplain. The White House sends a wreath, which is laid at the President's tomb. Townspeople, tourists, and descendants of the Coolidge family listen to a brief graveside prayer service followed by the playing of taps. Next to the president's grave are those of his father and his son, Calvin Coolidge, Jr., who died at the age of sixteen during his father's White House years.

Camel Market
Usually July

An important annual camel-trading fair in Guelmime (also spelled Goulimime or Goulimine), Morocco, a walled town that historically was a caravan center. Located on the northwest edge of the Sahara, the market is attended by the wanderers of the desert—the Shluh and the blue-veiled Tuaregs known as the Blue Men. The Tuareg men wear a blue *litham*, a double strip of blue cloth worn over the head and covering all but the eyes, sometimes giving their faces a blue tint. They also wear blue robes over their white *djellabahs*. The story is that an English cloth merchant visited the port and trading city of Agadir in the 1500s with calico dyed indigo blue. The Tauregs liked the blue cloth and have had a predilection for it ever since.

The camel market brings together thousands of these Blue Men and their camels. They come to sell and trade baby camels as well as animal skins and wool. Hundreds of tents are pitched, and there is constant activity and noise: camel races, shouted bartering, and at night performances of the erotic *guedra* dance.

See also BIANOU.

Camel Motorcycle Week *See* Motorcycle Week

Camel Races, International
Weekend after Labor Day

Possibly the only camel races in the United States, and a reminder of a peculiar nineteenth-century experiment. The races have been held since 1954 in Virginia City, Nev., the one-time mining town that was considered the richest place on earth in the 1860s. In 1991, a team from Alice Springs, Australia won the races.

The town is the site of the celebrated Comstock Lode, which yielded nearly $300 million in gold and silver in the two decades after its discovery in 1859. The wealth also gave the territory strategic importance: President Abraham Lincoln wanted Nevada as a state on the side of the North to support anti-slavery amendments and he also needed the mineral riches to finance the Civil War. Nevada became a state in 1864, and gold and silver were dug from the mines—with the help, briefly, of camels.

It was thought that camels could work like mules in the mines, and camels in the Federal Camel Corps were shipped to Nevada from Texas (where they were used in the army cavalry). The army had originally brought about 120 camels to the U.S. from Africa and Asia in the mid-1850's to carry cargo from Texas to California. But they didn't last long; their hoofs didn't adapt to the rocky terrain, so they were allowed to roam wild, and apparently died out.

There are some camels kept in town today, though, and others are imported for the races. The three-day race weekend now includes a Camel Hump Ball (a dance and barbecue); a parade with about seventy units, including belly dancers and bagpipe players; and a race of ostriches pulling chariots.

When the camel race was being held in 1961, the movie *The Misfits* was being filmed nearby.

Director John Huston came to the races, borrowed a camel, and won.

Camp Fire Founders' Day
March 17

The organization originally known as the Camp Fire Girls was founded on March 17, 1910, around the same time that the Boy Scout movement was getting its start in Great Britain (*see* BOY SCOUTS' DAY). Now it is coeducational and is known as Camp Fire Boys and Girls. The organization stresses self-reliance, and membership is divided into five different age levels, ranging from Sparks (pre-school) to Horizon (grades 9-12). Skilled adults work with these young people in small groups, helping them to become acquainted with nature's secrets and to learn a variety of crafts. Interaction with adults is also emphasized as a way of learning about career choices, hobbies, and other interests.

Camp Fire's founding is observed by the group's members as part of **Camp Fire Boys and Girls Birthday Week**. The Sunday nearest March 17 is **Camp Fire Boys and Girls Birthday Sunday**, and is a day when Camp Fire Boys and Girls worship together and participate in their church or temple services.

Canada Day
July 1

The British North America Act went into effect on July 1, 1867, uniting Upper Canada (now called Ontario), Lower Canada (now Quebec), New Brunswick, and Nova Scotia into a British dominion. Canadians celebrate this day—which was formerly known as **Dominion Day**—with parades and picnics, somewhat similar to FOURTH OF JULY festivities in the United States.

In Detroit, Michigan and Windsor, Ontario, which are on opposite sides of the Detroit River and are connected by a vehicular tunnel and the Ambassador Bridge, this is also the day on which the **International Freedom Festival** is held. A salute to both countries, the festival includes a powerboat race, sky-diving exhibitions, baton-twirling and kite-flying competitions, and an old-fashioned hootenany.

Canadian National Exhibition
August–September

The first Canadian National Exhibition was held in 1879 in Toronto. The fair moved briefly to Ottawa, but returned to Toronto and was called the **Toronto Industrial Exhibition** until 1921, when the name was changed to reflect its nationwide appeal. Located on the the shores of Lake Ontario, about ten minutes from downtown Toronto, the fairgrounds occupy 350 acres of lawns, gardens, pavilions, and Victorian-style buildings. Events include an air show, a horse show, a Scottish World Festival, and celebrity appearances. The Exhibition claims to be the oldest and largest of its kind in the world.

Canberra Day
Third Monday in March

Canberra, the capital city of Australia, was founded on March 12, 1913. Unusual in that it is one of the few world capitals planned from the ground up, the city and its giant ornamental pond, Lake Burley Griffin, were built out of a depression in a dusty plain about 200 miles southwest of Sydney.

The city's founding is celebrated on the third Monday in March each year, which marks the end of the ten-day Canberra Festival. The festival is an outdoor community event that encompasses everything from hot-air balloon rides and a "street bed" derby (in which wheeled beds are raced through the streets), to opera and "A Tribute to Elvis Presley."

Candelaria *See* Candlemas

Candlemas (Candelaria)
February 2

After observing the traditional forty-day period of purification following the birth of Jesus, Mary presented him to God at the Temple in Jerusalem. An aged and devout Jew named Simeon held the baby in his arms and said that he would be "a light to lighten the Gentiles" (Luke 2:32). It is for this reason that February 2 has come to be called Candlemas (or Candelaria in Spanish-speaking countries) and has been celebrated by the blessing of candles since the eleventh century. In the Eastern Church it is known as the **Feast of the Presentation of Christ in the Temple**; in the Western Church, it's the **Feast of the Purification of the Blessed Virgin Mary.** In the United States, February 2 is also GROUNDHOG DAY; in Great Britain it is said that the badger comes out to test the weather. The old rhyme is as follows;

If Candlemas Day be dry and fair,
The half of winter's to come and mair.
If Candlemas Day be wet and foul,
The half of winter's gone at Yule.

Cannes Film Festival
May

The **International Film Festival** held in the resort city of Cannes on the French Riviera is probably the best known of the hundreds of film festivals held all over the world each year. Sponsored by governments, industry, service organizations, experimental film groups, or individual promoters (see SUNDANCE FILM FESTIVAL), these festivals provide filmmakers, critics, distributors, and cinema enthusiasts an opportunity to attend showings of new films and to discuss current trends in the industry. The festival at Cannes is held at the Palais des Festivals, and its founding in 1947 marked a resurgence for the film industry, which had been shattered by World War II. The festival has also been responsible for the growing popularity of foreign films in the United States.

Other important film festivals are held in Berlin; Karlovy Vary, Czech Republic; London; San Francisco; New York; Chicago; and Venice. Some cater to the films of just one country, some to specific subjects, and some are special festivals for student filmmakers.

Cape Vincent French Festival
Saturday preceding July 14

Cape Vincent, New York is in the Thousand Islands, where Lake Ontario meets the St. Lawrence River, an area with a strong French heritage. At one time, there was so much feeling for Napoleon among the local residents that they built a cup-and-saucer style house (a local architectural style in which the ground floor is wider than the second floor) where they hoped he might decide to spend his exile. However, it was one of Napoleon's followers, Le Roy de Chaumont, who first settled here in the 1800s.

Launched in 1968, the festival immediately drew an astounding number of visitors, many of them French Canadians. It takes place, appropriately enough, on the Saturday before BASTILLE DAY and features a wide variety of French foods as well as a pageant and a parade of decorated carts. A French Mass is held at St. Vincent de Paul's Church, and the evening ends with a waterfront display of fireworks.

Captain Brady Day
Second week in July

The body of water around which the village of Brady Lake, Ohio was built has more than aesthetic value to the residents. Captain Samuel Brady an American frontiersman who fought in the Revolutionary War and was a scout in what was then called the Northwest Territory, escaped a group of Wyandotte Indians by hiding under the surface of the lake and breathing through a hollow reed. The importance of this event is reflected in the fact that both the community and the lake were named after Captain Brady, and every summer (on a date that has not yet been firmly fixed), the escape is re-enacted on the shores of the lake.

When the level of Lake Brady began to drop suddenly in the late 1970s, the residents pulled together to deal with the problems triggered by the water shortage rather than trying to sell their homes in anticipation of falling real estate values. The Captain Brady Day celebration has become an important unifying event for the people of Brady Lake, who view the lake as a symbol of their solidarity and peaceful way of life.

Carabao Festival
Third week of May
A feast in honor of San Isidro Labrador (St. Isidore the Farmer), the patron saint of the Filipino farmer, held in Pulilan, Bulacan province, the Philippines. The feast also honors the *carabao*, or water buffalo, the universal beast of burden of the Philippines. Farmers scrub their carabao then decorate them with flowers to parade with the image of San Isidro. A carabao race is held, and at the finish line, the animals kneel and are blessed by the parish priest. The festival is also marked by exploding firecrackers and the performance of the Bamboo Dance, where dancers represent the tinikling bird, a menace to the rice crop. Among the games played is *palo sebo*—climbing a 'greased pole' to get the prize at the top.

Carberry Day
Friday the 13th
The students and faculty at Brown University in Providence, Rhode Island celebrate the fictitious academic exploits of Professor Josiah Stinkney Carberry every Friday the 13th. It all began in 1929, when a young faculty member at Brown posted a notice saying that J. S. Carberry would give a lecture on "Archaic Greek Architectural Revetments in Connection with Ionian Phonology" at eight o'clock on a certain evening. A retired professor of Latin spotted the hoax and decided to join in the fun by inserting the word "not" between "will" and "give." After that, the joke took on a life of its own, and the ubiquitous Professor Carberry began to send postcards and telegrams with news of his latest exotic research trips. Articles under his name began appearing in schol-

arly journals and, in 1966, Brown gave Carberry a bona fide M.A. degree-awarded, of course, *in absentia.*

On Carberry Day, small brown jugs appear around the campus, and students and teachers fill them with change. The money goes to a book fund that Professor Carberry has set up "in memory of my future late wife, Laura."

Caricom Day
On or near July 4
CARICOM stands for the "Caribbean Community and Common Market," an organization established on July 4, 1973 for the purpose of supporting a common market, coordinating foreign policy, and promoting cooperation among the thirteen member states of the Caribbean: Antigua and Barbuda, Bahamas, Barbados, Belize, Dominica, Grenada, Guyana, Jamaica, Montserrat, St. Kitts-Nevis, St. Lucia, St. Vincent, and Trinidad and Tobago. Caricom Day is celebrated on or around July 4 in Barbados, Guyana, and St. Vincent. In Antigua and Barbuda, it is celebrated on the first Saturday in June.

Carling Sunday
March 8–April 11 in West; March 21–April 24 in East
The fifth or PASSION SUNDAY in LENT, possibly from 'care.' It is traditional in Great Britain to eat a dish of parched peas cooked in butter, called a *carling*, thought to be in memory of the corn Jesus' disciples picked on the Sabbath.

Carnaval de Quebec
Ten days starting the first Thursday in February
A ten-day winter festival that has been held in Quebec City, Canada since 1955, Carnaval has become a world-famous tourist attraction for winter enthusiasts. In addition to the international snow sculpture contest, there is a hazardous ice canoe race across the St. Lawrence River, motorcycle races on ice, and a snowmobile competition. The festival is also the setting for the International Pee-Wee Hockey Tournament, in which teams from all over Canada and the United States compete.

An interesting feature of this festival is the way it is financed. A principal source of income for the Carnaval Association is the candle sale or "bougie." People who buy the bougies increase the chances that their representative "duchess" (and there are a number of duchesses chosen from all over Quebec) will be selected as Carnaval Queen. They also get a chance to participate in a giant lottery. More than ten thousand people participate in the sale and distribution of candles on "Bougie Night."

Carnaval Miami
First full two weeks in March

The biggest event in Miami, Fla. honoring Hispanic culture. Held since 1938, it was estimated that 1.2 million people attended in 1991. The highlight and grand finale of the festival is the famous Calle Ocho Open House. This is non-stop, wall-to-wall entertainment along twenty-three blocks of Southwest Eighth Street (*Calle Ocho*): forty stages with more than 200 troupes offering live music, dancing, and folkloric performances. There are more than 600 vendors of ethnic food. Other events are the Miss Carnaval Miami beauty contest; a grand *paseo* or parade with floats, limbo dancers, samba groups, and steel bands from the Caribbean; a footrace; a laser display; fireworks; and concerts of international stars.

Carnea (Karneia, Karnea, Carneia)
August

The Carnea was one of ancient Sparta's three principal religious festivals—the other two being the Hyacinthia and the Gymnopaidiai—which were observed in many parts of the Peloponnesus as well as in Cyrene, Magna Græcia, and elsewhere. It was the ultimate expression of the cult of Apollo Karneios, the ram god of flocks and herds and of fertility in general. It was held during the month of Carneus (August) and dates back to 676 B.C. The Carnea was both a vintage festival and a military one, Apollo being expected to help his people both by promoting the harvest and by supporting them in battle. Young men called *staphylodromoi* 'grape-cluster-runners' chased after a man wearing garlands. It was considered a good omen for the city if they caught him and a bad one if they didn't.

No military operations could be held during this festival, and it is said that the Spartans might not have been defeated by the Persians at Thermopylæ if the Carnea hadn't prevented the movement of their main army.

Carnival
Varying dates, from Epiphany to Ash Wednesday Eve

The period known as Carnival—from Latin *carnem levare* 'to take away meat' and 'a farewell to flesh'—begins anytime after EPIPHANY and usually comes to a climax during the last three days before ASH WEDNESDAY especially on MARDI GRAS.

It is a time of feasting and revelry in anticipation of the prohibitions of LENT.

Carnival is still observed in most of Europe and the Americas. It features masked balls, lavish costume parades, torch processions, dancing, fireworks, noise-making, and of course feasting on all the foods that will have to be given up for Lent. Ordinarily Carnival includes only the Sunday, Monday and Tuesday before Ash Wednesday (see FASCHING), but sometimes it begins on the preceding Friday or even earlier. In Brazil, Carnival is the major holiday of the year.

See also CARNIVAL; SHROVE TUESDAY.

Carnival in Brazil
Between January 30 and March 5; five days preceding Ash Wednesday

CARNIVAL is the largest popular festival in Brazil, the last chance for partying before LENT. The most extravagant celebration takes place along the eight miles of Copacabana Beach in Rio de Janeiro, where, since the 1930s, the parades, pageants, and costume balls go on for four days, all accompanied by the distinctive rhythm of the samba. The whole city is decorated with colored lights and streamers, and impromptu bands play on every street corner. Banks, stores, and government offices are closed until noon on ASH WEDNESDAY.

The high point of the **Carioca** (as the natives of Rio are known) **Carnival** is the parade of the samba schools (*Escola de Samba*), which begins on Carnival Sunday and ends about midday on Monday. The samba schools are neighborhood groups, many of whom come from the humblest sections of Rio, who develop their own choreography, costumes, and theme songs. The competition among them is as fierce as the rivalry of top sports teams. A single samba school can have as many as two to three thousand participants, so the scale of the parade can only be described as massive. People spend months learning special dances for the parade, and must often raise huge sums of money to pay for their costumes, which range from a few strategically-placed strings of beads to elaborate spangled and feathered headdresses. Each samba school dances the length of the Sambadrome, a one-of-a-kind samba stadium designed by Oscar Niemeyer and built in 1984 to allow eighty-five thousand spectators to watch the samba schools dance by. Viewing the parade from the Sambadrome is usually an all-night affair.

In recent years, more and more of Carnival has moved into clubs, the Club Monte Libano being one of the most famous. The Marilyn Monroe look-alike contest held by transvestites on Sugarloaf Mountain is among the most unusual events.

Carnival in Malta
Preceding Ash Wednesday
Five days of pre-Lenten festivities in Malta, a custom since the 1500s. There are some festivities in the villages, but the main activities are in the capital city of Valletta. Here the traditional events include a parade with floats, brass bands, and participants wearing grotesque masks, and open-air folk-dancing competitions. A King Carnival reigns over the festival.

Carnival in the U. S. Virgin Islands
Last two weeks in April
Although CARNIVAL is a long-standing Caribbean tradition, the celebration waned somewhat in the U. S. Virgin Islands from around the time of World War I, when the islands were still under Danish rule, until the 1950s. But nowadays the Carnival observance in St. Thomas ranks second only to the TRINIDAD AND TOBAGO CARNIVAL. It begins with the opening of Calypso Tent, a week-long calypso song competition for the coveted title of "Calypso King." This is followed by another week of festivities, which include the crowning of a Carnival Queen, children's parades, and a J'Ouvert morning tramp. The celebration winds up with one of the most elaborate all-day parades in the Caribbean, featuring the Mocko Jumbi Dancers. These are colorful dancers on seventeen-foot-high stilts whose dances and customs derived from ancient cult traditions brought to the islands by African slaves.

Carnival in Trinidad and Tobago *See Trinidad and Tobago Carnival*

Carnival in Venice
Beginning between February 3 and March 9; ending on Shrove Tuesday night
The CARNIVAL celebration in Venice, Italy is more sophisticated and steeped in tradition than the gaudy MARDI GRAS celebrations in New Orleans and Rio de Janeiro (see CARNIVAL IN BRAZIL). Costumes for the event are often drawn from the stock characters of Italian popular theater during the sixteenth through eighteenth centuries—including Harlequin, a masked clown in diamond-patterned tights; Punchinello, the hunchback; and Pierrot, the sad white-faced clown adapted by the French from the commedia dell'arte. There are also traditional costumed characters such as *La Bautta* (the domino), *Il Dottore* (the professor or

doctor of law), and the Renaissance count or countess.

Italian university students, usually in more innovative costumes, pour into Venice by the trainload. As ASH WEDNESDAY draws near, the pace of the celebration picks up with a number of spectacular costume balls. The annual charity ball at Teatro La Fenice, for example, is known for attracting the rich and famous, including a number of movie stars and European artistocrats.

Carnival Lamayote
February–March; preceding Ash Wednesday
CARNIVAL, the biggest holiday of the year in Haiti, is distinguished from other Carnival celebrations by the preparation of wooden boxes, decorated with tissue paper and paint, known as *lamayotes*. Haitian boys put a "monster"—usually a mouse, lizard, bug, or other small animal—inside these boxes. During Carnival they dress up in masks and costumes and try to persuade people to pay them a penny for a peek inside their box.

Carnival of Binche
Seven weeks preceding Shrove Tuesday
The most famous pre-Lenten carnival in Belgium and one of the most unusual in Europe. Festivies in Binche, a town of 10,000 population, begin seven weeks before LENT starts and culminate on MARDI GRAS with day-long rites of elaborately costumed, orange-throwing clowns called *Gilles*, which means roughly 'fools' or 'jesters'. Some 200,000 visitors come for the Mardi Gras weekend.

The Gilles—about 800 men and boys—wear suits stuffed with hay and decorated with appliqued rearing lions, crowns, and stars in the Belgian colors of red, yellow, and black. Heavy bells hang at their waists, and their headresses, four feet tall and weighing up to seven pounds, are topped by ostrich plumes. In the early morning, the Gilles wear masks with green spectacles and orange eyebrows and moustaches, but these are doffed later in the day when the ostrich headdresses go on. The rites start at daybreak when the Gilles gather in the main square of Binche. To the beating of drums, they march and dance through the streets, stomping their wooden shoes and pelting spectators with oranges. Fireworks at midnight officially end the carnival, but dancing often goes on until dawn of Ash Wednesday.

The most accepted legend explaining the carnival traces its origins to a fete in 1549. Spain had just conquered Peru, and Mary of Hungary, regent of the Netherlands, gave a sumptuous reception at her Binche palace for her nephew, Philip II of Spain. Supposedly, the costumes of the Gilles are patterned on the wardrobe of the Incas, and the thrown oranges represent the Incan gold. A document of 1795 is the earliest to describe the mask of the Gilles.

Some people have suggested that the English word 'binge' comes from Binche.

Carnival of Oruro
Between end of January and early March; week preceding the beginning of Lent

The CARNIVAL celebrations in Oruro, Bolivia continue for an entire week and include music, dancing, eating and drinking, and offerings to *Pachamama* or Mother Earth. But the highlight is the parade that begins with a motorcade of vehicles carrying gold and silverware, jewels, fine embroideries, and old coins and banknotes. Next are the Diablos, wearing plaster-of-Paris horns, painted light bulbs for eyes, mirrors for teeth, and hair from the tails of oxen or horses. They are led by Lucifer and two Satans and surrounded by five dancing she-devils. Next are the Incas, who represent historical figures from the time of the Spanish conquest, and the Tobas, who perform war dances. The llama drivers or llameros are next, followed by the Callahuallas or witch doctors, and a number of other companies, each with its own distinctive costumes and role in the procession. The parade ends with the entry of all the masked groups into the church to hear Mass in honor of the Virgen del Socavón.

Carnival Thursday
Between January 29 and March 4; Thursday preceding Shrove Tuesday

This was the day on which pre-Lenten celebrations, such as CARNIVALS, traditionally began, ending several days later on SHROVE TUESDAY night. These celebrations often take the form of wild revelry, which is perhaps why it was also referred to as **Mad Thursday.**

Caruaru Roundup
September

Roundups started out as nothing more than the yearly task of bringing the cattle together in the winter for branding. But in Brazil they have developed into folkloric celebrations involving the participation of hundreds of cowboys who compete in "downing the steers." The Caruaru Roundup in the state of Pernambuco is one of the largest. In addition to steer-roping contests, viola players and

repentistas (verse improvisers) entertain the people with their music and rhyming descriptions of the day's activities. Local food specialities are served during the three-day event.

Casals Festival
Early June

A two-week music festival **held** in San Juan, Puerto Rico to celebrate the memory of Pablo Casals (1876–1973), the world-renowned Spanish-born cellist and conductor. An outspoken opponent of Fascism and the regime of Francisco Franco, he was forced to leave Spain and move to France in 1936. Twenty years later he moved to Puerto Rico, the birthplace of his mother. There he initiated this music festival.

Through the years internationally known artists, among them Rudolf Serkin, Andrés Segovia, Arthur Rubenstein, Isaac Stern, and Yehudi Menuhin, have appeared at the festival. Programs offer a variety of composers, from Bach to Bartok.

Castroville Artichoke Festival
Third weekend in September

One of the oldest agricultural festivals in California, held in Castroville, which calls itself the "Artichoke Center of the World." The two-day festival began in 1959 with a barbecue and parade; there is still a parade, and the lead float traditionally carries the Artichoke Queen and a huge green artichoke replica. Other events include a firefighters' muster, a coronation dinner dance, an artichoke recipe contest, and an artichoke eating contest. Food booths offer artichoke cookies and french-fried artichokes. Attendance is about 50,000.

Castroville, founded in 1863 by Juan Bautista Castro, was an agricultural community from the start. In 1888, sugar beets became an important crop on the land west of Castro's settlement. When beet prices declined in 1921, Andrew J. Molera, the owner of the land, decided to grow artichokes, which were new to the U.S. market. He provided the plants for the first crop and leased the acreage to farmers. By 1925, more than 4,000 acres of artichokes were being cultivated, and by 1929 artichokes were the third largest cash crop of the Salinas Valley.

Cats, Festival of the *See* Kattestoet

Cavalcata Sarda
Last Sunday of May

This famous procession—or *cavalcata*—was originally held in Sassari, Sardinia more than nine hundred years ago to celebrate a victory over Saracen invaders. Today the procession consists of costumed groups from over one hundred Sardinian villages. Wearing the traditional dress of their region, participants in the Cavalcata Sarda often ride through the streets in ox-drawn carts. After the procession is over, the celebration continues with singing and dancing.

Celebration, Days of *See* St. Genevieve, Jour de Fête à

Central City Summer Festival
First week in July to mid August

A festival of opera, operetta, and cabaret in the one-time mining town of Central City, Colo. Performances of two operas and one American operetta are staged in the Old Opera House, built in 1878 and since restored to its original Victorian elegance. On opening night, "flower girls" present the audience with fresh flowers, which are thrown on stage to the cast at the end of the performance.

Inaugurated in 1932, the **Opera Festival** was not only the first summer opera festival in the country but also the first to espouse singing opera in English, a tradition that continues. *The Ballad of Baby Doe*, an opera that depicts the love story of the real-life silver king, Horace Tabor, who left his wife for the beautiful and much younger Baby Doe, was commissioned by Central City.

Cabaret opera is presented on Saturdays and Sundays in the historic Teller House next to the Opera House. This was once the grandest hotel in the west, built in 1872, host to President Ulysses S. Grant and other notables.

One of the presentations is *Face on the Barroom Floor*, which was commissioned on the hundredth anniversary of the opera house. The saloon of the Teller House is the site of the "face" made famous in the poem by H. Antoine D'Arcy. The poem tells the story of the drunken vagabond who comes into the bar, asks for whisky, and explains that he was once a painter who fell in love with beautiful Madeline—and that she was stolen away by his friend. "That's why I took to drink, boys," the vagabond says, and then offers to draw Madeline's portrait on the barroom floor:

> *Another drink, and with chalk in hand the vagabond began*
> *To sketch a face that well might buy the soul of any man.*
> *Then, as he placed another lock upon the shapely head,*

> *With a fearful shriek, he leaped and fell across the picture—dead.*

Central Maine Egg Festival
Fourth Saturday in July

This one-day event in Pittsfield, Maine was started in 1972 by two journalists who were tired of hearing about their state's potato crop and wanted to focus attention on central Maine's egg and chicken industry. Today its primary attraction is the world's largest skillet—a three-hundred-pound teflon-coated frying pan, ten feet in diameter, that is used to cook more than four thousand eggs for those attending the festival breakfast. The giant skillet, designed and donated by the Alcoa Corporation, is stored in an airplane hangar.

A festival highlight is the World's Largest Egg Contest, in which only chicken eggs can be entered. Since entries come from all over the world, special tests must often be conducted to reveal imposters. The winning egg is plated with gold. Other events include parachute-jumping with chickens, a chicken flying contest, and a chicken barbecue.

Chakri Day
April 6

A national holiday in Thailand to commemorate the enthronement of Rama I, who founded the Chakri Dynasty in 1782. He was born Chao Phraya Chakri in 1737, and had become Thailand's leading general when a palace coup took place in Thon Buri. Officials invited the general to assume the throne; he did, and one of his first acts was to move the capital across the river to Bangkok. The dynasty he established has headed the country to this day, although the end of absolute monarchy came in 1932. The king was given the title Rama after his death. Ceremonies on April 6 honor his deeds and the founding of Bangkok as the capital.

Chalk Sunday
First Sunday of Lent

In rural Ireland it was at one time customary to mark unmarried persons with chalk as they entered the church on the first Sunday of LENT. Because Roman Catholics were not permitted to hold weddings during Lent, those who were still unmarried at the beginning of the Lenten season had to remain so until EASTER—if not longer. Back when it was less common for young people to stay single well into their twenties and thirties, marking them with chalk was a way of chiding them for their unmarried status.

Chanukah *See* Hanukkah

Chaomos
December 21, the winter solstice

The December festival of the Kafir Kalash people, who live in valleys in the northwestern corner of Pakistan, about twenty miles north of Chitral. The festival honors Balomain, a demigod who once lived among the Kalash and did heroic deeds. Every year, his spirit comes to the valleys to count the people, collect their prayers, and take them back to Tsiam, the mythical land where the Kalash originated, and to Dezao, the omnipotent creator god.

The celebration begins with the purification of women and girls: they take ritual baths, and then have water poured over their heads as they hold loaves of bread cooked by the men. A man waves burning juniper over the head of each woman, murmuring, "*Sooch*" ('Be pure'). On the following day, the men and boys are purified. They, too, take ritual baths and are then forbidden to sit on chairs or beds until evening when the blood of a sacrificed goat is sprinkled on their faces. The celebration continues with singing and chanting, a torchlight procession, dancing, bonfires, and festive eating of special bread and goat tripe.

Kalash means 'black,' and the people (thought to have descended from Alexander the Great) are called that because of the women's black robes. The Kafir Kalash are among the people who live in neighboring Afghanistan in the area called Nuristan ('land of light'). This entire region was once known to the Muslims as Kafiristan ('land of infidels'), but in 1896 the Afghan Kafirs were forcibly converted to Islam. The Kafir Kalash still maintain their old religion, a mixture of animism and ancestor—and fire—worship. Their pantheon of gods, besides Desao, includes Sajigor, god of shepherds, Mahandeo, god of honeybees, and Surisan, who protects cattle.

Chaomos is one of the four annual festivals of the Kalash; others are the spring festival in mid-May, the harvest festival in mid-August, and the autumn festival that marks the walnut and grape harvest.

Charleston Sternwheel Regatta
Ten days ending on Labor Day

A celebration of its river-town history by Charleston, W.V.. The highlights are the sternwheel and power-boat races on the Kanawha River. There are also forty other events including concerts, parades, car shows, a distance run, and the "Anything That Floats Race." There is free nightly entertainment by internationally known artists. The regatta began in 1971 and now attracts about a million spectators.

Charro Days Fiesta
Between January 31 and March 4; Four days, beginning on the Thursday of the weekend before Lent

The pre-Lenten festival known as Charro Days has been held each year since 1938 in the border towns of Brownsville, Texas and Matamoros, Mexico, on opposite sides of the Rio Grande. A major border-crossing point, the two towns have a rich Spanish-Mexican heritage which is reflected in the fiesta. Male residents of the two cities wear the *charro* costume—a cross between the costume worn by the Spanish dons who once ruled Mexico and the Mexican horseman's outfit. Women wear the *china poblana*—a regional costume once worn by a little Chinese girl who was befriended by the Mexicans and has since become a kind of fairy princess to them.

Fiesta events take place in both Brownsville and Matamoros, and include a huge children's parade, costume dances in the street, rodeos, bullfights, and other events with Mexican and Latin themes. The festival has been known to attract as many as 400,000 visitors, many of whom wear costumes and participate in the events.

Cheesefare Sunday
Between February 8 and February 28; the day before Lent begins in the East

In the Orthodox Church, the day before the beginning of Great Lent is called Cheesefare Sunday because it is traditionally the last day on which any dairy products—including eggs, cheese, milk, and yoghurt—may be eaten until Easter. See also Meat Fare Sunday, Shrove Tuesday, Ash Wednesday.

Cherokee Strip Day
September 16

September 16, 1893 was the date of the last and largest of the "land runs" that opened western Indian territories to white settlement. The Cherokee Strip encompassed more than six million acres of mostly grassy plains where white homesteaders wanted to graze their animals. Anyone who wanted to claim and settle the 160-acre parcels had to line up on the morning of September 16 and race to plant his flag at a chosen spot. The lure of free land attracted an estimated 100,000 prospective settlers, mostly young men who could withstand the harsh climate.

Cherokee Strip Day is a festival day in Oklahoma—particularly in the communities of Ponca City, Enid , and Perry —towns that sprang up as a result of the 1893 run. The celebrations last several days and include parades, picnics, dances, and rodeos. (See OKLAHOMA DAY.)

Cherry Blossom Festival
Late March–early April

The **National Cherry Blossom Festival** in Washington, D.C. is held whenever the cherry trees planted around the Potomac River Tidal Basin bloom—usually between March 20 and April 15. The three thousand trees were a gift to the city of Washington from the city of Tokyo, Japan in 1912, and today they are the focal point of a six-day festival celebrating the friendship between the two countries. Most of the original trees died because the water in the Basin flooded their roots. Their replacements were more carefully planted and now thrive. Dates for the festival are set a year in advance to avoid coinciding with EASTER and Holy Week observances.

The week-long festival has been in existence since 1948, although earlier celebrations included re-enacting the original planting and crowning a Cherry Blossom Festival Queen. Today the festivities include formal receptions for the fifty-two festival princesses (representing the 50 states, the District of Columbia, and the territory of Guam) and a Cherry Blossom parade through downtown Washington.

The Cherry Blossom Festival in Hawaii is an annual Japanese cultural celebration held in Honolulu, Hawaii, usually from mid-February until the first week in April. The beauty of cherry blossoms is almost sacred in Japan, but the cherry blossoms of this festival are purely symbolic; cherry trees don't grow in Hawaii. The festival offers a variety of events: presentations of Kabuki drama, traditional Japanese dances, martial arts, and Japanese films as well as demostrations of such arts as weaving and paper-doll making. The celebration was created in 1953 by the Honolulu Japanese community to "bridge the cultural gap by sharing with others the essence of the Japanese heritage."

See also HANAMI.

Cherry Festival, National
Second week in July

An annual event since 1926, Michigan's National Cherry Blossom Festival takes place in Tra-

verse City, "The Cherry Capital of the World," where seventy percent of the world's red cherries are grown. Traditionally held for a full week in July, the time of the cherry harvest, the festival features both traditional and offbeat events involving cherries: cherry pie eating and cooking contests, a cherry wine competition, displays of cherries and cherry products, free tours of the cherry orchards, a cherry smorgasbord luncheon, and the weighing-in of the world's largest cherry.

The festival began in 1924 with a ceremony to bless the cherry blossoms and ensure a good crop. Now it draws upwards of half a million visitors and includes three major parades, national high school band competitions, canoe races, and a water ski tournament among the more than one hundred different events. Former President Gerald R. Ford, a Michigan native, officiated at the festival in 1975.

Chesapeake Appreciation Days
Last weekend in October

This two-day celebration in Annapolis, Maryland focuses on the skipjacks—the working sailboats that have dredged the Chesapeake Bay for oysters since the early nineteenth century. A featured event is the skipjack race which spectators can watch from the beach at Sandy Point State Park, near the twin-span Chesapeake Bay Bridge, because the boats' shallow draft and movable centerboard enable them to race close to shore. Other festival events include an oyster cooking contest, regional arts and crafts, and an air show. But it is the skipjacks—unique to the Chesapeake—that most people come to see, as these classic sailing craft have been largely replaced by power vessels. Skipjack races are also held off Deal Island on Maryland's Eastern Shore on LABOR DAY.

Chester Greenwood Day
First Saturday in December

Chester Greenwood (1858–1937) made his first pair of "ear protectors" when he was fifteen years old. He was granted a patent in 1877 and established an entirely new industry in his home town of Farmington, Maine, where he continued to refine the design and manufacture of what we now know as earmuffs. By 1918 he was making 216,000 pairs a year, and by 1932 checks and plaids were added to the standard black velvet covering.

Although Greenwood was involved in a number of other business ventures in Farmington and was granted his last patent—for a tempered steel lawn rake—only a few months before he died, it is for his ear protectors that he is primarily remembered. Farmington residents celebrate Chester Greenwood Day on the first Saturday in December (Greenwood was born on December 4) with a parade, flag raising ceremony, and a foot race.

Chestertown Tea Party Festival
Third weekend in May

When the British passed the Boston Port Act closing the Port of Boston until complete restitution had been made for the tea destroyed during the Boston Tea Party, it unleashed a wave of anger throughout the American colonies. Shortly after the news reached Chestertown, Maryland, the brigantine *Geddes* dropped anchor in Chestertown harbor on May 13, 1774. Word went out that the *Geddes* was carrying a small shipment of tea, and ten days later a group of local residents boarded the ship and dumped the tea in the Chester River.

Every year during the Chestertown Tea Party Festival the rebellion is reenacted. The local merchants gather at the town park, where they voice their opposition to the British tax on tea. The crowd winds its way down High Street to the river, where the "colonists" board a ship—usually a reproduction of an historic vessel—and throw its cargo of tea (and some of its crew) into the river. Other festival events include a colonial parade with fife and drum corps, exhibits and demonstrations of eighteenth century American crafts, walking tours of Chestertown, clog dancing and fiddling, horse-and-carriage rides, and tall ship cruises. Typical Eastern Shore foods are served, such as Maryland fried chicken, barbequed ribs, "chitlins," crab cakes, she-crab soup, and fried clams.

Cheung Chau Bun Festival
Late April or early May, date decided by divination

One of the most spectacular events in Hong Kong, celebrated only on Cheung Chau, which means 'Long Island' in Chinese and is one of the outlying islands of Hong Kong. It is believed that restless ghosts roam the island during the seven days of the festival. Some believe they are the spirits of islanders massacred by nineteenth-century pirates. Others say they are the spirits of animals killed and eaten during the year. Whatever they are, the festival is held to placate them.

Three bamboo-and-paper towers, about forty-five feet high and covered with sweet pink and white buns, are dedicated to them. No meat or fish is eaten, and people burn paper replicas of houses, cars, and money.

At the island's Pak Tai Temple, rites are held to honor Pak Tai, "Supreme Emperor of the Dark Heaven." He is worshiped as a god of the sea who defeated a Demon King and the king's allies, a tortoise and a serpent. The temple holds many small wooden statues of Pak Tai, all with a tortoise under one foot and a serpent under the other.

In the highlight of the festival the images of the temple gods are carried in a procession of lion and dragon dancers, and children aged about five to eight who are costumed as legendary Chinese figures. These children are carried shoulder-high so that they seem to float above the procession.

Cheyenne Frontier Days
Last full week of July

What began in 1897 as an attempt to keep alive the sports and customs of the Old West has grown into a six-day festival that regularly attracts over 300,000 visitors. Cheyenne, Wyoming was one of the wealthiest cattle-raising cities in the world in the 1880s, and now it celebrates its colorful history by staging one of the world's largest oudoor rodeos. The festival also includes parades of covered wagons, stagecoaches, and other old-time vehicles; ceremonial Indian dances; the crowning of a "Miss Frontier" queen; and pageants recreating events from Cheyenne's past. Cheyenne residents make pancakes for all with batter mixed in a concrete mixer.

Chicago Jazz Festival
Four days preceding Labor Day

In the 1920s a four-block area along Chicago's State Street, known to the black community as "the Stroll," was the mecca of the jazz world. It was here that jazz took root in the city, establishing Chicago as a center for this uniquely American music. Shortly after the great composer-bandleader Duke Ellington died in 1974, a group of Chicago musicians got together to hold a concert in his honor; after that, the Ellington Concert became an annual event. A similar memorial concert was held for saxophonist John Coltrane in 1978, and the following year these two events merged with the jazz festival already being planned by the Jazz Institute of Chicago. Now it is the most extensive free jazz festival in the world, drawing an estimated audience of 400,000 and featuring such well-known artists as Sarah Vaughan, Ray Charles, Dave Brubeck, Herbie Hancock, George Benson, and Wynton Marsalis.

A number of major jazz events have occurred at the festival, such as the world premiere of Randy Weston's *African Sunrise* by Dizzy Gillespie and the Machito All-Star Orchestra in 1984, or the rendition of "Happy Birthday" sung in honor of Charlie Parker, the great jazz improviser, who was born on August 29, 1920 and died March 12, 1955.

Chief Seattle Days
Third weekend in August

A three-day inter-tribal festival to honor Chief Seattle 1786–1866, for whom Seattle, Washington, is named. He was head of the Suquamish and Duwamish Indian tribes in the Puget Sound area of Washington. His name in the *Lushootseed* language was See-ahth.

The festival is held at the Port Madison Indian Reservation in Suquamish, forty miles south of Seattle. Besides featuring traditional Indian dances and dancing and drumming contests, it has a distinctive northwestern flavor with salmon and clam bakes and canoe races. Other highlights are a horseshoe tournament, story-telling, and the election of a Chief Seattle Days Queen. The festival closes with the blessing of Chief Seattle's grave.

Chief Seattle and his father were both friendly to white settlers and helped them. He was the first to sign the Port Elliott Treaty in 1855, which set aside reservations for the Suquamish and other Washington tribes.

In a moving speech made in 1854 to a large group of Indians gathered to greet Isaac Stevens, the new United States Indian superintendent, Chief Seattle spoke of the passing away of the Indian tribes, fleeing at the approach of the White Man. "Let him be just and deal kindly with my people," he said, "for the dead are not powerless. There is no death, only a change of worlds."

It is uncertain that Chief Seattle actually uttered these words. The only known translation of Seattle's speech was made from the recollection of Dr. Harvy Smith thirty-three years later. The waters were made even muddier when, in 1971, Ted Perry, a screenwriter who now teaches at Middlebury College in Vermont, wrote a speech for the Chief that was included in a film on ecology. Mr. Perry knew the script was fiction, but others did not. Perry's apocryphal speech has been attributed to Chief Seattle ever since.

In 1992 a children's book based on an embellished version of Perry's script, *Brother Eagle, Sister Sky* by Susan Jeffers, made the New York Times Best Seller list and the great Chief Seattle slipped further into the mists of legend.

Childermas *See* **Holy Innocents' Day**

Children's Book Day, International
April 2

This day, which is observed by countries all over the world, was first suggested by the International Board on Books for Young People (IBBY). They chose **Hans Christian Andersen's birthday**, April 2, because the Danish author's stories—which include "The Little Match Girl," "The Steadfast Tin Soldier," "The Ugly Duckling," and "Thumbelina"—have been favorites among children of all nationalities. The celebrations include contests in which children illustrate their favorite books, and the adoption of foreign pen pals. Every two years the IBBY sponsors the Hans Christian Andersen medals, which are awarded to a children's book author and a children's book illustrator for their contributions to children's literature.

See also HANS CHRISTIAN ANDERSEN FESTIVAL

Children's Day *See* Kodomo-no-Hi; Urini Nal

Children's Day
Second Sunday in June

Many countries have set aside a day on which children are allowed to participate in church services, in government, and in various cultural and recreational activities. In the United States, Children's Day was first celebrated in June 1856 at the Universalist Church in Chelsea, Massachusetts. By 1868 its date had been set on a nationwide basis as the second Sunday in June.

Children's Day is also celebrated in Iceland, Indonesia, Japan (See KODOMO-NO-HI), Korea, Nigeria, and Turkey, although the dates vary from late April to mid-June. The Turkish Children's Day on April 23 gives four hundred students the educational opportunity to take seats in the national government in Ankara. The same thing takes place on a smaller scale in cities and towns all over the country.

Children's Day in Yugoslavia
December; three Sundays before Christmas

On a Sunday in early December known as **Dechiyi Dan** or Children's Day, parents in Yugoslavia tie up their children and refuse to release them until they have promised to be good. On the following Sunday, known as *Materitse*, Materice, or MOTHER'S DAY, the children tie up their mother, releasing her only when she has paid them with sweets or other goodies. On the third Sunday, known as *Ochichi*, Ocevi, or FATHER'S DAY, the children try to tie their father to his chair or bed. The ransom in this case is even higher, as the father must promise to buy them coats, shoes, dresses, or other expensive items before they let him go. These promises usually appear a short time later as CHRISTMAS gifts.

Children's Party *See* Kinderzeche

Chilympiad (Republic of Texas Chili Cookoff)
Third weekend in September

A chili cookoff in San Marcos, Tex. is called the "largest bowl o' red" competition in the world, which it probably is. From 500 to 600 chili chefs compete for the men's state championship, being judged on showmanship as much as recipes. (There is a smaller cookoff for women in Luckenbach in October.) Participation in the Chilympiad is a preliminary to entering the TERLINGUA CHILI COOKOFF in November. Besides the Chilympiad's gastronomic attractions, there are also concerts, arts and crafts, a parade, and carnival.

Chincoteague Pony Roundup and Penning
Wednesday before the last Thursday in July

The annual saltwater roundup of the famous wild ponies of Assateague Island off the Delmarva Peninsula. The volunteer firemen of Chincoteague Island, the largest inhabited island on the Eastern Shore of Virginia, become cowboys for a day: They ride to Assateague, round up as many as 250 or 300 foals, mares, and sires, and then guide them into the water to swim across the channel to Chincoteague. There the ponies are penned in corrals, and the next day some foals are sold at auction, and the rest of the herd swims back to Assateague.

Legend says the ponies, which are considered stunted horses rather than true ponies, are the descendants of mustangs that survived a shipwreck of a sixteenth-century Spanish galleon. Another story holds that the ponies were left behind by pirates who used the island as a hideout and had to leave in a hurry. Still a third (and most probable) version is that English colonists, having brought the ponies to the New World, turned them loose on Assateague and Chincoteague when they began to damage mainland crops.

The annual penning probably started with the colonists, who rounded up foals and yearlings to invigorate their workhorse supply. It took its present form in 1925 when the Chincoteague Volunteer Fire Company decided to add a fund-raising carnival to the regular pony penning.

Now a week of festivities surrounds the roundup, with midway rides, country music, and oysters and clams to eat. Tens of thousands come to watch the excitement from land and small boats.

A book featuring the event, *Misty of Chincoteague* by Marguerite Henry, was published in 1947 and became a children's classic. A movie based on the book appeared in 1960.

Chinese New Year *See* Lunar New Year

Ching Ming Festival *See* Qing Ming Festival

Chinhae Cherry Blossom Festival
Early April

A festival in Chinae, Korea, the headquarters of the Korean Navy, to enjoy the thousands of blossoming cherry trees and also to honor Korea's illustrious Admiral Yi Sun-shin. Admiral Yi defeated the Japanese in several sea battles during the latter's invasions of the late sixteenth century. He is famous for developing "turtle boats," the first iron-clad naval vessels, with twenty-six cannons on each side; though outnumbered, they proved superior to the Japanese boats. While the cherries bloom, there are daily events—a memorial service, parades, sports contests, music and dance performances, and folk games.

Chitlin' Strut
Friday and Saturday after Thanksgiving

A feast of chitlins or chitterlings (hog intestines), held in the small town of Salley, S.C. The affair features hog-calling contests, country music, arts and crafts, a parade, lots of chitlins (about 8,000 pounds are devoured each year), and chicken for those not enamored of chitlins. (Former president George Bush has said he is a chitlin fan.) Chitlins are prepared by cleaning them well, boiling them until they are tender, and then, after coating them in egg and crumbs, frying them in deep fat until they're crackling crisp.

Salley was named for Col. Dempsey Hammond Salley, who donated the site in the nineteenth century.

The Chitlin' Strut began in 1966 to raise money for the town's Christmas decorations. The strut now draws as many as 25,000 people, and Salley, with a population of 700, has used the revenues from it to pay for such necessities as trash cans, signs, and even a fire truck.

Choctaw Indian Fair
Begins first Wednesday after Fourth of July

Formerly known as the Green Corn Ceremony, this is a four-day annual gathering of the Mississippi band of Choctaw Indians. Held since 1949 in Philadelphia, Mississippi, it features, besides dances, crafts exhibits, pageantry, the Choctaw Stickball World Series. Choctaw stickball, the forerunner of lacrosse, is played with long-handled sticks with pouches at the ends for carrying and pitching a leather ball. It is called the "granddaddy of games," and is thought to be the oldest field sport in America. More than 20,000 visitors usually attend the fair.

Chongmyo Taeje (Royal Shrine Rite)
First Sunday in May

A Confucian memorial ceremony held at Chongmyo Shrine in Seoul, Korea, to honor the Yi kings and queens of the Choson Dynasty (1392–1910). The shrine, in a secluded garden in the center of Seoul, houses the ancestral tablets of the monarchs. Each year elaborate rites are performed to pay homage to them, and a number of royal descendants, robed in the traditional garments of their ancestors, take part. The rites are accompanied by court music and dance. The ceremony is a grand expression of the widespread Confucian practice of honoring ancestors, either at home or at their graves.

Christkindlesmarkt (Christmas Market) in Nuremberg
Early December through Christmas Eve

The biggest and best known of the CHRISTMAS markets of Germany. The market in Nuremberg has been held since 1697 in the city's *Hauptmarkt* ('main market'), the site of the famed 60-foot-high *Schöner Brunnen* ('beautiful fountain') and the 600-year-old redstone Church of Our Lady. More than 100 booths are set up to offer only goods directly related to Christmas—dolls, wooden soldiers, tinsel angels, picture books, and painted boxes. Food booths sell Nuremberg's specialties—*Lebkuchen*, or gingerbread, and *Zwetschgenmannlein*, which are little people-shaped confections made of prunes, figs, and raisins, with heads of painted walnuts. A post office branch is set up to cancel letters with a special stamp, and rides are offered in an old horse-drawn mail coach.

The three-week festival is inaugurated with choral singing, the pealing of church bells, and illumination of a crèche. A week or two before Christmas, some 10,000 people parade with lanterns to the Imperial Castle overlooking the city to sing carols.

Other major Christmas markets are held in a number of German cities. Munich has the oldest Christmas market; it has been held annually for about 600 years, and features daily musical programs. In Rothenburg-on-the Tauber, the market is a month-long "Winter's Tale" of 150 events that include stagecoach rides, plays, and concerts. In Berlin, a miniature village for children is featured.

Christmas
December 25

The most popular of the Christian festivals, also known as the **Feast of the Nativity of Our Lord**, Christmas (from "Christ's Mass") celebrates the birth of Jesus of Nazareth. The exact date of Jesus' birth is not known, and for more than three centuries it was a movable feast, often celebrated on EPIPHANY, January 6. The Western church chose to observe it at the end of December, perhaps as a way of countering the various pre-Christian festivals celebrated around that time of year. Some believe that Pope Julius I fixed the date of Christmas at December 25 in the fourth century. The earliest reference to it is in the Philocalian Calendar of Rome in 336. Although the majority of Eastern Orthodox churches have celebrated the Nativity on December 25 since the middle of the fifth century, those that still adhere to the old Julian calendar—called Old Calendarists—mark the occasion thirteen days later, on January 7. The Armenian Churches continue to celebrate OLD CHRISTMAS DAY on January 6, or Epiphany.

The Christmas season in the church begins on Christmas Eve and ends on Epiphany, unlike the commercial season that may begin any time after HALLOWEEN.

December 25th is a holy day of obligation for Roman Catholics, who must attend one of the three masses priests are permitted to say in honor of the occasion. These services are celebrated at midnight on CHRISTMAS EVE and at dawn and midday on Christmas.

As a holiday, Christmas represents a strange intermingling of both Christian and the pagan traditions it replaced. Many of the secular customs now associated with Christmas—such as decorating with mistletoe, holly, and ivy; indulging in excessive eating and drinking; stringing lights in trees; and exchanging gifts—can be traced back to early pagan festivals like the SATURNALIA and ancient WINTER SOLSTICE rites. Another example is burning the Yule log, which was part of a pre-Christian winter solstice rite celebrating the return of the sun in the middle of winter. Even the Christmas tree, a German custom introduced in Britain by Queen Victoria's husband, Albert, can trace its history back to ancient times, when trees were worshipped as spirits.

One of the most universal Christmas traditions is the crèche, a model of the birth scene of Christ, with Jesus in the manger, surrounded by the Holy Family and worshiping angels, shepherds, and animals. Many families have their own crèche, with the three Wise Men set apart and moved closer each day after Christmas until they arrive at the manger on EPIPHANY.

In Belgium, the manger also appears in shop windows, constructed of the material sold by the shop: bread at the bakery; silks and laces at dressmakers; a variety of materials from the hardware store; butter and cheese from dairies; and cravats and neckties at the haberdashers.

In Chile the crèche is called a *pesebre*. Some homes leave their doors open so people passing by can come in say a brief prayer to the *Niño Lindo* (beautiful baby).

In Italy it is a *presepio*, and is placed on the lowest shelf of a *ceppo*, which is a pyramid of shelves, lit with candles, used to display secular Christmas decorations and ornaments.

In Poland, where the crèche is called a *yaselko*, it is believed to be the origin of the Christmas folk play called the *King Herod play*, based on Herod's order to kill all male babies in Bethlehem (see HOLY INNOCENTS DAY). Thirteenth-century Franciscan monks brought the crèche to Poland. Eventually the wax, clay, and wooden figures were transformed into *szopka*, puppets that performed Christmas mystery plays, which told of the mysteries of Christ's life. Later, the monks acted the parts played by the puppets and were called "living *szopka*." In time, the plays were blended with characters and events from Polish history. The performers are called "Herods" and go from house to house in their village where they are invited in to sing carols, act, and later to eat and drink with the family.

In Burkina Faso, west Africa, until 1984 called Upper Volta, the population is mostly in Oua-gadougou, the government center, and there the children make nativities (manger scenes) around the entrance to their compound. They are ready on Christmas Day so friends and neighbors can come by and, if they like them, leave a few coins in the dish provided. Some are made of paper and set on a pedestal, others of mud bricks with a thatch roof, while others are in the form of the local round house and have the bricks covered with a coat of concrete and a masonry dome instead of thatch. All of this is ornately decorated with strings of plastic packing 'peanuts,' bits of shiny metal, tinsel, plastic, and flashlight bulbs. Some are modeled after pictures of European churches, but the child who can build a multi-storied nativity is thought very clever. On the wall of the compound behind the nativity is painted a white panel on which are affixed pictures of the Holy Family, crosses, hearts, arrows, stars, and anything else that comes to the mind of the young creator.

In Japan, since the end of World War II, Christmas has become a very popular holiday, even for non-Christians. Christmas dinner is replaced with a commercial Christmas cake, called "decoration cake," (dekoreshon keki), covered with ridges and waves of frosting. Grandfather Santa Claus brings the gifts, but stockings are hung on the pipe for the bathtub stove, which is the nearest equivalent to a fireplace in Japanese homes. NEW YEAR's postcards are much more important than Christmas cards, and the most elaborate use of evergreen trees is also saved for New Year's. Christmas parties are a kind of blending with *bonenkai* "closing of the year parties," which may only be attended by men and professional women: geishas, waitresses, entertainers. All women can attend Christmas parties, which is one of the reasons why the Japanese consider Christmas to be democratic.

Secular Christmas customs have continued to evolve. The Christmas card didn't become popular until nineteenth century England; Santa Claus' reindeer were an American invention at about the same time. Modern Christmas celebrations tend to focus on the worldly—with such "traditions" as the office Christmas party, sending out greeting cards, and "Christmas specials" on television taking the place of church services and other religious observances for many. The movement to "put Christ back into Christmas," has not lessened the enjoyment of this holiday as much for its social and commercial events as for its spiritual significance. The way Christmas is celebrated today is actually no worse—and in many ways much less excessive—than the hedonistic medieval celebration, where the feasting and revelry often extended all the way from Christmas to CANDLEMAS (February 2). In Austria, the crèche is not put away until CANDLEMAS DAY.

See also GANNA and POSADAS.

Christmas Eve
December 24

Christmas Eve or the **Vigil of Christmas** represents the culmination of the ADVENT season. Like CHRISTMAS itself, Christmas Eve celebrations combine both religious and secular events. Perhaps the most widely anticipated by children is the arrival of Santa Claus—known as *Sinterklass* by the Dutch settlers of New York, who were the first to introduce the idea of St. Nicholas' annual appearance on this day; the original Santa Claus was the tall, saintly-looking bishop Nicholas of Metz. It wasn't until the nineteenth century that he became the jolly, overweight, pipe-smoking figure in a red fur-trimmed suit that children in the United States recognize today. The modern Santa Claus was largely the invention of two men: Clement Moore, who in 1822 wrote his now-famous poem, "A Visit from St. Nicholas," and Thomas Nast, a cartoonist who did numerous illustrations of Santa Claus based on Moore's description. In any case, it is on Christmas Eve that Santa Claus climbs down the chimney and fills the children's stockings that have been hung by the fireplace mantel. Before going to bed children around the world leave milk and food out for the one who brings the presents, be it Santa Claus; the baby Jesus; the Christmas elf of Denmark; the Christmas goat of Finland, called *Joulupukki*; or the Swedish *tomte*, or little man, who resembles Puck or a leprechaun.

The midnight church service celebrating the birth of Jesus Christ is the main Christmas Eve tradition for many Christians of all denominations and even of non-believers, especially if there is a good organist, soloist, or choir. In most European countries, a large but meatless meal is eaten before church, for it is a fast day. Some families—especially those with grown children—exchange gifts on Christmas Eve rather than on Christmas day. Caroling—going from house to house singing Christmas carols—began in Europe in the Middle Ages. The English brought the custom to America, where it is still very popular.

In Venezuela after midnight on Christmas Eve, crowds of teenagers roller skate on the Avenida de los Caiboas. After an hour or so, they attend a special early Mass called Misa de Aguinaldos 'Mass of the Carols' where they're greeted at the door with folk songs. Then they skate home for Christmas breakfast.

In Newfoundland and Nova Scotia, Canada, mummers or *belsnickers* go from house to house. Once inside they jog, tell licentious stories, play instruments and sing, and generally act up until the householder identifies the person under the mask. Then the mummer takes off his or her costume and acts like a normal visitor.

In the nineteenth century in what is now New Mexico bundles of branches were set ablaze along the roads and pathways. Called *farolitos* and *luminarias* these small fires were to guide the Travelers to the people's homes on Christmas eve. The residents were ready to give hospitality to anyone on that night, especially Joseph and Mary with the Christ Child. They would await in faith for the Traveler's three knocks on their door.

But modern fire codes overtook the ancient faith and firefighters began to extinguish the small piles of burning pine branches for fear a spark would start an inferno. Small brown paper bags partially filled with sand and installed with a candle eventually replaced the open fires. Inevitably merchants began to sell wires of electric lights to replace the candles, and plastic, multi-colored sleeves to imitate lunch bags, and the modern luminarias began to appear at holidays like Halloween and the Fourth of July. But it is certain that the Travelers are not looking for a place in the inn on those nights.

Last-minute shopping is another Christmas Eve tradition, and stores often stay open late to accommodate those who wait until the last minute to purchase their Christmas gifts.

In Buddhist Japan, Christmas Eve is for lovers, a concept introduced by a Japanese pop star and expanded by trendy magazines. It is a Western rite celebrated with a Japanese twist. The day should be spent doing something extra special (expensive), and should end in a fine Tokyo hotel room, most of which have been booked since the previous January at exorbitant rates: the cheapest rooms going for about $270. Being alone on this night is comparable to being dateless on prom night in the United States.

Uncle Chimney is their version of Santa Claus. Youngsters may be treated to a $29 barrel of Kentucky Fried Chicken (10 pieces of chicken, 5 containers of ice cream, and salad) if their parents don't mind lining up for two hours. The reason for the chicken is that many Japanese think Colonel Sanders resembles Santa Claus. Another culinary tradition is strawberry shortcake with a plastic fir tree on top. This was introduced seventy years ago by a Japanese confectioner as a variant of plum pudding.

While the origins of this form of Christmas are unclear, many people say it dates from the 1930's, well before the United States occupation after World War II in 1945.

See also BEFANA, DÍA DE LOS TRES REYES, POSADAS, ST. NICHOLAS' DAY.

Christmas Market *See* Christkindlesmarkt

Christmas Pastorellas in Mexico
December 25–January 6

CHRISTMAS DAY in Mexico is traditionally a quiet family day, especially following the POSADAS season and the midnight Mass known as the *Misa de Gallo* or 'Mass of the Cock' that many attend on CHRISTMAS EVE. But Christmas in Mexico, which extends until THREE KINGS' DAY (EPIPHANY) on January 6, is also celebrated with *pastorellas* or pageants showing how the Wise Men and shepherds overcame obstacles to visit Jesus in the manger in Bethlehem.

These celebrations, which date from colonial days when Spanish missionaries used pageants as a way of teaching Mexicans the story of the Nativity, are performed throughout Mexico in public squares, churches, and theaters. Most of the pageants represent a humorous mix of tradition, politics, and social affairs.

Christmas Shooting
Christmas Eve and New Year's Eve

A very noisy custom in Berchtesgaden, Germany. About 200 marksmen gather at midnight above the Berchtegaden valley and shoot rifles and mortars for an hour. The salvos echoing off the mountains can be heard for many miles. It is believed that the custom began as a pagan rite to drive away evil spirits.

Christ the King, Feast of
Last Sunday in October (Roman Catholic); last Sunday in August (Protestant)

Pope Pius XI, in 1925, established the last Sunday in October as the Feast of Christ the King in the Roman Catholic church. The purpose of the feast is to place special emphasis on Jesus' earthly kingship. On this day his authority over all of hu-manity's political structure is asserted and homage is paid to him as the ruler of all nations. Some churches of the Anglican Communion and Protestants observe a day of the same name and for the same purpose on the last Sunday in August.

Chrysanthemum Festival
September–October

The Chrysanthemum Festival was the last of the five sacred festivals of ancient Japan. It extended over the ninth month and sometimes into the tenth month of the Buddhist lunar calendar, although the ninth day of the ninth moon was known as **Chrysanthemum Day**, primarily an occasion for paying visits to one's superiors. Also known as **Choyo**, the festival was a unique tribute to the gardening and artistic skills of the Japanese, who developed a method for growing chrysanthemums within a wire or bamboo frame in the shape of a human figure. The boughs were trained to grow in such a way that the blossoms formed only on the surface, covering the structure with a velvety coat of tiny flowers. The heads, hands, and feet of these more-than-life-size figures would be made of wax or paste, but their costumes were made entirely of chrysanthemums, with blossoms of different sizes and colors used to achieve as realistic an effect as possible.

Formerly, *kiku ningyo* exhibitions were numerous, and could still be seen in the parks of big cities in the early part of the twentieth century. But the cost of growing the flowers and erecting the figures became prohibitive and the exhibits eventually died out. In Japan, Korea, and Okinawa today, Chrysanthemum Day is a very minor holiday, observed in scattered locations by eating chrysanthemum cakes (a dumpling made from yellow chrysanthemum petals mixed with rice flour) and drinking chrysanthemum wine.

Chugiak-Eagle River Bear Paw Festival
Mid-July

A four-day community festival in the towns of Chugiak and Eagle River, near Anchorage, Alaska. Relatively new, it has established itself and achieved popularity with its Ugly Truck and Dog Contest, in which contestants compete for a combined score that rates the lack of beauty of both their vehicles and canine companions. Other events are a parade, a rodeo, arts and crafts displays, a beauty pageant, and carnival rides.

Chulalongkorn Day
October 23

A national holiday in Thailand commemorating

King Chulalongkorn, (Rama V) the king who abolished slavery and introduced numerous reforms when the country was still called Siam. He succeeded to the throne in 1868 when he was fifteen years old, was crowned in 1873, and ruled until his death in 1910. He had been a pupil of Anna Leonowens, who taught the young prince about Abraham Lincoln. The story of her stay in the royal court, and her teaching of the royal children and concubines, was told in Margaret Landon's book, *Anna and the King of Siam*. The book was the basis for the popular Broadway musical, *The King and I*.

Chung Yeung
Usually October; ninth day of ninth moon

A Chinese holiday, the second family-remembrance day of the year. It's customary, as on the festival of Qing Ming, for families to visit the graves of ancestors, tend their gravestones, and make offerings of food, which are eaten after the ceremonies are completed.

It's also traditional on this day for people to go to the hills for picnics and kite-flying. This is done because according to an ancient legend, a scholar was warned by a soothsayer that disaster would fall on the ninth day of the ninth moon. He took his family up into the mountains. When the family returned to their village, they found every living thing dead. They gave thanks that they had been spared. The custom of flying kites stems from the belief that kites carry misfortune into the skies.

The day is also known as **Ch'ung Yang, Double Nine Day**, and the **Festival of High Places**. It is a public holiday in some areas, including Hong Kong and Macau.

Ch'un-hyang Festival
May 20–24

A celebration in Namwon, Korea, to honor Ch'un-hyang, a symbol of female virtue. She is the heroine of the ancient Korean story *Ch'un-hyangjon*, which tells of the love between a commoner and nobleman. During the festival, her story is reenacted, and other events include a *p'ansori* 'narrative song' contest, a swinging competition, traditionally enjoyed by young women, and a Miss Ch'un-hyang beauty pageant.

Ch'un-hyang was the daughter of a *kisaeng*, or female entertainer, and she and a nobleman's son, Yi Mongnyong fell in love and were secretly married. Soon after, he was transferred from Namwon to Seoul. The new governor of Namwon was corrupt and licentious, and he wanted Ch'un-hyang. But even though she was beaten, she didn't give in to his advances. Finally Yi Mongnyong returned to Namwon as provincial inspector. He punished the governor and took Ch'un-hyang as his official bride. To Koreans, this is a favorite tale of love and fidelity and also a symbol of the resistance by common people to privileged classes.

Ch'usok *See* Mid-Autumn Festival

Cinco de Mayo
May 5

Cinco de Mayo or the **Fifth of May** is a national holiday in Mexico commemorating the Battle of Puebla on May 5, 1862, in which Mexican troops under General Ignacio Zaragoza defeated the invading French forces of Napoleon III. Although the battle itself represented only a temporary setback for the French, the Mexicans' victory against overwhelming odds gave them the confidence they needed to persevere until finally triumphing on April 2, 1867.

The anniversary of this event is celebrated not only in Mexico but in many American communities with large Mexican-American populations—especially in the southwestern states of Texas, Arizona, and southern California. The events include parades, patriotic speeches, bullfights, barbecues, and beauty contests. Olvera Street in Los Angeles is particularly known for its Cinco de Mayo celebration (see also POSADAS).

Circuit Finals Rodeo, National (Dodge National Circuit Finals Rodeo)
Four days ending with third Saturday in March

The finals competitions for cowboys competing in the regional circuit system of rodeos, held since 1986 in Pocatello, Idaho. Some 200 top cowboys and cowgirls of the Professional Rodeo Cowboys Association and the Women's Professional Rodeo Association competed in 1992 for their share of a $250,000 purse and gold championship buckles. Competitions for cowboys are in saddle bronc, bull riding, calf roping, bareback riding, team roping, and steer wrestling; the women compete in barrel racing. For youngsters aged four to seven, there's mutton bustin'—riding sheep. Opening ceremonies spotlight the Pocatello Rodeo Queen and her court. Post-rodeo parties are held each night. Attendance at the finals runs about 40,000.

The circuit system was introduced to allow weekend cowboys who can't compete full-time in rodeos to compete in one of twelve regions in the United States.

See also NATIONAL FINALS RODEO.

Circumcision, Feast of the
January 1

The feast of the Circumcision, which commemorates the circumcision of the infant Jesus on the eighth day after his birth, was first observed by the Eastern Orthodox and Roman Catholic churches in the sixth century or earlier, and was adopted by the Anglican church in 1549. It is known by a number of different names: Roman Catholics, who used to call it the **Octave of the Birth of Our Lord,** or the **Circumcision of Jesus,** now mark the day as the **Solemnity of Mary, the Mother of God.** Episcopalians call it the **Feast of the Holy Name of Our Lord Jesus Christ**—a reference to the fact that Jesus was officially given his name on this day. Lutherans refer to it as the **Feast of the Circumcision and the Name of Jesus.** And Eastern Orthodox churches call it the **Feast of the Circumcision of Our Lord.** Old Calendar Orthodox churches observe it thirteen days later in accordance with the Julian or Old Style calendar.

Círio de Nazaré
Second Sunday in October

The Brazilian festival known as the Círio de Nazaré is a great "Candle Procession," which attracts pilgrims from all over the country. It traditionally takes place on the second Sunday in October and winds through the city on its way to the Nazaré Basilica. There, the statue of Our Lady of Nazaré is venerated for fifteen days during the festival. The statue is carried on a wooden framework pulled by thousands of people as payment for prayers that have been answered by the saint.

Citizenship Day
September 17

Citizenship Day is an outgrowth of two earlier patriotic celebrations. As the anniversary of the signing of the Constitution of the United States in 1787, September 17 was first observed in Philadelphia shortly after the outbreak of the Civil War as **Constitution Day.** Then in 1940 Congress set aside the third Sunday in May as **"I Am an American" Day,** which honored those who had become U. S. citizens during the preceding year. The two holidays were combined in 1952 and called Citizenship Day.

A number of states and cities hold special exercises on September 17 to focus attention on the rights and obligations of citizenship. Schools make a special effort to acquaint their students with the history and importance of the Constitution. Naturalization ceremonies, re-creations of the signing of the Constitution, and parades are other popular ways of celebrating Citizenship Day. Several states observe the entire week in which this day occurs as Constitution Week.

Civil Rights Week *See* **Bill of Rights Day**

Clark Gable Birthday Celebration
Saturday closest to February 1

The American film actor William Clark Gable was born in Cadiz, Ohio on February 1, 1901. For almost a quarter of a century he was Hollywood's leading male star, playing such romantic heroes as Rhett Butler in *Gone With the Wind* (1939).

The Clark Gable Foundation, Inc. was formed in the actor's home town of Cadiz in 1985 for the purpose of preserving and promoting Gable's memory. Since 1987 it has hosted an annual celebration of Gable's birthday on or near February 1, an event that has been attended by John Clark, Gable's son; Joan Spreckles, his step-daughter; and a number of the original cast members of *Gone With the Wind.* There are booths for Gable memorabilia and showings of his films. The celebration is attended by several hundred collectors and fans.

The Foundation plans to rebuild the house in which Gable was born and to construct a theater-museum where the actor's sixty-seven films will be shown 365 days a year.

Clearwater County Fair and Lumberjack Days
Third weekend in September

An international lumberjack event that attracts loggers from throughout the world to little Orofino, Idaho (population 3,000). Goldminers came to Orofino to establish the state's first settlements in the 1860s, and more settlers came at the turn of the century to stake out timber claims. Lumbering is now a major part of Orofino's economy. Lumberjack Days began in the early 1940s as a local contest and kept growing.

The events begin on Thursday, a children's parade is held on Friday, and the lumberjack events come on the weekend. The logging competitions include log birling, ax-throwing, chopping, chainsaw events, a speed pole climb (130 feet), jack-and-jill sawing, and a skidding, or weight-pulling, contest. The cash prizes total more than $30,000 and attendance is about 6,000.

Coca-Cola 600
Memorial Day weekend

The longest race of the four big races of the NASCAR (National Association for Stock Car Auto Racing) Winston Cup circuit, held at the Charlotte (N.C.) Motor Speedway. The track, which opened in 1960, installed special lights in 1992 to be the first super speedway ever to have nighttime racing.

The winner of the 600 in 1992 was Dale Earnhardt, who won $125,100 for his speed. This was his second win in the 600, but he had won enough other races to be the number-one leader in purses at the end of 1990, when he had collected $12,827,634.

In the week preceding the 600, the Charlotte 600 Festival offers a variety of downtown events, including a parade.

See also DAYTONA 500, WINSTON 500, and SOUTHERN 500.

Cock's Mass *See* **Misa de Gallo**

Collop Monday
Between February 2 and March 8; Monday before Shrove Tuesday

In England, the day before SHROVE TUESDAY was called Collop Monday, a "collop" being a slice of meat or bacon. It was traditionally a day for getting rid of all the meat in the house in preparation for LENT.

Columbus Day
October, second Monday

When the Italian explorer Christopher Columbus persuaded King Ferdinand and Queen Isabella of Spain to provide financial backing for his plan to find a new route to the Orient by sailing west, he was confident that only about 2,400 miles of ocean separated the two continents—a gross underestimation, as it turned out. And when he first landed in the Bahamas on October 12, 1492, he believed that he'd reached the East Indies. Despite these errors in judgment, Columbus is credited with opening the New World to European colonization, and the anniversary of his landing on the Bahamian island of San Salvador is commemorated not only in the United States but in Italy and most of the Spanish-speaking nations of the world.

Also known as **Landing Day, Discoverers'**

Day (in Hawaii), DISCOVERY DAY, and in many Latin American countries as **Día de la Raza 'Day of the Race'**, the second Monday in October is celebrated in this country with parades, patriotic ceremonies, and pageants reenacting the historic landing. A mammoth parade up Fifth Avenue in New York City is a Columbus Day tradition.

In 1991, the spirit of political correctness affected Berkeley, California, as Columbus Day was cancelled in favor of Indigenous Peoples Day. Likewise, the Student Senate at the University of Cincinnati declared that myths about Columbus may not be studied or discussed—the University is "a Columbus-myth-free-campus."

Coming-of-Age Day *See* **Seijin-no-hi**

Common Prayer Day (Store Bededag)
Between April 18 and May 21; fourth Friday after Easter

A public holiday in Denmark, Common Prayer Day is a nationwide day of prayer which has been observed since the eighteenth century, when King Christian VII's prime minister, Count Johann Friedrich von Struensee, decided that one great day of prayer should replace the numerous penitential days observed by the Evangelical Lutheran Church, the state church.

The eve of **Store Bededag** is announced by the ringing of church bells. In former times, it was customary for Copenhagen burghers to greet the spring by putting on new clothes and strolling around the city ramparts. Then they went home and ate *varme hveder*, a small square wheat bread, served hot. Today, people still dress in their spring finery and eat the traditional bread, but now they walk along the famous Langelinie, the boulevard that faces Copenhagen's waterfront.

Common Ridings Day
Various dates in June

Many Scottish border towns hold a ceremony known as Riding the Marches in June or July. The marches are border districts between England and Scotland and England and Wales. The custom dates back to the Middle Ages, when it was often necessary to reconfirm boundaries destroyed by fire in order to retain royal charters. Originally this was done only as the need arose, but eventually it became a yearly event.

The two main observations of **Common Ridings Day** occur in Selkirk and Haywick in June. In Selkirk, the event is combined with a commemoration of the 1513 Battle of Flodden, in which King James IV of Scotland and ten thousand others were killed. The Royal Burgh Standard Bearer leads a cavalcade of two hundred riders around the borders of the town common.

Commonwealth Day
Second Sunday in March

From 1903 until 1957, this holiday in honor of the British Empire was known as **Empire Day** and was celebrated on May 24, Queen Victoria's birthday. Between 1958 and 1966, it was called **British Commonwealth Day.** Then it was switched to Queen Elizabeth II's official birthday in June (see QUEEN'S BIRTHDAY), and the name was shortened to Commonwealth Day. Since 1977 it has been observed annually on the second Sunday in March.

In Canada it is still celebrated on May 24 (or the Monday before) and referred to as **Victoria Day.**

Concordia Day
November 11

A public holiday on the island of St. Maarten in the West Indies, Concordia Day commemorates the 1648 agreement to divide the island between the Dutch and the French. To this day, St. Maarten (or St. Martin) is the smallest territory shared by two sovereign states, with only a stone monument and two hand-lettered signs marking the boundary.

Concordia Day celebrates the long-standing peaceful coexistence of the two countries by holding parades and a joint ceremony with French and Dutch officials at the obelisk border monument. November 11 is also the anniversary of the island's discovery in 1493 by Christopher Columbus, who named it after the saint on whose feast day it was discovered.

Confederate Memorial Day
Varies from state to state

Observed in memory of the Confederate soldiers who died in the Civil War, Confederate Memorial Day is widely observed in the southern United States. It grew out of a number of smaller, more localized responses to the bloodshed of the War between the States. In Vicksburg, Mississippi, for example, a group of women got together in 1865 to decorate the graves of more than 18,000 men who had been killed during the siege of Vicksburg. A similar event took place the following year in Columbus, Mississippi, where the women laid magnolia blossoms on the graves of the enemy soldiers as well.

The dates on which Confederate Memorial Day is observed vary from state to state, and are often linked to some local historical event. In Texas it is called **Confederate Heroes Day**, and is observed on January 19, Robert E. Lee's birthday (see LEE-JACKSON DAY).

Confucius's Birthday (Teacher's Day)
September 28

A time to commemorate the birth of the teacher Confucius, perhaps the most influential man in China's history. In Taiwan, the day is a national holiday. In Qufu, Shandong Province, China, the birthplace of Confucius, there is a two-week-long **Confucian Culture Festival**. In Hong Kong observances are held by the Confucian Society at the Confucius Temple at Causeway Bay near this date.

Confucius, the Latinized version of the name K'ung-fu-tzu, was born in 551 B.C. during the Warring States Period and developed a system of ethics and politics that stressed five virtues: charity, justice, propriety, wisdom, and loyalty. His teachings were recorded by his followers in the *Analects* and formed the code of ethics called Confucianism that is still the cornerstone of Chinese thought. It taught filial obedience, respect, and selflessness; the Confucian "golden rule" is "Do not do unto others what you would not want others to do unto you." Confucius died at the age of seventy-three in 479 B.C.

During the Cultural Revolution Confucianism lost favor, and in the late 1960s Red Guards defaced many of the buildings in Qufu. They have since been restored, and the festival held there from late September into October attracts scholars from China and abroad. The festival opens with a ceremony accompanied by ancient music and dance and includes exhibitions and lectures on the life and teachings of Confucius and on Chinese customs.

Commemorations in Taiwan take the form of dawn services at the Confucian temples. The Confucius Temple in Tainan was built in 1665 by Gen. Chen Yunghua of the Ming Dynasty and is the oldest Confucian temple in Taiwan.

Connecticut River Powwow
Weekend before Labor Day

A three-day festival organized since 1985 by five Connecticut tribes. Primarily an educational event, it is held in Farmington, Conn., and draws about 35,000 visitors.

The powwow features demonstrations of the

hunting ability of live birds of prey, including eagles and hawks. Other events include tribal dancing, drum playing, Indian story-telling, exhibits of Indian arts such as sculpture and pottery, and talks on environmental issues.

The tribes who organize the affair are the Schaghiticoke, Paucatuck Pequot, Mashantucket Pequot, Mohegan, and Golden Hill Paugussett.

Constitution Day in Norway
May 17

May 17, 1814 marks both Norway's declaration of independence from Sweden and the day on which its constitution was signed. At that time however, the king of Sweden still ruled Norway and true independence didn't come until 1905, when the union with Sweden was dissolved and Norway chose its own king. Nevertheless this day remains the great spring festival in Norway, and today it is celebrated primarily by young people. The children's procession in Oslo, the capital city, is the largest of many school parades throughout the country. Marching behind their school bands and banners, the children pass under the balcony of the Royal Palace in salute to the King. Students who are about to graduate from secondary school and enter the University cheer and spin their tasseled caps in the air on bamboo canes. In the afternoon, each neighborhood has a celebration of its own so that children who are too young to participate in the school parades may march near their homes. Everyone joins in the procession, waving Norwegian flags, leading dogs, and pushing baby carriages. Eventually they congregate in the town square to listen to patriotic speeches and play games.

May 17 has been celebrated since the 1820s and is sometimes referred to as **Norway's National Day** or **Norway's Liberation Day**.

Conversion of St. Paul, Feast of the
January 29

Saul of Tarsus, a highly-educated, devout Jew, was converted to Christianity on the road to Damascus not long after the death of Jesus Christ. Later he became known as Paul and through his life, his teachings, and his writings became the most influential leader in the history of the church. According to tradition, he was beheaded during Nero's persecution of Christians about the year 67.

The eight-day period ending on January 29 is known as the Week of Prayer for Christian Unity. Since 1908 it has been a time for interdenomina-tional prayer and worship. At St. Paul's Chapel in New York City, the oldest church building in Manhattan, the path through the graveyard that is routinely used as a shortcut between Broadway and Fulton Street is closed for forty-eight hours, beginning on the eve of the Feast of the Conversion of St. Paul.

At one time the weather on this day was linked to predictions about the coming year. Fair weather on St. Paul's day was said to presage a prosperous year; snow or rain an unproductive one. Clouds meant that many cattle would die, and a windy day was said to be the forerunner of war.

Coolidge, Calvin, Birthday Celebration
See **Calvin Coolidge Birthday Celebration**

Coptic New Year
September 11

Members of the Coptic Orthodox Church, the native Christian church in Egypt, celebrate the New Year on September 11 because it is the day on which the Dog Star, Sirius, reappears in the Egyptian sky, signalling the flooding of the Nile and the beginning of a new planting season.

To commemorate the martyrs of the church, red vestments and altar clothes are used on this day. A food of special significance on this day is the red date: red signifies the martyrs' blood, the white meat of the date symbolizes the purity of their hearts, and the hard pit represents their steadfast faith. The Coptic New Year is also celebrated by Canadians of Egyptian descent and by Egyptian communities elsewhere.

Corn Palace Festival
One week in mid-September

The world's only Corn Palace was built in Mitchell, South Dakota in 1892. It was home to the Corn Belt Exposition, designed to encourage farmers to settle in the area by displaying its corn and wheat crops on the building's exterior. A second and larger Corn Palace was built in 1905 to accommodate the growing crowds, and in 1937 a third Corn Palace was completed, this time with the addition of Moorish-looking minarets, turrets, and kiosks. The outside of the Palace is covered entirely with decorations consisting of dock, wild oats, bromegrass, blue grass, rye straw, and wheat tied in bunches. Corn of different colors, sawn in half lengthwise and nailed to the outside walls, is also used to complete the design, which changes every year. The decorating process usually begins in mid-summer and is completed in time for the festival.

Entertainment at the festival has reflected changing public tastes over the years. Stage revues in the 1920s gave way to the "big bands" of the '30s and '40s. Standup comedians and television entertainers in the '50s and '60s have yielded to country and western stars today.

Corpus Christi

Between May 21 and June 24; Thursday after Trinity Sunday

Also known as the **Feast of the Most Holy Body of Christ**, the **Day of Wreaths**, and in France, as the **Fête-Dieu**, Corpus Christi is a Roman Catholic festival that has been celebrated in honor of the Eucharist since 1246. In commemoration of the Last Supper on the day before Jesus' crucifixion, worshippers receive Communion and, in some countries, the consecrated bread (or Host) is paraded through the streets, held by the priests in a monstrance. In Spain and Provence, these processions can be quite elaborate, with saints and characters from the Bible following a path decorated with wreaths and strewn with flowers.

In Portugal the feast is known as **Día de Corpo de Deus** (Corpus Christi) and has been one of the major religious observances—both on the mainland and in the Azores—since medieval times. In the city of Ponta Delgada, on San Miguel in the Azores, the people make a flower-petal carpet almost three quarters of a mile in length. Over this carpet passes a colorful procession of high-ranking clergy and red-robed priests, who are followed by a group of first communicants (those who are to receive communion for the first time)-the young boys wearing dark suits and scarlet capes and the girls wearing white dresses and veils. The climax of the ceremony comes when the bishop raises the silver monstrance and exposes the Blessed Sacrament, the Body of Christ.

Cosby Ramp Festival

First Sunday in May

A festival started in 1951 to honor an obnoxious plant—the ramp. Held on Kineauvista Hill near Cosby, Tenn. (which is near Knoxville), the festival is touted as the first and largest of the ramp celebrations.

The ramp, related to the onion, is scientifically designated *Allium triccorcum lilaceae*. The name 'ramp' supposedly was a shortening of *rampson*, the name of a similar plant. Devotees of the ramp say it has a mouth-watering, sweet flavor with a hint of garlic; they also concede that it has an astoundingly strong smell—like that of a wild onion multiplied a thousand times. It was once used in medicinal tonics, the theory being that the odor was enough to ward off germs and certainly germy people. It is rich in vitamin C and was the first spring vegetable for mountain people. Ramp harvest festivals of an informal sort are an old Appalachian custom handed down from the Indians, who taught the European settlers how to cook ramps.

Several days before the festival, a group of ramp pluckers goes into the mountains to pick and clean the ramps. The festival lunch, of course, features fried ramp with eggs cooked with streaked meat, a kind of bacon. The festival music is bluegrass, gospel, and country, and the events include the crowning of the Ramp Prince and Princess and the Maid of Ramps. About 5,000 to 6,000 attend.

The Polk County Ramp Festival, a similar but smaller affair, is held in late April in Benton, Tenn. It has bluegrass music all day, and awards are given to the oldest and youngest ramp eaters, the largest family, and the person who has come the farthest distance. (In 1991, a visitor from Germany won.)

Cotton Bowl Game

January 1

This great college football game was inaugurated in 1937 and pits the Southwest Conference champion against another nationally ranked team. In 1993 Notre Dame faced Texas A&M and beat them 28-3 in the 72,000 seat Cotton Bowl stadium in Dallas, Texas.

Until 1993 the game was preceded by Cotton Bowl Week which offered a variety of activities and culminated in the Cotton Bowl Parade. Like other NEW YEAR'S DAY parades it was a lavish display of colorful floats and marching bands. The organizers of the Cotton Bowl couldn't secure a contract for television coverage of the parade and so it and Cotton Bowl week was canceled. However, the football game continues.

Cotton Carnival

Late May through early June

A two-week salute to King Cotton in Memphis, Tenn. The carnival began in 1931 during the Great Depression as an event to cheer-up the people. Its forebear was the Memphis Mardi Gras, which was started in 1872 to promote good because the Civil War and a yellow-fever epidemic had just about wiped out the city. Antebellum Memphis had been the site of the largest indoor port and cotton market in the South. Mardi Gras was discontinued in 1891, and Memphis has recovered, and is once again a busy port on the Mississippi, and as one of the world's biggest cotton markets annually trades more than four million bales.

A King and Queen Cotton are crowned a month before the carnival and rule over all the events. The official opening comes with a great river pageant featuring illuminated barges carrying the king and queen and their court of some 200 princesses and ladies-in-waiting. When the king and queen debark from the barge they are greeted by municipal and cotton-industry leaders and the Maid of Cotton, a young woman who has spent the previous year traveling to promote cotton clothing. The pageant is, after all, more than fun; it is a promotion for the cotton industry.

The days of the carnival are filled with parades, art exhibits, a week-long Music Fest with star performers on six outdoor stages, sports events, and such miscellany as crayfish boils, a masked ball, and tours of antebellum houses.

Cotton Row on Parade *See* **Crop Day**

Counting of the Omer *See* **Lag b'Omer**

Country Music Fan Fair, International
Early June

A week-long country feast of music at the Tennessee State Fairgrounds in Nashville, Tenn., also known as "Music City, U.S.A" and the home of the Grand Ole Opry. The twentieth anniversary of the Fan Fair was celebrated in 1991 with a "grand ole party" attended by country music's brightest stars. Yearly attractions are thirty or more hours of stage shows and concerts, autograph-and-picture-taking sessions with big-name stars, some 300 booths and exhibits, fan-club banquet dinners, and a celebrity auction that gives bidders a chance to buy such items as Junior Sample's overalls from TV's "Hee Haw" or Dolly Parton's boots. The Grand Master Fiddling Championship is held at Opryland U.S.A., a music-theme entertainment park.

The Grand Ole Opry was founded by George Dewey Hay, who was called "the Solemn Ole Judge," and began weekly radio broadcasts from Nashville in 1925. The music developed from ballads of rural laborers in the 1920s through the string bands and cowboy music of the 1930s into honky-tonk and rockabilly music after World War

II. In 1941, the Opry was staged live at the Ryman Auditorium in Nashville, and in 1974 it moved to Opryland U.S.A. This all led to the Fan Fair, which is billed as "The Closest Thing to Hillbilly Heaven."

Cowboy Poetry Gathering
January

A celebration of the old tradition of cowboy poetry—and of other cowboy art—in the buckaroo town of Elko, Nev.

Poetry by cowboys has a long history; cowboys traditionally recited poetry as they rode on cattle drives, but it was a private, little-known custom. A poem by Allen McCanless published in 1885 has these Shakespeare-echoing lines:
 . . . *My ceiling the sky, my carpet the grass,*
My music the lowing of herds as they pass;
My books are the brooks, my sermons the
*   stones,*
My parson's a wolf on a pulpit of bones . . .

The gathering, which began in 1985 with about fifty working cowboys, has become a six-day affair that now includes folk-music concerts, western dances, exhibits of cowboy gear, and workshops not only on writing but also on such topics as horsehair braiding and photography. In 1992, the Hispanic vaquero (cowboy) was honored with performances and exhibits. Poetry remains the heart of the festival, and the poets, all working ranch people include men, women, and children as young as six or eight. The poetry includes doggerel and limericks but is mostly in ballad form with narratives like those of Rudyard Kipling's.

Close to 300 cowboys, cowgirls, and ranchers participate, and between 6,000 and 8,000 people from all over the world attend the various events. Tickets go on sale in October and are instant sell-outs. The gathering has spawned other cowboy-poetry festivals throughout the west.

Hal Cannon, director of the Western Folklore Center in Salt Lake City, was the force behind the first gathering, and the center still sponsors it. The goals of the gathering are to represent the voice of working ranch people through their poetry, music, and folklife; to promote a dialogue between urban and rural people of the American west; and to nurture understanding between pastoral peoples throughout the world.

Cow Fights
April

The winner of the cow battles or **Kuhkämpee** held in the canton of Valais, Switzerland each spring is crowned Queen Cow of the village herds. Wearing a flower garland between her horns and a large bell hanging from a decorated collar, the Queen Cow leads a colorful procession of herdsmen and animals to their summer pasture in the mountains. (See also ALPAUFZUG, ALMABTRIEB.)

Craftsmen's Fair
August

Although craft fairs can be found all over New England during the summer months, the Craftsmen's Fair at Mt. Sunapee State Park in Newbury, New Hampshire is considered to be the oldest continuously held craft fair, dating back to 1934. Beginning on the first Tuesday in August and ending five days later, the fair features about three hundred craftspeople who sell their work and display their skills through demonstrations in such diverse areas as decoy carving, printmaking, weaving and spinning, basket making, embroidering, pipe making, and blacksmithing. Visitors to the **League of New Hampshire Craftsmen's Fair** can buy clothing, pottery, leaded glass, lampshades, character dolls, marionettes, jewelry, blown glass, leather goods, and just about any other craft they can imagine. There is also a juried craft exhibit, which is open only to members of the League.

Cranberry Harvest Festival
Two days in late September or early October

Also known as the **Massachusetts Cranberry Festival**, this annual event has celebrated the harvesting of cranberries in South Carver, Massachusetts since 1949. The idea for the festival came from Ellis D. Atwood, founder the the Edaville Railroad, and Robert Rich of Ocean Spray Cranberries. Rides through the cranberry bogs on the old Edaville steam train are still a popular festival attraction, as are the cranberry baking and pie-eating contests, the crowning of the Cranberry Queen, and performances by strolling musicians dressed as seventeenth century sailors singing old ballads and sea chanteys. The highlight of the festival, of course, is the harvesting of the cranberries themselves, which are a traditional part of the American and Canadian THANKSGIVING feasts.

Crane Watch
March–April

There are actually two events in Nebraska that celebrate the world's largest concentration of sandhill cranes: the Crane Watch in Kearney and **Wings Over the Platte** in Grand Island. Both take place during the six-week period in March and April when seventy percent of the world's sandhill cranes—over a half million birds—crowd a one-hundred-and-fifty-mile stretch of the Platte River between Grand Island and Sutherland. Arriving from west Texas, New Mexico, southern California, and central Mexico, the cranes rest and feed in the area before continuing their migration to Canada and Alaska.

The Fort Kearney State Historical Park serves as an information center for the many visitors who come to see the cranes, and there are guided tours to the most advantageous viewing areas. Events associated with the Crane Watch also include wildlife displays, outdoor photo seminars, and nature workshops.

Crawfish Festival
First weekend in May, on even-numbered years

A time to celebrate and eat the small crustaceans (also called crayfish and crawdads) in Breaux Bridge, La., a small Cajun village. Since 1959, by act of the state legislature, the village has been officially called Crawfish Capital of the World.

Crawfish is related to the lobster, and local folk say the crawfish is really the Acadian lobster that followed them to the bayou lands of southern Louisiana. The Cajuns are descendants of the French Canadians whom the British drove from the colony of Acadia (now Nova Scotia) in the eighteenth century. They still speak their own patois, a combination of French forms with words borrowed from American Indian, African, Spanish, English, and other languages; they often still live in small, self-contained communities.

The festival is a two-day event, featuring crawfish races (on a special circular table, with betting allowed), a parade, CaJune music night and day, a World Championship Crawfish Peeling Contest and a World Championship Crawfish Eating Contest. In the latter, contestants start out with a dishpan of five pounds of crawfish and eat for two hours. The record is thirty-three pounds. The prize is a trophy and crawfish to take home. As many as 100,000 visitors come to this village of 5,000 for the festival.

Creek Green Corn Ceremony
Late summer

A religious harvest festival, not open to the public, held in late summer by the Muskogee-Creek Indians on the ceremonial grounds in Okmulgee, Oklahoma. Each tribal group conducts its own

Green Corn Ceremony on one of twelve such Creek ceremonial grounds in the state.

The dances for the ceremony are performed not to the beat of drums, but to the rhythm of turtle and gourd rattles. Women are designated "shell-shakers," and they dance in groups of four with shells (or sometimes today with juice cans filled with pebbles) around their ankles. Children are included in ceremonies from the earliest age: women dancers with babies carry them into the ceremonial circle. One dance, known as the ribbon dance, honors women and is performed only by women and girls.

Other elements of the festival are stickball games and cleansing ceremonies, but the affair is essentially religious. To worship the Great Spirit, Creeks perform rituals relating to wind, fire, water, and earth.

Seminoles and Yuchis in Oklahoma also celebrate the Green Corn. In some ceremonies participants purge themselves with emetics and submit to ceremonial scratching on the legs and arms.

Cromm Dub's Sunday
First Sunday in August
In Irish folklore, Cromm Dub was a famous pagan idol that was destroyed on this day. Despite this, as late as the mid-nineteenth century, flowers were still being offered to Cromm Dub on Mount Callan in County Clare. It is for this reason that the Irish also called this day **Garland Sunday**. In ancient times, the flowers were probably preceded by more bloody sacrifices.

Cromwell's Day
September 3
As a British general, Puritan statesman, and Lord Protector of England from 1653–1658, Oliver Cromwell is remembered today more for his actions as a general and a statesman than for his efforts within the narrow field of Puritanism. Each year the Cromwell Association in England holds a special service near Cromwell's statue outside the Houses of Parliament on September 3. The date is particularly appropriate. It was on this day in 1650 that Cromwell won the battle of Dunbar, inflicting 3,000 casualties and taking 10,000 prisoners at a cost of only twenty British lives. It was on the same day a year later that he won a decisive victory at the battle of Worcester against the Scots. And it was also the day on which he died.

Crop Day (Cotton Row on Parade)
First Saturday in August

A salute to the historic Cotton Row business area of Greenwood, Miss. Cotton Row, listed on the National Register of Historic Places, has the nation's largest concentration of nineteenth-century cotton dealers' offices. These buildings are still in use and in their original architectural state. Of the original fifty-seven buildings in Cotton Row, twenty-four are currently occupied by cotton buyers and sellers, known as cotton factors. Greenwood today has one of the biggest cotton markets in the United States.

In the late 1800s, hundreds of thousands of acres of swamp land were opened for cotton production through a federal levee system. Front, Howard, and Main Streets, close to the Yazoo River, became the central point for cotton offices, banks, law offices, insurance companies, and the other businesses that supported the industry of cotton marketing and shipping.

Crop Day began in 1980 and has become the biggest outdoor event in the Mississippi Delta. It's a one-day affair, held early in August. This is a time when the cotton is high enough to fend for itself against the weeds and farmers can take a brief rest before the harvest. Activities include a street dance, a cotton-seed pulling contest, a cotton bale give-away, a bed race, a rubber duck race, a food fair, and sports events.

Crop Over
Late June–early July
This harvest festival in Barbados was originally celebrated in the 1800s by slaves at the end of the sugar-cane harvest. A procession of carts and animals decorated with flowers would bring the last load of cane to the plantation owner, who would then provide a feast for the laborers. One of the carts carried an effigy known as Mr. Harding made from sugar cane refuse and dressed in a black coat, top hat, and mask. The effigy represented the cruel gangdrivers and symbolized the hard times that lay ahead for the laborers until the next crop.

Today, Crop Over is a civic celebration, which was revived in 1973. It takes place during the last three weeks of June and usually ends on the first weekend in July. In rural areas of Barbados there are fairs, cane-cutting contests, open-air concerts, native dancing, and "stick licking"—a self-defense sport similar to fencing. On the first Saturday in July, the celebration moves to the island's capital, Bridgetown, which is transformed into a huge open-air bazaar where people can shop and listen to live bands. On Sunday a contest (known as the Cohobblepot) to select the Crop Over Queen is held at the National Stadium. Monday is the finale, known as the Kadooment, which includes the judging of costumed bands at the stadium and a five-mile procession from there to the Garrison Savannah, where a huge effigy of Mr. Harding is set on fire and pelted with stones.

Crossing of the Delaware
December 25

What is now known as Washington Crossing State Park is the site of the historic event that took place on CHRISTMAS night in 1776, when General George Washington and the Continental Army crossed the Delaware River just before the Battle of Trenton. **Washington's Crossing of the Delaware** is reenacted on December 25 each year, beginning at Washington Crossing, Pennsylvania (formerly McKonkey's Ferry) and ending on the opposite bank at Washington Crossing, New Jersey.

It was St. John Terrell, an actor, producer, and founder of the Music Circus at Lambertville, New Jersey, who inaugurated this observance in 1953, playing the part of George Washington himself for a number of years. The costumed actors who cross the river in a specially made Durham boat, similar to those originally used by Washington and his men, try to reproduce the scene exactly as it is depicted in the well-known painting by Emanual Leutze: Vermont's Green Mountain Boys sit in the bow, Gloucester fishermen from Massachusetts man the oars, and General Washington stands with one foot on the gunwale. The actor who portrays Lieutenant James Monroe carries the thirteen-star flag seen in the painting—an anachronism, since the flag had not been adopted in 1776.

Crow Fair
Third Weekend in August

One of the biggest powwows in the U.S., held since 1918 at Crow Agency, Mont., about sixty-five miles southeast of Billings. The fair, held Thursday through Sunday, is hosted by the Crow tribe but attracts thousands of other Indians (Peruvian Incas and Alaskan Eskimos were among those attending in 1991) who set up more than 1,000 tepees on the camp grounds.

Dancing at the fair includes not only traditional Plains Indian dances but also the Crow Hop, which is similar to a war dance and is unique to the Crows. It was originally a men's dance, but now women also take part, and all wear clothes of buckskin, feathers, quills, and bells to add a counterpoint to the drum beats. There are rodeos with

cash prizes, horse races, a relay of bareback riding, art exhibits, and demonstrations of such crafts as pipe-carving and jewelry-designing with turquoise and silver.

Crucifixion Friday *See* Good Friday

Crystal Night *See* Kristallnacht

Cuisinières, Fête des la
Early August

With the possible exception of the celebration at CARNIVAL, this is the most colorful event of the year in the French West Indian island of Guadeloupe. The **Women Cooks' Festival** begins with a morning service at the cathedral and a parade of women in Creole dress. The highlight of the festival is the five-hour feast prepared by the dozen or so members of the Association of Women Chefs. The Creole dishes they prepare include *blaffs* (a fish or shellfish dish in a sauce; the name comes from the sound made by the fish as it is plumged into boiling water), *boudins* (sausage), and *crabes farcis* (stuffed crabs). It has been said that "one fistful of the tiny hot peppers that are vital to Creole cooking is generally considered enough to blow up an average European city."

Culture Day *See* Bunka-no-hi

Cure Salée
September–October

The Tuareg, a largely nomadic ethnic group found primarily in Algeria, Niger, Mali, and Libya, converge with their camels and cattle on a place known as Ingal just after the first rains of the season arrive. An oasis in the Sahara region of northern Niger, Ingal has palm groves and date plantations, and is a favorite grazing ground. The **Salted Cure Festival** takes its name from the salt contained in the new grass, which is essential to the animals' diet. Each Tuareg group participating in the Cure Salée follows a very specific transhumance or seasonal migration route, some traveling hundreds of miles.

In Tamacheq, the language of the Tuareg, the event is known as **Tanekert** or **Tenekert**. The return of the rains is also celebrated with dancing, singing, and camel races.

Cynonfardd Eisteddfod
Last Saturday in April

When the Welsh began to emigrate to the United States during the latter part of the nineteenth century and the early years of the twentieth, many were drawn to the coal-mining areas of northeastern Pennsylvania. Among them was a minister, Dr. Thomas C. Edwards, who emigrated in 1870 and established a church society designed to teach the Welsh children English by having them read and memorize music, hymns, songs, poetry, and other literary selections in the tradition of the Welsh EISTEDDFOD. This group became known as the Cynonfardd Literary Society—the Cynon being a stream in South Wales where Edwards had lived as a child. Edwards patterned the society's activities after the Welsh National Eisteddfod, and by 1889 the Cynonfardd Eisteddfod was well established.

Believed to be the oldest continuous Eisteddfod outside of Wales and the only one of its kind in the United States today, the Cynonfardd Eisteddfod was originally held on March 17 or ST. PATRICK'S DAY, probably because the coal mines were closed on that day so the Irish miners could celebrate. Now it is held at the end of April, and the competition is limited to recitations and vocal and instrumental selections. Competitors range in age from under five years old to adults, and the prizes are generally modest—two dollars, for example, for the child under five years who sings the best "Twinkle, Twinkle Little Star," or fifty dollars for the prize-winning senior citizen who sings a Welsh hymn. Literary recitations include selections from the Bible, Henry Wadsworth Longfellow, and other well-known American authors. All performers in both the poetry and music competitions must memorize their selections.

Czech Festival, National
First full weekend in August
Wilber, Nebraska's annual Czech Festival is held in a town that has been designated by the U.S. Congress as the "Czech Capital of America." Patterned after the well-known Pennsylvania Dutch Festival in Kutztown (see KUTZTOWN FAIR), the purpose of the festival is to recognize contributions of Czech immigrants and to foster the Czech culture. Folk dance groups come from all over the state, and local residents wear Czech cos-

tumes and dance the *beseda* or polka in the streets. Foods prepared by the town's residents and served at the festival include a number of Czech specialties, such as roast duck, sauerkraut, dumplings, and *kolaches* (sweet buns). There is even a kolache-eating contest.

On the second day of the festival, awards are presented for special achievements in promoting both Nebraska and the Czech culture.

Czechoslovak Independence Day
October 28
The Republic of Czechoslovakia was founded on October 28, 1918, when the National Committee in Prague proclaimed independence from the Austrian Hapsburg emperors and took over the administration of an independent Czechoslovak state. They were supported in this move by President Woodrow Wilson, who sent a note to the Austro-Hungarian foreign minister urging that the various nationalities of the empire be allowed to determine their own political future.

Independence Day was widely celebrated in Czechoslovakia until the Communists seized power there in 1948 and turned it into a Soviet satellite. But it continued to be recognized in the United States with special banquets, addresses, religious services, cultural programs, and the laying of a wreath at the tomb of President Wilson at the Cathedral of St. Peter and St. Paul (also known as the National Cathedral or Washington Cathedral) in Washington, D.C. Communities with large Czech or Slovak populations such as New York City, Los Angeles, Wilber, Nebraska, and Newark, New Jersey also mark the occasion, but the division of the country into the Czech and Slovak republics has caused uncertainty about the way future celebrations will be handled.

This day should not be confused with Czechoslovak Liberation Day, a national holiday observed on May 9 to commemorate the country's liberation by the Soviet army and U.S. forces at the end of World War II.

D

Dædala

Spring

This is the name given to two festivals held in ancient Bœotia, which was a part of Greece, in honor of the reconciliation of Hera and Zeus. According to the myth, Hera and Zeus quarreled and Hera went away to Euboea and refused to return to his bed. To trick her into coming back and on the advice of Cithæron, Zeus dressed up a carved oak-trunk to resemble a bride and let it be known that he planned to marry Platæa, the daughter of Asopus. Hera was so angry she tore the clothes from the statue, discovered the deception, and was so pleased that the two were reconciled.

The **Little Dædala**, held every six years, involved going to an ancient oak grove and cutting down trees for images. Every sixty years the **Great Dædala** was held, and all Bœotia joined in the celebration. All the images that had been collected over the years during the Little Dædala were carried to the top of Mt. Cithæron, where they were burned on an altar along with sacrifices to Zeus and Hera.

Dahlonega Gold Rush Days

October (October 19–20 in 1992)

A celebratory reminder in Dahlonega, Ga., of the town's heyday as a gold-rush town. The nation's first major gold rush was here in 1828, and the area around Dahlonega boomed; a federal mint built in 1838 operated for twenty-three years and coined more than $6 million. Mining continued into the beginning of the twentieth century, and today visitors can pan for gold at several locations. The name of the town is pronounced dah-LON-a-gah; it is derived from the Cherokee name Talonega, meaning 'golden.' The festival includes arts and crafts exhibits, country cooking, and beard-growing and tobacco-spitting contests.

Dairy Festival

July

The dairy capital of Michigan is appropriately named Elsie in honor of the cow in Borden's ads, and although it has fewer than one thousand residents, there are twenty working dairy farms in the area. One of them is Green Meadow Farm, which boasts the largest herd of registered Holsteins in the United States.

For three days in July each year since 1986, the town of Elsie serves gallons of ice cream at bargain prices. Green Meadow Farm is open to visitors, and there are competitions in cow-milking, ice-cream-eating, and even milk-drinking, with competitors using a baby bottle. The fourteen-foot-tall fiberglass Holstein in the center of town is a popular place for the festival's twenty thousand visitors to have their photographs taken.

Dakota Cowboy Poetry Gathering

Memorial Day weekend

The Dakota Cowboy Poetry Gathering was founded by Bill Lowman, a cowboy poet who had attended a similar event in Nevada in 1985 (see COWBOY POETRY GATHERING) and decided that the badlands of North Dakota should host its own cowboy poetry festival. Two years later the first "Real Cowboy Review" was held in Medora, with forty poets and musicians participating. The crowds drawn to the event have continued to grow, and the performers often travel long distances to share their poetry, songs, and stories inspired by life on the ranch.

The Medora gathering prides itself on featuring only "the Real Ones"—those cowboys who "have spent a lifetime looking down the top of a cow." It tries to discourage "novelty cowboys, movie cowboys, or rodeo cowboys" who don't really live the life portrayed in their poems. This burgeoning interest in cowboy poetry is largely the result of research done by folklorists who wanted to draw attention to the cowboys' passion for rhyme and tale-spinning and to keep the tradition alive.

Dalai Lama, Birthday of the
July 6

This celebration is always held on July 6 for the birthday of the Dalai Lama, the spiritual and political head of Tibet. The name Dalai means 'ocean' and was given to the ruling lama in the sixteenth century by the Mongol leader Altan Khan. The title suggests depth of wisdom.

The present Dalai Lama, who was enthroned in 1940 at the age of five, is the latest in the line that began in the fourteenth century. Each Dalai Lama is believed to be the reincarnation of the preceding one, and when a Dalai Lama dies, Tibetan lamas search throughout the country for a child who is his reincarnation.

Tibet had been a sovereign country until 1949 when China invaded eastern Tibet and sporadic warfare followed. In 1959, a popular uprising exploded at Lhasa but was suppressed, and the Dalai Lama and most of his ministers and about 100,000 Tibetans escaped across the Himalayas. The Dalai Lama has lived since then in exile in Dharmsala, India. Today there are some 80,000 Tibetans in India, 30,000 in Nepal, and 3,000 in Bhutan.

The birthday is observed today by exiles in India with incense-burning ceremonies to appease the local spirits, family picnics, and traditional dances and singing. The incense-burning is a rite pre-dating Buddhism.

See also Universal Prayer Day.

Dance of Thanksgiving *See* Whe'wahchee

Dancing Procession
Between May 12 and June 15; Whit Tuesday

The **Sprangprocession** in Luxembourg has been held on Whit-Tuesday, which falls fifty-two days after Easter, for the past thirteen centuries in honor of St. Willibrord (St. Wilfred), the patron saint of Luxembourg, whose feast day is celebrated November 7. The dance that is performed by thousands of participants in the procession through the narrow streets of Echternach, has remained basically unchanged. It involves taking three steps forward and two back (or, according to some sources, five steps forward and three back), to the accompaniment of local bands playing the same melody that was played more than thirteen hundred years ago. The procession ends up in the Basilica, where the remains of St. Willibrord are buried.

There are a number of legends that attempt to explain the origin of the Dancing Procession. According to one of them, St. Willibrord came to Luxembourg from northern England to convert the people to Christianity. He saved them from a plague by promising that if they subjected themselves to physical punishment, the plague would end. The people danced to the same tune that is played today, hopping up and down until they were completely exhausted and, as promised, the plague disappeared.

Another explanation is that a Crusader returned from the Holy Land to discover that his dead wife's greedy relatives had taken over his property and branded him a murderer. As he was about to be hanged, he asked permission to play one last tune on his violin. The haunting melody mesmerized the onlookers, who started dancing and were unable to stop. The condemned man walked away from the scaffold, and the procession that is held each year is penance for his unjust condemnation.

Daniel Boone Festival
Eight days, beginning on the first Saturday in October

Held annually since 1948 in Barbourville, Kentucky, this week-long festival honors the frontiersman Daniel Boone (1734–1820), who in 1775 was the first to carve a trail through the Appalachian Mountains from eastern Tennessee all the way to the Ohio River. For fifty years Boone's "Wilderness Road" was the major route for settlers heading west.

An important part of the festival is the signing of the Cherokee Cane Treaty. Descendants of the original Cherokees who hid in the Smoky Mountains to avoid being forced to move to Oklahoma in 1838–39 sign a treaty each year that provides them with cane, which still grows along the Cumberland River, that they can use to make baskets. Other festival events include an old-fashioned barbecue featuring pioneer and American Indian foods, traditional Indian dances, a long-rifle shoot, and competitions in such activities as hog-calling, wood-chopping, and fiddling.

Dartmouth Winter Carnival
Weekend in February

The students of Dartmouth College in Hanover, New Hampshire have been celebrating Winter Carnival since 1910, when they decided to hold their own mini-Olympics to shake off the winter blues. Soon other colleges were invited to join in the athletic events, which included ski jumping and showshoe races. By the 1920s, there were so many parties and balls associated with the weekend that it was called "The Mardi Gras of the North."

The event became even more popular after it was featured in the 1939 movie "Winter Carnival." Students from other colleges, some as far away as Florida, came to Hanover to join in the fun, and eventually drunkenness and vandalism became a problem. Carnival events nowadays are limited to Dartmouth students and their guests. Teams from a dozen or so Northeastern colleges and universities compete in Nordic and Alpine skiing, ski jumping, hockey, basketball, gymnastics, and other sports. But the highlight for many is the snow sculpture competition on the Dartmouth green. Because snow has been so scarce in recent winters, the sculptors have had to rely on snow trucked in from nearby ski areas, scraped off parking lots, and recycled from skating rinks.

Dasain *See* **Durga Puja**

Data Ganj Baksh Death Festival
18–19 Safar
   A day of massive pilgrimages to the Mausoleum of Data Ganj Baksh in Lahore, Pakistan. Data Ganj Baksh, which means 'He Who Gives Generously,' was the name given to Syed Ali Abdul Hasan Bin Usman Hajweri (or Ali Hujwiri, or al-Hujwiri), a scholar and author who lived most of his life in Lahore and died in 1072. He wrote *Kashful Mahjub* (or *Kashf al-mahjub*), the oldest Persian treatise on Sufism. It is a text on the fundamentals of Sufism and it reviews Islamic mysticism, linking each famous master to a particular doctrine. Ali Hujwiri is one of the most popular saints in Pakistan, and every day hundreds of pilgrims pray at his shrine and ask for blessings and favors. On his *urs* (death festival), thousands throng to the shrine for celebratory activities and prayers.

Davis Cup
November–December
   The oldest international men's tennis competition, inaugurated in 1900 and credited with drawing world attention to the game. Tennis was then a young sport; the first U.S. national championship games were played in 1881. The competition was fathered by Dwight F. Davis, who was United States doubles champion with Harvard teammate Holcombe Ward in 1899–1901. Davis believed in-

ternational competition would boost the game's popularity, and had a thirteen-inch-high silver bowl crafted by a Boston silversmith; it was to be called the **International Lawn Tennis Challenge Trophy** but became known as the Davis Cup.

From the first, the championship was open to all nations. The first games, held at the Longwood Cricket Club in Chestnut Hill, Massachusetts, had only two contestants: a British Isles team and the American team (captained by Davis). The Americans won, 3-0. The Brits did better—but still lost—in 1902. In 1903, they won, and it was not until 1913 that the U.S. regained the cup.

There was growing interest in the cup. Four nations competed in 1919, and that number grew to fourteen in 1922 and twenty-four in 1926. From the start, teams have consisted of two singles players and a doubles team. There are five matches—four singles and one doubles. Each match is awarded one point, and the first team to win three points wins the cup. In women's tennis, the Federation Cup, inaugurated in 1963 and played each year in the spring, is considered the equivalent of the Davis Cup.

The United States dominated the Davis Cup in the 1920s, spurred by William T. ("Big Bill") Tilden 2nd, who was a member of the Davis Cup team for eleven years. France won in 1927, and went on to win in the next five years up through 1932. Great Britain was a power in the 1930s, and Australia and the United States dominated in the 1940s, 1950s, and 1960s; in the late 1970s and the 1980s the winners had a multi-national flavor. In 1980, Czechoslovakia became the first Communist country to win the Davis Cup. The United States won in 1990, but in 1991, playing in Lyons, France, the French team knocked out the champion U.S. team 3-1, and owned the cup for the first time in fifty-nine years. The French team (led by Guy Forget, Henri Leconte, and coach Yannick Noah) kissed, hugged, leapt over the net, lay down on the court, and danced a conga line. In 1992 the United States team defeated Switzerland to regain the cup.

Day of Judgment *See* **Rosh ha-Shanah**

Day of Peace, International
Third Tuesday of September
   The day of the opening session of the United Nations General Assembly, and a day proclaimed by the U.N. to promote the ideals of peace. The first official observance of the day was in Septem-

ber 1982, and *every year since then the Secretary-General of the United Nations has set a theme for the day. In 1991, the theme was "Light a Candle for Peace."*

At the United Nations the day is marked with a special message by the Secretary-General, who then rings the Japanese Peace Bell and invites people throughout the world to reflect on the meaning of peace.

Special events are organized in various countries, and in the United States, the mayors of a number of cities issue proclamations for the day.

Day of the Awakeners (Den na Buditelite)
November 1

A national holiday in Bulgaria, this day commemorates the patriots, writers, and revolutionaries who helped to ignite the spirit of Bulgarian nationalism. Thanksgiving services are held in churches, and elsewhere patriotic speeches, parades, and folk music mark this yearly event.

Day of the Blowing *See* Rosh ha-Shanah

Day of the Covenant
December 16

This South African holiday was established on December 16, 1838 in commemoration of the victory of the Voortrekkers over Dingaan and the Zulus. The "covenant" it refers to is the vow that Pretorius and the Voortrekkers made with God as they prepared for the Battle of Blood River: that if they were victorious, the day would be observed as a Sabbath and a church would be built in gratitude.

The original name for this holiday was **Dingaan's Day**. Then it was called **Day of the Vow** and, eventually, Day of the Covenant.

Day of the Covenant
November 26

A Baha'i holy day, commemorating the covenant Baha'u'llah, founder of the faith, made with humanity and his followers, appointing Abdu'l-Baha as the head of the Baha'i religion who would interpret Baha'i teachings. Adbu'l-Baha chose the date when followers requested an occasion to remember his importance.

Day of the Dead *See* All Souls' Day

Day of the Kings *See* Epiphany

Day of the Race *See* Columbus Day

Day of the Three Archbishops
January 30

In Greece during the eleventh century there was a popular controversy going on over which of the three fourth-century archbishops—Basil the Great, Gregory the Theologian, or John Chrysostom—was the greatest saint of the Greek Orthodox church. In 1081 Bishop John of Galatia resolved the problem by reporting that the three saints had appeared to him in a vision to say that they were all equal in the eyes of God. Their equality is celebrated on this day, which is also known as the **Holiday of the Three Hierarchs**. In Greek schools special exercises are held in honor of the three, who supported the classical Greek tradition at a time when many early Christians were opposed to all non-Christian literature.

Days of '76
First full weekend in August

This three-day celebration held each year in Deadwood, South Dakota is an attempt to revive the spirit of the gold rush days. It is timed to coincide as closely as possible with the anniversaries of the deaths of "Calamity Jane" Canary (August 1, 1903) and "Wild Bill" Hickok (August 2, 1876), two of Deadwood's most famous residents. The festivities begin with a three-mile-long historical parade that includes floats portraying the various stages of, and characters in Deadwood's history, from the earliest settlers to the coming of industry and tourism.

A highlight of the event is the reenactment of the capture and trial of Jack McCall, who shot the much-admired U.S. Marshal James Butler "Wild Bill" Hickok in the back, and who was eventually hanged. Visitors can tour long-abandoned gold mines and the cemetery where Calamity Jane, the famous frontierswoman, Wild Bill Hickok, and the brilliant young minister Henry Weston "Preacher" Smith are buried.

Daytona 500
February

The richest of the four biggest NASCAR (National Association for Stock Car Auto Racing) Winston Cup races. It's the final event of the sixteen day Speedweeks at Daytona International Speedway in Daytona Beach, Fla. The speedway is a 2.5-mile oval, and racers must complete 200 laps. In 1991, Ernie Irvan (dubbed "Swervin' Irvan" for his aggressive driving) was the unexpected winner. He averaged 148.128 miles per hour and collected $233,000 for the win. The all-time champion of the Daytona 500 is Richard Petty, who won seven times (1964, 1966, 1971, 1973, 1974, 1979, and 1981).

The Daytona Speedway, which has a seating capacity of 102,900, has been operating since 1959, but stock-car racing at Daytona dates back to 1936, and car racing has been going on here since the early days of cars. Between 1902 and 1935, thirteen automobile speed records were set on the beach by racing greats Barney Oldfield, Sir Henry Segrave, and Sir Malcolm Campbell, who broke existing records five times.

The speedway was the creation of William H. G. (Bill) France, a mechanic and racer who moved to Daytona Beach in 1934 in the heyday of beach racing. He gave up driving to organize and promote races, and in 1947 founded NASCAR. he had the idea of building the Daytona track in 1953, but financial and political problems delayed its opening until 1959. When he died in 1992, he was known as the father of stock-car racing.

Today the Speedway presents eight weeks of racing events. Speedweeks starts with the Sunbank 24, a twenty-four hour endurance race; this race and the 24 Hours of Le Mans (France) are the only two twenty-four hour races for prototype sports cars in the world.

The "crown jewels" of the NASCAR circuit are the Daytona 500, the WINSTON 500, the COCA-COLA 600, and the SOUTHERN 500.

D-Day
June 6

The day is also known as **Allied Landing Observances Day**. It marks the start of the Allied invasion of occupied France in 1944, which led to the final defeat of Hitler's Germany the following May. The assault, led by U.S. Gen. Dwight D. Eisenhower, was carried out by airborne forces and the greatest armada the world had ever known. About 3,000 ships transported 130,000 British, Canadian, and American troops across the English Channel to land on the beaches of Normandy, which are known historically by their invasion code names: Utah Beach, Omaha Beach, Gold Beach, Juno Beach, Sword Beach.

Airborne troops began parachuting into Normandy at fifteen minutes past midnight on June 6, and Landing Craft Transports plowed through the surf to spill troops onto the beaches starting at 6:30 A.M. About 10,000 troops were killed or wounded that day. Each year, simple ceremonies at the Normandy cemeteries commemorate the men who fell.

Dead, Feast of the *See* Samhain

Dead Rat's Ball *See* Bal du Rat Mort

Decorated Horse, Procession of the
Between May 21 and June 24; Corpus Christi

According to legend, during the Crusades the ship in which the French king was traveling and bearing the Eucharist, was wrecked on the beach at Brindisi, Italy. The local archbishop salvaged the sacred Host and carried it with him as he rode through the town on a white horse. To commemorate this event, the current Archbishop of Brindisi carries the Most Holy Sacrament in a procession that takes place on CORPUS CHRISTI each year. He rides at the head of the procession on a white horse caparisoned in gold, passing through galleries of silk draperies and a constant rain of flowers thrown by spectators. This event is sometimes referred to as the **Procession of the Caparisoned Horse**.

Corpus Christi is celebrated with flowers and colorful processions in other Italian towns and villages as well—those occurring at Genzano and Perugia being among the more spectacular.

Dedication, Feast of *See* Exaltation of the Cross; Hanukkah

Deepavali *See* Day of the Awakeners; Dewali

Deep Sea Fishing Rodeo
Weekend of July 4

The "World's Largest Fishing Rodeo," according to its promoters, and a four-day event staged from Gulfport, Miss. The Mississippi Gulf Coast area is reputed to be one of the world's best natural fish hatcheries, with an abundance of species of fresh-water, salt-water, and deep-sea game fish. The rodeo's fishing waters are the Mississippi Sound of the Gulf of Mexico, and the bayous and creeks within a range of 200 miles north of the Mississippi shoreline.

The rodeo began in 1949, and today attracts from 15,000 to 20,000 people, and entrants from forty-eight states. Prizes are awarded for the top weight in twenty-eight categories of fish. Besides fishing, there are also all the peripherals of a festival: arts and crafts exhibits, dances, a midway, fireworks, bands, and the coronation of a Rodeo Queen.

Defenders' Day
September 12

Defenders' Day, a legal holiday in Maryland, celebrates the anniversary of the battle of North Point during the War of 1812. The battle took place near Baltimore on September 12, 1814; two days later, the unsuccessful British attack on Baltimore's Fort McHenry inspired Francis Scott Key to jot down the words of "The Star-Spangled Banner." For this reason the two events are celebrated more or less in conjunction on September 12, a day that is sometimes referred to as **National Anthem Day**.

A fifty-six foot monument at Calvert and Fayette Streets in Baltimore commemorates the 1814 battle, and the star-shaped Fort McHenry is a national monument and an historic shrine. Defenders' Day is celebrated with a number of patriotic events, including an annual mock bombardment of the fort on the Sunday nearest September 12.

Den na Buditelite *See* **Day of the Awakeners**

Departure of the Continental Army
Saturday nearest June 19

On December 19, 1777 George Washington and twelve thousand of his Continental Army soldiers marched into Valley Forge, about eighteen miles north of Philadelphia to set up camp for the winter. The men were exhausted, hungry, and poorly equipped. Severe winter weather didn't make their stay at Valley Forge any easier, and they received only irregular supplies of meat and bread. Nearly two thousand of the men died from typhus, typhoid, dysentery, and pneumonia before the winter was over.

It was largely through Washington's leadership and the efforts of Baron Friedrich von Steuben (see VON STEUBEN DAY) that the dispirited army was turned into a well-trained, dependable fighting force by the following summer. The anniversary of the day the Continental army marched out of Valley Forge in pursuit of the British, who were moving toward New York, is still celebrated with an historic reenactment that takes place on or near June 19 at the Valley Forge National Historical Park each year.

Other historic events observed at Valley Forge include December 19, the anniversary of the army's arrival; Washington's Birthday Encampment Week in mid-February; and May 6, the French Alliance Day celebration.

Derby Day
Late May–early June

The most prestigious horse race in the world. The idea for the race arose at a dinner party in 1779 and was eventually named for the Earl of Derby, one of the guests who was present that evening. Derby Day is held annually at the Epsom Racecourse in Surrey, England, on the second day of the summer meeting, usually in late May or early June. Many companies in England give their employees the day off so they can join in the picnicking that takes place near the course.

Like its American counterpart, the KENTUCKY DERBY, the festivities surrounding the Epsom Derby last far longer than the race itself, which covers a mile-and-a-half and is over in just a few minutes. Only three-year-old colts and fillies can enter, which means that the race can never be won by the same horse twice.

De Soto Celebration
Mid–March

The celebration also known as **De Soto Landing Day** in Florida is in honor of the young Spanish explorer Hernando de Soto, who arrived on the west coast of Florida, probably near Tampa Bay and the present-day town of Bradenton in 1539. With his band of several hundred conquistadores (conquerors), de Soto set out on a 4,000 mile trek through the wilderness north to the Blue Ridge Mountains, across them, south along the Alabama River to present-day Mobile; across the Mississippi River into what is now Arkansas, and explored further to the south and west. It was the first time a European had explored the North American interior.

The De Soto Celebration held each year in mid-March in Bradenton goes back to 1939. A group of thirty-five costumed conquistadores reenacts de Soto's landing, coming ashore in longboats and skirmishing with the "Indians" in full view of a grandstand full of spectators. The conquest continues, with the "explorers" pressing onward until they reach Bradenton, where they raid the county courthouse. Most of the men in town grow beards for the occasion, which they then shave off in a race against time at the end of the festival.

Detroit/Windsor International Freedom Festival *See* **Canada Day**

Dewali (Divali, Deepavali, Festival of Lights)
First half of November; fifteenth day of the dark half of the Hindu lunar month of Kartika

The word *dewali* means 'a row or cluster of lights', and the week-long festivities are illuminated by lamps, fireworks, and bonfires. The holiday means different things in different parts of Asia. In northern India it marks the beginning of the Hindu New Year. In Gujarat and Malaysia families clean and whitewash their homes and draw elaborate designs (called *alpanas*) on their floors with colored powder to welcome Lakshmi, the Hindu goddess of wealth and prosperity. Then they set up rows of little clay lamps, decorating their courtyards, windows, and roofs with light in the belief that Lakshmi won't bless a home that isn't lit up to greet her.

In the Punjab and Mauritius, Dewali celebrates the coronation of Rama (a manifestation of Vishnu) after his conquest of Ravana, the ruler of Sri Lanka, who had stolen his wife. In West Bengal it is a Kali festival. In Maharashtra the lights fend off King Bali, the ruler of the underworld. The Jains commemorate the death of their great hero, Mahavira, on this day called Deva Dewali, in the city of Pava in Bihar. (See also MAHAVIR VAYANTI). In Nepal it is TIHAR, a multi-holiday that celebrates the New Year and Lakshmi, sisters honor brothers, and mandalas are prepared for each member of the family.

Dewali is as important to Hindus as CHRISTMAS is to Christians. It is celebrated by the world's 500 million Hindus with gift exchanges, fireworks, and festive (typically vegetarian) meals.

Dew Treading
Between April 30 and June 3; Ascension Day

Both city and country dwellers in the Netherlands continue to observe the old folk custom known as **Dauwtrappen** or 'dew treading' on ASCENSION DAY. People take their children to the fields—or, in the case of city dwellers, to the suburbs—to walk through the morning dew and gather spring flowers. According to an old superstition, the Ascension Day dew possesses supernatural growing and healing powers. In the country, it is customary for friends and neighbors to meet each other at an inn for a big breakfast afterward.

Día de Corpo de Deus (Corpus Christi)
See **Corpus Christi**

Día de la Santa Cruz (Day of the Holy Cross)
May 3

In Mexico the Day of the Holy Cross is primarily observed by miners, masons, and construction workers. They make elaborately decorated crosses and place them on the buildings where they are working. Anyone who is constructing a new building must throw a party for the workers on this day. Fireworks are set off and the occasion is treated as a fiesta.

See also EXALTATION OF THE CROSS.

Día de los Tres Reyes
January 6

Throughout most of Latin America, EPIPHANY is called *el día de los tres reyes* (**Three Kings Day** or **Day of the Wise Men**). It marks the end of the CHRISTMAS season that began on December 16 with POSADAS. In Mexico, on the night of January 5, the children stuff their shoes with hay and leave them out for the Wise Men to fill with sweets and gifts-much as children elsewhere leave their Christmas stockings out for Santa Claus to fill on CHRISTMAS EVE. And just as letters to Santa Claus are a popular custom in the United States, Mexican children often write letters to the Magi (the three Wise Men), listing their good deeds and suggesting what gifts they would like to receive.

In Venezuela, the children leave straw by their beds so that the Magi's camels will have something to eat. On the morning of January 6 they awake to find the straw gone and gifts delivered in its place.

See also TWELFTH NIGHT and BEFANA FESTIVAL.

Día del Puno
November 5

Many of the festivals celebrated by the Andean Indians of South America commemorate their Inca ancestors. Día del Puno, which is observed in Puno, Peru, reenacts the birth of Manco Capac and Mama Ocllo, the legendary founders of the Inca dynasty. A fleet of *balsas*—skiffs built from reeds or *totoras* and discarded as soon as they become waterlogged-gathers on Lake Titicaca and moves toward Puno. A royal barge carries the two Indians who play the parts of Manco Capac and Mama Ocllo. According to legend, these two were sent by their father, the Sun, to inhabit the Isla de Titicaca, one of the forty-one islands in the lake, and to become the first human rulers there. A ruined temple still marks the spot where this miraculous birth took place.

On shore, the festival features Indian musicians playing flutes and panpipes in the traditional costumes of the Quechua and Aymara Indians, and dancers twirling beaded strings.

Día de San Giuseppe *See* **St. Joseph's Day**

Día de San Juan *See* **St. John the Baptist's Day**

Día de San Lorenzo
August 10

St. Laurence of Rome was a deacon under Pope Sixtus II. According to legend, after the martyrdom of the Pope, St. Laurence was roasted alive on a gridiron. In the midst of his torture, it is said he suggested that his tormentors turn him over to ensure that he would be well-cooked. His feast day is August 10.

As the patron saint of Zinacantan, Mexico, San Lorenzo is honored with a five-day festival that takes place August 7–11 each year. The highlight is a dance performed by the *Capitanes* that involves rhythmic hops on one foot while the other is extended in front off the ground. Thousands attend the festival, which includes a huge open market and spectacular fireworks.

Dicing for the Maid's Money Day
Last Thursday in January

In the seventeenth century, dicing (throwing dice) for money was a favorite English pastime in which large sums of money could be won or lost. However, the annual dicing competition that still takes place in Guildford, England is for the relatively modest sum of eleven pounds, nineteen shillings. In 1674 a local resident named John How established a fund of four hundred pounds, which in his will he said he wanted invested and the proceeds distributed each year to a local "maid" or house servant who had served faithfully in the same position for at least two years. The will also stipulated that two servants should throw dice for the gift, and that the one who threw the highest number should receive the entire amount.

In the presence of the mayor, trustees, and assembled townspeople, the two women chosen to participate in this event each year take turns shaking the dice in a special hide-covered, silver-banded dice box which has been used for this purpose over the past century. According to the official Maid's Money receipt book, the recipients of the prize in recent years have been older women who have served faithfully in the same family for many years. But the gift was originally designed for young, unmarried women who might need the money for a dowry.

Dinagyang
Last weekend in January

A dancing-in-the-streets carnival on the island of Panay, Iloilo City, Philippines, held a week after the Ati-Atihan in Kalibo and the Sinulog in Cebu. Like these festivals, Dinagyang venerates the Santo Niño or Holy Infant. In Iloilo (pronounced ee-lo-*ee*-lo) the participation of tribal groups adds to the festival's color, but, unlike the exuberant Kalibo crowds, the spectators in Iloilo are quiet.

Dinosaur Days
Last week in July

A new celebration of very old bones: the dinosaur fossils that rest near Grand Junction, Colo. in the Dinosaur National Monument. About 140 million years ago, when the area of Grand Junction was semi-tropical, dinosaurs roamed here. In 1900, the remains of Brachiosaurus, one of the biggest of the dinosaurs, was found four miles west of downtown. Hence, the Dinosaur Days, which started in 1986 and consist of four days of festivities with a reptilian theme.

A foot race, called the Pterodactyl Trot for the ancient bird, starts things off and is followed by a parade of dinosaurs and cave men (anachronisms are allowed), a raft race on the Colorado River, and a street dance (with a rock band, of course) named the Stegosaurus Stomp. Other features are the T-Rex Tee-off, a golf game played in the wilds with oversize golf balls, and Kids' Day at the dinosaur quarry, during which paleontologists explain the dinosaur digs to children and help them make plaster molds of bones.

Dionysia (Bacchanalia)
Throughout the year

A festival in ancient Greece in honor of Dionysus (also called Bacchus), the son of Zeus and god of wine, fertility, and drama. There were a series of Dionysian festivals: the Oschophoria, the rustic Dionysia, the Lenaea, the ANTHESTERIA, the urban Dionysia and the most famous, the City or Great Dionysia.

The Great Dionysias were held in the spring (March or April) in Athens for five or six days, and their centerpieces were the performances of new tragedies, comedies, and satyric dramas. These took place in the Theater of Dionysus on the side of the Acropolis and were attended by people from throughout the country. The earliest tragedy that survives is *Persai* by Aeschylus, from the year 472 B.C. The dramatists and the actors and singers were considered to be performing an act of worship of the god, and Dionysus was thought to be present at the productions. The City Dionsyias were a time of general springtime rejoicing (even prisoners were released to share in the festivities) and great pomp. The statue of Dionysus was carried in a procession that also included representations of the phallus, symbolizing the god.

Dionysus was both a merry god who inspired great poetry and a cruel god; the Greeks realistically saw wine as something that made people happy and also made them drunk and cruel. Thus, like the god, his festivals seem to have combined contrasting elements of poetry and revelry.

The small rustic Dionysia were festive and bawdy affairs held in December-January at the first tasting of new wine. Besides dramatic presentations, there were processions of slaves carrying the phallus, the singing of obscene lays, youths balancing on a full goat-skin, and the like.

The Leneae, held in Athens in January-February included a procession of jesting citizens through the city and dramatic presentations. The Oschophoria ('carrying of the grape cluster'), held in the fall when the grapes were ripe, was marked by a footrace for youths.

Dipri Festival
March–April
A celebration held by the Abidji tribe in Gomon, Ivory Coast. The Abidjis are one of about sixty ethnic groups in the country, which became a French colony in 1893 and attained independence in 1960. First, relatives or neighbors meet on the evening before the celebration to reconcile their differences. Then, during the festival, the people go into frenzied trances as they are possessed by *sékés*—beneficent spirits—and stumble, dazed in the street. Some people, supposedly led by the spirits, plunge knives into their bodies and then, with the guidance of the sékés, are healed with poultices of raw eggs and herbs. This festival serves several purposes: it resolves conflicts between generations and in the community; it drives away evil spirits; it purifies the celebrants.

Discovery Day
August 2; November 19; December 5
There are a number of different days referred to by this name, all of which relate to the voyages of Christopher Columbus. In Trinidad and Tobago, August 2 is Discovery Day, in honor of Columbus' discovery of the two islands on his third voyage to the Western Hemisphere. In Haiti, Discovery Day is celebrated on December 5, commemorating its discovery by Columbus in 1492. And in Puerto

Rico, which was discovered by Columbus on his second voyage in 1493, Discovery Day is celebrated on November 19.

See also COLUMBUS DAY.

Distaff Day
January 7
After the twelve-day CHRISTMAS celebration ended on TWELFTH NIGHT or EPIPHANY, **St. Distaff's Day** was traditionally the day on which women resumed their chores, symbolized by the distaff, a tool used in spinning flax or wool. It was also called **Rock Day**, from the German word *rocken*—"rock" being another name for the distaff. The "spear side" and the "distaff side" were legal terms used to distinguish the inheritance of male from that of female children, and the distaff eventually became a synonym for the female sex as a whole. Distaff Day was not really a church festival, but it was widely observed at one time in England.

Although the women had to return to work after TWELFTH NIGHT was over, the men apparently had plenty of time to amuse themselves by setting the flax on fire, in return for which they would get buckets of water dumped on their heads.

Divali *See* Day of the Awakeners; Dewali

Divine Holy Spirit, Festival of the
May
This religious festival was first introduced in Brazil during the sixteenth century and is still celebrated today in many Brazilian cities. One of the most traditional celebrations takes place in Diamantina. The week-long festivities include Masses and fireworks, culminating in the "parade of the Emperor."

Divino, Festa do
Between May 9 and June 12; Saturday before Pentecost
Festa do Divino celebrations can be found in two of Brazil's most beautiful colonial-era towns: Alcântara and Paraty. The townspeople dress up in colonial costumes, with many playing the roles of prominent figures from Brazilian history. The climax is a visit from the "Emperor," who arrives with his servants for a procession and Mass at the church square. He frees prisoners from the town jail in a symbolic gesture of royal generosity, and strolling musicians known as *Folias do Divino* serenade the townspeople day and night.

Doan Ngu (Summer Solstice Day)
Fifth day of the fifth lunar month (June)

A celebration of the SUMMER SOLSTICE in Vietnam. Offerings are made to spirits and ghosts and to the God of Death to fend off epidemics. Human effigies are burned, providing souls to staff the army of the God of Death.

Dodge City Days
Late July

Dodge City's name alone is enough to conjure up memories of the Old West for the residents of Kansas and the surrounding states who come here to celebrate Dodge City Days every summer. Held annually for six days in late July, the main purpose of the festival is to keep the area's history alive. There are staged shootouts between "Marshal Dillon" and the bad guys, a rodeo, a horse show, and parades featuring costumed characters from the Old West on horseback.

First held in 1960, Dodge City Days now attracts crowds of up to 50,000—most of whom are tourists. In recent years the festival has featured entertainment by top country-and-western music stars, and the events have expanded to include a golf tournament, auto racing, and other decidedly non-traditional activities that have little to do with Dodge City's Old West heritage.

Dodge National Circuit Finals Rodeo
See **National Circuit Finals Rodeo**

Dog Days
July 3–August 11

Dog Days are the hottest days of the year in the Northern Hemisphere and usually occur in July and early August. In ancient times, the sultry weather in Rome during these months often made people sick, and they blamed their illnesses on the fact that this was the time of year when Sirius, the Dog Star, rose at about the same time as the sun. Because Sirius was the brightest star, it was thought to add its heat to the sun, producing hot, unhealthy weather. The ancients used to sacrifice a brown dog at the beginning of the Dog Days to appease the rage of Sirius.

Although there are many different ways of calculating which days in any given year are the dog days, and how long they last, it is impossible to be precise. Nowadays it is generally assumed that they fall between July 3 and August 11-slightly later than they occurred in ancient times.

Because of their association with the Dog Star, various beliefs have sprung up involving the be-havior of dogs during this period. In the sixteenth century it was believed that dogs went mad during the Dog Star season. Another name for this time of year, the **canicular days**, comes from the Latin word *canis* meaning "dog."

Doggett's Coat and Badge Race
August 1

Established in 1716 by Thomas Doggett, an actor and one of the owners of the Drury Lane Theatre in London, the **Waterman's Derby** is an annual rowing race held on the Thames River between Old Swan Pier and Cadogan Pier. Six young boatmen who have just completed their apprenticeship must row against the tide for a distance of four-and-a-half miles. The winner receives a new pair of breeches, an orange coat, and because the original race was to commemorate the crowning of King George I, a badge with the Hanoverian white horse on it. There are cash prizes as well: ten pounds for the winner, and six, five, four, three, or two pounds for the other rowers, according to the order in which they complete the race. When Doggett died in 1721, he left a legacy that would ensure the continuation of both the race and its prizes.

The race is administered by the Fishmongers' Company, of which Doggett was a member.

Dogwood Festival
April (April 3–12 in 1992)

A night-and-day celebration of the pink and white dogwoods (and azaleas) blooming everywhere in Atlanta, Ga. The founders of the first festival in 1936 thought the event could make Atlanta "internationally known for its beauty during the blooming of the dogwood trees and be the beginning of an annual pilgrimage to the Gate City of the South." The festival comes close to doing that, even though it lapsed during World War II, and didn't really get going again until 1968. Now this gala event each year attracts about 100,000 people who come not only to see the trees but also for numerous concerts, a hot-air balloon race, an architectural-design competition, a kite-flying exhibition, a street festival on famed Peachtree Street, a bike tour along a trail of dogwoods, and the annual Druid Hill Homes and Garden Tour, conducted on the first day of the festival. Children's activities include parades designed and carried out by children, theatrical performances, and a kite-making workshop. Trees are spotlit at night, and special tours of the lighted Dogwood Trail are offered.

Doleing Day
December 21

It was customary at one time in England on **St. Thomas's Day** for the poorer inhabitants of the parish to call on their wealthier neighbors and receive a gift or 'dole' of food or money. In return, they would give their benefactors a sprig of holly or mistletoe.

The custom of *going a-gooding*, as it was called, gave rise to the name **Gooding Day** in parts of Sussex; in other areas it was referred to as **Mumping (Begging) Day**, since those who had to beg were said to be 'on the mump.' The children would often spend St. Thomas's Day begging for apples.

Doll Festival *See* Hina Matsuri

Dol Purnima
Full Moon day of Phalguna

The Dol Purnima festival, celebrated throughout India by the followers of Krishna, occurs on the same day as the birthday of Chaitanya Mahaprabhu (1486–1534), also known as Gauranga, the sixteenth century Vishnavite saint and poet of Bengal, regarded as an incarnation of Krishna. It is therefore a significant festival for Hindus, who carry an image of Lord Krishna, covered with colored powder and placed in a swinging cradle, through the streets as they sing songs composed especially for the occasion.

Dom Fair
November through Christmas

The **Hamburger Dom** or Dom Fair is one of the most famous CHRISTMAS fairs in the world. It was named after its original location, which was in the open square in front of the Dom, or cathedral, in Hamburg, Germany. Today the fair is held in the Heiligengeistfeld or Holy Ghost Field in the center of town. It features booths filled with toys, gingerbread, crafts, and other temptations for holiday shoppers. The Dom opens in November and doesn't close until just before Christmas, giving shoppers from Hamburg and the surrounding area plenty of time to buy their gifts.

Dominican Republic Independence Day
February 27

In the 1830s Juan Pablo Duarte—known as "the father of Dominican independence"—organized a secret society known as *La Trinitaria* to fight the Haitians. After a long struggle, independence was finally declared on February 27,
1844. Although disorder, dictatorships, and intermittent peace characterized the Dominican Republic's history until the United States Marines occupied it from 1916 to 1924 to keep peace between rival political groups, February 27 is still observed as the country's Independence Day and is celebrated with parades and political meetings. The site of the proclamation, Independence Park, contains a shrine known as the *Altar de la Patria*, 'the nation's altar,' honoring the three founders of the Republic—Duarte, Ramón Mella, and Juan Sánchez Ramírez. Duarte's birthday, January 26, is also a public holiday, celebrated as Duarte Day.

Dominion Day *See* Canada Day

Dormition of the Mother of God *See* Assumption, Feast of the

Dosmoche
December–January; Moon 12, Day 28

This five-day **Tibetan New Year** festival begins with the erection of a large *dosmo* or magical pole decorated with pentagrams, stars, and crosses made out of string. The lamas make a food and drink offering to the Buddhas and the gods after the dosmo is in place. The following day is devoted to various prayers and rituals designed to drive away evil. The *lo si-sku-rim* or 'ceremony of the dying year' is held, during which dancers wearing hideous demons' masks try to scare off the hostile spirits. A similar custom involves throwing *tsamba* (toasted barley or wheat flour) until everyone is covered in white—a ceremony known as *Yangdrug* or 'the gathering of luck.' As evening falls, the dosmos is surrendered to the people, who have been waiting patiently to tear it down.

Double Seventh *See* Seven Sisters Festival

Double Tenth Day
October 10

A national holiday in Taiwan to commemorate the Chinese Revolution of Oct. 10, 1911. The revolt marked the end of the Ching, or Qing, Dynasty that had been established in 1644 by the Manchus, and it led to the founding of the Republic of China on Jan. 1, 1912.

It took the Ching rulers several decades to complete their military conquest of China and in 1683, when Taiwan became part of the empire, governed all of China. The Ching Court's period of glory was in the time of the first three emperors, but after 1795 the court began a slow decline. By the end of the nineteenth century, Japan and the Western powers had reduced China to what Sun Yat-sen called a "sub-colony," the court was weak and corrupt, and a group of national capitalists was fomenting uprisings. Sun Yat-sen was one of the leaders of this nationalistic group; he was a Jeffersonian figure who wanted a Western-style government with a parliament and separation of powers.

In October, 1911, a revolt in Wuhan (in the province of Hubei) succeeded, supportive uprisings broke out in other cities. The fall of the Manchus followed. Sun Yat-sen, who was in Denver, Colo., at the time of the October revolt, returned to Shanghai and was elected provisional president of the new republic. He is thought of today as the father of modern China, and his birthday on Nov. 12 is also a national holiday in Taiwan.

For several weeks before Double Tenth Day, the plaza in front of the Presidential Office Building in Taipei, Taiwan is illuminated. Here there are massive parades and rallies on the holiday, displays of martial arts, folk dancing, and other cultural activities. One of the world's most dazzling displays of fireworks is presented over an island in the middle of the Tanshui River.

See also SUN YAT-SEN'S BIRTHDAY.

Doughnut Tuesday *See* Shrove Tuesday

Dozynki Festival
August 15

For many Christians around the world, August 15 is the FEAST OF THE ASSUMPTION. But in Poland, it is also a time for celebrating the harvest. During the wheat harvest festival known as **Dozynki Pod Debami** or **Festival under the Oaks**, the reapers make wreaths out of grain, flowers, nuts and corn. When they present their wreaths to the master and mistress of the estate on which the wheat is grown, they are invited in for a feast, which is followed by dancing.

For Americans of Polish descent living in Orange County, New York—one of the richest onion-growing areas in the United States—the Dozynki Festival underwent a brief revival around 1940 under the name of **the feast of Our Lady of the Flowers**. In the village of Florida, the streets were banked high with piles of onions, and there was a huge parade with floats depicting the arrival of the Polish immigrants in America and various aspects of the onion production industry.

There was a costumed pageant in which the onion farmers presented the Lord and Lady of the Manor with a huge wreath of onions and flowers, followed by the Onion Dance, which had been created especially for the festival. Although a celebration of this magnitude was the exception, the Assumption had always been a holiday for the Polish onion farmers of Orange County.

Drachenstich (Spearing the Dragon)
Mid August

The performance of an open-air play, *Drachenstich*, in Fürth, Germany, in the Bavarian Forest. The climax of the play is a battle between a knight on horseback and a huge (about fifty feet long and ten feet tall), fire-spewing dragon. The knight, of course, wins—by thrusting his spear into the dragon's throat, thereby piercing a pig's bladder filled with ox-blood. Besides the dragon-sticking, the celebrations include various merrymaking events and a street procession. The play has been performed for about 500 years, and is thought to be based on a pagan legend or to be connected with religious processions.

Dragon Boat Festival (Tuan Yang Chieh)
Fifth day of the fifth month of the Chinese lunar calendar

Chu'ü Yüan (328–298 B.C.) was a Chinese poet and statesman of the Chou Dynasty who drowned himself in the Tungting Lake to protest the corruption and injustice of Prince Huai's court. The colorful dragon boat races that take place on lakes and rivers throughout China on this day are a re-enactment of the search for his body, which was never found. Although the shape of the boats has changed over time, most are narrow shells about a hundred feet long with a dragon's head at the prow and a drummer beating out the rhythm for his crew of up to fifty rowers.

It is said that rice dumplings were cast on the water to lure fish away from the martyr's body. Chinese populations in America and other countries celebrate the Dragon Boat Festival (also called the **Fifth Month Festival** or **Summer Festival**) by eating special dumplings made of steamed rice wrapped in banana leaves.

Dragon Boat International Races
Week after Dragon Boat Festival on fifth day of fifth moon

An international boat race held in Hong Kong usually a week after the traditional Chinese Dragon Boat Festival that commemorates the death of the poet Chu'ü Yüan. The dragon boats are built to strict specifications, and the crew may not exceed twenty-two, of whom one must be the drummer and one the steersman. Teams from throughout the world enter the races which raise money for the Community Chest of Hong Kong.

Dramatic Arts Festival at Avignon
July

The month-long **Festival Annuel d'Art Dramatique** was founded by 1947 by Jean Vilar, a well-known French actor and director. When he was invited to direct the first annual drama festival at Avignon, his approach was an innovative one, using bold movements and simplified sets on the large outdoor stage. His success at Avignon eventually led to his appointment as director of the Théatre National Populaire.

In addition to the festival's large theatrical productions, there are performances that recall the popular pageants of the Middle Ages. Some of the events take place in the city's many historical buildings, while others overflow into the streets. The Dramatic Arts Festival has made Avignon the kind of cultural center to which other Provençal towns aspire, and it regularly attracts a cosmopolitan crowd from all over Europe.

Drymiais
March 1–3

In Macedonia, the first three days of March are known as Drymiais and are associated with a number of superstitious beliefs. No trees are pruned or planted during this period because it is believed that they will wither. The same fate awaits trees that are pruned or planted during the last three days of March or on any Wednesday or Friday during the month.

The first day of March is traditionally considered to mark the beginning of spring. Macedonian mothers tie pieces of red and white yarn, twisted together, around their children's wrists on this day (see MARTENITZA). When they see a swallow, the children throw the skein of yarn to the bird as an offering, or place it under a stone. If they lift the stone a few days later and find a swarm of ants beneath it, they can expect a healthy and prosperous year.

Dukang Festival
December 15

A trade fair and festival held in Yichuan in the Henan province of China. This was the homeland of Dukang, who is supposed to have discovered alcoholic beverages 4,000 years ago (as Dionysus, in Greek mythology, invented wine). A Chinese folk tale tells of Dukang's beverage intoxicating the eight deities, and a poem contains the line, "Who other than Dukang can relieve me of my grief?" Dukang has become a synonym for liquor, and is also the name of a distillery in Yichuan.

The trade fair highlights not only wines and spirits but also cooking oil and food products, electrical appliances, dyes, and other manufactured goods. The festival features performances by opera troupes and dance ensembles.

Dulcimer Days
Third weekend in May

The hammered dulcimer is a stringed musical instrument in which the strings are beaten with small hammers rather than plucked with the fingers. It is a favorite with American folk musicians, many of whom gather in Coshocton, Ohio each year for the **Mid-Eastern Regional Dulcimer Championships**. The competition takes place near Roscoe Village, a restored 1830s canal town. In addition to the musical competition there are exhibits, workshops dealing with the hammered and mountain dulcimers—the latter being a narrow folk-zither with three to five metal strings—and jam sessions. The winners of the Dulcimer Days competition are given a chance to compete in the national competition held each year in Winfield, Kansas.

Dump Week, National
Thursday after Fourth of July–Labor Day

Kennebunkport, Maine is best known as a popular summer resort and as the summer residence of former U.S. president George Bush. But it is also the home of "America's Number One Dump." The Kennebunkport Dump Association, which was organized in 1965 by a local artist with a sense of humor, held the first observation of National Dump Week as a way of drawing attention to environmental issues. But the attitude of the event's organizers is decidedly tongue-in-cheek. There is a "Miss Dumpy" competition featuring young women dressed in Clorox bottles, beer cans, old newspapers, cottage cheese containers and other trash. Then there is the Giant Trash Parade featuring more than thirty floats made out of junk and illustrating various ecological themes. Beginning on the Thursday after the FOURTH OF JULY and extending through LABOR DAY in September, National Dump Week is actually a summer-long event.

Durga Puja
September–October (the waxing half of Hindu month of Asvina)

There are various Hindu festivals on the Indian subcontinent that celebrate the victory of good over evil.

The festival in Calcutta, India, in the state of West Bengal, India, honors Durga, who rides a lion and destroys demons. She is one aspect of the Mother Goddess and the personification of energy, and is famous for slaying the buffalo demon Mahisasura. During the ten days of Durga Puja, the city becomes one great festival, with deafening music and fireworks. Before the *puja* (a Sanskrit word meaning 'worship' or 'homage'), artisans have constructed clay figures over straw-and-bamboo frames, some of them ten feet high. Stages are set up for these figures in neighborhoods throughout the city, and for four days throngs of people admire the clay tableaux, often showing Durga on a lion slaying demons. (Artist Aloke Sen's images have become famous because his demons have the faces of ordinary men and women and represent such evils as lust, anger, vanity, and greed.) On the fourth night, the images, which are genuine works of art and have cost as much as $20,000, are taken down from the stages, placed on bamboo stretchers, and carried—to the music of hundreds of bagpipers and other musicians—to the banks of the Hooghly River and tossed in. As they float toward the mouth of the Ganges, they dissolve back into clay, straw and bamboo.

Navaratri
In the states of southern India this festival is known as Navaratri (nine nights), and also involves the worship of the goddesses Laksmi and Sarasvati. Laksmi is linked with wealth and good luck, and Sarasvati, associated with a river of that name, is associated with fertility as well as wisdom and education. The festival is a time for visiting friends and relatives, and houses are decorated with displays of toys and dolls and images of gods. In the state of Gujarat there are nine days of music and dancing devoted to the nine forms of the goddess Ambaji, as well as competitions of *garba* dancing.

Dussehra (Dashara)
In other parts of India the festival also celebrates the victory of Lord Rama over Ravana, and is known as Dussehra (Dashara).

During the ten days of Dussehra, scenes from the epic poem *Ramayana* are enacted. The epic tells the story of Lord Rama who wins the lovely Sita for his wife, only to have her carried off by evil ten-headed Ravana, demon king of Lanka. Ultimately, Rama slays Ravana, and the forces of good triumph over evil. The dramatizations with music, held throughout northern India, are considered at their best in Delhi. On the tenth day, immense effigies of demon Ravana, his brother, and his son (all of them stuffed with firecrackers) explode in dramatic bursts of flame and noise.

In the northern mountains of Himachal Pradesh, the festival begins with a procession of deities to the town of Kulu from the little hill temples of neighboring villages. Accompanying the deities are villagers blowing large horns, ringing bells, and beating drums. When a deity arrives in Kulu, it is placed before Raghunathji, the presiding god of Kulu Valley, who is in an honored position in a tent. Outside, there is folk dancing and music. On the final day of the festival, a bull is sacrificed as a gift to the gods.

Mysore, in the state of Karnataka, celebrates the victory of goddess Chamundi over demon Mahisasura with regal pomp. The palace of the maharajah is illuminated, there are torchlight and daylight parades, and deities on decorated barges in a floodlit lake. On the final day, there is a grand procession of magnificently caparisoned elephants, the camel corps, the cavalry, and the infantry.

Dasain
In Nepal, the festival is called Dasain, or Bada Dasain. It comes at the end of the long monsoon period when days are clear and the rice is ready for harvesting, and lasts for ten days.

In Nepal, Buddhists also celebrate this festival and special events are held at Buddhist shrines in Patan and Bhaktapur. The Nepalese also modify the Ramayana story to include the goddess Durga's victory over the forces of evil represented by the demon Mahisasura. Since Durga is bloodthirsty, there are thousands of animal sacrifices.

Before the festival begins, Nepalese clean their houses and set up ferris wheels and swings in their villages. On the first day of the festival, a water jug called a *kalash* is filled with holy water, and barley seeds are planted in cow dung on the outside of the jug. During the festival, the seeds are sprinkled with the water, and ceremonies are performed around it.

The first big day of the festival is the seventh

day, Fulpati, meaning 'day of flowers.' A royal kalash holding flowers is carried by Brahmin priests from the ancestral palace in Gurkha to Katmandu. Cannons boom, the king and queen review troops, and then revere the flowers at the Hanuman Dhoka Palace, the old residence of kings.

The eighth night is known as Kalratri, or 'black night.' At midnight, at Hanuman Dhoka, eight buffaloes and 108 goats are beheaded. During the next day, thousands of buffaloes, goats, and chickens are sacrificed in temples, military posts, and homes as people ask Durga for protection. Blood is sprinkled on the wheels of vehicles, and at the airport, a goat is sacrificed for each Royal Nepal Airlines aircraft.

The tenth day, Vijaya Dashami, commemorates the day that Durga (or Rama) appeared riding a lion to slay the Mahisasura (or Ravana). On this day, people wear the fresh shoots of the barley in their hair and visit older relatives to receive the red *tika* blessing on their forehead. In towns of the Katmandu Valley, there are masked dances and processions of priests carrying wooden swords, symbolic of the sword used to kill the buffalo demon.

Caitra Dasain, observed in the month of Caitra (March-April), is similar to Bada Dasain, but observed with less pomp. On this earlier occasion, the goddess Bhagavati is worshiped and animal sacrifices are made to her.

Dussehra *See* **Durga Puja**

Dutch Liberation Day
May 5
Liberation Day or **National Day** in the Netherlands celebrates the day on which the Nazi forces were driven out of Holland by the Allies in 1945. Although the Dutch had succeeded in remaining neutral during World War I, the country was invaded by the Nazis in May 1940 and rapidly overrun. Despite the occupation, however, the Dutch managed to make a significant contribution to the Allied cause by building up an effective resistance. The liberation of Holland in 1945, in which the resistance played a leading part, was an important step leading to the subsequent defeat of the Nazis.

Many Dutch cities hold military parades and special concerts on this day. A special service of commemoration is held in Amsterdam's Dam Square on May 5 each year.

Dzam Ling Chi Sang *See* **Universal Prayer Day**

E

Early May Bank Holiday *See* Bank Holiday

Earth Day
April 22

The first Earth Day was observed on April 22, 1970 for the purpose of drawing public attention to the need for cleaning up the earth's air and water and for conserving our natural resources. Since that time the idea has spread, and Earth Day is now observed regularly throughout the United States and in many other countries (though there were some years of slack observance until the late 1980s).

Typical ways of celebrating Earth Day include planting trees, picking up roadside trash, and conducting various programs for recycling and conservation. School children may be asked to use only recyclable containers for their snacks and lunches, and environmentally concerned families often try to give up wasteful habits, such as using paper towels or plastic garbage bags.

"Earth" days have been observed by other groups as well. The day of the VERNAL EQUINOX is also observed by some as Earth Day.

Easter
Between March 22 and April 25 in the West; April 4 and May 8 in the East; first Sunday after the first full moon on or following the vernal equinox

Easter is the principal feast of the Christian year, despite the popularity and commercialization that surrounds CHRISTMAS. According to the Gospel of St. John, Mary Magdalen came to the cave where Jesus had been buried and found the tomb empty. An angel of the Lord told her that Jesus had risen. The anniversary of his resurrection from the dead is joyfully celebrated by Christians every year with special services, music, candlelight, flowers, and the ringing of church bells that had remained silent during Lent.

For Orthodox Christians, the sorrow of Good Friday lifts with the service of the Holy Resurrection on Saturday night in a dimly lit church. At midnight, all lights are extinguished, the door to the altar opens and the priest, holding a lighted candle, appears and proclaims that Christ is risen. The congregants light their candles from the priest's, bells ring, people turn to each other and say, "Christos Anesti" ('Christ is risen'), and receive the reply, "Alithos Anesti" ('He is risen indeed'). In Cyprus, Greece, fireworks are set off, ships in ports blow their whistles and bonfires are built to burn Judas. People go home for a late dinner starting with red-dyed hard-boiled eggs and then a special soup and often cheese pie (*tiropita*). It's customary to tap the eggs against each other; whoever cracks the other's egg will have good luck in the coming year.

Customarily, there is feasting on lamb roasted on spits over open fires; other traditional foods are *kokoretsi*, a sausage made of lamb innards and herbs, and *lambropsomo*, an Easter bread with a whole red-dyed egg in the center. In the countryside, the feasting is accompanied by fairs and dancing in regional costume. Passersby are offered lamb and red eggs and wine and are toasted with "Christos Anesti".

Easter is a movable holiday whose day of observation has for centuries been painstakingly calculated. This is because its day of observance is determined initially by the lunar calendar (like PASSOVER), but then must be put into terms of the solar calendar. After many centuries of controversy among Christians, Western Christendom settled on the use of the Gregorian calendar (Eastern Christians use the Julian calendar only to determine Easter), determining that Easter shall be celebrated on the Sunday after the full moon on or after the vernal equinox. If the full moon is on a Sunday, Easter is held the next Sunday. In the East Easter can occur between March

22 and May 8, but it must come after PASSOVER has ended.

The name for Easter may have come from *Eostre*, the Teutonic goddess of spring and fertility, whose feast was celebrated around this same time. There is also a Germanic goddess named Ostara who was always accompanied by a hare-possibly the ancestor of our modern Easter Bunny. The association of both the rabbit and eggs with Easter is probably the vestige of an ancient springtime fertility rite.

Although Easter has retained a greater religious significance than CHRISTMAS, many children in the United States think of it as a time to get new Spring clothes, to decorate eggs, and to indulge in the chocolate and jelly beans that the Easter Bunny has left in their Easter baskets.

In Belgium, throughout Walloonia, the priest gives a number of unconsecrated priest's wafers to young children to sell to householders. The proceeds are given to the needy parish families, and the wafers are nailed over the front doors to protect the families from evil.

In Ethiopia, Easter is called Fasika.

Easter Egg Roll
between March 23 and April 26; Monday following Easter

Starting in the middle of the nineteenth century, it was customary for young children to roll EASTER eggs on the lawn of the capitol building in Washington, D.C. But Congress objected to the damage they inflicted on the grass and in 1878 stationed guards there to halt the practice. President Rutherford B. Hayes, who enjoyed children, said they could use the White House lawn. President Franklin D. Roosevelt stopped the custom during World War II, but then it was restored again in 1953 by President Dwight D. Eisenhower.

Today the Egg Roll takes place on the Ellipse behind the White House, and children up to age eight are invited to participate. In addition to rolling their own hard-boiled eggs, the children hunt for about a thousand wooden eggs—many of them signed by past presidents or celebrities—that have been hidden in the grass. A crowd of up to ten thousand adults and children gathers for the annual event, and sometimes the President greets the crowd from the balcony of the White House.

Easter Fires
Eve of Easter

A tradition of hillside fires on Easter eve in Fredericksburg, Tex. The tradition is thought to have begun many years ago, soon after the town's settlement by German farmers in 1846. A pioneer mother, to calm her children, told them the fires burning on the town's hillside had been lit by the Easter bunny to boil their Easter eggs. In reality, the fires were those of Indians who were watching the settlement—but since then, fires glow on the hillside every Easter.

Easter Monday
Monday after Easter

Although Easter Sunday is the culmination of Holy Week and the end of LENT, the following Monday (also known as **Pasch Monday**) is observed as a public holiday in eighty-two nations, perhaps to round off the long weekend that begins on GOOD FRIDAY. In London there is a big Easter parade in Hyde Park on this day.

A curious English tradition associated at one time with Easter Monday involved "lifting" or "heaving." Forming what children call a "chair" by crossing hands and grasping another person's wrists, the men would lift the women on Easter Monday—sometimes carrying them for a short distance down the street or to the village green—and on Easter Tuesday the women would lift the men. A similar retaliatory game involved taking off each other's shoes. This is thought to have a connection with the resurrection of Christ. Polish children play *smigus*, a water-throwing game.

Eastern States Exposition
Starts the second Wednesday after Labor Day

Also known as the **Big E**, an agricultural and industrial fair in West Springfield, Mass. It's sponsored by all six New England states and runs for twelve days. The first exposition in 1917 attracted 138,000 visitors; today attendance tops one million.

The exposition is known for its Avenue of the States, where each New England state has erected a permanent replica of its original State House. (The New Hampshire State House uses New Hampshire granite for its columns.) In the buildings are displays of state products, for example, Maine potatoes, New Hampshire maple syrup, Vermont cheese, Massachusetts cranberries, Rhode Island clam cakes, and Connecticut apples. The livestock show is the largest in the East, and the Eastern States Horse Show is one of the oldest and most prestigious equestrian events in the country. Besides hunters, jumpers, harness, and saddle horses, there are draft horses in dress harness.

Edinburgh International Festival
August–September

The capital city of Edinburgh (pronounced ED-in-bo-ro), Scotland, is transformed during the last two weeks of August and the first week of September each year, when it hosts what is probably the most prestigious arts festival in the world. Theater and dance companies, orchestras, chamber groups, and soloists from all over the world perform at the city's major venues, and there are art exhibitions and poetry readings as well. Many important new works have been commissioned specifically for the festival—one of the most famous being T.S. Eliot's *The Cocktail Party.*

A highlight of the festival, which has been held since 1947, is the traditional Military Tattoo performed nightly at Edinburgh Castle, which is perched high above the city on a rocky promontory. Marching bands from all over the world perform along with Scottish Pipe bands at the tattoo, which ends with a farewell song from a lone piper standing on the floodlit battlements.

There is also a "Fringe Festival" that goes on at the same time—an arena for new talent and amateur entertainers. Although student drama and street theater predominate, the quality of the productions in recent years has sometimes made it difficult to distinguish Fringe events from the 'official' ones. The number of Fringe performances has increased dramatically as well—from only a few in 1947 to over nine thousand in 1989. But the three defining features of the earliest Fringe events still hold true today: none of the performers are officially invited to take part; they must use small and unconventional theatre spaces; and they all assume their own financial risks, surviving or sinking according to public demand.

Edison Pageant of Light
Second Wednesday through third Saturday of February

Most people associate Thomas Alva Edison (1847–1931) with his famous laboratory in Menlo Park, New Jersey. But when he was thirty-eight years old, a widower and seriously ill, his doctors sent him to Florida for a long vacation. There he discovered giant bamboo growing along the Caloosahatchee River. He established his winter home in Fort Myers and planned to use the bamboo fiber to make filaments for his new incandescent electric lamp bulbs.

The Edison Pageant of Light held annually in Fort Myers for eleven days encompassing his birthday (see THOMAS EDISON'S BIRTHDAY), began

as a three-day event in 1938. Highlights of the festival include concerts, a formal ball, coronation of the King and Queen of Edisonia, a children's parade, a high school band competition, and exhibits of Edison's various inventions. The Grand Parade of Light—a nighttime procession of over one hundred bands, floats, and marching units—is the festival's grand finale. Edison's winter home and his Florida laboratory are open to the public year-round.

Egungun Festival
June

The Egungun is a secret society among the Yoruba people of Ede, Nigeria. The major Egungun festival takes place in June, when members of the society come to the market place and perform masked dances for the Timi or chief. The masks they wear represent ancestral spirits and may cover the whole body or just the face. It is considered dangerous to see any part of the man who is wearing the mask—an offense that was at one time punishable by death.

The masqueraders all dance simultaneously, although each has his own drum accompaniment and entourage of chanting women and girls. The festival climaxes with the appearance of Andu, the most powerful mask. It is believed that the spirits of the deceased possess the masqueraders while they are dancing, and although it promotes a feeling of oneness between the living and the dead, the festival also inspires a certain amount of fear.

Egyptian Days
Various, each month

In medieval times, there were two days each month that were considered to be unlucky. Although it is not known for sure why they were referred to as the Egyptian Days, it's possible that they were first computed by Egyptian astrologers or were somehow related to the Egyptian plagues. They were also known as the **Dismal Days**, from Latin *dies mali* 'evil days.'

The Egyptian Days were January 1 and 25, February 4 and 26, March 1 and 28, April 10 and 20, May 3 and 25, June 10 and 16, July 13 and 22, August 1 and 30, September 3 and 21, October 3 and 22, November 5 and 28, and December 7 and 22.

Eight Hour Day
Various

Each of Australia's states celebrates the improvements that have been made in working conditions with its own LABOR DAY. In Western Australia and Tasmania, where it's celebrated on March 5 and called Eight Hour Day, parades and celebrations commemorate trade union efforts to limit working hours. People still chant the unions' slogan: "Eight hours' labor, eight hours' recreation, and eight hours' rest!," which, by happenstance, is the basis of St. Benedict's Rule of Life for religious orders.

In Victoria, **Labour Day** is observed on March 11. In Queensland, it's May 6; in New South Wales and the Australian Capital Territory, it's October 7; in South Australia it's October 14. In New Zealand, Labour Day is observed on the last Monday in October.

Eisteddfod
First week in August
The **Royal National Eisteddfod of Wales** dates back to the fourth century. Its purpose is to encourage the preservation of Welsh music and literature, and only those who sing or write in Welsh may enter the competitions. The annual event opens with the blowing of trumpets, followed by all kinds of musical and literary contests—harp playing, solo and choral singing, dramatic presentations, and poetic composition. Prizes and degrees are awarded to the winners.

The National Eisteddfod is held in northern Wales one year and southern Wales the next. Other Eisteddfodau are held in Welsh communities from May to November.

Eka Dasa Rudra
Once every 100 years
A series of processions, ceremonies, and sacrifices held every 100 years at Pura Besakih, the 'mother temple' of Bali, Indonesia. The temple, which comprises about thirty separate temples honoring a great variety of Balinese gods, was probably built about a thousand years ago and is on the slopes of the volcano mountain, Gunung ('Mt.') Agung. On March 17, 1963, the Eka Desa Rudra was under way when Agung catastrophically erupted and killed more than 1,500 people. Since the sacrifices were interrupted, the Eka Desa Rudra was started again sixteen years later and completed in the period from late February to early May of 1979. Images of gods were carried nineteen miles down the mountain to be washed in the sea: entire villages gathered along the route. The climax came during the Taur rites when twenty-three priests offered prayers and sacrificed animals—ranging from an eagle to an anteater—to appease forms of Rudra, a demonic manifestation of Bali's supreme deity, Sanghyang Widhi.

Thousands of pilgrims traveled by truck and foot to Besakih. The complex Balinese religion blends Hindusim, Buddhism, and Animism.

Eldon Turkey Festival
Second Saturday in October
While most areas of the United States think about turkeys only as THANKSGIVING DAY approaches, it is a year-round concern for the turkey farmers of Eldon, Missouri and the surrounding area, where over two million turkeys are raised annually. There is also a large wild turkey population, which makes turkey hunting a popular local sport. Since 1986, Eldon has held a **Turkey Festival** designed to educate the public about domestic turkey production, turkey farming operations, and the health benefits of turkey food products. The festival is also an opportunity for numerous conservation and turkey hunting organizations to provide information on safe hunting practices, wild turkey calling techniques, and efforts to increase the wild turkey population.

Events at the October festival include turkey races (with the turkeys on leashes), a turkey egg toss, sales of turkey food products, and exhibits on the production of domestic turkeys.

Election Day
Tuesday following the first Monday in November
Americans vote for their president and vice president every four years on the Tuesday after the first Monday in November, and for their state senators and representatives on the same day every two years. United States senators are elected every six years, one third of them up for re-election every two years, and representatives every two years in the even-numbered years.

This date was set by Congress in 1845 to correct abuses caused by having allowed each state to appoint its electors any time before the date in December set for their convening. To encourage people to vote, Election Day is a legal holiday or half-holiday in many states and all territories, and employers in other states often give their employees the day off. But despite the easing of restrictions on who may vote and the unceasing efforts of the League of Women Voters and other civic organizations, the majority of Americans do not take advantage of what may be their most valuable privilege.

In England, the day when every constituency elects a representative is called **General Election Day**.

96

Elephant Round-Up
Third weekend in November

An internationally famous show of 100 trained elephants held annually in the provincial capital of Surin, Thailand. The Suay people of the area have traditionally captured and trained wild elephants to work in the northern Thailand teak forests. The Round-up gives the trainers the opportunity to demonstrate their elephants' intelligence, strength, and obedience. A tug-of-war is staged where elephants are pitted against 200 Thai soliders. There are also log-pulling contests, a soccer game with two teams of elephants kicking a giant soccer ball, and other stunts. A highlight is the spectacular array of elephants rigged out to re-enact a medieval war parade. Besides the elephant demonstrations, there are cultural performances and folk dancing.

Elfreth's Alley Fete Day
Early June

Elfreth's Alley is a well-preserved street of privately owned eighteenth-century homes in Philadelphia. It is the only street in the city that has not only survived architecturally, but is still lived in by the same kind of people who occupied it when the alley was first opened in 1702. The thirty houses on the street, dating from 1713 to 1811, have all remained private residences, with the exception of the Mantua Makers House, which is now a museum open to the public.

The idea of holding an "at home" day in early June dates back to 1934, when a group of residents formed the Elfreth's Alley Association. Now called **Fete Day**, it is a day on which many of the houses are open to visitors, with members of the Association acting as hostesses in Colonial dress. On Fete Day in 1963, the Alley's distinctive character and historical value were officially recognized by its designation as a Registered National Historic Landmark. Over the years the Elfreth's Alley Association has played an active role in renovating the street's cartway and brick sidewalks, as well as saving some of the houses from destruction.

Elfstedentocht
December, January, or February

The day of this famous ice skating race in the Netherlands depends on the weather and the thickness of the ice. In the eighteenth century, young men in the northern part of the country, known as Friesland, would try to skate all the canals that connected the province's eleven towns. Today the **Eleven Cities Race** covers the same 124-mile course, but increasingly mild winters have made its timing less dependable. As many as 16,000 men and women have competed in the race at one time, which takes several hours to complete.

Ellensburg Rodeo
September, Labor Day weekend

The richest rodeo in the state of Washington and also one of the top twenty-five rodeos of the Professional Rodeo Cowboys Association. Prize money in 1991 was more than $100,000, and an estimated 20,000 people visited Ellensburg on the weekend. Events include a parade and displays of hand crafts, especially weaving and bead work, by the people of the Yakima Indian nation. Yakimas, many in feathered headdress, open each performance of the rodeo with a solemn horseback ride down a steep hill that overlooks the arena.

Elvis International Tribute Week
Week including August 16

A week-long tribute in Memphis, Tenn., to rock and roll singer Elvis Presley—"The King of Rock and Roll." The tribute takes place largely at Graceland, the 15,000-square-foot mansion that Elvis called home and which is now his gravesite, museum, and a rock and roll shrine.

Born in 1935 in a two-room house in Tupelo, Miss., Elvis moved to Memphis when he was twelve, and came to fame in the 1950s with hits like "Hound Dog," "Don't Be Cruel," and "All Shook Up". As a white man singing a black sound; he swept the music world and helped create the Memphis Sound. He was charismatic and sexy and gyrated his hips while performing in a fashion that sent the females in his audiences into a screeching frenzy. This won him the nickname, "Elvis the Pelvis." When he first appeared on television on the "Ed Sullivan Show," the hip shaking was considered too erotic, and he was photographed only from the waist up. He appeared in thirty-three motion pictures and made forty-five recordings that sold over a million copies each. He died at Graceland of an overdose of prescription drugs on Aug. 16, 1977.

A candlelight vigil is held on the evening of Aug. 15 at Graceland. Thousands of Elvis' fans, each carrying a candle, pour through the gates and walk to the gravesite. Other events of the week include a Nostalgia Concert by singers and musicians who worked with Presley; a Sock Hop Ball for "flat-top cats and dungaree dolls," in which Elvis songs and other classics of the 1950s and 1960s are played; and an art exhibit and contest, with art depicting Elvis or his home. The Elvis Presley Memorial Karate Tournament draws about 500 competitors from all over the world and reflects Presley's interest in karate—he studied the martial arts for years and was the first movie star to use karate in films.

Emancipation Day *See* **Juneteenth**

Emancipation Day
January 1

President Abraham Lincoln issued his famous Emancipation Proclamation freeing the slaves on January 1, 1863. Although some states have their emancipation or "freedom" celebrations on the anniversary of the day on which they adopted the Thirteenth Amendment, the most widespread observance takes place on January 1 because it is both a traditional and a legal holiday in all the states. In Texas, and other parts of the south and southwest, the emancipation of the slaves is celebrated on June 19 or JUNETEENTH, the anniversary of the day in 1863 when General Gordon Granger arrived there to enforce Lincoln's proclamation.

Celebrations are more common in the southern United States, where they frequently center around public readings of the original Emancipation Proclamation, often in a rhythmic, dramatic style.

Emancipation Day in Trinidad and Tobago
August 1

For those of African descent living in Trinidad and Tobago—nearly half the existing population—August 1 has been observed as Emancipation Day since 1985, when it replaced Columbus' Discovery Day. A celebration of the abolition of slavery in the 1830s, the day begins with an all-night vigil and includes church services, processions past historic landmarks, addresses by dignitaries, and an evening of shows with a torchlight procession to the National Stadium.

Ember Days
Four times a year

The Ember Days occur four times a year, at the beginning of each of the natural seasons. Traditionally they are marked by three days of fasting and abstinence—the Wednesday, Friday, and Saturday following, respectively, ASH WEDNESDAY, WHITSUNDAY, EXALTATION OF THE CROSS, and ST. LUCY'S DAY. In 1966, the Roman Catholic church replaced them with days of prayer for various needs and withdrew the obligation to fast. The

Anglican Communion still observes them. The four weeks in which these days occur are called Ember Weeks, and the Friday in each of these weeks is known as **Golden Friday**. The word "ember" itself derives from an Old English word referring to the revolution of time.

Some scholars believe that the Ember Days originated with the old pagan purification rites that took place at the seasons of planting, harvest, and vintage. The idea of fasting on these days was instituted by Pope Calixtus I in the third century. By the ninth century it was observed throughout Europe, but it wasn't until 1095 that the dates were fixed. In the Roman Catholic Church and the Church of England, since the sixth century, priests have been ordained on an Ember Saturday.

Emmett Kelly Clown Festival
Early May

Houston, Missouri is the home town of Emmett Kelly, who was the world's most famous clown. Kelly was born on December 9, 1898 in Sedan, Kansas, but his Irish father moved the family to a farm near Houston when he was six years old. Kelly developed an interest in cartooning, and by the time he left Houston to seek work in Kansas City at the age of nineteen, he had gained a reputation as an entertainer with his "chalk talk" act, which involved telling a story while sketching on paper with colored chalk. Best known for his role as "Weary Willie," a sad-faced tramp dressed in tattered clothes who was originally one of his cartoon characters, Kelly worked for a number of circuses and in 1952 made his motion picture debut in "The Greatest Show on Earth". He died in Sarasota, Florida on March 28, 1979—opening day for the Ringling Bros. and Barnum & Bailey Circus in New York.

Houston's Emmett Kelly Clown Festival is still relatively new (1988), and is timed to coincide with the opening of the circus season in May. Among the seven or eight hundred clowns who participate in the two-day festival are Emmett Kelly's son (Emmett Kelly, Jr.) and grandson (Joseph Kelly), both of whom continue the "Weary Willie" tradition. In addition to the clown parade and performances of clown stunts and skits, there are a number of "chalk talk" storytelling events.

Empire Day *See* **Commonwealth Day**

Encaenia Day
June

In general terms, *encaenia* (pronounced en-SEEN-ya) refers to the festivities celebrating the founding of a city or the dedication of a church. But in Oxford, England, Encaenia Day—sometimes referred to as **Commemoration Day**—is the day at the end of the summer term when the founders and benefactors of Oxford University are commemorated and honorary degrees are awarded to distinguished men and women. The ceremonies take place in the Sheldonian Theatre, designed by Christopher Wren in 1669 when he was a professor of astronomy at the university. Based on a classical amphitheatre, the Sheldonian offers an exceptional and often-photographed view from its cupola of Oxford's spires and gargoyles.

Enkutatash
September 11

The **Ethiopian New Year** falls on the first day of the Ethiopian month of Maskarem, which is September 11 on the Gregorian calendar. It comes at the end of the rainy season, so the wildflowers that the children gather and the tall grass that the peasants use to cover their floors on this day are plentiful. Small groups of children go from house to house, singing songs, leaving small bouquets of flowers, and hoping for a handful of *dabo* or roasted grain in return. In some parts of Ethiopia it is customary to slaughter an animal on this day. For superstitious reasons this is either a white-headed lamb or a red chicken.

Entrance of the Lord into Jerusalem
See **Palm Sunday**

Epidauros Festival
Late June through August

Theatrical productions of ancient Greek tragedy and comedy at the theater built in the third century B.C. in Epidauros, Greece, about ninety miles southwest of Athens. This open-air theater, the best preserved in Greece, can seat 14,000, and the acoustics are so fine that those seated in the top row can hear a whisper on stage. The performances, also known as the **Festival of Ancient Drama**, are presented by the National Theater of Greece and the Northern Greece State and Art Theater. Summaries of the Greek language plays are available to the audience in English.

Epiphany Eve *See* **Twelfth Night**

Epiphany Eve in France
January 5

On the eve of Le Jour des Rois ('the Day of the Kings') it is customary in France to give food, clothing, money, and gifts to the parish poor. In

Alsace, the children go from door to door dressed as the Three Kings, asking for donations of eggs, bacon, and cakes. In Normandy, the children make their neighborhood rounds carrying Chinese lanterns and empty baskets, in which they hope to collect food, clothing, and money. In Brittany, someone dressed as a beggar leads a horse, decorated with ribbons and mistletoe, through the streets. There are empty baskets hanging from the saddle in which donations are carried. In Provence and some other parts of southern France, the children go out on Epiphany Eve to meet the Three Kings, carrying cakes and figs for the hungry Magi and hay for their camels. Even though they may not meet the Three Kings on the road, they can see their statues standing near the altar of the church, where an Epiphany Mass is celebrated at night.

Epiphany, Feast of the
January 6

One of the oldest Christian feasts, (celebrated since the end of the second century, before the establishment of the Christmas holiday), Epiphany (which means "manifestation" or "showing forth") is sometimes called **Twelfth Day, Three Kings' Day**, Dia de Los Tres Reyes (in Latin America), the **Feast of Jordan** (by Ukrainian Orthodox), or Old Christmas Day. It commemorates the first two occasions on which the divinity of Jesus was manifested: when the three kings (or wise men or Magi) came to worship the infant Jesus in Bethlehem, and when he was baptised by John the Baptist in the River Jordan and the Holy Spirit descended in the form of a dove and proclaimed him the Son of God. The Roman Catholic and Protestant Churches emphasize the visit of the Magi when they celebrate the Epiphany; the Eastern Orthodox churches focus on the baptism of Jesus. The blessing of lakes, rivers, and seas plays a central role in their celebrations.

In France **Le Jour des Rois** (the **Day of the Kings**), sometimes called the **Fête des Rois** or feast of Epiphany, is celebrated with parties for children and adults alike. The highlight of these celebrations is the *galette des rois* or 'cake of the Kings'—a round, flat cake which is cut in the pantry, covered with a white napkin, and carried into the dining room on a small table. An extra piece is always cut, which is traditionally called *le part à Dieu* or 'God's share' and is reserved for the first poor person who comes to the door. The youngest person in the room oversees the distribution of the pieces of cake, one of which contains a bean or tiny china doll. The person who finds this token becomes king or queen for the evening. He or she chooses a consort, and for the remainder of the evening, every move the royal couple makes is imitated and commented upon by the other guests, who take great delight in exclaiming, "The King drinks!" or "The Queen coughs!"

In many parts of France, the celebration begins on the evening of January 5 and involves collecting and distributing food and gifts for the poor (see EPIPHANY EVE IN FRANCE).

Now observed by a growing number of Protestants as well as Roman Catholics and Orthodox, Epiphany refers not only to the day itself but to the Church season that follows it—a season whose length varies because it ends when Lent begins, and that depends on the date of EASTER.

See also TWELFTH NIGHT, BEFANA FESTIVAL, FOUR AN' TWENTY DAY, TIMQAT, and ORTHODOX EPIPHANY.

Equal Opportunity Day
November 19
At the dedication of the Gettysburg National Cemetery in southern Pennsylvania on November 19, 1863, President Abraham Lincoln delivered the Gettysburg Address, a 270-word speech that is considered one of the greatest in American history, though it didn't receive much attention at the time. Equal Opportunity Day is observed at Gettysburg National Cemetery each year, where ceremonies commemorating Lincoln's address are held under the sponsorship of the Sons of Union Veterans and the Lincoln Fellowship of Pennsylvania. Sometimes this day is referred to as **Gettysburg Address Day**.

Esala (Asadha) Perahera (Arrival of the Tooth Relic)
Mid–June–mid-July; full moon of Asadha
A celebration in Kandy, Sri Lanka (formerly Ceylon), that lasts fourteen nights and pays homage to the sacred relic believed to be a tooth of the Buddha. Kandy, originally the capital of the independent kingdom of Kandy in the Sri Lankan highlands, is the site of the Dalada Maligava, or Temple of the Tooth, where the relic is kept. The celebration originated in the the fourth century when the king of Kandy declared that the tooth be paraded annually so people could honor it.

Processions are held each night for nine nights, and the tooth is paraded in an elaborate howdah (platform) on the back of an ornately decorated elephant. Dozens of richly caparisoned elephants follow, and there are also drummers beating big

bass drums and small tom-toms, horn blowers, the famous Kandyan dancers, acrobats, and torch bearers holding aloft baskets of blazing copra (coconut meat). Representatives of the major Hindu temples also are part of the processions.

Escalade (Scaling the Walls)
December 11
A celebration in Geneva, Switzerland, of the victory of the people of Geneva over the attacking French Savoyards. On the nights of Dec. 11 and 12 in 1602, the French soldiers tried to scale the city ramparts, but were ferociously turned back. Among the remembered defenders is Mère Royaume, who poured a pot of scalding soup on the head of a Savoyard soldier.

To mark the victory, people carrying torches and wearing period costumes and armor proceed through the old city on both banks of the Rhone River. Historic figures, like Mère Royaume, are always represented. Shops sell chocolates that look like miniature soup pots. These commemorate Royaume's courageous act. At several points on the route, the procession stops while a herald on horseback reads the proclamation of victory. The procession winds up at St. Peter's Cathedral, where the citizens sing patriotic songs and a huge bonfire concludes the celebration.

Esther, Fast of *See* Ta'anit Esther

Europalia
September–December
A festival held every other year since 1969 in Belgium to celebrate the artistic achievements of different countries. In 1991, it was Portugal's turn, and twenty exhibitions, 100 concerts, and other events attracted about 1.5 million visitors. The 1991 centerpiece exhibition was "Triumph of the Baroque," held at the Palais des Beaux-Arts in Brussels. It featured sculpture, paintings, and a silver carriage that was built to carry the Portuguese ambassador through Rome to the Vatican. There were also major exhibitions in Antwerp, Ghent, Charleroi, and Mons.

Evacuation Day
March 17; September 1; November 25
"Evacuation Day" has been used to describe a number of dates in history on which military forces have withdrawn from a city or country. The best known evacuation in the United States took place on March 17, 1776, during the early part of the American Revolution. British troops were forced out of Boston, when the British com-

mander, General Sir William Howe, conceded defeat to the American General George Washington in a move that he hoped would save the British fleet. Bostonians have been celebrating the day ever since. Because of the large Irish-American community in Boston, the popularity of this holiday is often attributed to its being conincident with St. Patrick's Day. Another well-known evacuation took place a few years later on November 25, 1783, when the British were forced out of New York City.

In England, "Evacuation Day" has also been used to refer to September 1, 1939 and the two days following, when over a million children and adults were evacuated from London and other cities considered to be likely targets for bombing during World War II.

Evamelunga
September 8

Evamelunga, which means **'The Taking Away of the Burden of Sin'** is Thanksgiving Day for the Christians in Cameroon. Families put on their best clothes and flock to the thatched-roof churches, which are decorated with flowers and palm leaves for the occasion. Church choirs and school choruses sing songs expressing gratitude for the arrival of the first missionary who brought them the story of Jesus in the late nineteenth century. After the church services are over, the feasting and singing continue late into the evening.

Exaltation of the Cross, Feast of the
*September 14; formerly May 3 by Roman
    Catholics*

So-called by the Eastern church, where it is one of the twelve great feasts, and is also known as the **Elevation**, **Recovery** or **Adoration of the Cross**. In the West, it is known as **Holy Cross Day** (by the Anglican Communion), the **Triumph of the Cross** (by Roman Catholics), and also the **Invention of the Cross** (from Latin *invenire* 'to find'). It commemorates three events: the finding of the cross on which Jesus was crucified, the dedication in 335 of the basilica built by Emperor Constantine enclosing the supposed site of Christ's crucifixion on Golgotha, and the recovery in 629 by Emperor Heraclius III of the relic of the cross that had been stolen by the Persians.

According to tradition, St. Helena, mother of Emperor Constantine, found the cross on a visit to Jerusalem, being enabled to identify it by a miracle. Many relics from the cross were distributed among the churches throughout the world. (In the late nineteenth century, Rohault de Fleury cata-

logued all the known relics in the world; he estimated that they constituted less than one-third of the size of the cross that was believed to have been used.) In addition, St. Helena discovered the four nails used in the Crucifixion, and the small plaque hung above Christ that bore the sarcastic inscription, INRI, Latin for Iesus Nazarenus Rex Iudaeorum 'Jesus of Nazareth, King of the Jews.' Two of the nails were placed in Constantine's crown, one was later brought to France by Charlemagne, and the fourth was supposedly cast into the Adriatic Sea when Helena's ship was threatened by a storm on her return journey.

On September 13, 335, bishops met in Jerusalem for the dedication of the basilica of the Holy Sepulchre built by order of Constantine. It is believed that the date was the anniversary of the discovery of the remains of the cross during excavations on the site of the Temple of Venus. On the fourteenth, a relic enshrined in a silver-gilt receptacle was elevated for veneration.

The relic was taken to Persia in 614 after the Persian army of King Chroesröes occupied Jerusalem. When Herakleios III of Constantinople defeated the Persians on the banks of the Danube in 629, he brought the sacred relic to Constantinople (now Istanbul). On September 14, 633 it was carried in a solemn procession to the Church of the Holy Wisdom (Hagia Sophia in Greek; Saint Sophia in English) where it was elevated for all to adore, recalling Christ's words, "And I, if I be lifted up from the earth, will draw all men unto me" (John 12:32).

Former names for this day are **Crouchmas** (**'Cross Mass'**), **Holy Rood Day**, and **Roodmas**, *rood* referring to the wood of which the cross was made.

In the Philippines, there is also a nationwide celebration commemorating the discovery of the Holy Cross of Calvary by St. Helena (formerly celebrated on May 3). It is known as **Santacruzan**. Nine-day pageants are held with local men and women playing the parts of Biblical characters. There are processions with floats of each town's patron saint and costumed young women and their escorts parade under flower-decked arches. In Lucban, Quezon Province, multicolored rice wafers, called *kiping*, are shaped into the form of fruits and vegetables and displayed as window ornaments.

See also Mascal, and Blessing of the Waters Day.

Excited Insects, Feast of
On or around March 5

Known as **Kyongchip** in Korea and as **Ching Che** in China, the Feast of Excited Insects marks the transition from winter to spring. It is the day when the insects awake from their long winter hibernation. In China, it is the day when "the dragon raises his head," summoning the insects back to life, and various rituals designed to placate the insects and assist Nature in the task of restoring fertility to the earth are performed. In Korea, this is one of twenty-four days in the lunar calendar year that indicate a change of season. Farmers sow their rice and wheat, and families lay flowers on the graves of their ancestors to welcome spring.

F

Fairbanks Winter Carnival
Third week in March

A week of festivities in Fairbanks, Alaska, highlighted by the North American sled dog races. Other events include dances, a parka parade, a campstove chili contest, a native potlatch, snow- and ice-sculpting contests, snowshoe races, musical and dramatic presentations, and a trade fair.

Fairhope Jubilee
Summer

A natural phenomenon greeted by the citizens of Fairhope, Alabama, with a rush to the shores of Mobile Bay. Fairhope, on a bluff over the bay, has two miles of beach. At a certain time, when the bay is calm and there is an east wind and a certain feel to the air, bottom-dwelling fish and crustaceans are trapped between a low-oxygen water mass and the shore. They become sluggish because of the shortage of oxygen and can't swim, so townsfolk rush out with buckets, cooking pots, crab nets, long poles, and wash basins to harvest them. The harvest may include flounder, shrimp, blue crab, stingrays, eels, and smaller fish such as shiners, anchovies, and hogchokers. It's impossible to predict when the phenomenon will occur except that it's always in the summer and usually in August; sometimes there is more than one occurence; sometimes it will happen five days in a row. This event depends on a number of very specific circumstances: an overcast day, a gentle wind from the east, a rising tide. Here's what happens: a deep-water pocket of very salty water stagnates and collects plant matter. This food supply and the warm temperatures cause a population explosion of microorganisms that consume great quantities of oxygen. A gentle east wind comes along and moves the upper-layer water offshore. Then the rising tide pushes the oxygen-poor bottom water toward the shore, and the bottom sea creatures are pushed in front of it. They act as though they're in a stupor because they're trying to get oxygen; they move slowly and don't try to swim. Eels will leave the water and burrow tail-first into the moist sand, leaving their heads in the air with mouths open.

Supposedly the event got its name because the first person seeing the marine migration called out, "Jubilee!"

Fallas de San Jose (Bonfires of St. Joseph) *See* St. Joseph's Day

Family Week
Begins on the first Sunday in May

In America Protestant churches, Roman Catholic churches, and Jewish congregations observe **National Family Week.** While each has its own way of celebrating this event, the emphasis is on the strength that a family can find in religion. Members of the congregation are encouraged to examine their own lives from the perspective of how they have contributed to the religious life of their families, and groups often meet to discuss how to deal with social conditions that are having an adverse effect on family life. National Family Week always begins on the first Sunday in May and leads up to MOTHER'S DAY and, among Christians, to the FESTIVAL OF THE CHRISTIAN HOME.

Many other countries observe a **Family Day**, as well, particularly in Africa. In Angola, Family Day is observed on December 25; in Namibia, December 26. Family Day is also the name by which EASTER MONDAY is known in South Africa.

Farvardegan Days
March 11–20; July; August

Also known as **Farvadin** or **Farvardin**, this is a Zoroastrian festival celebrated by the followers of Zoroaster in Iran and India. The ten-day **Remembrance of the Departed** is a festival in commemoration of the spirits of the dead (*fravashis*), who have returned to God or Ahura Mazda to help in the fight against evil. Parsi worshippers attend ceremonies for the dead on the hills in front of the

103

dakhmas (towers of silence) and at shrines in their homes.

Farvardegan is celebrated from the eleventh to the twentieth of March by the Fasli sect of the Parsis, in July by the Kadmi sect, and in August by the Shahenshai sect. Zoroaster (or Zarathushtra) was a Persian prophet and reformer in the sixth century B.C. whose teachings influenced Judaism, Christianity, and Islam. The largest Zoroastrian groups remaining today are the Parsis (or Parsees) of India and the Gabars of Iran.

Fasching
Between February 2 and March 8; The two days before Ash Wednesday

Known in southwest Germany as **Fastnacht**, in Mainz as **Fassenacht**, in Bavaria and Austria as Fasching, as **Karneval** in the Rhineland, and elsewhere as the **Feast of Fools**. This is a Shrovetide festival that takes place on the two days immediately preceding ASH WEDNESDAY, otherwise known as ROSE MONDAY and SHROVE TUESDAY. It features processions of masked figures, and is the equivalent of MARDI GRAS and the last day of CARNIVAL. Fastnacht means 'eve of the fast,' and the wild celebrations that typically take place during this festival are a way of making the most of the last hours before the deprivations of LENT.

In the Black Forest area of southern Germany, these pre-lenten festivities are called **Fastnet**. The celebrations date back to the Middle Ages and were developed by craftsmen's guilds. Today's carnival clubs (*Narrenzünfte*) still use the same wooden masks and traditional costumes in their parades as their ancestors did. The rites of Fasnet are distinctive: in Elzach, wooden-masked Schuddig Fools wearing red costumes and large hats decorated with snail shells, run through the town beating people with blown-up hogs' bladders; in Wolfach, fools stroll around in nightgowns and nightcaps; in Überlinger on the Bodensee and Villingen, they crack long whips, toss fruit and nuts to the children, and wear foxes' tails and smiling wooden masks. Carnival ends with *Kehraus* 'sweeping out.'

See also KARNEVAL IN COLOGNE.

Fasinada
July 22

A commemoration of a miraculous event on the tiny island of Gospa od Skrpjela (Our Lady of the Chisels) off Montenegro (formerly in Yugoslavia). The island, according to the story, was once noth-ing more than a rock. One stormy night, a shipwrecked sailor clung to the rock and vowed that if he survived he would build a church to the Virgin Mary. He did survive, and sailors dumped stones there until an island was formed; in the seventeenth century a church was built on the pile of rocks. The festival includes a procession to the island of boats decorated with garlands of flowers and loaded with rocks. The rocks are piled up to reinforce the shores of the island, and then the participants enjoy folk dancing and country sports and games.

Fast Day
Fourth Monday in April

At one time it was customary for the governors of the New England states to proclaim days of public fasting and prayer, usually around the middle of April. But after the Revolutionary War, enthusiasm for the custom began to wane. Because the day's spiritual significance had faded by the nineteenth century, Massachusetts abolished its Fast Day in 1895 and began to observe PATRIOTS' DAY in its place. Maine followed suit a few years later.

New Hampshire is now the only state that continues to observe Fast Day as a legal holiday, maintaining a tradition that can be traced back to 1679. No longer an occasion for abstinence, it is usually regarded as an opportunity for outdoor recreation and spring chores. Although the date is set by law, the governor of New Hampshire issues a yearly proclamation designating the day on which it will be observed.

Fastelavn
Between February 2 and March 8; Monday preceding Ash Wednesday

The Monday before LENT begins is a school holiday for children in Denmark. Early in the morning they enter their parents' bedrooms armed with "Lenten birches"—twigs covered with silk, crepe paper, or ribbon. As they poke or smack their parents they cry out, "Give buns! Give buns!"—referring to the traditional *Fastelavnsboller*, or Shrovetide buns, which their parents give them to put a stop to the beating. This custom probably has its roots in ancient purification rites, where people used to beat one another with switches to drive out evil. Various games are played with the buns, such as suspending one by string from a chandelier and trying to take a bite of it. Later in the day, the children dress up in costume and go from door to door, where they are given coins, candy, and more buns.

Fastens-een

Between February 3 and March 9; the day before Ash Wednesday

The eve or day before Ash Wednesday has been given a number of names in Scotland and Northern England, including Fastens-een, **Fastens-eve, Fastens-Even,** and **Fastens Tuesday.** All refer to the Lenten season that is about to begin, "Fasten Day" being the Old English form of "Fast Day." **Fastingong** was an early English expression for Shrove Tuesday, which was also called **Fastingong Tuesday.** In certain English dialects the word "fastgong" means "fast-going" or "approaching a time of fast."

No matter what the day is called, the day before Lent begins in the West is traditionally a time for carnival-like celebrations. See also Shrove Tuesday, Fasching, Carnival, Collop Monday.

Father's Day

3rd Sunday in June

Sonora Louise Smart Dodd from Spokane, Washington suggested to her minister in 1910 that a day be set aside for honoring fathers. Her own father was a Civil War veteran who raised his six children on the family farm after his wife died in childbirth. The Ministerial Association and the Spokane YMCA picked up on the idea, and in 1924 Father's Day received the support of President Calvin Coolidge. But it wasn't until 1966 that a presidential proclamation established Father's Day as the third Sunday in June. Although it began as a religious celebration, today it is primarily an occasion for showing appreciation through gift-giving.

Father's Day in Yugoslavia *See* **Children's Day in Yugoslavia**

Fat Tuesday *See* **Shrove Tuesday**

Fête des Géants *See* **Giants, Festival of the**

Fête Nationale *See* **Bastille Day**

Field Days, National

Second week of June

The largest agricultural show in New Zealand takes place for three days during the second week in June in Hamilton, and attracts visitors from more than forty countries. There are exhibits covering every type of rural activity, demonstrations of how to use the latest farm equipment, and contests in such areas as hay-baling, wire-fencing, tractor-driving, and helicopter log-lifting.

Other agricultural shows in New Zealand include the Agricultural and Pastoral Show at Auckland in late November, featuring New Zealand's largest livestock parade; the Annual Agricultural and Pastoral Show at Hamilton in late October, the country's largest dairy cattle and pig show; and the Canterbury Agricultural and Pastoral Show in mid-November. In a country that in 1990 had more than sixty million sheep and only 3.3 million people, these regional agricultural shows attract the kind of audiences that are usually associated with major athletic competitions. (See also Royal Show Days.)

Fiesta sa EDSA (People Power Anniversary)

February 25

A commemoration of the bloodless People Power Revolution in the Philippines on Feb. 22–25, 1986, in which the dictatorial regime of President Ferdinand Marcos was toppled. The revolution began because Marcos and Corazon C. Aquino both claimed victory in a presidential election filled with fraud and violence. Two key government officers, Minister Juan Ponce Enrile and Armed Forces Vice Chief of Staff Fidel Ramos, rebelled in protest of Marcos' oppression and demanded his resignation. They holed up at military camps at the Epifanio de los Santos Highway (EDSA), which borders Manila on the east. Pro-Marcos forces threatened to annihilate them, but two million unarmed people surged toward the camps. With offerings of flowers, food, and prayers, they provided a human shield and overcame the military's firepower. Fourteen years of Marcos' rule ended, and Corazon C. Aquino became the first woman president of the Philippines, (1986–92). The day is marked with ceremonies at the site of the revolution in Quezon City a part of metropolitan Manila.

Fifteenth of Av (Hamishah Asar be-Av)

between July 23 and August 21; 15 Av

During the time of the Second Temple in Jerusalem (dedicated between 521 and 517 B.C., destroyed in 70 A.D.), this was a Jewish folk festival in which the young women would dress in white and dance in the vineyards, and where young bachelors would come to choose their brides. There are a number of explanations for why the festival was celebrated this way. According to the *Talmud*, the fifteenth day of Av was the day when members of different tribes were allowed to intermarry. It was also the day when the cutting of trees to burn on the altar ceased, because the heat of the sun was diminishing and there was some concern that the trees wouldn't dry properly. It's also possible that the holiday was adapted from an ancient SUMMER SOLSTICE festival.

Although in modern times there have been attempts by the new settlements in Israel to turn this day into one of music and folk dancing, the idea doesn't seem to have caught on. The Fifteenth of Av is marked only by a ban on eulogies or fasting.

Fig Sunday
Between March 14 and April 18; Palm Sunday
The custom of eating figs on PALM SUNDAY gave rise to the name Fig Sunday or **Fig Pudding Day** in England, when children would buy figs and either eat them or bring them home to their mothers to make fig pudding. The name may have come from Christ's cursing of the barren fig tree, on the day after his entry into Jerusalem, as told in the eleventh chapter of the biblical Gospel of Mark.

Finnish Sliding Festival
Two days in February
Patterned after the traditional event in Finland that celebrates FAT TUESDAY before the beginning of LENT, the Finnish Sliding Festival or **Laskiainen** has been held in Aurora, Minnesota every winter for more than fifty years. It features two large ice slides which are constructed at the edge of Loon Lake. People bring their sleds or toboggans for an exciting ride down the slide onto the frozen expanse of the lake. For those who want more thrills, there is a *vipukelka* or 'wild sled' which resembles a kind of merry-go-round on ice.

Other activities at the weekend event include log sawing contests, Finnish music and dance performances, and traditional Finnish foods such as oven pancakes and pea soup.

Fireworks Day *See* Guy Fawkes Day

First-born, Fast of the
Between March 26 and April 23; 14 Nisan
The Fast of the First-born is the only fast in the Jewish calendar which is neither an atonement for sin nor a fast of petition. Observed only symbolically by firstborn male Jews on the day before PASSOVER, its main purpose appears to be to remind Jews of the Angel of Death's slaying of the Egyptians' firstborn sons and the miraculous escape of their own sons. The obligation to fast can be avoided by participating in a *siyyum*—the study of a particular passage of the Talmud.

First Day of Summer in Iceland
Thursday in April
In Iceland the First Day of Summer is second in importance only to CHRISTMAS and NEW YEAR'S DAY. It is observed on the Thursday that falls between April 19 and April 25, a time of year that marks the end of the long northern winter. The custom of giving gifts on this day was widespread by the middle of the nineteenth century, although they were usually home-made articles or, in some areas, a share of the fisherman's catch.

Special foods associated with the First Day of Summer include summer-day cakes—flat rye breads up to a foot in diameter—on top of which the day's share of food for each person would be piled. Since the turn of the century it has also been a popular day for young people to give speeches, poetry readings, and dramatic performances, or to engage in singing, dancing, and sports.

First-Foot Day
January 1
The custom of *first-footing*, or being the first to cross the threshhold of a home in the early hours of NEW YEAR'S DAY, was so popular in England and Scotland during the nineteenth century that the streets were often more crowded between midnight and one o'clock in the morning than they would normally be at midday. If the "First-Foot," traditionally a man, was to bring the family luck, he had to arrive with his arms full of cakes, bread, and cheese for everyone to share. He should be dark-haired, not fair, and must not have flat feet.

Today the custom may still be observed in Britain and in scattered areas of the United States.

First Monday Trade Day
Weekend of first Monday of each month
A colossal trading bazaar, originally known as **Horse Monday**, that each month brings 60,000 people to the small town of Canton, Tex. (population 2,800). This legendary affair in northern Texas had its origins in the 1860s when farmers began gathering in Canton on the first Monday of the month to sell or trade horses, hunting hounds, and other dogs. The event continued and grew. Now it starts on a Friday, runs through the weekend, and offers merchandise at 5,000 exhibition stalls.

Scottsboro, Ala., also has well-known First Monday Trade Days attended by thousands, and this custom is observed in most southern states. Commonly, the markets are held on the streets surrounding the county courthouse. Fiddling and storytelling are often part of the day's activities. The name for the event differs; in some places, it's **Court Day**. In Abingdon, Va., it's **Jockey Day** because of the horse races held along with the trading.

First Night in Boston
December 31

First Night originated in Boston as their annual New Year's Eve celebration of the arts. This city-wide festival was first held in 1976 to change the drinking and partying that have traditionally marked New Year's Eve celebrations in most American cities into a night of family entertainment. It has proved so successful that to date sixty-five other cities in the United States and Canada have followed Boston's lead.

To bring both inner city and suburban communities together 1,000 artists in Boston offer a wide variety of artistic events and performances at seventy indoor and outdoor sites in Boston's Back Bay, Beacon Hill, South End, Downtown, and Waterfront areas. In recent years as many as half a million residents and visitors have been drawn to places in the city where they would not normally walk after dark.

Fish Carnival *See* Groppenfasnacht

Flag Day
June 14

On June 14, 1777 the Continental Congress replaced the British symbols of George Washington's Grand Union flag with a new design featuring thirteen white stars in a circle on a field of blue and thirteen red and white stripes—one for each state. Although it is not certain, this flag may have been made by the Philadelphia seamstress Betsy Ross who was an official flagmaker for the Pennsylvania Navy. The number of stars increased as the new states entered the Union, but the number of stripes stopped at fifteen and was later returned to thirteen.

President Woodrow Wilson issued a proclamation that established June 14 as Flag Day in 1916, but it didn't become official until 1949. This occured as a result of a campaign by Bernard J. Cigrand and the American Flag-Day Association. It is a legal holiday only in Pennsylvania, but is observed across the country by displaying the American flag on homes and public buildings. Other popular ways of observing this day include flag-raising ceremonies, the singing of the national anthem, and the study of flag etiquette and the flag's origin and meaning.

Flag Day in Denmark
June 15

According to legend, the Danish King Valdemar set out to conquer the pagan Estonians and convert them to Christianity. During the night of June 15, 1219, the Estonians made a surprise attack on the Danish camp. As he raised his arms toward heaven to pray for help, the Danish archbishop discovered that as long as he could hold his arms up, the Danes were able to push back the enemy. But when they dropped from weariness, the Estonians gained ground. Eventually a red banner with a white cross floated down from the sky and, as the archbishop caught it, he heard a voice from the clouds say that the Danes would win if they raised this banner before their enemies. A messenger took the banner to King Valdemar and the Danes won the battle.

Schools, sports organizations, and Boy Scout troops in Denmark often hold Flag Day pageants on June 15 in which they re-enact the story of the *Dannebrog* (the Danish flag) and King Valdemar. The red and white flag can be seen flying everywhere on this day in honor of its miraculous first appearance.

Flag Day in Sweden
June 6

Constitution and Flag Day commemorates the adoption of the Swedish constitution on June 6, 1809 and the ascension of Gustavus I to the throne on June 6, 1523. It is observed throughout Sweden with patriotic meetings, parades, and the raising of flags. In Stockholm the main celebration takes place at the Stadium, where the Swedish national anthem is sung by a chorus of several thousand voices, and King Gustaf V awards flags to various schools, sports clubs, and other organizations. In the evening the celebration continues at Skansen, the oldest open-air museum in Europe.

Flagstaff Festival of the Arts
July

The major performing and visual arts festival of Arizona, held in Flagstaff on the campus of Northern Arizona University. The affair began in the early 1960s as a music camp, and became a full-fledged festival in 1966. It ran one week that year, and today is a four-week festival with more than forty-eight events: symphonic and chamber-music concerts, ballet, theater, film showings, and art exhibits. From 1966 to 1977, Izler Solomon directed and conducted the festival orchestra, which is composed of musicians from major U.S. orchestras.

Flemington Fair
Week before Labor Day

The **New Jersey State Agricultural Fair** held in Flemington for seven days at the end of August and continuing right through LABOR DAY is a traditional agricultural fair that was started by a group of local farmers in 1856, making it one of the oldest state fairs in the country. It features a statewide 4-H Lamb Show and Sale, a tractor pull, a horse and pony pull, and all types of car racing (mini-stocks, modified stocks, midgets, and super sprints). The fair also offers programs and exhibits of flowers, the 4-H organization, nurserymen, and various commercial enterprises.

Flitting Day *See* Moving Day

Float Festival
Night of full moon in Tamil month of Thai (mid-January to mid-February)

A festival held at the temple city of Madurai in the state of Tamil Nadu, India, to commemorate the birth of Tirumala Nayak, a 17th-century king of Madurai. The center of the festival is the Mariamman Teppakulam pond surrounding a temple on an island. Images of the goddess Meenakshi and her consort are floated on a flower-bedecked raft to the illuminated temple, and a spectacular array of lit floats move in procession around the pond, accompanied by music and chanted hymns.

Floating Lantern Ceremony (Toro Nagashi)
August 15

A Buddhist ceremony held in Honolulu, Hawaii, on the anniversary of the end of World War II. The festival is part of the annual Buddhist Bon season of July and August in which the spirits of departed ancestors are welcomed back to earth with prayers, dances, offerings, and by setting afloat some 2,000 colorful paper lanterns bearing the names of the dead.

See also OBON FESTIVAL.

Flood, Festival of the *See* Kataklysmos, Feast of

Flores de Mayo
May 31

Flores de Mayo ('May flowers') festivals take place throughout the Philippines during the month of May. Children make floral offerings and take them to their churches in the afternoon. Processions wind through the streets of the towns and villages, with girls wearing traditional costumes followed by their relatives and friends singing Hail Marys.

The festival culminates on May 31 with fiestas everywhere. In big cities like Manila, Flores de Mayo is one of the largest festivals of the year, featuring May Queens and fancy dress balls. In the smaller towns and villages, the last day of the month is a day to celebrate the birthday of their patron saint.

Floriade, the
Once every ten years, April–October

Once every ten years, the Netherlands organizes a World Horticultural Exhibition called the Floriade. The grounds for the exhibition are the Zoeteneer, outside Amsterdam. They cover 230 acres with lakes, gardens, theme pavilions, restaurants, and environmental displays—including a miniature Netherlands with dykes and canals that visitors can flood and drain at will. What has been billed as the greatest flower show on earth runs from early April through early October and attracts about three million visitors. Magnificent displays of bulbs and flowers, plants and trees, and fruits and vegetables are divided into seven thematic areas: transport, production, consumer, environment, future, world, and recreation. In addition to the many open-air activites, there are extensive indoor attractions in the numerous halls, greenhouses, and pavilions.

Flower Festival *See* Hana Matsuri

Fool Plough *See* Plough Monday

Fools, Feast of *See* Fasching

Footwashing Day
Sunday in early summer

According to the Gospel of John, before the Last Supper Jesus washed the feet of his disciples and instructed them to follow his example of humility and love. In some places, this practice is an important part of the celebration of the Eucharist. Although it was originally performed on MAUNDY THURSDAY, in most American Protestant sects it takes place at other times and occasionally at more frequent intervals.

For the mountain people of Kentucky, Footwashing Day takes place only once a year, but the preparations go on for weeks beforehand. On the day, the women take turns washing each other's feet and, on the opposite side of the church, the men do the same thing. Refreshment stands have been set up so children can eat while their parents are participating in the ritual. After the service, the people who live near the church invite the rest of the participants to eat with them.

Forefathers' Day
December 21, 22

Observed primarily in Plymouth, Massachusetts, and by various New England Societies throughout the country, Forefathers' Day commemorates the landing of the Pilgrims, who arrived in 1620 on the *Mayflower* and established the second English colony in North America. (The first colony successfully established was in Jamestown, Virginia in 1607.) The Old Colony Club of Plymouth was the first group to observe the anniversary in 1769, but since this was only fifteen years after the New Style Calendar went into effect, there was some confusion about how many days should be added to the original December 11 date of the landing. All dates before 1700 were supposed to have ten days added, and all dates after 1700 were supposed to have eleven days added. Somehow a mistake was made, and Old Colony Club members still celebrate Forefathers' Day on December 22. Wearing top hats and led by a drummer, they march down the main street of Plymouth. After firing a small cannon, they return to their Club for breakfast and toasts to the Pilgrims.

Transplanted New Englanders who have formed New England Societies in other parts of the country, however, observe the occasion on December 21, as does the General Society of Mayflower Descendants, which sometimes refers to it as **Compact Day.** The Pilgrim Society, which was founded in 1820 by a group of people interested in the history of Plymouth, holds its annual meeting on December 21 and serves a traditional dinner of succotash, stew, corn, turnips, and beans.

Forest, Festival of the *See* **Kiamichi Owa-Chito**

Forgiveness, Feast of
August 1–2

The **Festa del Perdono** or Feast of Forgiveness is observed annually in Assisi, Italy, where St. Francis built his humble hermitage, known as the *Porciúncola* ('little portion'), in the thirteenth century. It was here, on a small plot of land containing a ruined chapel that St. Francis experienced his religious conversion and began to preach and gather disciples. He restored the chapel and claimed it as his 'portion' or 'little inheritance.' In 1209 he received papal permission to establish the Franciscan monastic order, the Friars Minor, urging his followers to maintain the chapel as a sacred place. *Porciúncula* also refers to the plenary indulgence that used to be given to those who visited this sanctuary on August 2, the date set by Pope Honorius III in 1221. Although in the beginning the indulgence could only be gained in the *Porciúncula*, the privilege was eventually extended to all churches having a connection with the Franciscan order and the time for visiting the sanctuary was extended to the period between the afternoon of August 1 and sunset on August 2.

St. Francis instituted the two-day Feast of Forgiveness because it upset him that by going off to fight in the Crusades a sinful man could escape punishment in purgatory. Believing that there should be a more peaceful means to gain salvation, St. Francis received the Pope's permission for Roman Catholics to make an annual pilgrimage to Assisi to renew their relationship with the church.

The August 2 feast was brought to New Mexico by the early Spanish settlers, and it is still observed in the small town of Arroyo Hondo, about eighty miles north of Santa Fe. Although at one time it involved two processions—one beginning at the village church's main entrance and another, a quarter of a mile away, involving only members of the flagellant brotherhood—today the celebration in Arroyo Hondo that once drew large crowds has nearly died out.

See also FEAST OF ST. FRANCIS OF ASSISI.

Forty Martyrs' Day
March 10

The "Forty Martyrs of Sebaste" were Roman soldiers quartered in Armenia in 320. Agricola, the governor of the province, told them that under orders of the Emperor Licinius, they would have to make a sacrifice to the Roman gods. As Christians, they refused to do so. Agricola told them to strip themselves naked and stand on the ice of a nearby pond. All died from exposure during the night. They are greatly revered in the Eastern Christian Church. This day is observed in the Orthodox church in Syria as **'Id al-Arba'in Shahid**. In Greece, special foods are prepared: cake with forty layers of pastry, stew with forty herbs, forty pancakes, etc. In Romania, little cakes called *sfintisori* 'little mints' are baked and given to and received from every passer-by. *Coliva*, a cake of cooked corn and honey, is also traditional. Farm tools are readied for work, and hearth ashes are spread around the cottage to keep the serpent from entering (each home is said to have a serpent protecting it).

Founder's Day
May 29; April 6

Many organizations and institutions celebrate a Founder's Day. In London, the old soldiers at the Royal Hospital in Chelsea hold a Founder's Day parade on May 29, the birthday of Charles II, the hospital's founder and one of England's most popular monarchs. May 29 is also ROYAL OAK DAY.

In South Africa, Founder's Day honors the founders of the nation. It is observed on April 6, the day on which Jan Van Riebeek first landed at what would come to be known as Cape Town in 1652. It is also called **Van Riebeek Day**.

Four an' Twenty Day
January 18

When England and Scotland switched from the Julian to the Gregorian calendar in 1752, eleven days were dropped to make up for the additional time that had accumulated during the use of the Julian calendar. Four an' Twenty Day (or **Old Twelfth Day**) is a Scottish expression referring to the day on which TWELFTH DAY used to be celebrated before the switch.

Fourth of July *See* **Independence Day**

Fourth of July in Denmark
July 4

The Fourth of July celebration held in Aalborg, Denmark each year since 1912 was started by an American of Danish descent, Dr. Max Henius of Chicago. He bought two hundred acres of land in Rebild and deeded the land to King Christian X, with the stipulation that his fellow Danish-Americans be allowed to celebrate the Fourth of July there every year. The area is now a national park to which about thirty-five thousand people come to observe INDEPENDENCE DAY. A replica of the Liberty Bell is rung, the national anthems of both countries are sung by stars from the Royal Danish Opera, military bands perform, and there are bilingual readings of the Declaration of Independ-

ence and the Gettysburg Address. As a permanent shrine for Americans of Danish ancestry, there is a replica of the log cabin in which Abraham Lincoln lived as a young boy.

Fox Hill Day
Second Tuesday in August

For over a hundred years this day has been celebrated in Nassau, a seaside resort on the island of New Providence in the Bahamas, to mark the abolition of slavery. Most of the events take place at the Fox Hill Parade Ground about five miles from Nassau. Bahamian foods, singing, and dancing contribute to a carnival atmosphere, although there is a thanksgiving service in the local Baptist church in the morning that features gospel and Bahamian religious songs.

Fragrance of the Breeze *See* **Sham al-Nassim**

Frankenmuth Bavarian Festival
Second weekend and third week in June

Religious leaders in Bavaria sent a group of fifteen Franconians to Michigan's Saginaw Valley in 1845 to set up a mission for the Indians. Although the mission eventually moved elsewhere, the settlement known as Frankenmuth, meaning "courage of the Franconians," retained its Bavarian roots and soon attracted other German immigrants. In fact, for many years after the beginning of the twentieth century German remained the community's principal language.

The Frankenmuth Bavarian Festival held in June each year to celebrate the town's German heritage takes advantage of the town's Old-World atmosphere and Bavarian architecture, which includes a glockenspiel tower that plays traditional German melodies, while carved wooden figures depict the legend of the Pied Piper of Hamelin. There is also a replica of the nineteenth-century Holz Brücke, Frankenmuth's covered wooden bridge that spans the Cass River. The festival features a dance tent resembling a German *biergarten* with German dance bands and beverages, as well as farm tours, arts and crafts displays, a parade featuring the festival's Bavarian Princess, and well-known entertainers of German origin.

Frankfurt Book Fair (Buchmesse)
Second week in October

The world's largest annual trade show for the book-publishing industry, held annually for six days in Frankfurt, Germany. It attracts exhibitors from about 90 countries, and is attended by close to 250,000 people, of whom 8,000 to 8,500 are publishers, editors, and exhibitors.

Trade fairs have been a tradition in Frankfurt for at least 800 years, and, in even earlier times, its location on the Main River in the heart of the continent made the community a crossroads of trade. Book fairs were held in Frankfurt in the 16th century, when the city had become the center of German publishing. In 1579, the book fairs came under the supervision of the imperial censorship commission, and gradually the center of publishing shifted to Leipzig. The world wars severely restricted publishing in Europe, but the industry re-emerged after the war. Because Leipzig was in Soviet-controlled East Germany, the publishing trade center moved back to Frankfurt for the first time since about 1650. The book fair had been chiefly an event for German publishers before 1939, but it grew in a few years to be the world's preeminent book fair. In its present international form, the fair is officially dated to 1949.

Freeing the Insects
Late August–early September

There is a festival in Japan on May 28 during which vendors sell insects in tiny bamboo cages. Those who purchase the diminutive pets keep them in or near the house during the summer months so that can hear their songs in the evening. Then, on a day in late August or early September, they gather in public parks and at temples or shrines to set the insects free. When the creatures get their bearings, the former captors listen to them burst into their individual sounds.

The custom of freeing the insects, also known as the **Insect-Hearing Festival**, is more prevalent in rural areas. Although no one seems to know its exact origin, it is reminiscent of Italy's FESTA DEL GRILLO, where crickets are purchased in cages and kept as good luck tokens or harbingers of spring.

French Open (tennis)
May–June

Officially known as the **French Championships**, one of the four major tournaments that make up the Grand Slam of tennis. (The others are the Australian Open, the U.S. Open, and Wimbledon.) The French National Championship, played at the Stade Roland Garros in Auteil, France on red-clay courts, was instituted in 1891 but wasn't opened to players from other nations until 1925. It became an open (to both amateurs and professionals) in 1968.

In 1974, Bjorn Borg of Sweden, eighteen years

old, became the youngest French Open winner. He went on to become a six-time winner—1974, 1975, 1978–81—putting him ahead of the former champion, Henri Cochet, the winner in 1926, 1928, 1930, and 1932. In the women's division, the most-wins champions since 1925 have been American Chris Evert Lloyd (seven wins: 1974, 1975, 1979, 1980, 1983, 1985, and 1986) and Australian Margaret Smith Court (five wins: 1962, 1964, 1969, 1970, and 1973). In 1990, 16-year-old Monica Seles of Yugoslavia took the youngest-champion honors from Borg when she beat German Steffi Graf.

The year 1991 belonged to both the younger and the older athletes. Seles won three Grand Slam titles; she sat out Wimbledon because of shin splints. The excitement in France, though, was for the thirty-nine-year-old American Jimmy Connors, who reached the third round of the open while crowds chanted "Allez Jimbo." Connors was ranked the world's number-one male player for five years, from 1974 through 1978. The winner in 1991 was the twenty-one-year-old American Jim Courier.

Frisbee Festival, National
First weekend in September

The frisbee—a disc made of rigid plastic that soars through the air when thrown with a twisting movement of the wrist—has grown from a child's toy to a national pastime. In 1947 Californians Fred Morrison and Warren Francioni designed and constructed a plastic flying disk which improved upon the pie tins of the Frisbie Pie Company of Bridgeport, CT. (founded 1871) which had been tossed in a game of catch by Yale college students for decades. The name "Frisbee" was copyrighted by the Wham-O Manufacturing Company although it had been in use from the days of pie tins. At the National Frisbee Festival held on the Mall near the National Air and Space Museum in Washington, D.C. each year, enthusiasts come to watch frisbee exhibitions (including a special divison for frisbee-catching dogs) and to attend workshops with over two hundred instructors and world champions. The festival was originally organized by the Smithsonian with the help of Larry Schindel a frisbee champion—the idea being that such a festival would display another aspect of aerodynamics and relate to the exhibits at the Smithsonian Institution's National Air and Space Museum. But now Schindel organizes the festival himself.

One of the festival's goals has been to win a place in the Guinness Book of World Records by achieving "the big throw"—i.e., the largest number of frisbees in the air at once.

See also KITE-FLYING FESTIVAL.

Fritter Thursday
Between February 5 and March 11; day after Ash Wednesday

At one time in England, each day of the week during which LENT began had a special name: COLLOP MONDAY, SHROVE TUESDAY, ASH WEDNESDAY, Fritter Thursday, and KISSING FRIDAY. Fritter Thursday took its name from the custom of eating apple fritters—fruit-filled cakes fried in deep fat—on this day.

Frost Saints' Days
May 11, 12, 13

These three consecutive days in May mark the feasts of St. Mammertus, St. Pancras, and St. Servatus. In the wine-growing districts of France, a severe cold spell occasionally strikes at this time of year, inflicting serious damage on the grapevines. Although scientists claim that the unseasonable frost is caused by air currents blowing off a late breakup of polar ice in the north, French peasants have always believed that it is the result of their having offended one of the three saints, who for this reason are called the "frost saints."

In Germany, too, feelings toward these three saints are mixed, especially among those whose livelihood depends on agriculture. They call them "the three severe lords," and farmers believe that their crops are not safe from frost until May 13 has passed. French peasants have been known to show their displeasure over a cold snap at this time of year by flogging the statues and defacing the pictures of Mammertus, Pancras, and Servatus.

Full Moon Day *See* Magha Puja/Maka Buja

Furry Day
May 8

According to legend, there was a large stone that at one time blocked off the entrance to hell. One night Satan tried to steal the stone. But on his way through Cornwall, England, he was intercepted by the Archangel Michael, who forced him to drop the stone and flee. The town where he dropped it was called Helston (from Hellstone, or stone of hell), and for many years a large block of granite sat in the yard of a tavern there.

The people of Helston continue to celebrate the Archangel's victory, although no one is quite sure why they call this celebration "Furry Day." It may derive from the Gaelic word *fer* meaning "a fair," or from the Latin *feriae*, meaning "festival." Some think it's a corruption of "Flora's Day," a reference to the original Roman goddess of flowers. The day's festivities include the "Furry dance," which is performed in the streets by men in top hats and women in fancy dresses, and a trip to the woods in search of flowers and leaves. The original rock has long since been broken up into building stones and used for local construction.

Fur Trade Days
July

Chadron, Nebraska was at one time a frontier town with a reputation for lawlessness. Shoot-outs in the local saloons were a regular occurrence. But in 1893 a local newspaper came up with a way of putting the town's high spiritedness to better use. They organized the 1,000 Mile Horse Race from Chadron to Chicago—a publicity stunt that made Chadron a household name. Nine men, including one former outlaw, competed in the race. John Berry, the winner, reached Chicago in thirteen days, sixteen hours.

Today Chadron's frontier roots are celebrated in two annual events. Fur Trade Days, which takes place for three days in July, is an attempt to recreate the excitement of the town's active trading days in the mid-1800s. Activities include a buffalo stew cookout, horseshoe pitching and buffalo chip throwing contests, a pig roast, and a primitive rendezvous with a black powder shoot. The other event, which also takes place in mid-July, is the Buckskin Rendezvous, featuring such traditional events as tomahawk-throwing contests and demonstrations of hide tanning, flintlock marksmanship, and various camp activities.

G

Gai Jatra

First day of Nepalese month of Bhadra (August–September)

An eight-day carnival-type festival in Nepal, also known as the **Cow Festival**. It is sponsored by families who had deaths during the year and is intended to help the dead complete a smooth journey to heaven. Cows are believed to ease the journey and open the gates of heaven with their horns; therefore, during the festival, cows decorated with flowers and teenagers dressed as cows process through the streets. Dancing, singing, and performances satirizing the government and society are also part of the celebrations. These diversions stem from a legend that, after the death of a queen's child, the king sent clowns to console the queen.

Gallup Inter-Tribal Indian Ceremonial

Second week in August, Tuesday through Sunday

A major six-day inter-tribal celebration held at Red Rock State Park near Gallup, New Mexico. The ceremonial originated in 1922, and now more than fifty tribes from the United States, Canada, and Mexico participate. Average attendance is 30,000.

The ceremonial activities include competitive dancing, a barbecue, and all-Indian professional rodeos, in which cowboys compete for silver belt-buckle prizes in such events as calf-roping and bronco-riding. There are also three evenings of Indian ceremonial dancing, with the Hoop, Deer, Buffalo, and other dances performed by different tribes.

The markets here present some of the country's finest displays of Indian fine arts—Navajo rugs, kachinas, jewelry, pottery, basketry, beadwork, leatherwork, sculptures, and painting—there are also silversmiths, weavers, and potters at work on their crafts. On Saturday morning, downtown Gallup is the scene of the Ceremonial Parade, with tribal bands playing traditional and contemporary music. It is called the country's only all-Indian non-mechanized parade—all participants are walking, on horseback or in wagons. On Saturday night, a Ceremonial Queen is crowned.

Galungan

Determined by Wuku Calendar

A major ten day religious festival celebrated throughout the Indonesian island-province of Bali. This is a Hindu festival (Indonesia is largely Muslim except for Bali), but the Balinese also have their own supreme being, Sanghyang Widi (or Widhi). This god and all the other gods are thought to come to earth during the festival. Balinese festivals include rituals in the temples, where small thrones are symbolic seats for the gods to occupy; cock-fights, a combination of sport and gambling; offerings of foods, fruit, and flowers to the temple by the women; and card games, music, and dancing.

Numerous temple festivals are held during the year in individual Balinese villages, but Galungan is island-wide. The Wuku Calendar of 210 days is followed for festivals.

Galway Oyster Festival

Early September

In Galway, Ireland the opening of the oyster season is celebrated by bringing the first shellfish ashore to the accompaniment of fiddle music. A young woman chosen to preside over the day's activities as the Queen of Connemara presents the first oyster to the mayor, who stands on Clarenbridge Pier in his scarlet robes waiting to open and taste it. Banquets are held in the evening and local pubs serve oysters by the bucketful, washed down by beer.

Ganden Ngamcho *See* **Lights, Festival of**

113

Gandhi Jayanti (Mahatma Gandhi's Birthday)
October 2

A national holiday in India to commemorate the birth of Mohandas Karamchand Gandhi, who came to be known as Mahatma ('great soul') Gandhi. At this time pilgrimages are made from throughout the country to the Raj Ghat on the banks of the Yamuna River in Delhi where Gandhi was cremated. Many communities also hold spinning and weaving sessions in his honor.

Gandhi, often pictured in a simple white cotton robe at a spinning wheel, was the leader of the movement for Indian nationalism the twentieth century's great prophet of non-violence, and a religious innovator who encouraged a reformed, liberal Hinduism. He was born in 1869 in Porbandar, India and educated both in India and England. He went to South Africa as a young lawyer, was shocked by the racial discrimination, and led the African Indians in a non-violent struggle against repression. Returning to India, he became a dominant political figure, and, in the struggle for independence, was jailed several times. His protests often took the form of fasts.

In the 1930s, he worked for rural people trying to eradicate discrimination against the Untouchable caste and promoting hand spinning and weaving as occupations for the poor and as away to overcome the British monopoly on cloth. The ashram (a religious retreat center) he established near Ahmedabad became the center of his freedom movement. In the 1940s, he helped heal the scars of religious conflict in Bengal and Bihar; in 1947, his fasting put an end to the rioting in Calcutta. On January 30, on his way to an evening prayer meeting in Delhi, he was shot and killed by a Hindu fanatic. Albert Einstein was among his great admirers.

Ganesh Chathurthi
August–September; waxing Bhadrapada

A lively week-long festival to worship the elephant-headed Ganesh, the Hindu god of wisdom and success. He is also, the remover of obstacles, so he is also called Vighnesa, or Vighneswara. The festival is especially colorful in the Indian states of Tamil Nadu, Mahadashtra, Andhra Pradesh, and Karnataka, and is the best-known event of Bombay. Everyone pays homage to huge clay images of Ganesh made by highly respected artists and he is also propitiated with street performances, competitions, processions, and yoga demonstrations. In Bombay, at the end of the week of celebration, as sacred songs are chanted, an image is taken to the sea and immersed to ensure prosperity for both land and water.

Ganesh, the son of the gods Shiva and Parvati, so annoyed his father one day that Shiva cut off his head. But Shiva then repented, and replaced his head with that of an elephant. Today people ask for Ganesh's help in undertaking new projects.

The story behind the festival in Nepal is that the day, called **Ganesh Chata**, celebrates a bitter dispute between Ganesh and the moon goddess. Therefore, the Nepalese try to stay inside on this night and close out the moonlight.

Ganga Dussehra
May–June; Jyaistha

According to Hindu mythology, the Ganges River in India originally flowed only in heaven. In the form of a goddess, Ganga, the river was brought down to earth by King Bhagiratha in order to purify the ashes of his ancestors, sixty thousand of whom had been burned under a curse from the great sage Kapila. The river came down reluctantly, breaking her fall on the head of Shiva so that she wouldn't shatter the Earth. By the time she reached the Bay of Bengal, she had touched the ashes of the sixty thousands princes and fertilized the entire region.

On Ganga Dussehra day in the month of Jyaistha, Hindus who are able to reach the Ganges take a dip in the river to purify their sins and remedy their physical ills. The largest crowds assemble at Hardwar, Garh Muktesvar, Varanasi, and other locations on the banks of the Ganges that have legendary significance. Those who live far away from the Ganges immerse themselves in whatever river, pond, or sea they can get to on this day.

All Hindus hope to bathe in the Ganges at some point during their lives, and when they die, their ashes are immersed in its holy water to assure peace for their souls.

See also KUMBH MELA.

Gang Days *See* Rogation Days

Ganna (Genna)
January 7

The CHRISTMAS celebration in Ethiopia, which is officially called **Leddat**, takes place on January 7 (see OLD CHRISTMAS). But it is more popularly known as Ganna, after the game that is traditionally played by boys, young men, and occasionally elders, only on this day. According to legend, the shepherds were so happy when they heard about the birth of Jesus that they used their hooked staffs to play *ganna*—a game similar to field hockey.

Gansabhauet
November 11 (St. Martin's Day)

An old and peculiar festival involving a dead goose, held only in the country town of Sursee, Switzerland. A dead goose is hung by its neck in front of the town hall, and young men draw lots to take turns trying to knock it down with a blunt saber. (*Gansabhauet* means 'knocking down goose.') The young men, blindfolded and wearing a red robe and a big round mask representing the sun, get only one try at the bird. While the men whack at the goose, children's games take place: they scale a stripped tree, race in sacks, and compete in seeing who can make the ugliest face.

Gansabhauet was first mentioned in 1821. Its real origin is uncertain, although it is thought that it may have something to do with the old practice of handing over payment in kind to the landlord.

Garland Day
May 12; May 29

On May 12 or **Old May Day**, the children of the Dorset fishing village of Abbotsbury still "bring in the May." They do this by carrying garlands from door to door and receiving small gifts in return. The May garlands are woven by a local woman and her helpers, who are regarded as the town's official garland-makers. Each garland is constructed over a frame and supported by a stout broomstick, which is carried by two young people as they go about the village. Later, the garlands are laid at the base of the local War Memorial.

At one time this was an important festival marking the beginning of the fishing season. Garland Day used to center around the blessing of the wreaths, which were then carried down to the water and fastened to the bows of the fishing boats. The fishermen then rowed out to sea after dark and tossed the garlands to the waves with prayers for a safe and plentiful fishing season. This ceremony is probably a carry-over from pagan times, when sacrificial offerings were made to the gods of the sea.

Another Garland Day celebration is held in Castleton, Derbyshire on May 29 or SHICK-SHACK DAY. The Garland King (or May King) rides on horseback at the head of a procession of musicians and young girls, who perform a dance similar to the Helston Furry (see FURRY DAY). The

"garland" is an immense beehive-shaped structure that fits over his head and shoulders, covered with greenery and flowers and crowned with a special bouquet called the "queen." This is laid at the war memorial in Castelton's marketplace.

Gasparilla Pirate Festival
Begins on the Monday following the first Tuesday in February

In early February a 164-foot reproduction pirate ship sails up Florida's Tampa Bay and into the Hillsborough River with its cannons booming. About 500 costumed pirates lower themselves over the side and "capture" the city of Tampa and its mayor, raising the pirate flag over city hall. Thus begins the six-day **Gasparilla Pirate Invasion**, one of the nation's largest and best attended celebrations. The mock invasion is followed by a three-hour victory parade featuring members of a men's club known as Ye Mystic Krewe, who started the pirate festival in 1904.

The festival is named for José Gaspar, an eighteenth century Spanish pirate who terrorized the Florida coast from around 1783 until his death in 1821, when he wrapped a length of anchor chain around his waist and leapt into the sea brandishing his sword rather than be captured by a U. S. Navy warship.

Gawai Dayak
May–June

A harvest festival of the Dayak people of Sarawak, Malaysia, on the northern coast of Borneo, and a public holiday there. The celebrations have remained essentially the same for centuries. They take place in longhouses, the bamboo-and-palm-leaf structures built on stilts that are shared by twenty or thirty families. At midnight on the eve of Gawai Dayak, a house elder or bard conducts the chief ritual: while sacrificing a white cock, he recites a poem to ask for guidance, blessings, and a long life. Other events include the selection of the most beautiful man and woman to be king and queen of the harvest, dancing, a feast of rice, eggs, and vegetables, and the serving of traditional *tuak*, 'rice wine'.

Gedaliah, Fast of (Tsom Gedalyah, Tzom Gedaliahu)
Between September 8 and October 6; 3 Tishri, (first day following Rosh Ha-shanah)

When Nebuchadnezzar, the Babylonian king, destroyed Jerusalem and the First Temple, and carried away most of the Jews into slavery in 586 B.C., he left behind a few farmers and families under the supervision of a Jewish governor named Gedaliah ben Ahikam to clean up after the army and to administer affairs in the devastated land. Eventually some Jews who had managed to hide out in the hills came back to the area and joined the thousand or so who had been left behind.

Things progressed well until a few hot-headed traitors, who accused Gedaliah of collaborating with the enemy, murdered him and the small garrison of soldiers Nebuchadnezzar had stationed there. Many of the farmers took their families and fled in terror to Egypt; the rest were either killed or taken to Babylon, bringing about Judah's final collapse. The Fast of Gedaliah commemorates the man who was assassinated at a time when he was needed most.

Geerewol Celebrations
Rainy season—late June to mid September

Elaborate week long festivities held by the Wodaabe people of Niger as a kind of male beauty contest. The festivities also serve the important purpose of allowing young men and women to meet prospective mates outside their circle of cousins.

There are two main dances to the celebrations, the *yaake* and the *geerewol*. The *yaake* is the dance for demonstrating charm. The men paint their faces with pale yellow powder and borders of black kohl around their eyes; they also shave their hairline to heighten the forehead. They dance in a line, leaning forward on tiptoe to accentuate their height, and contorting their faces with rolling eyes, pursed lips, and inflated cheeks. Their charm and personality is judged based on these expressions. The *geerewol* is held to select the most beautiful men. In this dance the men line up wearing beads on their bare chests and turbans adorned with ostrich feathers on their heads. For a couple of hours they chant and jump and stomp while selected young unmarried women kneel and scrutinize them. These women are the judges; eventually they walk toward the dancers and indicate their favorites by swinging their arms.

The *Geerewol* celebration ends at sunrise after an entire night of dancing when the host group presents the departing guests with roasted meat.

General Clinton Canoe Regatta
May

Originally a recreation of the historic trip down the Susquehanna River by General James Clinton during the Revolutionary War, this well-known canoe regatta now has three divisions, one for pro-

fessionals and two for amateurs, based on the type of canoe used. The professional race, which has gained national recognition as the **World Championship Flat Water Endurance Race**, is the longest one-day race of its kind and covers a seventy-mile stretch of the river between Cooperstown and Bainbridge, New York. When it was first held in 1962, it was a one-day affair, but now the regatta and the events associated with it extend for three-and-a-half days over the MEMORIAL DAY weekend. There are cash prizes, and the event attracts canoeists from Canada, Michigan, Minnesota, and Wisconsin.

In addition to the races, a carnival and many other activities for spectators are held at General Clinton Park. It was, in fact, money raised by the races that enabled the Bainbridge Chamber of Commerce to purchase the riverfront land on which the park now stands.

Genna *See* Ganna

George Washington Birthday Celebration in Alexandria, Virginia
Third Monday in February and weekend preceding

An array of activities in Alexandria, Va., including the nation's largest parade honoring the Father of His Country. Alexandria calls itself Washington's hometown; he kept a townhouse there, was one of the city's original surveyors, organized the Friendship Fire Company, and was a vestryman of Christ Church Parish and Charter Master of Masonic Lodge No. 22. A reminder of the president's association with the Masons is the George Washington Masonic National Memorial, a 333-foot-tall replica of the ancient lighthouse in Alexandria, Egypt.

Celebrations of Washington's birthday have been held in Alexandria since the president's lifetime. The first parade to honor him was in 1798, when he came from his Mt. Vernon home to review the troops in front of Gadsby's Tavern

The present-day festivities get off to an elegant start on Saturday night with a banquet followed by the George Washington Birthnight Ball in Gadsby's Tavern, a duplication of the birthday-eve parties held in Washington's lifetime. People wear eighteenth-century dress, and the banquet toasts to Washington are usually delivered by people who are prominent in current events and who reflect Washington's military background. In 1991, Gen. Colin Powell, chairman of the U.S. Joint Chiefs of Staff proposed the toast. His name and face became widely known during the Persian Gulf War of 1991.

Sunday brings a Revolutionary War enactment and the running of a 10-K road race. On Monday is the big parade. It lasts two hours and usually draws about 75,000 spectators. George and Martha Washington are depicted, along with other colonial personages. The paraders include a number of Scottish bagpipe groups (the city was founded by Scots), Masonic units, equestrian groups, color guards, fife and drum corps, and horse-drawn carriages.

See also Washington's Birthday.

Georgia Day
February 12

Also known as **Oglethorpe Day**, February 12 commemorates the day in 1733 when James Edward Oglethorpe and 120 other Englishmen landed in Savannah, Georgia to establish a new colony. The earliest settlers observed the day by firing salutes and offering toasts in Oglethorpe's honor. For almost two hundred years thereafter, the celebrations were confined to major anniversaries of the event, and it wasn't until 1933 that February 12 became a "special day of observance" in the Georgia schools. In 1965 the anniversary of the state's founding was officially proclaimed Georgia Day and celebrated as a day-long event in Savannah.

Savannah's celebration has now grown into an eight-day event sponsored by more than eighty organizations. On February 12, there is a procession through the historic town, a number of wreath-laying ceremonies, and an Oglethorpe banquet. Since 1966 there has been a reenactment of Oglethorpe's landing, with costumed residents playing the roles of Georgia's first European settlers and of the American Indians who greeted them upon their arrival.

Georgia Peanut Festival
Ten days ending second week in October

A harvest festival paying tribute to Georgia's top crop is held in Sylvester, the Peanut Capital of the World. More peanuts are produced in the region around Sylvester than anywhere else in the state, and Georgia accounts for nearly half the United States peanut production and supplies five percent of the world's total production; furthermore, Georgia's peanuts are a $2.5 billion industry. Thus Sylvester's title of Peanut Capital. In other countries, the end products of peanuts are usually oil and meal; Georgia's harvest is largely

used for salted and roasted peanuts and in peanut butter.

This festival, which comes at the end of the peanut harvest time, began in 1964. Highlights through the years have included an appearance by George Bush in 1979 to kick off his unsuccessful drive for the Republican presidential nomination, and the making of the World's Largest Peanut Butter and Jelly Sandwich in 1987. The sandwich measured twelve and a half feet by twelve and a half feet.

Events of the festival include a beauty pageant to choose a Little Miss Peanut, Junior Miss Peanut, and Georgia Peanut Queen; a peanut-syrup-and-pancakes eating contest; a peanut-recipe contest for school children; concerts; clogging exhibitions; a kiddy parade, and a grand parade (the state's largest commodity parade) with 150 to 200 entries, including floats, horses, antique cars, and people dressed as peanuts.

Geraldine R. Dodge Poetry Festival
September

Since the first **Dodge Poetry Festival** was held in 1986, the biennial gathering has grown into a three-day event that draws upwards of 5,000 people—including television crews—for what has been described as "a grueling but exhilarating marathon of poetry activity." Readings, panel discussions, and talks by some of America's most famous poets have made the restored village of Waterloo in rural southern New Jersey synonymous with the word "poetry" for the students, writers, and interested spectators who flock to the festival, which is sponsored by the Geraldine R. Dodge Foundation. Mrs. Dodge was a local philanthropist.

Many of the events take place outdoors and include music, food, and strolling performers, giving the whole affair the flavor of a bona fide festival rather than the typical writers' conference. Coverage of the Dodge Festival by the award-winning PBS series "The Power of the Word," hosted by Bill Moyers, is thought to have contributed to the festival's broad public appeal.

Geranium Day
Early April

Since the 1920s this has been a day in England to collect money for the blind. It represents a joint effort by a number of charities dedicated to helping the blind and is organized by the Greater London Fund for the Blind. Although at one time real geraniums were given to those who made dona-

117

tions, today contributors receive a sticker with a red geranium on it. The choice of the geranium—a flower without a strong scent—seems unusual as a symbol for the blind, but it may have been chosen simply because the poppy (see POPPY DAY) and the rose (see ALEXANDRA ROSE DAY) were already being used for fund-raising purposes. It may also have been chosen for its symbolic meaning: consolation.

Gettysburg Civil War Heritage Days
Last weekend in June and first week in July

The Battle of Gettysburg on July 1–3, 1863, marked a turning point in the American Civil War. It was here that General Robert E. Lee's Confederate army of 75,000 men and the 97,000-man Northern army of General George G. Meade met by chance when a Confederate brigade sent there for supplies observed a forward column of Meade's cavalry. The ensuing battle did not end the war, nor did it attain any major military goals for either the North or the South. But the Confederate army was turned back, and it never recovered from its losses. With 51,000 casualties and 5,000 dead horses, the Battle of Gettysburg ranks as the bloodiest battle in American history.

Every year since 1983 the anniversary of the battle has been commemorated with a nine-day festival at the Gettysburg National Military Park. Civil War reenactment groups in authentic uniforms, carrying nineteenth-century weapons of the type used in the battle, demonstrate infantry tactics and drill, cavalry drill, and soldiers' occupations and pastimes. There are also band concerts, a Civil War battle reenactment, lectures by nationally known historians, and a Civil War collectors' show featuring antique arms and uniforms, documents, books, photographs, and personal effects from pre-1865 American military history.

Ghanta Karna
July–August; 14th day of waning half of Sravana

This day commemorates the death of Ghanta Karna or 'Bell Ears,' a monster who wore jingling bells in his ears so that he'd never have to hear the name of Vishnu. In Hindu mythology he caused death and destruction wherever he went, until a god in the form of a frog persuaded him to leap into a well, after which the people clubbed him to death and dragged his body to the river for cremation.

Also known as the **Festival of Boys** because young boys play a primary role in the celebration of Ghanta Karna's death, this day is observed in

Nepal by erecting effigies at various crossroads and making passers-by pay a toll. After they've spent the day collecting tolls and preparing for the Ghantakarna funeral, the boys tie up the effigy with a rope and throw it in the river. Sometimes the effigy is set on fire before being thrown in the water. Young girls hang tiny dolls on the effigy of Ghanta Karna to protect themselves from the monster.

Children also sell iron rings on this day and use the money to buy candy. It is believed that those who have iron nails in the lintels of their homes, or are wearing an iron ring will be protected from evil spirits in the coming year.

Ghent Floralies
April or May, every five years (1990, 1995 . . .)

The famous flower festival of Ghent (Gent, Gand), Belgium, held every five years in the Flanders Expo Hall. More than 450 horticulturists from around the world show their best products to be judged for cash prizes. The showing attracts about 700,000 visitors.

Ghent is the center of a thriving horticultural industry, and the *floralies* began in 1809 at the Frascati Inn where fifty plants were arranged around a bust of Napoleon. In 1814, it is believed that John Quincy Adams and other United States delegates visited the flower show; they were staying in Ghent during negotiations preceding the signing of the Treaty of Ghent, which ended the War of 1812.

See also LOCHRISTI BEGONIA FESTIVAL.

Giant Lantern Festival
December 23–24

A highlight of CHRISTMAS in the Philippines. In San Fernando, Pampanga, giant lanterns of colored paper and *capiz* shells, some twelve feet in diameter, are lit and carried in a parade. The event attracts crowds of people from Manila and nearby provinces.

Giants, Festival of the
Fourth Sunday in August

One of Belgium's more distinctive and colorful pageants, held in Ath (Aat) and highlighting the "Marriage of the Giants." The origins of the festival are a little vague, but the giants—Goliath and his bride, strong-man Samson, a warrior named Ambiorix, and several others—are supposed to date from about 1450. A giant horse, Bayard, is a fixture of the procession.

The giants, twenty-foot-tall figures made of

wicker and cloth, are paraded through the streets; men are underneath the figures and see where they're going by by peering out through peepholes. Goliath wears a helmet and breastplate, his bride has orange blossoms in her hair, Samson carries a broken column. After they lumber through the streets, Goliath and his lady are married.

Along with the giants is legendary Bayard. The story is that four brothers, the sons of Aymon, were carried by the mighty steed Bayard as they fled the wrath of Charlemagne. The horse and its riders were tracked to a high cliff above the Meuse River; the horse gave a tremendous leap and carried the riders to safety across the river. The replica of the horse weighs about three-quarters of a ton and is propelled by a dozen men while four boys ride on its back.

Besides the procession, the day is marked by the shooting of muskets, revelry, eating, drinking, and dancing.

Giants, Festival of the (Fête des Géants)
Begins on the Sunday following July 5
The huge figures that are often carried in procession through the streets of France used to be made of wicker supported by a light wooden frame, but their modern counterparts are usually made of plastic.

For three days and nights during the Fête des Géants in Douai, France, the figure of Gayant is carried through the streets to the accompaniment of drums and church bells. About twenty-five feet tall and wearing a military uniform, Gayant is followed by his wife, who is twenty feet high and always dressed in the latest fashion. Then come their three children—Jacquot, Fillion, and the baby, Binbin. The giants leave their home on Rue de Lambres and go to the Town Hall to salute the mayor, after which they continue on to the Place D'Armes and take part in the carnival festivities.

Another famous procession of the giants takes place in the city of Lille on WHIT MONDAY, when more than a hundred of these fabulous creatures are carried through the streets of the town.

Giglio, Festa del *See* Lily Festival

Gilroy Garlic Festival
Third weekend in July
A celebration of garlic in the California town, located in Santa Clara County, that calls itself the Garlic Capital of the World. The claim is made because 90 percent of America's garlic is grown and processed in the area. Humorist Will Rogers once described Gilroy as "the only town in America where you can marinate a steak by hanging it on the clothesline."

The highlight of the festival is Gourmet Alley with seventy-five food booths that use eight tons of garlic in preparing various garlic-flavored dishes, including garlic ice cream,. Other events are a Great Garlic Cook-off and Recipe Contest, arts and crafts exhibits, a Tour de Garlique bicycle race, and a barn dance.

Ginseng Festival
September 5–7
A celebration of ginseng in Fusong, a county in the Changbai Mountains of China and the largest ginseng grower in the country. The twisted roots of the ginseng, an herb, have for centuries been considered a cure for many ills and an aphrodisiac. The people of Fusong have traditionally celebrated the ginseng harvest, and in 1987 the government officially set aside three days for both a festival and a trade fair of ginseng products. The festival features performances of yangko, dragon, and lion dances; story-telling parties with a ginseng theme; art and photo exhibits, and a fireworks display. The trade fair has exhibits not only of ginseng products but also of Chinese medicines and local crafts.

Gion Matsuri (Gion Festival)
July 17
The best known festival in Japan and the biggest in Kyoto. It began in the year 869 when hundreds of people died in an epidemic that swept through Kyoto. The head priest of the Gion Shrine, now called the Yasaka Shrine, mounted sixty-six spears on a portable shrine, took it to the Emperor's garden, and the pestilence ended. In gratitude to the gods, the priest led a procession in the streets. Except for the period of the Onin War (1467–1477), which destroyed the city, the procession has been held ever since.

There are events related to the festival throughout July but the main event is the parade of elaborate, carefully preserved floats on July 17. There are twenty-nine *hoko* 'spears' floats and twenty-two smaller *yama* 'mountains' floats. The immense *hoko* weigh as much as ten tons and can be thirty feet tall; they look like wonderfully ornate towers on wheels. They are decorated with Chinese and Japanese paintings and even with French Gobelin tapestries imported in the seventeenth and eighteenth centuries. Just under their lacquered roofs musicians play flutes and drums. From the rooftops of the floats two men toss straw good-luck favors to the crowds. The *hoko* roll slowly on their big wooden wheels, pulled with ropes by parade participants.

Yama floats weigh only about a ton, and are carried on long poles by teams of men. Life-size dolls on platforms atop each float represent characters in the story the float depicts.

The towns of Hakata (Fukuoka Prefecture), Narita (Chiba Prefecture), and Takayama (Gifu Prefecture) have imitated the Kyoto celebration and now have their own "Gion" festivals.

See also Aoi Matsuri and Jidai Matsuri.

Giorno dei Morti, Il *See* **All Soul's Day**

Girl Scout Day
March 12

The anniversary of the founding of the American Girl Scouts by Juliette Gordon Low (1860–1927) in Savannah, Ga., in 1912. The day is the focal point of Girl Scout Week, which begins on the Sunday before March 12 and is observed by Girl Scout troops nationwide in various ways—with community service projects, anniversary parties, and plays. The eightieth anniversary in 1992 was celebrated with various events, including the kick-off of a national service project on the environment.

Glorious Twelfth, the
August 12, July 12

August 12 is the legal opening of the grouse season in Scotland. If the twelfth falls on a Sunday, **Grouse Day** is the following day. Because grouse-shooting has always played such a central role in the life of the Scottish gentleman, the occasion is referred to as the Glorious Twelfth and is observed as a social event by Scots around the world.

Another day that is sometimes referred to by this epithet is Orange Day, which falls on July 12.

Goddess of Mercy, Birthday of the
Between March and April, 19th day of the 3rd moon; between October and November, 19th day of the 10th moon

A celebration of Kuan Yin, the *Bodhisattva* 'Buddha-to-be' of infinite compassion and mercy. One of the most beloved of Buddhist deities, he or she is accepted not only by Buddhists but also by all Japanese, Chinese, and Koreans. This deity has been depicted as both masculine and feminine

and sometimes as transcending sexual identity (with soft body contours but also a moustache). The *Lotus Sutra,* or scripture, says Avalokitesvara (the deity's Sanskrit name, meaning 'the lord who looks in every direction') is able to assume whatever form is needed to relieve suffering. He/she exemplifies the compassion of the enlightened, and is known in Tibet as *Spyan-ras gzigs* 'with a pitying look'. Kuan Yin, the Chinese name, means 'regarder of sounds,' or of the voices of the suffering. The Japanese word for the deity is pronounced like Kannon.

Women especially celebrate Kuan Yin. In Malaysia, hundreds of devotees bearing joss sticks, fresh fruit, flowers, and sweet cakes gather twice a year at temples dedicated to Kuan Yin in Kuala Lumpur and Penang to pray for her benevolence. (She is feminine there and in China, Korea, and Japan.) At the old temple at Jalan Pitt, Penang, puppet shows are staged in celebration of her. In Hong Kong, Kuan Yin is honored on the nineteenth day of the sixth moon at Pak Sha Wan in Hebe Haven.

See also Sanja Matsuri.

Gold Discovery Days
Five days, including the last weekend in July

This five-day festival celebrates the beauty of the Black Hills and the discovery of gold on July 27, 1874 near the present-day city of Custer, South Dakota. The scientific expedition led by General George Custer confirmed the growing speculation about gold in the area and opened the way for a steady influx of eager prospectors. The festival includes a street fair, hot-air balloon rally, baseball tournament, and musical productions. But the highlight of the event is the Paha Sapa Pageant held on the fourth day (Saturday), which recreates this important era in South Dakota's history.

Part one of the pageant depicts the *Paha Sapa* or sacred land of the Sioux Indians. Part two portrays the lure of gold and the coming of Custer's expedition. In part three the Sioux display their rich cultural heritage by performing ancient ceremonial dances. At the end of the pageant, the entire cast—many of whom have participated since they were children—reappear in special costumes to create a "living flag" of the United States.

Golden Chariot and Battle of the Lumecon, Procession of the
Trinity Sunday (between May 17 and June 20)

An ancient commemoration in Mons, Belgium,

of the delivery of the town from the plague in 1349. In the morning, a golden chariot carrying a reliquary of St. Waudru is drawn by white horses through the city, followed by clerics and girls dressed in brocades and lace. In the afternoon, St. George, mounted on a steed, fights the dragon (the *lumecon*), a terrible-tailed beast called Doudou. The battle represents the triumph of good over evil. Before the fight starts, spectators sing the "Song of the Doudou" while carillons ring. Much boisterous merrymaking and feasting culminates in the evening with a pageant presented by 2,000 actors, musicians, and singers.

See also ST GEORGE'S DAY IN BULGARIA.

Golden Days
Third week in July
A celebration in Fairbanks, Alaska, of the discovery of gold here on July 22, 1902, and the Gold Rush days that followed. This is the largest summertime event in Alaska. Its ten days of activities include "Fairbanks in Bloom," billed as the farthest-north flower show, a Rubber Ducky race, beard and hairy-leg contests, drag races, a golf tournament, concerts, and a grand parade.

There's also a Felix Pedro look-alike contest. Felix Pedrone (remembered as Felix Pedro) was the Italian immigrant who first found gold on a creek near what is now Fairbanks.

Golden Friday *See* Ember Days

Golden Spike Anniversary
May 10
A reenactment of the completion of America's transcontinental railroad on May 10, 1869, at Promontory Summit, Utah held since 1952. It is supposed to be historically accurate, but differs from accounts of the time, which greatly varied because the crowds kept the members of the press from actually seeing the ceremony. Not only this, some reporters wrote their stories days before the event occured.

Today, preliminary events start at 10 A.M., and at 12:30 P.M. two trains, the Central Pacific's "Jupiter" and Union Pacific's "119" (reproductions of the original locomotives that were present in 1869), steam from opposite directions on the track and meet at the site of the ceremony where men in period dress speak. Then the Golden Spike and three other spikes are tapped into a special railroad tie; at 12:47 an ordinary iron "last spike" is driven into the last tie to connect the railroads

and the message "D-O-N-E" is sent by ham radio to the California State Railway Museum in Sacramento. Originally the message "D-O-N-E" was telegraphed (along lines strung beside the railroad) to San Francisco and Philadelphia. There is then much noise of train whistles, bands playing, and people shouting and hurrahing. A second reenactment is performed at 2 P.M.

There were four ceremonial spikes at the original ceremony. One was the famous Golden Spike; it was engraved on the top, "The Last Spike," and on one side, "May God continue the unity of our Country as the Railroad unites the two great Oceans of the World." That spike was made by San Franciso jewelers from $350 worth of gold supplied by David Hewes, a contractor friend of Central Pacific President Leland Stanford.

The other spikes were a second gold spike, not engraved, a silver spike from Nevada, and an iron spike from Arizona that was clad in silver and topped with gold.

There was also a polished laurel-wood tie for the ceremonial last tie. Four holes had been augured in it, and the ceremonial spikes were tapped into the holes. (Nobody tried to drive a soft gold spike into a hardwood tie.) The engraved Golden Spike and the silver spike are in the possession of Stanford University, and the iron spike from Arizona belongs to the Smithsonian Institution. The second gold spike and the hardwood tie have been lost, probably during the San Francisco Earthquake of 1906. The spikes used in the reenactments are replicas.

The building of the transcontinental railroad was a prodigious feat. It was started in 1863, with the Central Pacific working eastward from Sacramento and the Union Pacific laying tracks westward from Omaha. The Central Pacific crews faced the rugged Sierras almost immediately, and also had to have every rail, spike, and locomotive shipped around Cape Horn. Union Pacific had easier terrain, but its crews were harassed by Indians. The Union Pacific crews were Irish, German, and Italian immigrants, Civil War veterans, and ex-slaves. California's labor pool had been drained by the gold rush, so the railroad imported 10,000 Chinese who became the backbone of the labor force.

Golondrinas, Fiesta de las *See* Swallows of San Juan Capistrano

121

Good Friday

Between March 20 and April 23; Friday before Easter

There are several theories as to why the day commemorating Jesus' crucifixion is called "Good" Friday. Some scholars think it's a corruption of "God's Friday," while others interpret "good" in the sense of "observed as holy," or to signify that the act of the Crucifixion is central to the Christian view of salvation. It is called **Great Friday** by Orthodox Christians, but it's not surprising that the Friday before EASTER is sometimes referred to as **Black Friday** or **Sorrowful Friday.**

This day has been in the Christian calendar even longer than Easter. And although it was neglected for a long time by Protestant churches, Good Friday has again come into almost universal observance by Christians. From noon to three o'clock many western Christian churches in the U.S. hold the *Tre Ore* 'Three Hours', (from Italian, referring to the last three hours Jesus hung on the cross), a service based on the last seven things Jesus said on the cross. Many churches also observe the day by re-enacting the procession to the cross as in the ritual of the Stations of the Cross.

In every Orthodox church, the *Epitaphios*, a gold-embroidered pall representing the body of Christ, is laid on a special platform, which is smothered in flowers. During the evening service, the platform is carried out of the church in a procession. The faithful follow, carrying lighted candles and chanting hymns. At squares and crossroads, the procession stops for a prayer by the priest.

Long Friday is another name for Good Friday. In Norway, this day is called **Langfredag**; in Finland, **Pitkäperjantai** or Long Friday because it was a day of suffering for Christ.

See also PLEUREUSES.

Goombay Summer Festival *See* **Jonkonu Festival**

Goschenhoppen Historians' Folk Festival

Second Friday and Saturday of August

The Goschenhoppen region of Pennsylvania, in what is now Montgomery County, was settled in the early eighteenth century by Mennonite, Schwenkfeddian, Lutheran, Reformed, and Catholic farmers and artisans, most of whom were Dutch or German immigrants. It remains one of the oldest and most "authentic" Pennsylvania German communities in America. The Goschenhoppen Historians, a group founded in 1964 to study and preserve the culture of the Pennsylvania Dutch and related groups, hold an annual Folk Festival at the Goschenhoppen Park in East Greenville every summer to educate the public about life in this area during the eighteenth and nineteenth centuries and to preserve the traditional skills of the Pennsylvania Dutch and German people.

Since 1967, when the first Folk Festival was held, the Historians have made every effort to keep the festival as educational and as non-commercial as possible. One of the most interesting aspects is the participation of schoolchildren, who are recruited as apprentices or helpers for the craft demonstrators at the festival. By actively participating in the demonstrations, these young people learn traditional skills that might otherwise die out. These include: blacksmithing, fish net making, pewtering, gunsmithing, chair caning, rope making, weaving, and thatch and tile roofing.

See also KUTZTOWN FAIR.

Grandfather Mountain Highland Games and Gathering of Scottish Clans

Second full weekend in July

This largest and best-known Scottish event in America, held since 1956 on Grandfather Mountain near Linville, N.C., opens with a torchlight ceremony. On Friday there's a piping concert, followed by a *ceilidh*, or concert of Scottish folk music, followed by a Scottish country dance gala. On Saturday competitions are held throughout the day for Highland dancing, piping, drumming, Scottish fiddling, track and field events, and other athletic events including tugs-of-war. Entertainment includes sheep-herding demonstrations and performances by pipe bands and Scottish performing artists. Another *ceilidh* and the Tartan Ball round out the day. Sunday opens with a worship service. Then more competitions and entertainment including the colorful Parade of Tartans.

Grand National

Last Saturday in March or first Saturday in April

The world-famous steeplechase, run at the Aintree race course in Liverpool, England. It was started in 1839 by William Lynn, owner of the Waterloo Hotel in Liverpool, as a means of attracting hotel patrons. The first races were at Maghull just outside Liverpool, but the course was moved to Aintree in 1864 and remained unchanged until 1961 when a railing was erected to keep spectators off the course. The next change was in 1990 when the slope at the infamously hazardous Becher's Brook jump was modified because so many horses had been killed there.

The course is 4-1/2 miles and has sixteen bush fences, of which fourteen are jumped twice. The fences average 5'-3" high, and a horse can brush through about ten inches of them. All have ditches either on the take-off or landing side. The race is limited now to forty starters, and usually there is a full field. Of the starters, rarely do as many as half finish, and sometimes only as few as three or four. Horses have to qualify by winning three other set races in England, although any horse that wins the Maryland Hunt Cup is automatically eligible to run.

Probably the greatest horse to run the Grand National was Red Rum, a big, strong horse that won in 1973, 1974, and 1977. In 1973, Red Rum set a record for the fastest time—9 minutes, 1.90 seconds—that still stood in 1991.

The race became widely known to the general public with the 1944 movie *National Velvet* based on the 1935 bestseller by Enid Bagnold. It starred Mickey Rooney, playing an ex-jockey, and Elizabeth Taylor as Velvet Brown, the girl who trains "The Pi" for the Grand National steeplechase. When the jockey scheduled to ride proves unsuitable, Velvet cuts her hair and rides to victory herself, but is disqualified when it's discovered she's a girl. Only men could ride originally, but today women are eligible.

Grandparents' Day
First Sunday after Labor Day

Grandparents' Day is a far more recent invention than MOTHER'S DAY or FATHER'S DAY. It was fostered by Marion McQuade, and established by President Richard M. Nixon's proclamation on September 6, 1979. It is observed throughout the United States on the first Sunday after LABOR DAY, except in Massachusetts, where it is observed on the first Sunday in October.

There are a number of ways in which grandparents can be honored and their Day celebrated. One is to invite real or 'adopted' grandparents to school for the day, where they participate in their grandchildren's classes or special assembly programs. Gift-giving is not as widespread on this day as it is on Mother's Day or Father's Day.

See also BABIN DEN.

Grant's Bluegrass Festival
Early August

The oldest and largest bluegrass festival west of the Mississippi, held for five days near Hugo, Okla. The festival began in 1969, organized by Bill Grant as an extension of jam sessions in his home. Attendance the first year was less than 1,000; now more than 20,000 show up. There are band and instrument contests for all ages, non-stop entertainment from 10 A.M. until midnight each day, and jam sessions at all hours.

Grant Wood Art Festival
Second Sunday in June

American artist Grant Wood (1892–1942) is best known for his painting, "American Gothic," of a dour-looking farmer holding a pitchfork as he stands with his daughter in front of their nineteenth century Gothic revival farmhouse. The annual Grant Wood Art Festival in Stone City-Anamosa, Iowa celebrates the area's heritage as "Grant Wood Country" with juried art exhibits, children's and adults' "Art Happenings," dramatic and musical presentations, and guided bus tours of Stone City.

Born in Anamosa, Wood traveled to Europe several times, where he was exposed to Flemish and German primitive art. But he eventually returned to Iowa to paint the scenes he knew best in the clean-cut, realistic style for which he became famous. He established an art colony in the Stone City valley in 1932–33, and replicas of the colorful ice wagons used as housing by the students and instructors serve as a backdrop for the exhibits of contemporary artists during the festival.

The original "American Gothic"—one of the most widely parodied paintings in the world—is on display at the Chicago Art Institute.

Grape Festival
Labor Day weekend

The highlight of the Grape Festival held each year in Nauvoo, Illinois is the historical pageant known as **The Wedding of the Wine and Cheese**. It tells the story of a young French boy who left his unfinished lunch in a limestone cave to keep it cool and then forgot to pick it up. He returned months later and discovered that the bread had grown moldy and spread through the cheese, creating the first blue-veined Roquefort cheese. In the pageant there is a marriage ceremony celebrating the union of cheese and wine in which a magistrate reads the marriage contract, places it between the wine (carried by the bride) and the cheese (carried by the groom), and circles all three with a wooden hoop symbolizing the wedding ring. The festival also includes parades, a grape stomp, and historical tours.

In the late 1840s Nauvoo was occupied by French and German Icarians, members of a socialist sect whose creed was "From each according to his ability and to each according to his need." It was the Icarians who brought wine-making to the area, and several of their original wine cellars are still used to make the blue cheese that this festival has celebrated for over fifty years. A similar festival is held in Roquefort, France.

Grasmere Sports
Third Thursday in August
This annual event in England's Lake District began in the 1800s to encourage Cumberland and Westmorland wrestling, but it has since expanded to include other traditional lake district sports. The wrestling competitors stand chest to chest and lock arms behind each other's back. The aim of this subtle form of combat is to throw the opponent to the ground—a goal that many wrestlers struggle all day to achieve while other events are going on elsewhere. Fell running (a *fell* is a highland plateau), another traditional sport, is an all-out race to the top of the nearest mountain and back. Hound trailing, which reflects the Lake District's importance as a center for fox hunting, is done on foot with packs of hounds who run across the fells after their prey. Up until 1974, when Cumberland and Westmorland were combined to form Cumbria County, competition between the two rival counties had been fierce.

Great American Brass Band Festival
Mid–June
A weekend recreation of the golden age of brass bands in America, held at Centre College in Danville, Ky. About a dozen bands from throughout the country and Canada play Sousa march music, ragtime, and jazz in the New Orleans funeral-march style. A highlight is a band playing over-the-shoulder instruments of the Civil-War period; the music blew to the rear of the band so it could be heard by the troops marching behind. The festival begins with a hot-air balloon race, and music then continues through the weekend.

Great American Duck Race
Fourth weekend in August
A uniquely American event started in 1979 in Deming, N.M. just to make a little whoopee. Up to eighty live ducks race for cash prizes in an eight-lane chute. There are races which include politi-

cians' heats and a media heat. Other events in the week preceding the duck races are a parade, a gun and knife show, dances, a Mexican rodeo, an arts and crafts exhibit, an outhouse race, a tortilla toss, a pageant of people dressed like ducks, and a duck contest in which ducks are dressed like people. Race participants come from several states; spectators now number about 20,000, almost double the population of Deming.

Great American Smokeout
Third Thursday in November
It was the *Surgeon General's Report on Smoking and Health* that first gave impetus to grassroots efforts to discourage the smoking of cigarettes. As far back as 1971, the town of Randolph, Massachusetts had asked its residents to give up tobacco for a day. In 1974 the editor of the *Monticello Times* in Minnesota led the first mass movement by smokers to give up cigarettes, calling it "D-Day" for "Don't Smoke." The idea spread quickly throughout Minnesota and skipped west to California in 1977, where it became known as the Great American Smokeout. The following year it was observed nationwide for the first time, under the sponsorship of the American Cancer Society.

The Smokeout focuses attention not only on cigarette smokers but, more recently, on smokeless tobacco users as well. Activities are generally light-hearted-rallies, parades, obstacle courses, contests, skits, parties, etc.—and designed to keep smokers away from their cigarettes for an entire day, in the hope that they will continue the effort on their own. The Cancer Society encourages nonsmokers to "adopt" smokers on this day and support them as they go through withdrawal from nicotine—a drug that is said to be as addictive as heroin. Schools are particularly active in observing the Smokeout, teaching young people that the easiest way to avoid the health problems associated with smoking is never to start. Businesses, hospitals, and other organizations also sponsor programs and activities designed to increase public awareness of the hazards to which both smokers and those who breathe their smoke are exposed—particularly lung cancer.

In 1990, an estimated 7.4 million people quit for the day, and 4.9 million were still not smoking three days later.

Great Fifteenth, the
15th day of first lunar month
The Great Fifteenth marks the end of the New Year holiday season in Korea and is considered the last opportunity to ensure good luck for the

coming year. The number nine is considered lucky on this day, and people routinely repeat their actions nine times—particularly children, who compete with each other to see how many "lucky nines" they can achieve before the day is over.

It is common to celebrate the Great Fifteenth with kite flying and kite fighting, which is done by covering the strings with glass dust and then crossing them so that they rub together as they fly. The string held by the more skillfully maneuvered kite eventually cuts through the string of the less successful kite, sending it crashing to the ground.

Another popular sport on this day is the tug-of-war. In some areas, an entire town or county is divided into two opposing teams. It is widely believed that the winning side will have a good harvest and will have protection from disease in the coming year.

Great Friday *See* **Good Friday**

Great Lapp Winter Fair
Four days in February
The Lapps or Samis are a nomadic people of ancient origin who still make their living keeping reindeer herds in the northernmost regions of Norway, Sweden, and Finland, and on the Kola Peninsula of the Soviet Union. They started holding the **Great Sami Winter Fair** in Jokkmokk, Lapland more than a hundred years ago, and have continued to hold it in February because this is the time of year when they bring their reindeer to this area. The four-day event draws many visitors who are curious about the Sami culture. It includes the marking of the reindeer, reindeer roundup demonstrations, and the sale of special Sami foods and handicrafts.

Great Locomotive Chase Festival
First weekend in October
A three-day celebration in Adairsville, Ga., to commemorate the storied Civil War locomotive chase that led to the execution of six Union soldiers by the Confederates.

The chase came on April 12, 1862, after the Yankee spy, James J. Andrews, stole the Confederate engine named "The General," along with three boxcars and the tender. His plan was to burn the rail bridges between Atlanta, and Chattanoonga, in order to cut Confederate supply lines. Andrews swiped the locomotive at Big Shanty (Kennesaw), Georgia and roared off, stopping to cut telegraph wires and tear up tracks. In due time

W. A. Fuller, conductor of "The General", who had been having breakfast when his train was stolen, realized something was missing and set off in a handcar with Anthony Murphy. In Adairsville, they boarded the locomotive "Texas," and barreled after "The General" and Andrews, who was trying to reach the bridge at Resaca, to burn it. The drivers of "The General" kept throwing things on the track to derail the "Texas", but the "Texas" kept in pursuit. Finally, the Yankee raiders were out of fuel and had nothing left to throw on the track; arriving in Ringgold, Andrews ordered his men to jump and run. They did, but all were apprehended. Andrews and six others were tried and hanged; others were taken as prisoners until being exchanged, and later they received medals from the Union army. The Confederates won the accolades of the Army of the Confederacy. In 1927, Buster Keaton made the movie, *The General*, based on the chase, and in 1956, a Disney movie, *The Great Locomotive Chase*, later retitled *Andrews' Raiders*, retold the old story.

Events of the festival include showings of the locomotive-chase movies, a grand parade, beauty pageants, fireworks, and gospel singing. There are also such contests as three-legged races, a marshmallow-spitting contest, a bean-bag toss, a balloon toss, and a tug of war. Attendance is estimated at more than 10,000.

Great Monterey Squid Festival
Memorial Day weekend
A two-day celebration of the squid industry in Monterey, Calif. The main attraction is squid prepared in every imaginable way: fried, broiled, sauteed, marinated, barbecued; Siciliano-, Cajun-, or Greek-style; as (or in) ceviche, fajitas, pizza, chowder, and empanadas. There are also numerous exhibits, films, and demonstrations to let spectators learn more than they ever wanted to know about the lives of squid, and how they are caught and prepared for eating. Squid balloons (they have lots of trailing legs) are sold, and entertainment includes music, clowns and mimes, and crafts exhibits.

Monterey is the home of Cannery Row, made famous in John Steinbeck's novel of that name, and of the Monterey Bay Aquarium, one of the largest aquariums in the world.

Great Saturday *See* **Holy Saturday**

Great Schooner Race
Friday following July 4
The Great Schooner race is part of a four-day

festival in Rockland and Thomaston, Maine known as **Schooner Days**. Held since 1977, the race features schooners from the Maine Windjammer Association and a number of other large sailing ships—usually twenty-five to thirty in all. The race begins at Isleboro Island and ends in Rockland, where the boats parade through Penobscot Bay. On land, there are arts and crafts exhibits, entertainment by musicians and storytellers, children's activities and a harbor fireworks display. Visitors can sample a variety of seafood or take a harbor cruise.

Great Spring Festival of the Toshogu Shrine *See* **Toshogu Haru-No-Taisai**

Great Sunday *See* **Palm Sunday**

Great Thursday *See* **Maundy Thursday**

Greek Independence Day (Greece)
March 25

A national holiday in Greece to celebrate the anniversary of the country's proclamation of independence in 1821 after four centuries of Turkish occupation. The war that followed went on until 1829 when finally the Turkish sultan recognized the independence of Greece. The day is marked with church services and military parades—an especially impressive parade is held in Athens. Greek communities in other parts of the world also observe the day. In New York City, Greek Independence is celebrated on the Sunday nearest to March 25th, with a parade up Fifth Avenue.

Green River Rendezvous
Second Sunday in July

A reenactment in Pinedale, Wyo., of the days when mountain men, Indians, and traders came together to transact business, trade, drink, holler, and celebrate. The first rendezvous (gathering) of trappers was held on the Green River, near the present Wyoming-Utah border. After trading posts were established, the rendezvous became less important. The last of these colorful gatherings was held in 1840. A two-hour pageant recreating these rendezvous has been presented by the Sublette County Historical Society since 1936. Celebrations are held over three days, and other events include black-powder shoots and barbecues.

The trappers, traders and explorers who came to be known as mountain men were a distinctive breed who numbered in their ranks the legendary Jim Bridger, the scout and Indian agent Kit Carson, and William Sublette, who established the area's first trading post. They were satisfying the demand for fur and especially for beaver; the beaver hat was supreme in the world of fashion at the start of the nineteenth century. Besides trapping beaver, they also planted the American claim to much of the territory of the American West. For most of the year, they trapped on the tributaries of the Green River, but for several weeks each summer when there was no beaver trapping, they came out of the wilderness and met at a rendezvous site. Trade goods—blankets, coffee, sugar, gunpowder, and cheap whisky—were brought from Missouri by pack animals and trade wagons, and the trappers brought their beaver skins. It was a time of more than trading: on one occasion Jim Bridger rode around in a suit of armor that had been brought to him from Scotland. The rendezvous brought together a concentration of explorers and frontiersmen, and provided a stepping stone for the settlers who followed. The rendezvous and the era of the mountain men came to an end in the 1840s when the whims of fashion shifted from beaver hats to silk hats, and the race for beaver furs was over.

See also MOUNTAIN MAN RENDEZVOUS.

Green Teej *See* **Teej**

Green Thursday *See* **Maundy Thursday**

Grey Cup Day
Mid–November

The best teams from the Eastern and Western Conferences of the Canadian Football League play against each other in an annual event similar to the SUPER BOWL in the United States. It is called Grey Cup Day after the trophy that is awarded to the winning team—a cup donated by former Canadian Governor-General Earl Grey in 1909.

Parties are held throughout the country so that fans can get together to watch the big game on television. In sports and social clubs, it is not uncommon to set up two televisions so that rival supporters can each watch their own team. Like its American counterpart, the Super Bowl, the Grey Cup is an occasion for widespread drinking and rowdiness.

Grillo, Festa del
Between April 30 and June 3; forty days after Easter

In most European countries, ASCENSION DAY is a holiday when families go to the country to have picnics or just to spend the day outdoors. On Ascension Day in Florence, Italy crowds gather in the Cascine—a public park along the banks of the Arno—to celebrate the Festa del Grillo or **Cricket Festival**, the chirping cricket being a traditional symbol of spring. Food stalls are set up in the park and there are balloons and other souvenirs for sale.

Although people used to catch their own crickets, today they can buy them in brightly painted wood, wicker, or wire cages, where they are kept with a large lettuce leaf to sustain them. The children carry their crickets through the park and later hang the cages outside their windows. If the *grillo* sings to them, it means they'll have good luck.

Groppenfasnacht (Fish Carnival)

Between March 1 and April 4; Laetare Sunday (three weeks before Easter), every three years (1988, 1991 . . .)

A Lenten celebration in the village of Ermatingen, Switzerland that takes its name from the *Gropp*, a fish a few inches long caught only in the Ermatingen area. The event dates to the time when fishermen celebrated the breaking up of the ice in the spring because they could return to catching fish. Every three years a committee of villagers organizes a procession in which children dress as frogs and dwarfs and follow a float that carries a huge *Gropp*, while men march along carrying antique fishing implements. Smaller versions of the procession are held during the intervening years.

Grotto Day

August 5; July 25

In England during the late eighteenth and early nineteenth centuries, oysters were not considered the rare delicacy they are today and were, in fact, one of the common staples of fishermen's diets. The large number of oysters eaten at that time meant there were lots of shells around. On St. James's Day, which was observed on August 5 before the Gregorian or New Style Calendar came into use and on July 25 after, children used the shells to construct small decorative grottoes. Perhaps these were to represent the shrine of St. James in Spain. Sometimes the children begged for pennies as a reward for their efforts. Most of this grotto-building took place in London, and the custom continued right up to the 1950s. St. James the Great was one of the Apostles and brother to St. John the Evangelist, and the scallop shell was his emblem.

Groundhog Day

February 2

There was a medieval superstition that all hibernating animals—not just groundhogs—came out of their caves and dens on CANDLEMAS to check on the weather. If they could see their shadows, it meant that winter would go on for another six weeks and they could go back to sleep. A cloudy day meant that spring was just around the corner. It was the early German settlers known as the Pennsylvania Dutch who attached this superstition to the groundhog. In Germany it was the badger, and in England, France, and Canada it was the bear who was believed to make similar predictions about the weather.

The most famous forecaster in the United States is Punxsutawney Phil, a legendary groundhog in north-central Pennsylvania believed to be nearly a century old. There is a club whose members trek up to Phil's burrow on February 2 and get the news directly from him. Unfortunately, weather researchers have determined that over the years the groundhog has been correct only 28 percent of the time.

Gualterianas, Festas

Four days, beginning on the first Sunday in August

The **Festivals of St. Walter** take place in Guimarïes, the twelfth-century capital of Portugal. The celebrations, which date back to 1452, include magnificent processions, fireworks, animal fairs, and displays of food and merchandise; music, ranging from brass bands to modern jazz, can be heard all over the town.

St. Walter (or São Gualter), the town's patron, is represented by an image of a young Franciscan monk who stands in the nave of Senhor dos Passos (Our Lord of the Way of the Cross), the blue-and-white-tiled church that overlooks the town's public garden. During a Sunday night procession known as the *Procissão Gualteriana*, the image of the saint is carried from the church through the decorated streets of Guimarães while thousands of spectators gather to watch. The procession is followed by a night of fireworks, folk dancing in regional costume, and great activity at the shooting galleries and side shows that line the streets. The festival culminates on Wednesday with the *Marcha Gualteriana*, a midnight procession of twelve allegorical floats.

Guardian Angel, Festival of the *See* Schutzengelfest

Guavaween
Last Saturday of October

A parade and block party with a Latin flavor in Ybor City, a two-square-mile area in Tampa, Fla. Ybor City grew around the cigar factory established in 1886 by Cuban Vicente Martínez Ybor. From the steps of the factory, José Martí, sometimes called the George Washington of Cuba, exhorted the cigar workers to take up arms against Spain. The area still has a Latin flavor, and *Guavaween* is an event to celebrate the culture and have a good time. The parade, with twenty to fifty bands, is led by a woman portraying the mythical "Mama Guava" doing the "Mama Guava Stumble." Many paraders wear costumes lampooning national figures. After the early-evening parade, there is partying until the wee hours. Attendance is about 150,000.

Guelaguetza, La
Third and fourth Monday of July

Also known as **Los Lunes del Cerro** or **Mondays of the Hill**, this huge dance festival is held in Oaxaca, Mexico on the last two Mondays of July. Costumed dancers from different *oaxaquena* tribes perform in a hilltop arena built exclusively for this event. Seats for the nationally televised festival are expensive, and many of the visiting dance groups must stay in local missions. Although the event is geared mostly to tourists, it represents a unique opportunity to see regional dances from all the Mexican states.

Gunpowder Plot Day *See* Guy Fawkes Day

Gustavus Adolphus Day (Gustaf Adolfsdagen)
November 6

Gustavus Adolphus was the king of Sweden (1611–1632) who laid the foundations of the modern Swedish state and turned the country into a major European power. By resolving the long-standing constitutional struggle between the crown and the aristocracy, he was able to achieve sweeping reforms in the fields of administrative organization, economic development, and particularly education. Among other things, he created the *Gymnasia* in 1620, which provided for secondary education in Sweden, and gave the University of Uppsala the financial support it needed to flourish.

King Gustav II was killed during the Thirty Years' War while leading a cavalry charge at the Battle of Lützen on November 6, 1632, turning a tactical victory into a national tragedy for the Swedes. The anniversary of his death is observed throughout Sweden with patriotic demonstrations—particularly in Skansen, Stockholm's outdoor museum. Enormous bonfires are built on Reindeer Mountain and processions of students carry lighted torches through the museum grounds.

Gutzon Borglum Day
August 10

On this day in 1927, sculptor John Gutzon de la Mothe Borglum, began carving the faces of four American presidents out of Mount Rushmore in the Black Hills of South Dakota. He chose this site because of its smooth-grained granite and the way it dominated the surrounding terrain. It took fourteen years to bring the mountain sculpture to its present appearance, but because of delays caused by lack of funds and bad weather, only six-and-a-half years were actually spent in carving. Gutzon Borglum died before the national memorial could be completed, but his son Lincoln continued to work on the project until funds ran out in 1941. Since that time no additional carving has been done, nor is any further work planned other than maintenance of the memorial.

The four presidents whose faces emerge from the granite cliffs were chosen as symbols of the birth and growth of the United States during its first 150 years. George Washington signifies the struggle for independence and the birth of the republic, Thomas Jefferson the idea of representative government, Abraham Lincoln the permanent union of the States and equality for all citizens, and Theodore Roosevelt the twentieth-century role of the U. S. in world affairs.

August 10 is observed at Mount Rushmore each year with patriotic music and speeches. The fiftieth anniversary celebration in 1991 included a formal dedication of the monument and a summer-long extravaganza featuring appearances by former presidents, television personalities, and famous South Dakotans.

Guy Fawkes Day
November 5

On the night of November 4, 1605, thirty-six barrels of gunpowder were discovered in a cellar beneath the Houses of Parliament in London. The conspirators of the so-called Gunpowder Plot, who planned to blow up King James I and his government to avenge their laws against Roman Catholics, were discovered and arrested, and on January 31 eight of them were beheaded. While

Guy Fawkes didn't originate the plan, he was caught red-handed after someone tipped off the king's ministers. And he was among those whose heads were displayed on pikes at London Bridge.

The following year, Parliament established November 5 as a national day of thanksgiving. Children still make effigies of Guy Fawkes and ask passers-by for money ("Penny for the guy") which they spend on fireworks. The effigies are burned in bonfires that night, and fireworks traditionally fill the skies over Britain in remembrance of the failure of the Gunpowder Plot.

Gynaecocratia
January 8

The Greek title of this observance is a word that means female rule or government. This stab at feminist revolt is of long tradition in northern Greece where it is common for women to do all the household work and for most men to take life easy in cafes. Today in the villages of Komotini, Xanthi, Kilkis, and Serres, that standard is reversed for a day when Gynaecocratia is celebrated. The women gather in village cafes to socialize, while the men stay at home cleaning house, tending the babies, and generally looking after household tasks. At dusk, the men join their wives in celebrations.

H

Haghoghy Ortnootyoon *See* **Blessing of the Grapes**

Hagodol
Between end of March and Mid–April; the Sabbath before Passover

The Sabbath just before PASSOVER is called Hagodol. It commemorates the Sabbath that preceded the escape from Egypt, of which Passover is the memorial. As recorded in the Old Testament book of Exodus, each Jewish family had been ordered by Moses to set aside a lamb to be sacrificed—an order which they carried out with considerable fear, because the lamb was held sacred by the Egyptians. As the Egyptians were preparing to punish this sacrilege, God destroyed every first-born among the Egyptians, including humans and animals. In the subsequent confusion, the Jews were able to make their famous exodus, ending more than four hundred years of slavery. The day on which the miracle occurred that made their escape possible is also called the **Great Sabbath**, or the **Day of Deliverance**.

Haile Selassie's Coronation Day
On or near November 15

The Rastafarians (or Ras Tafarians), members of a politico-religious movement among the black population of Jamaica, worship Haile Selassie I, 'Might of the Trinity,' original name Makonnen Tafari (1892–1975), the former emperor of Ethiopia, under the name Ras (Duke) Tafari. Rastafarians consider the Ethiopian emperor the Messiah and son of God, and the champion of their race. Their beliefs, which combine political militancy and religious mysticism, include taboos on funerals, second-hand clothing, physical contact with whites, the eating of pork, and all magic and witchcraft.

The Rastafarians' most important celebration is the anniversary of Haile Selassie's Coronation Day, which occurred on November 2, 1930. The dedication of babies to Ras Tafari, recitations, and singing are typically part of the celebrations on this day.

Hajj *See* **Pilgrimage to Mecca**

Hakata Dontaku
May 3–4

The largest festival in Japan held in Fukuoka City (Fukuoka Perfecture) during Golden Week, the first week in May. This festival attracts more than two million spectators every year because Golden Week is a national holiday encompassing CHILDREN'S DAY and INDEPENDENCE DAY.

The festival originated in the Muromachi Period (1333–1568) as a procession of the merchants of Hakata, an old section of Fukuoka City, paying their new year visit to the *daimyo*, or feudal lord. The name of the holiday curiously is thought to have derived from the Dutch word *Zondag*, meaning 'Sunday,' which was broadened to mean 'holiday,' and corrupted into *Dontaku*.

The festival highlight is a three-hour parade with legendary gods on horseback, floats, and musicians playing samisens (a three-stringed instrument similar to a guitar), flutes, and drums.

Half Moon Bay Art and Pumpkin Festival
Weekend after Columbus Day

A festival highlighted by a Great Pumpkin Weigh-Off, held since 1971 in Half Moon Bay, Calif. The weigh-off winner gets $2,500; the recipient in 1991 was Cindi Glasier of Denver, Colo., whose pumpkin was a hefty 602 pounds. Other festival features are a Great Pumpkin Parade, arts and crafts, food concessions selling pumpkin bread, pumpkin crepes, pumpkin ice cream, and pumpkin strudel, and entertainment that includes live music, puppet shows, magicians, jugglers, clowns, and professional pumpkin carvers. There are competitions in pumpkin carving and pie eating.

Pumpkins have been grown in the Half Moon Bay area for decades but were used for cattle feed until the 1920s when two farmer brothers decided to try them as human food. That began a surge in pumpkin popularity. The pumpkin festival has also surged; attendance is estimated at 300,000.

Halifax Day
On or about April 12

Also known as **Halifax Resolves Day**, **Halifax Resolutions Day**, **Halifax Independence Day**, or **Halifax Resolutions of Independence Day**, this is the day on which, in the spring of 1776, North Carolina's delegates to the Second Continental Congress were given permission to join with representatives from other colonies in declaring their independence from British rule. As the first official sanction of separation from Great Britain, the Halifax Resolutions laid the groundwork for the American Revolution. It is a legal holiday in North Carolina.

Halloween
October 31

Halloween has its ultimate origins in the ancient Celtic harvest festival, SAMHAIN, a time when people believed that the spirits of the dead roamed the earth. Irish settlers brought their Halloween customs—which included bobbing for apples and lighting jack-o'-lanterns—to America in the 1840s.

In the United States children go from house to house in costume—often dressed as ghosts, skeletons, or vampires—on Halloween saying, "Trick or treat!" Though for the most part the threat is in jest, the "Trick" part of the children's cry carries the implication that if they don't receive a treat, the children will subject that house to some kind of prank, such as marking its windows with a bar of soap or throwing eggs at it. Most receive treats in the form of candy or money. But Halloween parties and parades are popular with adults as well. Because nuts were a favorite means of foretelling the future on this night, **All Hallows' Eve** in England became known as **Nutcrack Night**. Other British names for the day include **Bob Apple Night, Duck (or Dookie) Apple Night, Crab Apple Night, Thump-the-door Night,** and **Apple and Candle Night** (Wales). In the United States it is sometimes referred to as **Trick or Treat Night**.

See also MISCHIEF NIGHT, HALLOWEEN IN NEW ORLEANS.

Halloween in New Orleans
October 31

A spooky and macabre celebration in New Orleans, La., when costumed revelers parade up and down Bourbon Street and actors dressed as legendary characters are on the streets to narrate their grisly histories. The sheriff's Haunted House in City Park is a standard feature, and a Ghost Train rolls through the park while costumed police officers jump out of bushes to spook the riders. The Voodoo Museum usually offers a special Halloween ritual in which people may see true voodoo rites. Walking tours take visitors to such haunts as Le Pretre House, where a Turkish sultan and his five wives were murdered one night in 1792; it is said that their ghosts still have noisy parties.

On a more solemn note, the St. Louis Cathedral holds vigil services on Halloween, and several Masses on All Saints' Day. On the afternoon of that day, the archbishop leaves the cathedral for St. Louis Cemetery No. 1 to bless the newly scrubbed and decorated tombs.

Hambletonian Harness Racing Classic
First Saturday in August

Harness racing's most prestigious race for three-year-old trotters, the Hambletonian is a test of both speed and stamina. Currently held at the Meadowlands Racetrack in East Rutherford, New Jersey, the race dates back to 1926. It is always held on the first Saturday in August and is preceded by a week of other races, with purses ranging from $225,000 to $600,000. The purse for the one-mile Hambletonian race is $1.2 million, and the winner usually goes on to take a divisional title.

Hamishah Asar be-Av *See* **Fifteenth of Av**

Hamishah Assar Bi-Shevat *See* **Bi-Shevat**

Hana Matsuri (Flower Festival)
April 8

A celebration of the Buddha's birthday, observed in Buddhist temples throughout Japan. The highlight of the celebration is a ritual known as *kambutsu-e*, in which a tiny bronze statue of the Buddha, standing in an open lotus flower, is anointed with sweet tea. People use a small bamboo ladle to pour the tea, made of hydrangea leaves, over the head of the statue three times. The custom is supposed to date from the seventh century, when perfume rather than tea was used.

Festivities often include a procession of children carrying flowers, sometimes accompanied by a white elephant made of papier mâché.

See also VESAK.

Hanami
March and April

The word *hana* means 'flower' in Japanese, and *hanami* means 'flower viewing'. However, appreciation of the cherry blossom in Japan is almost a religion, and therefore *hanami* has come to refer specifically to cherry blossoms. The pink-and-white blooms last for two weeks, and in that time people swarm to the parks to picnic, play games, tell stories, and dance. Often companies organize *hanami* for their employees. The season usually starts at the end of March in Kyushu, in early April in the Tokyo area, and in late April in the north of Japan. The most famous viewing place is Yoshinoyama near Nara, where it is said one thousand trees can be seen at a glance.

See also CHERRY BLOSSOM FESTIVAL.

Handsel Monday
First Monday of the year; first Monday after January 12

A social rather than a religious holiday, Handsel Monday was an important holiday among the rural people of Scotland. 'Handsel' was something given as a token of good luck, particularly at the beginning of something; the modern house-warming gift would be a good example. Thus Handsel Monday was an occasion for gift-giving at the start of the new year, and it remained a Scottish tradition from the fourteenth until the nineteenth century. Eventually it was replaced by BOXING DAY, and the custom of giving farm laborers and public servants some extra money or a small gift on this day continues.

Because Handsel Monday was so widely celebrated among the rural population, many Scottish peasants celebrated **Auld Handsel Monday** on the first Monday after January 12, reflecting their reluctance to shift from the Old Style or Julian calendar to the New Style or Gregorian calendar.

Han'gul Day
October 5

This day commemorates the invention of the Korean alphabet by scholars under the direction of King Sejong of the Yi Dynasty in 1446.

The Han'gul system consists of fourteen consonants and ten vowels. The symbols for consonants are formed with curved or angled lines; the symbols for vowels are composed of vertical or horizonal straight lines with short lines on either side. Although Sejong made Han'gul the official writing system for the Korean language, it was not used by scholars or upper-class Koreans until after 1945, when Japanese rule came to an end and the influence of Confucianism and Chinese culture waned.

The reign of Sejong (1418–1450) was a golden age in Korea producing, besides the alphabet, the encyclopedic codification of medical knowledge and the development of new fonts of type for printing. (The technique of movable-type printing was developed in Korea in 1234, 200 years before Johann Gutenberg's invention in Germany.)

The day is celebrated with Confucian rituals and Choson-period court dances performed at Yongnung, the king's tomb, in Yoju, Kyonggi. Yoju also stages the King Sejong Cultural Festival, which is part of a three-day Grand Cultural Festival, with chanting and processions at Shilluksa Temple, farmers' dances, games such as tug of war, and a lantern parade. In some areas, there are calligraphy contests for both children and adults.

Ceremonies are also held at the King Sejong Memorial Center near Seoul.

Hans Christian Andersen Festival
July–August

Sometimes referred to as the **Hans Christian Andersen Plays,** this month-long event features dramatizations of the Danish author's works at the Open Air Theater in the Funen Village in Odense. It began in 1965 with the Danish actor Freddy Albeck, who dressed up like Andersen and did dramatic readings of his stories for children. Eventually it turned into a real theater event with both professional and child actors as well as a small orchestra. Prominent Danish producer Erik Bent Svendlund took over as manager of the festival in 1974, and he is still adapting Andersen's stories for the stage. About fifty children are chosen each year to act in the productions.

Lasting almost a month, the festival offers hour-long performances of such classic stories as *The Ugly Duckling, The Tinder Box, Little Claus and Big Claus,* and *Simple Simon,* and draws about thirty thousand spectators, many of them foreign tourists.

See also INTERNATIONAL CHILDREN'S BOOK DAY.

Hans Christian Andersen's Birthday
See **Children's Book Day, International**

Hanukkah (Chanukah)

Between November 25 and December 26; from 25 Kislev to 2 Tevet

Hanukkah commemorates the successful rebellion of the Jews against the Syrians in the Maccabean War of 162 B.C., but the military associations of this festival are played down. What is really being celebrated is the survival of Judaism. After the Jews' victory, they ritually cleansed and rededicated the Temple, then relit the menorah or 'perpetual lamp'; hence one of the other names for this celebration, the **Feast of Dedication** (Hanukkah means 'dedication' in Hebrew). The story is told that although there was only enough consecrated oil to keep the lamp burning for one day and it would take eight days to get more, the small bottle of oil miraculously lasted for the entire eight days. It is for this reason that Hanukkah is also known as the **Festival** or **Feast of Lights.**

Jewish families today celebrate this holiday by lighting a special Hanukkah menorah, a candelabrum with holders for eight candles, one for each day of celebration, plus a ninth, the shammash or 'server,' used to light the others. One candle is lit on the first night, two on the second, three on the third, through to the eighth night when all are lit. A special prayer is recited during the lighting, and while the candles burn it is a time for songs and games, including the four-sided toy called the dreidel. Other customs include the giving of gifts, especially to children, and decorating the home-much like the CHRISTMAS celebrations in Christian homes at this same time of year.

Hanuman Jayanti

March–April

Hanuman, the Monkey-God and a central figure in the great Hindu epic the *Ramayana*, helped Rama rescue his wife Sita from the demon Ravana; for this Rama decreed the two always be worshiped together. He is revered by Hindus all over India in the form of a monkey with a red face who stands erect like a human. His birth anniversary is observed in the month of Caitra (March–April) with celibacy and fasting, and reading of *Hanuman-Chalisa*. Hindus visit his temples, of which there are many, to offer prayers on this day and to re-paint his image with vermilion.

See also MONKEY GOD, BIRTHDAY OF THE.

Harbin Ice and Snow Festival

January 5–February 5

An extravaganza of ice sculptures in the port city of Harbin, the second largest city of northeast China. The sculptures, using themes of ancient legends and stories and modern historic events, depict pavilions, towers, temples, and mythic animals and persons. Located in Zhaolin Park, they shimmer in the sun by day, and at night are illuminated in a rainbow of colors. Theatrical events, art exhibitions, and a photo exhibition mark festival time, and wedding ceremonies are often scheduled at this time in the ice-filled park.

Harbor Festival

June–July

New York City's Harbor Festival is a good example of a festival that started as a one-time event—the bicentennial celebration on July 4, 1976, known as "Operation Sail," when tall ships from all over the world sailed into New York Harbor. This was so successful that local promoters decided to make it an annual event. Although the eighteen tall ships that came to the city in 1976 do not return every year, there is a Great Parade of Ships that includes both military and commercial vessels sailing up the Hudson River. The festival ends on the FOURTH OF JULY with a magnificent fireworks display. The Harbor Festival's many cultural, sporting, ethnic, and maritime events take place not only in Manhattan but in Brooklyn and Staten Island as well.

Operation Sail 1992 was a celebration of the 500th anniversary of Christopher Columbus' voyage to the New World. Thirty-four tall ships from twenty-four countries, accompanied by replicas of Columbus' three ships, the *Nina*, the *Pinta*, and the *Santa Maria* followed the eleven-mile parade route through New York Harbor. The dissolution of the Soviet Union allowed Russia to send four ships to the event, including the 400 foot *Sedov*, the longest of the tall ships. The total cost for the weekend was $12 million, but it generated $100 million in revenue for city businesses.

Hard Crab Derby, National

Labor Day weekend

The first **Hard Crab Derby** was held in 1947. A local newspaper editor dumped a few hard shell crabs into a circle on Main Street in Crisfield, Maryland. The crab that scurried to an outer circle first was declared the winner and its owner was awarded a trophy. There doesn't seem to have been any motivation for the race other than the wish to compete with the other derbies that had already been established for horses, automobiles, etc.

Today the National Hard Crab Derby attracts hundred of entries. The Governor's Cup Race, in which entries representing the fifty states compete, takes place on the Saturday of LABOR DAY weekend. There is also a boat docking contest, a fishing tournament, a plastic container boat regatta, and a soft crab cutting and wrapping contest. Fireworks, beauty contests, band concerts, drill team exhibitions, and professional entertainment complete the three-day festival.

Hari-Kuyo (Festival of Broken Needles)
February 8 or December 8

A requiem service for needles held throughout Japan. The ceremony of laying needles to rest harks back to at least the fourth century A.D. Today the services are attended not only by tailors and dressmakers but also by people who sew at home. Traditionally, a shrine is set up in the Shinto style, with a sacred rope and strips of white paper suspended over a three-tiered altar. On the top tier are offerings of cake and fruit, on the second tier there is a pan of tofu, and the bottom tier is for placing scissors and thimbles. The tofu is the important ingredient; people insert their broken or bent needles in it while offering prayers of thanks to the needles for their years of service. In the Buddhist service, special sutras are recited for the repose of the needles. Afterwards, the needles are wrapped in paper and laid to rest in the sea.

A hari-kuyo is held in Kyoto at the Buddhist Temple Horinji on Dec. 8, and in Tokyo one is held at Asakusa Kannon Temple on Feb. 8.

Harvard-Yale Regatta *See* Yale-Harvard Regatta

Harvest Home Festival
Autumn

Many countries celebrate the end of the summer harvest or the "ingathering" of the crops with a special feast. What became known in England as Harvest Home or **Harvest Thanksgiving** was called the **Kirn** in Scotland (from the churn of cream usually presented on the occasion), and probably derived from the ancient LAMMAS DAY celebrations. Eventually it gave rise to the **Harvest Festival** in Canada and THANKSGIVING in the United States.

The autumn harvest feast was usually served in a barn, a tent, or outdoors and was preceded by a church service. Although the earliest harvest feasts were served by a farmer or landowner to his laborers, eventually one big feast for the entire parish became the norm.

See also SZURET.

Harvest Moon Days
Full moon nearest September 23

Harvest Moon Days refer to the period of the full moon that falls closest to the AUTUMNAL EQUINOX, or September 23. This is traditionally a time for countries in the northern hemisphere to hold their annual harvest festivals. (See HARVEST HOME FESTIVAL.)

Hatch Chile Festival
Labor Day weekend

A tribute to the green chili (as it is more commonly spelled outside of New Mexico), New Mexico's state vegetable. The small town of Hatch is the center of the chili-growing industry in the southwestern part of the state. At festival time, the aroma of freshly harvested chilis permeates the town, and a marvelous variety of chilis in all forms can be purchased: fresh green chilis, from the mildest to the hottest; dried red chilis in ornamental braids called *ristras*; red chili powder; chili bread, chili salsa, chili jelly, chili wine, and chili con carne. Besides food, the festival features the crowning of a Green Chile Queen, a skeet shoot, a fiddling contest, a cookoff, and a *ristra*-making contest.

Haxey Hood Game
January 6

This centuries-old tradition in Haxey, England can be traced back more than six hundred years, when Lady Mowbray, whose husband owned a large portion of the parish of Haxey, lost her hood to a sudden gust of wind and thirteen local men struggled gallantly to retrieve it. She showed her appreciation by staging an annual reenactment of the event, which is believed by some to be the origin of rugby, an English sport that combines soccer with American football.

The game known as **Throwing the Hood**, which takes place on OLD CHRISTMAS DAY (January 6) each year, involves a Lord (who acts as umpire and master of ceremonies), thirteen Plough-Boggins (presumably named for the way the original thirteen men turned up the soil in their efforts to capture the hood), a Fool, and as many others as care to participate. After several warm-up rounds with sham hoods, the real contest begins. The participants wrestle over a piece of leather stuffed with straw, coins, and other fil-

135

lings. The winners carry it back to their village pub, where a victory celebration takes place. Later, the Boggins go from house to house, singing and collecting money for the celebration.

Hay-on-Wye Festival of Literature
Late May

This ten-day celebration of words and language has been held in Hay-on-Wye, Wales since 1988. It offers ten days of comedy, theater, and musical performances in addition to conversations, debates, lectures, interviews, and readings by poets and fiction writers. The festival regularly features some of the most widely known Welsh, Irish, English, European, and American writers in the world, including Margaret Atwood, Doris Lessing, John Mortimer, William Golding, Anthony Hecht, Joseph Heller, and Jan Morris. Musical performances have included the Welsh National Opera Male Choir and the English Shakespeare Company.

A series of master classes in poetry, short story, and television screenwriting has recently been established for young published or produced writers attending the festival. The master classes include a week of intensive work under the supervision of such renowned writers as Joseph Brodsky, who won the Nobel Prize for Literature in 1980, and the famous Welsh poet and short story writer Leslie Norris.

Heaving Day *See* Easter Monday

Heinz Southern 500 *See* Southern 500

Helen Keller Festival
Last weekend in June

A three-day festival in Tuscumbia, Ala., to honor Helen Keller and her remarkable life. Born in Tuscumbia in 1880, she was left blind, deaf, and mute by illness at the age of nineteen months. After Helen's parents appealed to Alexander Graham Bell for help in educating the child, twenty-year-old Anne Mansfield Sullivan, partially blind and a graduate of the Perkins School for the Blind in Boston, arrived and taught the child by pressing objects and a manual alphabet into Helen's palm. Helen learned to read and write and later graduated cum laude from Radcliffe College. She became widely known for her writings, and toured the world to promote opportunities for other blind and deaf persons. Samuel L. Clemens (Mark Twain) was so moved by her spirit that he likened Miss Keller to Joan of Arc.

Festival events include art exhibits, stage shows, musical entertainment, sports tournaments, a parade, and historic tours. At Miss Keller's birthplace, Ivy Green, visitors can see the pump at which Helen learned her first word, "water."

The house contains a library of Braille books, a Braille typewriter, and other mementos.

"The Miracle Worker," the play by William Gibson about Helen Keller and Anne Sullivan, has been presented since 1962 on Friday and Saturday nights in late June and July on the grounds of Ivy Green. The play opened in New York in 1959, won the Pulitzer Prize in 1960, and was made into a movie in 1962.

Hemingway Days Festival
The week of July 21

A week-long celebration of Ernest Hemingway, the American novelist and short-story writer, in Key West, Fla. The festival has been held since 1980 during the week of Hemingway's birthday, July 21, 1899. Hemingway made his home in Key West at one time, and his novel, *To Have and Have Not* (1937), is set there. He was awarded the Pulitzer Prize in fiction in 1953 for his short heroic novel about an old Cuban fisherman, The Old Man and the Sea, and he received the Nobel Prize for Literature in 1954.

At the center of the festival is the Writer's Workshop and Conference, with a schedule of fiction, poetry, and stage and screenwriting. A short-story competition, with a first-place prize of $1,000, drew a total of 972 submissions in 1991. Lorian Hemingway, the writer's granddaughter and a writer herself, is the coordinator of the story contest. Other events include a radio trivia contest, a Hemingway look-alike contest, a storytelling competition, arm wrestling, and a party and concert at the Hemingway Home and Museum.

Hemis Festival
Usually in June or July

A three-day Buddhist festival at the Hemis Gompa in the mountain state of Ladakh in northern India. This is the largest *gompa* (monastery) in Ladakh and has gold statues, huge stone monuments of Buddha, called stupas studded with precious stones, and an impressive collection of *thangkas*, or big scroll religious paintings. The festival celebrates the birthday of Guru Padmasambhava, the Indian Buddhist mystic who introduced Tantric Buddhism to Tibet in the eighth century. Tradition says he was a native of Swat (now in Pakistan), an area noted for magicians. Tradition also says he brought on an earthquake in Tibet to get rid of the demons who were delaying the building of a monastery.

The festival attracts people from throughout the mountain areas of Kadakh and Tibet—Muslims and Hindus as well as Buddhist, all dressed in their most colorful clothes. A fair springs up, with stalls selling confections, gems, and crafts.

The highlight of the festival is the Devil Dance of the monks. Demon dancers are costumed as satyrs, many-eyed monsters, fierce tigers, or skeletons, while lamas portraying saints wear miters and opulent silks and carry pastoral crooks. These good lamas, ringing bells and swinging censers, scatter the bad lamas, as they all swirl about to the music of cymbals, drums, and ten-foot-long trumpets. The dance is a morality play, a battle between good and evil spirits, and also expresses the idea that a person's helpless soul can be comforted only by a lama's exorcisms.

Heritage Holidays
Mid–October

A five-day celebration of the history of Rome, Ga., which, like its Italian namesake, was built on seven hills. There is also a bronze replica of the Capitoline Wolf outside City Hall. This Roman statue depicting a she-wolf nursing the legendary founders of Rome, Romulus and Remus was given to the town in 1929 by Benito Mussolini.

Heritage Holidays, however, looks back to different times: it features a re-creation of the famous ride of John Wisdom, who has been called the Paul Revere of the South. During the Civil War, Rome was important to the Confederacy as a rail and manufacturing center. Wisdom, a native of the city who was living in Alabama, was delivering mail when he heard that Yankee soldiers were headed for his hometown. He rode the sixty-seven miles to Rome in eleven hours, wearing out five horses and a mule. The men of Rome set up two old cannons, and the Yanks decided the town seemed too heavily fortified. They surrendered to a smaller Confederate force following them.

Features of the heritage days are a wagon train, parades, riverboat rides, concerts, and a major arts and crafts fair.

Higan
March 20 or 21 and September 23 or 24

A week of Buddhist services observed in Japan at the spring and autumn equinoxes (see VERNAL EQUINOX; AUTUMNAL EQUINOX)when day and night are of equal length.

Both equinoxes have been national holidays since the Meiji Period (1868–1912). Before World War II, they were known as *koreisai*, 'festivals of the Imperial ancestors.' After the war, when the national holidays were renamed, they became simply spring equinox and autumn equinox.

Higan is the seven-day period surrounding the equinoxes. It means 'the other shore,' and refers to the spirits of the dead reaching Nirvana after crossing the river of existence. Thus Higan is a celebration of the spiritual move from the world of suffering to the world of enlightenment and is a time for remembering the dead, visiting, cleaning, and decorating their graves, and reciting *sutras*, Buddhist prayers. O-hagi, rice balls covered with sweet bean paste, and sushi are offered. It is traditional not to eat meat during this period. Emperor Heizei instituted the celebration in 806 A.D., when he ordered a week-long reading of a certain sutra for the occasion.

In Okinawa it is a home thanksgiving festival. Barley (omugi) or barley cakes with brown sugar are eaten with prayers for good fortune.

High Holy Days *See* **Rosh ha-Shanah; Yom Kippur**

Highland Games
Dates vary

Originally impromptu athletic competitions carried out in the Scottish Highlands as part of a clan gathering, highland games are now held all over the world, usually under the auspices of a local Caledonian society. Although the Jacobites put an end to the clan assemblies in 1745, the tradition of the games survived, and the first of the modern gatherings was held ninety years later at Braemar (see BRAEMAR HIGHLAND GATHERING). Today there are about forty major gatherings in Scotland alone, as well as in Tauranga, New Zealand, and in several American communities such as Goshen, Connecticut and Alexandria, Virginia where there is a strong Anglo-Scottish presence.

Events at most Highland gatherings include flat and hurdle races, long and high jumps, pole vaulting, throwing the hammer, and tossing the weight (a round stone ball). A uniquely Highland event is tossing the caber, a tapered fir pole that must be thrown so that it turns end over end and comes to rest with the small end pointing away from the thrower. Competitors who toss the weight or the caber must wear the kilt or traditional Scottish costume. There are also competitions in bagpipe music and Highland dancing.

Hilaria
March 15

The ancient Romans celebrated the **Festival of Hilaria**, the "mother of the gods," each year on the IDES (15th day) of March. Part of the festival involved bringing offerings to the temple. When Christianity replaced the old pagan culture, legend has it that the Festival of Hilaria was adapted to fit the new church's needs and became known as MOTHERING SUNDAY in England. Eventually it was shifted from mid-March to mid-Lent, and it was observed as a time for young men and women living away from home to visit their parents.

Hill Cumorah Pageant
End of July

Billed as the largest outdoor pageant in the United States, the Hill Cumorah Pageant is based on the Bible and the *Book of Mormon* and is presented by the Church of Jesus Christ of Latter-Day Saints (popularly called Mormons) in Palmyra, New York for nine consecutive evenings (excluding Sunday and Monday) beginning on the third weekend in July. The drama, entitled "America's Witness for Christ," tells the story of the people who lived on the North American continent between 600 B.C. and 421 A.D., and how Christ taught these ancient Americans his gospels after his resurrection in Jerusalem. Presented on twenty-five hillside stages, each showing of the pageant can accommodate an audience of 15,000. More than five hundred people participate in the pageant on a volunteer basis.

Hill Cumorah is believed to be the site where, in 1823, the angel Moroni instructed Joseph Smith, the first prophet of the Mormon Church, to look for the secret records, written upon gold plates, that told about the ancient inhabitants of North America—American Indians that the Mormons believe were descended from the Israelites via the tribe of Joseph. Smith was told that the plates were hidden in a hill named Cumorah, located between Palmyra and Manchester, New York. But it was nearly four years before Moroni gave Smith permission to remove the plates and begin their translation. They would eventually be published as the *Book of Mormon* in 1830.

An impressive feature of the pageant is the water curtain that is used during the "vision" scenes.

Hina Matsuri (Doll Festival)
March 3

A festival for girls, celebrated in homes throughout Japan since the Edo Period (1600–1867) when doll-making became a highly skilled craft.

A set of ten to fifteen dolls (*hina*), usually unmatched family heirlooms from various generations, is displayed on a stand covered with red cloth, the stand having at least three and up to seven steps. Dressed in elaborate antique silk costumes, the dolls represent the prince and princess, ladies-in-waiting, court ministers, musicians, and servants. Replicas of ornate furnishings are part of the display, as are miniature dishes of foods offered to the prince and princess. People visit each other's homes to admire the dolls.

In parts of Tottori Prefecture, girls make boats of straw, place a pair of paper dolls in them with rice cakes and, after displaying them with the other *hina*, set them afloat on the Mochigase River. This custom supposedly dates back to ancient times when dolls were used as talismans to exorcise evil; a paper doll cast into a river signified the washing away of human misfortune.

Hippokrateia Festival
August

A celebration of Hippocrates, the "Great Physician," on Kos, the Greek island where he was born in about 460 B.C. A number of ancient manuscripts bear the name of Hippocrates; the best known of these is the *Aphorisms*, a collection of short discussions on the nature of illness, its diagnosis, prognosis, and treatment. The Hippocratic oath, an ethical code attributed to Hippocrates, is still used in graduation ceremonies at many medical schools. In it, the physician pledges to refrain from causing harm, and to live an exemplary personal and professional life.

Throughout antiquity, Kos attracted the sick and infirm who came for healing at the Shrine of Asclepius, the god of medicine. Today the island is a popular resort, featuring fine beaches, the ruins of Roman baths, a Greek theater, and a museum with a huge statue of Hippocrates. The festival includes performances of ancient drama, concerts, a flower show, and a reenactment of the Hippocratic oath.

Hiroshima Peace Ceremony
August 6

A ceremony held each year since 1947 at the Peace Memorial Park in Hiroshima, Japan, in memory of the victims of the atomic bomb that devastated the city in 1945. (The day was Aug. 5 in the United States, Aug. 6 in Japan.) It was the first time in history that a weapon of such destruction had been used. The American B-29 Superfortress Enola Gay carried the bomb, called "Little Boy." The day is sometimes called **Atomic Bomb Day**, but this refers more accurately to the anniversary of the first atomic bomb test on July 16, 1945 at Alamogordo Air Base in New Mexico.

In announcing the bombing, President Harry S Truman said, "The force from which the sun draws its power has been loosed against those who brought war to the Far East." The immediate death toll was 60,000, at least 75,000 more were injured, and the bomb wiped out more than four square miles—60 percent of the city. One man on the mission described its explosion as a bright, blinding flash followed by a "black cloud of boiling dust" and above it white smoke that "climbed like a mushroom to 20,000 feet." Three days later, on Aug. 9, a second A-bomb, called "Fat Man," was dropped on Nagasaki, razing the center of the city and killing 39,000. On Aug. 15, Japan surrendered, ending World War II.

The peace ceremony is held in the evening, when the city's citizens set thousands of lighted lanterns adrift on the Ota River and prayers are offered for world peace. Other memorial services are also held throughout the world at this time.

Hobart Cup Day

On or near January 23

There are a number of famous horse-races in Australia each year that are observed as holidays in the states where they take place. Hobart Cup Day is a holiday in Southern Tasmania, while Northern Tasmania observes **Launceston Cup Day** a month later. In South Australia, Adelaide Cup Day is celebrated in May. And the MELBOURNE CUP, the country's richest handicap race, is held on the first Tuesday in November.

Hobart Regatta Day

February

The **Royal Hobart Regatta** is a two-day aquatic carnival that includes sailing, rowing, and swimming events as well as fireworks and parades. It is a holiday in Southern Tasmania, Australia, and is held on the Derwent River sometime in early February during Australia's summer season. Hobart is the capital of Tasmania, Australia's southernmost state.

A similar holiday in Northern Tasmania is observed on the first Monday in November and is called **Recreation Day.**

Hobby Horse Parade *See* **Minehead Hobby Horse Parade**

Hobo Convention

Three days in August

The small, rural town of Britt, Iowa (population 2,000) seems an unlikely location for a convention of hobos—the unwashed but colorful riders of America's empty boxcars—but for three days each summer its residents play host to this diminishing segment of the population. From across the nation the hobos come to Britt, where they receive free food, sleeping accommodations in empty boxcars, and the adoration of more than 20,000 visitors who want to find out what a hobo's life is really like. There is a parade, an arts fair, carnival rides, races, and music. But the real action centers on the hobo camp set up by festival organizers on the outskirts of town, where visitors can hear the life stories of these men who have chosen to travel the country unencumbered by family or property.

The hobos are quick to distinguish themselves from tramps and bums. As one explains, "A hobo wants to wander, but he always works for his meals . . . a tramp wanders, but never does any work; a bum just drinks and wanders." The first Hobo Convention was held in Britt in 1900, and during the 1930s the event attracted hundreds of hobos. But their ranks are thinning, and today the town is lucky if thirty or forty real hobos show up.

Hocktide

Between April 5 and May 9; second Monday and Tuesday after Easter

Also known as **Hock Days**, the second Monday and Tuesday after EASTER in England was in medieval times and in Hungerford, Berkshire till the present day, associated with collecting dues or rents and money for the church, particularly in rural areas. There were a number of traditional methods for demanding money, most of them light-hearted rather than threatening. For example, people were often tied up with ropes and had to pay for their release, giving rise to the name **Binding Tuesday.** Or rope might be stretched across the road to stop passers-by, who would then have to pay before they were allowed to continue. In parts of Berkshire, two 'Tutti-men' in top hats and morning coats—a 'tutti' being a small bouquet of flowers—would go from house to house carrying a 'tutti-pole' decorated with flowers and ribbons. There was also an orange scatterer who threw oranges to the men, old women, and children to keep them busy while the tutti-men went from house to house demanding both money and a kiss from the lady of the house. In Yorkshire, children were still celebrating **Kissing Day** as recently as the 1950s—widely believed to have derived from hocktide customs.

Hocktide was also one of the QUARTER DAYS.

Hogmanay
December 31

In Scotland and the northern part of England, the last day of the year is known as Hogmanay. There are a number of theories as to where the name comes from—one of them being that it derives from the ancient Scandinavian name for the night preceding the feast of Yule, *Hoggu-nott* or *Hogg-night*. Another is that is comes from the French expression, *Au gui l'an neuf* ('To the mistletoe this New Year'), a reference to the ancient ceremony of gathering mistletoe (*gui* in French).

Scottish children, often wearing a sheet doubled up in front to form a huge pocket, used to call at the homes of the wealthy on this day and ask for their traditional gift of an oatmeal cake. They would call out "Hogmanay!" and recite traditional rhymes or sing songs in return for which they'd be given their cakes to take home. It is for this reason that December 31 was also referred to as **Cake Day**.

Hoi Lim Festival
13th day of first lunar month (usually February)

An alternating-song contest, held in Ha Bac Province of Vietnam. This is a courtship event, in which girls and boys of different villages carry on a singing courtship dialogue. The singers take part in what is a vocal contest with set rules; one melody, for example, can only be used for two verses of the song, and therefore there is considerable improvising. The story-lines of the songs tell of daily events. Young men and women practice them while they are at work in the rice fields or fishing.

Hola Mohalla
February–March

A Sikh festival celebrated in Anandpur Sahib, Punjab, India, on the day after Holi, the colorful water-tossing springtime festival. Mock battles with ancient weapons are staged, and there are also exhibitions of traditional martial arts like archery and fencing. The Sikh religion was founded in the state of Punjab in the late fifteenth century, and the majority of Sikhs now live there.

Holi
Late February and March; 14th of waxing Phalguna

A colorful and boisterous Hindu spring festival in India. This is a time of shedding inhibitions: People smear each other with red and yellow powder and shower each other with colored water shot from bamboo blowpipes or water pistols. Restrictions of caste, sex, age, and personal differences are ignored. Bhang, an intoxicating drink made from the same plant that produces marijuana, is imbibed, and revelry reigns.

The name of the festival derives from the name of the wicked Holika. According to legend, an evil king had a good son, Prince Prahlad, who was sent by the gods to deliver the land from the king's cruelty. Holika, the king's sister, decided to kill the prince with fire. Believing she was immune to fire, she held the child in her lap and sat in flames. But Lord Krishna stepped in to save Prahlad, and Holika was left in the fire and burned to death. On the night before the festival, images of Holika are burned on huge bonfires, drums pound, horns blow, and people whoop.

Another tale, related to the practice of water-throwing, is that the small monkey god Hanuman one day managed to swallow the sun. People were sad to live in darkness, and other gods suggested they rub color on one another and laugh. They mixed the color in water and squirted each other, and Hanuman thought this was so funny he gave a great laugh, and the sun flew out of his mouth.

There is also the story that the Mongol Emperor Akbar thought everyone would look equal if covered with color, and he therefore ordained the holiday to unite the castes.

The celebrations differ from city to city. In Mathura, Lord Krishna's legendary birthplace, there are especially exuberant processions with songs and music. In the villages of Nandgaon and Barsnar, once homes of Krishna and his beloved Radha, the celebrations are spread over sixteen days. And on Besant, people set up a twenty-five-foot pole called a *chir* to begin the celebrations and burn it at the end of the festival.

In Bangladesh the festival is called **Dol-Jatra**, the **Swing Festival** because a Krishna doll is kept in a swinging cradle (*dol*). In Nepal it is called **Rung Khelna** 'playing with color.' They build a three-tiered, twenty-five-foot high umbrella and at its base people light joss sticks, and place flowers and red powder. Instead of squirting water, they drop water-filled balloons from upper windows.

In Suriname it is **Holi Phagwa** and also the **Hindu New Year**.

Holland Festival
June 1–23

Since Holland (the Netherlands) didn't really have a single composer who could be honored by a festival in a specific city or town-such as the Mozart Festival in Salzburg, Austria (See SALZBURG FESTIVAL) or Germany's Wagner Festival in Bayreuth, (see BAYREUTH FESTIVAL) it was decided in 1947 to have a single festival focused on three major cities—Amsterdam, Rotterdam, and the Hague/Scheveningen—that would cover a wide range of artistic and cultural activities and at the same time draw top international artists to the Netherlands. The Holland Festival lasts twenty-three days in June, with most of the 150 programs being held in the three large cities but with some events taking place in smaller cities and towns. The festival offers not only performances of orchestral and choral works but opera, ballet, theater, and film as well.

Each year a different country is selected as a theme. In 1992, for example, the focus was on Russian and Baltic music, and many top musicians from the former Soviet Union were invited to participate.

Hollyhock Festival *See* **Aoi Matsuri**

Holmenkollen Day
Second Sunday in March

The Holmenkollen International Ski Meet is a week-long Norwegian winter festival held at Holmenkollen Hill outside Oslo. It is the main winter sports event of the year and it covers all types of skiing-cross-country racing and jumping as well as downhill and slalom. The world's best skiers meet here to compete for highly coveted prizes.

The high point of the festival comes on Holmenkollen Day, when over a hundred thousand spectators, headed by the King and the Royal Family, gather at the famous Holmenkollen Hill to watch the ski-jumping event, which has been held here since 1892. Competitors swoop down the 184-foot jump, and the one who soars the farthest wins the coveted King's Cup.

Holocaust Day (Yom Hashoah)
Between April 8 and May 6; 27 Nisan

Holocaust Day or **Yom Hashoah** was established by Israel's Knesset (parliament) as a memorial to the six million Jews slaughtered by the Nazis between 1933 and 1945. It is observed on the twenty-seventh day of the month of Nisan, the day on which Allied troops liberated the first Nazi concentration camp at Buchenwald, Germany in 1945. It is a commemoration that is observed by many non-Jewish people around the world.

Holy Blood, Procession of the
Between April 30 and June 3; Ascension Day

A major religious event in Bruges, Belgium to venerate the Holy Blood of Christ that was brought back from the Second Crusade by Thierry d'Alsace, Count of Flanders.

Thierry's bravery in Jerusalem in the battles against the Saracens was legendary. As a reward for his courage, King Baudouin entrusted the count with a vial of a few drops of blood supposed to have been from Christ's wounds and collected from under the cross by Joseph of Arimathea. When Thierry returned to Bruges on April 7, 1150, there was a great celebration: flowers were strewn in the streets, people waved the banners of the city trades, city dignitaries welcomed the heroic count, and the Holy Reliquary was taken in solemn procession to the Chapel of St. Basile.

The present procession commemorates that original one, although it was not a regular celebration until 1820. Today, the activities begin at 11 A.M. with a Pontifical Mass in the cathedral. The procession gets under way at 3 P.M., lasts about an hour and a half, and closes with a blessing by the bishop.

As the celebration gets under way, every church bell peals in this usually quiet city. Through living tableaux, the procession tells the story of the Bible from the fall of Adam and Eve, on through Abraham and Moses and to the New Testament stories of ST. JOHN THE BAPTIST, the birth of Christ, the Last Supper, and the Crucifixion on Calvary. Some dozen groups also depict the triumphant return of Thierry d'Alsace to Bruges. When the procession has returned to Burg Square, where it began, the Bishop of Bruges lifts the relic of the Holy Blood and blesses the crowd. Visitors come to Bruges from all over the world for the procession.

See also SAN GENNARO, FEAST OF.

Holy Cross Day *See* **Día de la Santa Cruz; Exaltation of the Cross**

Holy Day of Letters
May 24 in the West; May 11 in the East

This Bulgarian religious festival honors two brothers, Saint Cyril and Saint Methodius, missionaries to Moravia. St. Cyril invented the Slavic alphabet known as the Cyrillic alphabet in 855 and they are both widely regarded as the country's patrons of education and culture. In 1980, Pope John Paul II declared them patrons of Europe. The brothers started out preaching Christianity in what is now the Czech and Slovak Republics, but their followers fled to Bulgaria when they were persecuted, and Cyrillic became the official alphabet there. It is still used in the former Soviet Union, Serbia, and other Slavic countries as well.

Special Masses and student parades are held throughout Bulgaria on this day, which is also known as **Saints Cyril and Methodius' Day**. An impressive High Mass, celebrated at the cathedral in Sofia, is one of the festival's highlights.

Holy Family, Feast of the
January; Sunday after Epiphany

In the Roman Catholic church the Holy Family—Jesus, Mary and Joseph—is thought to provide the perfect example of what the family relationship should be like. But it was not until the seventeenth century that the Holy Family was venerated as a family, and the feast itself was not officially instituted until 1921. Its popularity spread rapidly, and it is now celebrated by Roman Catholics all over world. Each of the three members of the sacred household at Nazareth are also honored as individuals on their own feast days.

Holy Friday *See* Good Friday

Holy Ghost, Feast of the
March–July

Holy Ghost Season, or **Altura Do Espírito Santo**, has been celebrated in the Azores since the late fifteenth century. There are actually two types of celebration: the *bodo* or banquet and the *função* or function. *Bodos* are held in rural *Impérios*—elaborately painted one-room buildings that are used only once a year for the festival celebration. The *bodo* is a large-scale public festival that includes a Mass; a procession and coronation of young children; the ceremonial distribution of meat, bread, and wine; an auction; and a number of secular activities including singing competitions and bullfights. The *função* is a small-scale celebration held in private homes. It represents the payment of a personal promise to the Holy Ghost and a series of ritual exchange events, culminating in the coronation of an Emperor, the distribution of gifts to the poor, and a communal meal.

Although Holy Ghost season falls primarily between EASTER and TRINITY SUNDAY, urban Impérios have extended the season to July by staggering their celebrations so that the crowns, brocade flags, and other paraphernalia needed for the festival can be shared among the various Brotherhoods. Although observation of the feast has nearly disappeared in continental Portugal, it has been carried to Brazil, Canada, Bermuda, and the United States by Portuguese immigrants.

The Holy Ghost celebrations are based on the story of Queen Isabela of Portugal, who loved the poor and pleaded with God to help her starving people. When two ships laden with cattle and grain miraculously appeared in a Portuguese harbor, the Queen served a banquet to the poor and continued this yearly ceremony as an expression of gratitude to God.

Holy Innocents' Day
December 28

Also known as **Innocents' Day** or **Childermas** this day commemorates the massacre of all the male children two years and under in Bethlehem as ordered by King Herod, who hoped that the infant Jesus would be among them. Not surprisingly, this day has long been regarded as unlucky-particularly for getting married or undertaking any important task. Edward IV of England went so far as to change the day of his coronation when he realized it would fall on December 28.

In ancient times, the "Massacre of the Innocents" was re-enacted by whipping the younger members of a family. But over the years the tables turned, and in some countries it has become a day when children play pranks on their elders. In Mexico, Childermas is the equivalent of APRIL FOOL'S DAY.

Holy Kings' Day *See* Epiphany

Holy Maries, Festival of the *See* Saintes Maries, Fête des

Holy Saturday
Between March 21 and April 24 in West; between April 3 and May 7 in East; the day before Easter

Saturday eve before EASTER, also called **Easter Even**, is the last day of HOLY WEEK and brings the season of LENT to a close. In the early church, this was the major day for baptisms. Many churches, especially those of the Anglican Communion, still hold large baptismal services on Holy Saturday. It is also known as the **Vigil of Easter** in reference to the fact that Jesus' followers spent this day, after his crucifixion on GOOD FRIDAY, waiting. The Easter or Paschal Vigil, the principal celebration of Easter, is traditionally observed the night of Holy Saturday/Easter Day in many churches today. Another name for this day is the **Descent into Hell**, because it commemorates Jesus' descent into and victory over hell.

Slavic Orthodox Christians bring baskets of food to the church for the Blessing of the Pascha (Easter) Baskets on Holy Saturday. The baskets are filled with the foods from which people have abstained during the Lenten fast and which will be part of the Pascha feast. For the Mexican inhabitants of Los Angeles, California, Holy Saturday is the day for a colorful ceremony known as the Blessing of the Animals, which takes place at the old Plaza Church.

Holy Thursday
Between April 30 and June 3; forty days after Easter

Holy Thursday usually refers to MAUNDY THURSDAY, but in parts of rural England, it traditionally refers to ASCENSION DAY, the day on which Jesus Christ ascended into heaven. The English custom of "well dressing," which may have had its roots in a pagan festival, became associated with Holy Thursday in 1615. There was a severe drought in Derbyshire that year and most of the wells and streams dried up. The only wells that still had water were at Tissington, where people came to get water for their livestock. From that time onward, a special thanksgiving service was held there on Ascension Day, and Tissington became known as "the village of holy wells."

The well-dressing ceremony developed into a full-fledged festival in the nineteenth century. After delivering his sermon, the vicar would lead a procession to the wells, which were nearly hidden by screens of fresh flowers fastened to wooden frames. A simple ceremony, asking God to bless and keep the waters pure, was followed by a country fair that included gypsy fortune-tellers and dancing around a Maypole.

Holy Week
Between March 15 and April 18 in the West; between March 28 and May 1 in East; the week preceding Easter

Holy Week, the seven days beginning with PALM SUNDAY that precede EASTER, is the most solemn week in the Christian year. It includes MAUNDY THURSDAY, GOOD FRIDAY, and HOLY SATURDAY. The Germans call Holy Week **Still Week** or **Silent Week**, and some Americans call it **Passion Week**, although the season known as Passiontide actually refers to the preceding week.

Passion Sunday is the fifth Sunday in LENT (the Sunday *before* Palm Sunday), but since Holy Week was also referred to as Passion Week, this apparently led to the identification of Palm Sunday with Passion Sunday. Since 1970 the Roman Catholic church has considered the two names to be synonymous, although in 1956 the two Sundays were designated the First Sunday and Second Sunday of the Passion. Another name for the fifth Sunday in LENT is Judica Sunday, from the Introit for the day.

See also SEMANA SANTA IN GUATEMALA.

Homowo (Hunger-Hooting Festival)
between August and September

A harvest festival of thanks to the gods of the Ga (or Gan) people. *Homowo* means 'starved gods,' and the festival commemorates the good harvest the Ga were given in ancient times. This harvest came after the famine they endured while travelling to their present home in Ghana. The festival begins on Thursday and those who have moved away are called Soobi, 'Thursday people,' because that's the day they arrive home for the festival. The following day is the yam festival and the day of twins. All twins who are dressed in white are specially treated all day. Each day there are processions, songs, and dancing until the great day arrives: Homowo, or the Hunger-Hooting Festival and open house.

Most homes have enough food in them for a week during the festival. Fish are abundant in Ghana at this time of year, so, palm-nut soup and kpokpoi or ko are the festal foods. The latter are made from steamed, unleavened corn dough mashed and mixed with palm oil. The chiefs and elders sprinkle the ko everywhere people have been buried, then go to the prison and manually feed the warders. The following day they visit friends and relatives, reconciling and exchanging NEW YEAR's greetings.

Hong Kong Arts Festival
Last three weeks in January

An annual celebration of the arts in Hong Kong, held since 1972. Artists from around the world appear for a diverse program that includes opera, orchestral concerts, chamber music, jazz, dance, and theater and mime. The 1992 program scheduled a presentation of the opera Tosca with an international cast, as well as a performance of the 400-year-old Kunju Opera, the oldest surviving form of theater in China, by the Shanghai Kunju Opera Troupe.

Hope Watermelon Festival
Third weekend in August (Thursday through Sunday)

Best known as the birthplace of United States President Bill Clinton, Hope, Ark. is also "Home of the World's Largest Watermelons" and hosts the only watermelon festival featuring giant watermelons.

They are indeed large. Hope watermelon growers have been competing to grow the biggest since the 1920s. In 1925, Hugh Laseter created a sensation with a record 136-pounder that was exhibited for a few days and then sent to President Calvin Coolidge. The watermelons kept getting bigger. The 1928 champion was 144-3/4 pounds and was sent to the Rexall Corp. in Boston, Mass., where it "created quite a bit of excitement," according to old accounts. The first 200-pound melon was grown in 1979 by Ivan Bright and his son Lloyd; seeds from it went for $8 each. That melon broke a forty-four year record held by O. D. Middlebrooks, who had grown a 195-pound melon. (It was sent to actor Dick Powell.) In 1985, Lloyd Bright's ten-year-old son Jason produced a 260-pound watermelon that was recorded in the *1992 Guinness Book of World Records*. These melons attain their great size because of the quality of the soil, an early greenhouse start, and careful pruning. Hope farmers also grow average-size watermelons, weighing thirty to forty pounds.

The Hope Watermelon Festival originated in 1926, lapsed with hard times, was revived in 1977, and has been held annually ever since with attendance at about 75,000. There has been nationwide television and press coverage because of the colossal melons. This is a festival of real down-home Americana: ice cream socials, a big fish fry, softball, a dog show, tug-o'-war, juggling, sack races, arm wrestling, an air show, horseshoe pitching, and a hula-hoop contest. The watermelon events include a watermelon toss, a melon decorating competition, a melon eating contest, a melon seed spitting contest, and a melon judging and auction. While he was governor of Arkansas, Mr. Clinton visited the festival to compete in the Watermelon 5K Run.

Hopi Snake Dance
August or early September

The grand finale of ceremonies to pray for rain, held by individual Hopi tribes in Arizona every two years. Hopis believe their ancestors originated in an underworld, and that their gods and the spirits of ancestors live there. They call snakes their brothers, and trust that the snakes will carry their prayers to the Rainmakers beneath the earth. Thus the Hopi dancers carry snakes in their mouths to impart prayers to them.

The ceremonies, conducted by the Snake and Antelope fraternities, last sixteen days. On the eleventh day preparations start for the snake dance. For four days, snake priests go out from their village to gather snakes. On the fifteenth day, a race is run, signifying rain gods bringing water to the village. Then the Antelopes build a *kisi*, a shallow pit covered with a board, to represent the entrance to the underworld. At sunset on the fifteenth day, the Snake and Antelope Dancers dance around the plaza, stamping on the *kisi* board and shaking rattles to simulate the sounds of thunder and rain. The Antelope priest dances with green vines around his neck and in his mouth—just as the Snake priests will later do with snakes.

The last day starts with a footrace to honor the snakes. The snakes are washed and deposited in the *kisi*. The Snake priests, each accompanied by a whipper and catcher, dance around the *kisi*. Then each priest takes a snake and carries it first in his hands and then in his mouth. The whipper dances behind him with his left arm around the dancer's neck and calms the snake by stroking it with a feathered wand. After four dances around the plaza, the priests throw the snakes to the catchers. A priest draws a circle on the ground, the catchers throw the snakes in the circle, the Snake priests grab handfuls of them and run with them to turn them loose in the desert.

And the snake dance is over, and rain will come.

Hora at Prislop
Second Sunday in August

A dancing festival held at Mount Prislop at the Transylvania-Moldavia border in Romania. The dancers of the hora carry big rings that symbolize the friendship of the people of the regions of Moldavia, Maramures, and Transylvania. The top artistic groups gather at Prislop Pass to present a parade in colorful folk costumes and then a program of songs and dances, ending with the lively peasant horas. Typical food dishes of the area are served and folk art is on display.

Horn Dance, The
Monday following first Sunday after September 4

The ancient Horn Dance, believed by many to have originated in Norman times, is performed at Abbots Bromley, a small village in Staffordshire, England as part of the Wakes Monday celebration each year. Wakes Monday, the day after the first Sunday following September 4, was at one time part of the Old St. Barthelmy Fair. But the Horn Dance is all that remains of the original three-day festival. Although some believe it was once an ancient fertility dance, the Horn Dance probably had something to do with hunting rights and customs in nearby Needwood Forest.

A dozen local men, ranging in age from twelve to more than fifty, dress in sixteenth-century foresters' costumes. Six of them carry reindeer antlers mounted on short wooden sticks. There is also a Hobby Horse, a man dressed as a woman who plays the role of Maid Marian, a Fool carrying an inflated bladder on a stick, and a young archer who snaps his bow in time with the music—originally provided by a pipe and tabor but nowadays by a concertina and a triangle.

Beginning at the parish church, the men dance their way around the parish boundaries, stopping to perform at homes and farms along the way. The six deerman, three of whom carry white antlers and three black, take turns "charging" each other while the Hobby Horse prances, the Fool shakes his bladder at the spectators, and Maid Marian takes up a collection. The dancing is over by evening, when everyone adjourns to the local pub or goes home to eat Wakes Cakes, "fair rock candy"—sugar-coated sticks of candy—and brandy snap cookies.

In the United States, what is referred to as the **Abbots Bromley Horn Dance** is frequently performed as part of a CHRISTMAS pageant or TWELFTH NIGHT celebration.

Horse, Festival of the
October

A nine-day celebration of horses in Oklahoma City, capital of Oklahoma, which calls itself the Horse Capital of the World and boasts more horses per square mile than any other state. Highlighting the festival are the pari-mutuel Thoroughbred races at Remington Park. Other equine events are professional rodeo at Lazy E Arena in nearby Guthrie, the world's largest indoor rodeo

arena; indoor polo; a showcase of breeds; the National Miniature Horse Show, and a horse basketball tournament. Accompanying these activities are a celebrity golf tournament, a country and western concert, and other entertainment by nationally known stars.

Many of the events are hosted by the National Cowboy Hall of Fame and Western Heritage Center, which houses the eighteen-foot statue, *The End of the Trail*, by James Earle Fraser, a thirty-three-foot statue of Buffalo Bill, art works by Charles M. Russell and Frederic Remington, and portraits of western television and movie stars, including, of course, John Wayne.

Hortobágy Bridge Fair and International Equestrian Festival
July

A showcase of Hungary's fine horses and riders on the Hortobágy, part of the Great Plain of Hungary. The festival also celebrates the famous nine-arched bridge, built in 1833, that crosses the Hortobagy River and is the longest stone bridge in the country.

The Hortobágy National Park is 150 square kilometers in the grassy *puszta* ('prairie') of the Great Plain near the historic city of Debrecen. During the Turkish occupation that began in the fourteenth century the area was depopulated, and in the eighteenth century it was used for breeding horses, cattle, and sheep. The equestrian fair is held outside the city and features the famed Lipizzaner horses (from Austrian stock) in dressage exhibitions, the *csikós* (Hungarian cowboy) in colorful embroidered riding costume, carriage parades, pulling contests for draft horses, and other equestrian events. There are also crafts fairs and a peasant market.

Hosay Festival
February–March

To Muslims of the eastern hemisphere, the **Hussein Festival** is a solemn occasion commemorating the massacre of Hussein and his brother Hassan, grandsons of the prophet Muhammad, on the tenth day of the month of Muharram in 680 (see ASHURA). But in Trinidad and Tobago, where the Hosay (or Hussein) Festival was first celebrated in 1884, the traditional procession of mourning has been mixed with various European, African, and Indian rituals to form a celebration that is far from somber.

The most popular processions are held between February and March in the towns of St. James,

Curepe, Tunapuna, Couva, and Cedros. The festival usually begins with a procession of flags symbolizing the beginning of the battle of Kerbela, in which Hussein and Hassan were killed. On the second day dancers wearing *Tadjahs*—small minaretted tombs made of bamboo, colored tissue, tinfoil, crepe paper, mirrors, and coconut leis—parade through the streets to the accompaniment of African drummers in a ritual that is reminiscent of CARNIVAL (see TRINIDAD AND TOBAGO CARNIVAL).

The highlight of the festival occurs on the third night, when the large Tadjahs, some of which are six feet tall, are carried through the streets. There are also two moons, representing Hussein and his brother, carried by specially trained dancers. These large crescent-shaped structures are studded with sharp blades and carried on the dancers' shoulders. At midnight, the two moons engage in a ritual embrace to a chorus of cheers from the onlookers.

Hoshana Rabbah
Between September 27 and October 24; 21 Tishri

On each of the first six days of the Jewish SUKKOT festival, a single stanza of the *Hoshanat* litany is recited (except on the Sabbath) and the congregation circles the reader's platform carrying the four species: a palm branch, citron, three myrtle twigs, and two willow branches, gathered into a bouquet. But on the seventh day or **the Great Hoshana**, the congregation makes seven circuits around the altar, after which the four species are laid down and a bunch of five willow branches is picked up and beaten on the ground three times to symbolize humanity's dependence on rain.

Because Hoshana Rabbah is considered the last possible day on which one can seek forgiveness for the sins of the preceding year, the morning service on this day is very solemn. According to Jewish tradition, on YOM KIPPUR God seals the Book of Life and thus each individual's fate for the coming year. YOM KIPPUR falls on the tenth day of Tishri. But since the Middle Ages, Hoshana Rabbah has been regarded as an extension of the deadline for Divine judgment. According to an old Jewish folk belief, notes fell from Heaven on this day informing people of how they had been judged. The traditional Yiddish greeting, *a gute kvitl* 'May you receive a good note', reflects this belief. There is also a popular superstition claiming that a man who doesn't see his shadow on this night is fated to die in the coming year.

Hospital Day, National
May 12

Although Florence Nightingale (1820–1910), the famous nurse and public health activist, spent most of her life in England, it is in the United States that the anniversary of her birth has been celebrated since 1921 as **National Hospital Day**. Originally a day set aside in honor of the woman who made nursing a respectable profession and who revolutionized the way hospitals were run, the May 12 observance was expanded to a week-long event in 1953 so that hospitals could use it to plan and implement more extensive public information programs. Currently sponsored by the American Hospital Association, **National Hospital Week** provides an opportunity to recognize employee achievements, to educate the community about the services hospitals offer, and to keep the public up-to-date on technological advances in the health care field.

In nineteenth century England, it was customary for each community to designate a **Hospital Saturday** and a **Hospital Sunday**—a time to collect money for local hospitals both on the streets and in the churches. Hospital Saturday later became ALEXANDRA ROSE DAY.

Hot Air Balloon Championships, National
Late July–early August

The **U. S. National Hot Air Balloon Races** take place over a ten-day period in late July-early August at the campus of Simpson College in Indianola, Iowa. Their purpose is not only to select America's national champion but to select the hot air balloon team that will represent the United States in the World Hot Air Balloon Championships. When the event was first held in 1970, only eleven balloonists participated, but now there are close to two hundred participants and as many as 250,000 spectators. There are several flights or "tasks" involved in each race, designed to test the pilot's skill in handling his or her balloon. New tasks are added regularly as the sport becomes more demanding. As a result of the races, Indianola has come to be known as the balloon capital of the nation.

Houses and Gardens, Festival of
March–April

One of the nation's oldest and most prestigious house tours, held from March to mid-April in Charleston, S.C. This 300-year-old city has been bombarded by land and sea, devastated by an earthquake, and battered by hurricanes, but it remains a place known for splendid wrought-iron embellished architecture. The port city has seventy-three pre-Revolutionary buildings, 136 late eighteenth-century structures, and 600 others built before the 1840s. Among the more interesting areas is Cabbage Row, the model for Catfish Row in DuBose Heyward's novel *Porgy*, on which George Gershwin's opera *Porgy and Bess* was based.

More than 100 homes and gardens, full of blooming azaleas and camellias, are usually included in the festival, which dates from 1947. It features both afternoon and evening candlelight tours, and special candlelight galas with music and wine.

Houston Livestock Show & Rodeo
Last two weeks in February

The nation's largest livestock show, with some 20,000 entries, held in the famous Astrodome of Houston, Tex. The show is a reminder of the nineteenth-century days when Houston's shipping trade was based on timber, cotton, and cattle. Things get under way with a downtown parade, and the agenda then includes celebrity entertainers, a rally of hot air balloons, and a chili cookoff.

Huey P. Long Day
August 30

Huey Long was the colorful and often controversial governor of Louisiana from 1928 until 1932. Although he was impeached only a year after he'd been elected, he refused to yield the governorship to his lieutenant governor, a political enemy, and held on to the office until someone he liked better was elected. By then he'd been elected to the U. S. Senate, where he took what many considered to be an extreme stand on the redistribution of wealth, and openly rebelled against the administration of Franklin D. Roosevelt, a fellow Democrat.

In 1934–35 Long reorganized the Louisiana state government and set up what amounted to a dictatorship for himself. He exercised direct control over the judiciary, the police, firefighters, schoolteachers, election officials, and tax assessors while still serving as a U. S. Senator. As he was leaving the state capitol building on September 8, 1935, he was shot and killed by Dr. Carl Weiss, the son-in-law of one of his many political enemies.

Despite his controversial political activities, Long was revered by the rural people of the state, who supported his Share-Our-Wealth Society promising a minimum income for every American family. His birthday, August 30, has been observed as a legal holiday in Louisiana since 1937.

Human Rights Day *See* Bill of Rights Day

Human Towers of Valls
June 24

On St. John's Day in the Catalan city of Valls, a touring acrobatic company or *comparsa* presents the **Xiquets de Valls**, or 'human towers of Valls.' The acrobats form human towers or pyramids with four to six men at the base and one or more children at the top. The towers can extend to eight times a man's height, and they are formed to the musical accompaniment of the *gralla* or native oboe. There is a point during the performance at which the children on top salute, the music ceases, and the entire structure stands immobile for several seconds before collapsing gracefully to the ground.

Humor and Satire Festival, National
Late May–early June

Gabrovo, Bulgaria may seem an unlikely place for the only festival in the world devoted to humor. This town, founded by a blacksmith in the fourteenth century, has a longstanding reputation for stinginess, and many jokes are told about the length to which its inhabitants will go to avoid spending money. The first humor festival was held there in 1967 in hopes of attracting tourism to the area. Now it is a ten-day event that features a procession of people dressed as their favorite comic figure, a parade of satiric floats, and competitions to see who can get the best laugh. More than a thousand participants from fifty countries— mostly cartoonists, filmmakers, sculptors, artists, and performers specializing in humor and satire— take part in the festival each year, which attracts more than ten thousand spectators.

Hundred Drums Festival *See* Wangala

Hunger-Hooting Festival *See* Homowo

Hungry Ghosts, Festival of
August–September; full moon or 15th day of seventh lunar month

A Buddhist and Taoist festival probably dating back to the sixth century and Confucius, observed in China as well as throughout the rest of eastern Asia. It is believed that during this month the souls of the dead are released from purgatory to roam the earth. In Taiwan the day is called "open-

147

ing of the gates of Hell." This makes it a dangerous time to travel, get married, or move to a new house. Unhappy and hungry spirits—those who died without descendants to look after them or who had no proper funeral (because they were killed in a plane crash, for example)—may cause trouble and therefore must be placated with offerings. Therefore people burn paper replicas of material possessions like automobiles, furniture, clothing, and paper money ("ghost money") believing that this frees these things for the spirits' use. Joss sticks are burned, and offerings of food are placed on tables outside the people's homes. Prayers are said at all Chinese temples and at Chinese shops and homes, and *wayang* (Chinese street opera) and puppet shows are performed on open-air stages.

Families in Vietnam remember the souls of the dead by visiting their graves. It is known as **Yue Lan**, **Vu Lan Day**, **Day of the Dead**, and **Trung Nguyen**. The festival, the second most important of the year after TET, is observed throughout the country in Buddhist temples and homes and offices. To remember the dead, families perform the *dan chay*, an offering of incense at graves. An altar at home is prepared with two levels—one for Buddha with offerings of incense, fruit, and rice, and one for departed relatives, with rice soup, fruit, and meat. It is considered best if offerings include the *tan sinh*, three kinds of creatures—fish, meat, and shrimp—and the *ngu qua*, five kinds of fruit. Money and clothes made of votive papers are also burned at this time.

Hunters' Moon, Feast of the
End of September, early October

October was traditionally the time when the *voyageurs* or traders came to Fort Ouiatenon (in what is now Lafayette, Indiana) to trade their goods, gossip with the local French settlers, and generally relax and enjoy themselves before setting out on their next journey. Ouiatenon was home not only to the Ouiatenon Indian tribe but also to a number of French families from Canada. The Feast of the Hunter's Moon attempts to reenact as accurately as possible the events that took place there during the mid-eighteenth century.

The two-day festival, which was first held in 1968, begins with the arrival of the voyageurs by canoe on the Wabash River. Events include Indian chants, French folk songs, demonstrations of traditional crafts, and the cooking of typical French and Indian foods over an open fire.

Hurling the Silver Ball
Sunday nearest or Monday following February 3

St. Ia (Eia, Ives) is the patron saint of St. Ives, Cornwall. She was one of a group of Celtic missionary saints believed to have reached the southwestern tip of England miraculously by crossing the Irish Sea in a millstone boat. They made a safe landing at the place where St. Ives now stands, and there are parishes and churches throughout Cornwall named after them.

St. Ives celebrates **Feast Monday**, the day after the Feast of St. Ia on February 3, by playing an ancient game known as hurling. In this case the ball is made of cork encased in silver, which is believed to be very old and is kept in the town clerk's office during the year. The mayor begins the game by tossing the silver ball against the side of the parish church, which is dedicated to St. Ia. Children then take over, tossing the ball back and forth in what might be described as a kind of "hand football." The game stops promptly at twelve noon, and whoever has the ball in his or her possession at that time receives a cash prize or a medal. The festivities continue in the afternoon with more sporting events, and there is a municipal ball in the evening.

Hurricane Supplication Day
Fourth Monday in July

Observed in the U. S. Virgin Islands—St. Croix, St. Thomas, and St. John—Hurricane Supplication Day marks the beginning of the hurricane season. Special church services are held to pray for safety from the storms that ravage these and other Caribbean islands. The custom probably dates back to the "rogation" ceremonies which began in fifth century England—the word *rogare* meaning 'to beg or supplicate.' Rogations usually followed a frightening series of storms, earthquakes, or other natural disasters, although sometimes they took place annually on the ROGATION DAYS that preceded ASCENSION DAY.

At the end of the hurricane season in October there is a **Hurricane Thanksgiving Day**. Again, church services are held so that the islanders can give thanks for being spared the destruction of a major storm.

Husain Day *See* Ashura

I

Ibu Afo Festival
On or around March 20

The Igbo people of Nigeria celebrate their NEW YEAR'S EVE around March 20 with a solemn ceremony marking the end of the old year and heralding the arrival of the new. The council of elders who fix the annual calendar determine the exact hour at which the year will end. When it arrives, a wailing noise signals the departing year, and children rush into their houses, lock the doors to avoid being carried away by the old year as it leaves, and bang on the doors to add to the din. As soon as the wailing dies down, the doors are thrown open and everyone greets the new year with spontaneous applause.

Icelandic Festival
Late July–early August

The Icelandic Festival or **Islendingadagurinn** held in Gimli, Manitoba each year is one of the oldest ethnic festivals in Canada, dating back to 1890. The Icelandic settlers who emigrated to Canada after their homes in Iceland were destroyed by volcanic eruptions in 1875 wanted to do something to preserve their heritage and customs, and the current festival continues to reflect this interest in Icelandic culture. The events include theater programs, choral singing, song writing, and poetry competitions. Participants dress in native Icelandic costumes and eat traditional foods such as smoked lamb and *skyr*, which is similar to yoghurt. In recent years a regatta and air show have been added to the more traditional events, which extend over a three-day period during the last week of July or the first week in August.

Iceland Independence Day
June 17; December 1

Iceland was proclaimed an independent republic on June 17, 1944. Sometimes referred to as **National Day,** the anniversary of this event is also the birthday of Jon Sigurdsson, the nation's nine-teenth century leader. A varied program of parades, sporting competitions, outdoor concerts and shows, speeches, and amusements culminates in the evening with dancing in the streets of Reykjavik and other towns.

Another National Day is December 1, the anniversary of the 1918 treaty recognizing Iceland as an independent state under the Danish crown. This is now largely a student celebration.

Ice Worm Festival
Weekend after first Friday in February

A zany mid-winter festival to celebrate the emergence of the ice worm in Cordova, Alaska, where the winters are long and dark and give rise to thoughts of things like ice worms. The highlight of the three-day festival is the procession of a 150-foot-long ice worm (it has a dragon's head) followed by 500 or so paraders. Other events include variety shows, skeet shooting, ski events, a survival-suit race, a beard-growing contest, beauty pageants, and dances.

The celebration began in 1961 as a way to shake off the winter blahs, and the legend was born then that an ice worm hibernates during the winter in the Cordova Glacier but starts to hatch or wake up in early February. The worm has gained international fame, and the festival draws great crowds of people.

Idaho Regatta
Last weekend in June

A full-throttle three-day event on the Snake River at Burley, Idaho. Burley's population of 9,000 is doubled for the regatta which is a qualifying race for the American Power Boat Association Western Divisional Championship. A hundred speedboats in eleven inboard limited classes compete for a share of $35,000 in cash prizes—and a mink coat. The regatta has been held for seventeen years, and each year, a coat has been donated as a prize by Lee Moyle, one of the founders of the regatta, and an owner of the Don and Lee Moyle Mink Farm. Boats are entered from throughout the country. They include seven-liter, hydroplanes, super–stock, and pro–stock, KRR flatbottoms, Comp Jets, and stock hydros.

Idaho Spud Day
Third week in September

A celebration of the potato in Shelley, Idaho. The potato has come to be thought of as *the* crop of Idaho, but the state actually has a number of other important crops: wheat, hay, oats, barley, beans, peas, sugar beets, and fruits. Nonetheless, the spud gets the hurrahs with a six-day festival (even though it's called a day) that began in 1928 and includes a parade, potato-picking and horse-shoe-throwing contests, and, of course, potatoes fried, baked, scalloped, mashed, etc. Five thousand free baked potatoes are given to visitors.

'Id (Eid) al-Adha (Feast of Sacrifice)
Three days during Dhul-Hijjah

This most important feast of the Muslim calendar is the concluding rite of those performing the Hajj or PILGRIMAGE TO MECCA. It is also known as **'Id al-Kabir**, the **Great Feast.** For those not on pilgrimage, Id al-Adha is a three day festival celebrating Ibrahim's (Abraham) willingness to obey Allah by killing his son, believed by Muslims to be Ishmael, and not Isaac as written in the Old Testament. Muslims consider Ishmael to be the forefather of the Arabs. According to the Koran, Ibrahim had an ax poised over the boy when a voice from Heaven told him to stop. He was allowed to sacrifice a ram instead. Many Muslim families re-enact this show of faith by sacrificing a cow, a ram, or a lamb on this day, using a portion of it for the family feast and donating one- or two-thirds to the poor. In Turkey this day is called the **Kurban** 'sacrificial' **Bayram**. In northern Central Africa it is called **Tabaski**. It is an official government holiday in Chad and Cameroon.

'Id (Eid) al-Fitr
First day of Shawwal

Also known as the **Feast of Fast-Breaking** or the **Lesser Feast**, 'Id al-Fitr marks the end of the month-long fast of RAMADAN and the beginning of a three-day feast. It is the second most important Islamic holiday after 'ID AL-ADHA. The 'Id prayer is performed by the whole community at an outdoor prayer ground ('*musalla*') or *mosque*. Then people put on new clothes, children are given presents, and everyone visits relatives and friends. It is the time when everyone asks pardon for all the wrongs of the past year. Village squares have carnival rides, puppet shows, and candy vendors. It is called **Lebaran** or **Hari Raya** by Indonesians, Thais, and Malaysians. In Turkey, where it is called the **Candy Festival** or **Seker Bayrami**, this is the day on which children are given candy or money wrapped in handkerchiefs. In Pakistan the special treat associated with this day is *saween*, a spaghetti cooked in milk and sugar, and sprinkled with almonds, pistachios, and dates. In Malaya, where it is called **Hari Raya**, they hold open houses. It is the new custom to have one's non-Muslim friends visit to foster more understanding between the different ethnic groups. The Muslims in turn will visit the Chinese during LUNAR NEW YEAR, the Hindus during DEWALI, and the Christians at CHRISTMAS.

In West Africa, a Mande feast of the virgins has been added to this feast. In western Guinea, young men and women parade all night with floats of animals and boats, singing and dancing; small children sing for presents.

Ides
Various

In the ancient Roman calendar, the ides fell on the fifteenth day of March, May, July, and October, and on the thirteenth day of the other months. The Roman emperor Julius Caesar was assassinated on the Ides of March in 44 B.C., and Shakespeare's famous reference to this day in his play *Julius Caesar*—"*Beware the Ides of March*"—is probably the best-known use of the term.

The ancient Romans specified a particular day in the month by relating it to the next calends, ides, or nones. For example, "six days before the Ides of June" meant June 8, since the ides in June fell on the thirteenth.

Calends, sometimes spelled kalends, refers to the first day of the month, from which the days of the preceding months were counted backward. The order of the days in each month were publicly proclaimed on the calends. For example, "the sixth of the calends of April" meant March 27th, or the sixth day before the first day of April (counting April 1 as the first day.)

The Greeks didn't use the term, which is why the phrase 'on (or at) the Greek calends' is a synonym for 'never.' Occasionally calends was used to mean **Settlement Day**, since the first of the month was usually the day on which debts were settled.

The nones fell on the ninth day before the ides.

In March, May, July, and October, the nones occurred on the seventh of the month because the ides fell on the fifteenth. In all the other months, the nones occurred on the fifth day because the ides fell on the thirteenth.

Iditarod Trail Sled Dog Race
Early March

The world's longest and toughest sled dog race, across the state of Alaska from Anchorage on the south-central coast to Nome on the south coast of the Seward peninsula on the Bering Sea just south of the Arctic Circle. It commemorates a 650-mile mid-winter emergency run to take serum from Nenana to Nome during the 1925 diphtheria epidemic. The race, which began in 1973, follows an old frozen-river mail route, and is named for a deserted mining town along the way.

About seventy teams compete each year, and the winner is acclaimed the world's best long-distance dog musher. The race is completed in about two weeks. In 1985, Libby Riddles, twenty-eight, was the first woman to win the race, coming in three hours ahead of the second-place finisher. It took her eighteen days. Susan Butcher won in 1986, and again in 1987, 1988, and 1990. In 1991, Rick Swenson battled a howling blizzard on the last leg to win and become the first five-time winner (1977, 1979, 1981, 1982). His 1991 prize money was $50,000 out of the $250,000 purse. Martin Buser was the winner in 1992 with a record time of ten days, nineteen hours, and seventeen minutes. Jeff King was the winner in 1993.

Mushers draw lots for starting position at a banquet held in Anchorage a couple of days before the race. Each musher, with a team of eight to eighteen huskies, can expect to face thirty-foot snowdrifts and winds of sixty miles an hour.

A number of events are clustered around the running of the race. At Wasilla, near Anchorage, Iditarod Days are held on the beginning weekend of the race, and feature softball, golf on ice, fireworks, and snow sculptures. Anchorage stages an International Ice Carving Competition that weekend, with ice carvers from around the world creating their cold images in the city's Town Square. At Nome, the Bering Sea Ice Golf Classic, a six-hole golf tournament, is played on the frozen Bering Sea during the second week of the race.

Iemanjá Festival
February

A major festival in the Rio Vermelho district of Brazil. *Maes-de-santo* and *filhas-de-santo* (priests and priestesses) sing and dance from daybreak on, summoning *Iemanjá* (the goddess of the ocean) to the festival. Offerings are placed in boats and carried down to the sea, where they are set afloat. Thousands of people flock to the coast for the festivities.

See also NEW YEAR'S EVE IN BRAZIL.

Igbi
Sunday nearest February 5

Because February 5 is the day that the sun shines for the first time on the village of Khora, and then on Shaitli in the Dagestan region of Russia, the Tsezy (Didoitsy) people celebrate this event marking the middle of winter with a festival known as Igbi. The name comes from the plural of the Tsezian word *ig*—a ring-shaped bread similar to a bagel—and the baking of these ritual breads plays a central role in the celebration, which involves a number of masked and costumed characters playing traditional roles. Six *botsi* or wolves carrying wooden swords go from house to house collecting the igbi that the women have been baking in preparation for their arrival. The bagels are strung on a long pole known as the *giri*, and those who fail to cooperate are hit with the swords or have their shoes filled with wet snow and ice. The children get up early on this day, which is now observed on the Sunday nearest February 5 so they don't have to miss school, and go through the village collecting the igbi that have been made especially for them.

Igbi is also a day of reckoning. All through the year the young organizers of the feast have kept notes of the good and bad deeds of the villagers. Now after all the igbi have been collected, there is a ceremony in the center of the village in which the *kvidili*—a traditional figure wearing an animal-skin mask resembling no known animal; lately it looks like a horse with horns and a big mouth like a crocodile—reads out the names of those who have committed a transgression (such as public drunkenness) during the year. The unlucky ones are dragged to the river and immersed up to their knees through a hole in the ice. Those who are congratulated for their good deeds are handed an ig. At the end of the festival, the *kvidili* is symbolically slain with a wooden sword.

I Madonnari Italian Street Painting Festival
Memorial Day weekend

An ancient Italian tradition of street painting, brought to Santa Barbara, Calif. in 1987. Some 200 professional and amateur artists create chalk "paintings"—both reproductions of old masters and original designs—on the Old Mission courtyard. Artist Kurt Wenner has been known for his *trompe l'oeil* paintings in which he transforms sidewalks into fountains or chasms. In 1988, his *Dies Irae*, or 'Day of Wrath,' was a maelstrom of struggling bodies. He used 200 sticks of chalk for *Dies Irae*.

In Italy in the sixteenth century, vagabond artists created sidewalk works of chalk art. Because they often painted the Madonna, they were known as *madonnari*. Artists still follow the tradition in the Italian village of Grazie di Curtattone, and Santa Barbara's "I Madonnari" is considered the village's "sister festival." The art works, masterful as they are, are gone in a week's time.

Imbolc (Imbolg)
February 2

One of the "Greater Sabbats" during the Wiccan year, Imbolc celebrates the coming of spring and the recovery of the Earth Goddess after giving birth to the Sun God at YULE. "Wicca" is the name used by believers in neo-Pagan witchcraft because it doesn't carry the stigma that the terms "witch" or "pagan" carry.

The Greater Sabbats (or Sabbaths) take place four times a year, on February 2, April 30, July 31, and October 31 (see SAMHAIN). In ancient days, they were huge get-togethers that involved dancing, singing, and feasting which went on all night. Revolving around the changing of the seasons and the breeding of animals, they served as a way to give thanks for the bounties of the earth. Other names for Imbolc include the **Feast of Pan, Feast of Torches, Feast of Waxing Lights,** and **Oimelc.**

Immaculate Conception, Feast of the
December 8

Theological controversy surrounded this festival for centuries, though popular celebration of it dates to at least the eighth century. The argument hinged on the meaning of the word "immaculate," which in this context refers to the belief that Jesus' mother Mary was conceived without original sin, the basic inclination toward wrongdoing that originates from the sin of Adam. Many leading theologians, including St. Thomas Aquinas, questioned the Immaculate Conception. Although for many years it remained open for debate, in 1854 Pope Pius IX proclaimed it to be an essential dogma of the Roman Catholic Church, and since that time the Feast of the Immaculate Conception has celebrated God's choice of Mary to give birth to his Son. This is also a pious belief held by many Anglicans.

Impruneta, Festa del
Late October

The fair held at Impruneta, outside Florence, is one of the largest and noisiest of the autumn harvest festivals held all over Tuscany in October.

For weeks before the festival begins, the walls of Florence are covered with posters announcing when the fair will be held. Dating back three centuries, the *festa* originally celebrated the figure of the Virgin Mary which was believed to have been painted by St. Luke. But now it is primarily a celebration of the harvest and a last opportunity before winter to indulge in the area's special foods and the wines of the Elsa and Pesa valleys.

Chicken, pigeons, and suckling pigs are roasted on spits, and there are tables heaped with home-cured hams and loaves of country-style bread. Other foods associated with the fair include the paper-thin anise cookies known as *brigidini* and almond toffee, which is boiled in iron cauldrons.

Inauguration Day
January 20

From 1789 until 1933, the day on which the newly elected President of the United States began his term of office was March 4—now known as **Old Inauguration Day**. The day was changed to January 20 when the 20th Amendment to the Constitution was passed in 1933. When Inauguration Day falls on a Sunday, the oath of office is administered privately, but the public ceremonies are usually postponed until the following day.

The swearing-in of the President has been held at the east portico of the Capitol, building since 1817. At noontime, the chief justice of the United States administers the oath of office to the President, who then delivers an Inaugural Address. This is followed by a colorful Inauguration Parade through the streets of Washington, D.C. Inauguration festivities are usually somewhat more modest when a President is elected for a second term or when a change in the presidency does not involve a change in the ruling political party.

In the evening inaugural balls are held in a number of different locations, and the President and the First Lady try to make a brief appearance at each of them. William Henry Harrison was the first American president to dance at his own inaugural ball, but the exertion proved too much for him. Already suffering from his exposure to the stormy weather during his record-breaking inaugural address (one hour and forty-five minutes), he later developed pneumonia and died within a month.

Inconfidência Week
April

The *Inconfidência* was a colonial uprising for Brazilian independence from Portugal at the end of the eighteenth century. It is celebrated today by paying tribute to Joaquim José da Silva Xavier— also known as Tiradentes or 'tooth-puller' because of his occasional practice of extracting teeth— who became a martyr for independence when the uprising was put down and he was executed.

The Inconfidência Week festivities include performances by orchestras, bands, and choirs, and athletic competitions. The city of Ouro Preto is honorarily restored to its former position as state capital of Minas Gerais during the festival.

Incwala
December or January

The most sacred of the national ceremonies of the independent kingdom of Swaziland. Held in the royal village of Lobamba, it is a six-day ritualized festival of song, dance, folklore, and martial display, focusing on the king as the source of fertility and the symbol of power and unity. During the main ceremony, warriors dance and chant to persuade the king (who has secluded himself) to return to his people. He finally appears wearing a black-plumed headdress, dances the king's dance, eats part of a pumpkin, and throws away the remainder as a symbol of the harvest.

The main musical instruments of the Swazis are rattles, buckhorn whistles, long reed flutes, and the shield, used for percussion.

Independence Day, Finland
December 6

Sweden and Russia contended for Finland for almost 700 years. The Finnish people lived under Russian control beginning in 1809. The Finnish nationalist movement grew in the 1800s, and when the Bolsheviks took over Russia on Nov. 17, 1917, the Finns saw a time to declare their independence. They did so on Dec. 6 of that same year. This day is a national holiday celebrated with military parades in Helsinki and performances at the National Theater. It is generally a solemn occasion that begins with a parade of students carrying torches and one flag for each year of independence.

Independence Day (Fourth of July)
July 4

In Philadelphia, Pennsylvania on July 4, 1776, the Continental Congress approved the final draft of the Declaration of Independence. John Hancock, the president of the Congress was the first to sign the document, using a clear and distinctive hand, thus giving rise to the expression "John Hancock" for one's signature.

As the most important national holiday in America, Independence Day, often called the **Fourth of July,** is traditionally celebrated with fireworks displays, family picnics, parades, band concerts, and patriotic speeches. It is observed throughout the United States and U.S. territories.

Independence Day, Jamaica
First Monday in August

The island of Jamaica became an independent nation with loose ties to the British Commonwealth on August 6, 1962. Before that it had been a founding member of the Federation of the West Indies, a group of Caribbean islands that formed a unit within the Commonwealth of Nations. Allegiance to the British gradually gave way to the emergence of a national identity, and the federation was dissolved.

A public holiday throughout the island, Independence Day is celebrated with traditional music and dancing, and agricultural, arts, and crafts exhibits.

Independence Day, Liberia
July 26

This especially important Liberian holiday is celebrated with a parade, a party for the diplomatic corps in Monrovia, and a grand ball in the evening. Similar events are held throughout the country. The day commemorates the signing of the Declaration of Independence in 1847 by the various settlements of the country, establishing the first independent black republic in Africa. The nation that is now Liberia was settled in the early 1800s by freed American slaves under the auspices of the American Colonization Society. The capitol city, Monrovia, is named after United States President James Monroe. The first settlers arrived on Providence Island in 1822. Other settlers followed, and they united in 1838. After independence elections were held, and Joseph Jenkins Roberts was elected the first president in January 1848.

Independence Day, Malta
September 21

A nationwide celebration of Malta's independence achieved on this day in 1964. Malta was under the control of various political entities from its earliest days. In the early nineteenth century, the Maltese acknowledged Great Britain's sovereignty, but through the years various constitutions were in force, and in the twentieth century, self-government was repeatedly granted and suspended. Malta's heroic stand against the Axis in World War II won a declaration that self-government would be restored at the end of the war, and indeed self-government under another constitution was granted in 1947. It was revoked in 1959, restored in 1962, and independence finally granted in 1964. Ten years later, on Dec. 13, 1974, Malta became a republic.

Independence Day is celebrated with parades and festivities throughout the country.

See also Victory Day.

Independence Day, Tanzania
December 9

A celebration of the independence from the British in 1961 of Tanganyika, which merged with Zanzibar in 1964 to become Tanzania. The day is a national holiday celebrated with parades, youth leagues marching before the president at the stadium in Dar-es-Salaam, school games, cultural dances, and aerobatics by the Air Force.

Independence Day, Zimbabwe
April 18

The major holiday in Zimbabwe, which means 'stone dwelling' in Bantu. An independent constitution was written for Zimbabwe in London in 1979. The country was then known as Southern Rhodesia. Independence followed on April 18, 1980, with the first national budget adopted in July 1980. Robert Mugabe was the first prime minister.

Cecil Rhodes formed the British South Africa Company in 1889 to colonize the region, and European settlers began arriving in the 1890s. Rhodes' company governed the country until 1922 when the 34,000 European settlers chose to become a self-governing British colony. In 1923, Southern Rhodesia was annexed by the British Crown. In the fight for independence in the 1970s, black guerrilla organizations launched sporadic attacks and thousands died in the warfare. The white minority finally consented to multiracial

elections in 1980, when Mugabe won in a landslide.

Independence Day is celebrated in every city and district of the nation with political rallies, parades, traditional dances, singing, and fireworks.

Independence, Mexico, Festival of
September 15, 16

The **Fiesta Patrias** celebrates the anniversary of Mexico's independence. Although the festival itself goes on for the greater part of a week, it comes to a dramatic climax at eleven o'clock on the night of September 15 in Mexico City as crowds of merrymakers wait for the President to appear on the balcony of the National Palace and proclaim the famous *Grito de Dolores* (the 'cry of Dolores')—the 'call to freedom' that the priest Miguel Hidalgo y Costilla of the town of Dolores used to rouse the peasant population to fight for their independence in 1810. The people respond by cheering *Viva México!* and shooting off pistols and fireworks.

The Festival of Independence is celebrated in smaller communities throughout Mexico in much the same way, with the local mayor reciting the *Grito de Dolores* at precisely eleven o'clock.

The following day is Independence Day, which is celebrated with fireworks, the ringing of cathedral bells, and a huge military parade. One of the big events on Independence Day is the drawing for the National Lottery. Tickets are inexpensive, and the winner becomes an instant millionaire. Almost everyone watches the drawing on television or listens to the radio to see who wins.

Independence Movement Day *See* Samil-jol

Indianapolis 500
May; Sunday of Memorial Day weekend

The "Greatest Spectacle in Racing", popularly known as the **Indy 500**, is actually the culmination of a month-long event. It begins the first week in May with the Mayor's Breakfast and parade around the Indianapolis Motor Speedway, the two-and-a-half mile oval track on which the race takes place. Then there are qualifying races to determine who will participate in the final **Indianapolis 500 Mile Race**, which is held on the Sunday before MEMORIAL DAY. On the day before the big race, there is a 500 Festival Memorial Parade that draws more than 300,000 spectators to the streets of downtown Indianapolis and features floats, musical groups, and celebrities. The race itself, which has been held in Indianapolis since 1911, regularly attracts about 450,000 spectators to the 559-acre speedway, in addition to four thousand media people and a nationwide television audience. The Indy is said to be the largest one-day sporting event in the world. The official track record belongs to Robert Guerrero whose one-lap speed was 232.482 mph. This speed won Guerrero the pole position for the start of the 1992 race, but he crashed into a wall during a warm-up lap and had to leave the race.

The Indy racing car is fueled with a blend of fuels (such as methanol and nitromethane) and usually powered by a turbo charged engine. Officially, the Indy 500 is a testing-ground for devices that will eventually be used in passenger cars. The annual race has been credited with such automotive improvements as the rearview mirror, balloon tires, and ethyl gasoline.

Indian Market
Third weekend in August
A showplace for traditional and contemporary Indian art, held on the Plaza of Santa Fe, N.M. The market is the oldest and largest juried competition among Indian artists. It originated as part of the 1922 Fiesta de Santa Fe and continued and grew out of concern that the art forms of the Indian pueblos (villages) were disappearing.

Today more than 800 Indians enter the competition, largely from the nineteen New Mexico pueblos and the Apache, Navajo, Hopi, and Ute tribes of the Southwest. Besides the booths of art works, there are numerous food booths, offering such Indian specialties as green chile on fried bread. Indian dances are performed at the courtyard of the Palace of the Governors. A poster-signing ceremony and a benefit art auction precede the market days.

Indra Jatra
September–October; end of Bhadrapada–early Asvina
The most important festival of Nepal, combining homage to a god with an appearance by a living goddess. The festival, lasting for eight days, is a time to honor the recently deceased and to pay homage to the Hindu god Indra and his mother Dagini so they will bless the coming harvests. It furthermore commemorates the day in 1768, during an Indra Jatra (*jatra* means 'festival'), that Prithwi Narayan Shah conquered the Katmandu Valley and unified Nepal.

Legend says that Indra, the god of rain and ruler of heaven, once visited the Katmandu Valley in human form to pick flowers for his mother. The people caught him stealing flowers. Dagini, the mother, came down and promised to spread dew over the crops and to take those who had died in the past year back to heaven with her. The people then released Indra and they have celebrated the occasion ever since.

Before the ceremonies start, a fifty-foot tree is cut, sanctified, and dragged to the Hanuman Dhoka Palace in Katmandu. It represents Shiva's lingam, the phallic symbol of his creative powers and shows he's come to the valley. As the pole is erected, bands play and cannons boom. Images of Indra, usually as a captive, are displayed, and sacrifices of goats and roosters are offered.

Three gold chariots are assembled in Basantpur Square, outside the home of the Kumari Jayanti, the living goddess and vestal virgin. She is a young girl who was selected to be a goddess when she was about three years old, and she will be replaced by another girl when she begins to menstruate. This indicates she is human. Two boys playing the roles of the gods Ganesh and Bhairab emerge from the Kumari's house to be attendants to the goddess. Then the goddess herself appears in public for the first time, walking on a carpet so her feet don't touch the ground. The crowds go wild. The king bows to the Kumari, and the procession moves off to the palace where it stops in front of the twelve-foot mask of the Bhairab. This is the fearsome form of Shiva in Nepal and is displayed only at this time. The Kumari greets the image and rice beer pours from its mouth. Those who catch a drop of the beer are blessed, but even more are those who catch one of the tiny live fish in the beer.

In the following days the procession moves from place to place around Katmandu. Masked dancers perform every night at the Hanuman Dhoka square dramatizing each of the earthly incarnations of Vishnu. On the final day of the festival the great pole is carried to the river.

Innocents' Day *See* Holy Innocents' Day

Inti Raymi Fiesta
June 24
The **Inti Raymi Festival**, also known as the **Inti Raymi Pageant, Sun Festival,** or **Feast of the Sun**, is an ancient MIDSUMMER DAY festival celebrated by the Incas in Peru on June 24. The ancient Indians, whose empire at one time ex-

tended along the Pacific coast of South America from the northern border of modern Ecuador to the Río Maule in central Chile, believed that their land lay at the center of the earth. They honored Inti Raymi, their sun god, at the foot of La Marca Hills, not far from where the actual equator is now known to be. Their religion embraces both Christian and pagan elements, and they still believe that the sun and moon have god-like powers.

The original Inti Raymi celebration involved animal sacrifices performed by the shaman or priest at the top of the hill of La Marca when the sun reached its zenith at the solstice. Today the main celebration takes place in Cuzco, the Incan twelfth-century capital, where there is a special procession and mock sacrifice to the sun, followed by a week-long celebration involving folkloric dances, tours of archeological ruins, and regional arts and crafts displays. Bonfires are still lit in the Andes Mountains to celebrate the re-birth of the sun, and the Incas burn their old clothes as a way of marking the end of the harvest cycle.

Invention of the Cross *See* Exaltation of the Cross

Iowa State Fair
Eleven days through last Sunday in August

One of America's foremost state fairs, celebrating agriculture and featuring a life-size cow sculpted out of 600 pounds of sweet butter. Held for eleven days at the fairgrounds in Des Moines, and attracting close to a million people each year, the fair is famous for having inspired the Phil Stong novel *State Fair* and three movies based on the novel. Will Rogers starred in the first movie. The second and third were musicals by Rodgers and Hammerstein and included the now-standard songs "It Might As Well Be Spring" and "It's a Grand Night for Singing."

The fair is also famous for its cow made out of butter. The breed represented varies from year to year. It's kept in a display case cooled to forty degrees. The most frequently asked question at the fair information booth is, "Where's the butter cow?" (Answer: in the Agriculture Building.)

Sheep are an important feature at the fair, reflecting the fact that Iowa has more sheep farms than any other state. Sheepshearing contests are popular; champions can shear a sheep in ninety seconds. The big boar contest is also popular; the winning animal always weighs in at more than half a ton. There are other competitions as well: checker playing, horseshoe pitching, fiddling, and rolling-pin throwing.

The first Iowa state fair was held in 1854. Memorable moments in the intervening years include the spectacular crash of two trains, one labeled Roosevelt and the other Hoover, which were throttled up at opposite ends of a track. They roared down on each other, crashed, and exploded. The year was 1932, when the presidential candidates were Herbert Hoover and Franklin D. Roosevelt.

The fair underwent a period of rapid change between 1880 and 1930, expanding to encompass such activities as horse and auto racing, biplane stunt-flying, high-diving horses, and auto-to-airplane transfers. The American aviator Charles Lindbergh visited the fair in 1927, soon after his triumphant nonstop solo flight across the Atlantic.

Ironman Triathlon Championships
Saturday nearest the full moon in October

An extraordinarily grueling international athletic contest held since 1978 in Kailua-Kona on Hawaii Island. It consists of a 2.4-mile swim, a 112-mile bicycle race, and, for the final leg, a standard 26.2-mile marathon run. Close to 2,000 stout-hearted men and women participate, preceding the races with a Thursday-night party in which they stoke up on carbohydrates. Originally contestants swam, biked, and ran for the fun and challenge of the event, but cash prizes are now awarded at a banquet the day after the triathlon. The event is scheduled for the Saturday nearest the full moon in October so that more beach is exposed at low tide, and there is more light from the moon at night. This is the original, but no longer the toughest such contest: double ironmen now challenge triathletes.

Irrigation Festival
First full weekend in May

The oldest continuous festival in Washington, held since 1896 in Sequim. Originally known as "May Days," the festival celebrated the opening of the first ditch to bring water from the Dungeness River to the arid Sequim prairie. In the early days there were horse races, dancing, a keg of beer hidden in the brush, and tables loaded with food. After a few years, Maypole dances with girls in frilly dresses, were a big attraction. The first queen of May Day was chosen in 1908; the first parade was held in 1918; the first queen's float was built in 1948; and a descendant of a pioneer family has been honored as the festival's Grand Pioneer since 1960.

Today, thousands come for a week of activities: a grand parade, a loggers' show, a high-school operetta, crafts and flower exhibits, dances, a horseshoe-pitching tournament, music, and the Ditchwalkers Clam and Spaghetti Dinner.

Islamic New Year *See* Nawruz

Israeli Independence Day
between April 16 and May 14; 5 Iyyar

Known in Hebrew as **Yom ha-Atzama'ut**, this day commemorates the proclamation of independence by Palestinian Jews and the establishment of a provisional government in Israel on May 14, 1948, (5 Iyyar 5708 on the Jewish calendar). It is observed with parties, performances, and military parades as well as religious rituals, which include the reading of Psalms. In the United States, Jews celebrate Israeli Independence Day by attending concerts, films, parades, Israeli fairs, and other public events. An "Israeli Day Parade" is held in New York City, but it doesn't always take place on the fifth day of Iyyar.

A popular custom on this day for Israelis is to walk at least a short distance somewhere in the country where they have never walked before.

Isthmian Games
First month of spring

Athletic competitions held in ancient times at Corinth in Greece. They were held every second year beginning in 581 B.C., with contests in various events, including gymnastics, horse racing, and poetry (the last was open to both men and women). The prize was a crown of celery.

There are differing stories as to the origin of the games; one legend says they were founded by Theseus after he killed the robber chief Sinis. The games were one of the four great national Greek festivals, the others being the Olympic, Pythian, and Nemean games. The Isthmian games were especially popular because they offered more amusements than the other three festivals.

See also NEMEAN GAMES, OLYMPIC GAMES, and PYTHIAN GAMES.

Italian Festival
Late May

A weekend festival in McAlester, Okla., in Pittsburgh County, a coal-rich area that drew miners of Italian heritage in the 1880s. The town began as a tent store owned by J.J. McAlester, who discovered and mined the coal here. He was later lieutenant governor of the state. The descendants of the Italian miners celebrate their heritage with folk music, dances, costumes, arts and crafts, and, of course, food, lots of it: 12,000 meatballs, 6,000 sausages, and 200 gallons of spaghetti and sauce.

Itul
Early December

This highly regarded ritual is a ceremonial dance performed by the Kuba people who live in the Congo. It takes place on an infrequent basis, not only because the costs and preparation involved are so extensive but also because it can only be held with the King's authorization; the only sponsors (and funders) may be the children of a king. An *itul* performed for a king is held in the dance area of the palace and is considered more refined because the King's wives are professional dancers and singers. If the itul is open to the public, it takes place in the plaza in front of the palace. Although it is usually held in December, the dates can vary.

The preparations can take up to several months, but the dance itself lasts only a few hours. The villain's role is danced by someone dressed as an animal, and the plot on which the dance is based combines both traditional episodes and those that have been adapted to whatever animal is chosen. The dance is performed in two parts over two consecutive days. The first part mourns the destruction caused by the enemy-animal, and the second part deals with its capture and killing. There is a chorus of women kneeling in the center who perform the songs and provide a rhythmical accompaniment by beating calabashes or gourd drums on the ground. The dancers move counterclockwise around the chorus, and the king watches the spectacle from a special shelter set off to one side.

The Itul is considered so important that once the word spreads that the ceremony is taking place, Kuba people from all over rush to attend it. It is revived from time to time by kings who fear that their traditional power is being threatened by modern secular life.

Ivy Day
October 6

October 6 is the anniversary of the death of Charles Stewart Parnell (1846–1891), the famous Irish statesman and leader of the Home Rule Party. He entered the House of Commons when he was only twenty-nine and quickly established a reputation for hostility to England and all things English. He became a hero to the Irish poor, many of whom would try to touch his clothes or kiss his hands and knees when he walked through a crowd.

Parnell fell out of public favor somewhat when he became involved in a divorce case in 1890, and the trauma of rejection by so many of his countrypeople is thought to have contributed to his early death in 1891. But he is a symbol of Irish pride and independence, and his name appears frequently in Irish literature, particularly the poetry of William Butler Yeats and the short story in James Joyce's *Dubliners* called "Ivy Day in the Committee Room." It is somewhat ironic that the sprig of green ivy traditionally worn on this day—chosen by Parnell himself as an emblem—is a color he apparently intensely disliked.

J

Jackalope Days
Late June

Four days of celebration in Douglas, Wyo., to honor the jackalope, an elusive animal that is a cross between a jackrabbit and an antelope (according to the legends of Wyoming's Converse County). The jackalope might be mistaken for a large rabbit except for its antlers, and it might be identified as a small deer except for its rabbit-like shape. The jackalope was first seen in 1829 by Roy Ball, a trapper, who was denounced as a liar. Some people still doubt its existence, despite the evidence of numerous stuffed heads on barroom walls. The jackalope is rarely seen because it is a shy animal, and comes out of hiding only for breeding with the commonly seen and hornless females, called does, which look like ordinary rabbits. But it breeds only during electrical storms, at the precise moment of the flash when most people are not out wandering around. A ten-foot replica of a jackalope in Centennial Jackalope Square in Douglas attests to the cultural importance of this critter.

Events of Jackalope Days include a downtown carnival, rodeos, a street dance, a parade, the crowning of a rodeo queen, and sports competitions.

Jackson Day *See* Battle of New Orleans Day

Jacob's Pillow Dance Festival
June–August

The second oldest dance festival in the United States (after the BENNINGTON DANCE FESTIVAL), the Jacob's Pillow Dance Festival takes place for ten weeks every summer at the historic Ted Shawn Theatre near Lenox, Massachusetts. Edwin Myers ("Ted") Shawn was an innovative modern dancer and cofounder, with his wife Ruth St. Denis, of Denishawn, the first American modern dance company. In 1933, at his farm named Jacob's Pillow, he founded the Jacob's Pillow Dance Festival as a summer residence and theatre for his male dancers. After the group disbanded, Shawn turned Jacob's Pillow into a dance center of international importance—a place where not only ballet but modern and ethnic dance could be presented. Top dancers from all over the world give regular performances throughout the summer to packed houses.

James Whitcomb Riley Festival
Early October

James Whitcomb Riley (1849–1916), a poet best known for his nostalgic dialect verse, is honored in his home town of Greenfield, Indiana with a three-day festival held around his birthday on October 7 each year. Most of the events are held near the Riley Birthplace Museum, the house where the poet spent his childhood, although there are poetry contests, programs in the local schools, and parades through the streets of downtown Greenfield as well.

The festival was started in 1911 by Minnie Belle Mitchell, an author who wanted schools and literary clubs to observe the poet's birthday. The governor of Indiana proclaimed October 7 as **Riley Day** soon afterward, and Riley attended the celebration in 1912, finding himself smothered in bouquets of flowers as his car paraded down the street.

Today Riley is best remembered for such poems as "When the Frost is on the Punkin," "The Raggedy Man," and "Little Orphan Annie," which later inspired both the Raggedy Ann and Andy dolls as well as the Orphan Annie comic strip, which was successfully brought to Broadway as the musical *Annie*.

Jamhuri (Kenya Independence Day)
December 12

The biggest of the national holidays in Kenya, observed to commemorate the full independence of Kenya from the British in 1963. A year later, the country became a republic with Jomo Kenyatta the first president. The day is celebrated nationwide but with special events in Nairobi—speeches by the President and other officials, parades, fireworks, and *ngomas*, 'dances' performed in public plazas.

Jamshedi Naoroze (Jamshed Navroz)
March 21

The **Zoroastrian New Year** is observed at the VERNAL EQUINOX among the Parsis in India, who are the descendants of the original Zoroastrian immigrants from Iran (Persia). All the men dress in white, while the women wear colored clothing. Ritual bathing, worship, and the exchange of gifts are part of the celebration.

See also NAW RUZ.

Janai Purnima *See* Raksha Bandhan

Janmashtami (Krishnastami; Krishna's Birthday)
August–September; new moon of Bhadrapada

One of the most important Hindu festivals, celebrating the birthday of Lord Krishna, the eighth incarnation of Vishnu, and the hero of both rich and poor. Throughout India it is a fast day until the new moon is sighted. Then there are ceremonies and prayers at temples dedicated to Krishna. Rituals include bathing the statue of the infant Krishna and then placing his image in a silver cradle with playthings.

In Mathura, where Krishna was born, there are performances of Krishna Lila, the folk dramas depicting scenes from Krishna's life. In the state of Tamil Nadu, oiled poles called *ureyadi* are set up, a pot of money is tied to the top, and boys dressed as Krishna try to shinny up the pole and win the prize while spectators squirt water at them. In Maharashtra, where the festival is known as **Govinda**, pots containing money and curds and butter are suspended high over streets. Boys form human pyramids climbing on each others' shoulders to try to break the pot. These climbing games reflect stories of Krishna, who as a boy loved milk and butter so much they had to be kept out of his reach.

In Nepal, a religious fast is observed on Krishnastami, and Krishna's temple at Lalitpur is visited by pilgrims. People parade in a procession around the town and display pictures of Krishna.

Numerous rich legends tell of Krishna's life. He is supposed to have been adored as a child for his mischievous pranks—tricking people out of their

freshly churned butter, or stealing the clothes of the cow maidens, called *gopis*, while they bathed in the river. Later, he used his flute to lure the *gopis* to amorous dalliances. He also defeated the 100-headed serpent Kaliya by dancing it into submission. Paintings, sculpture, and classical dances depict the many episodes of his life. Portraits of him as a child often show him dancing joyously and holding a ball of butter in his hands. Most often he is shown as the divine lover, playing the flute and surrounded by adoring women.

Jefferson Davis's Birthday
First Monday in June

The only president of the Confederate States of America, Jefferson Davis was captured and imprisoned after the Civil War but never brought to trial. Since he refused to ask the federal government for a pardon, he went to his grave deprived of the rights of citizenship, including all of his former privileges and properties. It wasn't until October 17, 1978 that his citizenship was restored, posthumously, by President Jimmy Carter when he signed an Amnesty Bill designed to "finally set at rest the divisions that threatened to destroy our nation."

Davis's memory is honored by many white southerners in the United States, and his birthday (June 3) is a legal holiday in Alabama, Florida, Georgia, Mississippi, South Carolina, and Texas. In Kentucky, Louisiana, and Tennessee, it is observed as CONFEDERATE MEMORIAL DAY, a time when the graves of Confederate soldiers are decorated and memorial ceremonies are held. At Arlington National Cemetery in Virginia, the Confederate Memorial Services are held each year on the Sunday nearest June 3, and a speaker usually pays tribute to those who died while serving the Confederacy. Another important ceremony is the Massing of the Flags, which is held at the Jefferson Davis Monument in Richmond, Virginia. The flags of the various Southern states are presented in the order in which they seceded from the nation.

Jerez de Frontera Festival *See* Vendimia, Festa de la

Jeshn (Afghan Independence Day)
Late August

A week-long celebration of Afghanistan's independence from British control, observed throughout the country but with special ceremonies in Kabul. The Treaty of Rawalpindi, signed on August 8, 1919, gave Afghanistan the right to conduct its own foreign affairs. It was the formal conclusion of the brief Third Anglo-Afghan War, which actually ended in May, 1919, but August is a slack agricultural period in Afghanistan and therefore a time when more people can celebrate a holiday.

The holiday is observed with parades, dancing, games, music, and speeches by government figures. For example at Nawruz, buzkashi matches (the Afghan version of polo) are played, and customarily there are also wrestling matches and tent-pegging contests, based on cavalry maneuvers of past centuries. Often the period of Jeshn is used for major policy announcements. In 1959, one of the more significant events of modern Afghanistan occurred during Jeshn. Prime Minister Mohammad Daoud and other ministers and cabinet and royal-family members appeared on the reviewing stand with their wives and daughters exposing their faces. This was a highly dramatic event; until then, women in public always wore the *chadri* (an ankle-length tent-like gown and veil that totally covers the head and face, with only a mesh slit to see through). This marked the beginning of abolishing the required chadri, and now most urban upper-class women go about without a veil.

Despite the unsettled conditions in Afghanistan, since the withdrawal of the Soviet military, the independence day celebrations continue. In 1992 the holiday was observed on August 18.

Jidai Matsuri (Festival of the Ages)
October 22

One of the three great festivals of Kyoto, Japan, and also one of the more recent, commemorating the founding of the city as capital in the year 794. A procession of more than 2,000 picturesquely costumed people depict the epochs or ages in Kyoto's history. They parade from the Imperial Palace to the Heian Shrine, which was built in the eighteenth century as a dedication to the emperors who established Kyoto (then called Heian-kyo) as the capital. The capital was moved in 1868 to Tokyo, and the festival stems from that time. Among the paraders is one representing Gen. Toyotomi Hideyoshia, a patron of the arts under whom Kyoto flourished. He reunified the country after a period of civil war in the Azuchi-Momoyama Period (1573–1600). Wearing full armor, he reenacts an official visit to the Emperor.

See also AOI MATSURI and GION MATSURI.

Jimmie Rodgers Festival
Last full week in May

A country music festival in Meridian, Miss., to salute the life and music of Jimmie Rodgers on the anniversary of his death on May 26, 1933. Rodgers was born in Meridian in 1897 and left school at fourteen to work on the Mississippi and Ohio Railroad; later, in his singing career, he was known as the "Singing Brakeman." He learned to play the guitar and banjo, and learned the blues from black railroad workers. Mr. Rodgers' music blended blues with the sounds of country, work, hobo, and cowboy songs. In 1925, because tuberculosis prevented him from working any longer for the railroad, he became a performer, and quickly a best-selling recording artist. Today he is considered the Father of Country Music. Among his recordings that had a lasting influence on popular singers were "Blue Yodel No. 1," "Brakeman's Blues," and "My Time Ain't Long." The Jimmie Rodgers Memorial and Museum in Meridian has exhibits of his guitar, concert clothing, and railroad equipment he used.

The week-long festival highlights top musical stars, and features a talent contest and a beauty contest.

Joan of Arc, Feast day of
May 30; May 9

The second patron saint of France (the first is St. Denys) and one of the best known of all the saints, Joan of Arc—whom the French refer to as Jeanne d'Arc, the "Maid of Orleans," for the role she played in saving the city of Orleans from the British in the fifteenth century—was a young, pious peasant girl from the village of Domremy. In 1428 she heard the voices of St. Michael, St. Catherine, and St. Margaret telling her to help the Dauphin, Charles VII, recover his kingdom from the British. Her mission was accomplished within fifteen months, but Joan was captured by the king's enemies, tried for witchcraft and heresy, and burned at the stake in Rouen on May 30, 1431.

St. Joan's Day is celebrated on May 30 everywhere except in the city of New Orleans, Louisiana, where she is honored on May 9, the day after the anniversary of her dramatic rescue of the French city for which New Orleans was named. In France, the **Fête de Jeanne d'Arc** is observed with special ceremonies in Rouen and Orleans, where the streets are decorated with banners, garlands, and portraits of the teenage girl who was canonized in 1920, five centuries after she led the

French forces to victory and brought about the coronation of Charles VII at Rheims.

Jodlerfests (Yodeling Festivals)
Summer (end of May through September)

Regional festivals of the art of yodeling are held in the summer months throughout the northern German region of Switzerland. Every two years a national Jodlerfest is held. In 1991, it was in Engelberg and brought together not only yodelers from all over the country but also about 150 players of the Alphorn, a 10-15 foot wooden horn with a haunting sound.

The regular annual festivals are held outdoors and feature yodeling clubs, and sometimes solists, who usually yodel without musical accompaniment. The themes of the songs are related to the mountains and the cows and the herdsman's life and loves.

Technically, yodeling is a type of singing in which high falsetto and low chest notes alternate. It is supposed to have originated in Switzerland as a way for Alpine cowherds to call from meadow to meadow or to urge on their cows. However, yodeling is also found in other mountain areas in China and North and South America, and among the Pygmies of Africa and the Aboriginal people of Australia.

John Canoe *See* Jonkonnu Festival

Johnny Appleseed Festival
Third weekend in September

A legend in his own time, John Chapman—better known as "Johnny Appleseed"—was born in Leominster, Massachusetts on September 26, 1774. Although facts about his early life are hard to come by, there is a story that he fell in love with a woman named Dorothy Durand, and that the families of the two lovers were bitter enemies. When Dorothy's family moved West, Johnny followed. But she died of a broken heart before he found her, the legend says, and many years later he returned to place apple blossoms on her grave.

Chapman knew that there was money to be made in the apple nursery business. By the 1790s he was planting apple trees in western Pennsylvania, and by the turn of the century, he'd moved on to Ohio. He had an uncanny knack for selecting the most advantageous spot near a new settlement, begging or leasing a plot of land to plant his trees, and then selling the saplings to frontier farmers. Ironically, his trees and apples were never of the best quality, because he refused to improve his stock by grafting superior branches onto his seedlings. One settler in Fort Wayne, Indiana, where Chapman arrived in 1834, complained that his apples were "so sour they would make a pig squeal." It was supposedly in Fort Wayne that he died in 1845, although no one is certain exactly where he is buried.

Chapman has been commemorated in Fort Wayne since 1974 with a two-day fall festival held at Johnny Appleseed Park. The festival includes traditional music and entertainment, demonstrations of pioneer arts and crafts, visits to the alleged gravesite, and discussions with "The Living Lincoln," who talks with visitors about the social issues of the period in history he shared with Johnny Appleseed.

Jonkonnu Festival (John Canoe)
December 26; January 1

The **Jonkonnu Parade and Festival**, held in Nassau's native quarter combines elements of MARDI GRAS, mummer's parades, and ancient African tribal rituals. It is held on December 26, BOXING DAY, and January 1, NEW YEAR'S DAY. Masqueraded marchers wearing colorful headpieces and costumes that have taken months to prepare dance to the beat of an Afro-Bahamian rhythm called Goombay, which refers to all Bahamian secular music. The music is played by a variety of unusual native instruments, including goat skin drums, lignum vitae sticks, pebble-filled "shak-shaks," and steel drums. The name comes from a number of sources. Historically, it referred to the drumbeats and rhythms of Africa, which were brought to the Bahamas by slaves. The term was used during jump-in dances, when the drummer would shout "Gimbey!" at the beginning of each dance. The Ibo tribes in West Africa have a drum they call Gamby, from which the name goombay probably derived. The Jonkonnu parade, which begins at four o'clock in the morning and continues until sunrise, is followed by the judging of costumes and awarding of prizes. There are Jonkonnu parades in Freeport and the Family of Out Islands as well.

In Belize and parts of Guatemala the John Canoe masqueraders dance from house to house. Their wire-screen masks are painted white or pink, have staring eyes, red lips, black eyebrows, and thin moustaches for men; they are accompanied by two drums and a women's chorus.

In Jamaica, Jonkonnu is featured also at political rallies and Independence Day celebrations. There are "root" and "fancy dress" troupes, the latter being more sedate. Their procession contains Courtiers; a King and Queen preceded by a Flower Girl; Sailor Boy who uses a whip to keep the audience in line; Babu, an East Indian cowboy with a long cattle prod; and Pitchy Patchy, the latter three being more boisterous than the courtiers. The "root" Jonkonnu parade features Amerindians and Warriors, the former dancing with a throbbing rhythm and more body movement; Whore Girl who raises skirts or Belly Woman who shakes her belly in time with the music; and Cowhead and other animal characters who butt the crowd to keep it in line. "Root" Jonkonnu is usually found in remote villages far from large towns or cities.

There are a number of theories as to where the name "Jonkonnu" came from. One is that the festival was started by a West African tribal chief named Jananin Canno, or by the American folklore figure Johnny Canoe. Another is that it comes from the French expression *gens inconnus*, or 'unknown people,' which would seem to refer to the masked dancers. The Jonkonnu Festival is celebrated in Jamaica as well.

Jonquil Festival
Third weekend in March

A three-day (Friday through Sunday) festival to enjoy about 10,000 jonquils in Old Washington Historic State Park in the town of Washington, Ark. The first of these jonquils and daffodils were planted by pioneer families who came here along the Southwest Trail that ran from Missouri to Texas. Washington was the home of the state government after Union troops took Little Rock, Ark. during the Civil War. It is also where James Black, a blacksmith, forged the original Bowie knife for Jim Bowie in 1830 or 1831.

This festival focuses on the history of Washington; the Pioneer Washington Restoration Foundation, established in 1958, has restored buildings that recreate the period of the early 1800s. Tours are given of these historic buildings. Other events are folk-music concerts, food vendors selling funnel cakes (round, greasy, flat cakes made by pouring dough through a funnel onto a grid and sprinkled with powdered sugar) as well as hot dogs and lemonade, an arts and crafts show, blacksmithing, and a special worship service on Sunday morning. The festival attracts about 60,000 vistors.

Jordan, Feast of *See* Epiphany

Jordbruksdagarna
Late September

The town of Bishop Hill, Illinois was founded in 1846 by a group of Swedes fleeing religious persecution in the Old World. Their leader, Erik Jansson, sailed across the Atlantic with twelve hundred followers, crossed the Great Lakes on steamers, and walked 150 miles to form the colony named with the English translation of Jansson's birthplace in Sweden. Cholera took its toll on the settlers, but their biggest setback was Jansson's murder in 1850. Without his leadership, the colony entered a period of rapid decline and, since it was bypassed by the main railroad line, time stood still there for about a century. As a result, many of the historic buildings remained undisturbed, and in 1984 Bishop Hill was designated a National Historic Landmark.

Many of the descendants of the original colonists still live in Bishop Hill or nearby towns, and they continue to celebrate a number of traditional Swedish holidays. One of these is Jordbruksdagarna or **Agricultural Days**, a two-day celebration featuring harvest demonstrations, nineteenth century crafts and children's games, and ample servings of Colony Stew. The residents of Bishop Hill also celebrate Lucia Nights (see LUCIADAGEN), when young women dressed as "Lucias" serve refreshments in the shops and museums.

Jour des Rois, Le *See* Epiphany

Jousting the Bear
March 10

Although jousting normally involves two knights charging each other on horseback with lances, the custom has been changed somewhat in Pistoia, Italy, where **La Giostra dell' Orso** is held in March each year. Twelve horsemen representing the town's four districts join in a procession to the Cathedral Square, each accompanied by a group of costumed attendants. They compete against each other in pairs, racing at a gallop toward the effigies of two bears holding targets in their outstretched paws. Points are won by hitting the targets, and the most successful knight is proclaimed Knight of the Golden Spur of Pistoia.

Jousting Tournament
Third Saturday in June and second Sunday in October

A tournament for "knights" on horseback sponsored by The National Jousting Hall of Fame and held since 1823 in Mount Solon, Va. It's reputed to be America's oldest continuous sporting event.

The tourney, recalling the knights of old, is held at the Natural Chimneys Regional Park, where rock formations resemble castle towers.

Jousting contestants gallop full-tilt down an eighty-yard course as they try to spear and pluck with their lances three steel rings from crossbars; this exercise is called "running at the ring." The rings are as small as one-quarter-inch in diameter. Jousting has been practiced in the United States since the seventeenth century. Tournaments are also held in Maryland, South Carolina, Virginia, and West Virginia, but the Virginia spectacle is the oldest and the most prestigious. Accompanied by parties, these are high social points of the year. About 150 jousters run at the rings at the Mount Solon tournaments.

Juhannus (Midsummer Day)
Saturday nearest June 24

A celebration in Finland of the SUMMER SOLSTICE, and of the feast of St. John. Like a medieval holiday, people celebrate at the lake shores where they build bonfires and dance all night. Since this is the longest day of the year, special late performances are held at open-air theaters in many town. There are also dances at hotels.

Many customs are remnants of pagan times. In earlier times, the bonfire was supposed to reveal the future. Birch-tree branches are brought into the homes to insure future happiness. Even buses and office buildings are adorned with birch branches. On the Aland Islands, tall poles are decorated with flowers and leaves, and supper tables are decorated with birch and garlands of flowers. The church made the festival St. John's Day, but the celebration has more pagan overtones than Christian.

See also MIDSUMMER DAY.

Juneteenth
June 19

Although President Abraham Lincoln (see LINCOLN'S BIRTHDAY) signed the Emancipation Proclamation on January 1, 1863, it wasn't until two years later that the word reached the slaves in Texas. General Gordon Granger arrived in Galveston on June 19, 1865 with the intention of forcing the slave owners there to release their slaves, and the day has been celebrated since that time in eastern Texas, Louisiana, southwestern Arkansas, Oklahoma and other parts of the Deep South under the nickname "Juneteenth."

Observed primarily in African-American communities, Juneteenth festivities usually include parades, picnics, and baseball games. Although Juneteenth observances can be found as far west as California, many blacks who originally came from east Texas and surrounding areas choose to return home on the weekend nearest the nineteenth of June. (See also EMANCIPATION DAY.)

Juvenalia
Three days in June

During the Juvenalia festival each year in Cracow, Poland, the students of Jagiellonian University take over the city for three days. After the mayor hands over the keys to the city, they dress up in costumes and masks and parade through the streets making fun of anything they choose. This celebration goes back to a medieval tradition, when new students at the university had to pay a tax to older ones as part of their ritual entry into college life—much like the "hazing" that goes on in fraternities and sororities at American colleges.

K

Kamakura Matsuri (Snow Hut Festival)
February 15–17

Held in northern Japan in the Akita Prefecture, at the time of year when there is deep snow on the ground. The original purpose of the festival was to offer prayers for a good rice crop to Suijin-sama, the water god.

In Yokote and other towns of the region, children build *Kamakura*, snow houses about six feet in diameter resembling Eskimo igloos. They furnish the huts with tatami mats and a wooden altar dedicated to Suijin-sama and have parties in them, while families gather to drink sweet sake and eat rice cakes and fruits. The rice cakes are made in the shape of cranes and turtles, traditional symbols of longevity, and of dogs called *inukko* and thought to guard against devils.

A similar Kamakura Festival is held in Tokamachi in Niigata Prefecture on Jan. 14.

Kamehameha Day *See* King Kamehameha Day

Kan-Ben
August–September; waning half of Photrobot

The fifteen-day period known as **Prachum-Ben** in Cambodia is dedicated to rituals for the dead. It occurs during the rainy season when skies are usually overcast, and the darkness seems an appropriate time for Yama, the Hindu God of the Underworld, to let the souls of the dead visit their families. The traditional offering to the dead consists of *ben*—special cakes made of glutinous rice mixed with coconut milk and other ingredients-arranged on a platter around a centerpiece and placed on a pedestal. Sometimes the rice is formed into a cone called bay bettbor, with flags, flowers, and joss sticks used to decorate the top. During this time a monk says prayers at the tombs of the dead.

Karnea *See* Carnea

Karneval in Cologne
New Year's Eve until Ash Wednesday

Pre-Lenten activities are especially festive in Cologne, Germany. The celebration begins officially on the eleventh day of the eleventh month at 11:11 p.m., when CARNIVAL societies throughout Germany begin their public activities with singers submitting their latest songs and speakers telling funny tales. The date was originally the end of a fasting period ordered by the church.

During the period from early January until the beginning of LENT, the festival calendar is filled with 300 costume balls, performance of original songs and humorous speeches, and numerous smaller affairs sponsored by such special interest groups as skittle clubs and the rabbit breeders' association. The humorous talks began in 1829, and today audiences clap hands in a slow rhythm to show their approval and whistle to express their disapproval.

These events lead up to the final "crazy days" (Tolle Tage) just before ASH WEDNESDAY. During this time, the Lord Mayor of Cologne receives the Triumvirate of Carnival—Prince Carnival, the Cologne Virgin (who, according to tradition, is played by a man), and the Cologne Peasant. The prince represents the prince of joy, the peasant the valor of the men of the town, and the virgin the purity of the city of Cologne, whose city walls the enemy never breached. The prince gets the keys to the city and rules the city until Carnival ends. On *Weiberfastnacht*, or 'Women's Carnival,' the Thursday before Ash Wednesday, women take control and cut off the tie of any men within reach. This is revenge—women were excluded from Karneval in the nineteenth-century. On Sunday, there are school and suburban parades. Rose Monday is the day of Carnival's mammoth parade with decorated floats, giant figures, and bands. Police from surrounding districts are on duty and join the crowds in singing and dancing. On Shrove Tuesday, there are more parades, and crowds cheer the prince and his attendants. That evening, the Carnival season ends with a ball in Gürzenich Hall, the city's fifteenth-century festival hall. The prince returns the keys of the city, and normalcy is back. On Ash Wednesday, people traditionally eat a fish dinner, and so the restraint of Lent begins.

See also FASCHING.

Kartini Day
April 21

An Indonesian national holiday and commemoration of the birth in 1879 of Raden Ajeng Kartini, one of the country's national heroes and a pioneer in the emancipation of Indonesian women. Throughout Indonesia women wear national dress to symbolize their unity and the nation enjoys parades, lectures, and various school activities.

Lady Kartini, the daughter of a Javanese nobleman who worked for the Dutch colonial administration, was exposed to Western ideas when she attended a Dutch school. When she had to withdraw from school because she was of noble birth, she corresponded with Dutch friends telling of her concern both for the plight of Indonesians under colonial rule and for the restricted lives of Indonesian women. She married in 1903 and began a fight for the right of women to be educated and against the unwritten but all-pervading Javanese law, *Adat*. She died in 1904 at the age of twenty-five after the birth of her first child. Her letters were published in 1911 under the title, *Door duisternis tot licht* ('Through Darkness into Light'), and created support for the Kartini Foundation, which opened the first girls' school in Java in 1916.

Karwachoth
October–November; Karttika

Observed by married women in all Hindu families, the Karwachoth festival is a day-long fast in honor of the Hindu god Siva and goddess Parvati, whom they hope will bring prosperity and long life to their husbands. It is also a time for mothers to bless their married daughters and present them with gifts. Virgins and widows are not allowed to participate in the celebrations, which begin at dawn when the women bathe and put on new clothes. The day is devoted to worshipping Siva and Parvati, and the fast is broken at night when the moon rises.

See also VATA SAVITRI

Kasone Festival of Watering the Banyan Tree
Mid–April–May; Kasone full moon

The most important of the twelve Burmese festivals of the months, **Kason Fullmoon Day**—sometimes known as **Buddha Day**—celebrates the birth and the enlightenment of the Buddha at the foot of the banyan tree. Buddhists gather at monasteries and precept halls to practice meditation, to make charitable donations, and to observe the precepts of Buddhism. Another ritual associated with this day is the pouring of water, both individually and collectively, to celebrate the preservation of the banyan tree. Because Kasone is a hot, dry month, fish are often transferred from streams, ponds, and tanks to places where there is more water.

Kataklysmos, Feast of (Festival of the Flood)
Between May 10 and June 13; coincides with Christian Pentecost

A religious and popular festival celebrated only on Cyprus, with its roots in both the Bible and Greek mythology. The Greek word katalysmos, meaning 'flood,' refers to the Bible's story in the book of Genesis, and a Greek creation story.

In Genesis 6:5-9:1, God decided all humankind was corrupt and that he would bring a flood to destroy all life—except for Noah, his wife, their sons and their sons' wives, and the male and female of every beast and fowl. Noah built an ark for this menagerie, and they all lived on it while it rained for forty days and forty nights, eventually landing, it is thought, on Mt. Ararat. (See also ASHURA.) When the flood ended, God told Noah and his family to be fruitful and replenish the earth.

In the Greek story, Zeus decided to destroy the earth because of human wickedness. Floods covered the earth, leaving only a spot of dry land on top of Mt. Parnassus. After it had rained nine days and nine nights, a great wooden chest drifted to the spot. Within it were Deucalion, the son of Prometheus, and his wife Pyrrha. Prometheus, knowing the flood was coming, had told his son to build the chest and embark in it.

Coming down from the mountain into a dead world, Deucalion and Pyrrha heard a voice telling them to "cast behind you the bones of your mother." They realized the earth was the mother, and stones her bones. They began to throw the stones, and the stones took human shape. They were called Stone People, and rescued the earth from desolation.

Biblical scholars have suggested that the flood described in Genesis is based on the one from ancient Mesopotamian literature, especially in the Gilgamesh Epic, whose hero is called Ut-Napishtim. In this story, the gods bring on the flood because mankind is so noisy they cannot sleep. After the flood, Ut-Napishtim is made a god.

The Katalysmos festivities, held in seaside towns, usually last from Saturday through Monday. They include games, folk dancing, boat races, swimming competitions, feasting, and the singing of *tchattista*, improvised verses sung in competition. The most popular custom is throwing water at one another on Monday to symbolize the purification of both body and soul. Larnaca is especially known for its celebration of Kataklysmos, and other celebrations are held in Limassol, Paphos, Polis, Agia Napa, and Paralimni.

Kattestoet (Festival of the Cats)
Second Sunday in May, every three years (1994, 1997 . . .)

A peculiar celebration to commemorate historic events involving cats, held in Ypres (Ieper), Belgium. There are different stories about how the festival began. One story says that in 962, Baudoin III, count of Flanders, threw several live cats from his castle tower to show that he wasn't awed by cats. The animals had historically been worshiped as creatures related to witches, and Baudoin, a recent Christian convert, was demonstrating that he didn't believe in such pagan ideas.

Another story is that cats in great numbers were needed in the Middle Ages to battle mice and rats. The Cloth Hall, where yearly sales of cloth and garments were held, attracted mice, and cats were set free to devour the mice. But once the sales were over, the rodent problem disappeared and there was a cat problem. The solution seemed to be to hurl the live cats from the belfry.

In the celebration today, about 2,000 people, dressed as cats, witches, and giants, march in a parade to the tune of bagpipes. Floats depict the history of the town and of feline figures—Puss in Boots, the Egyptian cat-headed goddess Bast, and others. The climax of the celebration comes when a jester throws toy witches and stuffed cloth cats from the town belfry.

Keaw Yed Wakes Festival
Sunday of or following August 24

Keaw Yed means 'cow's head' in Lancastrian dialect and *Wakes* refers to the annual feast held in Westhoughton, Lancashire on the Sunday of or following ST. BARTHOLOMEW'S DAY, August 24. Dating back more than four hundred years, the Wakes started out as a religious festival featuring a grand rushbearing procession in which a cart filled with new rushes to replace those used in the church pews moved through the town, ending up at the church where special services were held. After the sermon, the children were given "rush money" to spend at the fair. But over time, the rushbearing ceremony faded and the festival became primarily an opportunity for merrymaking. The foods traditionally served at the festival included pork pasties and frumenty (often called furmenty or furmety), a porridge made from boiled wheat seasoned with sugar, cinnamon, and raisins. Today it is more common to find pies made of chicken, beef, or pork—often with a small china doll baked inside—and brandy snaps, or paper-thin wafers rolled into small hollow cylinders and served with tea.

There have been several attempts to explain the association of the cow's head with the Wakes. One story says that some of the town's wealthier citizens donated a cow to be publicly roasted and distributed to the poor. But rivalry between two factions in town led to a brawl, and the cow's head went to the victors, who were then referred to as "Keaw Yeds" by their rivals.

Keiro-no-ki (Respect-for-the-Aged Day)
September 15

A national holiday in Japan set aside as a day to honor the elderly. At community centers entertainments are held and the guests are given small keepsakes and gifts of food—for example, rice cakes dyed red and white, the traditional Japanese colors of happiness.

Kent State Memorial Day
May 4

When the students at Kent State University in Ohio decided to hold a rally to protest the incursion of U. S. military forces into Cambodia during the Vietnam War, no one thought it would end in a national tragedy or that it would mark a turning point in public opinion about the war. But when the Ohio National Guard started firing indiscriminately at the crowd, four Kent State students were killed and nine were wounded—one of whom was paralyzed from the waist down. The next year, three students were convicted on rioting charges, but the eight guardsmen involved in the tragic incident were never tried. A lawsuit brought by the parents of the slain and wounded students ended in an out-of-court settlement.

A candlelight vigil takes place at the Kent State campus every year on May 4, the anniversary of the 1970 shootings. It begins at midnight on May 3, when a candlelight procession winds its way around the campus and stops in a parking lot near the university's Prentice Hall. There, for the next twelve hours, rotating teams of sentinels stand in the places where Allison Krause, Sandy Scheuer, Bill Schroeder, and Jeff Miller were killed. The vigil is coordinated by the May 4 Task Force, a group led by a Kent State graduate and dedicated to promoting campus awareness and preventing a repetition of the violence. Although the university refused to discuss the tragedy for ten years after it occurred, nowadays it is commemorated openly—to the point where the May 4 Memorial is featured prominently in the college catalog and a course is offered on "May 4th and its Aftermath." There are four permanent scholarships named for the dead.

Kentucky Derby
First Saturday in May

The greatest and most glamorous horse race in America, run since 1875 in Louisville, Ky. Also known as the *Run for the Roses* because of the garland of roses draped on the winning horse, it is a 1-1/4-mile race for three-year-old Thoroughbreds and is the first race in the Triple Crown; the others are the Preakness and the Belmont Stakes. The site of the race is hallowed Churchill Downs, the track known for its twin spires, built in 1895.

The race is usually run in slightly over two minutes, but in 1964, Northern Dancer was the first to win the Derby in two minutes flat. In 1973, the great Secretariat, fondly known as Big Red, won in 1:59 2/5. That remains the only time the Derby was raced in less than two minutes. Ridden by Ron Turcotte, Secretariat then went on to take the Triple Crown, exploding from the pack to win the Belmont by an unprecedented thirty-one lengths.

The Derby took its name from the English horse race that was started in 1780 by the twelfth Earl of Derby, and Kentuckians hoped to duplicate the social panache of the Epsom Derby. They did, in a different way. The Derby became Louisville's major social occasion of the year; women to this day wear their most stylish hats to the racetrack, and there are numerous lavish Derby breakfasts and parties. Traditional food includes Kentucky ham and beaten biscuits. And, of course, the Derby

wouldn't be the Derby without mint juleps, the bourbon-and-mint drink served in cold silver julep cups or in special iced commemorative glasses at the track. Parties are not confined to Louisville; throughout the country and the world, Derby parties are held to watch the race on television. Stephen Foster's "My Old Kentucky Home," the official state song, is played as the horses parade to the post, and spectators in Louisville and far away stand and sing and (sometimes) dab their eyes.

Attendance at Churchill Downs is usually 120,000 to 130,000 people—most of them watching what they can from the infield and a select few, often including royalty, from Millionaires Row high in the clubhouse.

Derby Day is the finale of the ten-day Kentucky Derby Festival—a series of events that include a sternwheel steamboat race on the Ohio River, a Pegasus parade, fireworks, concerts, and a coronation ball.

Landmark events of past Derbies:

The first win by a filly, Regret, was in 1915. She paid $7.30 to win. The only other filly to win was Genuine Risk in 1980; the pay-out was $28.60.

The first woman to ride the Derby was Diane Crump in 1970; fourteen years later, P. J. Cooksey was the second woman jockey.

In 1978, Steve Cauthen, an eighteen-year-old wunderkind known as The Kid, rode to the roses on Affirmed, the latest Triple Crown winner.

Incidental information: the two most winning jockeys have been Eddie Arcaro and Bill Hartack, who have each won five Derbies. Aristides was the name of the horse who won the first Derby.

Keretkun Festival
Late autumn

The Chukchi people of northeastern Siberia hold a two or three day celebration in late autumn known as the Keretkun Festival, in honor of the "owner" of all the sea animals on which they depend for their livelihood. The purpose of the festival is to symbolically return all the animals that had been killed during the hunting season to the sea, thus replenishing the resource that had been plundered. Objects used in the celebration include a special net made out of reindeer tendons, painted oars, statues of birds, and a small wooden image of Keretkun, which is burned at the end of the festival.

A similar festival is held by the Koryak people, another group that depends upon sea animals for their survival. The **Seal Festival** is held at the end of the hunting season in November, and the participants plead with the animals they'd killed to return to the sea and let themselves be caught again next year. The dead animals were represented by stylized likenesses made out of seaweed.

Keukenhof Flower Show
Late March–late May

The world's largest flower show takes place in Lisse, Holland, at the Keukenhof, a former fifteenth-century estate and hunting lodge that has been turned into a park dotted with lakes. As many as five or six million bulbs blossom here between late March and the end of May, either in hothouses or in the flowerbeds that border the ponds and fountains. There is a museum in Lisse devoted to the history and cultivation of bulbs, and young girls (*meisjes*) in fifteenth-century dress sell guidebooks to help acquaint visitors with the eight hundred varieties of tulips, hyacinths, and daffodils that fill the seventy-acre park with color. Thousands of people flock to the gardens each spring, although some prefer to view the bulbs from the windows of the Leiden-Haarlem train.

Kewpiesta
Third weekend in April

The Kewpie doll, which was very popular in the 1920s and 1930s, was the creation of Rose O'Neill, a writer, artist, and sculptor from the Ozark region of Missouri. Modeled on her baby brother, the kewpie doll had a pointed tuft of hair at the top of the head. The annual four-day event known as Kewpiesta is held in Branson, about ten miles south of O'Neill's homestead. Planned and sponsored by members of the National Rose O'Neill Club, the festival includes tours of O'Neill's birthplace, a Kewpie doll look-alike contest, and special displays in store windows. It is held in April, which is the month during which O'Neill died in 1944 as well as the start of the tourist season in the Ozarks.

Khamis al-Amwat
Thursday after Easter

Also known as **Dead Remembrance Thursday**, the observation of this day by Muslims was instituted by Saladin the Magnificent (1137–1193) to offset the widespread celebration in Jordan of EASTER by the Christians and of PASSOVER by the Jews. It is a day to visit cemeteries and to give colored eggs to children. Before World War II, it became a three-day holiday, which included

a visit to the shrine of Moses **Ziyarit al-Nabi Musi** , or simply **al-Ziyara** 'the Visit'.

In Jerusalem on Saturday of HOLY WEEK (see HOLY SATURDAY), Muslims hold the feast of Nebi Mousa for the same reason. Peasants from the countryside arrive in great numbers and go to the mosque near the Dome of the Rock. Old green war banners are unfurled and there is a parade to the shrine of Moses near the Dead Sea which can last for several hours.

Khordad Sal
March 21; July 13; August 15

The Parsis of India, descendants of the original Zoroastrian immigrants from Iran (Persia), celebrate the birthday of their founder on this day. Zoroaster (or Zarathushtra, or Zarathustra) was a sixth century Persian prophet and religious reformer whose ideas combined both monotheism and dualism in the worship of Ahura Mazda, the Wise Lord, and his evil opponent, Ahriman. The largest group of Zoroastrians today can be found in India, where they are known as Parsis (or Parsees), although there are still isolated groups of Zoroastrians in Iran.

Zoroaster's birth is observed on March 21 by the Fasli sect of the Parsis, on July 13 by the Kadmi sect, and on August 15 by the Shahenshai sect.

Kiamichi Owa-Chito (Festival of the Forest)
Third weekend in June

A celebration of southeastern Oklahoma's forest industry and of the culture of the Choctaw Indians of the area, held in Beavers Bend State Park near Broken Bow. Shortleaf and loblolly pines are abundant in the region, which is the heart of Oklahoma's timberland. The mistletoe, Oklahoma's state flower, also flourishes here. The Forest Heritage Center in the park has exhibits that include pertified logs, tools of the forest industry, and dioramas.

Sporting events of the festival include canoe races, archery, horseshoe throwing, and log birling (log rolling). Other activities range from contests in tobacco spitting and turkey and owl calling to a photography show and musical entertainment—gospel singing, fiddling, and bluegrass.

Kiddies' Carnival
Between January and March; the week before Carnival

Trinidad and Tobago, in the West Indies, is the

only country that sponsors a CARNIVAL celebration specifically for children, based on the pre-Lenten Carnival celebrations for adults. The week before Carnival begins, there is a big parade in which groups of children choose a theme (such as "Arabian Nights") and dress up in costumes illustrating their theme. They sing and dance to calypso or do the "jump-up," a free-style dance that originated here.

Kiel Week
Last week of June

An international sailing regatta in Kiel, Germany, at which the world's leading yachters compete. Craft of all sorts—sail, motor, and muscle-powered—race on the waters of the Kiel Fjord. Kiel, once the chief naval port of Germany, is a center of inshore and deep-sea fishing, and was host for the sailing races of the 1972 OLYMPIC GAMES.

Kinderzeche (Children's Party)
Saturday before the third Monday of July

A festival in Dinkelsbühl (Bavaria), Germany, to honor the children who saved the town during the Thirty Years' War of 1618–1648. In 1632, according to legend, the Swedish commander, a Colonel Sperreuth, threatened destruction of the town (which endured eight sieges during the war). The town council was debating its response, when a gatekeeper's daughter named Lore proposed gathering a group of children together to appeal to Sperreuth. The council agreed to let her try. As the Swedish troops rode into town, the children sang, and Lore with her small band of children appeared before the commander, knelt, and asked his mercy. The commander's heart softened; he spared the town, and told the citizens, "Children are the rescuers of Dinkelsbühl. Always remember the debt of thanks you owe them."

The celebration today is a reenactment of the event, with participants (most of them Dinkelsbühl residents) in the costume of seventeenth-century town councilors and soldiers. Highlights of the festival are the parade of the Dinkelsbühl Boys' Band and a performance of a medieval sword dance, in which dancers stand atop a pedestal of crossed blades. About 300,000 visitors attend the festival.

Dinkelsbühl is about twenty miles from Rothenburg-on-the-Tauber, Germany, which also commemorates an event of the Thirty Years' War.

See also MEISTERTRUNK PAGEANT.

King, Birthday of His Majesty the
December 29

A public holiday to celebrate the birthday of Nepal's present ruler, King Birendra Bir Bikram Shah Dev. People from all over the country gather for a huge parade and rally on the Tundikhel parade grounds of Katmandu, Nepal. Troupes perform song and dance in traditional costumes, and fireworks round off the festivities.

Kingdom Days
Last weekend in June

This annual festival in Fulton, Missouri is based on a Civil War confrontation between a Union General and the local militia. On July 28, 1861, there was a battle near Calwood that left nineteen dead and seventy-six wounded. In an effort to spare Callaway County any further bloodshed, Colonel Jefferson Jones sent a letter to General John B. Henderson, commander of the Union military forces in northeastern Missouri. Jones requested that the county be left alone to conduct its own business and to control its own destiny. Henderson, perhaps fearing stiff resistance, agreed to the truce and signed the treaty that designated Callaway County a "kingdom," separate from both the U. S. and the Confederacy. No shots were fired, no one was injured, and the disagreements between the two military units were settled peacefully.

This event is only one of the historic reenactments that take place during the annual Kingdom Days festival. Others are more humorous, such as the "shotgun" Civil War-era wedding that took place in 1991. Other events include bed races, a "baby derby" in which babies up to eighteen months old crawl ten feet to the finish line, a hot-air balloon rally, and a pig-kissing contest.

King Kamehameha Celebration
June 11

A state holiday in Hawaii to celebrate the reign of the island state's first king, and the only public holiday in the United States that honors royalty.

King Kamehameha I, known as 'the Great' (1758–1819) was the son of a high chief. At his birth it was prophesied that he would defeat all his rivals. He originally was named Paiea, which means 'soft-shelled crab'. When he grew to manhood he took the name Kamehameha, meaning 'the very lonely one' or 'the one set apart'. By 1810 he had united all the Hawaiian islands and was undisputed ruler (1810–19). He promulgated the *mamalahoe kanawai* 'law of the splintered paddle,' which protected the common people from the brutality of powerful chiefs, and he outlawed human sacrifice. He made a fortune for his people with a government monopoly on the sandalwood trade. After his death, he was succeeded by his son, Kamehameha II.

Celebrations extend several days beyond the actual public holiday. Leis (Hawaiian floral necklaces) are draped on the king's statue across from Iolani Palace, formerly the home of Hawaii's monarchs and now the state capitol, in Honolulu, and there is another lei-draping at Kapaau, North Kohala. A floral parade travels from downtown Honolulu to Waikiki; it features a young man who depicts the king wearing a replic of the golden amo-feather cloak and Grecian-style helmet (the originals are kept in Honolulu's Bernice P. Bishop Museum and are displayed on this day). The parade also includes floats and princesses on horseback wearing the pa'u, satin riding dresses in the color of their island home. Other events include demonstrations of arts and crafts, a competition of chants and hulas, and a luau, or Hawaiian cookout.

King's Birthday
December 5

A national holiday to celebrate the birthday of Thailand's King Bhumibol Adulyadej, who has been the largely symbolic chief of state since 1950. Bangkok blooms with decorations, which are especially lavish in the area of the floodlit Grand Palace. Full dress ceremonies, including a Trooping of the Colors by Thailand's elite Royal Guards, are performed at the palace.

Kingsburg Swedish Festival
Third weekend in May (Thursday through Sunday)

A tribute to the Swedish heritage of Kingsburg, Calif. The event began in 1924 as a luncheon to commemorate the midsummer celebration of the harvest in Sweden. Today it's a full-fledged festival attracting about 25,000 visitors. Swedish costumes are worn and Swedish food is eaten—Swedish pancakes, Swedish pea soup, a smorgasbord. Events include a Parade of Trolls, raising of the May Pole, folk dancing, arts and crafts displays, a horse trot, and live entertainment.

Kissing Day
January 1

In the nineteenth century, the Chippewa Indians of Minnesota observed NEW YEAR'S DAY by giving and receiving a kiss or a cake—a custom they apparently picked up from the French-Canadians. The Puritan missionaries who came to Minnesota to convert the Indians to Christianity were aghast when the natives attempted to greet them in this way on New Year's Day, and eventually taught them to receive gifts and sing a New Year's hymn instead.

Kite Flying *See* **Tako-Age**

Klo Dance
Autumn

A harvest celebration among the Baoulé people of the Ivory Coast in western Africa, the *klo* dance takes place during the fall harvest season and is similar to TRICK OR TREAT NIGHT in the United States. Groups of young boys dressed from head to toe in strips of palm leaves go from house to house, dancing to the accompaniment of sticks beaten together. They ask for "treats"—yams, manioc, or peanuts—and sing a song of thanks if they are given any. But if they are refused, their "trick" is to sing teasing songs and to scold the woman of the house for being stingy. Afterward, the boys take their treats into the bush to eat them.

Klondike Gold Discovery Day
Monday nearest August 17

On August 17, 1896 George Washington Carmack discovered gold at Bonanza Creek in northwestern Canada's Yukon Territory. His discovery triggered a huge gold rush and an enormous influx of American miners and traders. More than thirty thousand poured into the Klondike region over the next couple of years, sparking the formation of Dawson and the construction of the Yukon narrow-guage railway. But the Klondike boom was short-lived, and by 1900 most of the miners had given up and were replaced by companies using mechanical mining techniques. To this day, mining remains the area's most important industry.

Also known as **Discovery Day**, this important event in Canada's history is observed as a holiday in the Yukon.

Klondike International Outhouse Race
Sunday of Labor Day weekend

First held in 1977, the Klondike International Outhouse Race takes place annually in the gold rush city of Dawson in Canada's Yukon Territory. A serious athletic event for some—and an opportunity for less serious competitors to indulge in what can only be described as "bathroom humor"—the race involves four-person teams, each pulling an outhouse on wheels. Many of the teams compete in outrageous costumes and cover their outhouses with appropriate graffiti or equip them with such modern-day comforts as telephones and carpeted seats.

There are two basic types of competitors: the serious runners, who train rigorously for the event and are sent off in the first heat of the three kilometer race; and those who never make it any further than the first bar on the course, or who reach the finish line from the wrong direction. There are awards for the best dressed as well as the fastest, and the grand trophy is a wooden outhouse with an engraved plaque.

Knabenschiessen (Boys' Rifle Match)
Second weekend in September

A marksmanship contest in Zurich, Switzerland, for boys aged twelve to sixteen. The custom dates to the seventeenth century when all boys were required to practice their shooting during summer holidays. The final rifle match was a kind of examination. Today, the boys use rifles like those they will be issued in the army. Prizes are awarded, and the winner is named King of the Marksmen. A huge amusement park is set up for the Knabenschiessen, and there is a parade and market.

Kodomo-no-Hi (Children's Day)
May 5

A national holiday in Japan that was known as Boys' Day from the ninth century, but became a day for both boys and girls in 1948. Today the day is observed largely with family picnics, but some still practice the old custom of flying wind socks in the shape of carp, a common Japanese food fish. Households with sons erect tall bamboo poles outside the home and attach streamers in the shape of carp for each son. The carp supposedly represents the strength, courage, and determination shown in its upstream journeys. The festivities are part of GOLDEN WEEK.

Koledouvane
December 24–25

Koledouvane is the ritual singing of Christmas carols that takes place in Bulgaria each year on December 24 and 25. The *koledari* 'carol singers' go from house to house and wish people good health and prosperity. Although their dress and ornaments differ from region to region, they always carry a *koledarka*, a long oak stick covered with elaborate carving.

A similar ritual, called Sourvakari, is carried out on NEW YEAR'S DAY. Those who go from house to house wishing people a Happy New Year carry

a decorated cornel (dogwood) twig, which they use to tap people on the back as they deliver their good wishes. The near coincidence of the two customs can probably be explained by the switch from the Julian to the Gregorian calendar. They have survived as separate celebrations, even though they are closely related in meaning.

Kopenfahrt (Barrel Parade)
Between February 3 and March 9; Shrove Tuesday

The **Kope Festival** on SHROVE TUESDAY has been observed by the salt miners of Lüneburg, Germany since the fifteenth century. Originally the *Kope*, a wooden barrel filled with stones, was dragged through the narrow streets of the town by *Salzjunker*, or young journeymen salters, on horseback. They were followed by a long procession of local officials, salt mine laborers, and townspeople. Today the **Kope Procession** has become a folk, rather than an historical, event. As the riders attempt to guide the Kope through the streets, trumpeters blast their instruments as loudly as possible in an attempt to unnerve the horses. Once the Kope is brought to the mouth of the salt mine, it is set on a huge pile of wood and burned. Following the bonfire is a ceremony initiating the Salzjunker into the Guild of Master Salters.

Some believe that the Kopenfahrt bonfire was originally a pagan ceremony symbolizing the Sun God's triumph over the forces of darkness. In any case, the ancient festival was revived in 1950 and is now a regular part of the old mining town's annual CARNIVAL celebration.

Krishna's Birthday *See* Janmashtami

Kristallnacht (Crystal Night)
November 9–10

When a seventeen-year-old Jew named Herschel Grynszpan assassinated the Third Secretary at the German embassy in Paris on November 7, 1938 to avenge the expulsion of his parents and fifteen thousand other Polish Jews to German concentration camps, it gave the German Nazis the excuse they had been looking for to conduct a *pogrom* 'organized massacre.' Crystal Night or **Night of the Broken Glass** gets its name from the shattered glass that littered the streets two nights later, when the windows of Jewish-owned shops and homes were systematically smashed throughout Leipzig and other German and Austrian cities in a frenzy of destruction that resulted in the arrest and deportation of about 30,000 Jews.

Crystal Night marked the beginning of the Nazis' plan to rob the Jews of their possessions and to force them out of their homes and neighborhoods. Although the so-called "Final Solution" (to kill all European Jews) had not been suggested at this point, the Nazis' actions on this night left little doubt as to what the fate of German Jews would be if war broke out. Today Jews everywhere observe the anniversary of this infamous event by holding special memorial services.

In Germany, Kristallnacht coincides with the anniversary of another famous, if very recent, event: the breaching of the Berlin Wall in 1989. The coincidence of the two observances is seen by many as symbolic of the conflicts of German history.

'Ksan Celebrations
Friday evenings, July and August
Dances and accompanying songs held by the 'Ksan Indians in a long house in the Indian Village in Hazelton, British Columbia (Canada). They are generally a celebration of the important things of life, such as breathing, and being at one with the cosmos.

The dances are said to go back to pre-history; they were revived in 1958, and the 'Ksan dancers have since performed in New York City, San Francisco, Seattle, Kansas City, and even Australia.

Box-shaped skin drums provide the beat for the dances. Songs, besides being about cosmic events, are sometimes songs of marriage, songs of divorce, or what are known as "happy heart songs" about almost anything. Performers must be *Git 'Ksan*, meaning 'People of the 'Ksan.' (The 'Ksan is a river in the area.)

Because the homeland of the Git 'Ksan is far inland, it was overlooked by the Spaniards and Russians who explored the coast in the 1700s, and fur traders didn't stay here because the climate is too humid for good fur. As a result of this neglect, the 'Ksan culture has been maintained without outside influences.

Kuhio Day *See* Prince Kuhio Day

Kumbh Mela (Pitcher Fair)
Every 12 years on a date calculated by astrologers (most recently in February 1989)
Mass immersion rituals by Hindus near the city of Allahabad (the ancient holy city of Prayag) in north-central India. Millions of pilgrims gather to bathe at the confluence of the *Ganga* (Ganges River) and Yamuna Rivers, which is also where the mythical river of enlightenment, the Saraswati flows. The bathers wash away the sins of their past lives and pray to escape the cycle of reincarnation. *Sadhus*, or holy men, carry images of deities to the river for immersion, and the most ascetic sadhus, naked except for loincloths, their faces and bodies smeared with ashes, go in procession to the waters, escorting images borne on palanquins. The Ganges is not only a sacred river but is the source of all sacred waters. The junction of the three rivers at Allahabad is called the *sangam* and is considered by some the holiest place in India.

The *mela* ('fair') is thought to be the largest periodic gathering of human beings in the world; a vast tent city appears, temporary water and power lines are installed, and ten pontoon bridges are laid across the Ganges. Movies of Hindu gods and heroes are shown from the backs of trucks, and plays recounting Hindu mythology are performed. Merchants lay out all manner of goods.

The story behind the mela is that Hindu gods and *asuras* or 'demons' fought for a *kumbh*, or 'pitcher,' carrying *amrit*, the nectar of immortality. The god who seized the kumbh stopped at Prayag, Hardwar, Nasik, and Ujjain on his way to paradise. The journey took twelve days (longer than earthly days), and therefore the mela follows a twelve-year cycle.

A purification bathing ceremony called the **Magh Mela** is also held each spring in Allahabad. It is India's biggest yearly religious bathing festival. Although the Magh Mela attracts a million people, more or less, the Kumbh Mela dwarfs it!

Ku-omboko
February or March
Ku-omboko, which means 'getting out of the water,' is a floodtime festival observed by the Lozi people of Zambia. When the Zambezi River begins its annual flooding of the Barotzé flood plains, thousands of boats and canoes, led by the chief on his royal barge, make their way to higher ground. When the Lozi reach their new seasonal home at Limulunga, they celebrate with singing and dancing. In July, when the floods have receded, they return to the lowlands.

Kupalo Festival
June 24; Midsummer's day and night
A Ukrainian festival, dating back to pagan days

that is celebrated by young unmarried men and women, and boys and girls. The festival takes its name from the god of summer and fertility: Kupalo sleeps in the winter and each spring awakens and shakes the tree he's been under, making the seeds fall as a sign of the year's harvest. During the day and night of the celebration, boys and girls decorate a sapling tree with flowers, seeds, and fruit, call it Kupalo, and dance and sing special songs to please this image of the god.

In other events of the day, young women gather flowers to make a wreath that is tossed into a river; the spot where the wreath reaches shore indicates the family the girl will marry into. Another custom for girls is to make an effigy of Marena, the goddess of cold, death, and winter. After singing special songs, they burn or drown the effigy to cut the goddess's power over the coming winter; winters in Ukraine are very harsh.

Young men sometimes go into the forest to look for a special fern that only blooms (according to the legend) on the night of MIDSUMMER. They take with them a special cloth, white powder, and a knife. If they find the fern and are strong enough to ward off the enticements of wood nymphs, they draw a circle with the white powder and sit and wait for the fern to bloom. When it does, they cut the blossom with the knife and put the flower in the special cloth. They must never, ever, tell anyone they have found the fern, or they will lose the luck and power it gives. The people's rationale behind this story is that it explains why some people have more talent and luck than others.

The celebrations to a greater or lesser degree are popular in both Ukraine and among Ukrainians in the United States.

Kutztown Fair
Five days including 4th of July weekend

The **Pennsylvania Dutch Folk Festival** in Kutztown, Pennsylvania is an annual celebration of Pennsylvania Dutch foods, crafts, and customs. Although many people identify the "Pennsylvania Dutch" with the Amish people, the Mennonites or with the Holland Dutch, the name actually came from the Yankee pronunciation of *Deutsch*, meaning German. But the Pennsylvania Dutch are not simply transplanted Germans, either. Their folk culture is peculiarly American, and they encompass a number of national and religious groups.

The Kutztown Fair, sponsored by Franklin and Marshall College, acquaints visitors with all aspects of Pennsylvania Dutch culture. There are special foods—such as apple butter, *rivvel* soup (*rivvels* are like dumplings), and the fruit pies which the Pennsylvania Dutch claim to have originated. Traditional artisans featured at the fair include tinsmiths, pretzel-makers, candlemakers, cigarmakers, weavers, potters, and quilters. There are reenactments of a Pennsylvania Dutch funeral feast and demonstrations of *nipsi*—a complicated game that involves batting a piece of wood and then "bidding" the number of hops that the opposing team will require to get from where the wood landed back to home base. There is even a seminar on Pennsylvania Dutch cooking. One of the fair's most interesting figures is the *Fraktur* painter, who illuminates birth and baptismal records and book plates with bright colors and flowing scrollwork.

Kwanzaa
December 26–January 1

An African-American celebration of family and black culture, thought to be observed by 5 million Americans and perhaps 10 million others in Africa, Canada, the Caribbean, and parts of Europe. The holiday was created in 1966 by Maulana Karenga, chairman of the Black Studies Department at California State University in Long Beach.

In Swahili, Kwanzaa means 'first fruits of the harvest,' and first-fruit practices common throughout Africa were adapted by Karenga for the celebration.

Each day of the seven-day festival is dedicated to one of seven principles: *umoja* (unity), *kujichagulia* (self-determination), *ujima* (collective work and responsibility), *ujamaa* (cooperative economics), *nia* (purpose), *kuumba* (creativity), and *imani* (faith). Families gather in the evenings to discuss the principle of the day, and then light a black, red, or green candle and place it in a seven-branched candleholder called a *kinara* to symbolize giving light and life to the principle. On the evening of Dec. 31, families join with other members of the community for a feast called the *karamu*. Decorations are in the red, black, and green that symbolize Africa, and both adults and children wear African garments. Increasingly, colleges and museums are holding Kwanzaa events during some of the days. For example, in Chicago, an African Market is held on Dec. 28 by the Ujamma Family, a black self-help group. In New York City the American Museum of Natural History celebrates Kwanzaa with an African Marketplace, poetry folktales, and music.

L

Labor Day
First Monday in September

Although workers' holidays had been observed since the days of the medieval trade guilds, laborers in the United States didn't have a holiday of their own until 1882, when Peter J. McGuire, a New York City carpenter and labor union leader, and Matthew Maguire, a machinist from Paterson, N.J. suggested to the Central Labor Union of New York that a celebration be held in honor of the American worker. Some 10,000 New Yorkers paraded in Union Square, New York, on September 5 of that year—a date specifically chosen by McGuire to fill the long gap between INDEPENDENCE DAY and THANKSGIVING.

Although the first Labor Day observance was confined to New York City, the idea of setting aside a day to honor workers spread quickly, and by 1895 Labor Day events were taking place across the nation. Oregon, in 1887, was the first state to make it a legal holiday, and in 1894 President Grover Cleveland signed a bill making it a national holiday. The holiday's association with trade unions has declined, but it remains important as the day that marks the end of the summer season for schoolchildren and as an opportunity for friends and families to get together for picnics and sporting events.

Labour Day is celebrated in England and Europe on May 1. In Australia, where it is called EIGHT HOUR DAY, it is celebrated at different times in different states, and commemorates the struggle for a shorter working day. Labor Day is observed on the first Monday in September throughout the United States, in Canada, and in Puerto Rico.

Labour Day *See* Eight-Hour Day

Ladouvane
January 1; June 24

Ladouvane or the **Singing to Rings** is a Bulgarian fertility ritual. Young girls drop their rings, together with oats and barley (symbols of fertility) into a cauldron of spring water. The rings are tied with a red thread to a bunch of ivy, crane's bill, basil, or some other perennial plant, and the cauldron is left out overnight. Ritual dances are performed around the cauldron and the girls' fortunes are told.

In West Bulgaria, the Central Balkan Range, and along the Danube River, Ladouvane is observed on NEW YEAR'S EVE. In the rest of the country, it is observed on MIDSUMMER DAY.

Lady Day
March 25

The name in England for the ANNUNCIATION. This day was originally called **Our Lady Day**, a name that applied to three other days relating to the Virgin Mary: the IMMACULATE CONCEPTION (December 8), the NATIVITY OF THE VIRGIN (September 8), and the ASSUMPTION OF THE VIRGIN MARY (August 15). It commemorates the archangel Gabriel's announcement to Mary that she would give birth to Jesus, and is often referred to simply as The Annunciation. Lady Day is one of the QUARTER DAYS in England and Ireland when rents are paid and tenants change houses. In France it is called **Nôtre Dame de Mars** ('Our Lady of March').

Laetare Sunday *See* Mothering Sunday

Lajkonik
Between May 21 and June 24; first Thursday after Corpus Christi

The most popular folk festival in Krakow, Poland, Lajkonik or the **Horse Festival** has lost touch with its medieval roots, but is believed to commemorate the horseman who carried the news of the Tartar defeat during the thirteenth century Tartar invasions. A group of eighteen costumed people gathers in the courtyard of the Norbertine Monastery in a suburb of Krakow. They include a standard-bearer in the traditional dress

Lammas

of a Polish nobleman, a small band of musicians, and a bearded horseman in oriental costume riding a richly draped but rather small wooden hobby-horse. This is the Lajkonik, originally called the Horse or the 'Zwierzyniec Horse,' named for the town where the monastery is located, and now the unofficial symbol of Krakow.

After performing a ceremonial dance for the vicar and the nuns, the procession leaves the monastery and moves in the direction of the city. The horseman collects money from the crowds lining the streets, striking each contributor lightly with his baton to bring them good luck; they then join the procession. Eventually the parade ends up in the market square for the most important part of the ceremony. The city officials await the horseman on the steps of the town hall. He performs a dance for them, is rewarded with a purse full of money and a glass of wine, which he drinks to the health of the city.

The festival was first sponsored by the guild that funished wood to Krakow and the salt mines. Today the actors are from the Boatman Congregation who, since the Middle Ages, have floated timber down the Vistula River to Krakow.

Lammas
August 1
This was one of the four great pagan festivals of Britain and was originally called the festival of the **Gule of August.** It celebrated the harvest, and was the forerunner of America's THANKSGIVING and Canada's Harvest Festival. In medieval England, loaves made from the first ripe grain were blessed in the church on this day—the word *lammas* being a short form of "loaf Mass." Lammas Day is similar in original intent to the Jewish Feast of Weeks, also called SHAVUOTH or **Pentecost**, which also came at the end of the PASSOVER grain harvest. A fifteenth-century suggestion was that the name derived from 'lamb' and 'Mass,' and was the time when a feudal tribute of lambs was paid.

Along with CANDLEMAS, WALPURGIS NIGHT, and HALLOWEEN, Lammas is an important day in the occult calendar. In the Scottish Highlands, people used to sprinkle their cows and the floors of their houses with menstrual blood, which they believed was especially potent against evil on this day. It was also one of the QUARTER DAYS in Scotland, when tenants brought in the first new grain to their landlords.

A phrase used from the sixteenth to the nineteenth century, "at Latter Lammas Day," meant 'never.'

Landing of d'Iberville
Last weekend in April
A commemoration of the landing in 1699 of Pierre LeMoyne d'Iberville at a spot on Biloxi Bay that is now Ocean Springs, Miss. The arrival of d'Iberville and 200 colonists established the Louisiana Colony for King Louis XIV of France; the territory stretched from the Appalachians to the Rocky Mountains, and from Canada to the Gulf of Mexico. D'Iberville built Fort Maurepas here, the first significant structure erected by Europeans on the Gulf Coast.

A replica of the fort is the backdrop for the reenactment of the landing. This pageant boasts a costumed cast representing both the notables of d'Iberville's fleet as well as the welcoming Biloxi Indians. The part of d'Iberville is always played by a celebrity, usually from the political world. However, in 1984, Col. Stuart A. Roosa, an Apollo 14 astronaut, played the explorer. In the enactment, d'Iberville with his officers debarks and wades ashore, plants a cross in the sand, and claims the land for Louis XIV. The Indians, at first wary, invite the French to their village to smoke a peace pipe. The reenactment was first staged in 1939.

The celebration begins on Friday night with a covered dish supper at the civic center. Saturday night, there is a formal-dress historic ball and pageant, with the presentation of d'Iberville, his officers, and the Cassette Girls. These were young orphan women who had been taught by Catholic nuns in Paris; they made the long trip to the Gulf Coast to become the brides of the men settled in the territory. They were called Cassette Girls because of the cases each carried that contained their trousseaus. The reenactment takes place on Sunday and is followed by a grand parade. There are also exhibits, and street and food fairs.

Landsgemeinden
Last Sunday of April
An open-air meeting to conduct cantonal business, held once a year in Appenzell, in the canton of Appenzell Inner-Rhoden, in Switzerland. At the meeting, citizens vote on representatives for cantonal offices and on budget and tax proposals. Voting is by raised hands.

The assembly is tradition that dates back to the very early days of the Swiss state. Women wear richly embroidered national costumes and men wear their swords. Other districts in central and eastern Switzerland also have these assemblies, each with distinct customs. In Stans, for example, the blowing of a horn signals the time to walk to the meeting place outside the town; the horn is a reminder of the ancient call to battle.

Landsgemeinden has echos in the town meetings of the United States.

See also TOWN MEETING DAY.

Landshut Wedding

Late June and early July, every three years (1989, 1992 . . .)

A pageant in Landshut (Bavaria), Germany, that recreates a lavish fifteenth-century wedding: that of Duke George the Rich of Bavaria and Polish Princess Hadwiga, which took place in 1475. There were 10,000 guests, and records state that they ate 333 oxen, 275 fat pigs, 40 calves, and 12,000 geese.

Today the festivities are spread over three weeks, with the wedding reenactions on weekends—a play and dances on Saturdays; the historical wedding procession, followed by a concert, on Sundays. During the week, historical dances are performed, and some 1,000 residents dressed as medieval burghers roam the streets. There are also jesters parading, armored knights on horseback, and wandering minstrels.

Lantern Festival (Yuan Hsiao Chieh)

Fifteenth day of first lunar month (usually February); 4th day in Tibet

A festival of lights that ends the CHINESE NEW YEAR celebrations and marks the first full moon of the new lunar year.

In China, it's traditional for merchants to hang paper lanterns outside their shops for several days before the full-moon day. On the night of the festival, the streets are bright with both lanterns and streamers, and people go out in throngs to see the displays. The most popular lanterns are cut-outs of running horses that revolve with the heat of the candles that light them. Other customs include eating round, stuffed dumplings and solving "lantern riddles"—riddles that are written on pieces of paper and stuck to the lanterns. In many areas, children parade with lanterns of all shapes and sizes. It's also thought to be a good night for young women to find husbands. In Penang, Malaysia, single women in their best dresses stroll along the city's promenade, and some parade in decorated cars followed by musicians.

Tibetan Buddhists celebrate the day as Monlam or Prayer festival, and in Lhasa, the butter sculptures of the monks are famous. In China's Gansu Province, the Lhabuleng Monastery is the site of sculptured butter flowers made by the lamas and hung in front of the main scripture hall. On the day before the full moon, a dance is performed by about thirty masked lamas to the music of drums, horns, and cymbals. The protagonists are the God of Death and his concubines; they dance with others who are dressed as skeletons, horned stags, and yaks.

In 1990, the Taipei Lantern Festival was first held in Taiwan's capital city, and in 1991, a million people came for the three-day festival. It's held at the Chiang Kai-shek Memorial Hall and features high-tech lanterns with mechanical animation, dry-ice "smoke," and laser beams. The 1990 and 1991 theme lanterns were modeled after the Chinese zodiacal animals for those years—the dragon in 1990 and the goat in 1991. Sculptor Yuyu Yang produced a dragon that was forty feet high with a skin of a stainless-steel grid and 1,200 interior light bulbs that shone through to make it look like a gigantic hand-made paper lantern. Laser beams shot from the dragon's eyes, and red-colored smoke spewed from the mouth. In 1991, he created three thirty-three-foot-high goats made of acrylic tubes with colored lights shining from the inside. The festival also offers musical and folk-art performances, a procession of religious and folk floats, and troupes of performers entertaining with martial-arts demonstrations, stilt-walking, and acrobatics.

In Hong Kong, anyone who has had a son during the year brings a lantern to the Ancestral Hall, where the men gather for a meal.

The Lantern Festival is supposed to have originated with the emperors of China's Han dynasty (206 B.C.–221 A.D.), who paid tribute to the universe on that night. Because the ceremony was held in the evening, lanterns were used to illuminate the palace. The Han rulers imposed a year-round curfew on their subjects, but on this night the curfew was lifted, and the people, carrying their own simple lanterns, went forth to view the fancy lanterns of the palace.

Another legend holds that the festival originated because a maid of honor (named Yuan Xiao, also the name of the sweet dumpling of this day) in the emperor's household longed to see her parents during the days of the Spring Festival. The resourceful Dongfang Shuo decided to help her. He spread the rumor that the god of fire was going to burn down the city of Chang-an. The city was thrown into a panic. Dongfang Shuo, summoned by the emperor, advised him to have everyone leave the palace and also to order that lanterns be hung in every street and every building. In this way, the god of fire would think the city was already burning. The emperor followed the advice, and Yuan Xiao took the opportunity to see her family. There have been lanterns ever since.

Lanterns Festival
30th Ramadan

A trader known as Daddy Maggay introduced the custom of parading with lanterns in Freetown, Sierra Leone during the 1930s. The original lanterns were simple hand-held paper boxes, lit from within and mounted on sticks. They were carried through the streets of Freetown in celebration of the twenty-sixth day of RAMADAN, also known as the **Day of Light** or **Lai-Lai-Tu-Gadri**, when the Koran was sent to earth by Allah (see LAYLAT AL-QADR).

As the years passed, the celebration—and the lanterns—grew larger. Heavy boots, originally worn as protection from the crowds, came to be used to produce drum-like rhythmical beats on the paved streets since some Muslims discourage using drums. Maggay's group were called bobo, the name for their distinctive beat. Neighborhood rivalries, based on competition in lantern-building, often erupted in violence. By the 1950s the Young Men's Muslim Association had taken over the festival in hopes of reducing the violence through better organization. The lanterns—which by that time were elaborate float-like structures illuminated from within and drawn by eight-man teams or motor vehicles—were divided into three categories for judging: Group A for ships; Group B for animals and people; and Group C for miscellaneous secular subjects. Prizes were awarded to the top three winners in each group, based on creativity and building technique.

Latter-Day Saints, Founding of the Church of
April 6

April 6, 1830 is the day on which Joseph Smith formally established the Church of Jesus Christ of the Latter-Day Saints in Fayette, New York. Three years later the anniversary of the Church's founding was celebrated for the first time, with a meeting of about eighty people on the Big Blue River in Jackson County, Missouri. After that, there were no "birthday" celebrations until 1837, when a "general conference" was held to conduct church business and to observe the anniversary. Eventu-

ally the idea of holding an annual conference became an established custom, and it was always scheduled to encompass the April 6 founding date.

Launceston Cup Day *See* Hobart Cup Day

Laylat al Miraj
Twenty-seventh day of Rajab

Laylat al Miraj commemorates the ascent of the Prophet Muhammed into heaven. One night during the tenth year of his prophecy, the angel Gabriel woke Muhammad and traveled with him to Jerusalem on the winged horse Burak. There he prayed at the site of the Temple of Solomon with the Prophets, Abraham, Moses, Jesus and others. Then, carried by Gabriel, he rose to heaven from the rock of the Temple Mount, where the Dome of the Rock sanctuary now stands. Allah instructed him regarding the five daily prayers that all Muslims must observe. Muslims today celebrate the evening of the twenty-seventh day of Rajab with special prayers. This day is also known as the **Night Journey**, or the **Ascent**.

Laylat al-Qadr
One of the last ten days of Ramadan

Laylat al-Qadr commemorates the night in 610 during which Allah revealed the entire Koran or Muslim holy book to Muhammad. It was then that the angel Gabriel first spoke to him, and was thus the beginning of his mission. These revelations continued throughout the remainder of his life. Children begin studying the Koran when they are very young, and they celebrate when they've read all 114 chapters for the first time. Many adults try to memorize the entire Koran. The common belief that this day occurred on the 26th or 27th of Ramadan has no Islamic base. It seems to have originated in Manicheism where the death of Mani is celebrated on the 27th of the fasting month. This day is also known as the **Night of Power** or **Night of Destiny**.

See also LANTERN FESTIVAL.

Lazarus Saturday
Between March 27 and April 30; Saturday before Palm Sunday

In Russia and in all Orthodox churches, the Saturday before PALM (or Willow) SUNDAY is set aside to honor Lazarus, whom Jesus raised from the dead. Pussywillows are blessed at the evening service in the Russian Orthodox church, and the branches are distributed to the worshippers, who take them home and display them above their ikons. It was an ancient folk custom for people to beat their children with willow branches—not so much to punish them as to ensure that they would grow up tall and resilient like the willow tree.

On this day in Greece, Romania, and the former Yugoslavia, groups of children carry willow branches from house to house and sing songs and act out the story of Christ raising Lazarus from the dead. In return, they receive gifts of fruit and candy. They believe the resurrection of Lazarus is symbolic of the renewal of spring, which is why the *Lazarouvane* (the celebration of ST. LAZARUS' DAY in Bulgaria) focuses on fertility and marriage.

Leap Year Day
February 29

The earth actually takes longer than 365 days to complete its trip around the sun—five hours, forty-eight minutes, and forty-five seconds longer, to be precise. To accommodate this discrepancy, an extra day is added to the Gregorian calendar at the end of February every four years (but not in "century" years unless evenly divisible by four hundred, e.g., 1600 and 2000, but not 1700). The year in which this occurs is called Leap Year, probably because the English courts did not always recognize February 29, and the date was often "leaped over" in the records.

There's an old tradition that women could propose marriage to men during Leap Year. The men had to pay a forfeit if they refused. It is for this reason that February 29 is sometimes referred to as **Ladies' Day** or **Bachelors' Day**. Leap Year Day is also **St. Oswald's Day**, named after the tenth-century archbishop of York, who died on February 29, 992.

See also SADIE HAWKINS DAY.

Lei Day
May 1

This is a celebration of Hawaii's state symbol of friendship. In 1928 Mrs. John T. Warren came up with the slogan, "Lei Day is May Day," and the holiday has been held then ever since. The events of the day include state-wide lei competitions. Leis are garlands made of flower blossoms, seeds, leaves, ferns, and pods. There is the crowning of a Lei Queen in Honolulu, and assorted exhibits and hula performances. The queen's coronation is accompanied by chanting and the blowing of conch shells.

On the day after the celebration, leis from the state-wide competitions are ceremoniously placed on the graves of Hawaii's royalty at the Royal Mausoleum in Nuuanu Valley.

Also see MAY DAY.

Leif Erikson (Ericson) Day
October 9

The Viking explorer known as Leif the Lucky or Leif Erikson (because he was the son of Eric the Red) sailed westward from Greenland somewhere around the year 1000 and discovered a place he named Vinland after the wild grapes that grew there. No one really knows where Vinland was, but some historians believe that Erikson landed in North America 488 years before Columbus sailed into the New World. The only evidence that this may have happened are a few Viking relics found in Rhode Island, Minnesota, and Ontario. In 1960, the site of a Norse settlement was discovered at L'Anse aux Meadows, at the northern tip of New-foundland. The site dates from about the year 1000, but it has not been definitively linked to Leif Erikson's explorations.

Because the date and place of Erikson's "discovery" of North America were uncertain, members of the Leif Erikson Association arbitrarily chose October 9 to commemorate this event—perhaps because the first organized group of Norwegian emigrants landed in America on October 9, 1825. But it wasn't until 1964 that President Lyndon B. Johnson proclaimed this as Leif Erikson Day.

States with large Norwegian-American populations—such as Washington, Minnesota, Wisconsin, and New York—often hold observances on this day, as do members of the Sons of Norway, the Leif Erikson Society, and other Norwegian-American organizations. October 9 is a commemorative day in Iceland and Norway as well.

Le Mans (motor race)
June

The motor racing circuit in the city of Le Mans, capital of the Sarthe department of France, has been the scene of important races since 1914, although it wasn't until 1923 that the first twenty-four-hour sports car race for which the course is now famous was held. Over the years the **Le Mans 24-hour Grand Prix d'Endurance** has had a significant impact on the development of sports cars for racing, resulting in some prototype sports cars that are not far behind Formula I racing cars in terms of power and speed. The original course was rough and dusty, with a lap distance of just under eleven miles. Eventually the road surface was improved, the corners were eased, and the lap distance was reduced to just over eight miles. Part of the course is still a French highway, now flanked by permanent concrete stands for spectators, and the pits, where refueling and repairs are done. A serious accident at Le Mans in 1955, in which a French driver and eighty-five spectators died, led to a number of course improvements.

The all-night racing at Le Mans is a favorite spectacle for motor racing fans. One of the major attractions is the opportunity to watch what goes on in the pits. Although most Grand Prix races can now be run without refueling or tire changing, the highly efficient work of the teams' mechanics still plays an important part in long-duration races like the one at Le Mans.

Lemuralia
May 9, 11, 15

In ancient Rome the *lemures* were the ghosts of the family's dead, who were considered to be troublesome and therefore had to be exorcised on a regular basis. The *lemures* were generally equated with larvae or evil spirits, although some people believed that the *lemures* included the *lares* 'good spirits' as well.

The Lemuralia or **Lemuria** was a yearly festival held on the ninth, eleventh, and fifteenth of May to get rid of the *lemures*. Supposedly introduced by Romulus, the legendary founder of Rome, after he killed his twin brother Remus, this festival was originally called the **Remuria**. Participants walked barefoot, cleansed their hands three times, and threw black beans behind them nine times to appease the spirits of the dead. On the third day of the festival, a merchants' festival was held to ensure a properous year for business. The period during which the Lemuralia was held—the entire month of May—was considered to be an unlucky time for marriages.

Lent
Begins between February 4 and March 10 in
West; between February 15 and March 21 in
East; 40 days, beginning on Ash Wednesday in
the West; beginning on the Monday seven
weeks before Easter in the East; and ending on
Easter eve
Self-denial during a period of intense religious devotion has been a long-standing tradition in both the Eastern and Western churches. In the early days, Christians prepared for EASTER with a strict fast only from GOOD FRIDAY until Easter morning. It wasn't until the ninth century that the

Lenten season, called the **Great Lent** in the East to differentiate it from the ADVENT fast called **Little Lent**, was fixed at forty days (with Sundays omitted)—perhaps reflecting the importance attached to the number forty: Moses had gone without food for forty days on Mt. Sinai, the children of Israel had wandered for forty years with little sustenance, Elijah had fasted forty days, and so did Jesus, between his baptism and the beginning of his ministry. In the Western church further extensions led to a no-longer-existing "pre-Lent" season, with its Sundays called SEPTUAGESIMA (roughly seventy days before Easter), SEXAGESIMA (sixty), and QUINQUAGESIMA (fifty)—all preceding the first Sunday of Lent, QUADRAGESIMA (forty).

The first day of Orthodox Lent is called **Clean Monday**.

For centuries the Lenten season has been observed with certain periods of strict fasting, and with abstinence from meat, and in the East, also from dairy products, wine, and olive oil, as well as "giving up" (for Lent) something—a favorite food or other worldly pleasure—for the forty days of Lent. Celebrations such as CARNIVAL and MARDI GRAS offered Christians their last opportunities to indulge before the rigorous Lenten restrictions.

See also MEAT FARE SUNDAY, DAIRY SUNDAY, SHROVE TUESDAY, ASH WEDNESDAY, MOTHERING SUNDAY.

Leonhardiritt (Leonard's Ride)
November 6, or nearest weekend

A celebration of St. Leonhard, the patron saint of horses and cattle, observed in various towns of Bavaria, Germany. Traditionally, processions of elaborately harnessed horses draw decorated wagons to the local church. Some people also bring their cattle to be blessed. A contest of whipcracking usually follows the procession. Among the towns where Leonard's Ride is held are Rottenbuch, Bad Fussing, Waldkirchen, and Murnau. November 6 is the name-day of the saint and the traditional day of the procession, but some towns now hold their rides on a weekend near that date.

Leyden Day
October 3

In 1574 the Dutch city of Leyden was besieged by the Spaniards. Thousands were dying from disease and hunger, but when a group of desperate citizens pleaded with the Burgomaster to surrender, he replied that he had sworn to keep the city safe and that it was better to die of starvation than shame. His stubbornness heartened the people, and on October 2 he had the river dikes cut so that the navy could sail in over the flooded fields and save the city. A statue of the heroic Burgomaster, Adrian van der Werff, was later erected in Leyden's Church of Saint Pancras.

According to legend, the first person to emerge from the beseiged city on October 3, 1574 was a young orphan boy. In the deserted Spanish camp, he discovered a huge pot of stew that was still hot. He summoned the townspeople, who enjoyed their first hot meal in several months. Known as *Hutspot met Klapstuk*, the mixture of meat and vegetables is still served on this day, along with bread and herring.

Liberation Day
August 15

A Korean commemoration of the surrender of Japan to the Allies in 1945, liberating Korea from Japan's thirty-five-year occupation. The day also commemorates the formal proclamation of the Republic of Korea in South Korea in 1948; there it is a national holiday.

See also SAMIL-JOL.

Lighting of the National Christmas Tree
A Thursday in December

On a selected Thursday night in December, the President of the United States lights the national Christmas tree at the northern end of the Ellipse in Washington, D. C. to the accompaniment of orchestral and choral music. The lighting ceremony marks the beginning of the two-week **Pageant of Peace**, a huge holiday celebration in the nation's capital that includes seasonal music, caroling, a Nativity scene, fifty state Christmas trees, and a burning Yule log.

Lights, Feast of *See* Hannukah

Lights, Festival of
Late November through early January

The biggest event of the year in Niagara Falls, New York is its Festival of Lights, which is held for six weeks during the CHRISTMAS holiday season. The falls themselves are illuminated, as are displays throughout the town featuring more than two hundred life-size storybook characters in dozens of animated scenes. There is an arts and crafts show, a toy train collectors' show, a boat show, a doll show, and magic shows. Musical events include performances by internationally known singers, gospel choirs, bell choirs, steel drum bands, jazz groups, and blues bands. During the festival more than half a million lights adorn the city which was the site of the world's first commercial hydroelectric plant in 1895.

Lights, Festival of (Ganden Ngamcho)
Twenty-fifth day of tenth Tibetan lunar month (usually November–December)

A festival in Tibet to commemorate the birth and death of Tsongkhapa (1357–1419), a saintly scholar, teacher, and reformer of the monasteries, who enforced strict monastic rules. In 1408 he instituted the Great Prayer, a NEW YEAR rededication of Tibet to Buddhism; it was celebrated without interruption until 1959 when the Chinese invaded Tibet. He formulated a doctrine that became the basis of the Gelug (meaning 'virtuous') sect of Buddhism. It became the predominant sect of Tibet, and Tsongkhapa's successors became the Dalai Lamas, the rulers of Tibet.

During the festival, thousands of butter lamps (dishes of liquid clarified butter called ghee, with wicks floating in them) are lit on the roofs and windowsills of homes and on temple altars. At this time people acquire spiritual merit by visiting the temples.

Lily Festival (Festa del Giglio)
Sunday following June 22

The Lily Festival in Nola, Italy, honors San Paolino, the town's patron saint. It began in the fourth century as a "welcome home" celebration when Paolino, who had placed himself in slavery to release a local widow's son, returned from Africa. Eight tradesmen representing the town greeted him by strewing flowers at his feet. Eventually the eight tradesmen were represented by sticks covered in lilies, and over the years the lily sticks (Italian *gigli*) grew longer and more ornate. Today they are from seventy-five to nearly a hundred feet high. Since they weigh fifty tons, it takes forty men to carry each one. After a traditional blessing is given, the crowd throws flowers into the air and begins a costumed procession that meanders through the narrow streets of the town, led by a boat carrying a statue of San Paolino and featuring the eight huge *gigli*, each of which is surrounded by its own symphony orchestra.

Limassol Wine Festival
Early September

An annual ten-day celebration of the wine of Cyprus, held in the Municipal Gardens of Limassol, the center of the wine-making industry. Wineries there compete to create the most original and decorative booths, and every evening pour out from barrels free samples of their wine. People sitting at picnic tables may watch exhibits of traditional wine pressing. There are also concerts and dance performances.

Lincoln's Birthday
February 12 and other dates

Abraham Lincoln, the sixteenth president of the United States, also called the Great Emancipator, the Rail Splitter, and Honest Abe, was born on Feb. 12, 1809. President throughout the Civil War, he is known for his struggle to preserve the union, the issuance of the Emancipation Proclamation, and his assassination less than two weeks after the Confederate surrender at Appomatox Court House in 1865.

A wreath-laying ceremony and reading of the Gettysburg Address at the Lincoln Memorial in Washington D.C. are traditional on Feb. 12. Because the Republican Party reveres Lincoln as its first president, Republicans commonly hold Lincoln-Day fund-raising dinners, as the Democrats hold Jackson-Day dinners.

Lincoln's actual birthday, Feb. 12, is a legal holiday in 14 states: California, Connecticut, Florida, Illinois, Indiana, Kansas, Kentucky, Maryland, Michigan, Missouri, New Jersey, New York, Vermont, and West Virginia. In Arizona, Lincoln's Birthday is observed on the second Monday in February. In 15 states, Lincoln's and Washington's birthdays are combined for a legal holiday on the third Monday in February called either Presidents' Day or Washington-Lincoln Day. Washington-Lincoln Day is observed in New Mexico on the third Monday in January.

Lindenfest
Second weekend in July

A six-hundred-year-old linden tree in Geisenheim, Germany is the center of this annual festival celebrating the new wine. As the oldest town in the Rhineland region, Geisenheim is renowned for its vineyards, and during the festival people come from all over the world to taste the wine, visit the vineyards, and make pilgrimages to Marienthal, a Franciscan shrine in a nearby wooded valley. The ancient linden tree is decorated with lights for the three-day festival, and folk dancing and feasting take place beneath its branches.

Literacy Day, International
September 8

Established by the United Nations to encourage universal literacy, this day has been observed since 1966 by all countries and organizations that are part of the United Nations system. It was a direct outgrowth of the World Conference of Ministers of Education in Teheran, which first called for the eradication of illiteracy throughout the world. Observances are sponsored primarily by UNESCO (United Nations Educational, Scientific and Cultural Organization) and include the awarding of special literacy prizes.

Prizes are also awarded by the International Reading Association, and the Japanese publisher Shoichi Noma to literacy programs that have made a significant difference. For example, in 1984 the Noma Prize was given to the Bazhong District in the People's Republic of China, where the literacy rate had been raised from ten percent to ninety percent over a thirty-five-year period.

Little Big Horn Days
Weekend nearest June 25

A commemoration in Hardin, Mont., of the old west and particularly of the most famous Indian-United States cavalry battle in history, Custer's Last Stand. An hour-long reenactment of that battle, known as the Battle of Little Big Horn, Battle of, is staged each night of the three-day festival near the actual site of the original battle which occured June 25, 1876. The is performed by more than 200 Indian and cavalry riders. Among them are descendants of the Indian scouts who rode with Colonel George Armstrong Custer, who led more than 200 men to battle and to death. The pageant is based on the notes and outline prepared by Joe Medicine Crow, a tribal historian, and was originally sponsored by the Crow Agency, administrator of the Crow Reservation. The first presentation of the drama was in 1964. It continued for a number of years before lapsing and then being restored to life in 1990.

Other events of the weekend are a historical symposium, traditional Indian dances, a black-powder shoot, a street dance, Scandinavian dinners, and a parade.

Little League World Series
Late August

Little League baseball began in 1939 with only three teams. It was incorporated under a bill signed into law by President Lyndon B. Johnson in 1964. Ten years later the law was amended to allow girls to join Little League teams. It is now played by over 2.5 million boys and girls between the ages of nine and twelve in forty-eight countries. The field is a smaller version of the regulation baseball diamond with bases sixty feet apart and a pitching distance of forty-six feet.

Every year in August the Little League World Series is held at Howard J. Lamade Field in Williamsport, Pennsylvania, location of the International Headquarters of Little League Baseball and home of the Little League Museum. First-round games are held on Monday, Tuesday, and Wednesday, with every team guaranteed a minimum of three games. Those who advance to the championship game end up playing as many as five games. The U. S. and International Championships are on Thursday, and Friday remains an open date, in case of rain. The series finale is played on Saturday.

World Series games are also held in August for Pony League Baseball (ages 13–14), Colt League (ages 15–16), and Palomino League (ages 17–18).

Living Chess Game (La Partita a Scácchi Viventi)
Second weekend in September in even-numbered years
Every two years the main piazza in Marchóstica, Italy is transformed into a giant chessboard. More than five hundred townspople wearing elaborate medieval costumes portray chessmen and act out a living game: knights in shining armor ride real horses, castles roll by on wheels, and black and white queens and kings march from square to square to meet their destinies. Thousands of spectators watch from bleachers, cheering loudly when a castle is lost and moaning when there is an impending checkmate. The local players begin rehearsing in March for the two-and-a-half hour performances. Some start out as pawns and over the years work their way up to become knights, kings, and queens.

The basis for the game is an incident that took place in 1454, when Lionora, the daughter of the lord of the castle, was being courted by two rivals. They challenged each other to a deadly duel but were persuaded to engage in a game of chess instead. Even today, the moves in the game are spoken in an ancient dialect, including the final *scácco matto!* (checkmate).

Llama Ch'uyay
July 31
The Llama Ch'uyay in Bolivia is the ritual force-feeding of "medicine" to llamas. On the eve of August 1, which the Andean Indians believe to be the day when the earth is at her most sensitive, the llamas are gathered together in a corral and, one at a time, they are forced to drink bottles of *hampi*, a medicine made from *chicha* and *trago*, (two kinds of liquor), sugar, barley mash, soup broth, and special herbs. A large male may consume more than five bottles, while baby llamas usually drink only half a bottle. Three bottles is considered a normal dose. After the animals drink their medicine, they are decorated with colored tassels made out of yarn. While men are feeding the llamas, women continually serve them chicha and trago. At the end of the ritual, whole containers of *chicha* are thrown onto the herd. A similar ritual is performed for horses on July 25, the feast of Santiago (see ST. JAMES'S DAY).

Lochristi Begonia Festival
Last weekend in August
A colorful celebration of the national flower of Belgium, held in Lochristi (six miles from Ghent), where 30 to 33 million flowering tubers are produced each year on more than 400 acres. For the festival, residents create enormous three-dimensional floral tableaux for the Floral Parade of Floats. These depict a different theme each year—for example, the world's favorite fairy tales. Besides the tableaux, arrangements of millions of yellow, red, orange, and white blossoms on beds of sand turn the town's main street into a carpet of flowered pictures. Other events are band concerts and tours to the begonia fields.

The tuberous begonia was originally a tropical plant. It takes its name from Michel Bégon, a French amateur botanist who was an administrator in the West Indies at the time of Louis XIV. The plant reached England in 1777, and Belgium began cultivating the begonia in the middle of the nineteenth century. Because the commercial value of the begonias comes from their tubers, or underground stems, the farmers of Lochristi discarded the blossoms before the festival was begun in 1946 and put them to good use.

See also Ghent Floralies.

Loi Krathong
Full-moon night in twelfth lunar month (usually mid-November)
An ancient festival held under a full moon throughout Thailand, and considered to be the loveliest of the country's festivals. After sunset, people make their way to the water to launch small lotus-shaped banana-leaf or paper boats, each holding a lighted candle, a flower, joss sticks, and a small coin. The aim is to thank Me Khongkha, Mother of the Waters, and wash away

the sins of the past year. Loi means 'to float' and Krathong is a 'leaf cup' or 'bowl'.

There are several legends linked to the origins of this festival. One holds that the festival began about 700 years ago when King Ramakhamhaeng of Sukhothai, the first Thai capital, was making a pilgrimage on the river from temple to temple. One of his wives wanted to please both the king and the Lord Buddha, so she created a paper lantern resembling a lotus flower (which symbolizes the flowering of the human spirit), put a candle in it, and set it afloat. The king was so delighted he decreed that his subjects should follow this custom on one night of the year. Fittingly, the ruins of Sukhothai are the backdrop on the night of Loi Krathong for celebrations that include displays of lighted candles, fireworks, folk dancing, and a spectacular sound-and-light presentation.

A second legend traces the festival to the more ancient practice of propitiating the Mother of Water, Me Khongkha. The coins in the lotus cups are meant as tokens to ask forgiveness for thoughtless ways.

In yet another story, the festival celebrates the lotus blossoms that sprang up when the Buddha took his first baby steps.

A similar celebration is held in Washington, D.C. at the reflecting pool near the Lincoln Memorial. Dinner and participation are by paid ticket, but anyone passing can watch the adult, child, and teen dances and the exhibition of martial arts; and after dark, the floating candles.

London Bridge Days
First full week in October
Given its location, this is one of the stranger and more unexpected festivals in all of the U.S. Held in Lake Havasu City, Ariz., in the Arizona desert, the festival is a week-long celebration of all things English and of the London Bridge that spans a channel of the Colorado River. This London Bridge was built in 1831 to span the River Thames in London, England. Opening festivities at the time included a banquet held on the bridge and a balloon ascending from it. Like its predecessor mentioned in the nursery rhyme, which was completed in 1209, this bridge was falling down until Robert P. McCulloch Sr. of the McCulloch Oil Corp. bought 10,000 tons of the granite facing blocks, transported then from foggy Londontown to sunny Arizona, rebuilt the bridge stone by stone, and dedicated it on Oct. 10, 1971. The Bridge Days are a commemoration of that reopening.

A replica of an English village next to the bridge is the center of festival activities. There are English-costume contests, a parade, a ball, musical entertainment, arts and crafts exhibits, and a "quit-rent" ceremony. Lake Havasu City is a planned community and resort on the banks of Lake Havasu, which is fed by the Colorado River and impounded by the Parker Dam.

Longest Day *See* Summer Solstice

Long Friday *See* Good Friday

Looking Glass Powwow
August
A powwow held by the Nez Perce Indians each August in Kamiah, Idaho, to celebrate the memory of Chief Looking Glass, who was killed in the Nez Perce War of 1877. Nez Perce (meaning 'pierced nose' and pronounced NEZ-purse) is the name given by the French to a number of tribes that practiced the custom of nose-piercing. The term is used now to designate the main tribe of the Shahaptian Indians who, however, never pierced their noses.

Other major annual powwows of the Nez Perce are the Epethese Powwow, held the first weekend in March in Lapwai, Idaho, to decide war dance championships; the Mat-Al-YM'A Powwow and Root Feast in Kamiah the third weekend in May, with traditional dancing; the Warriors Memorial Powwow the third weekend in June in Lapwai, honoring Chief Joseph and his warriors; and the Four Nations Powwow, held the last week in October in Lapwai.

Lord Krishna's Birthday *See* Janmashtami

Lord Mayor's Show
Second Saturday in November
The second Friday in November is **Lord Mayor's Day** in London, the day on which the city's Lord Mayor is admitted to office. The following day is the Lord Mayor's Show, a series of civic ceremonies that culminate in a parade to the Law Courts. At one time the Lord Mayor rode on horseback or traveled by state barge along the Thames, but today he rides from Guildhall to the Law Courts in a scarlet and gold coach drawn by six matched horses. This is the only time the mayoral coach is used; the rest of the time it is kept in the Museum of London.

Accompanying the coach is an honor guard of musketeers and pikemen in period dress, as well as many bands and numerous floats decorated to reflect the interests or profession of the new Lord Mayor. This colorful pageant dates back to the thirteenth century, when King John gave the citizens of London a charter stating that the Mayor was to be elected on September 29 and that he was to present himself either to the King or to the Royal Justices to be officially installed.

Losar
First day of first Tibetan lunar month; usually February or March

The new year in Tibet, according to the Tibetan calendar, which is in use throughout the Himalayan region; the date is determined by Tibetan astrologers in Dharmsala, India.

Before the new year, bad memories from the old year must be chased away, so houses are whitewashed and thoroughly cleaned. A little of the dirt collected is thrown away at a crossroads where spirits might dwell. A special dish called *guthuk* is prepared; in it are dumplings holding omens: a pebble promises life as durable as a diamond; cayenne pepper suggests a temperamental personality; a piece of charcoal would mean the recipient has a black heart. On the last day of the old year, monks conduct ceremonies to drive out evil spirits and negative forces. In one such ritual, the monks, in grotesque masks and wigs and exotic robes, perform a dance in which they portray the struggle between good and evil.

On the first day of the year, people arise early to place water and offerings on their household shrines. In the three days of the celebration, much special food and drink is prepared. This is a time of hospitality and merrymaking, with feasts, dances and archery competitions.

Tibet was invaded by the Chinese in 1949, and the Dalai Lama, the spiritual and political head of Tibet, has been in exile since 1959. Much of the Tibetan culture has been suppressed, but festivals are still observed in a modest way in Tibet and by Tibetans in exile.

Tibetan exiles in India celebrate Losar by flocking to the temple in Dharmsala where the Dalai Lama lives. On the second day of the new year, he blesses people by touching their heads and giving them a piece of red and white string. People tie the blessed string around their necks as a protection from illness.

In Bodhnath, on the eastern side of Katmandu, Nepal, crowds of Tibetan refugees visit the *stupa* there to watch lamas perform rites. Copper horns are blown, there are masked dances, and a portrait of the Dalai Lama is displayed.

See also LUNAR NEW YEAR, OSHOGATSU, SONGKRAN, TET, and THINGYAN.

Lotus, Birthday of the
24th day of the sixth lunar month

Although the Chinese celebrate the birthday of flowers in general (Moon 2, Day 12 or 15) and honor Wei Shen, the protectress of flowers (Moon 4, Day 19), the lotus is singled out for special attention because of its connection with Buddhism. The Birthday of the Lotus is observed at the time when lotuses bloom in the ponds and moats around Beijing, and people flock to the city to see them—much as they do in Japan and in Washington, D.C. during cherry blossom time (see CHERRY BLOSSOM FESTIVAL). Their blooms are a sign that prayers to the Dragon Prince have been answered and the summer rains will soon start. Special lanes for rowboats are cut through the thick layer of lotus blossoms that cover the lakes of the Winter Palace in Beijing.

Lou Bunch Day
Late August

An annual reminder of the rowdy gold-mining days of Central City, Colorado, held to honor the town's last madam. The day features bed races, a Madams and Miners Ball, and the selection of a Madam of the Year. In addition, there are tours of old mining rigs, and trains to take visitors into the heart of the mountains to see colorful veins of ore.

Central City was settled in the Gold Rush of 1859 and became known as the Richest Square Mile on Earth—some $75 million in gold was mined there. One of the miners was a man named John Gregory who dug up a fortune. New York newspaper editor Horace Greeley heard about Gregory Gulch and went west to take a look, after which he supposedly wrote, "Go west, young man". The phrase isn't found in his writings because this advice was first given by John Babsone Soulé in an article for Indiana's *Terre Haute Express*. Greeley reprinted the article in his *New York Tribune* under Soulé's byline; nevertheless Greeley has been remembered for the inspiring phrase and both Gregory and Soulé have faded into history.

Louisiana Shrimp and Petroleum Festival
Labor Day weekend

A celebration of an old industry and a newer one in Morgan City, La., which once called itself the

Jumbo Shrimp Capital of the World. In 1947, oil was discovered offshore, and it was decided to combine the tribute to shrimp with a tribute to oil.

The celebration was originally known as the Shrimp Festival and Blessing of the Fleet. It began in 1937 as a revival of the Italian custom of blessing fishing fleets before they set out to sea, but from the first it also included boat races, a dance, a parade, and free boiled shrimp. After the world's first commercial offshore well was drilled in the Gulf of Mexico below Morgan City, the shrimp industry was outstripped in economic importance by the petroleum industry, and petroleum seeped into the festival. The highlight, though, is still the Blessing of the Fleet and a water parade, with hundred of boats taking part. Other events of this festival, one of the state's premier affairs, are fireworks, an outdoor Roman Catholic Mass, arts and crafts displays, Cajun culinary treats, the coronation of the festival King and Queen, and a parade with floats.

Louisiana Sugar Cane Festival
Last weekend in September

A tribute to this important crop in New Iberia, La., which lies on the Bayou Teche. The Teche country is known as the "Sugar Bowl of Louisiana." The festival, which began in 1937 and now is participated in by thirteen of the seventeen sugar-producing parishes of the area, begins on Friday with a Farmers' Day. Highlights of the day are agriculture, homemaking and livestock shows, and a boat parade down Bayou Teche. On Saturday, there's a children's parade and the crowning of Queen Sugar at a ball, and on Sunday, the new Queen Sugar and King Sucrose reign over a parade. Other features are a blessing of the crops and a *fais-do-do*, a dance party.

Low Sunday
Sunday after Easter

The Sunday following the 'high' feast of EASTER, it is also known as **Quasimodo Sunday**, **Close Sunday**, or **Low Easterday**. "Low" probably refers to the lack of "high" ritual used on Easter, and not to the low attendance usual on this day. The name Quasimodo Sunday comes from the Introit of the Mass which is said on this day. In Latin it begins with the phrase *Quasi modo geniti infantes*- 'As newborn babes . . . ' The famous character Quasimodo in Victor Hugo's novel *The Hunchback of Notre Dame* is said to have been found abandoned on this day, which marks the close of Easter week.

Loyalty Day
May 1

The U. S. Veterans of Foreign Wars designated the first day of May as Loyalty Day in 1947. The intention was to direct attention away from the Communist Party in the United States, which was using U.S. MAY DAY rallies to promote its doctrines and sign up new members. The idea caught on, and soon Loyalty Day was being celebrated throughout the country with parades, school programs, patriotic exercises, and speeches on the importance of showing loyalty to the United States. In Delaware, for example, Loyalty Day was marked by a special ceremony at Cooch's Bridge, where the Stars and Stripes were first displayed in battle. And in New York City, the Loyalty Day parade routinely attracted tens of thousands of participants.

Dissent over American intervention in Vietnam eventually eroded the popularity of Loyalty Day, and in 1968 only a few thousand marchers turned out for the traditional parades in Manhattan and Brooklyn, while 87,000 people participated in the Vietnam peace march in Central Park. Loyalty Day was later replaced by LAW DAY.

Luciadagen *See* St. Lucy's Day

Lucy Stone Day
August 13

Lucy Stone (1818–1893) was a pioneer in the women's rights movement. When she married Henry Blackwell, she insisted on keeping her maiden name as a way of protesting the unequal laws applicable to married women. Although few women followed her example during her lifetime, she has since inspired many "Lucy Stoners," or women who do not change their names when they marry. Her birthday, August 13, is observed by members of the Lucy Stone League in New York City, an organization devoted to the study of the status of women.

Ludi
Various

Ludi was the word used for public games in ancient Rome. These were holidays devoted to rest and pleasure. The **Ludi Megalenses** were held every year from April 4–10 from 191 B.C. onwards in honor of Cybele, the Roman Mother Goddess, whose image had been brought to Rome in 204 B.C. The **Megalensian Games** were followed by the **Ludi Ceriales** in honor of Ceres, the ancient corn goddess, from April 12–19. Then came the **Ludi Florales** in honor of Flora, the goddess of flowers, from April 28–May 3. The Ludi Florales were followed by a period of hard work in the fields, and the next games didn't occur for seven weeks. The **Ludi Apollinares** , held in honor of Apollo, went on from July 6–13. The **Ludi Romani**, instituted in 366 B.C., lasted from September 4–19. And the **Ludi Plebei**, which were first held somewhere between 220 and 216 B.C., were held from November 4–17.

All in all, there were fifty-nine days devoted to these traditional games in the Roman calendar before the time of Sulla who became dictator of the Roman Republic in 82 B.C. They were considered to be the *dies nefasti*-days on which all civil and judicial business must be suspended for fear of offending the gods.

Luilak
Between May 9 and June 12; Saturday before Whitsunday

Luilak or **Lazybones Day** is a youth festival celebrated in Zaandam, Haarlem, Amsterdam, and other towns in the western Netherlands. The celebration begins at four o'clock in the morning on the Saturday before WHITSUNDAY, when groups of young people awaken their neighbors by whistling, banging on pots and pans, and ringing doorbells. Any boys or girls who refuse to get up and join the noise-making are referred to as *Luilak* or 'Lazybones,' a name that originated in 1672 when a watchman named Piet Lak fell asleep while French invaders entered the country. Thereafter he was referred to as *Luie-Lak* 'Lazy Lak.' In many parts of the country *Luilakbollen* or 'Lazybones Cakes,' traditionally baked in the shape of fat double rolls and served with syrup, are a specialty of the season.

Children often celebrate Luilak by making little wagons, often shaped like boots and decorated with branches and thistles, known as *luilakken*. Pulling the wagons over the cobblestone streets often generates enough friction to set the wheels smoking. The children then either watch while their luilakken go up in flames or else dump them in the canals.

In Haarlem, Luilak marks the opening of the celebrated Whitsun flower market in the Grote Markt at midnight.

Lumberjack World Championships
Last weekend in July

At the turn of the century Hayward, Wisconsin was one of the most active logging towns in the northern United States. Nowadays Hayward is known primarily as the site of the largest lumberjack competition in the country. Lumberjacks and logrollers from New Zealand, Australia, Canada, England, and the United States come to Hayward to compete in one- and two-man buck sawing, power sawing, a variety of chopping events, and the speed climbing contest, where loggers climb up and down a ninety-foot fir pole in less than thirty seconds. There is also a lumberjack relay race, with teams consisting of one speed climber, one "river pig" (logroller), two-man crosscut saw partners, and one standing cut chopper.

The three-day event takes place at the end of July in the Lumberjack Bowl, a large bay of Lake Hayward that was once used as a giant holding pond for the North Wisconsin Lumber Company and is now used for the World Logrolling Championships. The sport of "birling" or logrolling originated in New England and then moved west. Lumberjacks in overalls, woolen shirts, and high boots learned to maneuver a floating carpet of logs, using their pike poles to break up log jams. A working skill soon became a pastime and then a sporting event. Today's competitors dress in shorts and t-shirts or bathing suits and wear special birling shoes. Competitors stand on a floating log and try to roll each other off balance and into the water.

Lunar New Year
First day of first lunar month (usually late January or February)

The Lunar New Year has certain variations from country to country, but they all include offerings to the household god(s), house-cleaning and new clothes, a large banquet, ancestor worship, and firecrackers.

It is the most important and the longest of all Chinese festivals, celebrated by Chinese communities throughout the world. The festival, believed to date back to prehistory, marks the beginning of the new lunar cycle. It is also called the **Spring Festival**, since it falls between the WINTER SOLSTICE and SPRING EQUINOX. It is the day when everyone becomes one year older—age is calculated by the year not the date of birth.

Activities begin in the twelfth month, as people prepare food, clean their houses, settle debts, and buy new clothes. They also paste red papers with auspicious writings on the doors and windows of their homes.

On the twenty-fourth day of the twelfth month, each Kitchen God leaves earth to report to the Jade Emperor in heaven on the activities of each family during the past year. To send their Kitchen

God on his way, households burn paper money and joss sticks and give him offerings of wine. To make sure that his words to the Jade Emperor are sweet, they also offer *tang kwa*, a dumpling that finds its way to the mouths of eager children.

The eve of the new year is the high point of the festival when family members return home to honor their ancestors and enjoy a great feast. The food that is served has symbolic meaning. Abalone, for example, promises abundance; bean sprouts, prosperity; oysters, good business.

This is also a night of colossal noise; firecrackers explode and rockets whistle to frighten away devils—or the wild beast that tradition says was afraid of bright lights, the color red, and noise. The explosions go on till dawn, and continue sporadically for the next two weeks. In Hong Kong, it is traditional after the feast to visit the flower markets. Flowers also have symbolic meaning, and gardeners try to ensure that peach and plum trees, which signify good luck, bloom on New Year's Day.

On the first day of the new year, household doors are thrown open to let good luck enter. Families go out to visit friends and worship at temples. Words are carefully watched to avoid saying anything that might signify death, sickness, or poverty. Scissors and knives aren't used for fear of "cutting" the good fortune, and brooms aren't used either, lest they sweep away good luck. Dragon and lion dances are performed, with 50 or more people supporting long paper dragons. There are acrobatic demonstrations and much beating of gongs and clashing of cymbals.

An ancient custom is giving little red packets of money (called *hung-pao* or *lai see*) to children and employees or service-people. The red signifies good fortune, and red is everywhere at this time.

On the third day of the holiday, families stay home, because it's supposed to be a time of bad luck. On the fourth day, local deities return to earth after a stay in heaven and are welcomed back with firecrackers and the burning of spirit money. According to legend, the seventh day is the anniversary of the creation of mankind, and the ninth day is the birthday of the Jade Emperor, the supreme Taoist deity. He is honored, not surprisingly, with firecrackers.

In most Asian countries, people return to work after the fourth or fifth day of celebration. In Taiwan, New Year's Eve, New Year's Day, and the two days following are public holidays, and all government offices, most businesses, restaurants,

and stores are closed. The closings may continue for eight days.

By the thirteenth and fourteenth days, shops hang out lanterns for the Yuen Siu or Lantern Festival, the day of the first full moon of the new year and the conclusion of the celebration.

In Chinese, the lunar new year is known as **Ch'un Chieh**, or 'Spring Festival.' It was formerly called **Yuan Tan** 'the first morning', but the name was changed when the Gregorian calendar was officially adopted by the Republic of China in 1912. To differentiate the Chinese new year from the Western new year, January 1 was designated *Yuan Tan*. Today in China and in other Eastern nations, January 1 is a public holiday, but the Spring Festival is the much grander celebration.

Celebrations vary from country to country and region to region. In some towns in the countryside of Yunnan province in China, for example, an opera is performed by the farmers. The Chinese communities in San Francisco and New York City are especially known for their exuberant and ear-splitting celebrations. In China, celebrations were banned from the onset of the Cultural Revolution in 1966 until 1980 when dragons and lions once again appeared on the streets.

An old legend says that the lunar festival dates from the times when a wild beast (*nihn*, also the Cantonese word for 'year,') appeared at the end of winter to devour many villagers. After the people discovered that the beast feared bright lights, red, and noise, they protected themselves on the last day of the year by lighting up their houses, painting objects red, banging drums and gongs, and exploding bamboo "crackers."

In Vietnam, where the holiday is called **Tet**, the ancestors are believed to return to heaven on the fourth day, and everyone has to return to work. On the seventh day, the *Cay Neu* is removed from the front of the home. This is a high bamboo pole that was set up on the last day of the old year. On its top are red paper with inscriptions, wind chimes, a square of woven bamboo to stop evil spirits from entering, and a small basket with betel and areca nuts for the good spirits.

In Taiwan it is called **Sang-Sin**. Small horses and palanquins are cut from yellow paper and burned to serve as conveyances for the kitchen god.

The New Year's feast is first laid before the ancestor shrine. About seven o'clock, after the ancestors have eaten, the food is gathered up, re-heated, and eaten by the family. The greater the amount of food placed before the shrine, the greater will be the reward for the new year.

After the banquet, oranges are stacked in fives before the ancestor tablets and household gods. A dragon bedecked red cloth is hung before the altar. The dragon is the spirit of rain and abundance, and the oranges are an invitation to the gods to share the family's feasting.

In Korea **Je-sok** or **Je-ya** is the name for New Year's Eve. Torches are lit in every part of the home, and everyone sits up all night to "defend the New Year" from evil spirits. In modern Seoul, the capital, the church bells are rung thirty-three times at midnight.

While the foods may vary, everyone, rich and poor alike, has *duggook* soup, made from rice and containing pheasant, chicken, meat, pinenuts, and chestnuts.

Many games are played. Among the most unusual is girls seesawing. In early times Korean men stopped some of the sterner sports and forbade women to have any outdoor exercises. Korean girls then took to using a seesaw behind their garden walls. But they do it standing up—so as to get a possible glimpse of their boyfriend, as they fly up and down.

In Okinawa's villages there is the custom of new water for **Shogatsu**, the new year. About five o'clock in the morning youngsters bring a teapot of fresh water to the homes of their relatives. There a cupful is placed on the Buddhist god shelf, or the fire god's shelf in the kitchen, and the first pot of tea is made from it.

See also OSHOGATSU, LOSAR.

Lu Pan, Birthday of
Thirteenth day of the sixth moon (usually July)
A commemoration of the birth of the Taoist pa-tron saint of carpenters and builders. Born in 507 B.C., Lu Pan, a versatile inventor, is sometimes called the Chinese Leonardo da Vinci. In Hong Kong, people in the construction industry observe the day with celebratory banquets to give thanks for their good fortune in the past year and to pray for better fortune in the year to come. They also pay their respects at noon at the Lu Pan Temple in Kennedy Town.

Lu Pan, an architect, engineer, and inventor, is credited with inventing the drill, plane, saw, shovel, saw, lock, and ladder. His wife is said to have invented the umbrella. Because his inventions are indispensable to building, it is common practice at the start of major construction projects for employees to have feasts, burn incense, and offer prayers to Lu Pan so that he may protect them and the construction work from disaster.

Lupercalia
February 15

This was an ancient Roman festival during which worshippers gathered at a grotto on the Palatine Hill in Rome called the Lupercal, where Rome's legendary founders Romulus and Remus had been suckled by a wolf. The sacrifice of goats and dogs to the Roman deities Lupercus and Faunus was part of the ceremony. Luperci (priests of Lupercus) dressed in goatskins and smeared with the sacrificial blood would run about striking the women with thongs of goat skin. This was thought to assure them of fertility and an easy delivery. The name for these thongs—*februa*—meant "means of purification" and eventually gave the month of February its name. There is some reason to believe that the Lupercalia was a forerunner of modern Valentine's Day customs. Part of the ceremony involved putting girls' names in a box and letting boys draw them out, thus pairing them off until the next Lupercalia.

M

Macon Cherry Blossom Festival
Mid-March

A celebration of the blooming (traditional date of full bloom is March 23) of the Yoshino cherry trees in Macon, Ga., which calls itself the Cherry Blossom Capital of the World. Cherry trees in Macon date back to 1952 when William A. Fickling discovered a mystery tree on his lawn. It was identified as a Yoshino flowering cherry, a native of Japan. Fickling learned to propagate the trees, and began giving them to the community; today Macon has 170,000 Yoshino cherries given by the Fickling family: thirty times more than the number in Washington, D.C. The festival honors Fickling, known as 'Johnny Cherry seed,' and has as its themes love and international friendship.

The ten-day celebration, started in 1982, includes the 10-mile Cherry Blossom Trail, and now offers about 250 activities. Among the events are parades, a coronation ball, a fashion show, fireworks, concerts, a bed race, a cherry-dessert contest, and the fire department's Pink Pancake Breakfast. Macon has many antebellum mansions spared by Gen. William T. Sherman on his Civil War march to the sea so there are house and garden tours, a flower show, and a tea put on by the Federated Garden Clubs.

The city continues donating trees: about 15,000 are given to area residents for planting each spring.

Madeleine, Fête de la
July 22

The **Magdalene Festival** is observed in St. Baume, a forested region of Provence, on the anniversary of the death of Mary Magdalene, according to repudiated traditions the sister of Martha and Lazarus. A ninth century, unfounded legend has it that she set out from Palestine in a small boat and miraculously arrived on the shores of Provence. Wandering eastward from Les Saintes-Maries-de-la-Mer, she came to *la fôret de la Baume* 'the forest of the Cave,' a grotto where she spent thirty-three years living on wild roots and berries doing penance for her sins.

Thousands of pilgrims have visited *la Sainte Baume*, the holy cave, since the thirteenth century. Although July 22 is the most popular pilgrimage date, the shrine is visited throughout the year. At one time a journey to the grotto was considered especially important for engaged couples, who went there to ensure a fruitful marriage. Today young girls scramble up the wooded hillside to ask for the Magdalene's help in finding a husband.

Magellan Day
March 6

The island of Guam, largest and southernmost of the Mariana Islands in the Pacific Ocean, about three thousand miles west of Hawaii, was discovered on this date in 1521 by the Portuguese navigator Ferdinand Magellan. He named the island Ladrones, meaning 'thieves' because of the way the inhabitants behaved. The island was formally claimed by Spain in 1565, and was later ceded to the United States as a prize at the end of the Spanish-American War. Today, Guam is the site of major U. S. military installations.

Guamanians celebrate their island's founding on or near March 6 with fiestas and sailboating. This day is also known as **Discovery Day**.

Magha Puja (Maka Buja, Full Moon Day)
February; full moon night of Magha

An important Buddhist holy day celebrated in India, and in Laos (as **Makha Bouxa**) and Thailand, where it is a national holiday. The day commemorates the occasion when 1,250 followers ordained by the Buddha arrived by coincidence at Veluvan Monastery in Rajagriha, India to hear him lay down monastic regulations and predict his own death and entry with Nirvana in three months' time. On this day there are sermons in the temples throughout the day, and monks spend the day chanting. The people perform acts of merit-making, such as offering food to monks, and freeing captive birds and fish. After sunset, monks lead followers in walking three times around the chapels of monasteries. Each person carries flowers, glowing incense, and a lighted candle in homage to the Buddha. In Laos, the ceremonies are especially colorful at Vientiane and at the Khmer ruins of Wat Ph near Champasak.

Magh Sankranti
January–February; Magha

In celebration of the sun's movement back toward the northern hemisphere, the people of Nepal visit holy bathing spots on this day in the Hindu month of Magha. Some actually bathe in the shallow water, but the weather is usually quite chilly and most are content to splash water on their hands and faces and sprinkle it on their heads. People also spend the day sitting in the sun, massaging each other with mustard oil, which is used by mothers to bless their children. Foods traditionally served on this day include *khichari*, a mixture of rice and lentils; sesame seeds; sweet potatoes, spinach; and homemade wine and beer. Traditional gifts for the priests are a bundle of wood and a clay fire pot.

Magna Charta (Carta) Day
June 15

The Magna Charta was the "great charter" of English liberties, which the tyrannical King John I was forced by the English nobility to sign on June 15, 1215. Although this day does not appear in the official calendar of any church, it is a day of great religious significance throughout the English-speaking world. One of the forty-eight personal rights and liberties guaranteed by the Magna Charta was freedom of worship; in fact, the opening words of the document were, "The Church of England shall be free."

The Magna Charta is regarded as one of the most important documents in the history of political and human freedom. Although it may seem remote to Americans, who sometimes take freedom for granted, for the English this date marks the first time that the basic belief in the value of the individual was recognized by the ruling government.

Mahatma Gandhi's Birthday *See* **Gandhi Jayanti**

Mahavir Jayanti
March–April; 13th of waxing Chaitra

A major Jain festival in India, dedicated to Vardhamana Jnatrputra (c.540–468 B.C.), who came to be known as Mahavira, meaning 'great hero' of the Jains. The festival celebrates his birthday, and is marked with prayers, fasting, and recitations. The holiday is observed with special fanfare by eastern Indians at Pawapuri in the state of Bihar, where Mahavira was born near the modern town of Patna. Another large celebration is held at the Parasnatha temple in Calcutta.

Mahavira, a contemporary of the Buddha, is regarded by the Jains as the twenty-fourth and last in a series of *Tirthankaras*, or enlightened teachers or 'ford-makers', and present-day Jainism is traced to his life and teachings. For 12-1/2 years, he was an ascetic, wandering about, begging for food, and wearing little. Then he found enlightenment, became a *Jina* 'conqueror' and a Tirthankara. He taught for thirty years before he died. Jainism today continues to be an ascetic religion, practiced by about 3.5 million people. They reject any action that could harm a living being, and some, therefore, wear masks over their mouths to prevent the chance of breathing in and thus killing of an insect. Jains, with a strong literary tradition, have played an important role in conserving the writings of non-Jain Hindu authors.

See also DEWALI.

Maidens' Fair on Mount Gaina *See* **Tirgul de fete de pe muntele Gaina**

Maimona (Maimuna)
Between March 28 and April 25; day after Passover

The Jews of North Africa commemorate the twelfth century philosopher and rabbi, Moses Maimonides (1135 or 1138–1204), on the evening of the last day of PASSOVER and the day that follows. Since the news of Maimonides' death in 1204 reached many Jews during Passover, they were not able to mourn his passing, as custom would normally dictate, by eating bread and an egg. So they postponed it until the following day.

In Libya on this day, each family member receives the *maimona* (from an Arabic word meaning 'good fortune')—a small loaf of bread with an egg baked inside, which they eat with slices of lamb. In Morocco, everyone dresses up or wears a costume. Special displays of food are arranged on tables, including pitchers of milk and bowls of flour with eggs, broad green beans, stalks of wheat, and dates on top. Surrounding the bowls are honey, fruit, nuts, cookies, lettuce, wine, and a type of pancake known as *muflita*. After going to the synagogue, the people stop to bless their friends and sample the refreshments at each home. A lettuce leaf, representing prosperous crops, dipped in honey, symbolizing sweetness, is given to each guest. Wherever possible, people dip their feet in streams, rivers, or the sea.

Maine Lobster Festival
Four days including first weekend in August

Claiming to be the "Original Lobster Festival," the four-day event known as the Maine Lobster Festival has been held in the fishing port of Rockland since 1948. The festival's emphasis is on marine foods and exhibits, with special events such as lobster crate and trap hauling races, a Maine cooking contest, the crowning of a Maine Sea Goddess, and a lobster eating competition.

Although many towns in Maine hold annual lobster festivals, many have gone bankrupt by offering visitors all the lobster they can eat for a ridiculously low price. Although the prices have gone up, the lure of an inexpensive lobster meal remains one of the primary reasons people attend these festivals. At the Rockland festival, the price of the lobster meal is based on the current market price. But the lobster is fresh and it is steamed in the world's largest lobster cooker.

Maka Buja *See* Magha Puja

Making Happiness Festival
Ninth day of first Chinese lunar month

The **Tso-Fu** or 'making happiness' **Festival** is celebrated in Taiwan soon after the CHINESE NEW YEAR. The Happiness Master, headman, chief medium, and other villagers "invite the gods." They collect a number of gods who normally dwell in various shrines and private homes and bring them to the temple, accompanied by a hired band, children, gongs, and banners. Mothers of newborn sons pay their respects to the Heaven God by presenting *hsin-ting ping* or 'new male cakes.' The following day they distribute these cakes to every household except those occupied by other new mothers. Elaborate sacrificial rites are performed in the temple on this day and a special feast is held for villagers over sixty, other important guests, and women who have given birth to sons during the year. At the end of the festival, the gods that have been brought to the temple are returned to their shrines.

Malcolm X Day
Third Sunday in May

Malcolm X, whose original name was Malcolm Little (1925–1965), was an outspoken leader in the black nationalist movement of the 1960s. He converted to the Black Muslim faith while serving time in prison for burglary, and upon his release began touring the country on behalf of the Nation of Islam. In 1964 he was suspended from the sect and started his own religious organization. But hostility between Malcolm's followers and the rival Black Muslims escalated. He was assassinated at a rally in Harlem.

Because Malcolm X advocated violence (for self-protection) and had a reputation for fanaticism, his leadership was rejected by most of the other civil rights leaders of his day. But his birthday, May 19, is still observed in most major American cities with a large African-American population. In Washington, D.C. the celebration takes place on the third Sunday in May at Anacostia Park and regularly draws fifty to seventy-five thousand people. There is a showcase for local African-American talent and a commemorative ceremony with a speech. A community service award is given to a local citizen who has made a significant contribution to promoting racial harmony.

Mallard Ceremony
Every hundred years

The **Mallard Feast** or **Mallard Day** ceremony held once every hundred years at All Souls College in Oxford commemorates the college's founding in 1437. Henry Chichele, Archbishop of Canterbury at the time, wanted to establish a college at Oxford in memory of those who had perished in the wars between England and France. While he was considering where such a college might be located, he had a dream that when the foundations were being dug, a fattened mallard was found stuck in the drain or sewer. He decided to heed the omen and, when the digging began at the location specified in his dream, a huge mallard was indeed found—a sure sign that his college would flourish.

Although no one is sure exactly when the first commemoration of this event was held, the ceremony itself has remained unchanged. The Fellows of the college nominate the Lord of the Mallard. He in turn appoints six officers, who march before him carrying white staves and wearing medals with the image of the mallard engraved on them. When the Lord is seated in his chair, the officers carry him around the quadrangle three times and sing a traditional song. After that, they climb up to the college roof in a torchlight procession and sing the song again, loudly enough for most of the town to hear. Eventually they retire to their common rooms to drink wine and continue their merrymaking.

Mandi Safar
Second Moslem month (Safar)

A Muslim bathing festival unique to Malaysia. This day was originally believed to commemorate the last time Muhammad was able to bathe before his death. Muslims wearing bright colors visited beaches for a religious cleansing of the body and soul with water. There is no mention of the rite in the *Koran*, and orthodox Muslims consider it nothing more than a picnic. It continues as a merry holiday. The best known gathering places are the beaches of Tanjong Kling near Malacca and of Penang.

Manitoba Sunflower Festival
Last weekend in July

The Mennonites were members of an evangelical Protestant sect that originated in Europe in the sixteenth century and was named for Menno Simon, a Dutch priest. They began emigrating to North America in the late seventeenth century and lived primarily as farmers, retaining their German language. A number of Russian Mennonites settled in Manitoba, Canada, where their heritage is still celebrated in the towns along the so-called Mennonite Trail.

Because the Mennonites were the first to extract the oil from sunflower plants, the city of Altona in southern Manitoba has chosen to honor its Mennonite heritage with an annual **Sunflower Festival** during the last weekend in July. Since 1965 the festival has attempted to revive the Mennonite culture by offering performances of "low German" humor and by serving a number of Mennonite foods such as *schmaunfat*, *veriniki*, *pluma moose*, *borscht*, and *rollkuchen*. A special sunflower ice cream is made especially for the festival. Less "authentic" activities include the Great Ping Pong Ball Drop, motorcross races, pancake breakfasts, and a huge farmers' market.

Marbles Tournament, National
Late June

The annual National Marbles Tournament began in 1922, when Macy's Department Store in Philadelphia sponsored a promotional tournament. The Scripps-Howard Newspapers sponsored the event until 1955, when the city of Wildwood, New Jersey and a group of volunteers interested in preserving the game decided to sponsor the event jointly. Traditionally held for five days near the end of June in this New Jersey seaside resort town, the tournament features a competition among champions selected in elimination contests throughout the country. The national boy and girl champions each receive a trophy and a plaque as well as a $2,000 scholarship.

Although there are many games that can be played with marbles—such as Potsies, Poison, Passout, Chassies, Puggy, Black Snake, and Old Boiler (reportedly a favorite with Abraham Lincoln)—the game played in the national tournament is called Ringer. It is played by placing thirteen marbles in the form of a cross in a ten-foot circle. The marbles inside the circle are called "migs" or "miggles". Players alternate shots using a "shooter" or "taw," and the winner is the first one to shoot seven miggles out of the ring.

Mardi Gras
February–March; two weeks before Ash Wednesday

The most flamboyant of Mardi Gras (from French 'fat Tuesday') celebrations in North America, culminating in a riot of parades and throngs of laughing, drinking, dancing people in the streets of New Orleans, La.

The Mardi Gras celebrations symbolize New Orleans, "The City that Care Forgot," to most people. The festivities actually start on Jan. 6 (EPIPHANY) with a series of private balls. The tempo picks up in the last two weeks of the Carnival season, when the streets ring with thirty separate parades organized by organizations called *krewes*. The parades consist of marching jazz bands and lavishly decorated two-story floats carrying the costumed and masked krewe royalty who toss "throws" to pleading spectators; these are beads or bonbons or the coveted Mardi Gras doubloons. Each of the parades has fifteen to twenty floats, all decorated to express a certain theme. Two of the biggest and most elaborate parades, the Krewe of Endymion and the Bacchus parade, take place on the weekend before Mardi Gras. On the day of Mardi Gras, designated the "Day of Un-Rule," the traditional parades spotlight Rex, King of Carnival and Monarch of Merriment in the morning, and Comus, God of Revelry by torchlight at night. On that same evening the private balls of Rex and Comus are held. At midnight, the madness of Carnival ends, and Lent begins, and a million or so spectators and participants face sobriety.

New Orleans had its first organized Mardi Gras parade in 1857. It consisted of two floats and was presented by the first Carnival society, the Mistick Krewe of Comus, its name alluding to John Milton's masque *Comus*. The parade was apparently well received; it was one of the first local institutions revived after the Civil War.

Mardi Gras in New Orleans is the best known, but not the oldest Mardi Gras. A two-week pre-Lenten celebration in Mobile, Ala. stands alone as the oldest celebration of Mardi Gras in the country. It was first observed in 1703 by the French who had founded the port city the year before. When the Spanish occupied Mobile in 1780, they moved it to the eve of the TWELFTH NIGHT of CHRISTMAS and paraded in grotesque costumes and masks. The celebrations were suspended in the Civil War, but were revived in 1866 by Joe Cain, a town clerk who togged himself out as an Indian chief and rode through the streets in a charcoal wagon. The old Mardi Gras societies reappeared, and new ones evolved.

Today a different mystic society parades each evening in the two weeks before Lent, and balls are held that are open to everyone.

Mardi Gras itself, the day before Ash Wednesday, is a state holiday in Alabama.

Galveston, Texas has a twelve-day period of whoop-de-do leading up to the actual day of **Fat Tuesday** in this barrier-island city of Texas. About 200,000 spectators are attracted to the Mardi Gras festival, which was first held here in 1867. Though it died out at the turn of the century, it was revived in 1985. Growing bigger every year, this celebration features masked balls, royal coronations, Cajun dances, jazz performances, and, of course, numerous parades with dramatic floats.

See also SHROVE TUESDAY; CARNIVAL.

Marion County Ham Days
Late September
A weekend celebration of the famous Kentucky smoked ham, held in Lebanon (Marion County), Ky., since 1969. The affair started with a simple country ham breakfast served to about 300 people on the street; now about 50,000 folks show up. Breakfast (ham cured in Marion County, eggs, biscuits with local honey, fried apples) is still served on Saturday and Sunday, but there is more: a "PIGASUS PARADE" with more than 100 floats, a Pokey Pig 10-kilometer run, a crafts and antiques show, a hog-calling contest, a hay-bale toss, and a hot-air balloon race.

Maritime Day, National
May 22
The day chosen to commemorate the contribution of American commercial shipping is, appropriately, the day on which the *Savannah* left its home port in Georgia in 1819 to attempt the first steam-propelled crossing of the Atlantic. So unusual was it to see a steam-powered vessel in those days that when the *Savannah* passed the naval station at Cape Clear, Ireland, the authorities thought she was on fire and quickly dispatched a royal cutter to assist her. In reality, the *Savannah* was equipped with sails and only relied on her engines for about ninety hours of the journey.

It was President Franklin D. Roosevelt who first proclaimed May 22 as National Maritime Day in 1933. Since that time observations of this day have grown in popularity, particularly in American port cities. Ships are opened to the public, maritime art and essay contests are held, and parades and band concerts are common. Environmentalists sometimes take advantage of the attention focused on the country's maritime heritage on this day to draw attention to pollution and deterioration of maritime environments, particularly in large commercial ports like New York City.

Marksmen's Festival *See* Schutzenfest

Marlboro Music Festival
July–August
It was the noted violinist Adolf Busch who came up with the idea of establishing a summer community for musicians that would free them from the pressures and restrictions of concert life. Every summer since 1951, a group of artists from all over the world has gathered in Marlboro, Vermont to exchange musical ideas. The Marlboro Music School, which holds an eight-week session each summer, is primarily a place where students or those who are just starting out on their professional careers can study contemporary and classical chamber music. During the five-week festival, the general public has an opportunity to hear the results of their collaborations. But the primary emphasis at Marlboro is on rehearsing the works that the participants themselves have selected, rather than on performing them for the public.

Although many noted musicians have been associated with Marlboro, perhaps the best known is Pablo Casals, the world-famous cellist who conducted the Marlboro Festival Orchestra and taught master classes there from 1960 to 1973.

Maroon Festival
January 6

When Jamaica was a Spanish territory in the sixteenth century, African slaves were brought in to work the plantations. The Spanish, disappointed by the lack of gold on the island, eventually left and the former slaves fled to the mountains. During the seventeenth and eighteenth centuries, the island's British inhabitants were often harassed or attacked by the descendants of these well-armed and organized fugitive slaves, who were called Maroons (having been marooned or deserted by their owners). By 1738 the Maroons had been given permission to settle in the northern part of the island.

The annual Maroon Festival has been held since 1759 at Accompong on or near January 6. It is celebrated with traditional dancing and singing, maroon feasts and ceremonies, the blowing of the *abeng*, and the playing of maroon drums.

Marriage Fair
September

A mass engagement and marriage *moussem* 'festival' held in the remote village of Imilchil in the Atlas Mountains of Morocco. As many as 30,000 people of the Ait Hadiddou tribe, a Berber clan, gather for the three days of the *moussem*. This is a combined trade fair and pageant of public courtship, instant engagement, and the immediate exchange of marriage vows. The festival solves the problem of meeting a mate in a society where isolation is the norm: the men spend half a year moving with their flocks to upland pastures, while the women stay in the villages, planting crops and weaving rugs.

Families and their herds of sheep and donkeys stream onto the Imilchil plateau at dawn of the first day. They sell or barter their wool, meat, grain, and vegetables, while tradesmen set up tents of pottery, rugs, and tools. Musicians beat tambourines, games are played, and acrobats perform. The center of their Islam-influenced devotions is the tomb of the holy man Sidi Mohammed el Merheni. It's not certain when he lived but it's known that the marriages he blessed were happy.

The courtship proceeds with women wearing a peaked headdress and striped wool capes over white dresses. Their eyes are outlined with kohl and their cheeks are rouged. The prospective grooms, wearing white robes and turbans, weave in pairs through the clusters of brides-to-be. A man speaks to a woman, the woman nods assent, and if the family approves, the couple will enter the wedding tent to seek approval from a representative of the Ministry of Justice in Rabat. Brides who have not been previously married will leave the *moussem* with their fathers, and be welcomed by their grooms' families with a feast later in the year. Women who are divorcées or widows will go directly to live with their husbands. (Ait Hadiddou women are free to divorce and remarry.)

When a woman consents to marriage, she tells her suitor, "You have captured my liver." The Ait Hadiddou consider the liver to be the soul of love because it aids digestion and well-being.

Marriage of Goliath
Saturday before fourth Sunday in August

In many French and Belgian towns, people carry giants—towering figures representing various biblical, historical, or legendary characters—through the streets in their religious or historical processions (see FESTIVAL OF THE GIANTS). In Ath, Belgium, a giant was used for the first time in 1461 in the Procession of St. Julien. Other figures were added by local guilds over the years, and today the procession is known as **Les Vêpres de Gouyasse** because it portrays the marriage of Goliath, the biblical giant.

Wearing his helmet and breastplate, the giant's figure is carried to the Church of St. Julien, accompanied by Madame Goliath and escorted by other giants—including Samson, a symbolic figure known as Mademoiselle Victoire, and Ambiorix, the leader of a Gaulish tribe. Goliath and his bride stand on either side of the church door as town officials and others enter for the religious ceremony. Afterward, the battle of David and Goliath is reenacted at the Grand Place or market square.

Martenitza
March 1

Every year on March 1, the people of Bulgaria present each other with *martenitzas*—two joined tassels of red and white woolen thread resembling a simple Christmas decoration symbolizing health and happiness. The custom originated with the ancient Thracians, and the first *martenitzas* had silver or gold coins attached to them. Today it is most widespread in Bulgaria, although the Martenitza is also celebrated in southern Romania, Albania, Greece, and Cyprus.

The rites are varied. In some regions, the women dress completely in red on this day. In northeastern Bulgaria, the lady of the house tosses a red cloth over a fruit tree, or spreads a red woolen cloth on the fields for fertility. In stock-breeding areas, a red-and-white thread is tied to the cattle. Bulgaria is the only country where this particular fertility custom seems to have survived. In Greece the "March" is tied to the wrist or big toe of children to protect them from the March sun. They remove it when they see the first swallow or stork, signs of springtime. On Cyprus it is hoped that one's skin will be as red (healthy) as the string. In Canada, Bulgarian-Macedonians throw the string out for the first robins to use in their nest.

Martin Luther King's Birthday

Federal holiday: third Monday in January; birthday: January 21

In 1955 Rosa Parks, a black seamstress in Montgomery, Alabama refused to obey a bus driver's order to give up her seat to a white male passenger. She was fined $14 for her defiance of the Jim Crow (segregationist) law that required blacks to sit in the rear of buses, and if the bus were crowded, to give up their seat to a white. The incident led to a citywide bus boycott and raised its leader, the young black Baptist minister Dr. Martin Luther King, Jr., to national prominence.

King went on to establish the Southern Christian Leadership Conference, to win the Nobel Peace Prize, and to play an active role in the civil rights movement of the 1960s. He was in Memphis, Tennessee on April 4, 1968 organizing a strike of the city's predominantly black sanitation workers when he was shot to death at the age of 39 by James Earl Ray.

Martin Luther King Day is a federal holiday, the only one for a person who was not a president; federal government offices are closed on that day. It has become a focal point for recognition of African-American history and the American civil rights movement led by Dr. King. It is also a legal holiday in some states—among them Connecticut, Illinois, Kentucky, Maryland, Massachusetts, Michigan, New Jersey, New York, and Ohio—although it is sometimes moved to the nearest Monday. In Alabama it became **Martin Luther King and Robert E. Lee's Birthday**, observed on January 21. The same day in Virginia is called **Lee-Jackson-King Day**, combining Dr. King's birthday with those of Robert E. Lee and Andrew "Stonewall" Jackson. In schools, the day is often observed with special lessons and assembly programs dealing with Dr. King's life and work.

Martinmas
November 11

This is the feast day of St. Martin of Tours (316–397), one of the most popular saints of the Middle Ages. It is said that when he heard that he had been elected Bishop of Tours, he hid himself in a barn. A squawking goose gave away his hiding place, and the day is still celebrated with roast goose dinners. Another popular legend involves St. Martin's cloak, which he divided with his sword, giving half to a shivering beggar.

In Germany and northern Europe, Roman Catholics commemorate St. Martin while Protestants commemorate Martin Luther's baptismal day.

For rural people, Martinmas comes at a happy time of year: the crops are in, the animals have been slaughtered, the new wine is ready, and the hard work of summer and autumn is over. It's no surprise, then, that St. Martin is the patron saint of tavern keepers, wine-growers, and drunkards. There is a good deal of weather-lore associated with this day. Spells of mild autumn weather that Americans refer to as "Indian summer" are called "St. Martin's summer" or "a Martinmas summer" in Europe and England. It was once a QUARTER DAY. Nowadays, in England, this day is more remembered as Armistice Day (VETERANS' DAY).

In Belgium, where it is called **Sint Maartens Dag**, St. Martin's Day is a favorite holiday among the children. Like St. Nicholas (see ST. NICHOLAS' DAY), St. Martin visits them on the feast day eve bringing them gifts. On November 11 apples and nuts are tossed into children's rooms while they stand with their faces turned to the wall. *Gauffres*, or little waffle cakes, are particularly popular on St. Martin's Day.

This day is also an important festival in the Netherlands. There it is know as Beggar's Day and boys and girls serenade their neighbors and beg for goodies. In many towns the children light a bonfire and dance and shout around it. Then they march in processions with lanterns made from scooped-out turnips, carrots, or beets.

In other European countries, St. Martin's Day is regarded as a time to give thanks for the harvest and is often observed with feasting. Goose is the traditional meal. In Sweden, November 11 is known as **Martin's Goose Day** (Marten Gas). In France, *mal de Saint Martin* 'St. Martin's sickness' is the name given to the upset stomach that often follows overindulgence. There is also an impressive ceremony at St. Martin's shrine in Tours on this day.

Martinsfest
November 11

St. Martin's Festival in Germany honors both St. Martin of Tours (see ST. MARTIN'S DAY, MARTINMAS) and Martin Luther, the German theologian and leader of the Protestant Reformation. In Düsseldorf, a man dressed as St. Martin rides through the streets followed by hundreds of children. Many carry lanterns made from hollowed-out pumpkins. It is thought that the rites associated with St. Martin's Day may have originated as an early thanksgiving festival in honor of Freya, the ancient German goddess of plenty.

While German Roman Catholics honor St. Martin on this day, Protestants honor Martin Luther, who was born on November 10, 1483 and baptized on the 11th. In Erfurt, where Martin Luther attended the university, there is a procession of children carrying lanterns. This ends in the plaza in front of the cathedral and the Severi Church. With their lanterns the children form the "Luther rose," or the escutcheon of Martin Luther.

Martyrs of North America, Feast of the
October 19

The **Feast of the North American Martyrs** commemorates the death of eight priests who were killed by the Iroquois, mortal enemies of the Huron Indians with whom the priests had been working for thirty-four years. There was a great deal of missionary activity being carried out in what is now Canada and upstate New York during the 1600s, and many of the devoted missionaries who worked among the Indians in the area extending from Nova Scotia to the Great Lakes met with torture and often cruel death. The eight who are remembered on this day are John de Brébeuf and his companions, French Jesuits who died in 1649. They were canonized together in 1930, and a shrine was built for them at Auriesville, New York.

Marya
July–August; third day of the waning half of Sravana

When Gautama sat down under the Bo tree to await Enlightenment, Mara, the Buddhist Lord of the Senses and satanic tempter, tried a number of strategies to divert him from his goal. Disguised as a messenger, Mara brought the news that one of Gautama's rivals had usurped his family's throne. Then he scared away the other gods who had gathered to honor the future Buddha by causing a storm of rain, rocks, and ashes to fall. Finally, he sent his three daughters, representing thirst, desire, and delight, to seduce Gautama—all to no avail.

In the city of Patan, Nepal, a procession on this day commemorates the Buddha's triumph over Mara's temptations. A procession of three or four thousand people, carrying gifts, usually butter lamps, for Lord Buddha, moves through the city from shrine to shrine. Some wear masks and others play traditional Nepalese musical instruments. The devil dancers and mask-wearers in the parade often pretend to scare the children who line the streets by suddenly jumping out at them.

Maryland Day
March 25

Maryland Day or **Founder's Day** commemorates the landing of the first colonists there in 1634, and the first Roman Catholic Mass they celebrated. Named after Henrietta Maria, the consort of King Charles I of England, Maryland was the first proprietary colony on the American mainland. George Calvert, Lord Baltimore was appointed by the king as proprietor, and as a Catholic he hoped to establish a refuge for other Catholics, who had been persecuted in Anglican England. He was succeeded as head of the colony by his son, Cecilius Calvert, the second Lord Baltimore, who brought 200 more colonists over from England.

Maryland Hunt Cup
Last Saturday in April

A steeplechase that has been run in Maryland since 1894 and is considered the premier such horse race in America and one of the toughest steeplechases in the world. It's a timber race: the jumps are over stout post-and-rail fences rather than hedges as in the English GRAND NATIONAL. Since 1922, it has always been held in Glyndon, the locale of the Green Spring Valley Hounds, a hunt club. The course is four miles long and has twenty-two fences, none of which is jumped twice. The highest fence is the sixteenth at four-feet-ten, while the most spectacular, causing the most spills, is the four-feet-six-inch third fence, near the beginning of the race before the horses are well warmed up.

The first race was held to settle a dispute between two hunt clubs, Green Spring Valley Hounds and the Elkridge Hunt, over which had the better fox-hunting horses. Originally only for club members, the race was opened to all comers in 1903, and a rivalry between Pennsylvania and Maryland horses began and still endures. At the first race, a silver cup and $100 were awarded to the winner. Today there is still a cup, but the award has grown—$25,000 is now split among the top four finishers. Memorable horses have been Mountain Dew, a three-time winner in the 1960s; Jay Trump, also a three-time winner in the 1960s and the winner of the English Grand National in 1965; and Ben Nevis, twice a winner, who took seven seconds off the course record in 1978, a record that still stood in 1991. Ben Nevis, who also won the English Grand National, was a small horse but a spectacular athlete.

The Hunt Cup was originally only for men, but women were allowed to enter in the late 1970s, and in 1980 Joy Slater was the first woman to take the prize.

Tailgate parties are held before the race, and a hunt ball after it is attended by riders, trainers, jockeys, owners, and members of the two local hunt clubs. It's considered the social event of the season.

Marzenna Day
Saturday or Sunday nearest March 21

A festival day along the Vistula River in Poland, Marzenna Day is a spring ritual particularly enjoyed by young people. A *Marzenna* is a straw doll about three or four feet tall and dressed in rags, a striped shirt, a hat, and lots of ribbons. On this day near the first day of spring (see VERNAL EQUINOX), the townspeople, dressed in costume, accompany the Marzenna to the river and throw her in. Not only is this act a final farewell to winter, but it also recalls an old legend about a young man whose faith in one god was so great that he was able to save a girl who was about to be sacrificed to appease the gods of storms and floods. After the doll is thrown into the water, the people welcome spring with singing and dancing.

Maskal
September

A Christian festival in Ethiopia to commemorate the finding of the True Cross, the cross on which Christ was crucified. (*Maskal* means 'cross.') The celebration comes at the end of the rainy season in the Ethiopian spring, when fields are blooming with yellow flowers known as the maskal flowers. In communities throughout the nation, a tall pole called a *demara* is set up and topped with a cross. Families place smaller

demaras against the big one, and in the evening they are made into a huge bonfire. Religious ceremonies are performed around the bonfire, with songs and dancing. The ashes of the burned-out fire are considered holy, so the people place the powder of the ashes on their foreheads.

See also EXALTATION OF THE CROSS.

Master Draught Pageant *See Meistertrunk Pageant*

Master's Golf Tournament, The
First full week in April

Known to golf fans everywhere as **The Masters**, this annual tournament has been held at the exclusive Augusta National Golf Club in Georgia since it was first started there in 1934 by Bobby Jones, who designed the course. It has long been associated with names like Ben Hogan, Sam Snead, Arnold Palmer, and Jack Nicklaus. Former U. S. President Dwight Eisenhower, often played the course and stayed in a cottage to the left of the tenth tee that is still called "Ike's Cottage."

The qualifying rounds are held on Thursday and Friday of the four-day tournament, and the top forty-four finishers participate in the final round. The top twenty-four finishers are automatically invited back the next year and do not have to qualify over again. In addition to the cash prize, the winner of the tournament, which has been referred to as "golf's rite of spring," receives a trophy and a green blazer. Each year on the Tuesday night before the tournament, there is a Champions Dinner attended by past winners and hosted by the defending champion—all of them wearing their distinctive green jackets.

It wasn't until September 1990 that the Augusta National Golf Club admitted its first black member, Ron Townsend president of the Gannett Television Group. Had the Club refused to admit a black man, it is likely that the Masters would no longer have been held there, since the PGA (Professional Golfers' Association) now has rules forbidding discriminatory membership practices.

Matsu, Birthday of
Twenty-third day of third lunar month (mid April to mid May)

A celebration of the birthday of the Chinese deity Matsu (or Ma-cho or Mazu), the Goddess of the Sea who is venerated by fishermen for protecting them from storms and disasters at sea. People pay homage to her on her birthday at the Meizhou Mazu Temple on Meishou Island, Fujian

Province, China, on Taiwan, and in other Chinese communities.

One Chinese legend says that the goddess was born in about 960 and, because she never cried in the first month of her life, was named Lin Moniang, *moniang* meaning 'quiet girl.' She began to read when she was eight, became a believer in Buddhism at ten, studied magic arts when she was twelve, and at twenty-eight achieved nirvana and became a goddess. She is worshiped because she saved the lives of sailors. Courts in successive dynasties issued decrees to honor her with such titles as "Holy Princess" and "Holy Mother."

In Taiwan, the story is that Matsu, a girl from Hokkien province in China, took up the fishing trade to support her mother after her fisherman father died. One day she died at sea, and because of her filial devotion, she came to be worshiped as a deity. During World War II, when American planes started to bomb Taiwan, many women prayed to Matsu, and it is said that some women saw a girl dressed in red holding out a red cloth to catch the falling bombs.

She is known as A-Ma, or the Mother Goddess, on Macao. The legend there says A-Ma was a beautiful young woman whose presence on a Canton-bound ship saved it from disaster. All the other ships in the fleet, whose rich owners had refused to give her passage, were destroyed in a storm.

Whatever the story, people whose lives depend on the sea visit the goddess's temples on her birthday.

On Taiwan, the most famous celebration site is the Chaotien Temple in Peikang. Built in 1694, it is Taiwan's oldest, biggest, and richest Matsu temple. On Matsu's birthday, hundreds of thousands of people pour out of buses and arrive on foot at Peikang. Many of them make pilgrimages from the town of Tachia about sixty miles north, spending a week visiting about sixteen Matsu temples along the route. Peikang becomes so crowded it's hard to move, and the firecrackers are deafening. It has been estimated that 75 percent of all firecrackers manufactured on Taiwan are exploded in Peikang on the Matsu festival; afterwards the remnants of the firecrackers lie two inches deep on the streets.

See also TIN HAU FESTIVAL.

Matsu Festival
Moon 3, Day 23
The Chinese goddess Matsu studied Buddhist

and Taoist scriptures and performed many miracles during her brief life, which ended sometime between the ages of eighteen and twenty-eight. The name Matsu means "granny". She is the protectress of seamen, especially those who ply the dangerous Taiwan Strait. Her birthday is observed in Taiwan with a parade of the goddess and other gods through village streets, where altars bearing sacrifices of food and incense have been set up. A carnival-like atmosphere prevails on this day, with watermelon stalls, cotton candy stalls, and slingshot ranges set up along the roadside. The next morning, the entire village participates in an elaborate sacrificial rite in the temple, after which people return to their homes to hold feasts for their friends and relatives—often dragging acquaintances off the streets and urging them to come in and eat.

Maundy Thursday
Between March 19 and April 22 in West; between April 1 and May 5 in East; Thursday before Easter
Also known as **Green Thursday** in Germany from the practice of giving a green branch to penitents as a sign that their penance was completed; **Shere** or **Sheer Thursday,** meaning 'free from guilt'; **Paschal Thursday, Passion Thursday,** or **Holy Thursday,** it is the day preceding GOOD FRIDAY. It commemorates Jesus' institution of the Eucharist in the Last Supper, celebrated by Christians since the middle of the fourth century. The practice of ceremonial foot-washing in imitation of Jesus, who washed his disciples' feet before the Last Supper as a sign and example of humility and love, has been largely discontinued in Protestant churches. However, the Roman Catholic church and the Anglican Communion still celebrate the rites of Maundy Thursday, which may include handing out special coins known as "Maundy money" to the aged and the poor, instead of foot washing. Also on this day, the sacramental Holy Oils, or chrism, are blessed.

The name "Maundy" probably comes from the Latin *mandatum* 'commandment' referring to Christ's words after he washed the feet of his disciples: "A new commandment I give unto you, that you love one another as I have loved you." (John 13:34)

Mawlid al-Nabi (Maulid al-Nabi; Prophet's Birthday)
Twelfth day of the Islamic lunar month of Rabi al-Awwal
Mawlid al-Nabi celebrates the birth of Muham-

mad, the founder of Islam. Born in Mecca in 570, he was a shepherd and a trader who began to receive revelations from God when he was forty years old. Over the next twenty-three years he not only established a religion but brought an unprecedented political unity to Arab tribes. Muhammad's birth began to be observed as a public holiday about the twelfth century, except by conservative sects such as the Wahhabis who do not celebrate any human. They believe that to do so would detract from the worship of God. It is celebrated with the recitation of litanies in mosques, and with firecrackers and gift-giving throughout the Middle East. In Libya it is an official holiday; in Upper Volta it is called **Damba** and Indonesia **Sekartan**.

May Day
May 1

Many of the customs associated with the first day of May come from the old Roman Floralia, or festival of flowers. These include the gathering of branches and flowers on May Eve or early May Day morning, the choosing and crowning of a May Queen, and dancing around a bush, tree, or decorated pole, the Maypole. The sports and festivities that are held on this day symbolize the rebirth of nature as well as human fertility. In fact, the ritual drinking and dancing around the Maypole in colonial America so horrified the Pilgrim Fathers that they outlawed the practice and punished the offenders. This is probably why May Day has remained a relatively quiet affair in this country.

In Communist countries, May Day has been transformed into a holiday for workers, marked by parades that are an occasion for displaying military strength. The May Day Parade in Red Square, Moscow, has long been a spectacular example though less so in recent years with the dissolution of the Soviet Union and the resulting relaxation of Cold War tensions. Perhaps in reaction to such displays, Americans instituted LOYALTY DAY and LAW DAY on this same date. In Great Britain, May 1 is LABOUR DAY.

See also PREMIER MAI and VAPPU.

Mayfest, International
May

A five-day celebration of the arts—performing, visual, and literary—held in Tulsa, Okla. One of the largest festivals in the state, the event features a juried art fair and theatrical presentations. In the past, these varied works have been staged: *Three Penny Opera, Our Town,* and *Revenge of the Space Pandas.* There is also a variety of musical entertainment, and ethnic foods from all corners of the globe.

Mayoring Day
May

In England, this is the day on which the new mayor of a town or borough parades through the streets. If it takes place on a Sunday, it is often called **Mayor's Sunday** and is celebrated with a church service. In Rye, Sussex the old tradition of the "hot-penny scramble" is carried out on this day. The new mayor throws hot pennies to the children, who then scramble to pick them up. This custom probably dates back to the time when Rye minted its own coins and they were distributed while still hot from the molds.

Meat Fare Sunday
Between February 1 and March 7; eight days before Lent begins in the East

In the Orthodox Church, the second Sunday before the beginning of Great LENT is called Meat Fare Sunday because it is traditionally the last day on which meat may be eaten until EASTER. See also CHEESEFARE SUNDAY, SHROVE TUESDAY, and ASH WEDNESDAY.

Mecklenburg Independence Day
May 20

The citizens of Mecklenburg County, North Carolina, would like to think that their ancestors were the first to call for independence from the British when they adopted the Mecklenburg Declaration of Independence on May 20, 1775. But historians now believe that the resolutions calling for independence that had been sent to the Second Continental Congress in Philadelphia were never actually presented there—and, in fact, they question that the meeting ever took place.

Even though the Mecklenburg patriots may not have been the first to declare their independence from British rule, their actions represent an important step on the road to the American Revolution, and **Mecklenburg Declaration of Independence Day**, sometimes referred to simply as **Mecklenburg Day**, is still observed as a legal holiday in North Carolina.

Medora Musical
June–September

Theodore ("Teddy") Roosevelt, the twenty-sixth president of the United States, spent two years ranching in the Dakota Territory as a young man. When the Spanish-American War was declared in 1898, Roosevelt resigned his position as assistant secretary of the Navy under President William McKinley and organized the First Volunteer Cavalry, nicknamed the "Rough Riders," and took them to Cuba. His colorful exploits, particularly in the Battle of Santiago, made him a national hero.

Every night from mid-June through Labor Day in Medora, North Dakota there is a musical extravaganza known as the Medora Musical—a patriotic song-and-dance salute to Teddy Roosevelt and his Rough Riders. The musical is performed in a natural amphitheatre featuring an outdoor escalator to get people to their seats. The colorful buttes and ravines of the Bad Lands form a dramatic backdrop for the Broadway-class variety show.

Meenakshi Kalyanam
April; full moon of Phalguna

The marriage of the goddess Meenakshi, an incarnation of Parvati, and Lord Sundereswarar (also known as Lord Shiva), celebrated as part of the Hindu **Chitrai** (or **Chithirai**) **Festival** in Madurai, Tamil Nadu, India. The rituals are observed at the Meenaskshi Temple, one of the biggest temple complexes in India, most of it built between the twelfth and eighteenth centuries. There is a huge procession, with chariots carrying the temple images, dressed in special robes and jewels, through the streets. The people, in celebrating the marriage of the deities, also commemorate their own marriages.

In Malaysia and Singapore it is called **Panguni Uttiram** and also celebrates the marriage of Subramanya to Theivani, adopted daughter of Indra. In Malaysia, food is free to anyone all day. In Singapore, at the Sri Mariamman Temple, there is a fire-walking ceremony. A couple of days later there is a dancing procession led by a man balancing a flower-bedecked pot of yellow-colored water.

Meistertrunk Pageant (Master Draught Pageant)
Between May 8 and June 11; Whitsuntide

A celebration in the medieval town of Rothenburg-on-the-Tauber, Germany, to commemorate a gargantuan drinking feat in 1631. The pageant is staged for the four days ending on Whitmonday, and the play itself, Meistertrunk, is also performed on various occasions during the summer. The best known of the Bavarian history plays, *Meistertrunk* dramatizes a chronicled event of the Thirty Years' War: the town was threatened with destruction by Imperial troops led by the famed general, Johann Tserclaes Tilly. The general saw the state wine beaker and decided to play a game with the town's life at stake. If a council member could drink off the entire beaker of wine—about a gallon—in one draught, Tilly promised to spare the town. Burgomaster George Nusch accepted the challenge and emptied the beaker in one mighty gulp and the town was saved.

The play is performed out of doors with the entire town a stage. Tilly's troops are camped outside the city walls, and in the market square costumed children plead with the general. The same beaker that Nusch drained in 1631 is used in the reenactment.

A parade precedes the play, and the "Shepherds' Dance" is performed after it in the market square. The dance, dating to 1516, is in honor of St. Wolfgang, the patron saint of shepherds, and recalls the time a member of the shepherds' guild raced from his pastures to warn the city of the approach of an enemy.

Melbourne Cup Day
First Tuesday in November

The only public holiday in the world dedicated to a horse race, Melbourne Cup Day has been observed in Melbourne, Victoria, Australia since the first Cup race was held there in 1867. The event actually features seven races, including the grueling handicap race of just under two miles, which is run by some twenty Thoroughbreds for a purse worth about two million dollars. The story of Phar Lap, the legendary New Zealand Thoroughbred who won the Cup in 1930 after nearly being shot by unscrupulous gamblers, was made into a movie that made the Cup an event familiar to people all over the world.

Cup Day is not only a holiday in Australia, but is observed throughout the world in offices where Australians work. For those who attend, it is a particularly glamorous event. The champagne flows, huge sums of money are wagered, and the women wear lavish hats while the men turn out in grey top hats and dark morning suits. There are similar races held in other Australian states (see HOBART CUP DAY), but the Melbourne Cup is still the number one classic of the Australian horse-racing circuit.

Memorial Day
Last Monday in May

A legal holiday, formerly known as **Decoration Day**, proclaimed annually by the president to honor United States citizens who have died in war. Since 1950, by Congressional request, the day is also set aside to pray for permanent peace. Memorial Day is observed in every state but Alabama, which instead celebrates Confederate Memorial Day on the fourth Monday of April. (In all, eight states observe the Confederate holiday, and a ninth, Texas, makes Confederate Heroes Day a state holiday.)

Both religious services and patriotic parades mark the day's celebrations. In the national official observance, a wreath is placed on the Tomb of the Unknown Soldier in Arlington National Cemetery in Virginia. One of the more moving observances is at the Gettysburg National Cemetery in Pennsylvania, where schoolchildren scatter flowers over the graves of unknown soldiers of the Civil War.

The practice of decorating graves of war dead began before the close of the Civil War. However, an officially set day was established in 1868 when Gen. John A. Logan, Commander-in-Chief of the Grand Army of the Republic, issued an order naming May 30 as a day for "strewing with flowers or otherwise decorating the graves of comrades who died in defense of their country during the late rebellion." The day became known as Decoration Day, but as it was extended to include the dead of all wars, it took the name Memorial Day.

Merdeka Day
August 31

A national holiday in Malaysia to commemorate its *merdeka* 'independence' from British sovereignty in 1957. Parts of Malaysia were variously under the rule of foreign powers for centuries, but by the 1920s all the states eventually comprising Malaysia were ruled by Britain. The Federation of Malaya was founded in 1957 and Malaysia was formed in 1963.

The streets of towns and cities are decorated on this day, and there are numerous parades, exhibitions, and stage shows.

Merrie Monarch Festival
Week after Easter

A week of festivities in Honolulu honoring Hawaii's King David Kalakaua, who reigned from 1874 to 1891, and gave the United States exclusive rights to maintain a naval station at Pearl Harbor. The week's events, starting on Easter, close with the world's largest hula competition on the last three nights. The top hula schools (*hula halau*) compete in ancient and modern hula.

Mexico Independence Day *See Independence Festival of Mexico*

Mi-Carême
Between March 8 and April 11; fourth Sunday in Lent

This break from the strictness of the Lenten season is observed in France, Belgium, and various islands of the French West Indies—including Guadeloupe, St. Barthélemy, and Martinique. In Paris, it is celebrated with the **Fête des Blanchisseuses**, or laundresses, who choose a queen from each of the various metropolitan districts. The district queens and the queen of queens chosen by them ride through the streets on a float, followed by their costumed courtiers and ladies-in-waiting. There is a colorful ball for the washerwomen that night.

In Belgium, **Mid-Lent** or **Half-Vasten** is the day when the Count of Mid-Lent makes his appearance, rewarding good boys and girls with gifts.

Michaelmas
September 29 in the West, November 8 in the East

The **Feast of the Archangel Michael**, or the **Day of St. Michael and All Angels**, is a traditional feast day in the Roman Catholic, Anglican Communion, and Orthodox churches. The cult of St. Michael, traditionally regarded as the leader of the heavenly host of angels, probably originated in the East, then spread to the West by the fifth century. The Roman Catholic feast honors the archangels Michael, Gabriel, and Raphael, while in the East and the Anglican communion, Michael and all the angels are honored.

Churches dedicated to Michael can be found in Asia and throughout coastal Europe, usually in places where Michael is reputed to have saved the community from the threat of a monster or giant. The ninth century abbey Mont St. Michel, off the coast of Normandy, France once held the shield worn by Michael in his fight against the dragon.

There is an old saying that if you eat goose on Michaelmas you won't have to worry about money for a year. When tenants paid their rent on this day (see QUARTER DAYS), it was customary to include "one goose fit for the lord's dinner." Feasting on goose dinners is still part of the Michaelmas tradition, particularly in Ireland.

Michigan Brown Trout Festival
Third through fourth weekend in July

You don't have to be a professional charter captain or even a local fisherman to participate in the Michigan Brown Trout Festival, which has been held in Alpena on the shores of Lake Huron since 1975. The main event is the two-day Super Tournament, which pits boat against boat. It was won recently by someone who had never fished in the area before. Cash prizes are awarded to those who catch the largest fish (by weight) in each of five divisions—brown trout, salmon, lake trout, steelhead, and walleye—each day and over the course of the week-long festival.

Tens of thousands of people come to Alpena to enjoy not only the fishing competitions but the sailboat races, entertainment, and other festival events. The lucky person who catches Big Brownie, a specially-tagged brown trout, during the festival wins a $50,000 savings bond. But the luck that is familiar to fishermen everywhere has plagued those attending the festival as well: no one has ever collected.

Michigan is also home to the National Trout Festival, which dates back to 1933. About forty thousand fishermen and visitors come to the small town of Kalkaska, which has 275 miles of trout streams and 85 lakes stocked with brown, brook, rainbow, and lake trout. This festival is timed to coincide with the April opening of trout season.

Michigan Renaissance Festival
August–September for seven consecutive weekends

Visitors who walk through the turreted gates of the annual Renaissance Festival in Holly, Michigan are made to feel as if they're stepping back into the sixteenth century. The festival has a permanent, two-hundred-acre site which is set up to resemble a European village. Festival activities, which are designed to entertain as well as to educate, include theater, games, and equestrian events as well as displays and demonstrations of Renaissance crafts and cooking. The entire event, which takes place over seven consecutive weekends beginning in mid-August, is based on the theme of a harvest celebration in which visitors are encouraged to participate. They can try their hand at archery or dueling, sample roasted turkey drumsticks, observe the arts of glass-blowing, pewter-casting, and blacksmithing, and witness a Tournament of Chivalry in which costumed knights on horseback joust on the gaming field.

The popularity of Renaissance festivals began with their introduction in California during the 1960s. Such events are now held in Detroit, Minneapolis, Kansas City, and Largo and Sarasota, Florida, and in many other cities across the country. Attendance at the Holly festival has grown to more than 150,000 since it was first held in 1980.

Mid-Autumn Festival
Full moon nearest September 15; Fifteenth day of the eighth moon, Chinese lunar calendar

This festival to honor the moon goddess is a national holiday in China and a day celebrated, throughout the Far East, and in Asian communities all over the world. It is also known as the **Moon Cake Festival**. In Korea, it is called **Hangawi** or **Ch'usok**; in Vietnam **Trung Thursday**; in Hong Kong **Chung Ch'iu**; and in Taiwan **Tiong-chhiu Choeh**.

Family reunions are traditional on this day, giving it some resemblance to the American THANKSGIVING. People travel long distances to be together for exchanging presents, feasting, and eating moon cakes. The ingredients of the cakes and the celebration vary according to the region.

In Taiwan, people have picnics and climb mountains to have a better view of the moon. Besides eating moon cakes, people eat pomelos, or grapefruit. The Chinese word for grapefruit is *yu*, which sounds like the Chinese word for protection, and this is a time for praying to the moon god for protection, family unity, and good fortune. It's also a time for lovers to tryst.

In Malaysia, Vietnam, and other areas, it is a children's festival. They parade through the streets on the night of the festival with candle-lit paper lanterns, some of them white and round like the moon, others like all sorts of animals. Dancers parade with dragons made of paper and cloth, and firecrackers are lit after the parades. In Hong Kong children also carry paper lanterns, and many people spend the evening on the beaches watching the moon and the many bonfires that are lit on this night.

In Suzhou, China, a celebration is held in the Museum of Chinese Drama and Opera, with spectators seated at small porcelain tables where they eat moon cakes, drink jasmine tea, and watch a program of Chinese classical music, ballad-singing, acrobatics, and comic scenes from operas.

In Japan, the custom of *tsukimi*, or 'moon-viewing,' is observed at the same time as the Chinese festival—at the time of the full moon nearest Sep. 15. People set up a table facing the horizon where the moon will rise, and place offerings on the table to the spirit of the moon. These would include a vase holding the seven grasses of autumn, cooked vegetables, and *tsukimi dango,* moon-viewing dumplings made of rice flour. Moon-viewing festivals are held at Hyakkaen Garden, Mukojima, Tokyo, and on Osawa at Daikakuji Temple in Kyoto, where the moon is watched from boats with dragons on their bows.

There are twenty to thirty varieties of moon cakes, which in their roundness are symbolic of family unity. Some are made of lotus seed paste, some of red bean paste, some with mixed nuts, and some have a duck egg in the center. In some regions, the moon cakes are crusty, while in others they are flaky.

There are also varying versions of the origins of the festival, which is thought to go back to the ninth century. One version has it that the Chinese, looking at the dark side of the full moon, saw a hare or rabbit, which was able to make a potion for immortality. The festival was the rabbit's birthday, and people sold rabbits on the streets. Moon cakes were made to feed the rabbits. Another version says that the day marks the overthrow of the Mongol overlords in ancient China; the moon cakes supposedly hid secret messages planning the overthrow.

The more accepted version is that the day is a harvest festival at a time when the moon is brightest. At this time of year, as the weather gets colder, people want a day to rest and enjoy life.

Middfest International

Three days in late September–early October

Middletown, Ohio is home to the annual festival of international culture known as Middfest. Designed to promote world understanding, friendship, and peace, the festival highlights the culture of a different country each year. Performers, artists, and dignitaries from the featured country come to Middletown and stay with local families. During the week preceding the three-day festival, they perform in nearby communities, give talks, and demonstrate their art and skills. Countries that have been invited to participate since the festival's inception in 1981 include Luxembourg, Mexico, Egypt, Brazil, Japan, Switzerland, Canada, Italy, India, and Ireland. Included in the celebration are museum quality exhibits, ethnic dances, and menus from all over the world. Lectures, workshops, films, and special interest activities are also scheduled throughout Middfest weekend.

Mid-Lent

Between March 8 and April 7; fourth Sunday in Lent

In Italy **Mezza Quaresima** or Mid-Lent is a day of respite from the otherwise severe restrictions of LENT. Parties, dances, and street celebrations take place throughout the country, and many feature effigies of *Quaresima* that resemble a lean, witch-like old hag—in stark contrast to the fat man who represents CARNIVAL.

In Abruzzi, the effigy of Quaresima is pierced with seven feathers and suspended on a rope stretched across the street. On each Saturday in Lent the villagers pluck out one feather to signify the end of one of the seven weeks of the Lenten season.

Midnight Sun Festival

June 21

Celebrations of the summer solstice in Nome, Alaska, where the sun shines for better than twenty-two hours a day in the peak of summer. In Nome, the longest day of the year is feted on two days with a street dance, blanket toss, barbecue, Monte Carlo night (gambling), Eskimo dances, a parade, and a mock bank hold-up and jail. A river raft race has been held at midnight on June 21 since the 1960s. Various homemade rafts paddle down a one- to two-mile course on the Nome River, and the winning team claims a fur-lined honey bucket, which is passed on from year to year. A softball tournament, with about twenty men's and women's teams competing for trophies, precedes the day of the solstice. Games start at about 10 P.M.

Various places in Alaska celebrate the midnight sun in various ways: Skagway throws a dance, and at Tok, in 1990 the Frigid Poets Society began the practice of climbing a mountain to watch the sun not set.

In Fairbanks, a midnight baseball game is played without artificial lights. The home team Fairbanks Goldpanners (the name recalls the gold-rush days of early Fairbanks), is reputed to be one of the best semi-pro teams in the nation. The solstice is also marked with department store sales. On the day before the baseball game, there is a Midnight Sun Run, a ten-kilometer race attracting local and national runners, with refreshments and entertainment at the finish.

This excessive activity at midnight may be at least partly explained by the function of the pineal gland. In humans, this pinecone-shaped gland is thought to produce the hormone melatonin that cirulates through the body and triggers two reactions—drowsiness and reduced sex drive. Light inhibits melatonin production and thus makes it easier to do with less sleep when the sun shines. Hence, baseball games at midnight. (It is also a fact that 72 percent of Alaska babies are conceived between May and September.)

Midsummer Day
June 24, or nearest Friday

This ancient pagan festival of the Summer Solstice, originally kept on June 21, is celebrated in Europe and Scandinavian countries in much the same way as Beltane is celebrated in Ireland. Bonfires are still lit in some places on Midsummer Eve as a way of driving out evil and renewing reproductive powers. At one time it was believed that all natural waters had medicinal powers on this day, and people bathed in streams and rivers to cure their illnesses. Midsummer Day is also sacred to lovers. Shakespeare's romantic comedy, *A Midsummer Night's Dream* reflects the traditional spirit associated with this festival.

The Swedish begin their **Midsommar** celebration on Friday or Midsummer Eve and continue through Sunday. Every town and village sets up a maypole or *Majstang*, which is decorated with flowers, leaves, and flags. In Rattvik, Sweden on Lake Siljan, the festivities are held on a pier. The province of Dalarna, where some of Sweden's oldest wooden cottages have been preserved is a popular place to spend the Midsommar festival weekend.

The Swedes call Midsommar "the day that never ends" because the sun doesn't begin to set until 10:00 P.M. and it rises again at 2:00 A.M. In areas of Norway and Sweden that lie above the Arctic Circle, the sun shines brightly twenty-four hours a day for six weeks.

When June 24 was designated St. John the Baptist's Day by the church, the fires that had been associated with the pagan festival were reinterpreted to symbolize St. John, whom the Lord had called "a burning and shining light." But the pre-Christian elements surrounding Midsummer Day never really disappeared, and the Feast of St. John has long been associated with solstitial rites. This day is also one of the official Quarter Days in England.

See also Juhannus; Kupalo; St. Hans Festival; Inti Raymi Festival.

Midumu Ceremony
June–October

The Midumu ceremony is a masked dance ritual celebrating the end of the three-year initiation period for Makonde boys and girls. Although the Makonde originally lived in Malawi, Zambia, and Zimbabwe, they have migrated to Tanzania and Mozambique as well. Between June and October, the dry season, some of the Makonde men tell their families that they have been "called" to make a long journey. There is a public farewell ceremony, and then they disappear for ten to fifteen days. During this time they go from one village to the next and perform the masked dances of the Midumu ceremony, visiting the house of each new initiate and, after portraying various mythical stories in dance, receiving honey, meat, jewelry, and occasionally money in return.

The Midumu ceremony always begins at night during the time when the moon moves from the quarter to the half phase. It usually follows a happy event—such as a successful hunt, a good haul of fish, or a bountiful harvest.

Mihr, Festival of
February 5; forty days after Christmas

The Church of Armenia, proud of its ancient lineage and determined to retain its national character, has made it a point to keep a number of pagan ceremonies alive by investing them with Christian significance. This seems to be the case with the Festival of Mihr, the god of fire. This pagan spring festival was originally observed by lighting fires in Mihr's honor in the marketplace, and by lighting a lantern that burned throughout the year in the temple. When Christianity was introduced in Armenia early in the third century, fires were lit on this day in the church courtyards, and people danced around them or jumped through the flames.

The modern-day Armenian celebration of the Presentation of Christ in the Temple retains many elements of the pagan Festival of Mihr. In fact, the Armenian name for the month of February, *Mihragan*, is a reflection of the extent to which this ancient god and his festival have survived.

Mille Miglia
Early May

The three-day endurance rally in Italy for vintage racing cars known as the Mille Miglia or **Thousand Miles** began in 1927 as an all-out race, and it took about twenty hours to cover the course. By 1938, the roads had improved to the point where it took only about twelve hours, and the all-time record of ten hours, seven minutes, forty-eight seconds was set in 1955. This meant that the driver had to average nearly one hundred miles per hour on roads that normal drivers would hesitate to traverse at forty. A tragic accident in 1957, in which one of the racers, his navigator, and eleven spectators were killed, led to a ban against racing on public roads and brought the Mille Miglia to an abrupt halt.

The event was reorganized in 1977 with different rules. Although it still features vintage racing cars from the 1920s through the 1950s and the same roads, drivers are given three days—rather than ten hours—to cover the thousand miles. Driving in ordinary traffic, the competitors have to average a set number of miles per hour on thirty-four timed sections of the course, nineteen of which are driven over particularly challenging and scenic stretches of road.

The route begins in Brescia, goes east to Verona, and then southeast to Ferrera, where the drivers spend the night. Early the next morning they leave for Ravenna, follow the coast to Rimini, and then head into the mountains, where they must cover some of the most serpentine and beautiful roads in the world. The drivers spend the second night in Rome and on the third day make a twelve-hour dash back to Brescia via Viterbo, Siena, Florence, and Bologna.

Minehead Hobby Horse Parade
April 30–May 1

In England and Wales, hobby horses have been a part of celebrations welcoming spring as far back as anyone can remember. In the waterfront town of Minehead, Somerset, the "sailors' horse" has a boat-shaped frame seven to ten feet long, which is carried on the shoulders of a man whose body is concealed by a canvas curtain that hangs to the ground. His head is covered by a painted tin mask and a tall dunce cap. Through a slit in the canvas, he can reach out his hand for contributions from spectators. Hundreds of rainbow-colored ribbons stream from the top of the horse, fluttering in the wind as he cavorts about town to the accompaniment of a drum and an accordion. Most of the money that is collected by the hobby horse and his companions is spent in the local pub afterwards, although some of it is supposed to go to charitable causes.

On MAY DAY Eve the horse sets out promptly at midnight, ending up at Whitecross (a crossroads to the west of town where a maypole used to be erected) on May Day morning. Later in the afternoon the group goes to the nearby village of Dunster and pays its respects to the lord of the local castle. The hobby horse performs again in the square at Dunster that evening.

A similar ceremony is held in Padstow, Cornwall, where "Old 'Obby 'Oss" is a ferocious-looking monster with snapping jaws and sharp teeth. During the dance that represents the culmination of the Padstow ceremony, the horse goes through a ritualistic death and rebirth—an indication, perhaps, of the ceremony's roots in ancient fertility rites driving out winter and welcoming spring.

Minstrels' Carnival
January 1–10

The **Annual Minstrels' Carnival** in Cape Town, South Africa was inspired by the animated singing and dancing of the African-American musicians and singers of the United States. Bands are organized during the year, money is raised to purchase the materials needed for their costumes, and on NEW YEAR'S DAY, Second New Year (January 2), and the week or so that follows, the bands take over the city, displaying their costumes and performing their music in the streets.

This roisterous carnival is offset by string bands, who are decorously dressed, and parade with great dignity while playing sacred and other songs during the CHRISTMAS-New Year season.

Misa de Gallo (Cock's Mass; Simbang Gabi)
December 16–24

The start of the CHRISTMAS season in the Philippines, blending Christian tradition with the harvest thanksgiving of the ancient Filipinos.

As the first cockcrows are heard at dawn on Dec. 16, bells of the Roman Catholic churches ring, brass bands parade through towns, children fire small bamboo cannons, and skyrockets burst—all to awaken people for the Misa de Gallo, called Simbang Gabi in Tagalog. Each morning of the festival families walk to the dawn Mass. Then, on Dec. 24, there is a midnight Mass. After the services, the people congregate in food stalls that have been set up around church patios or go home for traditional breakfasts of rice cakes and ginger tea or cocoa.

Legend says the Mass started in the 1700s when a Spanish priest thought that blending native custom with Catholic ritual would help spread the faith. The Filipinos had long celebrated good harvests with festivals of thanksgiving, and the priest called the farmers together at harvest time to thank God for good fortune and to pray for a good harvest in the coming year.

Misas de Aguinaldos *See* **Christmas Eve**

Mischief Night
October 30, November 4

The idea of letting children have a "lawless night" originated in England, and was often celebrated on MAY DAY eve (April 30) or on HALLOWEEN. But in the mid-seventeenth century, when GUY FAWKES DAY (November 5) became a national holiday, Guy Fawkes Eve became the most popular night for mischief in England, Australia, and New Zealand, where it is sometimes called **Mischievous Night** or **Danger Night**.

Misisi Beer Feast
October; Twamo

The ritual harvest feast known as the **Misisi** takes place in Uganda after the millet harvest each year. The Sebei people make a beer out of the *misisi* 'grain that is left on the ground' after the millet stalks have been gathered and placed in granaries. Misisi also refers to the cobs of maize that are too small to be worth storing. In addition to beer, the feast includes maize meal, steamed plantains, and a bullock, ram or chickens. A special group of close relatives is invited to the feast, and the host's father (or some other elder) pours the beer from a libation gourd or *mwendet* and offers it to a friend, saying, "Please accept this beer; I am still alive and let us enjoy it together." Libations are poured with the right hand, inside the house or kraal, naming the host's father, brothers, mother, mother's brothers, grandparents, father-in-law, brothers-in-law, and all deceased members of the clan who still have living descendants. Libations are poured for the evil spirits with the left hand, outside the house or *kraal*, naming deceased relatives who are jealous because they never had children, or those who cursed them in life.

The Misisi Beer Feast is usually held during the month called Twamo, which is around the same time as the month of October. Mukutanik, an adaptation of Misisi, is held at CHRISTMAS. In areas of Uganda where the millet ripens sooner, it is held earlier.

Miss America Pageant
Labor Day week

What began in 1921 as an attempt by the Business Men's League of Atlantic City, New Jersey to keep tourists in town after LABOR DAY has developed into an American institution. The weeklong event that begins when the winners of the fifty state pageants arrive on Monday includes evening gown, swimsuit, and talent competitions; a parade along Atlantic City's famous boardwalk; and, on Saturday evening, final judging of the ten semifinalists and five finalists, culminating in the crowning of the new Miss America shortly before midnight. Bert Parks, who hosted the pageant on television for twenty-five years, was renowned for his patented rendition of "There She Goes," the song that is traditionally sung as the new Miss America walks down the runway in Convention Hall for the first time. In addition to a year of travel and lucrative personal appearances, the winner receives a $25,000 scholarship.

The Miss America Pageant has had its ups and downs over the years—notably the 1968 protests by members of the Women's Liberation Movement, who lit a symbolic fire in a trashcan and threw in a brassiere, some fashion magazines, and make-up—giving rise to the labelling of feminists as "bra-burners." Vanessa Williams, the first African-American to win the pageant, was also the first to be dethroned when it was revealed in July of 1984 that she had once posed nude for *Penthouse* magazine. But many former Miss Americas have gone on to achieve successful careers as models, actresses, or television personalities, or in public service—among them Phyllis George (Miss America 1971), Mary Ann Mobley (1959), and Bess Myerson (1945).

Miwok Acorn Festival
Usually weekend after fourth Friday of September

An annual two-day event of the Miwok (which means 'people') Indians, held at the Indian Grinding Rock State Historic Park near Sacramento, Calif. The park was a gathering place for Indians for thousands of years until Europeans settled there in 1848 at the time of the Gold Rush. This is an ancient harvest festival, largely religious, with ceremonial rites and traditional dances. It celebrates the acorn, just as Indians in the east have harvest festivals for the turkey, and in the south and southwest for corn. Acorns were a staple of the California Indians' diet, and were ground to make soup and meal for bread.

Mnarja (Imnarja; Feast of St. Peter and St. Paul)
June 29

The principal folk festival of Malta and a public holiday there, thought to have been originally a harvest festival. It is held in Buskett Gardens, a park with extensive vineyards and orange and lemon orchards not far from Mdina, Malta's medieval capital. The name of the festival is a corruption of Italian *luminaria*, meaning 'illumination,' since in long-ago times, the bastions around Mdina were illuminated by bonfires for the event. At one time, Mnarja was such a popular and important feast that a husband traditionally promised his bride on their wedding day that he would take her to Buskett on Mnarja-day every year.

Festivities begin on the eve of Mnarja with an agricultural show that continues through the next morning and folk-singing (*ghana*) and folk-music competitions. The traditional food of the evening is fried rabbit. On the following day, bareback horse and donkey races bring the feast to an end. The winners receive *pajjj* 'embroidered banners', which they donate to their town church.

See also SS. PETER AND PAUL'S DAY

Mochi No Matsuri
8th day of the twelfth lunar month

The **Rice Cake Festival** is a minor public holiday native to Okinawa. The rice cakes are red or white and cylindrical, about four inches long and one inch in diameter. They are wrapped in the leaf of the *sannin* plant or in sugar cane leaves. On the morning of the eighth day of the twelfth moon, the cakes are placed on a special shelf while prayers are said. Then they are served to guests or hung by string around the room.

Mohegan Homecoming
Third Sunday in August

The Mohegan Homecoming, which takes place in and around Norwich, Connecticut on the third Sunday in August each year, is a modern festival that has evolved from the pre-Columbian thanksgiving ceremony held by the Indians to thank their creator for the corn harvest. Up until 1941 the Mohegans held a Green Corn Festival, also known as the Wigwam Festival, but since that time the event has been billed as a "homecoming"—a time for Mohegan Indians living in all parts of the world to come home and renew their roots. It is an opportunity to conduct tribal business, such as the installation of new chieftains and medicine women, and to update one another on tribal matters. Foods served at the festival include succotash, clam chowder, and other New England specialties.

Mollyockett Day
Third Saturday in July

Mollyockett was a Pequawket Indian who lived among the early settlers of western Maine. Born between 1730 and 1740, she lived in the area now known as Bethel after 1770 and made frequent trips throughout the Androscoggin Valley and into northern New Hampshire, Vermont, and Quebec. She was known as an "Indian doctress" who treated the white settlers of New England as well. One of her most famous patients was the infant Hannibal Hamlin, whom she found near death and cured with warm cow's milk. He grew up to become Abraham Lincoln's vice president. Mollyockett was also known as a storyteller, famous for her tales of buried Indian treasure.

The local festival that is currently known as Mollyockett Day in Bethel, Maine started out in the 1950s as a fundraising event for families in need of assistance. In 1970 the name was changed in honor of the Indian woman whose generosity and self-reliance have become legendary. The festival includes a horseshoe tournament, parade, lumberjack competition, and frog-jumping contest.

Monaco Grand Prix
May

One of the last true road circuits, the Monaco Grand Prix winds through the streets of Monte Carlo, along the harbor, and through a tunnel. It is a Formula One motor race, which refers to very specific rules governing the car's weight, maximum number of cylinders, fuel, and engine cylinder capacity. First run in 1929, the Monaco Grand Prix has a lap distance of 1.95 miles with an unusually high number of corners, which demand constant gear-changes and maximum concentration from the drivers. In 1955 an Italian car skidded and ended up in the harbor, underscoring the dangerous and unusual nature of this race.

Formula One cars are single-seaters, although prior to the 1920s the mechanic rode in the car as well. The engine is located in the rear and the driver, protected by special clothing, a crash helmet, and goggles, steers with a very small wheel from a reclining position, to reduce air drag to a minimum. Grand Prix races are held all over the world and are approximately two hundred miles in length. But most, like the UNITED STATES GRAND PRIX, are now run on specially constructed courses designed to simulate road conditions.

Monkey God, Birthday of the
February 17 and September 12

A celebration by Chinese Taoists of Tai Seng Yeh, the popular Monkey God, who sneaked into heaven and acquired miraculous powers; he is thought to cure the sick and absolve the hopeless. He is the godfather of many Chinese children.

In Singapore, Taoist mediums go into a trance to let the god's spirit enter their bodies; then, possessed, they howl and slash themselves with knives, and scrawl symbols on scraps of paper that are grabbed by devotees. There are also puppet shows and Chinese street opera performances at Chinese temples.

See also HANUMAN JAYANTI.

Monlam (Prayer Festival)
Usually February; 4–25th day of first Tibetan lunar month

The greatest festival in Tibet follows the Tibetan New Year (Losar) celebrations, and commemorates the miraculous powers of Buddha. The two-week festival was started in the fifteenth century by Tsongkhapa, the great reformist monk, to ensure that the new year would be successful and prosperous. It is a time to attend examinations of and make offerings to monks, to light butter lamps, and above all to socialize, get the latest news, and watch sports events such as wrestling, archery, and horse racing. On the fifteenth day celebrants throng to Lhasa's famous Jokhang temple, where monks have created enormous butter sculptures. (See BUTTER SCULPTURE FESTIVAL.) A procession around the Barkor, the old city of Lhasa, carried a statue of Maitreya, the future Buddha.

When the Chinese denounced religious obervances in 1959, the festival died. It was revived again in 1986, and has been observed since, although not with the grandeur of the earlier days.

Monterey Jazz Festival
Third weekend in September

A three-day celebration of jazz held since 1958 outside Monterey, Calif. at the Monterey Fairgrounds where there is seating for 7,000. Jimmy Lyons, a West Coast disc jockey, is credited with starting the first festival, and since then it has attracted top jazz artists. Among the many who have appeared are Dizzy Gillespie, Woody Herman, Thelonius Monk, Gerry Mulligan, Odetta, and Pee Wee Russell. The festival has boasted a number of world premieres: Duke Ellington's *Suite Thursday*, Lalo Schifrin's *Gillespiana*, and Charles Mingus's *Meditations on Monterey* are a few of them.

The atmosphere is jazzy and cosmopolitan. Booths outside the arena sell food for every taste, from sweet-potato pies to tacos to beef teriyaki.

Montreal Jazz Festival
June–July

What has been called the most important cultural event in Canada and the largest jazz festival in the world, the **Festival International de Jazz de Montréal** has attracted some of the greatest names in jazz-including Miles Davis, Pat Metheny, Ray Charles, and Dizzy Gillespie. Close to a million people come to the festival, about one-fourth of them from outside Montreal. Although the first festival in 1980 featured only about twenty performances, a recent event had two thousand artists performing in three hundred concerts, which were recorded and broadcast in twenty-five foreign countries.

Montreal's streets are closed for the ten days of the festival to make room for the outdoor performances, which take place rain or shine, and represent a mix of traditional, modern, and innovative jazz.

Moon Day
July 20

The first man to walk on the moon was American astronaut Neil Armstrong. On July 20, 1969, he and his fellow astronaut Edwin E. "Buzz" Aldrin left the command module *Columbia* and landed the lunar module *Eagle* in the moon's Sea of Tranquillity. Armstrong's first words as he stepped out on the lunar surface were seen and heard by an estimated 600 million television viewers around the world: "That's one small step for a man, one giant leap for mankind."

Air Force Lieutenant Colonel Michael Collins, pilot of the *Columbia*, continued to circle the moon for the twenty-one-and-a-half hours during which Armstrong and Aldrin conducted their experiments. The information they collected about the moon's soil, terrain, and atmospheric conditions made an enormous contribution to knowledge of the universe and future space exploration. The Apollo 11 mission was completed eight years after President John F. Kennedy told Congress he believed that the United States could put a man on the moon before the decade ended.

Moors and Christians Fiesta

April 22–24

Moors and Christians fiestas are celebrated throughout the year all over Spain to commemorate various battles between the two groups. But it is the **fiesta of Alcoy** in the province of Alicante that is one of the most colorful. Coinciding with the feast day of St. George (see St. George's Day) on April 23, the fiesta commemorates the victory of the Christians over the Moorish leader al Azraq in 1276.

The three-day event begins on the morning of April 22 with the ceremonial entry of the Christians, symbolizing the forces who assembled to defend the town of Alcoy in the thirteenth century. The Moors arrive in the afternoon, dressed in exotic Oriental costumes. On April 23 the relic of St. George is carried in procession from his temple to the parish Church of Santa Maria, where a Mass is sung. On the third day the battle is reenacted and an apparition of St. George appears on the battlements of the castle.

In the fifteenth, sixteenth, and seventeenth centuries, fiestas of Moors and Christians were danced. It is believed that this type of celebration eventually crossed the sea to England and became the familiar Morris dance.

Moreska Sword Dance

July 27; every Thursday July–September

A ritual dance of the medieval knights that has been performed every July twenty-seventh for centuries in Korcula, the main town of the island of Korcula off the coast of the former Yugoslavia. The dance-cum-pageant, with many clashes of steel, symbolizes the battle against the Turks when Korcula was under the control of the kings of Bosnia in the late fourteenth century. A spirited and athletic dance, it has been performed in other parts of Europe, but only by men and the one woman in the pageant, all of whom were born on Korcula. Originally performed only on July twenty-seventh, it is now presented regularly in the tourist season.

From the fifteenth century, Korcula was under the control, successively, of Venice, Austria, France, Britain, again Austria, and Italy, until being ceded to Yugoslavia after World War I. It was under Italian occupation in World War II and liberated by Yugoslavian partisans in 1944–45. Marco Polo is supposed to have been born on Korcula.

Moriones Festival

Beginning between March 15 and April 18; Holy Week

One of the more popular and colorful of the many passion plays performed before Easter in the Philippines. Held in Marinduque with participants wearing masks and costumes of Roman soliders, Moriones focuses not on Jesus but tells the story of the legendary Roman centurion Longinus, who is said to have been blind in one eye. As he pierced the side of the crucified Jesus, a drop of the blood cured his blindness. The first thing he saw with both eyes was Christ's passage to heaven. According to the legend Longinus announced this good news. The Roman warriors, however, wanted to stop this report and captured him. The beheading of Longinus is the climax of the play.

Mormon Pioneer Day

July 24

After their founder, Joseph Smith, was murdered in 1844, the Mormons—members of the Church of Jesus Christ of Latter-Day Saints—moved westward from their settlement in Nauvoo, Illinois under the leadership of Brigham Young. When Young surveyed the Salt Lake Valley on July 24, 1847, he proclaimed, "This is the right place." Thousands of Mormon pioneers followed him over the next two decades, many of them pushing their belongings in handcarts. The original forty-acre plot with log houses where the Mormons settled is the modern Salt Lake City and the day on which Young chose the site is celebrated not only in Utah but in surrounding states with significant Mormon populations, such as Idaho, Arizona, Nevada, Wyoming, and California. Other states observe their own **Pioneer Day** at different times of the year.

Morris Rattlesnake Roundup

Second weekend in June

In 1956, when the first **Rattlesnake Roundup** was held in Morris, Pennsylvania, more than four hundred of the poisonous snakes were caught and sold to leather craftsmen and zoos. But their numbers have dwindled since that time, and the trend has been toward the protection of endangered species—even poisonous ones. Now only about twenty-five to thirty-five snakes are found each year, and by law they must be returned to the wild. The roundup is sponsored by the local fire department and about eighty hunters participate, catching the snakes with tongs and forked sticks. Most of the snakes are thirty to forty-five inches long.

Moshoeshoe (Moshoeshoe's) Day
March 12

Moshoeshoe (also called **Mshweshwe** or **Moshesh**) was a nineteenth century tribal leader in South Africa who organized a group of tribes to fight the Zulu warlord Shaka. He called his followers the Basotho (or Basuto) people, and although they succeeded in fending off the Zulu, they were eventually drawn into a war with the Europeans who started settling their territory. Moshoeshoe and the Basotho retreated into the mountains, and from this position they were able to keep the European invaders at bay. In 1868 the Basotho nation became a British protectorate known as Basutoland, and in 1966 it became the independent kingdom of Lesotho within the British Commonwealth.

The Basotho people continue to honor their founder on this day with sports and traditional music and dancing.

Most Precious Blood, Feast of the
Formerly July 1

In the Roman Catholic church, July was the month of the Most Precious Blood—referring to the blood of Jesus, which ever since the time of the Last Supper has been regarded by Christians as possessing redemptive power. But it wasn't until 1849 that a specific day was chosen for general observance of this festival. At that time Pope Pius IX was forced into exile while Rome was under attack by the French. One of his companions, who happened to be a general officer of the Fathers of the Most Precious Blood, tried to convince the Pope to promise that if he regained his papal lands he would establish this festival as a universal observance. The Pope, of course, said he didn't want to bargain with God, but that he would extend the festival to the whole church anyway. Since he reached this decision on the day before the first Sunday in July, it was originally the first Sunday that was dedicated to the Most Precious Blood. But Pius X moved the feast to the first day of July. In 1969 it was suppressed altogether and is no longer on the church calendar.

Mothering Sunday
March–April; fourth Sunday in Lent

It was the custom in seventeenth century England for Christians to pay their respects on the fourth Sunday in LENT to the "Mother Church" where they had been baptized. Also known as **Misers** or **Mid-Lent Sunday,** this day usually included a visit to one's parents—to "go a-mothering," as it was called back then. It was common practice to bring a cake or trinket for the mother of the family. In England the favorite gift was the simnel cake, a saffron-flavored fruitcake topped with almond paste.

In the Roman Catholic church and the Anglican Communion, the fourth Sunday in Lent is sometimes known as **Laetare Sunday**. The Introit of the Mass begins with the word "Rejoice" (Latin *laetare*), marking a slight respite in the solemn Lenten season, hence the terms **Mid-Lent Sunday** and **Refreshment Sunday**. Priests may wear rose-colored vestments to Mass, instead of the usual purple for Lent, so the day is also called **Rose Sunday** . Also on this day the Pope blesses the Golden Rose, an ornament resembling a spray of roses, symbolizing spiritual joy.

Mother-in-Law Day
Fourth Sunday in October

Modeled on the celebration of MOTHER'S DAY and FATHER'S DAY, **Mother-in-Law's Day** was first celebrated on March 5, 1934 in Amarillo, Texas, where it was initiated by the editor of the local newspaper. The observance was later moved to the fourth Sunday in October.

Mothers-in-law have never enjoyed the widespread respect and devotion that mothers have received over the years, and the rising divorce rate has given the whole concept of in-laws a less permanent place in the national imagination. This may be part of the reason why Mother-in-Law Day has failed to catch on like MOTHER'S DAY, FATHER'S DAY, and even GRANDPARENTS' DAY. But many people feel that mothers-in-law deserve a special day of their own, if for no other reason than for their good humor in enduring the many jokes that have been told about them.

Mother's Day
Second Sunday in May

The setting aside of a day each year to honor mothers was the suggestion of Anna M. Jarvis of Philadelphia, Pennsylvania whose own mother had died on May 9, 1906. She held a memorial service and asked those attending to wear white carnations—a gesture that soon became a tradition. By 1914 President Woodrow Wilson had proclaimed a national day in honor of mothers, and some people still wear carnations on the second Sunday in May—pink or red for mothers who are living and white for those who have died.

Sometimes Mother's Day is confused with MOTHERING SUNDAY, an English holiday that falls on the fourth Sunday in LENT. But Mother's Day is now observed in England as well, and the traditions associated with Mothering Sunday have been largely forgotten. A number of Protestant churches have designated this day as the **Festival of the Christian Home.**

See also ANTROSHT.

Mother's Day in Yugoslavia *See* Children's Day in Yugoslavia

Motorcycle Week (Camel Motorcycle Week; Bike Week)
First week in March

The largest motorcycle meet in the world, held for ten days in Daytona Beach, Fla. The event began in 1937, as an outgrowth of automobile races. These had been started years earlier on Daytona's Ormond Beach by Henry Ford, who had a mansion and was testing cars there. It was suspended for a few years in World War II, but the 50th anniversary was celebrated in 1991, with half a million people attending.

The highlight of the week is the Daytona 200 race, which attracts competitors from all over the world and is considered one of the most prestigious motorcycle road races in the world. Other race events include a three-hour U.S. Endurance Championship race and vintage motorcycle races on Classics Day. The events take place in the Daytona Beach Municipal Stadium, with a quarter-mile banked oval track, and on the Daytona International Speedway.

Motorcyclists come from around the world, and most bring their motorcycles with them. A popular feature of the week is a mammoth parade of over 5,000 motorcycles. Parade watchers include large contingents of elderly people, some of whom hold signs saying "Grandmothers Love Biking" and other slogans. Concerts and trade shows are held throughout the week.

Mountain Man Rendezvous
Labor Day weekend (Friday through Monday)

A celebration of nineteenth-century history at Fort Bridger, Wyo. This town was founded in 1842 as a trading post by mountain men Jim Bridger and Louis Vasquez. It was established as a stronghold by Mormons in 1853, and taken over by the United States Army in 1959. In the great westward migration, streams of wagon trains passed through Fort Bridger for points west.

The Mountain Man Rendezvous began in 1973 and today attracts about 45,000 visitors over four days. The days of 1820–1840 are reenacted with people in calico and buckskins, furs and feathers. A tepee village is set up where campers wear clothing of the period, and there is a traders' row where replicas of pre-1840 items are for sale. Other activities include competitions in tomahawk throwing and archery, costume and cooking contests, black-powder shoots, and Indian tribal dances.

See also GREEN RIVER RENDEZVOUS.

Mountain State Forest Festival
Late September through early October

A two-week celebration of the timber industry—one of West Virginia's biggest industries—in the small town of Elkins. The 55th annual festival was held in 1991, but the event actually has its origins in the 1930 three-day "fall homecoming" held to call attention to the area's scenic attractions. The festival was suspended during World War II. Today attendance tops 100,000.

A highlight of the festival is the crowning of Queen Silvia, who wears an elaborate embroidered velvet gown. Usually the governor crowns the queen, but in 1936, President Franklin D. Roosevelt did the honors. After his address, a pageant was presented that was based on the ancient Egyptian myth of creation.

Events today salute the timber industry but also include non-timber events. Hence, there are forestry and wood-products exhibits and lumberjack contests along with a pet show, horseshoe tournaments, archery and turkey-calling contests, a bed race, a cross-country motorcycle race, arts and crafts exhibits, hot-air balloon rides, and a mammoth buckwheat-cake and sausage feed. Buckwheat cakes are a local favorite. There are additionally several parades, including a fireman's parade with antique and modern fire equipment.

Mount Ceahlau Feast
Second Sunday in August

A folk event that has ancient roots, held at Durau, Romania, at the foot of Mount Ceahlau. The mountain was considered sacred to the Dacians, the ancestors of the present Romanians, and was the scene of their annual celebrations. In those days, people climbed to the summit to greet the sun with religious ceremonies and feasts. Today there are demonstrations of such sports as wrestling and foot racing, and exhibits and sales of folk art.

213

Moving Day
May 1; May 25

The idea of packing up one's belongings and changing residences on a particular day has been a tradition in many countries. In nineteenth century America, May 1st was the normal day for the inhabitants of Boston and New York to change their place of residence, since leases normally expired on this day.

In Scotland, it was called **Flitting Day** and took place on May 25. The decision of whether to "sit or flit" was up to the tenant, but "flitting" seemed to be more common. On Flitting Day they had to vacate their houses by noon, which often meant a great upheaval for the family during the preceding day or two. But apparently the novelty value of "flitting" outweighed the boredom of "sitting." In some parts of Scotland, this occurs on May 1, and is also called **Term Day**.

In Norway, Moving Day or **Flyttedag** takes place sometime during the autumn months. But rather than being a day for changing residences, it is a day when servants searching for employment flock to the larger towns and cities dressed in the costumes of their native villages. Sometimes they ride in small carts or wagons, piled high with painted trunks or bundles of clothing and other possessions. While city residents take advantage of this opportunity to interview their help for the coming year, the servants seeking employment often try to sell their produce, farm animals, and handicrafts on the street.

Moxie Festival
Second Saturday in July

Moxie, originally a nerve tonic, was invented in 1876 by Dr. Augustine Thompson of Union, Maine. In 1884 it became a carbonated beverage whose main ingredient was gentian root. The Moxie Festival in Lisbon, Maine began as an autograph session for Frank Potter, the author of "The Moxie Mystique," in 1982. Within a few years the event had grown to include a pancake breakfast, parade, car show, craft fair, chicken barbecue, and firemen's muster.

Although Moxie is no longer widely available, those who remember it describe it as a kind of precursor to Coca Cola. The drink can still be found in Maine, where it is quite popular. About ten thousand people attend the festival each year.

Mt. Cameroon Race
Last Sunday in January

The annual "mad race" up and down Mt. Cam-eroon (13,353 ft.) in the central African country of Cameroon. The race is the most difficult in Africa; the course is so steep that runners have to carry poles, and temperatures can vary from a humid 80 degrees F. at the start of the race to freezing at the summit. On the night before the race, local people make sacrifices to appease the mountain spirits. Thousands of spectators watch the race, in which about 250 runners usually participate; the winner's time can be under four hours.

Muharram *See* Nawruz

Mule Days
Memorial Day weekend

A raucous salute in Bishop, Calif. to that workhorse of the ages, the mule. Bishop is an outfitting point for pack trips and lies between California's two highest mountain ranges. The entire region depends on mules to transport people and gear into the High Sierra.

Mule Days was started in 1969 by mule-packers who wanted to have a good time and initiate their summer packing season. Now about 50,000 people show up in Bishop (population 3,500) for the Thursday-through-Monday celebration. A highlight is the Saturday morning 250-unit parade, billed as the world's largest non-motorized parade. It includes pack strings from local pack stations and national parks, a sheep-drawn wagon, llamas (used for sheepherding), and a rider on a Brahma steer. The pack loads demonstrate how mules haul such various necessities as machinery, wood, and outhouses into remote areas. Other events include mule-shoeing contests and such muleback cowboy events as steer roping and barrel racing. The weekend's wildest events are "packers' scramble", where about fifty packers scramble to catch mules, pack and saddle them, and race away with horses and cattle. About forty horses, two dozen cattle, and eighty mules raise the dust in the arena during the scrambles.

Draft horses and miniature horses also put in appearances, and there are mule shows and sales, western art, barbecues, and country dances. Motels are booked solid a year in advance. Ronald Reagan attended Mule Days in 1974 when he was California's governor.

Mules are the sterile progeny of male asses or donkeys and mares (female horses). The rarer offspring of male horses and female donkeys are called hinneys. Mules have been beasts of burden for at least 3,000 years.

Mummers' Parade *See* **New Year's Day**

Mushroom Festival

First weekend in May

Richmond, Missouri isn't the only town that claims to be the "mushroom capital of the world." Kennett Square, Pennsylvania, and Stover, Missouri share this distinction as well. But Richmond is known for its highly prized morel mushrooms, which resemble a deeply pitted or folded cone-like sponge at the top of a hollow stem. The highlight of the annual Mushroom Festival, which has been held in Richmond since 1980, is the Big Morel Contest. Mushroom hunters flock to the town's wooded areas in search of the morel, known as the "Golden Fleece of mushrooms" because it is hard to find and has never been successfully cultivated.

Widespread morel hunting during the festival has necessitated an informal code of ethics among hunters. The rules include asking permission to hunt on privately owned lands, avoiding damage to the delicate fungi by inadvertently "stomping" small morels concealed by leaves, and dividing the day's booty with one's fellow "morellers." Above all, the hunters must refrain from revealing where they found their prize-winning specimens.

Music and Dance Festival (Granada, Spain), International

June–July

One of the most important music and dance festivals in Europe, the Granada festival has been held for more than forty years. It features an array of international orchestras and performers in settings of incomparable grandeur, such as the Alhambra (a fourteenth-century palace built for the Moorish kings), the adjoining Renaissance palace of Charles V, and the theater of the Generalife Gardens.

Mut l-ard

May 17

This is believed to be the **first day of summer in Morocco**, and the word *mut l-ard* means 'death of the earth.' Various rituals performed on this day by different tribes are designed to ward off evil and danger. For example, it is believed that rising at dawn and taking a bath will strengthen the body, and there is a taboo against sleeping, which is believed to result in a loss of courage. A special dish made from barley, fresh milk or buttermilk, and the root of a plant called *bûzeffur* is prepared and eaten on this day in the belief that it will make the people strong and ward off evil. In some areas it is believed that a husband's affections will waver on this day, and that the wife should therefore make herself as attractive as possible by using cosmetics.

N

Naag Panchami

July–August; waxing Shravana

A Hindu festival celebrated throughout India and Nepal, dedicated to the sacred serpent Ananta, on whose coils Lord Vishnu rested while he was creating the universe. All snakes can bring wealth and rain, and unhappy ones can cause a home to collapse. Therefore milk and flowers are offered to snakes, especially cobras; snake deities; or painted snake images at shrines. Because snakes are also worn by Lord Shiva, hundreds of snakes are released at the Indian Shiva temples in Ujjain, where Shiva lived after destroying a demon, and in Varanasi, considered the religious capital of the Hindu faith. In Jodhpur, India, huge cloth *naags* 'cobras' are displayed.

Nadam

July 11; July 20–26

A Mongolian festival celebrating the NEW YEAR (**Tsagan Sara**) spotlights three major sports events. Its history goes back to the thirteenth century when Marco Polo described a gathering of 10,000 white horses. Mongolian chieftains, after meeting for parleys, competed in horse racing, archery, and wrestling, the "three manly games" for a Mongolian. Later, the fairs included women and were held in July or August when the pastures were lush and the horses well-fed. Today Nadam is held on July 11 in provinces throughout Mongolia. The chief Nadam is in the stadium in Ulan Bator. In Inner Mongolia (the Inner Mongolia Autonomous Region of China), Nadam is celebrated on July 20–26 on the Gogantala Pasture and at Lake Salim in the prefecture of Xinjiang. Other Nadams are held as people desire.

The fairs bring together the nomadic people who pitch a city of *yurts*, their cone-shaped felt tents. Wrestling is usually the first event; at Ulan Bator, several hundred participants make a grand entrance in special tight-fitting costumes that leave the chest bare, proving the wrestler is male. A legend has it that long ago many men were once defeated by a woman. Titles awarded to top wrestlers are Falcon, Elephant, Lion, and Titan, their prizes are silk scarves and horses. The second sport is archery, a sport of great antiquity—sixth-century Mongols hunted hares with bows and arrows while riding at full speed. Modern contests are both on foot and horseback. The last of the traditional sporting events is horse racing. In the National Nadam, the featured race is for children aged seven to twelve who cover a twenty mile cross-country course. When night falls, a bowed stringed instrument called a *matouqin* is played, and people sit by their yurts talking, dancing, and drinking aromatic butter tea and *kumys*, a drink made of fermented mare's milk.

Nagoya City Festival

October 10–20

An annual secular festival in Nagoya, Japan, started by the city's merchants to give thanks for their prosperity. It features a parade of about 700 participants depicting historical figures in period costume, among them Oda Nobunaga, Toyotomi Hideyoshi, and Tokugawa Ieyasu, the three feudal warlords who unified the country at the end of the sixteenth century.

Nanakusa Matsuri (Seven Herbs or Grasses Festival)

January 7

A Japanese ceremony dating back to the ninth century, also called Wakana-setsu or 'Festival of Young Herbs,' or Jin-jitsu 'Man Day' because it occurs on the zodiacal day for "man." After an offering to the clan deity in the morning, participants partake of nanakusa gayu, a rice gruel seasoned with seven different herbs that is said to have been served for its medicinal value to the young prince of the Emperor Saga (ruled 810–824). The herbs are shepherd's-purse, chickweed, parsley, cottonweed, radish, and the herbs called in Japanese *hotoke-no-za* and *aona*.

Napoleon's Day
May 5

Napoleon Bonaparte, emperor of France from 1804–1815, is one of the most celebrated individuals in European history and still has many admirers in France. Often referred to as "Le Corse" (from Corsica, where he was born) or "Le Petit Caporal" (the little corporal), for his short stature, Napoleon is best known for the zeal with which he pursued the military expansion of France and for his reforms, which left a lasting mark on the judicial, financial, administrative, and educational institutions of not only France, but much of western Europe.

After finally abdicating in favor of his son on June 22, 1815, Napoleon was exiled to the island of St. Helena in the southern Atlantic with a small group of followers. He died there on May 5, 1821 at the age of only 51. But his legend grew, and in 1840 his remains were taken from St. Helena back to Paris, where a magnificent funeral was held. He was finally entombed under the gold-plated dome of the Church of Saint-Louis, one of the buildings in the compound of the Hôtel des Invalides, where his descendants and admirers still congregate on May 5 each year to attend a commemorative Mass.

See also CAPE VINCENT FRENCH FESTIVAL.

Narcissus Festival
January or February

A celebration in Honolulu, Hawaii, to usher in the Chinese New Year. There is a queen pageant and a coronation ball, Chinese cooking demonstrations, food booths, and arts and crafts exhibits. A parade features lion dances and fireworks. The first Narcissus Festival was held in 1950, narcissus blossoms being chosen as a symbol of hope that Chinese culture would have a renaissance in Hawaii.

Also see CHINESE NEW YEAR.

Natchez Spring Pilgrimage
March, October

This thirty-day event held since 1932 in Natchez, Miss. attracts about 75,000 people to tour the county's antebellum houses. Women in hoop skirts welcome visitors to the mansions and their gardens of azaleas, camellias, olive trees, and boxwood hedges.

Natchez, situated on 200-foot bluffs overlooking the Mississippi River, was named for the Natchez Indians. It was founded by the French in 1716, and was the first settlement on the river. It had a golden era in the sixty years after Mississippi became a territory in 1798. The town was an important river port, and wealthy citizens had vast plantations and built magnificent homes. Thirty of these, some owned by descendants of the original families, are open for tours. They include such spectacular homes as Longwood, the largest octagonal house remaining in America, and Auburn, an imposing mansion with a free-standing stairway to the second floor.

Besides the tours, there are candlelight dinners in Magnolia Hall, a mansion that houses a costume museum, and presentations four times a week of the "Confederate Pageant," a lavish musical with local performers in costume presenting vignettes of the Old South. A satire of the pilgrimage, "Southern Exposure," is presented four times a week. "Southern Road to Freedom," presented by the Holy Family Choir, is a musical tribute to the struggles and victories of African-Americans in Natchez from colonial days to the present, and is performed three times a week.

During a month-long fall celebration in October, there is another mansion tour. During the three-week Natchez Fall Pilgrimage there are twenty-four homes open to tours. October also brings theatrical performances of classic melodrama, the Great Mississippi River Balloon Race, a street dance, and arts and crafts exhibits.

National Day, Romania
December 1

The national holiday of Romania, celebrated since 1990, after the fall of Nicolae Ceausescu, head of the Romanian Communist Party, with military parades, speeches and a holiday from work. This day marks the unification in 1918 of Romania and Transylvania and the formation of the Romanian state within its present-day boundaries. Romania's full independence had been recognized in 1878, but Transylvania had remained outside the new state. On December 1, a Romanian assembly passed the resolution of unity celebrated on National Day.

National Day, Singapore
August 9

A public holiday in Singapore to commemorate its independence. Singapore was the administrative seat for the Straits Settlements, a British crown colony, from 1867 until it was occupied by Japan in World War II. It was restored to Britain in 1945, became a part of Malaysia in 1963, and became independent in 1965. The holiday is celebrated with a spectacular parade, cultural dances, and fireworks.

National Finals Rodeo
Starting on first Friday in December

Rodeo's premier event, sometimes called the Super Bowl of rodeos, a ten day affair held since 1985 in Las Vegas, Nev. The National Finals Rodeo, which offered a record $2.45 million in prize money in 1991, is reserved for the top fifteen contestants in each of seven events: bareback riding, steer wrestling, team roping, saddle bronc riding, calf roping, women's barrel racing, and bull riding. The winners are considered the world champions in their event. There is also a world all-around champion. Twenty-two year old Ty Murray who made more than half a million dollars in three years as a Professional Rodeo Cowboy Association competitor, was the all-around champ in 1989, 1990, and 1991.

The national finals debuted in 1959 in Dallas, moved to Los Angeles in 1962 and to Oklahoma City in 1965, where it stayed until its move to Las Vegas twenty years later. Attendance is about 85,000.

The rodeo is preceded by the Miss Rodeo America Pageant. Events during the ten days of rodeo include a Professional Rodeo Cowboy Association convention and trade show, horsemanship competitions, the National Finals Rodeo Christmas Gift Show, a hoedown, cowboy poetry gatherings, style shows, a golf invitational, fashion shows, and dances. The World Champions Awards Banquet is the grand finale.

See also CIRCUIT FINALS RODEO.

National Foundation Day
October 3

A national holiday in Korea, also known as **Tangun Day**, to commemorate the founding of the Korean nation in 2333 B.C. by Tangun.

According to legend, Prince Hwan-ung left heaven to rule earth from Mt. T'aebaek. In his kingdom were a bear and a tiger who wished to become humans. Hwan-ung told them that if they remained in a cave for 100 days eating nothing but mugwort and garlic, they would become like people. The tiger got bored, but the bear lasted it out and became a beautiful woman. She and Hwan-ung bore a son called Tangun Wanggom, meaning Sandalwood King. When he grew up, he built his own city at the present site of P'yongyang (now the capital of North Korea) and called his new kingdom Choson, meaning 'morning fresh-

ness' or 'morning calm.' The book *Samguk Yusa*, written in 1289, records this story. The myth is important in that it links the Korean people with a heavenly origin.

The holiday is celebrated with ceremonies at the ancient rock Altar of Tangun, on the summit of Mt. Mani on Kanghwa Island, about twenty-five miles west of Seoul.

National Pike Festival
May–June

The National Pike Festival is literally the "world's longest festival": three hundred miles of events along Route 40 in southwestern Pennsylvania, western Maryland, and parts of West Virginia and Ohio. The original section of the road (or "pike"), from Baltimore to Cumberland, Maryland, was Thomas Jefferson's idea in 1806. The section between Cumberland and Wheeling, West Virginia was the first road to receive federal funding in 1811.

Since 1974 the festival has commemorated America's first transportation link from the East to the western frontier. It was originally designed as a Bicentennial event in Pennsylvania, but the idea caught on quickly and towns along Route 40 in nearby states were eager to add their own events. The festival begins on a weekend in mid-May in western Maryland and southwestern Pennsylvania and continues for four successive weekends in Wheeling, West Virginia; Belmont County, Ohio; Guernsey County, Ohio; and Muskingham County, Ohio. Wagon trains travel along the route known as the National Road or "the road that made the nation." When they set up camp for the night, there are bonfires and other entertainment to which the public is invited. Inns, taverns, tollhouses, and other historic buildings along the route host tours and special ceremonies. A Pony Express rider often meets the wagon train as it pulls into town.

National Western Stock Show
Mid–January

The world's largest livestock exhibition and the show of shows in Denver, Colo. This is a twelve-day trade show for the ranching industry, drawing visitors from throughout the U.S. as well as Mexico and Canada. On view at the stock show are more than 20,000 Hereford, Angus, Simmental, Shorthorn and Longhorn cattle. Plus Arabian, Morgan, draft horses, miniature and quarter horses, and ewes and lambs. Transactions in the millions of dollars are daily events; the livestock auctions as a matter of course can bring six figures for a single bull.

There are also daily rodeos, with more than 1,000 professional cowboys and cowgirls taking part in calf roping, bull and bronco riding, steer wrestling, and barrel racing. Sheep-shearing contests, displays for children, exhibits and sales of livestock supplies, and exhibitions of Western paintings are other features.

More than half a million people attend, among them ranchers wearing belt buckles with diamonds and boots with the value of diamonds.

Nations, Festival of (Minnesota)
Last weekend in April or first weekend in May

Minnesota's largest ethnic celebration, the Festival of Nations takes place in St. Paul, a city of great ethnic diversity. As many as sixty-five different ethnic groups participate in this event, which has been held since 1932 and features costumes, folk craft demonstrations, and cultural exhibits. Folk dance and music performances run continuously and showcase performers from Greece, Egypt, Ireland, Polynesia, Norway, Ecuador, Armenia, and many other countries. Spectators can also take twenty-minute language lessons in Russian, Swedish, Lao, Italian, and other tongues. Another festival event is the naturalization ceremony for five hundred new citizens.

Food is one of the festival's main attractions. There is sausage with kraut (Czech), chicken schnitzel in pita (Israeli), fafaatoo and sambusa (Oromo pople of Ethiopia and Kenya), fatiah spinach pie (Syrian), strawberry mousse with kirsch (French), and maple syrup tarts (Canadian). Visitors who are thirsty can find mango milk shakes (Indian), green tea (Japanese), and egg coffee (Finnish). Sidewalk cafés serve authentic food from more than four dozen countries.

Nations, Festival of (Montana)
Starting first Saturday of August for nine days

A celebration of the multi-ethnic heritage of Red Lodge, Mont. In its early days, Red Lodge was a coal-mining town where miners who came from a number of European nations established their own communities. This festival began in 1961 to honor the different ethnic traditions. Today there is dancing, singing, and eating. Special foods are served by representatives of England, Scotland, Ireland, Wales, Germany, Finland, the Scandinavian countries, Italy, and the several nationalities that made up the former Yugoslavia.

Nine days of events wind up with an All Nations Parade followed by a street dance.

Native American Day *See* **American Indian Day**

Nativity of Our Lord, Feast of the *See* **Christmas**

Nativity of the Blessed Virgin Mary, Feast of the
September 8

Only three births are celebrated in the whole Christian calendar: the Virgin Mary's, ST. JOHN THE BAPTIST's on June 24, and Jesus Christ's on December 25. Although it is not known where the September 8 date of Mary's birth originated, it seems to have been established by the end of the seventh century. In the Coptic and Abyssinian Churches, the first day of every month is celebrated as the birthday of the Virgin Mary.

There are a number of legends describing the Virgin Mary's birth. Most early works of art show Mary and her mother, Anne, surrounded by elaborate furnishings and ancient Hebrew decorations, with a choir of angels hovering overhead. There are more festivals in honor of Mary than of any other saint-among them the Feasts of the IMMACULATE CONCEPTION, the ANNUNCIATION, the PURIFICATION , and the VISITATION.

In Malta there is a regatta in the capital, Valletta, in celebration of the defeat of the Turks by the Knights of St. John of Jerusalem on this day in 1565, and the end of the Axis siege in 1943.

Navajo Nation Fair at Window Rock
Early September

A five-day gala billed as the "World's Largest American Indian Fair," held in Window Rock, Ariz., the capital of the Navajo Nation. More than 100,000 visitors attend the fair, which dates back to 1947. It features a parade through the Window Rock area and a rodeo with more than 900 cowboys and cowgirls from eight different Indian rodeo associations. Other events include horse races, an inter-tribal powwow, a Miss Navajo Nation competition, an Indian fry-bread contest, a baby contest, country and western dances, Indian song and dance competitions, and agricultural and livestock exhibits. Arts and crafts exhibits are always part of Navajo fairs: the Navajos are famous for turquoise-and-silver jewelry, sand paintings, and woven rugs. The art of weaving was taught to Navajo women, their lore says, by Spider Woman, one of the Holy People from the underworld.

The Navajo Reservation covers 17.5 million acres and is the largest in the United States. Other fairs are the Eastern Navajo Fair held in Crownpoint, New Mexico in late July; the Central Navajo Fair, Chinle, Ariz. in late August; Southwestern Navajo Fair, Dilcon, Ariz. in mid September; the Northern or Shiprock Navajo Fair, Shiprock, New Mexico, in early October, and Western Navajo Fair, Tuba City, Ariz. in mid October, and the Utah Navajo Fair in Bluff, Utah the second week in September.

Navratri *See* Durga Puja

Nawruz (Naw roz; No Ruz; New Year)
Beginning about March 21 for 13 days

The first day of spring and the first day of the Islamic new year (*nawruz* means 'new day') celebrated by all religious groups in Iran and Afghanistan. In India, it is celebrated by the Parsis as **Jamshed Navroz**. The holiday is pre-Islamic, a legacy of Zoroastrian Persia. It is also called **Ras al-Am**. In Afghanistan it is celebrated as **Nauroz**; and in Kashmir as **Nav Roz**.

The origins of Nawruz are obscure, but it is generally thought to be a pastoral festival marking the change from winter to summer. Legends have grown up around the holiday. In Afghanistan, where it is also **Farmer's Day**, an ugly old woman named Ajuzak is thought to roam around when Nawruz begins. If it rains on Nawruz, she is washing her hair, and the spring plantings will thrive. The Achaemenid kings (559–330 B.C.) are known to have celebrated Nawruz, probably with gift-giving.

Farmers decorate their cows and come into the city for an annual agricultural fair with prizes. Betting on kite flying is a sport for later in the day.

A special event, *jandah bala kardan* 'raising of the standard' is held on Nawruz at the tomb of Hazrat Ali in Mazar-i-Sharif in northern Afghanistan. The *jandah* 'standard' is raised in the courtyard of the shrine, and stays there for forty days. Thousands visit the shrine to touch the staff to gain merit, and the sick and crippled touch it hoping for cures. The standard comes down at a time when a distinct kind of red tulip blooms and then soon fades; at this time, people visit friends and wish each other long lives and many children.

Buzkashi, the national game of Afghanistan, is usually played on Nawruz, especially in Mazar-i-Sharif. *Buzkashi* means 'goat-grabbing,' and the object of the game is for a team of horse riders to grab the carcass of a goat placed in a pit, carry it around a goal post, and put it back in the pit. The game is supposed to have developed on the plains of Mongolia and Central Asia, sometimes using a prisoner-of-war instead of a goat; now a dead calf is usually used. It's a ferocious game occasionally producing fatalities; there are several hundred horsemen (*chapandaz*) on each team, and they gallop at breakneck speed, lashing at horses and each other with special buzkashi whips.

Special Afghan dishes on Nawruz are *samanak*, a dessert made of wheat and sugar, and *haft-mewah* 'seven fruits', a compote of walnuts, almonds, pistachio nuts, red and green raisins, dried apricots, and a fruit called *sanjet*.

In Iran, Nawruz is an event lasting thirteen days, during which people wear new clothes, give gifts, and visit friends and relatives. The banquet table holds seven foods starting with the letter S. Plates with sprouting wheat symbolize fertility, as do eggs, which are colored. Other symbols on the table are a mirror, candlesticks, and a bowl of water with a green leaf in it. The thirteenth day after No Ruz is Sizdah-Bedar 'thirteenth day out' and everyone picnics in the country or on rugs in city parks. The idea is to get out of their houses, taking any bad luck with them.

For the Baha'i, the day also marks the end of the nineteenth day fast, from March 2–20, when Baha'i abstain from food and drink from sunrise to sunset as a reminder that one's true nature is spiritual rather than material.

See also Bᴏᴇᴋᴇᴛ Jᴀᴛᴏᴀ.

See also Bisket Jatra.

NEBRASKAland DAYS
Third week in June

This week-long celebration of Nebraska's western heritage is held in North Platte, the home of Colonel William "Buffalo Bill" Cody. This famous buffalo hunter, U. S. Army scout, and Indian fighter eventually became a touring showman, organizing his first Wild West exhibition in 1883. His stars included Annie Oakley (see Annie Oakley Festival) and Chief Sitting Bull. Since 1965 the NEBRASKAland DAYS celebration has honored North Platte's most famous citizen by bestowing the Buffalo Bill Award on a well-known Western film star. Past winners have included Andy Devine, Gene Autry, Henry Fonda, Slim Pickens, and Wilford Brimley.

Other highlights of the festival include the Buffalo Bill Rodeo; the Frontier Revue, which tells the story of the West in song and dance; entertainment by top country and western performers; an equestrian show; and a Chuckwagon Pork Breakfast.

Nebuta Matsuri
August 2–7

The main festival of Aomori Prefecture in Japan, featuring processions of huge, elaborately painted papier-mâché figures called *nebuta*. The festival supposedly originated when Sakanoue-no-Tamuramaro (758–811) was sent here to put down a rebellion. He won by raising dummy soldiers along the skyline, making the enemy think his army was bigger than it was. Today in the capital city of Aomori, the *nebuta* figures, up to sixty feet wide and thirty feet high, depict birds and animals, fabulous creatures, and ferociously scowling warriors. Illuminated from within by candles, they glow as they are carried through the streets at nightfall. Spectators wear hats made of flowers and dance in the streets.

A similar but smaller festival is held in Hirosaki Aug. 1–7. Here, the *nebuta* are fan-shaped and depict warriors on one side and beautiful women on the other.

Nemean Games
Probably August

Ancient Greek games, one of four ancient Greek festivals involving games, held every second year in the sanctuary of Zeus in the valley of Nemea in the northeastern part at the Greek Peloponnesus. Little is known of these games before 573 B.C. Legend says they may have been originated by Hercules after he slew the lion of Nemea—one of his twelve labors. He killed the lion by driving it into a cave and strangling it. The games consisted of gymnastic, equestrian, and musical contests. Winners were crowned with a garland of wild celery.

See also ISTHMIAN GAMES, PYTHIAN GAMES, and OLYMPIC GAMES.

Nenana Ice Classic
Late February and early spring

Alaska's oldest tradition, a legal game that allows people to bet on when the massive ice cover on the Tanana River will break up. The Classic is kicked off in late February in Nenana (which has a population of about 570) with a winter carnival known as Tripod Days. At this time, a 1,500-pound spruce tripod is set into the ice of the Tanana River with a rope leading to a watchtower and clock. Two to three months later when the ice starts to move, a siren will sound, and when the tripod has moved 100 feet downstream, a meat cleaver stops the hands of the clock. This becomes the official time of the breakup. This setup of tripod, tower, clock, and cleaver has been the same since 1936 and has never failed.

Throughout Alaska, people place $2 bets in red gas cans with their predictions on the month, day, and hour of the ice's breakup. In early April, Nenana residents collect and sort the tickets. The earliest breakup ever recorded was April 20, 1940, at 3:27 a.m., and the latest May 20, 1964, at 11:41 a.m.

Wagering on the Nenana River ice began informally in 1906 when Jimmy Duke, owner of a roadhouse on the banks of the Tanana, started wagering with his chum Adolph "Two Cord" Nelson on the breakup day. In 1913, railroad engineers surveying the site for a bridge got in on the betting, and a pool started. In 1917, they started keeping records, and that year has been marked as the first official year of the Nenana Ice Classic. Now it's part of Alaskan lore, and the red betting cans are sometimes called the first spring flower. In 1990, 152,000 tickets were sold, and after deductions for taxes and expenses, the purse was $138,000.

Neri-Kuyo
August 16, every three years (most recently in 1990)

A Buddhist ceremony held every three years at Joshinji Temple in Tokyo, Japan, to celebrate the coming to earth of the Bodhisattvas. They are Buddhas-to-be who have undertaken a quest for enlightenment and have vowed to save all beings before they attain Buddhahood.

One of the best known vows taken by a Bodhisattva is this:
"Living beings are countless—
I vow to save them all.
Passions are inextinguishable—
I vow to extinguish them all.
Dharma truths are measureless—
I vow to master them all.
The Buddha-way is unexcelled—
I vow to attain it.

For the Neri-Kuyo in Tokyo, a curved wooden bridge is erected between two of the temple buildings, and local people dressed as Amitabha Buddha and twenty-four other Bodhisattvas file slowly across the bridge and back again. Wearing golden masks and haloes and fanned by attendants, they repeat this ceremony three times a day.

Nevis Tea Meeting
Full moon night in summer

The pageant known as the **Tea Meeting** held on the island of Nevis in the West Indies probably developed from church fund-raising events in the nineteenth century. The characters include a King, his Queen, and their court. The King and Queen sit on a stage while costumed members of the audience get up and perform for them-singing, dancing, reciting poetry, or giving a speech. Tea (or some other hot drink) is served and ceremonial fruit, cakes, and kisses from the King and Queen are auctioned off. Then the King and Queen and their court give ironic speeches, followed by more audience acts. If there is enough participation from the audience, the pageant can go on all night. It is common for scoffers in the back of the room to make loud and obscene comments throughout the performance.

Newala
December–January

A first fruits ceremony, before which the people are forbidden to eat certain new crops, the Newala ceremony in Swaziland takes place at the end of the year. It is a combination harvest and NEW YEAR'S festival. It is also a celebration of kingship, since according to tradition the king of Swaziland, the Ngwenyama or 'Lion,' has mystical powers and is believed to embody the nation's prosperity and fertility, thus he must have many wives and sire many children.

Events taking place during the ceremony, which lasts nearly a month, include the gathering of foam from the tops of waves and the collection of water from the major rivers by a group of *bemanti* or Swazi water officials. The day before they leave the king goes into seclusion. Young boys from all over the country who have reached puberty gather lusekwane, a type of acacia that is considered sacred, and bring it to the cattle pen. The climax of the Newala occurs when warriors, chanting sacred songs, dance around the *nhlambelo*, the king's sacred enclosure, persuading him to rejoin his people. The king feigns reluctance but eventually emerges: his face is blackened with medicines, he wears a headress of large black plumes, and a silver monkey skin belt, bright green grass covers his body. He improvises a dance before his people, and at one point he eats part of a special pumpkin known as the *luselwa* and throws the rest to one of his warriors. This is a signal that the new crops may now be eaten. The Newala ends with a huge bonfire which represents the burning of the past year. It is believed that rain will fall to quench the flames.

New Church Day
June 19

New Church Day refers to the Church of the New Jerusalem, founded in London in the late eighteenth century by the disciples of Emanuel Swedenborg, the Swedish scientist, philosopher, and theologian. In 1817, the General Convention of the New Jerusalem in the U.S.A. was founded in Philadelphia.

Swedenborg's followers believe that in 1757 there was a great judgment in the spiritual world, and that as a result the evil spirits were separated from the good and a new heaven was established. At that time Jesus called his apostles together and told them to preach the new doctrines in the new heaven, just as he had told them to do sixteen centuries earlier on earth. All of this took place on June 19 and 20. June 19 is also the date on which Swedenborg's disciples met in 1770 to organize the Church of the New Jerusalem. Every year on this day members of the New Church, called Swedenborgians, meet to conduct important church business and to commemorate the church's founding.

New Jersey Offshore Grand Prix
Four days in mid-July

Formerly known as the **Benihana Grand Prix Power Boat Regatta** and before that as the **Hennessy Grand Prix**, this four-day race is not only one of the largest offshore power boat races in the country but a festival as well, with a beauty pageant, band concerts, and fireworks taking place at the popular beach resort of Point Pleasant. The race itself takes place on a Wednesday and runs along the Atlantic coast of New Jersey from Asbury Park to Barnegat attracting more than 250,000 spectators to the state's beaches.

When the regatta was first held in 1964, it covered a 265-mile course around Long Island. But it was eventually moved to the Jersey shore, where there were more open beaches and clear waterways. In addition to the large number of on-shore spectators, about three thousand power boats watch the race from the water.

New Orleans Jazz and Heritage Festival
Late April to early May

A ten-day feast for the ears, the eyes, and the stomach, held in New Orleans "Crescent City", Louisiana. The festival's forerunner was the New

Orleans International Jazz Fest organized in 1968 to celebrate the city's 250th anniversary. Among the jazz greats on hand were Louis Armstrong and Duke Ellington. After it disbanded, George Wein, the founder of the famed Newport Jazz Festival, urged the initiation of a festival to celebrate the regional culture of New Orleans, and in 1970 it was under way. A high spot in the festival was the evening when Eubie Blake, then ninety-five years old, was honored as a ragtime and jazz pioneer; he played several of his own tunes, including "I'm Just Wild About Harry" and "Memories of You."

Today it brings together more than 4,000 musicians, artisans, and cooks who do their thing for more than a quarter of a million visitors. The concerts feature not only traditional and contemporary jazz, but also other music forms developed in New Orleans: ragtime, country, Cajun, zydeco, gospel, folk, and Latin. Food tents serve a multitude of indigenous foods, such as jambalaya, andouille, crawfish bisque, gumbo, frog legs, and so on. Hundreds of artisans also display their crafts.

Newport Harbor Christmas Boat Parade

December 17–23

A weeklong nightly parade of boats at Newport Beach, Calif., which has one of the largest concentrations of pleasure craft in the world—more than 9,000 boats are docked at the harbor. About 200 boats of all kinds, wildly decorated with lights that depict Santa Claus, snowmen, snowflakes, and other symbols of winter, join the parade. Some boats carry huge inflated figures (an enormous Grinch in an engineer's cap appeared in 1990) and many play music. The vessels range from rowboats to tugs to elegant yachts.

The floating parades actually started in 1908 as a Fourth of July spectacular. (The Fourth parades are no more.) John Scarpa, a real-estate broker was trying to sell some property, and to promote it he lit up a gondola and eight canoes with Japanese lanterns and paraded around the harbor. This developed into the Illuminated Water Parade, and was a highlight of the Fourth for years. In 1946, the city got a barge, put a tree and carollers on it, and towed it around the harbor, and that began the current December parades. They are considered the "granddaddy" of water parades, the biggest in the nation. About a million spectators watch them during the festival's seven days.

Newport Music Festival

Two weeks in mid-July

In 1969 the Metropolitan Opera in New York City decided to establish its summer home in Newport, Rhode Island. The fog and humidity, however, played havoc with the artists' delicate instruments, and it quickly became apparent that Newport wasn't the place for outdoor opera. But the grand rooms of its famed waterfront mansions provided an ideal setting for chamber music. Using members of the Metropolitan Opera Orchestra, the festival in its infancy paved the way for the "Romantic revival," which soon spread worldwide.

The Newport Music Festival still offers music of the Romantic era (1825–1900) but in recent years it has expanded its offerings and now presents a wide spectrum of composers and performers. Dozens of world premieres of forgotten or lost minor masterpieces by well-known composers, such as the four-handed *Andante Cantabile* by Debussy, have taken place here, as have the North American debuts of many now-famous international and American artists, such as the twelve year old Dimitris Sgouros. Up to forty-five concerts are presented during the two-week festival, which has developed a reputation for programs so rare and varied that they draw music-lovers from thousands of miles away.

Newport to Bermuda Race

Biennially in June

One of the oldest sailing races in the international calendar, the race from Newport, Rhode Island to Bermuda was initiated by Thomas Fleming Day editor and founder of *Rudder* magazine. At the time, most existing ocean races were for yachts of more than a hundred feet, and Day wanted to see a race for smaller yachts (less than forty feet overall). The first such race, in 1904, was run from Brooklyn, New York to Marblehead, Massachusetts, a distance of 330 nautical miles. The following year it went from Brooklyn to Hampton Roads, Virginia (250 miles). In 1906, the finish was in Bermuda.

The Bermuda races died out in 1910, but they were revived in 1923 under the sponsorship of the Cruising Club of America (CCA). Since 1924 the race has been sailed biennially in June. The starting point was moved from New London, Connecticut to Montauk, Long Island. But since 1936 the race has been run from Brenton Reef Tower off Newport to Mount Hill Light on St. David's Head, Bermuda—a distance of 635 miles. Sponsored jointly by the CCA and the Royal Bermuda Yacht

Club, the Newport to Bermuda Race is now part of the Onion Patch trophy series, which consists of this and three local, unnamed races.

New Year's Day
January 1

Celebrating the first day of the year on the first day of January is a relatively modern practice. Although the Romans began marking the beginning of their civil year on January 1, the traditional springtime opening of the growing season and time for major military campaigns still held on as the popular New Year celebration.

William the Conqueror decreed that the New Year commence on January 1, but practice in England was still variable. Even after the Gregorian calendar was adopted by all Roman Catholic countries in 1582, Great Britain and the English colonies in America continued to begin the year on March 25 in accordance with the old Julian calendar. It wasn't until 1752 that Britain and its possessions adopted the New Style calendar (Gregorian) and accepted January 1 as the beginning of the year. New Year's Day is a public holiday in the U.S. and in many other countries, and is traditionally a day for receiving visitors and recovering from New Year's Eve festivities. A favorite pastime in the United States is watching football games on television—especially the ROSE BOWL game in Pasadena, California, the COTTON BOWL in Dallas, Texas, the SUGAR BOWL in New Orleans, Louisiana, and the ORANGE BOWL in Miami, Florida. A number of parades are also televised on New Year's Day, one of the most famous being the MUMMERS' PARADE in Philadelphia, Pennsylvania. New Year's is a time for making resolutions for the coming year—promises that are loudly proclaimed and then often forgotten.

See also HOGMANAY; LUNAR NEW YEAR; ST. BASU; IBU AFO FESTIVAL; OSHOGATSU; SOL.

New Year's Day in the Former Soviet Union
January 1

NEW YEAR'S DAY has largely replaced CHRISTMAS as the major winter festival in the former Soviet Union. This was the day on which Grandfather Frost visited, bringing gifts for the children. Within the walls of Moscow's Kremlin, there was a huge party at the Palace of Congresses attended by as many as 50,000 children. Entertainment at the party included the arrival of *D'yed Moroz* or Grandfather Frost, wearing a white beard, red robe, and a hat trimmed in white fur and riding a Sputnik-drawn sleigh or some other outlandish

vehicle. There were also troops of folk dancers, magicians, clowns, and tumblers who performed for the children. Older Muscovites celebrated New Year's by attending dances at schools, clubs, theaters, and union halls. Outside of Moscow, the same festivities took place on a more modest scale.

Caviar, smoked fish, roast meats, and other treats were served in honor of the holiday. Among the many cakes and sweets served were *babka*, a yeast coffee cake made in a round pan, and *kulich*, a fancy fruitbread of Ukrainian origin made in three tiers to symbolize the Trinity.

New Year's Eve
December 31

The last day of the year is usually greeted with mixed emotions—joy and anticipation on the one hand, melancholy and regret on the other. Some celebrate by attending midnight church services, while others congregate in public places like Times Square in New York City, or Trafalgar Square in London, Glasgow's George Square or Edinburgh's Iron Kirk to count down the closing seconds of the old year. In the United States, people congregate at parties, some lasting all night, and many people spend New Year's Eve in front of the television watching other people celebrate. In recent years, celebrations in time zones other than Eastern have also been televised, so viewers nationwide can celebrate four times in one night, if they wish.

In Scotland, December 31 is known as **Old Year's Night** or **Hogmanay**. Although there are a number of theories about the derivation of the name, the tradition it refers to involves handing out pieces of oat-cake to poor children, who go from door to door calling out "Hogmanay!" In the United States, the Scottish song "Auld Lang Syne," with lyrics by poet Robert Burns, is sung at almost every New Year's Eve celebration, while in London, the Scots at St. Paul's Churchyard toast and sing.

See also OMISOKA.

In Denmark the New Year is "shot in" with a thunderous explosion of fireworks, rockets, and Chinese pistols. In the villages, the young people play pranks such as those done on HALLOWEEN in the United States.

Iceland has bonfires to clean up trash, and elf dances because elves are believed to be about on this night and might want to stop and rest on their way.

Neapolitans believe it brings luck to throw pots and dishes out the windows at midnight.

On the last two days of the year in Japan, a fire watch is implemented to prepare for the New Year, their most important holiday. Young men gather into groups then go to separate parts of the towns. They carry a clapper which they sound every few yards, crying out, "take care with fire."

Armenian families spend the night at home feasting. During the celebration, the neighbors, one at a time, lower a basket of presents down the chimney, then it is the recipients' turn to go to their neighbors.

Romanian boys used to go around to their neighbors with a *plugusorul*, a little plough, which is a remnant of the Roman *Opalia*, the festival to the goddess of abundance, *Ops*. Later they changed to a home-made drum that sounds like a bull, which is what pulls the plough through the meadow. They ring cow bells and crack whips and recite hundreds of verses of their country story at the top of their lungs.

See also FIRST NIGHT.

New Year's Eve in Brazil
January 31

One of the most exotic NEW YEAR'S EVE celebrations in the world takes place along the beaches of Brazil—particularly Copacabana Beach in Rio de Janeiro, where thousands of believers in *Umbanda*, the official religion of the city's poor meet to pay homage to the ocean goddess Iemanjá (Yemanjá). Dressed in white and carrying fresh flowers, candles, and *cachaça* (sugarcane alcohol), they flock to the beach around ten o'clock and lay out tablecloths surrounded by candles and covered with gifts for the goddess. Animal sacrifices are not uncommon.

The ceremony reaches its peak at midnight, when everyone rushes into the water—shrieking, sobbing, or singing—carrying their flowers and gifts for Iemanjá. If the waves carry their gifts out to sea, it means that the goddess was satisfied and they can go home happy. It is considered an ill omen if the ocean throws back their gifts.

See also IEMANJA FESTIVAL

New York City Marathon
First Sunday in November

The New York City Marathon began in 1970 as a race four times around Central Park. But in 1976, Fred Lebow and the New York Road Runners Club, the world's largest running club and the race's sponsor, decided to get corporate support, invite top runners from all over the world, and to run the course through all five New York boroughs. Unlike the BOSTON MARATHON, which is run primarily through the countryside and small towns, the New York course is urban, beginning at the tollbooth plaza at the end of the Verrazano-Narrows Bridge on Staten Island and progressing across the bridge through Brooklyn, Queens, Manhattan, and the Bronx before finishing in Manhattan's Central Park. About 25,000 runners compete in the race-including a number of handicapped competitors in wheelchairs—and over a million New Yorkers turn out to watch. In addition to cash prizes ranging from $20,000 for the first-place finishers to $2,500 for fifth place, more than $200,000 in bonuses are handed out each year.

The marathon has had a positive effect on New York City's public image, which has suffered because of its high crime rate and frequent clashes between ethnic groups. The runners who compete regularly in New York say that the crowds are enthusiastic and friendly, and city dwellers look upon it as a time to forget racial and ethnic differences and cheer the runners on.

Like most things in New York City, its marathon is amazing. Rosie Ruiz, well known for being disqualified for cheating in the Boston Marathon, was thrown out in New York for taking the subway to the finish line. On the positive side, Liz McColgan, the 10,000 meter champion from Dundee, Scotland, won the New York women's division in 1991 with a time of 2 hours 27 minutes 23 seconds. It was her first attempt at a marathon race.

Then there's race organizer Fred Lebow: although an avid runner he had never run New York until he was struck by brain cancer. Then in 1992, the cancer in remission, this sixty-year old Romanian-born escapee from the Holocaust finally ran the 26.2 mile course. His companion on his heroic run was his good friend and nine-time New York winner Grete Waitz of Norway. Lebow's time: 5 hours 32 minutes 34 seconds.

In 1992 Australian-born Lisa Ondieki set a new women's course record of 2:24:40 and won a $30,000 bonus in addition to the standard $20,000 purse and Mercedes-Benz automobile. Willie Mtolo, a twenty-eight year old Zulu from South Africa, won his first major international marathon in 1992. This was a special victory for him since he had been unable to compete outside his homeland until this year: South African athletes had suffered a twenty-one year political embargo. Mtolo's time: 2 hours 9 minutes 29 seconds.

Nganja, Feast of
April

A harvest festival in Angola, the Feast of Nganja is primarily celebrated by children. On a day in April, when the harvest is ripe, they go out to their family fields and gather some fresh corn. In small groups they go to the woods, where they build campfires and roast their corn on the cob. But the real excitement of the feast lies in the game that is played while the corn is being cooked. Without warning, a child from one group may jump up and steal the corn from another. The robbing and plundering is good-natured, although there are always a few children who end up with no corn at all.

A similar children's feast held in Angola during the harvest months of February, March, and April is known as the Feast of Okambondondo. This all-night celebration is held indoors, with the girls doing all the cooking and the meal itself being served in the kitchen just before dawn.

Nice Carnival
Twelve days beginning between January 22 and February 25, ending on Shrove Tuesday

Dating back to the fourteenth century and deriving, some believe, from ancient rites of spring, the CARNIVAL celebration in Nice, France is one of the Mediterranean resort town's most picturesque spectacles. It actually begins about three weeks before SHROVE TUESDAY with the arrival of King Carnival. The next two Saturdays and Sundays are filled with processions, confetti battles, fireworks, and masked balls. The procession of floats, each accompanied by marchers or riders on horseback wearing elaborate costumes, draws the largest crowd. On Shrove Tuesday, King Carnival is burnt in effigy on a pyre.

Night of the Radishes
December 23

A festival that dates from the nineteenth century that combines art, agriculture, and religion. It is held in the *zócalo*, or main square, in Oaxaca, Mexico, 300 miles south of Mexico City. The radish made its first appearance here during the Spanish colonial period, and in commemoration Oaxaqueños carve them into elaborate shapes and display them on **La Noche de Ratanos**. The radishes, the same red-skinned, white-fleshed roots commonly eaten in salads, grow to yam-size here and are each uniquely shaped by growing through the rocky soil.

Indian families harvest these vegetables, combine and sculpt them into elaborate forms and complex scenes depicting biblical scenes, especially the nativity of Jesus. Historical and Aztec themes are also represented. After the awarding of cash prizes and ribbons, a fireworks display caps the night.

During the festival and throughout the CHRISTMAS season, another custom is observed: people buy small pottery bowls filled with sweet fried dough called *buñuelos*, after they eat the dough, they fling the bowl violently to the ground. The walks become thick with pottery shards.

Night of the Shooting Stars
August 11

Meteors, also called shooting stars or falling stars, are seen as streaks of light in the sky that result when a small chunk of stony or metallic matter enters the Earth's atmosphere and vaporizes. A meteor shower occurs when a number of meteors enter the Earth's atmosphere at approximately the same time and place. The shower's name is usually derived from the constellation (or a star within it) from which the shower appears to originate.

Since the year 830 there has been an annual meteor shower known as **The Perseids** (because it appears to originate in the constellation Perseus) that arrives annually on the night of August 11. Observers everywhere except the South Pole can see as many as sixty meteors an hour streak across the sky on what is often referred to as "the Night of the Shooting Stars."

Night Watch, the
July 13

La Retraite aux Flambeaux or the Night Watch is a half-holiday in France that is celebrated on the eve of BASTILLE DAY. The lights in Paris are darkened in remembrance of the day in 1789 when the Bastille fell. Colorful processions of soldiers, patriotic bands, and people bearing torches and Chinese lanterns march through the streets, followed by crowds of spectators. The procession usually ends at the home of a prominent citizen, who offers the torch- and lantern-bearers something to drink.

Niman Festival
July

The Niman or **Going Home Ceremony** takes

place in the Hopi Indian pueblos of northeastern Arizona. After entering the pueblos in February, the *kachinas* or ancestral spirits (impersonated by men wearing elaborate masks) leave again in July. During the six months when they are present in the pueblo (see POWAMÛ FESTIVAL), the kachinas appear in a series of dances, of which the Niman is the last. For the Going Home Ceremony, up to seventy-five dancers representing kachinas spend an entire day singing and dancing. They give bows, arrows, and other gifts to the boys and kachina dolls to the girls before returning to their mountain homes.

Nine Imperial Gods, Festival of the
First nine days of the ninth lunar month

As celebrated today in Singapore, the Festival of the Nine Imperial Gods derives from an ancient Chinese cleansing ritual. The festival begins with a procession to a river or the sea to invite the Nine Imperial Gods to descend from the heavens into an urn filled with burning benzoin. The urn is then carried to the temple and put in a place where only Taoist priests and Buddhist monks are allowed to enter. Nine oil lamps representing the gods are hung from a bamboo pole in front of the temple. They are lowered and then raised again to signify that the gods have arrived. The ground below the lamps is purified every morning and afternoon with holy water. Worshippers enter the temple by crossing a specially constructed bridge, symbolizing the belief that they are leaving the evils of the past year behind.

Chinese operas known as *wayang* shows—some of which take two or more days to complete—are often performed during the nine days of the festival. On the ninth day, the sacred urn with the burning ashes is brought out of the temple and taken in procession back to the water's edge, where it is placed in a boat. The observers wait for the boat to move, indicating that the gods have departed—but what often happens is that other boats turn on their engines to churn up the water and send the gods on their way.

Nippy Lug Day
Between February 6 and March 12; Friday following Shrove Tuesday

A "lug" at one time referred to the ear-flap of a man's cap, but in Scotland and Northern England it became a synonym for the ear itself. In nineteenth century Scotland, schoolchildren called their teachers "nip-lugs" because they often pulled their pupils' ears as a disciplinary measure. In Westmorland, England it was traditional at one

time for children to pinch each other's ears on the Friday following SHROVE TUESDAY, giving rise to the name Nippy Lug Day.

Nisei Week
August (August 1–9 in 1992)

An annual Japanese festival in the Little Tokyo area of Los Angeles, Calif. Little Tokyo is the social, cultural, and economic center for the Japanese and Nisei community of southern California. The Nisei are people of Japanese descent born and raised in the United States. Held since the 1940s, this festival features a parade, a carnival, Japanese folk dancing, celebrity appearances, and a prince and princess pageant. There are special exhibits of bonsai, flower arranging, doll making, tea ceremonies, and other Japanese arts. Sports competitions and demonstrations include jiu-jitsu and karate. Attendance is about 50,000.

Noc Swietego Andreja *See* St. Andrew's Eve

Nones *See* Ides

Norsk Høstfest
October

All five Scandinavian countries—Denmark, Finland, Iceland, Norway, and Sweden—are represented at the annual Scandinavian heritage festival known as Norsk Høstfest that has been held in Minot, North Dakota since 1978. The festival includes performances by top entertainers, one of which is selected by the previous year's ticketholders as the "People's Choice" and many of whom are either Scandinavian or Americans of Scandinavian descent. There are also Swedish accordian players, Scandinavian folk dancers, and Lakota flute players, who perform at the Høstfest complex on North Dakota's state fairgrounds in Minot. The complex includes five stages, forty food booths, and dozens of demonstration areas for craftsmen and artisans—among them the highly skilled *rosemalers* 'folk painters'. The Viking Age Club sets up an authentic encampment to show how the North Plains Scandinavian settlers lived.

Food is a big part of the five-day festival, which features traditional Scandinavian delicacies. More than sixty thousands visitors come to Minot to sample Swedish sweet bread, søt suppe (fruit soup), potet klub (potato dumpling), Icelandic cake, rømmergrøt ('red porridge', a rhubarb pudding), Danish kringle (pretzel-shaped cooky), lefse (a thin, sweet cake spread with butter and cinnamon and folded over), and lutefisk (boiled cod). A similar Scandinavian festival, the Hjemkomst Festival, is held in June in Fargo.

North American Indian Days
Second week in July

One of the largest gatherings of United States and Canadian Indian tribes, held in Browning, Montana, the hub of the Blackfeet Indian Reservation in the northwest mountains of the state. Tepees are pitched on the powwow grounds for four days of traditional Indian dancing, games, sports events, and socializing. There are also exhibits of arts and crafts—beadwork, quill and feather work, moccasins and other leather goods.

Northern Games
Mid-July

A showcase for traditional Inuit and Indian sports and culture, the Northern Games are held in the Northwest Territories of Canada for four days in July each year. They feature traditional dances, drumming competitions, arts and crafts displays, and the "Good Woman" Contest, which gives Northern women a chance to demonstrate their skill in such areas as animal skinning and bannock baking. The games are held in a different part of the Northwest Territories each year, and draw competitors from Alaska, Yukon Territory, and Labrador as well.

North Pole Winter Carnival
Early March

A weekend to celebrate winter in North Pole, Alaska, a suburb of Fairbanks. North Pole was named by Con Miller, a man who bought a Fairbanks trading post in 1949. When he cleaned it out, he found a Santa Claus suit and started wearing it on trips to the interior to buy furs and sell supplies. A few years later he built a new trading post southeast of Fairbanks, called it Santa Claus House, and named the town around it North Pole. The town now has a government and a post office. It also has the winter carnival which features the North Pole Championship Sled Dog Race, a dog weight-pulling contest, carnival rides and games, food booths, crafts bazaars, and live entertainment.

Northwest Folklife Festival
Memorial Day weekend

An international four-day festival started in 1972 in Seattle, Wash., that draws performers and artisans from Washington, Oregon, Idaho, Alaska, and the province of British Columbia. The emphasis is on amateur performers and ethnicity with some 55 ethnic groups represented. Events include music and dance on twenty stages; demonstrations by artisans of such skills as leather tanning, boatbuilding, blacksmithing, and broom making; and an Ethnic Food Village that offers food from more than thirty nations.

The festival spans the Memorial Day weekend, starting on Friday and winding up on Monday.

Nuestra Senora de Peñafrancia, Feast of
Third week of September

A grand fiesta devoted to Our Lady of Peñafrancia, held in Naga City on the Bicol peninsula in the Philipppines. Some 200 years ago a Spanish official attributed the recovery of his ill daughter to the lady, and built a shrine to her in Naga City, starting the devotion to her that has lasted into the present.

This is the biggest festival of the Bicol region; it starts with a nine-day novena at the Naga Cathedral. A procession then carries the image of the Virgin to a pagoda on a festooned barge, which is surrounded by a flotilla of smaller boats. The people on the smaller boats chant prayers and hymns as they proceed along the river. Meanwhile, on the shore, pilgrims from other Bicol provinces kneel and pray as the barge passes by. When the water-borne pagoda has finished its journey, there are shouts of "Viva la virgen!" and the image is taken back to its shrine.

Nyambinyambi
Spring

The annual planting festival called the **Rain-Calling Ceremony** or Nyambinyambi is observed by the Kwangali people of Namibia, who believe that the land must be cleansed before the rain can fall and the fields can be planted. The chief sends his grandson out to cut down a tree, which is erected at the entrance gate to the *kraal* or village. The people lay their planting tools, seeds, pumpkins, and hunting weapons at the base of the tree and pray to the god known as Karunga or Kalunga to bring them a plentiful harvest and a good hunting season. In the Songhay's region of Niger, this is called **Genji Bi Hori** 'Black Spirit Festival'. They also pray that rain will fall soon after the ceremony, which is believed to rid the country of bad luck.

The Songhay rain-bringing ceremony is held at the end of the hot-dry season. Known as **Yenaandi** 'the act of cooling off' or the **Rain Dance**, it is usually held on a Thursday, the *Tooru* 'gods' sacred day, and is addressed to the four principal Tooru deities: Dongo, the god of thunder; Cirey, the god of lightning; Moussa Nyori, the god of clouds and wind; and Hausakoy, the god of blacksmithing.

Nyepí
About March 21

The people of Bali in Indonesia celebrate the VERNAL EQUINOX and the NEW YEAR by driving the devils out of the villages and then observing a day of stillness, known as Nyepí. It is believed that when spring arrives and the rainy season ends, the Lord of Hell, Yama, sweeps the devils out of Hades, which then fall on Bali making it necessary to purify the entire island. First the evil spirits are lured out of their hiding places with an elaborate offering of food, drink, money, and household utensils. Samples of every seed and fruit, and of every animal used as food are all laid out in an eight-point star representing the Rose of the Winds. Then the evil spirits are driven out of the village by the strong incantations and curses of the priests, and by the people who run through the streets with their faces and bodies painted, lighting firecrackers, carrying torches, beating the trees and the ground, and banging drums, tin cans, and anything else they can find to make noise to drive the demons away. Cockfighting plays an important role in the ceremony, because blood is believed to cleanse the impure earth.

The following day, Nyepí, marks the start of the New Year and the arrival of spring. It is observed with the suspension of all activity: no cooking or fires, no sexual intercourse, and no work of any kind are permitted.

O

Oath Monday
July

A centuries-old custom in Ulm, Germany, that combines politics and pageantry. Each year in July, the burgomaster, or mayor, gives a policy speech in the market square, listens to the public discussions, and then, after the ringing of a bell, takes an oath swearing to stand "for rich and poor" in all matters "of the public weal."

Events then shift to the Danube River and a waterborne parade called the *Nabada*. Rafts and boats are decorated with tableaux of papier-mâché figures that satirize local and regional politics. With them are floating bands and private boats. Later, back on land, a medieval pageant is presented.

The oath-taking began in 1397 when the city was on the verge of bankruptcy. The nobles, who had been running the city, agreed to sit down with representatives of the guilds—groups of merchants and craftsmen. At the close of the negotiations, the guilds had a majority on the city council, the citizens had the right to a hearing before major city decisions were made, and the Solemn Oath was established, ending the privileges of the aristocracy.

Oberammergau Passion Play
May through September, once every decade in years ending in zero

The most famous of Passion Plays, held since the 17th century in the small woodcarving village of Oberammergau, Germany, in the Bavarian Alps.

The play, depicting the story of Christ's suffering, crucifixion, and resurrection, is presented in six hours by a cast of about 1,500. All performers are villagers, and the 600 with speaking parts are required to have been born in Oberammergau. The role of Mary is traditionally played by an unmarried woman. Close to half a million people attend the productions, which are staged in an open-air theater seating 5,000.

Legend says that the play was first performed in 1634 in fulfillment of a vow. The plague was sweeping Europe, and the Oberammergau elders swore to God that they would reenact the Passion of Christ if he would spare the remaining villagers; already a fifth of the population had been lost. The plague passed by, and the play has been performed since then (shifting to decennial years in 1700), except in 1870 during the Franco-Prussian War and in World War II. In modern times, the play has aroused protests that the 1860 text has anti-Semitic overtones.

Obon Festival
July 13–15; August 13–15

Also called the **Festival of the Dead**, this is the time when the dead revisit the earth, according to Japanese Buddhist belief. Throughout Japan, in either July or August, depending on the area, religious rites and family reunions are held in memory of the dead. On the first evening of the festival, small bonfires are lit outside homes to welcome the spirits of ancestors. A meal, usually vegetables, rice cakes, and fruit, is set out for the spirits, and for two days they are spoken to as though they were present. On the final day (Jul. or Aug. 15), farewell dumplings are prepared, and another bonfire is lit outside the house to guide the spirits back. The climax is the *Bon-Odori* 'Dance of Rejoicing,' folk dances held in every town by the light of paper lanterns, to comfort the souls of the dead. Some Bon-Odori dances are especially famous—one being the AWA ODORI of Tokushima, which is accompanied by puppet shows and groups of musicians parading night and day.

At midnight some families gather the left-over rice cakes and food and take them to the waterfront. They are placed in a boat two or three feet long, made of rice straw with a rice straw sail; a lit paper lantern is on the bow and burning joss sticks at the stern. The breeze carries the boats, sustaining the spirits on their outward trip.

Obon celebrations are also held in Japanese communities throughout the world. About 500 people usually take part in the Bon-Odori in Chicago in July, and there are noted celebrations in several California cities.

See also DIA DE LOS MUERTOS.

Obzinky
Late August or early September

There are two harvest celebrations in the Czech and Slovak Republics. One of them, known as Posviceni, is the church consecration of the harvest. The other, Obzinky, is a secular festival where the field workers celebrate the end of the harvest by making a wreath out of corn, ears of wheat or rye, and wildflowers. Sometimes the wreath is placed on the head of a pretty young girl, and sometimes it is placed in a wagon along with decorated rakes and scythes and pulled in procession to the home of the land owner. The laborers present the wreath and congratulate their employer on a good harvest, after which they are invited to participate in dancing and feasting at the farm owner's expense. Foods served at the feast traditionally include roast pig, roast goose, and *Kolace*—square cakes filled with plum jam or a stuffing made from sweetened cheese or poppy seed. Beer and slivovice, a prune liquor, accompany the food.

The woman who binds the last sheaf is known as the *Baba* 'old woman' in some areas. In others, the Baba is a doll made from the last sheaf of grain and decorated with ribbons and flowers. Like the wreath, the Baba is carried in procession to the landlord's home, where it occupies a place of honor until the next harvest.

A similar harvest festival, known as the **Nubaigai,** is held in Lithuania. Here, too, a *Boba* is borne in procession to the farm; sometimes the worker who bound the last sheaf is wrapped up in it. But the harvest wreath is carried on a plate covered with a white linen cloth, and as the procession advances, the reapers sing an old song about how they rescued the crop from a huge bison that tried to devour it.

October War of Liberation Anniversary
October 6

In Syria, the anniversary of the Arab-Israeli War of 1973 is celebrated on October 6, the day the hostilities started with a surprise attack by Syrian and Egyptian forces that caught the Israelis off guard during the Jewish fast of YOM KIPPUR. Although the Arab armies were turned back, they inflicted heavy casualties on Israel and reclaimed some of the land they had lost in the Six Day War. Also known as **Tishrin** after the month of October in which the war started, the celebration tends to play up the Arab soldiers' role in the war with special television broadcasts glorifying the conflict, art exhibits, plays, films, concerts, rallies, and wreath-laying ceremonies. No mention is made of the fact that six thousand Syrians died in the conflict, or that Israeli troops reached the outskirts of Damascus.

In Egypt, October 6 is **Armed Forces Day**, commemorating the Egyptians' role in the October War. Anwar Sadat, the hero of that war, was assassinated on October 6, 1981 while viewing the Armed Forces Day parade.

Odo Festival
December–August, biannually

The Odo festival marks the return of the dead (*odo*) to visit the living in the northern Igbo villages of Nigeria. Lasting in some places from December until August, the festival has three distinct stages: the arrival of the odo, their stay with the living, and their departure. The first stage is observed with ritual celebrations and festivities welcoming the returning spirits of the dead. Then there is a stretch of six or more months during which the spirits of the dead interact with their living relatives and visit their ancestral homes. Their final departure is a very emotional affair (see AWURU ODO FESTIVAL), since they will not return for two more years.

Odo plays, featuring certain stock characters identified by their costumes and the manner in which they interact with the audience, are usually performed at the return and staying stages of the odo journey. Most of the roles are played by men, while the women function as chorus members and sometimes as spectators. The performers wear costumes traditionally made from plant fiber, leaves, beads, and feathers, although more durable cloth costumes are becoming more common in contemporary Odo plays. A musical accompaniment, featuring xylophones, drums, and rattles is known as *obilenu* music, meaning 'that which lies above.'

Odwira
September

A celebration of the national identity by the Asante (or Ashanti) people of Ghana, once known as the Gold Coast. The festival originated centuries ago as a time for people to assemble after the yam harvest, and was wrongly called the Yam Festival by non-Africans.

The kingdom of Asante, which is now the region of Asante, became rich and powerful in the late 1600s under its first ruler, *Asantahene* ('King') Osei Tutu. He is believed to have initiated the festival with the additional purpose of reinforcing the loyalty of the subjugated chiefs. The nation he built up withstood the British until 1901. He built a palace at Kumasi, and to further strengthen the nation, he and a priest, Okomfo Anokye, introduced the legendary Golden Stool. Supposed to have been brought down from heaven, it was thought to enshrine the nation's soul and became a symbol of the bond among all Asante people. Tutu also set down laws for life and religion. Much of this culture still survives.

During Odwira, the national identity is reinforced with purification ceremonies: a priest in each town prepares a purification bundle of certain tree branches and shoots, and in the evening carries it out of town and buries it. The Golden Stool is carried in a procession and placed on a throne without touching the ground. Huge umbrellas to protect participants from the sun add to the color of the procession. Drums and horns provide music.

Ohio River Sternwheel Festival
Weekend after Labor Day

A sternwheeler is a boat propelled by a paddle wheel at the stern or rear of the vessel. At one time they were a common sight along the Ohio River, although many have fallen into decay or have been turned into floating restaurants. The riverfront town of Marietta, Ohio is home to two of the sternwheelers that remain in working order and is the site of an annual Sternwheel Festival celebrating the era of the riverboat (mid to late 1800s). Anywhere from eighteen to twenty-five sternwheelers arrive in Marietta during the first week in September for the festival, which begins on the Friday after LABOR DAY. Outdoor concerts, calliope music, entertainment by singers and dancers, and the crowning of Queen Genevieve of the River take place on Saturday, and on Sunday there are sternwheel races. Two of the largest and best-known sternwheelers, the *Delta Queen* and the *River Queen*, participate in the festival every year.

Oklahoma Day
April 22

After forcing the Indians to move west of the Mississippi River during the early decades of the nineteenth century, Congress set aside a vast area including all of what is now Oklahoma and called it the Indian Territory, telling them the land would be theirs forever. But eventually the U. S. government reneged on its policy in response to pressure from railroad companies and land-hungry homesteaders. Part of the Indian Territory was opened to white settlement by allowing "land runs" in which homesteaders raced across the border to stake their claim to 160-acre plots offered free of charge. Those who managed to sneak across the line before the official opening were called "sooners," which is how Oklahoma came to be nicknamed "the Sooner State." The land run of April 22, 1889 paved the way for the organization of the Oklahoma Territory in 1890, and for Oklahoma's statehood in 1907.

Also known as **Oklahoma 89ers Day**, the celebrations on April 22 focus on the town of Guthrie, the site of the original land office about eighty miles from the starting border. In 1915, the "89ers," as the original participants came to be called, re-enacted the land rush, and each year Guthrie observes its anniversary with an 89ers festival. Elsewhere in Oklahoma, the day is celebrated with parades, rodeos, and events based on the "land rush" theme. See also CHEROKEE STRIP DAY.

Oklahoma Historical Day
October 10

The early history of Oklahoma is replete with stories about a French family named Chouteau. Major Jean Pierre Chouteau and his half-brother René Auguste monopolized the fur trade with the Indians, and in 1796 Chouteau established the first permanent non-Indian settlement within the boundaries of what is now Oklahoma when he built a cabin to serve as a headquarters and trading post in Salina. Chouteau's birthday, October 10, became a legal holiday known as Oklahoma Historical Day in 1939, and a major annual celebration is held in Salina each year.

Okmulgee Pecan Festival
Third weekend in June

A nutty festival in Okmulgee, Okla. that made the *Guinness Book of World Records* in 1988 for the world's largest pecan pie. The pie had a diameter of forty feet, and it weighed about 16 1/2 tons. Even with the help of the culinary arts department of the Oklahoma State University Technical Branch in Okmulgee this was an enormous task. So in 1990 the big event was a pecan cookie with a diameter of thirty-two feet and a weight of 7,500 pounds. That was a bit of a chore, too. In 1991, it was decided to keep it simple and celebrate with the "World's Largest Pecan Cookie and Ice Cream Party." More than 15,000 cookies and 5,000 single servings of vanilla ice cream were served.

Okmulgee, a name that means 'bubbling waters' in the Creek language, is the capital of the Creek Nation. It is also an area that raises a lot of pecans; some 600 acres near Okmulgee are devoted to growing pecans. The festival began in 1984 and has been voted one of the top ten festivals in the state. Besides big pecan concoctions, it offers a carnival, a pecan bake-off, a pie-throwing booth, arm wrestling contests, the crowning of a Pecan Prince and Princess, and a turtle race.

Okpesi Festival

September

The Igbo people of Nigeria believe that failure to perform this annual rite will bring bad luck not only to the individual but to the entire community. It must be carried out by every male child whose father has died, for it is a ceremony in honor of the Igbo ancestors, or *ndioki*. Also known as **Itensi**, the ritual begins with a blood sacrifice of cocks, after which the blood is spread on wooden altars built specifically for the purpose. The sacrifice is followed by a feast during which communion is achieved both among the living and between the living and the dead.

See also ODO FESTIVAL.

Oktoberfest

September–October

The first Oktoberfest was held on October 17, 1810, in honor of the marriage of Crown Prince Ludwig of Bavaria to Princess Therese von Saxe-Hildburghausen. Since that time it has become, above all else, a celebration of German beer. The Lord Mayor of Munich opens the first barrel, and the sixteen-day festival begins. Both citizens and tourists flock to this event, which is marked by folk costume parades in which brewery horses draw floats and decorated beer wagons through the streets. Oktoberfest celebrations modeled on the German festival are also held in United States cities.

Old Christmas Day

January 6 or 7

In addition to being the FEAST OF THE EPIPHANY, January 6 is known as Old Christmas Day. When England and Scotland switched over from the Ju-

lian to the Gregorian calendar in 1752, eleven days were dropped to make up for the calendar discrepancy that had accumulated with the use of the Julian calendar. In all subsequent years, CHRISTMAS arrived eleven days early. Many people, especially in rural areas, had trouble accepting the loss of these eleven days, and continued to recognize the holidays of the Julian calendar as Old Christmas, Old CANDLEMAS, Old MIDSUMMER DAY, etc. The Ukrainians celebrate this holiday on January 7.

See also RUSSIAN ORTHODOX CHRISTMAS.

Old Fiddler's Convention

Second week in August

A three-day concert in the small town of Galax, Va., that spotlights old-time music in an outdoor setting. The convention was organized in 1935 as a fund-raising event by members of Moose Lodge No. 753 and was dedicated to "keeping alive the memories and sentiments of days gone by." About 25,000 people now attend.

Hundreds of contestants take part, competing for cash prizes and trophies in categories that include guitar, mandolin, dulcimer, dobro, clawhammer and bluegrass banjo, clog or flatfoot dancing, and folk singing.

Old Hickory's Day *See* Battle of New Orleans Day

Old Saybrook Torchlight Parade and Muster

Second Saturday night in December

In 1970 the Colonial Saybrook Fifes and Drums, under the leadership of Bill Reid, revived the tradition of a Christmas torchlight parade. In early December each year, in colonial America, the village militia would muster with their fifes and drums and march to the town green carrying torches and lanterns. When they heard the fifes and drums pass, the townspeople would follow behind the militia, also carrying torches and lanterns, to the green where a community meeting and carol sing would take place. It is thought that the event originally commemorated ADVENT.

Old Saybrook, Connecticut (population 10,000) is located at the mouth of the Connecticut River on Long Island Sound and was settled in 1635. It is the only community in the United States that is known to have revived this tradition.

The modern-day procession follows the traditional ritual with no less than fifty-eight fife and drum corps from as far away as Virginia, New

Jersey, and New York made up of thirty-five people per unit on average, plus support groups. The corps are sometimes led by Santa Claus himself and the marchers often augment their colonial-style costumes with seasonal decorations. For example, Christmas lights sparkle on tricornered hats, and silver tinsel hangs from flintlock rifles. The fifes and drums play not only colonial martial music but also the joyous and peaceful songs of Christmas. Citizens of the town and thousands of visitors join the march carrying torches and lanterns to the town green for a community carol sing led by the high school band.

Old Silvester
December 31, January 13

The custom known as **Silvesterklausen** (or Chlause) in the small town of Urnäsch, Switzerland is performed both on December 31, New Silvester (*silvester* means 'New Year's Eve' in the part of Switzerland where German is spoken), and on January 13, or Old Silvester. The two dates reflect the change from the Julian or Old Style calendar to the Gregorian or New Style calendar in 1582. The men of the village, wearing masks, costumes, and heavy harnesses with bells, walk in groups from house to house—or, in the surrounding countryside, from one farm to the next—singing wordless yodels. The friends and neighbors who receive them offer them a drink before they move on to the next house. The yodelers are usually so well disguised that their neighbors don't recognize them.

Old-Time Country Music Contest and Festival, National
Labor Day weekend

Created by Bob Everhart as part of America's bicentennial celebration in 1976, the National Old-Time Country Music Contest and Festival in Avoca, Iowa is now the largest gathering of public domain music-makers and listeners in the United States. Sponsored by the National Traditional Country Music Association, the festival's purpose is to preserve the music that, in Everhart's words, has been "prostituted, violated, diluted, and in many instances altered so dramatically that it is no longer recognizable as a traditional American art form." There are more than thirty competitions in such varied musical genres as ragtime, polka, Cajun, mountain, folk, cowboy, Western, swing, yodeling, and gospel. The festival also includes songwriting contests and the National Bluegrass Band Championships. Non-musical events include a railroad spike driving contest and a recreation of an 1840s fur-trading village.

Old-Time Fiddlers' Contest, National
Third week in June

A major musical event in the United States, held for a full week in Weiser, Idaho, where fiddling was first heard in 1863. A way station was established that year at Weiser, and people traveling through in covered wagons stopped for rest and recreational fiddling. In 1914, the first fiddling contest was held, but interest petered out until 1953 when Blaine Stubblefield, a fiddle fan and member of the local Chamber of Commerce, initiated a fiddling competition. In 1963, in conjunction with Idaho's Centennial, the competition officially became the National Old-Time Fiddlers' Contest. Awards are given for the national champion in several categories; this is big-time fiddling, with contestants having won their spot through competitions in other states. Besides music, there are all-you-can-eat breakfasts, a parade, old-fashioned melodrama, street dancing, and sing-alongs; another attraction is the National Fiddlers' Hall of Fame here. Attendance is about 10,000.

Ole Time Fiddlers' and Bluegrass Festival
Memorial Day Weekend; last weekend in May

A festival for genuinely old-time fiddlers, held in Union Grove, N.C. The festival was organized in 1970 by Harper A. Van Hoy as a serious musical venture, and admission is limited to 5,000 people to attract those who want to hear what Van Hoy has called the "purest mountain music this side of the Mississippi."

A special contest category is for fiddlers who must meet these criteria: they are over fifty-five years old, have had no formal musical training, and have learned from fiddlers older than themselves. There are competitions for all the major instruments of traditional American music, including autoharp, banjo, fiddle, harmonica, and mandolin. Workshops are conducted for most of the instruments played in competition, as well as in shape-note singing, story-telling, clog dancing, and children's folk music. Additionally, there are arts and crafts and food.

Olympic Games
Every four years (1988, 1992 . . .)

The world's oldest sports spectacular, the first known Olympiad was held in 776 B.C. in Olympia, Greece. It is believed the festivals began before 1400 B.C. The modern games, held roughly every four years in different countries, were revived in 1896 by Baron Pierre de Coubertin of France. Those 1896 summer games took place in Athens, with thirteen nations sending about 300 male athletes to compete in forty-two events and ten different sports. Now about 160 nations send thousands of male and female athletes to the Summer Olympics, and hundreds of millions watch the events on television. Some winter sports were included in early years of the modern Olympics, but the Winter Games as a separate event didn't begin until 1924. Now about 1200 male and female athletes, representing some sixty nations take part in them.

In ancient Greece, four national religious festivals—the Olympic Games, the Pythian Games, the Nemean Games, and the Isthmian Games—were major events; the Olympic Games, honoring Zeus, were especially famous. Records tell of Olympic Games every four years from 776 B.C. to 217 A.D. when, with Greece under Roman domination, the games had lost their religious purpose and the athletes vied only for money. They were abolished by the Roman emperor Theodosius I. It is generally believed, however, that the festival consisted not only of sporting contests, but of the presentation of offerings to Zeus and other gods. At first, these were simple foot races; later the long jump, discus- and javelin-throwing, wrestling, boxing, *pancratium* (a ferocious combination of boxing and wrestling), and chariot racing were added. Poets and dramatists also presented works. The games opened with trumpet fanfares and closed with a banquet.

Modern Olympics comprise Summer Games, held in a large city, and Winter Games, held at a resort. Beginning in 1994, the games will still be on a four-year cycle, but two years apart: Winter Games in 1994 and 1998, Summer Games 1996 and 2000. There are twenty-three approved sports for the Summer Games and from fifteen to twenty-three may be included. The Winter Games consist of seven approved sports, all are included.

Today, the opening ceremonies highlight a parade of the athletes led by those from Greece, in honor of the original Games, followed by the athletes from the other nations, in alphabetical order according to the spelling in the country's language; the host country enters last.

After the Games are declared open, the dramatic lighting of the olympic flame occurs. A cross-country relay runner, carries a torch first lit in Olympia, and ignites the flame that burns for the fifteen–sixteen days of the games. Thousands of runners, representing each country between Greece and the host country, take part in the four-week torch relay. This is followed by a spectacular

production of fireworks, strobe lights, fly-overs, music, dance, and assorted entertainment.

The Winter Games of 1992, held in Albertville, France, were historic in their reflection of dramatic political changes. The Soviet Union had broken up in August, 1991, and athletes from five former Soviet republics competed as representatives of the Commonwealth of Independent States or United Team, and the Olympic flag, not that of the USSR, was raised for the winners.

The first- and second-place medals are both made of silver but the first place has a wash of gold; the third-place medal is bronze.

The Olympics are supposed to be nonpolitical but have been marked (and marred) by politics. In 1936, Adolf Hitler, who called blacks an inferior race, opened the Olympics in Berlin, Germany, as a propaganda show. It was thus a great triumph for humanity when Jesse Owens, a black man from Ohio State University, won four gold (first place) medals. He won the 100- and 200-meter dashes and the running broad jump, and was on the winning 400-meter relay team. Hitler ducked out of the stadium so he wouldn't have to congratulate Owens.

In 1972, the Games in Munich, Germany, were struck with horror: eleven Israeli athletes were killed by Arab terrorists.

The 1980 Games were opened in Moscow by Communist Party chairman Leonid I. Brezhnev, but athletes from the United States, Canada, West Germany, Japan and 50 other countries didn't particpate. Their countries boycotted the event in protest of the Soviet invasion of Afghanistan.

Prominent Olympics participants have included: Jim Thorpe, an American Indian and one of the greatest all-round athletes of all time, won gold medals for the decathlon and pentathlon in 1912. The following year, he was stripped of the medals when an investigation showed he had played semiprofessional baseball. He died in 1953, and the medals were restored to his family in 1982.

Paavo Nurmi, known as the "Flying Finn," won nine gold medals in long-distance running in three Olympics—in 1920, 1924, and 1928. On an extremely hot day at the Paris Summer Games in 1924, Nurmi set Olympic records in the 1,500-meter and 5,000-meter runs. Two days later he won the 10,000-meter cross-country race. In 1928, he set a record for the one-hour run, covering eleven miles and 1,648 yards. His 1924 wins were considered the greatest individual performance in the history of track and field.

The Norwegian skater Sonja Henie, won three gold medals—in 1928, 1932, and 1936. In 1924, at the age of eleven, she was the youngest Olympian contestant ever (she finished last that year). She thrilled crowds by incorporating balletic moves into what had been standard skating exercises.

Emil Zatopek, a Czech long-distance runner, who won three gold medals in 1952 and set Olympic records for the 5,000- and 10,000-meter races and for the marathon.

Jean-Claude Killy, known as "Le Superman" in his native France, won three gold medals in Alpine ski events at Grenoble, France, in 1968.

Mark Spitz, a swimmer from California, became the first athlete to win seven gold medals in a single Olympics (1972). He set world records in four individual men's events, and won the remaining medals in team events. These teams also set world records. Spitz, twenty-two at the time, was so popular for a while that his photo was a pinup poster.

Omak Stampede and Suicide Race
Second weekend in August

Three days of professional rodeo in Omak, Wash. What makes this different from other rodeos is the World Famous Suicide Race which has been featured on the television program, "Ripley's Believe It or Not." This is a terrifying hoof-thundering gallop by twenty mounted horses down an almost vertical hill, across the Okanogan River, and then into the rodeo arena. Four of these races are held, one after each rodeo performance.

The rodeos top off a week of activities which include Indian ceremonies, dances, and stick games, a type of gambling, at an Indian tepee village. (Much of the town of Omak is on the Colville Indian Reservation, the name Omak comes from the Indian word *omache*, meaning 'good medicine.') Other events are a Not Quite White Water Raft Race, a western art show, a grand parade, and a kiddies' parade, and dances. Attendance is 20,000 to 30,000.

Omisoka
December 31

New Year's Eve in Japan is observed by settling financial accounts (*kake*), eating a special noodle dish known as *okake*, which is hot soup over noodles, and taking a hot bath followed by a well-earned rest. Widely celebrated on December

31, Omisoka marks the end of the preparations for New Year's celebrations, which go on for the next three days. It is a popular time for visitors to drop in to exchange NEW YEAR's greetings over cups of hot *sake* and decorated *mochi* cakes.

The city of Ashikaga, fifty miles north of Tokyo, is the site of the 1200-year-old Saishoji temple, headquarters for the Akutare Matsuri, the 'naughty festival' or 'festival of abusive language'. On New Year's Eve there, participants walk (or take a bus) up a dark mountain road led by a man blowing a *horagai*, a shell that is supposed to fend off bad tidings. Some carry lanterns and wear cardboard hats bearing the picture of Bishamonten, one of the seven gods of fortune in Japanese Buddhism. The Saishoji temple was built in honor of this god.

The festival originated more than 200 years ago so repressed workers could let off steam; therefore this is not simply a midnight stroll. Those hiking toward the temple atop the 1000-foot-high hill scream curses into the night. They curse politicians, teachers, bad grades, low pay, and any other complaints of modern daily life in Japan. They release the pent-up frustrations with words they would never say directly to anyone. *Bakayaro* is the word most frequently heard. It means 'you idiot' or sometimes, 'goddamn it'.

After the forty-minute walk the crowd storms into the temple, the bell is rung, prayers are offered, and of course the cursing continues. But when the new year arrives at midnight the curses end and more typical celebration begins. Then the celebrants turn to another unique ceremony: when the priest calls the name of each worshipper, the individual kneels with a wide red lacquer bowl at his or her lips. Sake is then poured onto the person's forehead, runs across their face, into the bowl and is consumed. All this occurs while the priest reads the worshiper's personal wishes for the new year to the pounding of a taiko drum. This ceremony is supposed to ensure that happiness will flow in the new year.

See also OSHOGATSU.

Omizutori Matsuri (Water Drawing Festival)
March 1–14

Religious rites that have been observed for twelve centuries at the Buddhist Todaiji Temple in Nara (Akita Prefecture) in Japan. During this period of meditative rituals, the drone of recited sutras and the sound of blowing conchs echo from the temple. The high point comes on March 12, when young monks on the gallery of the temple brandish burning pine-branch torches, shaking off burning pieces. Spectators below try to catch the sparks, believing they have magic power against evil.

At 2 A.M. on March 13, the ceremony of drawing water is observed to the accompaniment of ancient music. Buckets are carried to a well, the first water of the year is drawn, and offered to the Buddha. Then the monks perform a final dramatic fire dance to the beating of drums.

For many Japanese, the Omizutori signals the start of spring.

Ommegang
First Thursday in July

A medieval pageant presented on the Gran' Place of Brussels, Belgium, and one of Belgium's most popular attractions. The pageant in its present form dates only from 1930, the year of the centenary of Belgium, but it is a reenactment of the Ommegang of 1549. And that Ommegang had gone back at least to 1359, when it was first recorded.

The word *ommegang* is from the Flemish words *om* 'around' and *gang* 'march', and was a word used for processions around monuments. The present Brussels Ommegang is linked to the story of Béatrice Soetkens.

The year was 1348. Béatrice, a poor but honest woman, was told by the Virgin Mary to go to Antwerp to get a miracle-making statue. Béatrice ordered her husband to start rowing his boat to take her to Antwerp, and there she was able to get the statue, despite the interference of the sexton. On the way back to Brussels, her husband, exhausted, had to stop rowing, but the drifting boat safely arrived in Brussels at a spot where archers practiced. A Church was built there, and every year the statue was carried around under the protection of the "Grand Serment," the Archery Guild.

That was the start of the Ommegang. At first wholly religious, in time profane elements were mingled. The royal princes were admirers of the Ommegang, and details of the 1549 Ommegang are known through the works of Juan Christobal Calvete de Estrelle, the chronicler of Philippe II, son of Charles V. The 1549 Ommegang was dedicated to Charles.

The Ommegang disappeared after 1810, but has been the same since its 1930 revival. It is preceded by strolling musicians, followed by a parade of people representing the magistrate and various city officials; the court of Marie of Hungary, with pages, ladies-in-waiting, and a hunting group of dogs and falcons; and the Court of Charles V, with mounted knights bearing banners. Many of those representing the court figures are descendants of the original noble families.

Then the actual procession takes place led by the Knight of Peace and the Theban trumpets. Participants include trade groups with floats, archers and crossbowmen, and stilt walkers and groups of dancers and Gilles (clowns) dancing around symbolic animals: the horse Bayard and the four sons of Aymon surrounded by eagles, a pelican, unicorn, dragon, lion, and serpent.

See also GIANTS, FESTIVAL OF THE, BELGIUM.

Onam
August–September

A harvest festival and a celebration of ancient King Mahabalia in the state of Kerala in India. This is Kerala's biggest festival, lasting ten days, and featuring dancing, feasting, and displays of elaborately designed carpets of flowers. It's famous for the races of so-called snake boats held at Champakulan, Aranmula, and Kottayam. The boats are designed in all shapes—with beaks or kite tails—and have crews of up to 100 men who row to the rhythm of drums and cymbals.

The festival honors King Mahabalia, who was sent into exile in the nether world when gods grew jealous of him. He's allowed to return to his people once a year, and the boat races, cleaned homes, carpets of flowers, clapping dances by girls, and other events are the welcome for him.

Onion Market *See* Zibelemarit

Onwasato Festival
August

Observed by the Ibo people of Nigeria, the Onwasato Festival marks the beginning of the harvest season and is celebrated by feasting on the new crops, particularly yams. The highlight of the festival is the thanksgiving ritual in which the senior member of each family kills a fowl in the Obu (the father's sitting-house), sprinkles the blood on the Okpensi (the family symbol), and gives thanks to the family's ancestors. The feathers are then removed and scattered on the threshold of the compound—a sign that the people have forsaken all evil for the coming season. Of all the many fowl that are killed, one is roasted and set aside, while the others are used for the first day's feasting. On the second day of the festival, all the members of the extended family meet in the senior member's Obu and share the fowl that has been set aside in a ritual known as the 'handing round of fowl' or *Inya Okuku*.

Opening of Parliament *See* **State Opening of Parliament**

Open Marathon, International
Mid–October
A modern-day marathon run by men and women athletes of all ages. The race retraces the course of the Greek soldier Pheidippides who ran from the battlefield at Marathon to Athens to bring news of the Athenian victory over the Persians, a distance of about twenty-five miles. The starting line today is in the village of Marathon and the finish line is at the Olympic Stadium in the heart of Athens.

A mound in Marathon marks the grave of 192 Athenian soldiers killed in the 490 B.C. victory.

Orange Bowl Game
January 1
One of the older post-season college football games, first played in 1935, in which the champion of the Big-Eight Conference meets another nationally ranked team at the 74,224-seat stadium in Miami, Florida. The game is preceded by a New Year's Eve King Orange Jamboree Parade along Biscayne Boulevard. A parade more on the satirical side is the King Mango Strut held each year near Jan. 1 in Coconut Grove, Florida.

Orange Day (Orangemen's Day)
July 12
Sometimes referred to simply as **The Twelfth** or **The Glorious Twelfth**, this is the anniversary of the Battle of Boyne, which took place in Ireland on July 1, 1690, when the old Julian calendar was still in use. Ireland was under English rule at the time, and the trouble began when James II, who was Roman Catholic, was deposed in 1668 and his throne was given to William of Orange, a Protestant. Each side raised an army of about 30,000 men, and the two clashed on the banks of the Boyne River. The Protestants won a decisive victory, but that was hardly the end of the conflict. The Catholics formed underground societies designed to restore the line of James, and the Protestants countered by forming the Orange Order, committed to maintaining the link with Protestant England. As Irishmen left Ireland and England for the New World, lodges of Orangemen were

formed in Canada and the United States, where Orange Day is still observed by Protestant Irish.

Orthodox Epiphany
January 6
The celebration by the Orthodox Christian Churches of the baptism of Jesus in the River Jordan and the manifestation of his divinity when a dove descended on him. For Orthodox Christians around the world it is called **Blessing of the Waters Day**. In honor of the baptism of Christ, the church's baptismal water is blessed, and small bottles of the holy water are given to parishioners to take home. In many American cities, the priest leads the congregation to a local river which he blesses. Many places throughout the world mark the day with a blessing of the waters and immersion of a cross in seas, lakes, and rivers. At the port of Piraeus, Greece, the local priest throws a cross into the sea, and the diver who retrieves it is thought to be blessed with good luck in the coming year.

In pre-revolutionary Russia, priests and church officials led a procession to the banks of streams or rivers, breaking the ice and lowering a crucifix into the water. Those brave enough to jump into the icy waters to recover the crucifix were thought to be especially blessed. In the north, diving for the cross is frequently done on September 14 (See EXALTATION OF THE CROSS), when the water is warmer.

The holy day of the Epiphany is celebrated in colorful fashion in Tarpon Springs, Fla., at one time a sea sponge center with the largest sponge market in the world. The community has a strong Greek influence, going back to the beginning of the twentieth century when sponge divers from Greece came here to take part in the growing sponge industry. On Epiphany, up to 100 young men from Greek Orthodox churches compete in diving for a gold cross. The cross has been tossed in the bayou by the chief celebrant from the town's St. Nicholas Greek Orthodox Church, and the person who retrieves it will be specially blessed.

Events of this holiday begin the day before with a blessing of the sponge fleet. The next morning, after Mass and a blessing of the waters, there is a parade of school and civic groups led by ecclesiastical dignitaries in their vestments. Many of the paraders wear Greek costume. After the parade, when the cross has been retrieved, the day becomes festive, with bouzouki music, dancing, and feasting, especially on roast lamb. Epiphany has been observed in this manner at Tarpon Springs since 1904, and now attracts about 30,000 people.

In Greece, Epiphany is one of the country's most important church days, especially in the port towns where diving for the cross takes place. After mass, on the eve of Epiphany in Cyprus, priests visit houses to cleanse them from demons known as *Kalikandjiari*. According to Cypriot tradition, these evil spirits appear on earth at Christmas, and for the next twelve days play evil tricks on people. On the eve of their departure, people appease them by throwing pancakes and sausages onto their roofs, which is where the demons dwell.

Oshogatsu (New Year's Day)
January 1

This is the "festival of festivals" in Japan, actually celebrated for several days. Government offices, banks, museums and most businesses are closed from NEW YEAR'S DAY, a national holiday, through Jan 3.

From the middle of December, streets are decorated with pine and plum branches, bamboo stalks, and ropes festooned with paper. Traditional home decorations are small pine trees with bamboo stems attached, which are placed on either side of the front entrance to represent longevity and constancy. For weeks before New Year's, people clean house and purchase new clothes for the children; this is also a time for exchanging gifts, sending greeting cards, and paying off personal debts.

On NEW YEAR'S EVE, people wearing kimonos fill the streets as they go to visit shrines. But many more—an estimated seventy million people in 1991—watch the "Red and White Song Contest" on the Japanese publicly owned television station. This marathon song festival, first organized in 1950, has become an indispensable ritual of the New Year. The show, lasting up to 4-1/2 hours, had fifty-six performers in 1991, including an orchestra playing Mozart, a group singing Okinawan folk music, and a female singer in a gown of feathers that made her look like a bird; as she finished her song she flapped her arms and flew away, suspended by a wire. Each performer is a member of a team. The Red team is women, the White team men. When the performances are over, the audience and a panel of judges decide which team won.

The TV show ends shortly before midnight in time for an older tradition: the tolling of the great bells in Buddhist temples at midnight. Priests strike the bells 108 times, a reminder of the 108

human frailties or sins in Buddhist belief. By the end of the 108 strokes of the bell, the impure desires of the old year have been driven away.

An ancient folk ritual of a very different sort is observed on the Oga Peninsula, Akita Prefecture, on New Year's Eve. Young men play the part of hairy devils called *Namahage*, dressing in grotesque red and blue masks and straw cloaks. They stomp through the streets shouting, "Any wicked people about?" and then pound on people's doorways, the idea being to frighten children and newly-married women so that they won't be lazy. After being admitted to a home, they sit down for rice cakes, first scaring the wits out of children with stories of what will happen to them if they are naughty.

On New Year's Day, it's traditional to pray at the household altar and to eat special foods, for example, steamed rice that has been pounded into small round, gooey cakes called *mochi*. Herring roe is eaten for fertility, black beans for health, dried chestnuts for success, and porgy and prawns are omens of happiness.

Business resumes on Jan. 4, and the holiday period is over on Jan. 7 when decorations come down as part of the festival of Nanakusa.

See also LUNAR NEW YEAR.

Our Lady Aparecida, Festival of
May 11

Brazil's patron saint, the Virgin Mary *Aparecida* 'she who has appeared' , is honored with a ten-day festival in the city near Sao Paulo that bears her name. Legend has it that after a poor day's catch, fishermen cast their nets into the Paraiba do Sul River and pulled up a small statue of the Virgin Mary, carved out of black wood. When they cast their nets again, they came up full of fish. This was the first miracle attributed to the saint, and the city of Aparecida with its beautiful church built to house the statue is now the destination of many pilgrimages.

Our Lady of Carmel, feast of
July 16

Our Lady of Carmel, (the Madonna del Carmine) is the patroness of the city of Naples. Her festival is celebrated with dancing, singing, and magnificent firework displays. Brightly decorated wax replicas of human body parts used to be sold at booths near the church, and people suffering from various physical ailments appealed to the Madonna to restore their health by offering her these replicas of the diseased portions of their bodies.

Her feast is also observed by Italian-Americans in the United States. In New York City, novenas, anointing of the sick, processions, and special Masses are held at the Church of Our Lady of Mount Carmel beginning on July 4 and ending with High Mass and a procession on the sixteenth. The Italian section of New York City around 115 St. is decorated with green, red, and white lights during the festival, and people can buy sweets, fruits, strings of chestnuts, and all kinds of food every night during this time.

Our Lady of Fatima Day
July 13

This Portuguese holiday commemorates the appearance of the Virgin Mary to three children aged from ten to thirteen from the village of Fatima in 1917. The first appearance to the dos Santos children—Lucia, and her cousins Jacinto, and Francisca—took place on May 13, 1917, when they heard the sound of thunder and "a young girl" appeared to them from the top of a nearby tree. No one really took their story seriously, however, until the same thing began to occur on the thirteenth of every month. Each time the children went to see the Virgin, they were accompanied by an increasingly large crowd of adults. She appeared to them for the last time on October 13, in the presence of about seventy thousand onlookers, when she revealed she was Our Lady of the Rosary. She told them to recite the rosary daily, and asked that a church be built for her.

Eventually the cult of Our Lady of Fatima spread, a basilica was built, and pilgrimages to the isolated shrine became common. Two great pilgrimages take place each year on May 13 and October 13, with smaller groups making their way to Fatima around the thirteenth day of each month in-between. July 13 is considered Our Lady of Fatima Day because it was two months after the Virgin's first appearance that a large number of adults witnessed the same miracle: the sun seemed to dance, tremble, and finally fall. It took twenty years for the event to be investigated, authenticated, and the cult granted acceptance by the Pope.

Our Lady of Guadalupe, Fiesta of
December 12

Nuestra Señora de Guadalupe is the patron saint of Mexico, and on December 12 thousands of pilgrims flock to her shrine at the famous Church of Guadalupe outside Mexico City. This great religious festival commemorates the appearance of the Virgin Mary on Tepeyac hill just north of present-day Mexico City. According to legend, she identified herself to an Indian convert named Juan Diego in the early morning of December 9, 1531, and told him to tell the bishop to build her a shrine there. When the bishop refused to believe the story, the Virgin filled Diego's homespun blanket with Castillian roses, which did not normally grow in Mexico, as proof of his vision. When Juan opened the blanket to show the bishop the roses, they had vanished. In their place was an image of Mary on the blanket. It soon adorned the newly built shrine and has hung there for four centuries without any apparent deterioration or fading of colors.

The story of Juan Diego and the Virgin is reenacted in a puppet show each year, and relics of Our Lady of Guadalupe are sold in the streets. It is said that only the French shrine at Lourdes and the one at Fatima attract as many pilgrims.

She is the patron saint of Peruvian students, and of all of Central and South America. In El Salvador, it is called *Día del Indio* ('Day of the Indian').

Our Lady of Nazaré Festival
September 8–18

Nazaré has been called "the most picturesque town in Portugal," and thousands of tourists flock here every summer to paint, film, and photograph the quaint fishing village. The Church of Our Lady of Nazareth was built near the place where the Virgin Mary saved the life of Fuas Roupinho, who was pursuing a white deer when a sudden sea mist arose and caused him to lose his bearings. The Virgin halted his horse in its tracks—a hoof-print is still visible—and, as the mist cleared, Roupinho discovered that he was on the brink of a cliff, three hundred feet above the ocean. Today the town is built on two levels, the lower one extending along the beach. A pilgrimage chapel overlooks the town from the upper level.

The name *Nazaré* comes from a statue of the Virgin brought back here from Nazareth, the childhood home of Jesus, by a monk in the fourth century. The annual ten-day festival that takes place in the town's main square begins on September 8, the anniversary of the miracle, and includes bullfights, musical concerts, and folk dancing. Some of the best and most dangerous fishing in all of Portugal goes on here. Fishermen have to negotiate a treacherous barrier reef with a difficult swell that often capsizes entire boats with their crews. Therefore, the Nazaré fishermen, who carry the Virgin's statue on their shoulders in three festive processions, are the focus of the event.

Our Lady of Sorrows Festival

Friday, Saturday, and Sunday closest to August 20

The pilgrimage to the church of Our Lady of Sorrows or Nossa Senhora da Agonia in Viana do Castelo, Portugal, is one of the country's most colorful religious festivals. Sometimes called the **Pardon of Our Lady of Sorrows**, it includes a procession in which the image of Our Lady is carried over carpets of flowers. Participants also enjoy fireworks on the River Lima, a parade of carnival giants and dwarfs, bull-running through the barricaded streets, and regional singing and folk dancing.

Our Lady of Victories Day *See* Victory Day

Oxi Day

October 28

A national holiday in Greece to commemorate the Greeks saying *"oxi"* (Greek for *no*, pronounced "O-hee," with guttural h-sound) in 1940 to Italy's attempted incursion ordered by their Fascist dictator, Benito Mussolini. The day is observed with military and school parades.

On the morning of Oct. 28 in 1940, the Italian ambassador to Greece called on Gen. Ioannis Metaxas, the self-appointed prime minister, to demand that Italian troops be allowed to occupy certain strategic areas in Greece. Metaxas curtly responded, "Oxi." The Italians invaded, but were routed by the Greeks.

Ozark Folk Festival

First week in November

An off-the-beaten-track affair in Eureka Springs, Ark., first held in 1948 to preserve the music and folklore of the Ozarks. For two or three days, musicians, mostly nonprofessional, gather to play mountain music on fiddles, banjos, jackass jawbones, harmonicas, dulcimers, and other non-electrified instruments. Only traditional Ozark music is allowed, and that means it must be at least seventy years old. Some of the music dates back to Elizabethan times. Also on the menu are performances by jig, clog, and square-dance groups, crafts displays, a Gay Nineties costume parade, and a Festival Queen contest.

Eureka Springs, about fifty miles north of Fayetteville, is the oldest health spa in the Ozarks, and the winding streets and houses are much the same as they were in the 1880s.

P

Padi Harvest Festival
May 30–31

A festival and public holiday in Labuan Territory and the state of Sabah in Malaysia. The festival is celebrated by the Kadazan people (also known as Dusun), the largest indigenous ethnic group in Sabah, which lies on the northern tip of Borneo. Originally headhunters, they were the first native group in Borneo to use the plow. Irrigated (not flooded) rice is their principal crop, and the harvest is a ritual dedicated to the *Bambaazon*, or rice spirit. If the harvest has been good, this is a thanksgiving, and if it has been poor, the ritual is an appeasement of the spirit. The Kadazans are animists or shamanists, believing that spirits reside in natural objects, and the rituals are conducted by shamanist priestesses. Besides the solemn aspects of the festival, there is much merrymaking and free flowing of rice wine.

Padstow Hobby Horse Parade *See* Minehead Hobby Horse Parade

Palio, Festival of the
July 2, August 16

The **Palio of the Contrade** is a horse race that has been held in Siena, Italy, twice a year since the thirteenth century. Each of Siena's seventeen *contrade* 'ward organizations,' which now are social clubs but in the Middle Ages were rival military companies, hires a professional jockey and selects his attendants. Each *contrade* also has its own animal symbol, flag, color, museum, church, and motto. In medieval costume and with banners flying, the riders form a procession which carries the *Palio,* or silk standard painted with an image of the Virgin Mary, through the city streets.

The race itself is run in the city's main square, the Piazza del Campo. There is intense rivalry, distrust, cheating, fixing, bribery, and frequent fights. The jockeys ride bareback, each holding a whip which he can use on his opponents' horses as well as on his own. Riders for the finalist *contrade*

race three times around the Piazza, and the winning *contrada* receives the *Palio* to hang on its church until the next festival. Revelry and merrymaking continue until dawn, and the winning jockey is honored with a victory dinner.

The second big race, held on August 16, is known as Madonna del Voto Day in honor of the Virgin Mary.

Palio of the Goose and River Festival
June 28–29

In the Middle Ages the Leap of the Goose was a test of swimming skill for the local boatmen in Pavia, Italy. Now it is a combined rowing and swimming relay race held the end of June each year. Competitors leap from a raft at the end of the race and try to reach a goose suspended in air. Geese apparently played an important part in the city's history, acting as sentries when Pavia was besieged by the Gauls. In the procession through the streets of Pavia that precedes the competition, live geese are carried in cages.

There is also a Tournament of the Towers in which teams of six men from each of the city's nine wards try to knock down each other's wooden towers in a mock battle. A final battle involves the Beccaria Tower, which can only be approached by gangplanks. The winners set the tower on fire.

Palm Sunday
Between March 15 and April 18 in the West; between March 28 and May 1 in the East; the Sunday preceding Easter

During the Jewish PASSOVER celebration Jesus rode into Jerusalem and was given a heroes' welcome by the people, who had heard of his miracles and regarded him as the leader who would deliver them from the domination of the Roman Empire. They carried palm branches, a traditional symbol of victory, and spread them in the streets before him, shouting "Hosanna, glory to God" (John 12:12,13). Palms are still used in church services on this day, which is the beginning of Holy Week, and Jesus' triumphal entry into Jerusalem is often re-enacted with a procession—the most impressive being the one in Rome, where the Pope, carried in St. Peter's chair, blesses the palms.

At the end of the service, the palms are distributed to the congregation. In some countries, where palms are not available, branches of other trees-particularly pussy willow, olive, box, yew, and spruce-are used. They are later hung up in houses for good luck, buried to preserve crops, or used to decorate graves. Other names for this day include **Passion Sunday**, **Fig Sunday**, **Willow Sunday**, **Branch Sunday**, **Blossom Sunday**, and **Rameaux** in France.

Pan American Day
April 14

April 14, 1890 is the day on which the First International Conference of American States adopted a resolution forming what is now known as the Organization of American States (OAS). The member countries include Argentina, Bolivia, Brazil, Chile, Colombia, Costa Rica, Cuba, the Dominican Republic, Ecuador, El Salvador, Guatemala, Haiti, Honduras, Mexico, Nicaragua, Panama, Paraguay, Peru, the United States, Uruguay, and Venezuela. The purpose of the OAS, which has remained basically unchanged since that time, is to strengthen peace and security in the Western Hemisphere by promoting understanding among the various countries of North, Central, and South America. The International Union of American Republics (now called the Pan American Union)—the central permanent agency and general secretariat of the OAS—designated April 14 as Pan American Day in 1930, and it was first observed the following year.

Although each member country holds its own celebration, it is at the Pan American Union building in Washington, D.C. that one of the largest observances takes place. Students from all over the Western Hemisphere travel to Washington where, against a backdrop of flags in the courtyard of the House of the Americas, they perform a program of folk songs and dances. Ceremonies are also held in Miami and in other cities with large populations from Latin American countries.

Panathenaea
July, August

The most important of the ancient Greek festivals, celebrated in Athens in honor of Athena, the patron goddess of that city. The lesser festival was held every year, and the Great Panathenaea every fifth year with much greater pomp. The date was the twenty-eighth Hecatombaeon (July or August), considered Athena's birthday.

In the yearly celebrations, there were musical and athletic contests, animal sacrifices, and a procession. The procession of the Great Panathenaea was an especially grand affair and is pictured on a frieze of the Parthenon. The *peplus*, a garment with an embroidered depiction of the battle of the gods and the giants, was rigged like a sail on a ship with wheels and carried through the city to the Acropolis. The procession included priests leading a train of animals that would be sacrifices, maidens carrying sacrificial implements, warriors, old men with olive branches, and horses. The festival ended with the sacrifice of oxen and a banquet.

Pancake Day
Between February 3 and March 9; Shrove Tuesday

For the people of Olney, England and Liberal, Kansas, Pancake Day is more than another name for Shrove Tuesday. The old custom of making pancakes on the Tuesday preceding Ash Wednesday has survived in the form of a Pancake Race. Ladies of both towns run a 415-yard course, flipping pancakes as they go. Participants must wear a skirt, an apron, and a headscarf, and must toss their pancakes in the air three times as they run. The winner of the Kansas race is announced by a transatlantic phone call to Olney immediately after it is over.

The Olney race dates back to 1445. According to the legend, a housewife who was making pancakes heard the bell summoning her to church and was in such a hurry that she ran along the road with the frying pan still in her hand. The Liberal, Kansas race has been run since 1950. It only lasts about a minute, but it draws a good deal of media attention and is followed by pancake eating contests, a parade, and children's races.

Panchadaan
August–September; third day, waning half of Bhadrapada; July–August; eighth day, waxing half of Sravana

The **Alms Giving festival** in Nepal is based on the ancient Buddhist text, the Dangatha chapter of Kapidawdan, stating that those who donate food and clothing to beggars on this day will be blessed with seven great gifts: health, happiness, longevity, wisdom, wealth, fame, and children. All Buddhists, rich or poor, go from door to door in

244

large groups begging for alms. They are usually well-received in Nepalese homes—even non-Buddhist people give food or money to the Buddhist beggars on this day.

In Patan and elsewhere in Nepal, Panchadaan is observed on the eighth day of the waxing half of Sravana. In Katmandu and Bhadgaon, it is observed on the third day of the waning half of Bhadrapada.

Pardon of Nossa Senhora dos Remédios
Early September

Both religious and secular activities play a part in the pilgrimage to the **Sanctuary of Our Lady of the Remedies** in Lamego, Portugal, a small town known for its port wine and smoked ham. Great numbers of pilgrims climb the monumental staircase up to the Baroque church, but the highlight of the festival is the Triumphal Procession on the last day, in which thousands of country people in local costume participate. There is also a battle of flowers, a folklore festival, fireworks, sports contests, and handicraft exhibitions.

Pardon of Ste. Anne D'Auray
Last weekend in July

In the seventeenth century in Brittany, St. Anne, mother of the Virgin Mary, appeared to a peasant named Yves (or Yvon) and told him that she wanted to see her ruined chapel rebuilt. Yves reported this to his bishop, who at first refused to believe him, but eventually changed his mind. Soon afterward, a broken image of St. Anne was found in a field nearby, and people started making contributions so that the effigy could be enshrined. A church was built in Auray and soon it became a place of pilgrimage for believers all over France.

The **Pardon of St. Anne** remains one of Brittany's most picturesque festivals. On their knees, twenty thousand devout Roman Catholics mount the *Scala Santa* or sacred stairway leading to the chapel containing St. Anne's statue. Many Bretons attending the festival wear the ornate headdresses and embroidered costumes for which their province is famous. They come to pay homage to St. Anne and pray she will grant their requests.

Parentalia
February 13

This was an ancient Roman festival held in honor of the *Manes* or souls of the dead—in particular, deceased relatives. It was a quiet, serious

occasion, without the rowdiness that characterized other Roman festivals. Everything, including the temples, closed down for a week, and people decorated graves with flowers and left food—sometimes elaborate banquets—in the cemeteries in the belief that it would be eaten by the spirits of the deceased. The last day of the festival, known as the **Feast of Peace and Love**, was devoted to forgiveness and the restoration of friendships broken during the preceding year.

Paris Air and Space Show
June, odd-numbered years in

The biennial **Salon Internationale de l'Aéronautique et de l'Espace** is held at Le Bourget Airport just outside of Paris-the airfield where Charles Linbergh landed after his historic nonstop flight from New York in 1927. It attracts more than half a million visitors who come to see exhibits of aircraft, launching and ground equipment, missile propulsion units, navigational aids, anti-aircraft detection devices, and other aeronautic equipment.

On the last day of the eleven-day event there is a special flying demonstration which has occasionally been marred by spectacular crashes. In 1989, for example, a Soviet MiG-29 flying only 580 feet above the ground in a maneuver designed to display its slow-speed handling suddenly plummeted earthward, burying its needle-shaped nose eight feet into the rain-softened turf before bursting into flames. The pilot was fortunate enough to have ejected in time and sustained only minor injuries.

The thirty-ninth biennial Paris Air Show was held in 1991, just a few months after the Persian Gulf War and a worldwide recession had threatened to scuttle the event. But the role played by high technology aircraft in the Allied victory over Saddam Hussein attracted a record number of exhibitors—approximately 1700 from thirty-eight countries—and spectators.

Paro Tshechu
Early spring on a date set by the lamas

One of the most popular festivals of Bhutan, a principality northeast of India in the Himalayas, is held in the town of Paro. (*Tshechus* means 'tenth day' and relates to the birth of the Buddha. It is used as 'festival' is used in English.)

The Paro festival is held over five days to commemorate the life and deeds of Padmasambhava. Known in Bhutan as Guru Rinpoche, he was a mystic who brought Buddhism to Bhutan from Tibet. The purpose of this festival is to exorcise evil influences and to ensure good fortune in the coming year. The highlight of Paro events comes before dawn on the last day when a huge appliqued scroll known as the *Thongdrel* is unfurled from the top of the wall of the *Dzong* (the monastery and district center). It is displayed to onlookers in the courtyard until just before the first rays of the sun touch it. The Thongdrel is said to have the power to confer blessings and provide surcease from the cycle of existence. It is a type of *thangka* (a religious scroll of any size), and is so big that it covers the three-story wall of the Dzong, and it depicts the life of the Guru Rinpoche, his various peaceful manifestations, and his consorts.

Dressed in their best clothes, people bring dried yak meat and *churra*, a puffed rice dish to the Dzong and watch masked dancers. A series of dances, called *cham*, are performed for the festival. One of these, the Black Hat Dance, tells of the victory over a Tibetan king who tried to wipe out Buddhism; those who watch the dance are supposed to receive great spiritual blessings. The Dance of the Four Stags commemorates the vanquishing of the god of the wind by Guru Rinpoche. The god rode on a stag, and the guru commandeered the stag as his own mount. Another dance, the Deer Dance, tells the story of Guru Rinpoche, teaching Buddhism while traveling through the country on the back of a deer. The dances are performed by monks who play the roles of deities, heroes, and animals dressed in brilliantly colored silks and brocades. They wear carved wooden or papier mâché masks symbolizing the figure they portray.

The dances are accompanied by the music of drums, bells, gongs, conch-shell trumpets, and horns. Some horns are so long that they touch the ground.

Other activities include folk dancing and singing and lewd performances by clowns called *atsaras*. Many of the dances and performances are typical of Tibetan Buddhist traditions also observed in Tibet and the Ladakh area of India.

Partita a Scácchi Viventi, La *See* **Living Chess Game**

Partridge Day
September 1

This is traditionally the day on which the partridge hunting season opens in England. Just as Grouse Day in Scotland (see THE GLORIOUS TWELFTH) was often referred to as St. Grouse's

Day, Partridge Day was sometimes called **St. Partridge's Day**.

Paryushana
August–September; Bhadon in the Hindu calendar

Like most other Jaina festivals, the Paryushana festival is observed by focusing on the ten cardinal virtues: forgiveness, charity, simplicity, contentment, truthfulness, self-restraint, fasting, detachment, humility, and continence. Believers ask those whom they may have offended to forgive them, and friendships that have lapsed during the year are restored.

The Paryushana festival is observed all over India in the month of Bhadrapada (August–September), but on different dates. The Svetambara Jainas observe it for eight days, and then the ten-day celebration of the Digambara Jainas begins.

Pasch Monday *See* **Easter Monday**

Pascua Florida Day
On or near April 2

Although no one knows for certain the date on which Ponce de León discovered Florida in 1513, it is widely believed that he first stepped ashore somewhere between St. Augustine and the mouth of the St. Johns River on April 2. He named the newly discovered land Pascua Florida because it was Eastertime. *Pascua* is a Spanish word meaning 'Easter,' and *Florida* means 'flowering' or 'full of flowers.' In Scotland and Northern England, another name for EASTER was Pasch Day; among Orthodox Christians it is called Pascha.

The Florida state legislature designated April 2 **Florida State Day** in 1953, but when it falls on a Saturday or Sunday, the holiday is observed on the preceding Friday or the following Monday. The week ending on April 2 is known as Pascua Florida Week, a time when both school children and adults are encouraged to attend special programs devoted to the area's discovery and history.

Passion Saturday *See* **Holy Saturday**

Passover
Begins between March 27 and April 24; 15–21 (or 22) Nisan

Also known as **Pesach** or the **Feast of Unleavened Bread**, Passover is an eight-day celebration (seven days in Israel and by Reform Jews) of the deliverance of the Jews from slavery in Egypt. It is one of the three pilgrim festivals (see also SHAVUOT and SUKKOT.) According to the book of Exodus, when Pharaoh refused to let Moses lead the Jews out of Egypt, God sent a number of plagues—including locusts, fire, and hailstones—but Pharaoh still was unmoved. A tenth and final plague, during which the Angel of Death was sent to kill the Egyptians' first-born sons, finally persuaded Pharaoh to relent. All the Jews had been instructed to sacrifice a lamb and sprinkle the blood on their doorposts so that the Angel would "pass over" and spare their sons.

Jewish families today eat a ceremonial dinner called the *seder* at which they retell the story of the Exodus from Egypt and eat various symbolic foods—including meat of the paschal lamb, bitter herbs (recalling the harsh life of slavery) and wine (symbolizing the fruitfulness of the earth). The *matzoh*, a flat, unleavened bread, is meant to symbolize the haste with which the Jews left: they didn't have time to let their bread rise before baking it. In strictly religious Jewish homes today, all foods made with leavening are prohibited during this season.

See also HAGODOL; FAST OF THE FIRST-BORN.

Patrickmas *See* St. Patrick's Day

Patriots' Day
Third Monday in April

The battles of Lexington and Concord, Massachusetts, marked the beginning of the American Revolution on April 19, 1775. This is a legal holiday in Massachusetts and Maine. Although no one really knows who fired the first shot on the Lexington green—"the shot heard 'round the world" in the words of Ralph Waldo Emerson—the British proceeded from Lexington to Concord, where there was a second bloody confrontation at North Bridge.

Residents of Maine and Massachusetts have observed Patriots' Day since the eighteenth century with costume parades, flag-raising ceremonies, and reenactments of the battles and the famous rides of Paul Revere and William Dawes, who were sent to warn their comrades in Concord of the British troops' approach. The BOSTON MARATHON, one of the most famous of the world's marathon races, is run each year on Patriot's Day from Hopkinton, Massachusetts, to the Back Bay section of Boston. Sometimes this day is referred to as **Lexington Day** or **Battles of Lexington and Concord Day.**

Paul Bunyan Show
First full weekend in October

Paul Bunyan is the mythical hero of lumberjacks in the United States, and many tall tales have been passed down about his adventures with Babe the Blue Ox and Johnny Inkslinger. Among other things, these tales describe how he created Puget Sound and the Grand Canyon, and how his hotcake griddle was so large that it had to be greased by men using sides of bacon for skates. The first Bunyan stories were published in 1910, and within fifteen years he had become a national legend.

Since 1952 the **Paul Bunyan Festival,** sponsored jointly by the Ohio Forestry Association and Hocking College in Nelsonville (which grants an Associate Degree in Forestry) has focused on wood products and forestry conservation. It is the lumber industry's opportunity to familiarize visitors with the journey wood takes from the forest to finished products, and an opportunity for both professional and student lumberjacks to test their skills in chopping and sawing. Teams of draft horses compete in a log skidding contest—an operation that is performed today by heavy machines—and turn-of-the-century steam logging equipment is on display. Billed as the largest live forestry exposition in the East, the show gives visitors an opportunity to see both traditional and modern logging techniques in action.

Payment of Quit Rent
September 29

One of London's oldest and most unusual events, the annual payment of the Quit Rent takes place at the Royal Courts of Justice on MICHAELMAS DAY, September 29. The ceremony symbolizes the city of London's payment to the Crown for two parcels of land: the first, known as The Forge, is thought to have been the old tournament ground for the Knights of the Templars, who rented it in 1235 for an annual payment of horseshoes and nails. The second, a piece of land in Shropshire known as The Moors, came into the city's possession during the reign of Henry VIII and was rented from the Crown for an annual payment of a billhook and a hatchet.

During the first part of the ceremony, the City Solicitor counts out six huge horseshoes from Flemish war horses and sixty-one nails. He gives them to the Queen's Remembrancer, who keeps them in his office until the following year. During the second part, the City Solicitor demonstrates how sharp the blades of the billhook and hatchet are by cutting up a bundle of faggots or twigs.

These, too, are presented to the Queen's Remembrancer, who is dressed in his wig and ceremonial robes.

Payson Rodeo
Mid August

A rodeo and parade and general wild-west three-day weekend in the cowboy-and-cattle country of Payson, Ariz. The first Payson rodeo was held in 1885, and it's been held ever since with no interruptions, not even for war, making it the world's oldest continuous Professional Rodeo Cowboys Association rodeo. Events of the weekend include the parade with floats, dancers, and cowboys; country music, a chili cookout, and arts and crafts. Total attendance is usually about 30,000.

Peanut Festival, National
Mid–October

A two-week festival in Dothan, Ala., honoring the peanut, a multimillion-dollar crop in Alabama. A highlight is the Goober Parade, for which the streets are paved with peanuts by a giant cement mixer that moves along the line of march throwing out a ton of peanuts, while parade watchers scramble for them. It is said the parade attracts as many as 350,000 spectators. Other events include the selection of Peanut Farmer of the Year, a cooking contest of peanut dishes, crafts exhibits, fireworks, a beauty pageant, and a greased-pig contest, with the pigs coated with peanut oil, of course.

The festival began in 1938, was discontinued during World War II, and resumed in 1947. Revenues from the festival help the economy not only of Dothan but of neighboring areas of Florida and Georgia. Plains, Ga., the home of peanut farmer and former President Jimmy Carter, is just over the state border.

The peanut and its potential became nationally if not internationally known because of the work of George Washington Carver, who in 1896 became head of agricultural research at Tuskegee Institute in Tuskegee, Ala. His research program ultimately developed 300 derivative products from peanuts, including cheese, flour, inks, dyes, soap, and cosmetics. The research was crucial to the South's economy; the peanut crop freed farmers of their dependence on cotton, which depleted the soil and could be wiped out by boll weevils. When Carver arrived in Tuskegee, the peanut was not recognized as a crop; within the next fifty years, it became the South's second cash crop after cotton.

Pearl Harbor Day
December 7

The anniversary of the Japanese raid on Pearl Harbor in 1941, bringing the United States into World War II and widening the European war to the Pacific.

The bombing, which began at 7:55 A.M. Hawaiian time on a Sunday morning, lasted little more than an hour but devastated the American military base on the island of Oahu in the Hawaiian Islands. Nearly all the ships of the U.S. Pacific Fleet were anchored there side by side, and most were damaged or destroyed; half the bombers at the army's Hickam Field were destroyed. The battleship USS Arizona sank, and 1,177 sailors and marines went down with the ship, which became their tomb. In all, the attack claimed more than 3,000 casualties—2,403 killed and 1,178 wounded.

On the following day, President Franklin D. Roosevelt addressed a solemn Congress to ask for a declaration of war. His opening unforgettable words: "Yesterday, December 7, 1941—a date which will live in infamy—the United States of America was suddenly and deliberately attacked by naval and air forces of the Empire of Japan." War was declared immediately with only one opposing vote, that by Rep. Jeannette Rankin of Montana.

In the months that followed, the slogan "Remember Pearl Harbor" swept America, and radios repeatedly played the song of the same name with these lyrics:

"*Let's remember Pearl Harbor, as we go to
  meet the foe,*
"*Let's remember Pearl Harbor, as we did the
  Alamo.*
"*We will always remember, how they died for
  liberty,*
"*Let's remember Pearl Harbor, and go on to
  victory.*"

Many states proclaim a Pearl Harbor Remembrance Day, and each year, services are held on December 7 at the *Arizona* Memorial in Pearl Harbor. The marble memorial, built over the sunken USS *Arizona* and dedicated in 1962, was designed by architect Albert Preis, a resident of Honolulu who was an Austrian citizen in 1941 and was interned as an enemy alien.

In 1991, on the fiftieth anniversary of the attack, commemorations were held over several days in Hawaii.

The observations began on Dec. 4, designated

as Hawaii Remembrance Day. Ceremonies recalled the death of civilians in downtown Pearl Harbor. One of them was Nancy Masako Arakaki, a nine-year-old Japanese-American girl killed when anti-aircraft shells fell on her Japanese-language school.

On Dec. 5, Survivors Day, families of those present in Pearl Harbor in 1941 attended ceremonies at the Arizona Memorial. Franklin Van Valkenburgh, the commanding officer of the USS Arizona, was among those remembered; he posthumously won the Medal of Honor for his heroism aboard ship.

Dec. 6 was a Day of Reflection, intended to focus on the gains since the war rather than on the losses of the day.

On Pearl Harbor Day itself, President George H.W. Bush, who received the Distinguished Flying Cross for heroism as a Navy pilot in the Pacific during World War II, spoke at ceremonies beginning at 7:55 A.M. at the Arizona Memorial. Other dignitaries were all Americans, with no foreign representatives invited out of political prudence. Other events included a parade, a flyover by jet fighters, an outdoor concert by the Honolulu Symphony presenting the premiere of *Pearl Harbor Overture: Time of Remembrance* by John Duffy, and a wreath-laying service at the National Memorial Cemetery of the Pacific in the Punchbowl overlooking Honolulu. And finally, at sunset on Pearl Harbor Day, survivors and their families gathered at the Arizona Visitors Center for a final service to honor those who died aboard the battleship in 1941.

Pendleton Round-Up and Happy Canyon

Second full week in September

One of the best-known rodeos in the West, held since 1910 in the small ranch town of Pendleton, Ore. The home of internationally known saddle makers, Pendleton is also the heart of Oregon's wheat-producing region. The week-long round-up started as a celebration of the end of the wheat harvest. Happy Canyon was inaugurated four years later when two local men decided the entertainment at a local fair was of poor quality and too expensive. The Happy Canyon shows at first depicted historical episodes and evolved into the present-day Happy Canyon Pageant, a presentation by Northwest Indian tribes that features a tepee encampment and ceremonial dancing. Nowadays, each day of the rodeo begins with a cowboy

breakfast (ham, eggs, flapjacks) at Stillman Park and ends with the pageant.

In between, the rodeo features the standard competitions approved by the Professional Rodeo Cowboys Association—bronco riding, bareback riding, Brahma bull riding, steer wrestling, and calf and steer roping. Additionally, there are wild-horse and stagecoach races and wild-cow milking.

Penitents, Procession of the

Last Sunday in July

A religious procession in Veurne (Furnes), Belgium, in which penitents in coarse robes and hoods walk barefoot through town, many carrying heavy wooden crosses. The procession, to the sound of drumbeats, is interspersed with scenes depicting Biblical events. In some, costumed people dramatize Old and New Testament characters. In others there are carved wooden figures on platforms. At the end of the procession bishops parade carrying the Sacred Host, and as the Sacrament passes, spectators quietly kneel. After the procession is over there is a *kermess*, or fair, in the marketplace. The celebration traditionally draws large crowds.

Two legends account for the origins of the procession. One says that it dates back to 1099 when the Crusader, Count Robert II of Flanders, returned from Jerusalem with a fragment of the True Cross. The other traces it to 1644 when townsfolk carried crosses in a reenactment of the last walk of Jesus before his crucifixion. The procession was to seek intercession against the plague and an outbreak of war between the Spanish and French.

Pennsylvania Day

On or near October 24

The state of Pennsylvania was named for William Penn, who was born in London on October 24, 1644. As a young man he joined the Quakers, who were at that time considered a radical religious group, and eventually he used his inheritance from his father to establish a Quaker colony in the New World. He put a great deal of thought and planning into how his colony would be governed, and insisted that the colonists treat the Indians with respect. The colony thrived, its population growing from about a thousand in 1682 to more than twelve thousand seven years later.

Pennsylvanians have always held large celebrations on major anniversaries of Penn's birth, and in 1932 the governor proclaimed October 24 as **William Penn Commemoration Day,** or simply **Penn Day**. This day was also commemorated with a special pageant held in Jordans, Buckinghamshire, England, where Penn and his family are buried. Since that time celebrations have tended to be local rather than statewide. In recent decades, the week of October 24 has been celebrated as **Pennsylvania Week**.

Any observation using his name would undoubtedly have made William Penn turn over in his grave, as he was outspoken in his opposition to the practice of naming streets, cities, states, or anything else after people.

Pentecost
Between May 10 and June 13 in West; between May 24 and June 27 in East; seventh Sunday (fifty days) after Easter

As recorded in the New Testament in Acts 2, it was on the fiftieth day after Easter that the Apostles were praying together and the Holy Spirit descended on them in the form of tongues of fire. They received the "gift of tongues"—the ability to speak in other languages—and immediately began to preach about Jesus Christ to the Jews from all over the world who had flocked to Jerusalem for the Feast of SHAVUOT. (Pentecost, from the Greek word meaning 'fiftieth,' is also one of the names for the second of the three Jewish PILGRIM FESTIVALS.) Christian Pentecost thus became not only a commemoration of the Holy Spirit's visit but is the birth of the Christian church. Interestingly is was on roughly this same day, centuries earlier, that Moses received the Ten Commandments on Mt. Sinai and the Jewish religious community got its start.

The English call it **White Sunday**, or **Whitsunday**, after the white garments worn on Pentecost by the newly baptized. Although it is not certain when Pentecost began to be observed by Christians, it may have been as early as the first century. The period beginning with the Saturday before Whitsunday and ending the following Saturday is known as **Whitsuntide**, or in modern times simply as **Whitsun**.

Whitsunday has been linked to pagan spring rites, such as the English custom of morris dancing and the drinking of "Whitsun ale." In Scotland, Whitsunday was one of the QUARTER DAYS. In Estonia and Finland eggs are dyed as at Easter because their hens don't lay until this time. In Germany it is called **Pfingsten**, and pink and red peonies, called *Pfingstrosen* 'Whitsun roses' are the symbols along with birch trees. Some churches lower a carved dove into the congrega-

tion and call this "swinging the Holy Ghost." Cattle are decorated and an overdressed person is said to be "dressed like a Whitsun ox." A holdover pagan game is called 'hunting the green man' *'Laubmannchen'*—a young man dressed in leaves and moss hides and children hunt him.

See also PINKSTER DAY.

People Power Anniversary *See* Fiesta sa EDSA

Peppercorn Ceremony
Day near April 23

This ceremony has been a tradition on the island of Bermuda since 1816, when a lease to the State House in St. George (the seat of Bermuda's government from 1620–1815) was granted to the mayor, aldermen, and common council of St. George in trust by the members of the Masonic Lodge for the annual rent of one peppercorn. The date for the annual rent payment was originally December 27, the feast of ST. JOHN THE EVANGELIST, but it was changed to the **most** suitable day nearest April 23, ST. GEORGE'S DAY, in honor of the patron saint for whom the town is named.

On the day of the Peppercorn Ceremony, the governor of Bermuda arrives at the State House with great pomp in a horse-drawn carriage, is welcomed by the mayor of St. George, and receives a key to the State House for the purpose of holding a meeting of Her Majesty's Executive Council, which upholds the conditions of the lease. The rent of one peppercorn is delivered on a velvet pillow and members of the Executive Council proceed to the State House for their meeting.

The old State House building, with mortar made of turtle oil and lime, was constructed in 1619 and is believed to be the first stone building in Bermuda. Until the capital was moved to Hamilton in 1815, Parliament met there. Bermuda's Parliament is the third oldest in the world (after Iceland and England).

Perahera Procession *See* Esala Perahera

Perchtenlauf
January 6

The Perchtenlauf in Austria is usually held on EPIPHANY, but in some areas it is celebrated at a later date. The *Perchten* are old masks, usually of witches and fearsome animals, that have been handed down from generation to generation. People wearing the masks run through the village beating drums, ringing bells, singing, shouting, and making as much noise as possible to scare winter away—an ancient custom that can be traced back to pre-Christian times. Another tradition associated with the Perchtenlauf is the cracking of whips-again, an attempt to drive out winter.

Dancing also plays a part in the celebration. The *Perchtentanz* takes place when the procession of masked figures stops in the main square of the village and everyone begins to dance wildly, making even more noise than before. The Perchten dances of Imst and Thaur in Tyrol are particularly well known for their brightly colored old masks.

Percíngula, La *See* **Forgiveness, Feast of**

Pffiferdaj
First Sunday in September
A typical Alsatian festival of medieval origin, Pffiferdaj—also known as the **Day of the Strolling Fiddlers** or **Fiddlers' Festival**—is celebrated in the city of Ribeauvillé, France, an area widely known for its wines. In the Middle Ages the Ribeaupierre family started a musicians' union here, and every September the musicians of Alsace gathered to pay homage to the lord of Ribeaupierre by forming a procession to the church of Notre Dame du Dusenbach.

Today the custom continues. Wine flows freely from the fountain in front of the Town Hall and a procession of fiddlers and other musicians, often playing old instruments, makes its way through the town. Their costumes and floats recall life in the Middle Ages.

Phagwa
Full moon in March
The Hindu festival of Phagwa celebrates the VERNAL EQUINOX and the start of the HINDU NEW YEAR. In Trinidad and Tobago, a Carnival spirit has gradually pervaded the festivities, which now combine both secular and religious elements and are no longer confined to Hindus. The celebration includes bonfires (to symbolize the destruction of Holika, the evil sister of King Hiranya Kashipu) and Chowtal singing competitions, which mix religious and secular music and are heavily influenced by calypso. The spraying of *Abeer* powder, a red vegetable dye made into a bright fuchsia liquid, gives everyone's hair and skin a tie-dyed effect.

Band competitions, similar to those held at Carnival (see TRINIDAD AND TOBAGO CARNIVAL) are

held at several locations throughout the island. There are also reenactments of the legend of Holika, complete with oriental costumes, crowns, jewelry, and flowers.

Phra Buddha Bat Fair
March
An annual festival at the Phra Buddha Bat temple (the Shrine of the Holy Footprint), a hill temple near Saraburi, Thailand, where the Holy Footprint of the Buddha is enshrined. This is one of the most sacred places in Thailand, and pilgrims throng here during the festival to pay homage. The festival features performances of folk music and a handicraft bazaar.

Pickle Festival
Third weekend in August
The small town of Linwood, Michigan is a center for pickle growing and processing. Since 1977 it has hosted a three-day festival in honor of its native product. Because so many local residents grow their own cucumbers and develop their own pickling recipes, there is a pickle canning contest. Another popular event is the pickle eating contest. Competitors are timed to see how long it takes them to unwrap and eat a pickle. The first one who is able to whistle afterward wins.

Pied Piper Open Air Theater
Sundays, June through mid-September
A dramatization of the legend of the Pied Piper of Hameln, presented on an open-air stage in Hamelin (Hameln), Germany.

According to the legend, in 1284 Hamelin was infested with rats. A stranger appeared, wearing an outlandishly colored (pied) coat, and he promised to free the town of its plague of vermin if they would pay him a set sum of money. The town agreed, and the piper began playing his pipes, and all the rats and mice came out of the houses and gathered around the piper. He led them to the Weser River, walked into it, and they followed him and were drowned. But the citizens refused to pay the piper. He left, angry. On June 26, he returned, dressed as a hunter and wearing a red hat. He played his pipes, and this time children followed him. He led 130 children out of the town and to the Koppenberg hill where they disappeared—forever. Only two children remained behind. One was blind, and couldn't see where the children went, and one was dumb.

Research tends to discredit the legend. One theory is that the ratcatcher was Nicholas of Cologne, who led thousands of German children on the disastrous Children's Crusade in 1212. Another holds that the story stemmed from the arrival of a labor agent who lured many young men to Bohemia with the promise of good wages.

Fortunately, the people of Hamelin don't let research get in the way of a good story. Today, the children of Hamelin are the principal performers in the play, and their number is limited to 130 in keeping with the legend.

Robert Browning, the English poet who wrote the poem, "The Pied Piper of Hamelin," to amuse a sick child, described the vermin this way:
"Rats!
"They fought the dogs and killed the cats,
"And bit the babies in the cradles,
"And ate the cheeses out of the vats,
"And licked the soup from the cooks' own ladles . . . "

When the piper arrived and began to play, Browning wrote,
" . . . out of the houses the rats came tumbling.
"Great rats, small rats, lean rats, brawny rats,
"Brown rats, black rats, gray rats, tawny rats
. . .
"Brothers, sisters, husbands, wives—
"Followed the Piper for their lives."

And then when the piper led the children off to Koppenberg, a portal opened wide, the piper and the children entered, and—
"When all were in to the very last,
"The door in the mountain-side shut fast."

Pig festival
Various

For the Bundi people of Papua New Guinea, the pig festival is an event of enormous importance that encompasses dozens of social ceremonies and political events. Among other things, it is a time when tribe members must settle their debts. There are many behind-the-scenes discussions and debates involving money, as well as opportunities to trade and exchange goods. Marriage ceremonies, initiation ceremonies, bride-price payments, menstruation and courtship ceremonies also take place during the period of the Pig Festival. The *kanam*, a Bundi dance performance that depicts the life of the animals and birds that live in the forest, is frequently performed at pig festivals.

Pig's Face Feast
Sunday following September 14

A number of explanations have been offered for the custom of eating pig's face or pork-chap [*sic*] sandwiches on the Sunday following HOLY CROSS DAY (September 14) in the Cotswold village of Avening, England. One involves the love of Matilda, who later became the wife of William the Conqueror, for Brictric, Lord of Gloucester. When Brictric refused to reciprocate, Matilda married William and then, as Queen, ordered Brictric's imprisonment and, eventually, his death. She later repented and built a church at the place where Brictric had once ruled as lord of the manor. The church was completed on September 14, Holy Cross Day, and the Queen is said to have held a boar's head dedication feast. The wild boars were so delicious that the people of Avening continued to celebrate their church dedication by eating the same meat. Another legend says that the feast commemorates the slaying of a troublesome wild boar, which took place on or around this date.

Today there is an evening anniversary service in the church at Avening, after which the villagers participate in an eleventh-century banquet headed by Queen Matilda and other historic characters in period costume. Pork sandwiches are also served in the local pubs.

Pilgrimage of the Dew
Between May 8 and June 11; Friday before Pentecost to Tuesday following

This colorful procession, known as the **Romería del Rocío** or Pilgrimage of the Dew, begins during the week preceding WHITSUNDAY in the towns and villages of Andalusia, Spain. The pilgrims' destination is the church of El Rocío in Almonte, where a small statue of the Virgin known as *La Blanca Paloma* or 'the White Dove' resides. They travel in two-wheeled, white-hooded farm carts, drawn by oxen wearing bells, flowers, and ribbon streamers. Some of the carts are set up as moving shrines to the Virgin, and the pilgrims themselves are dressed in regional costumes.

On Whitsunday the pilgrims file past the church of El Rocío and pay homage to La Blanca Paloma. There are fireworks at midnight, followed by dancing and singing until dawn. On Monday the image of the Virgin is carried in solemn procession through the streets of Almonte. Being chosen to bear the statue on one's shoulders is considered a special privilege, eagerly sought by those who wish to receive special indulgence during the coming year. The procession is accompanied by the chanting of priests and the shouts of the pilgrims, who call out "Viva la Blanca Paloma!" as they wend their way through the town.

See also ROMERÍA OF OUR LADY OF VALMEY.

Pilgrimage to Mecca (Hajj)

8th–13th Dhu-l-Hijjah

At least once in a lifetime, every Muslim man or woman (if she is accompanied by a male protector) with the means and the opportunity to do so is expected to make a pilgrimage to Mecca, the city in Saudi Arabia where Muhammad was born. It is one of the "five pillars" (fundamental duties) of Islam, and must be performed during the special pilgrimage season. The Koran says the founder of this pilgrimage was Abraham. The pilgrims wear two sheets of seamless white cloth and perform elaborate rites at the Grand Mosque of Mecca and in the immediate vicinity, requiring about six days to complete. The focal point is the Kaaba, a fifteen-foot-high stone structure that stands in the center court of the Grand Mosque of Mecca. In one corner of the court is the Black Stone, believed to have been brought by the angel Gabriel to Moses when he was rebuilding the Kaaba. It is a symbol of eternity because of its durability. These are not worshiped, but are a sanctuary consecrated to God, and toward which all Muslim prayers are oriented. Among the stages of the Pilgrimage are walking around the Kaaba seven times, sacrificing a ram, ox, or camel, gathering at the Mount of Mercy and "standing before God" from noon to sunset, and throwing pebbles at three pillars at Mina, which represent Satan's tempting Abraham not to sacrifice his son. (See ID AL-ADHA)

It is not uncommon for two million or more Muslims to participate in the pilgrimage, which has forced Saudi Arabia and other countries to explore new methods for freezing, preserving, and distributing the meat that is produced by so many sacrifices. At the end of the pilgrimage, it is customary to visit the tomb of Muhammad at Medina before returning home.

Returning pilgrims, wearing the green scarf of the Hajj, are met by family and friends who have rented taxis and decorated them with palm branches and the families' best rugs. The pilgrim's house has been decorated with palm-leaf arches, and sometimes outlined with lights. In Kurdish and Egyptian villages, the doorways will also have designs suggesting the journey. Then a feast and party finish the welcome home.

Pilgrimage to Moulay Idriss

Late August or September

The most important *moussem*, or 'festival,' in Morocco is held in the holy city of Moulay Idriss. Moulay Idriss I was the eighth-century imam who united the Berbers and founded the city of Fez and the first dynasty of Morocco; he is supposed to have had 500 wives, 1,000 children, and 12,000 horses. His burial place is the white Mausoleum of Moulay Idriss. The town named for him grew up around the tomb after his death.

This *moussem* consists of several weeks, alternating prayers and celebrations. A feature is the *fantasia*, a great charge of horses and costumed riders who fire their rifles into the air and perform equestrian stunts as they gallop. There are also bazaars and singing and dancing.

Pilgrimage to Shrine of Father Laval

September 8

An annual pilgrimage by thousands of people of all faiths to the shrine of the Roman Catholic priest, Père Jacques Désiré Laval, in Port Louis, Mauritius. Father Laval came to Mauritius in 1841 and devoted himself to the spiritual improvement of the emancipated slaves until his death in 1864. The pilgrimage is held on the day of his death. It originated on the day the priest was buried, when more than 30,000 weeping people followed his bier as he was taken for burial opposite the Ste. Croix Church. A monument to him has since been erected there. Many Masses are celebrated at the shrine on the memorial day, starting early in the morning. A vigil ends the day. Miracles of healing are attributed to Father Laval, who was beatified in 1979 in Rome by Pope John Paul II.

Pilgrim Festivals

various

The ancient Israelites were expected to celebrate three pilgrim festivals: PASSOVER, SHAVU'OT, and SUKKOT. They are referred to in Hebrew as the *shalosh regalim* 'three (foot) pilgrimages' because the Bible commanded that they be observed "in the place the Lord your God will choose." Adult males over the age of thirteen traditionally made a pilgrimage to Jerusalem on these three occasions. But after the Temple there was destroyed, the law requiring pilgrimages lapsed. The obligation to rejoice on the three pilgrim festivals—by eating meat, drinking wine, and wearing new clothes—continued.

Today, Jews come from all over the world to spend these festivals in Jerusalem. But now they tend to be sorrowful voyages, made for the purpose of mourning the destruction of the Temple. It is for this reason that Jews traditionally gather at the Wailing Wall—the only remaining retaining wall of the Temple Mount, site of the First and Second Temples, built during the first century BC in the reign of Herod.

Pilgrim Thanksgiving Day in Plymouth
Last Thursday in November

Ten thousand visitors flock to Plymouth, Massachusetts on THANKSGIVING DAY to watch the annual procession from Plymouth Rock to the First Parish Church, where the congregation sings the same psalms sung by the original Pilgrims more than three-and-a-half centuries ago. Each marcher represents one of the fifty-one men, women, and children who survived the 1621 trip from England aboard the *Mayflower* to form the settlement known as Plimoth Plantation.

At eleven o'clock on Thursday morning in front of Memorial Hall, the crowds line up for the first seating of the town's traditional public Thanksgiving dinner, modeled after the 1621 harvest meal shared by the town's earliest settlers. About fourteen hundred people participate in the four successive dinners put on by the Plymouth Chamber of Commerce, which serves up one ton of turkey, five hundred pounds of mashed potatoes, five hundred pounds of squash, and four hundred pounds of Indian pudding.

The modern-day Plimoth Plantation is an outdoor living-history museum that recreates life in a 1627 Pilgrim village. Costumed actor/historians carry out many of the same activities performed by the original Pilgrims, such as sheep-shearing, building houses, planting crops, weeding gardens, and cooking.

Pi Mai *See* Songkran

Pinkster Day
between May 10 and June 13; Fifty days after Easter

When PENTECOST (Whitsunday) became part of the Christian calendar in Northern Europe, the name underwent numerous transformations. In Germany it became *Pfingsten*, and the Dutch called it *Pinkster*. When the Dutch settled in New York, they called the feast of Pentecost "Pinkster Day."

By the beginning of the nineteenth century, Albany had become a center for this celebration, which took place on Capitol or "Pinkster" Hill and consisted of a week-long carnival dominated by

the city's African-American population. It is said that their African-inspired dancing and music horrified the staid Dutch settlers, and by 1811 Pinkster Day had been legally prohibited by the New York state legislature.

Pirates Week
Last week in October

A Cayman Islands festival celebrating the history of Grand Cayman, at one time a favorite haunt for pirates and buccaneers. The entire island is transformed into a pirate encampment for the week-long festival. There is a mock invasion of George Town, parades, pageants, and the crowning of a pirate queen. Everyone dresses up in costumes, and the singing, dancing, and food fairs that are held throughout the island all revolve around a pirate theme.

The Cayman Islands—from the Spanish *caimán*, meaning 'alligator'—were first sighted by Columbus in 1503. Although frequented by Spanish, English, and French ships, they were not claimed by anyone until they were ceded to the British in 1670 and settlers started arriving. Before long, the islands' remote location made them an ideal stopover for pirates.

Pitcher Fair *See* Kumbh Mela

Pitra Visarjana Amavasya
September–October; Asvina

During this two-week festival in India, no male family member is allowed to shave, nor is it permissible to cut hair, pare nails, or wear new clothes. It is a time for honoring ancestors by making special offerings of food and water, especially *khir* or rice boiled in milk. Brahmans or members of the highest Hindu caste are often invited to partake of these special foods in the belief that they will ensure that the offerings reach the souls of departed family members. It is usually the eldest son or senior member of the family who performs the rituals associated with this festival.

Pjodhatid
Early August

A three-day "people's feast," celebrated in the Vestmannaeyjar area of Iceland. The festival commemorates the granting of Iceland's constitution on July 1, 1874, which permitted the nation, long under the control of Denmark, to handle its own domestic affairs. Because of foul weather, the island people of Vestmannaeyjar weren't able to attend the mainland celebration, so they held their own festival at home a month later. They've been holding this month-late celebration ever since.

Most of the festivities take place in Herjolfsdalur on Heimaey Island. Enormous bonfires are built, there are sporting events, dancing, singing, and eating and drinking. People come from the mainland for this event, so the island is filled with campers.

Plague Sunday
Last Sunday in August

When the plague reached the village of Eyam, Derbyshire, England in 1665, three-fourths of the town's population was wiped out. But under the leadership of Vicar Mompesson, the villagers displayed both courage and selflessness, voluntarily isolating themselves from other villages in the parish and requesting that their food and medical supplies be dropped off at a point outside the village. The disease eventually became so virulent that the vicar had to hold open-air services for his dwindling congregation in a place up in the hills known as Cucklet Dell.

Every year on the last Sunday in August, a procession of clergy, standard bearers, choir members, and musicians forms at Eyam's parish church and slowly proceeds up the road leading toward the Dell. Hundreds of villagers, tourists, hikers, cyclists, and parents with baby carriages fall in behind them, finding seats on the grassy slopes of the Dell's natural amphitheatre. A simple sermon pays tribute to the plague victims and the thirty-five villagers who survived.

Pleureuses, Ceremony of
Good Friday

A GOOD FRIDAY ceremony at the Church of Romont in Switzerland. Held since the 15th century, the ceremony begins with a reading from the Bible of the Passion of Christ (the last seven days of his life). The congregation then begins its procession through the village streets. The weepers or mourners (the *Pleureuses*) are veiled in black attire resembling nuns' habits, and walk slowly behind a young girl portraying the Virgin Mary. She walks behind a penitent wearing a black hood and carrying a large cross. The mourners carry the symbols of the Passion on scarlet cushions: a crown of thorns, a whip, nails, a hammer, tongs, and St. Veronica's shroud (Veronica was a woman in the crowd who, as Christ passed her carrying the cross, wiped his face and his image was, according to legend, imprinted on the cloth). During the procession, the town resounds with chants and prayers.

Plough Monday
January, first Monday after Epiphany

An ancient rustic English holiday, also called **Fool** or **Fond Plough** or **Fond Pleeaf**, of obscure origins that survived into the late 1800s. It is thought to have started in the days of the medieval Roman Catholic Church, when farmers, or ploughmen, kept candles called plough-lights burning in churches before the images of saints. Once a year, either on the Monday after Epiphany (before ploughing begins), or at the end of Lent (to celebrate the end of ploughing), they gathered in villages to ask for money to pay for the plough-lights. The Reformation of the sixteenth century ended this homage to saints, but not the day's celebration as a time to return to labor after the CHRISTMAS festivities. By the nineteenth century, the day was observed with music, dancing, processions, and collecting money through trick-or-treat type means. "The Bessy"—a man dressed up to look ridiculous in women's clothing—and "The Fool," wearing animal skins or a fur cap and tail, solicited money from door to door so they could buy food and drink for their merry-making. The ploughmen dragged a beribboned plough from house to house, shouting "God speed the plough," and if a home owner failed to make a contribution, they ploughed up his front yard. The money collected was spent not on plough-lights but on ale in the public houses. The custom of blessing the plough on the prior day, Plough Sunday, was still observed in some areas in the twentieth century.

Plow, Festival of the
June 25

Saban Tuy or the Festival of the Plow celebrates the founding of the famous Tatar Autonomous Soviet Socialist Republic on this date in 1920. Originally a Mongolian spring farming celebration, the festival is held in Kazan on the Volga River in what is now Russia. The events include climbing a greased pole to reach a cock in a cage on top and "smashing the crocks," a variation of Pin-the-Tail-on-the-Donkey in which a blindfolded player who has been spun around several times tries to smash a set of earthenware crocks containing prizes. The highlight of the festival is a horse race across the plains in which the riders are blindfolded.

Polar Bear Swim Day
January 1

Since 1920 a group of hardy swimmers has celebrated NEW YEAR'S DAY by plunging into the frigid waters of Vancouver's English Bay. As crazy as it sounds, the custom has spread to the United States, where chapters of the American Polar Bear Club have established themselves in a number of states known for their cold winter weather. In Sheboygan, Wisconsin, more than three hundred daring swimmers—many of them in costume—brave the ice floes of Lake Michigan to take their New Year's Day swim. About three or four thousand spectators stay bundled up on the beach and watch. The Sheboygan event has gradually expanded into a day-long festival, with a brat-fry, a costume contest, and live entertainment.

Polish Constitution Day
May 3

May 3, known in Poland as **Swieto Trzeciego Maja**, is a patriotic holiday honoring the nation's first constitution, adopted in 1791. It introduced fundamental changes in the way Poland was governed, based on the ideas of the French Revolution, and represented an attempt to preserve the country's independence. Although the May 3rd Constitution (as it was called) represented a great advance for the Polish people, it also aroused the anxieties of neighboring countries and eventually led to the Second Partition two years later.

Polish Liberation Day
July 22; January 17

A national holiday in Poland, July 22 marks the day on which the KRN (National Home Council) established the Polish Committee of National Liberation (PKWN) in 1944, the first people's government in the country's thousand-year history. The PKWN manifesto issued on this date proclaimed that complete liberation from the Nazis and the freeing of ancient Polish lands on the Baltic Sea and Odra River were its first priorities, as well as the democratization of the country's social and political life.

In the city of Warsaw, January 17 is observed as Liberation Day. It was on this day in 1945 that the city was freed from Nazi oppression by Soviet troops. Special ceremonies are held at the Monument to the Unknown Soldier in Warsaw's Victory Square.

Polish Solidarity Day
August 31

This marks the day in 1980 when the Polish labor union Solidarity or *Solidarnosc* was formed at the Lenin Shipyards in Gdansk. Under the leadership of Lech Walesa, an electrician at the shipyard, seventeen thousand workers had staged a strike earlier in the year to protest rising food prices. An agreement was finally reached between the Gdansk strikers and the Polish Communist government, allowing free unions to be formed, independent of the Communist Party. Solidarity was formally founded on September 22 and consists of about fifty labor unions. But when the union stepped up its demands, staging a series of controlled strikes throughout 1981 to pressure the government for free elections and economic reforms, Premier Wojciech Jaruzelskiwas subjected to even greater pressure from the Soviet Union to put a stop to the group's activities. On December 13, 1981 martial law was declared, the fledgling union's legal status was terminated, and Walesa was put under arrest. He was released in November 1982, and martial law was lifted six months later.

After almost a decade of struggle, Solidarity was finally granted legal status on April 17, 1989, clearing the way for the downfall of the Polish Communist Party. The Polish labor union's successful struggle marked the beginning of similar changes in other Communist-bloc countries in Europe, many of whom overthrew their Communist leaders and took the first steps toward establishing more democratic forms of government. Solidarity's founding is celebrated not only in Poland but by Polish-Americans in the United States, with demonstrations and programs in support of Polish workers.

Pongal
December–January; Pausa

A colorful three-day harvest and thanksgiving celebration in southern India, honoring the sun, the earth, and the cow. It is called Pongal in the state of Tamil Nadu; in Andhra Pradesh, Karnataka, and Gujarat, it is known as **Makara Sankranti**.

The first day is called Bhogi Pongal and is for cleaning everything in the house. On the second day, freshly harvested rice and *jaggery* 'palm sugar' are put to boil in new pots. When the mixture bubbles, people cry out, "Pongal!" ('It boils.') The rice is offered to Surya, the sun god before people taste it themselves, thus the second day is called Surya Pongal. The third day, called Mattu Pongal (Festival of the Cow), village cows and oxen are bathed, decorated with garlands of bells, beads, and leaves, and worshipped. In villages near Madurai, the festival of Jellikattu takes place. Bundles containing money are tied to the sharpened horns of bulls. The animals are paraded around the village and then stampeded. Young men who are brave enough try to snatch the money from the bulls' horns.

In Ahmedabad in the state of Gujarat, the celebration is a time of competitive kite-flying, and is termed the **International Kite Festival**. The skies are filled with kites, and kite makers come from other cities to make their multicolored kites in all shapes. As darkness falls, the battle of the kites ends, and new kites soar aloft, each with its own paper lamp, so that the sky is filled with flickering lights.

Pony Express Ride
August

When the Pony Express riders made their first run between St. Joseph, Missouri and Sacramento, California on April 3, 1860, carrying mail on horseback was already routine between eastern Pennsylvania and the "frontier" settlements of Greensburg and Pittsburgh. Since 1788 postal patrons in Armstrong and Butler counties had been paying a minimum of eight cents and a maximum of thirty-five cents to mail a single-page letter, depending on the distance. Although the image of the Pony Express popularized by Hollywood includes Indians and bandits in hot pursuit, its reality in Pennsylvania was the opposite. It was a low-paid and often boring occupation whose main hazards were bad roads and cut-throat competition from stage lines.

Since 1989 a group of Pennsylvania towns once linked by the post riders has staged a two-day recreation of the event known as the **Crooked Creek Pony Express Ride**. The route starts in Adrian and ends in Kittanning, with about ten stops at post offices along the way. A brief ceremony is held at each post office to swear in the rider and to commemorate the history of the early days of postal delivery. The thirty-three riders chosen to participate are judged for the authenticity of their costumes and tack at the end of the eighty-mile route. These "post riders" should not be confused with the later legendary Pony Express riders of the American West.

Pony League World Series *See* **Little League World Series**

Pooram
April–May

One of the most spectacular festivals of southern India, this is a ten-day celebration in Trichur (Kerala) dedicated to Lord Shiva. People fast on the first day of the festival and the rest of the days are devoted to fairs, processions, and fireworks displays. The highlight of the pagentry comes when an image of the deity Vadakkunathan is taken from the temple and carried in a procession of about 100 temple elephants ornately decorated with gold-plated mail. The Brahmans riding them hold colorful ceremonial umbrellas and whisks of yak hair and peacock feathers. The elephants lumber through the pagoda-shaped gateway of the Vadakkunathan temple and into the village while drummers beat and pipers trill. Fireworks light the skies until dawn.

Poppy Day *See* **Veterans' Day**

Portland Rose Festival
First weeks in June

A twenty-six-day salute to the rose in Portland, Ore., and certainly one of the sweetest-smelling festivals anywhere.

The "City of Roses" has been putting on a rose festival since 1907 and claims now to produce the biggest celebration of the rose in the world. To justify such a claim, the festival offers more than sixty events. These include an air show, band competitions, fireworks, a hot-air balloon race, tours and cruises on visiting U.S. and Canadian Navy ships, and boat, ski, and Indy-class car races. The salute starts with the coronation of the Rose Queen, and continues with parade after parade, including a starlight parade, called the second largest lighted parade in the United States, the largest children's parade, and the climax, a grand floral parade, with dozens of rose-bedecked floats. On the final days of the festival, the Portland Rose Society stages the Rose Show, the oldest and largest rose show in the country, with about 20,000 individual blossoms exhibited.

Portland is thought to have started its life as a rose city in the early nineteenth century, when traders brought with them seeds of the wild rose of England. It flourished as the Oregon Sweet Briar. Settlers brought more roses, and then in 1888, Mrs. Henry L. Pittock held a rose show in her front yard, and that evolved into today's festival.

The parade is one of two major floral parades in the country, the other being the better known TOURNAMENT OF ROSES in Pasadena, Calif., every New Year's Day.

Posadas
December 16–24

This nine-day CHRISTMAS celebration in Mexico commemorates the journey Mary and Joseph (the parents of Jesus) took from Nazareth to Bethlehem. Reenacting the couple's search for shelter (Spanish *posada*) in which the infant Jesus might be born, a group of "pilgrims" will knock on someone's door and ask the owner to let them in. Although they may initially be refused, the master of the house finally invites them to enter and the Posadas party begins. The children are blindfolded and given a chance to break the *piñata* (a clay or papier-mâché animal that hangs from the ceiling and is filled with candy and toys) by swinging at it with a stick. The *posadas* are repeated for nine evenings, the last occurring on CHRISTMAS EVE.

The *Misa de Gallo* or Mass of the Cock (so-called because it's held so early) ends after midnight, and then there are fireworks and, in some towns, a special parade with floats and tableaux vivants representing biblical scenes.

In small Mexican villages, there is often a procession led by two children bearing images of Joseph and Mary riding a burro. The adult members of the group carry lighted tapers and sing the Litany of the Virgin as they approach each house. There is also a famous posadas celebration on Olvera Street in Los Angeles.

Poson

May–June; full moon of Jyaistha

This festival, also called **Dhamma Vijaya** and **Full Moon Day**, celebrates the bringing of Buddhism to Sri Lanka (formerly Ceylon). It is second in importance only to Vesak. The story of this day is that King Devanampiya Tissa, who was chasing a deer in the forest of Mihintale when someone called out his name. He looked up and saw a figure in a saffron-colored robe standing on a rock with six companions. The robed figure was the holy patron of Sri Lanka, Arahat Mahinda, the son of Emperor Asoka of India, who was a convert to Buddhism from Hinduism. He had sent his son and companions as missionaries to Ceylon in about 251 B.C. Mahinda converted King Devanampiya Tissa and the royal family, and they in turn converted the common people. Mahinda, who propagated the faith through works of practical benevolence, died in about 204 B.C.

While the holiday is celebrated throughout Sri Lanka, the major ceremonies are at the ancient cities of Anuradhapura and Mihintale. There, historical events involving Mahinda are reenacted, streets and buildings are decorated and illuminated, and temples are crowded. In Mihintale,

people climb to the rock where Arahat Mahinda delivered his first sermon to the king. An important part of the festival is paying homage to the branch of the Bodhi Tree brought to Sri Lanka by Mahinda's sister Sanghamita (See SANGHAMITA DAY). This is the tree that Gautama sat under until he received enlightenment and became the Buddha.

Possum Festival

Last Saturday in June

The annual Possum Festival in Arcadia, Louisiana was first held in 1982. Rodney Cook, the festival's founder and the head of Possums Unlimited (P.U.), initiated the event to commemorate the victims of the many "one-car, one-possum collisions" that take place on Louisiana's roads each year. Although only two or three hundred people attended the first festival, it now attracts up to four thousand roadkill enthusiasts annually. They come to hear the preach-off, at which various clergymen (ordained or self-appointed) preside over a possum funeral, and to participate in such events as a weed-arranging competition—using containers suitable for being thrown from a speeding pickup.

During the rest of the year, Cook and his P.U. organization are kept busy promoting some of the little-known ways in which possums can be beneficial. Among other things, they advertise compass possums—so named, according to Cook, because hunters carry them and if they get lost, all they have to do is turn the possum loose and follow it to the nearest road.

Potato Days

October

In Norway during the fall potato harvest, it was customary to give children a week off school to help in the fields. Norwegian farmers would put in a request for a certain number of children and feed them during their week of employment. Although this arrangement is no longer as common as it was up until the 1950s, children still help harvest the potatoes on their families' farms, and the traditional fall vacation is still known as the potato vacation or *potetserie*.

A similar arrangement can be found in the United States, especially in states where there are many small farms producing a single crop. In northern Maine, children also harvest potatoes and in Vermont some schools give their students time off to help pick apples.

Powamû Festival
February

The Hopi Indians believe that for six months of the year ancestral spirits called the *kachinas* leave their mountain homes and visit the tribe, bringing health to the people and rain for their crops. The Hopi who live at the Walpi Pueblo in northeastern Arizona celebrate the entry of the Sky Father (also known as the Sun God) into the pueblo in February by dramatizing the event in a festival known as Powamû. The Sky Father, represented by a man wearing a circular mask surrounded by feathers and horsehair with a curved beak in the middle, is led into the pueblo from the east at sunrise. There he visits the house and kiva (underground chamber used for religious and other ceremonies) of the chief, performing certain ceremonial rites and exchanging symbolic gifts.

A similar sequence of events is performed in July during the NIMAN FESTIVAL. At this time the Sky Father is ushered out of the pueblo. In the intervening months, it is assumed that he remains in the village or nearby, making public appearances in masked dances from time to time.

Prayer Festival *See* Monlam

Preakness Stakes
Third Saturday in May

The ten-day **Preakness Festival** or **Maryland Preakness Celebration** culminates in the running of the Preakness Stakes, the "middle jewel of the Triple Crown" of horseracing—the other two being the KENTUCKY DERBY and the BELMONT STAKES. Held at Baltimore's Pimlico Race Course, the Preakness was first run on May 27, 1873. The festival leading up to the race includes hundreds of recreational, educational, and cultural events-including a hot air balloon competition, a schooner race in Baltimore Harbor, and a celebrity golf tournament.

Premier Mai
May 1

In France the celebration of MAY DAY is inextricably linked to flowers. It is considered good luck to wear lilies-of-the-valley on this day, and it is believed that any wishes made while wearing the flowers are bound to come true. Sometimes sprays of pressed lilies are sent to distant friends and loved ones. In southern France the flower vendors sell lilies-of-the-valley on every street corner.

The **First of May** has political overtones in France as well, and many working people assert their freedom by taking it as a holiday even though their employers do not officially recognize it as such. Political demonstrations, speeches, and parades are common on this day-similar to MAY DAY celebrations in England, Russia, and other countries.

See also VAPPU.

Presentation of the Blessed Virgin Mary, Feast of the
November 21

The feast of the Presentation of the Blessed Virgin was first celebrated by the Greeks about the eighth century and was not adopted by the Roman Catholic church until the later Middle Ages; no one is quite sure when this festival was first introduced. As related in the apocryphal Book of James, it commemorates the presentation of the three-year-old Mary in the Temple to consecrate her to the service of God. Many have confused this festival with the Feast of the Presentation of Christ in the Temple, otherwise known as CANDLEMAS.

Presidents' Day
Third Monday in February

The passage of Public Law 90-363 in 1968, also known as the "Monday Holiday Law," changed the observance of WASHINGTON'S BIRTHDAY from February 22 to the third Monday in February. Because it occurs so soon after LINCOLN'S BIRTHDAY, many states—such as Hawaii, Minnesota, Nebraska, Wisconsin, and Wyoming—combine the two holidays and call it Presidents' Day or **Washington-Lincoln Day**. Some regard it as a day to honor all former presidents of the United States.

Pretzel Sunday
Between March 8 and April 7; fourth Sunday in Lent

On **Bretzelsonndeg** in Luxembourg, it is the custom for boys to present their sweethearts with decorated pretzel-cakes. If a girl wants to encourage the boy, she reciprocates with a decorated egg on EASTER SUNDAY. If the pretzel-cake is large, the egg must be large, also; a small cake warrants a small egg.

The custom is reversed during Leap Year (see LEAP YEAR DAY), when the girls give cakes to the boys on Pretzel Sunday and the boys return the favor with eggs at Easter. Married couples often participate in the exchange of cakes and eggs as well.

Primrose Day
April 19

Benjamin Disraeli, Earl of Beaconsfield, novelist, and twice Prime Minister of England, died on this day in 1881. When he was buried in the family vault at Hughenden Manor, near High Wycombe, Queen Victoria came to lay a wreath of primroses, his favorite flower, on his grave. Two years later the Primrose League was formed to support the principles of Conservatism which Disraeli had championed. Although the League has lost much of its influence since World War I, it still has a large membership. Primrose Day is observed in honor of Disraeli and his contribution to the Conservative cause.

Prince Kuhio Day
March 26

Prince Jonah Kuhio Kalanianaole was a young man when the Hawaiian monarchy was overthrown in 1893. As a member of the royal family, he fought for the restoration of the monarchy and spent a year as a political prisoner. He lived abroad for a number of years after his release, but eventually returned to his native land and was elected as the first delegate to represent the Territory of Hawaii in the U.S. Congress in 1903. He was reelected and served ten consecutive terms until his death in 1921.

Because he worked so hard to preserve the old Hawaiian customs and traditions and to take care of the dwindling number of Hawaiian natives, Prince Kuhio has been revered by his people. His birthday is commemorated on the island of Kauai, where he was born, with a week-long Prince Kuhio Festival during the latter part of March. The festival pays tribute to him by featuring such traditional Hawaiian events as outrigger canoe races, hula dancing, and performances of Hawaiian music.

Prince's Birthday
August 15

A national holiday in Liechtenstein. This sixty-two-square-mile country gets almost 25 percent of its revenue from selling postage stamps. The country is a constitutional monarchy headed by Prince Franz Joseph II, who turned over actual power to his son, Hans-Adam, in 1984. It was founded at the end of the seventeenth century when Johann Adam von Liechtenstein, a wealthy Austrian prince, bought land in the Rhine valley from two bankrupt counts. In 1719 he obtained an imperial deed creating the country. That date is considered the official birth of the nation. Members of the Liechtenstein family have ruled the country ever since.

Franz Joseph II was born on Aug. 16, 1905, but his birthday is celebrated on Aug. 15, the day of the FEAST OF THE ASSUMPTION. Celebrations take place in the capital city of Vaduz. People come from the countryside for the festivities which include an open house at the prince's home and castle, Schloss Vaduz; dancing in the streets; special food in the cafes; and fireworks in the evening.

Prinsjesdag
Third Tuesday in September

The state opening of Parliament in the Netherlands takes place on the third Tuesday in September at the thirteenth century Ridderzaal or Knights' Hall in The Hague. Queen Beatrix rides to Parliament in a golden coach drawn by eight horses. She is received by the two houses of Parliament—the Upper House and the Lower House, corresponding to the Senate and the House of Representatives in the United States—to whom she addresses her speech outlining the government's intended majority program for the coming year.

A similar day is observed in Great Britain. (See STATE OPENING OF PARLIAMENT)

Professional Secretaries' Day
Wednesday during last full week of April

Professional Secretaries Week was started in 1952 by Professional Secretaries International (PSI), an organization devoted to the education and professional development of secretaries, executive assistants, information specialists, and office managers. It takes place during the last full week in April, with Professional Secretaries' Day observed on Wednesday. Many PSI chapters sponsor special events throughout the week-such as educational seminars or luncheons with guest speakers for secretaries and their bosses—but Wednesday is the day when managers and executives are supposed to give their office support staff a special token of their appreciation.

How do secretaries want to be recognized on this day? According to a PSI survey, most of them want a bonus, a raise, or time off. What do they get? Lunch or dinner is the most common form of recognition, followed by flowers, gifts, and gift certificates.

Prophet's Birthday *See* **Mawlid al-Nabi**

Prudence Crandall Day
Saturday of Labor Day weekend

The official celebration of Prudence Crandall Day in Canterbury, Connecticut only dates back to 1987, but Crandall herself has been recognized for some time as a pioneer in the education of young African-American girls. Born in 1803 in Hopkinton, Rhode Island and educated at the Friends' School in Providence, she established a private academy for girls in Canterbury in 1831. Although her school was widely recognized as one of the state's best, she lost many of her white patrons when she admitted a young African-American girl. Rather than bow to social pressure, she opened another school for "young ladies and little misses of colour"—an act for which she was socially ostracized.

Eventually the Connecticut legislature passed a Black Law (repealed in 1838), which prohibited setting up schools for nonresident African-Americans in any Connecticut city or town without the local authorities' approval. Crandall ignored the new law and was arrested, tried, and convicted. Although the verdict was reversed by the court of appeals in July 1834, this only served to strengthen the opposition of the people of Canterbury. Crandall moved to Illinois later that year with her husband, a Baptist clergyman. In a belated attempt to make amends, Connecticut provided Crandall with an annuity. She died in Kansas in 1890.

Prudence Crandall Day events include craft demonstrations from the 1830s, period children's games, and at least one activity directly relating to Crandall herself. One year, for example, an actor portraying Crandall gave an interpretation of her character. Most of the festival events are held at the Prudence Crandall Museum, located in the house where Crandall lived and taught.

Puck's Fair
August 10–12

A traditional gathering that dates back hundreds of years, Puck's Fair is a three-day event held in Killorglin in County Kerry, Ireland. A large male goat is decorated with ribbons and paraded through the streets on the first day, which is known as Gathering Day. The goat, known as King Puck, presides over the fair from his "throne," an enclosure on a three-story platform in the town square. The main event of the second day, known as Puck's Fair Day, is a livestock show. On the third day, known as Scattering Day or Children's Day, King Puck is led out of town to the accompaniment of traditional Irish music.

Gypsies in large numbers attend the fair, selling, trading, telling fortunes, and playing wonderful Irish music.

Pulaski Day
October 11; first Monday in March

Count Casimir Pulaski was already a seasoned fighter for the cause of independence when he first arrived in America in 1777 to help General George Washington and the Continental Army overthrow the British. While still a teenager he had fought to preserve the independence of his native Poland, and when he was forced to flee his country he ended up in Paris. There he met Benjamin Franklin and Silas Deane, who were impressed by his military background and arranged for him to join the American revolutionaries.

Although he was put in charge of the mounted units and given the title Commander of the Horse, Pulaski had trouble maintaining his soldiers' respect. He spoke no English and was unwilling to take orders from anyone, including Washington. Eventually he resigned from the army and raised an independent cavalry corps, continuing his fight for the colonies' independence. It was on October 11, 1779 that the Polish count died while trying to free Savannah, Georgia from British control.

The President of the United States proclaims October 11 as Pulaski Day each year, and it is observed with parades and patriotic exercises in communities in Georgia, Indiana, Nebraska, and Wisconsin. It is a legal holiday in Illinois, observed on the first Monday in March. The biggest Pulaski Day parade takes place in New York City on the Sunday nearest October 11, when over one hundred thousand Polish-Americans march up Fifth Avenue.

Punky (Punkie) Night
October 28, 29, or last Thursday in October

In the village of Hinton St. George, Somerset, it is traditional for both children and adults to walk through town carrying "punkies," or lanterns, made from carved-out mangel-wurzels or mangolds, a variety of beet, with candles in them. Some say that the custom originated when parish women made crude vegetable lanterns to guide their husbands home after a long evening at the local pub. October 28 was traditionally the date for the Chiselborough Fair, and it was not uncommon for the men to drink too much and get lost in the fields on their way home.

Although this custom is observed in other English towns, the celebration at Hinton St. George is by far the best established. There is a procession of children carrying punkies through the streets, begging for money, and singing the "punky song." A prize is given out for the best carved punky. There is no evidence that the name "punky" came from "pumpkin," but the custom is very similar to what takes place on HALLOWEEN in the United States, where carved, candlelit pumpkins are displayed in windows and on doorsteps.

Purification of Mary, Feast of the *See* Candlemas

Purim

Between February 25 and March 25; 14 Adar; second Adar in leap year

Six hundred years before the Christian era, most of the Jews were slaves in Persia. The Persian prime minister Haman, who generally hated the Jews and particularly hated a proud Jew named Mordecai, persuaded King Ahasuerus (Xerxes I) to let him destroy the empire's entire Jewish population. Haman cast lots (*pur* is Akkadian for 'lot') to find out which day would be the most auspicious for his evil plan, and the lots told him that things would go especially well on the fourteenth of Adar. This is why Purim is also called **The Feast of Lots.**

The king did not realize that his own wife, Esther, was Jewish, and that Mordecai was her cousin, until she pleaded with him to spare her people. Haman was hanged, and his position as prime minister was given to Mordecai.

Ahasuerus granted the Jews an extra day to vanquish Haman's supporters, so the rabbis decreed that in Jerusalem and other walled cities, Purim should be celebrated on 15 Adar called *Purim Shushan*, Hebrew for 'Susa', the Persian capital. In leap year, the 14th (or 15th in Jerusalem) Adar is known as *Purim Katan*, 'the lesser Purim.'

The Old Testament Book of Esther, is read aloud in synagogues on the eve and morning of Purim, and listeners drown out every mention of Haman's name by jeering and stamping their feet. Purim is also a time for sharing food with friends and for charity to the poor.

See also PURIMS, SPECIAL.

Purims, Special

Just as Jews throughout the world celebrate their escape from the evil plot of the Persian prince Haman (see PURIM), many individual Jewish communities commemorate their deliverance from specific calamities by observing their own Purims. The **Padua Purim**, for example, observed on 11 Sivan, celebrates the Jews' deliverance from a major fire in 1795. The **Baghdad Purim**, observed on 11 Av, celebrates the conquest of Baghdad by the Arabs and the defeat of the Persians. The **Snow Purim**, observed on 24 Tevet, celebrates the major snowstorm in Tunis that caused extensive damage and injury elsewhere but left the Jewish quarter of the city untouched. And the **Hitler Purim**, observed in Casablanca on 2 Kislev, commemorates the city's escape from German domination during World War II.

Pushkar Mela

October–November; full moon of Karttika

A camel fair and one of the best known of the Hindu religious fairs of India, held at Pushkar, the place where a lotus flower slipped out of Lord Brahma's hands. Water sprang up where the petals fell and created the holy waters of Pushkar Lake. A temple to Brahma on the shore of the lake is one of the few temples in India dedicated to Brahma. Pushkar is in the state of Rajasthan, a vast desert area dotted with oases and populated with wild black camels.

The commercial side of the fair features the sale of about 10,000 camels. Sheep, goats, horses, and donkeys are also sold there. Countless stalls offer such camel accoutrements as saddles and blankets embellished with mirrors, bangles, brass utensils, and brass-studded belts. Camel races are a highlight. In the "camel rush," people jump onto camels and the camel that holds the most people wins a prize.

On the night of the full moon (*Karttika Poornima*), devotees bathe in the waters of the lake and then make offerings of coconut and rice at the Brahma temple.

Pythian Games

Mid August

The ancient Greek games considered next in importance to the Olympic Games. From 586 B.C., they were held every four years on the plain near Delphi. Competitions in instrumental music, singing, drama, and recitations in verse and prose were primary, but there were also athletic and equestrian contests modeled on those at Olympia. The prize was a crown of bay leaves.

Also see ISTHMIAN GAMES; NEMEAN GAMES; OLYMPIC GAMES.

Q

Qing Ming Festival (Ching Ming Festival)

April 5 or 6, fourth or fifth day of the third moon

A day for Chinese throughout the world to honor their dead. *Ching Ming* means 'clear and bright,' and refers to the weather at this time of year. It is a Confucian festival that dates back to the Han Dynasty (206 B.C. to 221 A.D.), and it is now a Chinese national holiday. It is computed as 105 days after the WINTER SOLSTICE, Tong-ji. The day is observed in the countryside with visits to ancestral graves to sweep, wash, repair, and paint them. Offerings of food, wine, incense, and flowers are made, firecrackers are set off, and paper money is burned at the graveside, so that the ancestors will have funds to spend in the afterworld. (The Chinese traditional belief is that the afterlife is quite similar to this life, and that the dead live a little below ground in the Yellow Springs region.) In ancient China, people spent Qing Ming playing Chinese football and flying kites. Today, they picnic and gather for family meals. In the cities, though, it has been changed to a day of patriotism with placement of memorial wreaths only to Chinese revolution heroes in a few state-run public cemeteries.

The day is also called **Cold Food Day** (in Korea, Han Sik-il; in Taiwan, Han Shih) because, according to an ancient legend, it was taboo to cook the day before.

In Taiwan, yellow paper strips about 3 X 2 inches, are stuck in the ground of the grave, as is shingling. This symbolically maintains the home of one's ancestors. Then the prayers and food offerings are done.

See also FESTIVAL OF HUNGRY GHOSTS.

Quadragesima Sunday

Between February 8 and March 14; first Sunday in Lent in West

The name for the first Sunday in LENT is derived from the Latin word meaning 'fortieth.' The first Sunday of the Lenten season is forty days before EASTER. The other "numbered" Sundays, all in pre-Lent, are Quinquagesima ('fiftieth'), Sexagesima ('sixtieth'), and Septuagesima ('seventieth'). These are reckoned by an approximate number of days before Easter; only Quadrigesima is close to the actual count. These names and Pre-Lent are no longer used, the calendar now referring to the number of Sundays after EPIPHANY, e.g. first Sunday after Epiphany, second Sunday after Epiphany, and so on until Ash Wednesday, then first Sunday in Lent.

Quarter Days

Various

The four traditional quarter days in England, Ireland, and Wales are LADY DAY (March 15), MIDSUMMER DAY (June 24), MICHAELMAS (September 29), and CHRISTMAS DAY (December 25). They mark off the four quarters of the year and the times at which rents and other payments are due. It was also customary to move into or out of a house on a quarter day.

In Scotland the quarter days are CANDLEMAS (February 2), WHITSUNDAY (seventh Sunday after Easter), LAMMAS (August 1), and MARTINMAS (November 11).

Québec Winter Carnival

Ten days in early February

Winter carnivals are common throughout Canada, but the celebration of winter that has been held since 1954 in Québec City ranks among the great carnivals of the world. It begins with the Queen's Ball at the Château Frontenac, a hotel resembling a huge medieval castle in the center of the city, and a parade of illuminated floats. The International Ice Sculpture Contest, featuring artists from several northern countries, is held at Place Carnaval. More than forty thousand tons of snow are trucked in to construct a large snow castle, which is illuminated at night and which serves as a mock jail for those who fail to remain smiling throughout the celebration. Bonhomme Carnaval, the festival's seven-foot-high snowman mascot dressed in a red cap and traditional sash, roams the streets teasing children and looking for people to lock up in the Ice Palace. The festival drink is caribou, a blend of white alcohol and red wine.

An unusual festival event is the race of steel-bottomed boats on the semi-frozen St. Lawrence River. Each boat has a team of five, and its members must maneuver around ice floes and occasionally drag their boats over large patches of ice.

Queen Juliana's Birthday
April 30

Juliana Louise Emma Marie Wilhelmina, born on this day in 1909, was queen of the Netherlands from 1948 until 1980, when she voluntarily abdicated in favor of her oldest daughter, Beatrix. Although she has aroused controversy from time to time—especially by employing a faith healer in the 1950s and by letting two of her four daughters marry foreigners, she was a popular monarch whose birthday is still celebrated throughout the Netherlands with parades, fun fairs, and decorations honoring the queens of the House of Orange.

Queen's Birthday
Second Saturday in June

Queen Elizabeth II was born on April 21, 1926, but her birthday is officially observed on the second Saturday in June by proclamation each year (it may be changed if the weather is really foul). A good explanation for the discrepancy in dates is that the April weather is notoriously bad in London.

The celebration includes Trooping the Colour. The "colour" referred to here is the regimental flag. When British soldiers went to battle, it was important that they be able to recognize their flag so they could rally around it. "Trooping the Colour" was a marching display put on for new recruits so they would know what their regiment's flag looked like.

In 1805 the ceremony became an annual event to celebrate the king or queen's official birthday. Today, a different regiment is chosen each year to parade its flag before Queen Elizabeth II, who sits on horseback and inspects the troops in their brightly colored uniforms as they pass before her in London's Horseguards Parade, a large open space in Whitehall. Then she rides in a carriage back to Buckingham Palace. Although the event attracts thousands of tourists, many Londoners turn out for the traditional ceremony as well.

Queen's Birthday is a national holiday in Australia, where it is celebrated on a Monday in early June. It was first observed there in 1788, not long after the country was settled. June 4, the birthday of King George III, was set aside at that time as a holiday for convicts and settlers. After George V died in 1936, the date of his birth, June 3, was set aside to honor the reigning king or queen.

Queen's Birthday in Thailand
August 12

A nationwide celebration in Thailand of the birthday of Her Majesty Queen Sirikit. Throughout the country, buildings are decorated to honor the queen, but the most splendid are in Bangkok, where buildings and streets are brilliant with colored lights.

Queen's Day
November 17

This is the day on which Queen Elizabeth I ascended to the throne in 1558 upon the death of her sister, Queen Mary I. Often referred to as the Virgin Queen because she never married, Elizabeth reigned for forty-four years—a period that came to be known as the Elizabethan Age because it marked England's rise as a major European power in commerce, politics, and the arts.

The anniversary of her coronation was celebrated for more than three hundred years after her reign ended, primarily as a holiday for those working in government offices. After the Gunpowder Plot was exposed in 1605, two years following Elizabeth's death, the day was marked by anti-papal demonstrations, which included burning the pope in effigy. **Queen Elizabeth's Day** eventually merged with the celebration of GUY FAWKES DAY.

Quilt Festival, National
August–September

Silver Dollar City, the site of the National Quilt Festival, is a theme park built in 1960 near Branson, Missouri. It is set up to resemble a late nineteenth-century working community, with a resident colony of craftspeople, street performers and musicians, shops, and restaurants. It is home to more than fourteen different festivals and special events throughout the year, including the National Crafts Festival (September–October) and the American Folk Music Festival (June).

The National Quilt Festival takes place for two weeks in late August and early September. In addition to displays and demonstrations by some of America's premier quiltmakers, there is an antique quilt auction, a "wearable art" competition, hands-on workshops and seminars for student quilters, and sales and displays of the latest in quilting equipment and supplies. The festival, which has been held at Silver Dollar City since 1982, also features a "Wallhanging Challenge" in which a select group of quiltmakers from across the United States are asked to design and produce a wall quilt working within a prescribed size limit and using a specially chosen group of fabrics.

Quinquagesima Sunday *See*
Quadragesima Sunday

Quintaine, La
Second Sunday in November

St. Leonard, the patron saint of prisoners, is honored each year in the French town of St.-Léon-ard-de-Noblat by a ceremony in which thirty men carry the *quintaine*, a three-foot-high box painted to resemble a prison, to the church to be blessed. Afterward they mount it on a post and strike it with mallets as they gallop by on horseback. Fragments of the smashed *quintaine* are said to bring good luck and to make hens lay eggs.

Quirinalia
February 17

Quirinus was an ancient Roman deity who closely resembled Mars, the god of war. His name is associated with that of the Quirinal, one of the seven hills on which Rome was built and the site of an ancient Sabine settlement that was the seat of his cult. Eventually Quirinus was identified with Romulus, one of the legendary founders of Rome, and his festival on February 17, the Quirinalia, coincided with the date on which Romulus was believed to have been deified. This festival was also associated with the advent of spring warfare, when the shields and weapons of the army which had been purified and retired for the winter, were brought out. The temple dedicated to Quirinus on the hill known as the Quirinal was one of the oldest in Rome.

R

Rabindranath Tagore, Birthday of
May 7

A commemoration of the works of Rabindranath Tagore (1861–1941), the great poet, philosopher, social reformer, dramatist, and musician of Calcutta, India. Born into a family of painters, writers, and musicians, Tagore possessed all these talents. In 1913, he was the first non-European to win the Nobel Prize for Literature. The Tagore family has been important in India's cultural history from the nineteenth century and is especially revered in Calcutta. Rabindranath Tagore's birthday is celebrated with a festival of his poetry, plays, music, and dance dramas. There are discussions at schools of his ideas on education and philosophy, and screening of films based on Tagore's short stories and novels made by filmmaker and Calcutta native, Satyajit Ray.

Race Relations Sunday
Sunday nearest February 12

This day is observed on the Sunday nearest Abraham LINCOLN'S BIRTHDAY because of the role he played in freeing the slaves during the Civil War. Up until 1965 it was sponsored by the National Council of Churches, but since that time, sponsorship has been taken over by individual denominations within the National Council. A number of Roman Catholic groups observe Race Relations Sunday as well, and some Jewish organizations observe it on the preceding Sabbath. Although it was originally conceived in 1924 as an opportunity to focus on improving relations among all races, the longstanding racial conflict between whites and African-Americans in the United States has made this the focal point in recent decades.

There are a number of other observances dealing with race relations at this same time in February. The NAACP (National Association for the Advancement of Colored People) was established on Lincoln's Birthday in 1909, and members of this organization combine the observance of Race Relations Sunday with their organization's founding and with the birthday of the black abolitionist and early human rights activist Frederick Douglass on February 7, 1817.

See also BROTHERHOOD SUNDAY.

Race Unity Day
Second Sunday in June

A day observed worldwide by Baha'is and others with meetings and discussions. The day was begun in 1957 by the Baha'i National Spiritual Assembly in the United States, with the purpose of focusing attenion on racial prejudice.

The Baha'is see racism as a major barrier to peace, and teach that there must be universal recognition of the oneness of all humans to achieve peace.

Ragbrai
Mid–July

A bicycle ride (not race) across the state of Iowa that is billed as the oldest, longest, and largest bicycle touring event in the nation and possibly the world. The sponsor from the start has been the *Des Moines Register*, and "Ragbrai" stands for the **Register's Annual Great Bicycle Ride Across Iowa**. The field is limited to 7,500, and participants are chosen through a drawing.

The ride began in 1973 when Don Kaul, a *Register* columnist who worked out of Washington D.C., was challenged by another columnist, John Karras, to bicycle across the state to learn about Iowa. The challenge was accepted, and both decided to ride. Karras wrote an article telling about the plan and inviting readers to go along: at the start of the race, there were 300 riders, and 115 rode the distance. One of these was eighty-three-year-old Clarence Pickard, who rode a women's bike from border to border.

The ride was intended as a one-time event, but interest was such that it continued the next year

. . . and the next, when it got the Ragbrai name. The route is different each year but always from west to east. Distances average 462 miles; the longest was the 540 miles of Ragbrai XIII in 1985. According to tradition, riders dip their rear tires in the Missouri River at the start of the tour and seven days later dip their front tires in the Mississippi River when they finish. Multi-day touring rides have been organized in other states since Ragbrai started.

Raksha Bandhan (Janai Purnima; Brother and Sister Day)
July–August; Sravana

A day celebrated in north India by brothers and sisters to reaffirm their bonds of affection. A sister ties colorful threads or amulets called *rakhis* on her brother's wrists, and places vermilion paste on his forehead while praying he may be deathless. The brother in turn give his sister gifts—a piece of jewelry or money—while promising to protect her. In families of only boys or only girls, children ask a friend or relative to be their brother or sister.

In Nepal it is a festival for both Hindus and Buddhists, which they may even attend in each others temples. The Brahmins put the golden threads around everyone's wrist; it is worn until Dewali. The *Janai* 'sacred threads,' which all Brahmins and Chhetris wear around their neck, are also changed. This is a three-strand thread necklace signifying the three basic qualities of Nature, or the Hindu Trinity: Brahma, Vishnu, and Shiva.

Ramadan
Ninth month of the Islamic calendar

The month of Ramadan traditionally begins with the actual sighting of the new moon, marking the start of the ninth month in the Islamic lunar calendar. Authorities in Saudi Arabia are relied upon for this official sighting. With the exception of children, the sick, and the very old, devout Muslims abstain from food, drink, smoking, sex, and gambling from sunrise to sunset during this period.

This holiest time in the Islamic year commemorates the time when the Koran, the Islamic holy book, is said to have been revealed to Muhammad. This occurred on LAYLAT AL-QADR, one of the last ten nights of the month. Fasting during the month of Ramadan is one of the Five Pillars (fundamental requirements) of Islam. It is a time for self-examination and increased religious devotion—similar to the Jewish period from ROSH HA-SHANAH to YOM KIPPUR and the Christian LENT.

West Africans have a two-day carnival, similar to SHROVE TUESDAY, before Ramadan starts.

Because it is based on the Islamic lunar calendar, which does not use intercalated days to stay aligned with the solar calendar's seasons, Ramadan moves through the year, occurring in each of the seasons over time.

The **Fast of Ramadan** ends when the new moon is again sighted and the new lunar month begins. It is followed by the ID AL-FITR, Festival of Breaking Fast, which lasts for three days and is marked by feasting and the exchange of gifts.

Ramanavami (Ram Navami)
March–April; 9th of waxing half of Chaitra

The Hindu festival of Ramanavami celebrates the birth of Rama, who was the first son of King Dasaratha of Ayodhya. According to Hindu belief, the god Vishnu was incarnated in ten different human forms, of which Rama was the seventh. He and his wife, Sita, are venerated by Hindus as the ideal man and wife. Because Rama is the hero of the great religious epic poem, *The Ramayana*, Hindus observe his birthday by reciting stories from it. They also flock to the temples, where the image of Rama is enshrined, and chant prayers, repeating his name as they strive to free themselves from the cycle of birth and death.

Ramayana Ballet
May through October; four successive full-moon nights in each month of the dry season

The most spectacular dance-drama on the island of Java, Indonesia, is held on an open-air stage at the Prambanan Temple near Yogya. The ballet is a contemporary abbreviated version of the Hindu Ramayana epic, unfolding over the four nights to tell the story of Prince Rama banished from his country to wander for years in the wilderness. More than 100 dancers and players of *gamelans* 'percussion instruments' present spectacles of monkey armies, giants on stilts, and clashing battles. The rich carvings—lions and Ramayana scenes—of the Prambanan temple complex in the background are spotlighted by the moon.

Rara (Ra-Ra)
February–April; weekends in Lent

In Haiti the celebration of CARNIVAL is known as Rara for the groups of people who come down from the hills to dance in processions on the weekends throughout LENT and particularly during EASTER week. It begins by calling on Legba, who appears as Carrefour, the guardian of thresholds and crossroads. Each Rara band consists of a musical group, a band chief, a queen with attendants, a women's choir, and vendors selling food. The group's leader often dresses like a jester and twirls a long baton known as a *jonc*. On SHROVE TUESDAY night, the Rara bands perform a Bruler Carnival in which they carry out the ritual burning of various carnival objects then making a cross on their forehead with the ashes. Rara has deep ties with voodoo and its resemblance to other Carnival celebrations is only superficial.

Rath Yatra
July–August; month of Sravana

An outpouring of tens of thousands of pilgrims to honor Lord Jagannath, Lord of the Universe, in Puri, in the state of Orissa, India. Jagannath, worshiped primarily in Orissa, is a form of Krishna (though the term applies also to Vishnu), and the Jagannath temple in Puri is one of the largest Hindu temples in the country. During the festival, wooden images of Jagannath, his brother Balabhadra, and his sister Subhadra are taken in procession in three huge chariots or carts that look like temples and are called *raths*. They go from the Jagannath Temple to be bathed at Gundicha Mandir, a temple about a mile away; the gods are installed there for a week before being brought back to the Jagannath Temple. This is such a popular festival because all castes are considered equal, and everyone has to eat the food prepared by low caste men at the shrine.

The main chariot has a striped yellow and orange canopy forty-five feet high and sixteen wheels seven feet in diameter. It is occupied by scores of riders and pulled by thousands of devotees. Because the moving chariot becomes an inexorable force that could crush anything in its path, the name of the god entered the English language as "juggernaut."

The festival is also known as the **Jagannath Festival** or **Car Festival**. Others are held in Varanasi, in Serompore, near Calcutta, and other areas, but the most impressive Rath Yatra is at Puri.

Ratification Day
January 14

Most people associate the end of the Revolutionary War with the surrender of Lord Cornwallis at Yorktown, Virginia in 1781. But it was almost two years later that the **Treaty of Paris** was signed. It then had to be ratified by the Continental Congress and returned to England within six months. As members of the Congress arrived in Annapolis, Maryland to ratify the treaty, it became apparent that they needed delegates from two more states to constitute a quorum. With prodding from Thomas Jefferson, the delegates from Connecticut finally arrived, and South Carolina Congressman Richard Beresford was dragged from his sickbed in a Philadelphia hotel room. Once everyone was assembled, the treaty was quickly ratified on January 14, 1784, and the American Revolution was officially ended. But it was still too late to get it back to England by the March deadline, since an ocean crossing took at least two months. Fortunately, Britain was willing to forgive the delay.

The Old Senate Chamber in Maryland's historic State House at Annapolis has been preserved exactly as it was when the ratification took place. On January 14, the same type of flag that was displayed in 1784—with twelve stars in a circle and the thirteenth in the center—flies over the State House and many other buildings in Annapolis. The ceremony that takes place inside varies from year to year, but it often revolves around a particular aspect of the original event. One year, for example, the original Treaty of Paris was put on display in the rotunda.

Rato (Red) Machhendranath
April–May; Vaisakha

This chariot procession is the biggest event in Patan, Nepal. The festival honors Machhendranath, the god of rain and plenty, who is worshipped by both Hindus and Buddhists in different incarnations, and has shrines at both Patan and in the village of Bungamati, a few miles south of Patan. The festival, held when the monsoon season is approaching, is a plea for plentiful rain.

The image of the god, a carved piece of red-painted wood, is taken from the shrine in the Pulchowk area at the start of the festivities and paraded around the city in several stages on a wheeled chariot. The chariot is a huge wooden wagon that is towed by hundreds of devotees. Finally, after a month of being hauled about, the chariot is dismantled, and the image is conveyed to Bungamati to spend six months at the temple there.

A similar but shorter festival, the Sweta (or White) Machhendranath, is held in Katmandu in March or April. The image of the god is taken from the temple at Kel Tole, placed on a chariot and pulled from one historic location to another. When it arrives in the south of the city, the chariot is taken apart, and the image is returned to its starting place.

Rat's Wedding Day
Day 19, first lunar month

The Rat's Wedding Day is observed in some Chinese households on the nineteenth day of the first moon. It is customary to go to bed early so that the rats have plenty of time to enjoy themselves. Food is left out for them in the hope that it will dissuade the more ravenous rodents from disturbing the householder's kitchen. If a very large rat takes up residence in a house, it is regarded as the "Money Rat" and is treated well on this day, for its arrival indicates that the householder will prosper.

Ravinia Festival
June–September

Chicago's twelve-week festival of music, theater, and dance takes place in Highland Park, one of the city's northern suburbs. Although today the festival can boast performances by some of the world's most distinguished conductors, soloists, symphony orchestras, and dance companies, its history since 1904 has been punctuated by periodic financial crises and, in the 1940s, a fire that destroyed the Ravinia Park pavillion. But since that time the festival has rebounded, expanding to include pop, jazz, and folk music as well as several weeks of theater performances. Nearly half a million people attend the festival each year.

Red Earth Native American Cultural Festival
First weekend in June

One of the largest such events in the country, held in Oklahoma City and drawing participants from more than 100 American Indian tribes. The three-day festival features arts and crafts, dancing, parades, foot races, and seminars.

The name Oklahoma means 'red people,' being derived from two Choctaw words, *okla* 'people,' and *humma* 'red.' Thirty-five tribes with tribal councils now live in Oklahoma. Their population is more than 175,000, the second largest of any state in the nation.

Redentore, Festa del
Third Sunday in July

The **Feast of the Redeemer** is celebrated in Venice, Italy—one of only two remaining national religious festivals surviving in the republic of Venice. (The other is at the church of the Salute on the Grand Canal, which also commemorates deliverance from the plague, but is more religious in nature.) It commemorates the end of the plague in the late sixteenth century, when the people of Venice dedicated a church on Guidecca Island to Jesus the Redeemer and vowed to visit it every year. They continue to keep their promise by building a bridge of boats across the Guidecca and Grand canals, across which worshippers can walk back and forth during the celebration. At dawn, the boats all go out to the Lido to watch the sun rise over the Adriatic Sea. During the festival the cafés, shops, canals, and the church are decorated with lights. When the bridge of boats closes at around nine o'clock, a fireworks display begins.

Services inside the Church of the Redentore, which include Masses commemorating the redeeming power of Jesus, are quite solemn in comparison to what is going on outside—a festival that has been described as the "Venetian Bacchanal."

Red Waistcoat Festival
First or second weekend in July

The **Festa do Colete Encarnado** or Red Waistcoat Festival celebrates the *campionos*—the cowboys who watch over the bulls in the pasturelands of the Ribatejo in Portugal, and who traditionally wear red vests, green stocking caps, blue or black trousers, and red sashes. Supposedly the best bulls for bullfighting are those that have been allowed to roam freely in the vast, rich pastures for which this part of the country is famous, and bullfights play a big part in the festival. But unlike bullfighting elsewhere, no one gets hurt and it's against Portugese law to kill the bull.

A highlight of the festival is the traditional running of the bulls through the streets of Vila Franca de Xira, where the three-day festival takes place, which is about twenty miles from Lisbon. In addition to bullfighting, there are folk dances, fireworks, and various competitions for the *campionos*, including the Ribatejan fandango, a competitive dance for men only.

Reed Dance
Late August

The Reed Dance is the culmination of a week-long coming-of-age ceremony for young girls in Swaziland. They gather in the royal city of Lobamba and spend several days along the riverbank gathering reeds for the Queen Mother. They use the reeds to rebuild the screens that surround the Queen Mother's *kraal* or enclosure. The Reed Dance is performed for the Queen Mother near the end of the ceremony, when the girls, dressed in bead skirts and beautiful jewelry, perform complicated steps done in perfect time, tossing reeds high into the air. Since the Reed Dance, also known as **Umhlanga**, is not a sacred ceremony, visitors are welcome to watch.

Reformation Day
October 31

When Martin Luther, a German monk and religious reformer, nailed his ninety-five "theses" (or propositions) to the church door in Wittenberg on October 31, 1517, his only intention was to voice his opinions about certain practices and customs in the Roman Catholic church, in the hope that someone would engage him in a public debate. Instead, so many people agreed with his ideas that they spread throughout western Europe and touched off a religious revolt known as the Reformation. As a result, many Christians broke their centuries-old connection with the Roman Catholic church and established independent churches of their own, prime among them being the Lutheran Church. October 31 is observed by most Protestant denominations as Reformation Day, and the preceding Sunday is known as **Reformation Sunday**. In Germany the day is sometimes referred to as **Luther's Theses Day**.

Regatta between Harvard and Yale *See* Yale-Harvard Regatta

Regatta of the Great Maritime Republics
First Sunday in June

The great maritime republics of Italy for which this event is named are Pisa, Genoa, Amalfi, and Venice. Although they no longer enjoy the wealth and power of medieval days, the four cities commemorate their former greatness with a friendly battle for supremacy of the seas off the coast of Pisa. The contest takes the form of an historic regatta in which longboats representing each of the republics race for a prize.

Another event held on this day in Pisa is the *Gioco del Ponte* or 'Battle for the Bridge,' which also goes back to the thirteenth century. Following a medieval procession, two teams in full costume take part in a traditional competition which involves a reversal of the usual tug-of-war. Twenty-four men from each team line up behind a mechanism on rails and push. The first team to make a "goal" on the opposing side wins, and this is repeated five times.

Reggae Sunsplash
August

The largest reggae event in the world takes place for four nights each August at the Bob Mar-

ley Centre in Montego Bay, Jamaica. Described as the "Jamaican version of Woodstock," the annual festival features the world's best-known reggae performers as well as salespeople hawking such island specialties as curried goat, bammy and fish, sugarcane, and jelly coconut. Held since 1978, **Sunsplash** has been plagued by organizational problems. But it still qualifies as one of the world's premier musical events, attracting up to 50,000 people.

Reggae originated as the music of the Jamaican poor, reflecting social discontent and the Rastafarian movement. Jamaican-born reggae star Bob Marley, who died of brain cancer at the age of 36, transformed the island-bred music into an international craze. He is venerated in Jamaica much as Elvis Presley is in the United States, and his former house and studio in Kingston, called Tuff Gong, is still a center for some of the more serious reggae music being produced today. One of the festival's most memorable moments occurred in 1981, when American superstar Stevie Wonder sang a moving tribute to Bob Marley following his death earlier that year.

Reindeer Driving Competition
Third week in March

The Lapp people who live in the northern part of the Scandinavian countries round up their herds of reindeer between December and March every year to count, sort, slaughter, and mark their animals in much the same way that cattle and sheep are rounded up in the United States and elsewhere. Round-ups usually last from one to three days and often include athletic competitions. During the third week of March in Inari, Finland, men and women compete on cross-country skis as they try to herd a hundred reindeer over a three-and-a-quarter-mile course. The fastest time wins the competition.

Repotini *See* Ropotine

Republic Day in India
January 26

An important national festival in India celebrating the day in 1950 when India's ties with Britain were severed and the country became a fully independent republic. The holiday is marked with parades and much celebration in all the state capitols, but the celebration in Delhi is especially grand. There is a mammoth parade with military units, floats from each state, dancers and musicians, and fly-overs. The festivities in Delhi actually last for about a week, with special events of all sorts in auditoriums and hotels.

England's Queen Victoria had been proclaimed Empress of India in 1877, and it wasn't until 1947 that India won its long fight for freedom. The India Independence Act was passed by the British Parliament in July 1947, and by August 15 the Muslim nation of Pakistan and the Hindu nation of India had become independent dominions. Lord Mountbatten served as governor general during the transition period. When a new constitution came into effect in 1950 his governor-generalship ended, and India stood fully independent. Independence Day on Aug. 15 is also a national holiday, but is observed chiefly with speech-making and none of the grandeur of Republic Day.

Republic Day in South Africa
May 31

A referendum held in South Africa on October 6, 1960 narrowly approved the formation of the Republic of South Africa, although "coloured" voters were excluded as part of the country's long-standing policy of racial segregation known as apartheid. The closeness of the vote—52.14 percent in favor, 47.42 percent opposed—reflected the mixed feelings of both the Afrikaners and the British settlers, although the former generally supported the idea. The Union of South Africa became the Republic of South Africa on May 31, 1961, thus severing its long-standing ties to the old British Empire. Also on this date in 1902 the Boer War ended. The Treaty of Vereeniging was signed by representatives of the South African Republic and the Orange Free State who had been waging war with Great Britain since October 12, 1899. Eight years later the Union of South Africa was inaugurated, uniting the Cape of Good Hope, Natal, the Transvaal, and the Orange Free State.

Republic Day in Turkey
October 29

The Turkish Republic was founded by Mustafa Kemal Atatürk in 1923 after the fall of the Ottoman Empire. Kemal was named the first president on October 29, a full republican constitution was adopted the following April, and all members of the Ottoman dynasty were expelled from the country. Although Islam remained the state religion for several years, this clause was eventually removed from the constitution and in April 1928, Turkey became a purely secular state.

The public celebration, which lasts for two days, includes parades, music, torchlight processions, and other festivities in honor of the founding of the republic. The largest parades are held in Ankara and Istanbul.

Repudiation Day
November 23

The Stamp Act of 1765 forced the American colonies to pay a tax on various official documents and publications, such as legal papers, liquor permits, lawyers' licenses, and school diplomas. The tax on newspapers and pamphlets was particularly burdensome, as it was based on the number of printed sheets and advertisements in each publication. The tax had to be paid in British pounds sterling, which made it even more expensive. In defiance of the new law, the court of Frederick County, Maryland declared that it would carry on its business without the tax stamps required by the Act. In March 1766, the Act was rescinded.

The date on which the Stamp Act was repudiated, November 23, has been observed for many years as a half-holiday in Frederick County to commemorate this courageous act. It is customary for the Daughters of the American Revolution (DAR) to meet in the courthouse on this day and to listen while the clerk of the circuit court reads the original 1765 decision.

Respect-for-the-Aged Day *See* Keiro-no-ki

Resurrection Day *See* Easter

Resurrection, feast of the *See* Easter

Return Day
Thursday following Election Day

In the early nineteenth century, the rural residents of Sussex County, Delaware had to travel all the way to Georgetown, the county seat, to cast their ballots on ELECTION DAY. The roads were rough, the weather was often bad, and many of the men were uneasy about leaving their families behind. In 1828 the General Assembly adopted new election laws establishing polling places in the "hundreds," as the political subdivisions of the county were called (probably referring to the early English "group of 100 hides," the number of land units necessary to support one peasant family). While this spared voters from having to travel, they had no way of finding out the results of the election because there were no county newspapers. The tabulations were rushed to Georgetown by couriers, and the results were read two days later from the courthouse steps. Many of the farmers in the surrounding areas would take a day off and travel to Georgetown with their families to hear the announcement and to join in the festivities, which included cockfights, band concerts, and open-air markets. The winning candidates were often carried around the town green in an impromptu victory celebration.

Of course there is no longer any need to wait two days to hear election results. But the residents of Georgetown continue the tradition, which includes a formal announcement of the results on the Thursday after the Presidential Election Day. There are parades, picnics, military displays, and, of course, politicking. Both the winners and the losers circulate among their supporters. Street vendors sell roast oxen, which has been cooked on a spit, and there is a parade down Market Street reminiscent of the days when farmers would arrive in town in their wagons and ox-drawn carts.

Reversing Current, Festival of the (Water Festival)
Late October or early November

A festival to celebrate a natural phemomenon in Cambodia. Tonle Sap, a lake, is connected to the Mekong River by the Tonle Sap River which normally flows south from the lake. But in the rainy season, from mid-May to mid-October, the flood-swollen Mekong backs up and flows backward through the Tonle Sap River into the lake. The depth of the lake jumps from seven feet to thirty-five feet, and the total surface quadruples. The normal southward flow returns when the dry season starts. (Because of the phenomenon, the Tonle Sap lake is an extremely rich source of freshwater fish.)

The festival, held at the time when the Tonle Sap returns to its normal direction, is a time of fireworks and merrymaking and races of pirogues, or long canoes, at Phnom Penh.

Revolution Day
November 7

The commemoration of the October Revolution of 1917 when the Bolsheviks overthrew the Russian government by seizing power in Petrograd (formerly St. Petersburg, later to be Leningrad, and in 1991, after the collapse of the Communist Party, renamed St. Petersburg). The coup took place on Nov. 7 (Oct. 25 on the Julian calendar) and through the years was celebrated as a national holiday to mark the start of the Soviet regime. Celebrations were particularly lavish in Moscow, with grand military parades and fly-

overs and the Soviet leadership reviewing the parade from atop the Lenin Mausoleum. In Leningrad, the Soviet Baltic fleet sailed up the Neva to drop anchor across from the Winter Palace.

All this ended in 1991. With the Soviet Union disintegrating, the state holiday was still in place, but marches and demonstrations were banned in Moscow. In the newly renamed St. Petersburg, Mayor Anatoly A. Sobchak attended Russian Orthodox services (formerly forbidden) with the Grand Duke Vladimir Kirillovich Romanov, son of a cousin of the last czar.

Rhode Island Independence Day
May 4

Rhode Island was the first and only state to declare its independence from England entirely on its own. Relations between the colony and its British rulers had deteriorated rapidly after the 1772 incident in which Rhode Island colonists boarded and burned the British revenue cutter *Gaspée*, which had been patrolling the coastal waters in search of local smugglers. On May 4, 1776 both houses of the General Assembly renounced the colony's allegiance to Great Britain—a full two months before the rest of the colonies followed suit on July 4 (see INDEPENDENCE DAY). Rhode Islanders celebrate this event during May, which is Rhode Island Heritage Month, with flag-raising ceremonies, cannon salutes, and parades of local patriotic, veterans', and scouting organizations.

Ridvan, Feast of
April 21–May 2

A Baha'i celebration to commemorate the twelve-day period in 1863 when the Baha'i founder Baha'u'llah (which means 'Glory of God') made the declaration that he was God's messenger for this age—the one foreseen by the Bab to be a prophet of the same rank as Abraham, Moses, Jesus, Muhammad, Buddha, Krishna, and Zoroaster. The first, ninth, and twelfth days of the period are holy days when work is suspended. The celebration starts at sunset, April 20, the eve of Ridvan.

When he made his declaration, Baha'u'llah was staying outside Baghdad at a garden he called *Ridvan*, meaning Paradise. On the first day, he declared his manifestation to his family and close associates. On the ninth day other followers joined him, and the declaration of his station became public knowledge. On the twelfth day, he left the garden.

Nineteen years earlier, the Bab had prophesied

that one greater than he would come; Baha'u'llah's proclamation stated that he was the "promised one." He set forth the form of the Baha'i religion, teaching the unity of all religions, and the unity and brotherhood of all mankind. He wrote more than 100 works of sacred literature.

River Kwai Bridge Week
Last week in November

A commemoration in Kanchanaburi, Thailand, of World War II's infamous Death Railway and the River Kwai (Khwae Noi) Bridge. Between 1942 and 1945, more than 16,000 Allied prisoners of war and 49,000 impressed Asian laborers were forced by the Japanese to build a railway through the jungle from Bangkok, Thailand, into Burma, and it is said that one person died for every railway tie on the track. At the Kanchanaburi War Cemetery, commemorative services are held every April 25 for the 6,982 American, Australian, British, and Dutch prisoners of war buried there.

The bridge became known as a symbol of the horrors and futilities of war through the novel *The Bridge Over the River Kwai* by Pierre Boulle and the movie based on it, *The Bridge on the River Kwai*. During the week-long events, the reconstructed bridge (it was bombed during the war) is the setting for sound-and-light presentations, and there are also historical exhibitions and rides on World War II-era trains.

Rizal Day
December 30

A national holiday in the Philippines commemorating the execution of the national hero, Dr. José Rizal, on this day in 1896. Flags fly at half-mast throughout the country, and special rites are led by the president at the 500-foot obelisk that is the Rizal Monument in Manila.

Rizal, born in 1861 in the Philippines, was a doctor who studied medicine in Spain, France, and Germany. He was also a botanist, educator, man of letters, and inspiration for the Philippine nationalist movement. Writing from Europe and denouncing the corrupt ruling of the Philippines by Spanish friars, he became known as a leader of the Philippine reform movement. He returned to the Philippines in 1892 and founded a nonviolent reform movement, as a result of which he was deported to the Philippine island of Mindanao, where he established a school and hospital. Rizal had no part in the nationalist insurrection, but nevertheless he was arrested, tried for sedition, and executed by a firing squad. On the eve of his execution, he wrote the poem *Mi Ultimo Adiós*, 'My Last Farewell.' The poem, in the original Spanish and translated into other languages, is transcribed on a marble slab near the Rizal Monument.

Road Building
April

In areas of Nigeria where the Igbo live, especially Mbaise, there is a festival in April known as **Emume Ibo Uzo** or Road Building. It is a time for everyone in the community to get together and maintain the major thoroughfares by clearing and levelling them. This festival was particularly important in the days before government-sponsored road building became common.

Robert E. Lee Day
Third Monday in January

The Confederate General Robert Edward Lee was born on January 19, 1807. He was in charge of the military and naval forces of Virginia during the Civil War, building a reputation as a brilliant military strategist and a man who inspired great loyalty among his troops. By the time he was appointed general-in-chief of all the Confederate armies, the South's defeat was imminent. Lee's subsequent surrender to General Ulysses S. Grant at the Appomattox Court House in 1865 marked the end of the war.

In 1889 Georgia became the first state to make Lee's birthday a legal holiday. Other states observing Lee's birthday each year include Alabama, Arkansas, Florida, Kentucky, Louisiana, Mississippi, North Carolina, South Carolina, and Tennessee. While Texas observes Lee's birthday as **Confederate Heroes Day**, in Virginia it is combined with the birthdays of Andrew "Stonewall" Jackson and Martin Luther King (see MARTIN LUTHER KING'S BIRTHDAY) and called **Lee-Jackson-King Day**.

Robigalia
April 25

The ancient Romans knew how much damage certain fungi could do to their crops, but they attributed these diseases to the wrath of the gods. Robigus was the Roman god who personified such blights, and the annual festival known as the Robigalia was designed to placate him. It was believed that prayers and sacrifices made on this day, April 25, would head off the mildew, rust, wilt, and other blights that so often devastated their crops.

Rocket Festival *See* Bun Bang Fai, Boun Bang Fay

Rogation Days

Between April 30 and June 3; Monday, Tuesday, and Wednesday preceding Ascension Day

Since Medieval times the three days before As-CENSION DAY (called Holy Thursday in Great Britain) have been known as Rogation Days (from *rogare*, 'to pray'). Both the Roman Catholic and Protestant churches set them aside as days of abstinence and prayer, especially for the harvest. In many churches in the United States **Rogation Sunday**, the fifth Sunday after EASTER, has been known as **Rural Life Sunday** or **Soil Steward-ship Sunday** since 1929—a day when the religious aspects of agricultural life are emphasized. It is also known as **Cantate Sunday** because the Latin Mass for this day begins with the first words of Psalm 98, *Cantate Domino* 'Sing to the Lord.'

The Rogation Days also had a secular meaning at one time in England, where they were called **Gang Days** or **Gange Days**—from the Saxon word *gangen* meaning 'to go.' There was a custom of walking the parish boundaries during the three days before Holy Thursday (Ascension Day), the procession consisting of the priests and prelates of the church and a select number of men from the parish. Later these Rogation Days were set aside for special local celebrations. In nineteenth century Dorsetshire, for example, a local festival called the Bezant was held each year on **Roga-tion Monday**.

Roger Williams Day

February 5

Roger Williams was the founder of the American Baptist Church. Born in Wales, he arrived in the Massachusetts colony on this day in 1631 and soon found himself in profound disagreement with the local Puritans. The latter admitted no distinction between crime and sin, while Williams contended that the civil authorities only had a right to punish those who had committed a civil offense. The argument led to a court trial in 1635, and soon afterward Williams was banished from the colony. He fled south to what is now called Providence and founded the Rhode Island colony. Under his leadership, the people of Rhode Island were the first to establish a Baptist congregation on American soil (in 1638) and the first to build a community based on the principle of religious liberty.

Baptists in the United States still celebrate the day of his arrival in America. On the Sunday nearest Rhode Island Independence Day, May 4, the First Baptist Meeting House in Providence holds its annual Forefathers Service, honoring Williams as its founder and often using the eighteenth century order of worship.

Romería of Our Lady of Valme

October 17

The Romería (pilgrimage) of Our Lady of Valme involves a cross-country pilgrimage. The image of Our Lady of Valme is kept in the parish church of Dos Hermanas, but on this day she is carried in an elaborate procession to the shrine of Valme, on a hill overlooking Seville . Legend has it that King Ferdinand III stopped here on his way to free Seville from the Moors. He prayed to the Virgin Mary, "valme" (bless me), and promised a sanctuary for her if he were successful.

Accompanied by children in carriages, decorated floats, local men on horseback carrying silver maces, and Andalusian cavaliers and their ladies in regional dress, the cart bearing the statue of the Virgin Mary dressed in a blue velvet cloak is drawn by oxen with gilded horns and garlands of flowers around their necks. The pilgrims walk behind, and there is laughter, hand-clapping, and singing with tambourine accompaniment. Every so often fireworks are set off so the pilgrims in Valme can judge the progress of the procession. It takes about three hours to reach the sanctuary, then the cavaliers open the gates, everyone rushes inside, the statue is carried in at shoulder height, and the Mass begins. Afterwards, there is dancing, singing, and drinking until sunset, when the image is escorted back to Dos Hermanas.

Other well-known romerías include The Virgen de la Cabeza (Andalusia, late April), The Virgen de la Pena (Huelva, last Sunday in April), the Romería del Rocio (see PILGRIMAGE OF THE DEW), the Romería of Pedro Bernardo (Ávila, September 5–17), and La Dandelada (Ávila, second Sunday in September).

Ropotine (Repotini)

Between April 7 and May 18; third Tuesday after Easter

This Romanian festival is celebrated exclusively by women, who take advantage of this day to turn the tables on their husbands. It is the one day of the year when women are the masters: they eat, drink, and make merry, and they can punish men for any slights they may have suffered. The spring ceremony known as Repotini can be traced back to the ancient Roman festival known as Repotia, although no one seems to know where the custom of treating men harshly on this day got started. The women get together and make household utensils out of straw and clay, particularly a shallow baking dish for bread known as the *tzesturi* used to bake rolls and cakes which they hand out to children and the poor "to keep away wars."

Rosary, Festival of the
First Sunday in October

The rosary is a string of beads used by Roman Catholics to count a ritual series of prayers consisting of fifteen *Pater Nosters* 'Our Father,' the Lord's Prayer, and a hundred and fifty *Ave Marias* 'Hail Marys'. The rosary is divided into fifteen decades—each decade containing one Pater Noster marked by a large bead and ten Ave Marias marked by ten smaller beads. As the prayers are recited, the beads are passed through the fingers, making it easier to keep track of the sequence.

The Festival of the Rosary, observed on the first Sunday in October, was established by Pope Pius V under the name of Santa Maria de Victoria (St. Mary of Victory). But the name was changed by Gregory XIII to Festival of the Rosary. Among the events for which the faithful give thanks on this day is the victory of Prince Eugene over the Turks at Belgrade in 1716.

Rose Bowl Game
January 1

The oldest and best known of the post-season college-football bowl games, held in Pasadena, Calif., the home of the TOURNAMENT OF ROSES. The first Rose Bowl game was played in 1902 between Michigan and Stanford; the Michigan Wolverines, coached by Fielding H. "Hurry Up" Yost, demolished the Indians, 49-0. Yost was known for his "point-a-minute" teams, and the Michigan eleven had racked up 550 points in eleven winning games, unscored on and untied, before the bowl encounter. Willie Heston, one of the great all-time backs, led the team to victory.

Football gave way to chariot races after that first game, but football came back to stay in 1916. Among the notable highlights in the years since then was the wrong-way run in 1929. The University of California was playing Georgia Tech. Roy Riegels the center and captain of California's Golden Bears, picked up a Tech fumble, started toward the Tech goal line, and then, facing a troop of Tech defenders, cut across the field and started toward his own goal line, sixty yards away. Players on both sides gaped. Finally Benny Lom, a Bears halfback, ran after Riegels and grabbed him at the three-yard line. Tech players bounced him back to the one. California tried a punt, but it was blocked and the ball rolled out of the end zone.

The officials declared a safety, and Georgia Tech won the contest by one point.

Since 1947, the Rose Bowl has brought together the champions of the midwest Big Ten and Pac Ten (Pacific Ten) Conferences. Numerous other bowl games have come along since 1902: Miami, New Orleans, Dallas, and El Paso, Tex., started games in the mid-1930s, and by the 1980s there were sixteen bowl games in late December or on NEW YEAR'S DAY.

See also Tournament of Roses.

Rose Monday (Rosenmontag)
Between February 2 and March 8; Monday before Lent

Germany is famous for its CARNIVAL celebrations, which reach a climax on Rose Monday, the day before SHROVE TUESDAY. Over four hundred Carnival balls are held in Munich alone, and Rose Monday celebrations are held in Cologne, Düsseldorf, Mainz, Münster, and Berlin as well. In addition to balls and parades, which take place in small towns as well as the cities, the day is observed by singing songs, often with haunting tunes, that have been composed especially for Carnival.

Because it is the last time for hi-jinks before LENT, **Rosenmontag** is characterized by a free-for-all atmosphere in which the normal rules of behavior are relaxed. It is not uncommon, for example, for people to go up to strangers on the street, and kiss them.

The German name for the day, *Rosen Montag* 'Roses Monday', is a mispronunciation of the original name *Rasen Montag*, 'rushing Monday' or 'live it up Monday.'

Rose of Tralee Beauty Contest
Late summer

The village of Tralee in County Kerry is famous for a festival that is unique in Ireland: the annual beauty contest for the "Rose of Tralee." Lasting for a week in late summer, the festivities begin with the playing of a harp by a woman belonging to a Kerry family in which harp-playing has been a traditional occupation for generations. There are also horse races and competitions in singing, dancing, and storytelling, but it is the beauty contest that draws the most attention. Contestants come from Ireland, Britain, the United States, and even Australia, although the winner must be of Kerry descent.

"The Rose of Tralee," a popular Irish ballad,

was written by William Pembroke Mulchinock, who lived just outside the village of Tralee and fell in love with a girl who was a servant in one of the nearby houses. To put a stop to the relationship, his family sent him to India, where he served as a soldier for three years. He returned to Tralee just in time to see the funeral procession of the girl he loved, who had died of a broken heart. In the public park just outside of Tralee there is a memorial to the ill-fated lovers.

Rosh ha-Shanah
Between September 6 and October 4; 1 and 2 Tishri

Rosh ha-Shanah marks the beginning of the **Jewish New Year** and is the first two of the ten High Holy Days that conclude with YOM KIPPUR, the Day of Atonement. Unlike the secular NEW YEAR'S DAY observance, this is a solemn season during which each person is subject to review and judgment for the coming year. It is a time of prayer and penitence, and is sometimes called the **Day of Remembrance** or the **Day of Blowing the Shofar**. The story of Abraham is read in the synagogue, and the blowing of the *shofar* 'ram's horn' serves as a reminder that although Abraham, in obedience to God, was willing to sacrifice his son, Isaac, God allowed him to sacrifice a ram instead. The plaintive sound of the shofar is also a call to penitence.

Orthodox Ashkenazim (Jews whose ancestors came from northern Europe) observe the ceremony of Tashlikh, a symbolic throwing of one's sins into a body of water, on the first day of Rosh ha-Shanah; Kurds jump into the water; kabbalists shake their garments to "free" themselves from sin. All debts from the past year are supposed to be settled before Rosh ha-Shanah, and many Jews ask forgiveness from friends and family for any slights or transgressions of the concluding year.

Jews celebrate the New Year by eating a special rounded loaf of challah bread, symbolic of the continuity of life, as well as apples dipped in honey, symbols of sweetness and health.

Rousa, Feast of
Between April 29 and June 2, 25 days after Easter

In parts of Greece, the **feast of Mid-Pentecost**, which occurs on the twenty-fifth day after EASTER, is called the Feast of Rousa (or Rosa). On this day a special ceremony is performed to ward off scarlatina or scarlet fever. The children bake rolls out of flour, butter, honey, sesame oil, and other ingredients which they have collected from their neighbors. Along with other foods, these are eaten at a children's banquet, which is followed by singing and dancing. Central to the ceremony, however, is the baking of special ring-shaped cakes, which can only be made by a girl whose name is unique in the neighborhood and which must be baked in a specially built oven.

After the banquet is over, these ring-shaped cakes are divided among the children and hung up to dry. If any of the children who participated in the feast come down with scarlet fever or any similar disease, a piece of the cake is pounded and sprinkled over their skin, which has already been smeared with molten sugar, honey, or sesame oil. This is believed to be an infallible cure.

While the name of this feast is widely believed to come from the crimson rash that accompanies scarlet fever, it may also be a remanent of the old Roman festival known as Rosalia or Feast of the Roses.

Rousalii
Between May 17 and June 20

In Romania, TRINITY SUNDAY is better known as Rousalii, after the three daughters of an emperor who were ill-treated during their life on earth and, when they became goddesses, set out to cause misery and mischief wherever they could. The Romanian peasants believe that during the period from Trinity to ST. PETER'S DAY (June 29), the Rousalii roam over the earth, causing high winds and storms. People may be caught up in whirlwinds, or children may be snatched from the arms of their mothers if they venture outdoors or travel any distance from home.

On the eve of Rousalii, it is traditional to place a twig of wormwood under your pillow. Because medicinal herbs supposedly lose their potency for several weeks after Rousalii, it is considered unwise to gather any herbs from the fields until at least nine weeks have passed.

Royal Ascot
Mid–June

The racecourse on Ascot Heath in Berkshire, England, is the site of a world-famous horse race also called the **Royal Meeting**, that was initiated in 1711 by Queen Anne. The Royal Ascot race meeting goes on for four days in June each year and culminates in the event known as the **Ascot Gold Cup**, an almost-two-mile race for horses more than three years old. Although the Gold Cup race was established in 1807, the original cup was stolen a hundred years later.

A major social and fashion event as well as a sporting one, the Royal Ascot race is usually attended by the British sovereign and receives widespread media coverage. It has even given its name to a type of broad neck-scarf worn by the well-dressed English gentleman at the races.

Royal Easter Show
March–April; Easter holiday

The largest and best-attended of the Australian agricultural fairs, the Royal Easter Show was first held in 1822 as a way of promoting the country's agricultural industry and helping people sell their products. Now it attracts more than a million visitors each year and has expanded to include sports competitions, fashion and flower shows, and celebrity performances, in addition to the usual agricultural and industrial exhibits.

The show has been held at the Moore Park Showground in Sydney every year since 1882, although it was canceled during the 1919 influenza epidemic and during World War II, when the showground was occupied by the Australian army. Sponsored by the Royal Agricultural Society of New South Wales, the Royal Easter Show attracts more than six hundred exhibitors each year and is similar to some of the larger American state fairs, such as the IOWA STATE FAIR and the EASTERN STATES EXPOSITION.

See also ROYAL SHOW DAYS.

Royal Oak Day *See* Shick-Shack Day

Royal Ploughing Ceremony
Early May

An ancient Brahman ritual held on a large field near the Grand Palace in Bangkok, Thailand. It celebrates the official start of the annual rice-planting season and ensures an abundant rice crop. The king presides over the rituals, in which the participants wear scarlet and gold costumes and oxen wear bells.

The Brahmans are a small group in Thailand, numbering only a few thousand families, but they have considerable influence. Royal and official ceremonies are almost always performed by them. The national calendar is prepared by Brahmans and the royal astrologers. Brahman rites blend with those of Buddhism, the dominant Thai religion.

Royal Show Days
Various

More than five hundred agricultural shows are held in Australia each year, but the annual Royal shows, held in each of the state capitals, are famous for their outstanding livestock, agricultural, and industrial exhibits as well as their competitive events. More than four-and-a-half million people visit **the Royals** each year.

The **Brisbane Royal Show**, noted for its unusual display of tropical plants and flowers from all over the state of Queensland, is held in August. The **Hobart Royal Show** is held in mid-October. The **Royal Melbourne Show**, the **Royal Adelaide Show**, and the **Perth Royal Show** are held in September. The ROYAL EASTER SHOW, held at Sydney's seventy-one acre show grounds in early to mid-April, is the most popular of the country's Royal shows. All of the Royals feature attractions such as sheep dog trials, wood chopping, and tree-felling contests, and the uniquely Australian camp drafts—an unusual rodeo event in which cattle are driven over a course that tests both horse and rider.

Other agricultural show days include **Alice Springs Show Day, Tennant Creek Show Day, Katherine Show Day**, and **Darwin Show Day**-all observed in the Northern Territory during the month of July.

Royal Shrine Rite *See* Chongmyo Taeje

Roy Rogers Festival
Wednesday-Saturday, first weekend in June

With his wife Dale Evans, Roy Rogers was one of America's best known singing cowboys. The couple starred in a television series, "The Roy Rogers Show," which was popular during the 1950s and featured his horse, Trigger, and dog, Bullet. Since 1984 Rogers has been honored in his hometown of Portsmouth, Ohio with an annual festival sponsored by the Roy Rogers-Dale Evans Collectors Association. The four day event includes displays of Roy Rogers memorabilia, tours of Roy Rogers' boyhood home, and special performances by old-time Western stars such as Lash LaRue, "King of the Bullwhip." There are showings of Roy Rogers' films and television programs, and Western memorabilia collectors set up booths to sell and exchange their wares. Proceeds from the annual event go into a Roy Rogers Scholarship Fund that pays for a needy student to attend Shawnee State University in Portsmouth. Rogers' son, Roy (Dusty) Rogers, Jr. a cowboy singer in his own right, often attends the festival.

Running of the Bulls
Sunday following August 15

The running of the bulls that takes place on the Sunday following the FEAST OF THE ASSUMPTION in Huamantla, Mexico is considered to be far more dangerous than the famous running of the bulls in Pamplona, Spain during the SAN FERMIN FESTIVAL. This is because the bulls are released from cages in nine different locations, making it almost impossible for those who are trying to outrun the bulls to anticipate the direction from which they are coming or the path that they are likely to follow through the maze of streets that lead to the arena. In Pamplona, the bulls are all released in one location, and they follow a well-known route to the bullring.

This particular running of the bulls dates back to the time when the Spanish conquistadores first brought cattle to Mexico, and the custom of running the bulls through the streets of Huamantla was observed every year until it began to fade around 1700. A group of local people revived the tradition in the 1920s as part of the **Assumption Fiesta**.

Rushbearing Festival
July–August

The custom of rushbearing in England dates back over a thousand years, perhaps to an ancient Roman harvest festival. Young girls would cover the floor of the parish church with rushes and fasten elaborate flower garlands to the walls. After the invention of floor coverings eliminated the need for rushes, the original ceremony gradually evolved into a flower festival, similar to MAY DAY celebrations, with sports, folk dancing, and floral processions.

Modern-day rushbearing ceremonies still take place in Musgrave, Ambleside, Grasmere, and Warcop in Westmorland, although Grasmere claims to be the only community where the rushbearing tradition has remained unbroken since ancient times. The poet William Wordsworth was largely responsible for keeping the custom alive there during the early nineteenth century. He and his sister Dorothy lived at Dove Cottage in Grasmere from 1799 until 1808.

Most rushbearing festivals begin with a procession of children carrying flower garlands and wood-framed bearings with rushes woven into traditional designs and ecclesiastical emblems. When they reach the parish church, they scatter rushes over the floor and arrange the garlands and bearings around the altar and against the church walls. There is a religious service, after which the entire village participates in sports, Maypole dancing, and other festivities. Most rushbearing events take place in July and August, usually on the Saturday nearest ST. ANNE'S DAY (July 26) or St. Oswald's Day (August 5).

Russell, C. M., Auction
Third weekend in March

An art auction, a celebration of western artist Charles M. Russell, and a western-style good time in Great Falls, Mont., where Charley Russell had his home and studio. The affair began in 1969 to raise money for the C. M. Russell (as he signed his paintings) Museum, which was then just getting started. Events include seminars, dance demonstrations by the Blackfeet Indians, an exhibit of paintings and sculpture of western artists and an auction of their works, and a Quick Draw, in which artists have thirty minutes to draw any subject they want. Their quick draws are then auctioned. There is also a chuckwagon brunch, and a Charley Russell Birthday Party (he was born March 19, 1864, and died in 1926).

Charley Russell, a cowboy artist who was also the author of a collection of stories and sketches, *Trails Plowed Under*, depicted the early days of cowpunchers and Indians in Montana and Wyoming. In an introduction to *Trails Plowed Under*, Will Rogers wrote that there will never be "the Real Cowboy, Painter and Man, combined that old Charley was . . . " Charley Russell wrote about himself: "I am an illustrator. There are lots better ones, but some worse." His paintings now are coveted by collectors and worth millions.

Russian Orthodox Christmas
January 7

This celebration of the birth of Christ is observed by the Russian Orthodox Church under the Julian calendar. The calendar trails behind the Gregorian calendar by thirteen days.

Before the 1917 Revolution, the Orthodox CHRISTMAS was widely observed in Russia, Ukraine, Byelorussia, and Georgia. After the Revolution, churches were closed and people practicing religion were persecuted. In 1991, after the Soviet Union had been officially dissolved, Christmas was observed openly and as a state holiday in Russia for the first time in seventy years.

In Moscow, banners were strung up and Nativity scenes were displayed in Red Square. On radio and television, there were nonstop programs telling the Christmas story and showing villagers wearing embroidered folk costumes and carrying tambourines as they made the rounds to offer Christmas bread at every house. On CHRISTMAS EVE, tens of thousands jammed Red Square for performances by choirs and bellringers, and gala fireworks over the multi-colored onion domes of St. Basil's Cathedral. Midnight Masses were celebrated in churches. At the Kremlin, a Christmas charity ball was held to raise money for orphan children.

Before the Revolution, Christmas in Russia was a great feast celebrated with decorated trees, strolling carolers, and gifts. There was a legend of "Father Frost" or "Grandfather Frost," who wore a red robe and black boots, and had a long white beard. Tchaikovsky's "Nutcracker Suite" was, of course, associated with the holiday. When Joseph Stalin was in power some of the aspects of the old Christmas like the tree and the gifts from Father Frost were added to the New Year's celebrations. Then January 7 became a holiday observed only by those who dared to go to church.

See also RUSSIAN WINTER FESTIVAL; OLD CHRISTMAS DAY.

Russian Winter Festival
December 25–January 5

A festival of arts and a time of holiday partying largely in Moscow, Russia, and somewhat less grandly in other cities of the former Soviet Union. In Moscow, there are circuses, performances of Russian fables for children, and other special theatrical presentations as well as traditional outdoor parties with troika rides, folk games, and dancing around fir trees. On New Year's Eve, children wait for gifts from "Father Frost" or "Grandfather Frost," who wears a red robe and black boots and has a white beard, and his helper Snow Girl.

In the past, Father Frost was associated with CHRISTMAS, but religious holidays were stamped out after the 1917 Revolution. In 1992, old traditions were being revived after the dissolution of the Soviet Union, and Father Frost may again become a Christmas figure.

S

Saba Saba Day
July 7

July 7 marks the day when the ruling party of Tanzania, known as TANU or Tanganyika African National Union, was formed in 1954. The TANU Creed is based on the principles of socialism as set forth in the TANU Constitution. Also known as **Saba Saba Peasants' Day** or **Farmers' Day**, it is officially celebrated in a different region of the country each year with traditional dances, sports, processions, rallies, and fairs.

Tanzania, perhaps best known as the home of Mt. Kilimanjaro, was formed in 1964 when Tanganyika merged with Zanzibar.

Sacred Heart of Jesus, Feast of the
Between May 22 and June 25; Friday after Corpus Christi

The feast of the Sacred Heart of Jesus is a solemnity (of the greatest importance) in the Roman Catholic church celebrated on the Friday after CORPUS CHRISTI. It is devoted to the symbol of Jesus' love for all humanity and is a religious holiday in Colombia, South America.

Sacrifice, Feast of *See* 'Id (Eid) al-Adha

Sadie Hawkins Day
Usually first Saturday in November

A day when spinsters can legitimately chase bachelors; if caught, the men are obliged to marry their pursuers. Artist Al Capp invented the unpretty but hopeful Sadie Hawkins and her day in his comic strip, *L'il Abner*, some time in the 1930s. In the following decades, Sadie Hawkins Days, usually featuring dances to which males were invited by females, were popular on school campuses. Celebrations are rarer now.

Capp's long-running *L'il Abner*, named for its good-looking but not-too-bright hero, injected the hillbilly characters of Dogpatch into American culture.

Safari Rally
Easter weekend

This grueling four-day auto race takes place on a 2,550-mile circuit over unpaved roads. Starting outside Nairobi, Kenya, the route is considered the toughest in the world; the roads climb in and out of the Great Rift Valley and there are severe changes in climate. Furthermore, it's the rainy season when the race is held, and can turn the roads into virtual swamps. There are usually about 100 entrants, and fewer than ten to twenty finish.

The rally began as part of the celebrations marking the coronation of Queen Elizabeth II in 1953 and was called the Coronation Rally. It generated such interest that it was continued and renamed the East African Safari, with Kenya, Uganda, and Tanzania on the route. Since 1974, it has been confined to Kenya. Nairobi gets rally fever at this time of year. The city is hung with flags, and cars sprayed to look like rally cars zoom around the streets. Thousands of spectators watch the race at various points along the route.

Saffron Rose Festival
Last Sunday in October

Saffron, the world's most expensive condiment, is harvested from the stigmas of the autumn-flowering *Crocus sativus*. Much of the world's saffron comes from Spain's La Mancha region, and it is used to flavor French bouillabaisse, Spanish paella, cakes, breads, cookies, and the cuisines of East India, the Middle East, and North Africa. It takes 35,000 flowers to produce one pound.

The Saffron Rose Festival held in the town of Consuegra each year celebrates this exotic crop, which must be harvested by hand so that the valuable stigmas are not crumpled. Hosted by a national television personality, the celebrations include parades and contests, traditional folk dancing, and the crowning of a pageant queen. Costumed characters from Cervantes' seventeenth century novel *Don Quixote* stroll among the crowds who flock to Consuegra for the fiesta.

Sailors' Day *See* **Sjomannadagurinn**

St. Agatha Festival
February 3–5

Sant' Agata is especially revered in Catania, Sicily, where her relics are preserved in a silver casket. The beautiful young Sicilian virgin was put to death in 251 because she refused to yield to the advances of a Roman prefect. Among the tortures she endured was having her breasts cut off, and to this day she is the patron saint of nursing mothers and women suffering from diseases of the breast.

On February 3, 4 and 5 each year, a silver bust of Saint Agatha wearing a jewel-encrusted crown is carried in procession from the Cathedral to Catania's various churches. Included in the procession are the *ceri*, huge wooden replicas of candlesticks which are carved with episodes from the saint's martyrdom. The streets are lined with streamers and flowers, and illuminated by strings of colored lights after dark. The festival ends with a fireworks display in the piazza.

St. Agnes' Eve
January 20

The eve of St. Agnes' Day (Jan 21) has long been associated with various superstitions about how young girls might discover the identity of their future husbands. According to one such belief, a girl who went to bed without any supper on this night would dream of the man she was to marry. John Keats used this legend as the basis for his well-known poem, "The Eve of St. Agnes," in which a young maid dreams of her lover and wakes to find him standing at her bedside.

St. Agnes herself was martyred early in the fourth century, when she was only twelve or thirteen years old, because she had consecrated herself to Christ and refused to marry. She was later named the patron saint of young virgins. In art St. Agnes is often represented with a lamb or sometimes with a dove with a ring in its beak.

St. Andrew's Day
November 30

St. Andrew, the brother of St. Peter, was the first apostle called by Christ, but he is primarily known today as the patron saint of Scotland, though he was also chosen to be patron saint of Russia. According to the apocryphal and unreliable Acts of St. Andrew, he went to Greece, and having converted the proconsul's wife there, he

was condemned to be crucified. Fastened to an X-shaped cross by cords rather than nails, he eventually died of thirst and starvation.

St. Andrew's association with Scotland didn't come about until four centuries after his death, when some of his relics were brought there. Although there are a number of churches throughout England and Scotland that bear St. Andrew's name, many associate it with the famous St. Andrew's golf course near Dundee. Some Scots continue the custom of wearing a "St. Andrew's cross" on November 30, which consists of blue and white ribbons shaped like the letter X. The tradition for this form of a cross began no earlier than the thirteenth century.

This is the Laplanders' major feast and a time for weddings and meeting new people.

St. Andrew's Eve (Noc Swietego Andreja)
November 29

The **Eve of St. Andrew's Day** is a special night for young Polish girls who want to find husbands. They play *Andrzejki* or 'Andrew's games,' a kind of fortune-telling. Young girls break off dry branches from cherry trees, place them in wet sand, and tend them carefully for the next few weeks. If the branch blooms by CHRISTMAS, it is believed that they will marry within the year. Pouring liquid wax into cold water is another popular method of foretelling their romantic futures. The shapes into which the wax hardens often provide clues with which they can read their fate. The boys try to foretell their own futures on St. Catherine's Eve (November 25).

The patron saint of both Russia and Scotland (see ST. ANDREW'S DAY), St. Andrew's name means "manly" or "courageous," making him an appropriate target for the appeals of young girls seeking lovers. *Andrzejki* are popular among Polish-Americans as well, where they include peeling apples to see what letter the apple-peel forms when thrown over the peeler's left shoulder.

Austrian peasant women also forced fruit tree branches, but they brought them to Christmas Mass and believed they gave them the ability to see all the witches in the congregation.

St. Anne's Day
July 26

In 1650 a group of Breton sailors built a tiny frame church at the place where the town of Beaupré, Quebec now stands, in honor of St. Anne, the traditional name for the mother of the

Virgin Mary, and wife of Joachim (neither of their names appears in the Bible). The sailors had been caught in a vicious storm at sea and vowed that if St. Anne would save them, they would build her a sanctuary at the spot where their feet first touched land. In 1658 the people of the village built a new and larger church, and it was then that the first of St. Anne de Beaupré's miraculous cures took place, when a local man suffering from rheumatism came to the church and walked away in perfect health. Since that time thousands of cures have been reported at the Basilica of Sainte Anne de Beaupré, which has been called the "Lourdes of the New World" after the famous shrine in France.

St. Anne is the patron saint of Canada. The pilgrimage to her shrine in Beaupré is one of the major pilgrimages on the North American continent. Gypsies from Canada and the United States also arrive to celebrate Santana ('St. Anna'). They camp on the church property, prepare a *slava* feast of special foods for and prayers to St. Anne, and visit their families.

St. Anthony of Padua, Feast of
June 13

St. Anthony of Padua lived in the thirteenth century. He is the patron saint of people who lose things, and of children. He has also become, like St. Francis of Assisi, a patron saint of animals. In the days before automobiles, everyone in Rome sent his horses and mules to St. Anthony's Church to be blessed on this day. The Feast of St. Anthony is also celebrated by many Puerto Rican communities, as well as by American Indians in the southwestern United States. In New Mexico, for instance, traditional Indian dances are held on **San Antonio's Day** in the pueblos at Taos, San Juan, Santa Clara, San Ildefonso, Sandia, Cochiti, and elsewhere.

One of the most outstanding celebrations is held in New York City's Greenwich Village. St. Anthony's Shrine Church on West Houston and Sullivan Streets, in the heart of one of the original 'Little Italy' sections of New York, boasts the oldest Italian Roman Catholic congregation in the city and is the site of a ten-day festival that combines religious observance and the carnival atmosphere of a street fair. Masses are held all day on June 13, and a procession bearing the statue of St. Anthony through the streets begins at seven o'clock that evening. Thousands of people are drawn to the festival, which extends from the weekend before the actual feast day through the weekend following it.

In the village of El Pinar, Spain, a novena ends with the Rosary on St. Anthony's eve. Then a fiesta begins with a parade of huge papier-mâché heads of historical and imaginary characters (called *gigantes* 'giants' and *cabezudos* 'bigheads', on ten-foot-tall wire frames and dressed in long robes. This parade is accompanied by a band playing *pasodobles* (a quick, light march often played at bullfights). Boys toss firecrackers, small children hide in terror, fireworks are set off, street dancing begins, and carnival booths are set up. On the thirteenth, the parade begins at 9 A.M. After a noon High Mass, the statue of St. Anthony is paraded through the village for three hours. The band plays and pairs of men in two lines dance the *jota* (a complex dance using the rhythm of bootheels and castanets). When the dancers tire, they are replaced by eager onlookers. At their return to the church, they block the door to keep St. Anthony from going in so the dancing can go on. Parishioners lay money at the feet of the statue for the support of the church for the coming year.

St. Anthony of Padua was born in Lisbon, Portugal in 1195, and is the patron saint of Portugal. The festivities held here in his honor begin on the evening of June 12 with an impressive display of *marchas*, walking groups of singers and musicians, who parade along the Avenida da Liberdade. The celebration continues the next day with more processions and traditional folk dancing.

Throughout the month of June, children in Lisbon prepare altars in the saint's honor, covering boxes and tables with white paper and decorating them with candles and pictures of St. Anthony. They beg "a little penny for San António" from passersby, but the money—once used to restore the church of San António da Sé after its destruction by an earthquake in 1755—is now put toward a children's feast.

Because he is considered the matchmaker saint, St. Anthony's Eve is a time when young people write letters asking António for help in finding a mate. Another custom of the day is for a young man to present the girl he hopes to marry with a pot of basil concealing a verse or love letter.

St. Anthony the Abbott, Feast of
January 17

Saint Anthony the Abbott, one of the earliest saints, loved both animals and children. His feast day is celebrated in Mexico and other parts of Latin America by bringing household pets and livestock into the churchyard, where the local priest blesses them with holy water. All the animals are carefully groomed and often decorated with ribbons and fresh flowers.

In some Latin American cities, the **Blessing of the Animals** takes place on a different day-often on HOLY SATURDAY, the day before EASTER. People of Hispanic descent living in the United States often celebrate the Blessing of the Animals on this day as well. In Los Angeles, the procession of animals to Our Lady of the Angels Church follows a cobblestone path that was laid by Mexican settlers more than two hundred years ago.

St. Barbara's Day
December 4

In parts of France, Germany, and Syria, St. Barbara's Day is considered the beginning of the CHRISTMAS season. In southern France, especially in Provence, it is customary to set out dishes holding grains of wheat soaked in water on sunny window sills. There is a folk belief that if the "St. Barbara's grain" grows quickly, it means a good year for crops. But if it withers and dies, the crops will be ruined. On CHRISTMAS EVE, the grain is placed near the crèche as a symbol of the coming harvest. There is a similar custom in republics Czech and Slovak and Germany, where cherry branches are placed in water and tended carefully in the hope that they will bloom on Christmas Eve. In Syria, St. Barbara's Day is for feasting and bringing food to the poor.

In Poland, St. Barbara's Day is associated with weather prophecies. If it rains, it will be cold and icy on Christmas Day; if it's cold and icy, Christmas will be rainy.

St. Barnabas' Day
June 11

Before England adopted the Gregorian calendar in 1752, June 11 was the day of the SUMMER SOLSTICE. In addition to being the longest day of the year, it was also St. Barnabas' Day (or **Barnaby Day**), and this association gave rise to the old English jingle, "Barnaby bright, Barnaby bright, the longest day and the shortest night." It was customary on this day for the priests and clerks in the Church of England to wear garlands of roses and to decorate the church with them. Other names for this day were **Long Barnaby** or **Barnaby Bright**.

St. Basil, Feast of
January 1

NEW YEAR'S DAY and the feast day for Agios Vasilis (St. Basil) are one and the same in Greece and Cyprus, and for all Orthodox Christians in the world. Celebrations begin on New Year's Eve when Agios Vasilis is believed to visit each house, blessing the people and their belongings and animals, and bringing presents to the children. Nowadays, the parish priest goes around and blesses the homes of his flock.

On New Year's Day, a cake called the *Vassilopita* 'St. Basil's bread' is ceremoniously sliced, according to varying traditions going back to Byzantine times. Usually the first slice is cut for Jesus Christ, the next is for the house, and the following for absent family members. A coin has been baked in the cake, and the person finding the coin will be the luckiest member of the family that year.

St. Basil was a monk and church father who left many influential writings, including a defense of the study of pagan writings by Christians. He was born about the year 329 and was declared a saint soon after his death on Jan. 1 of the year 379 in Caesarea (in present day Israel).

St. Blaise's Day
February 3

The association of St. Blaise (or Blase, or Blasius) with the blessing of throats can be traced to a number of sources. According to one story, as he was being led to his own execution in 316, he miraculously cured a child who was suffering from a throat infection. Another story has it that he saved the life of a boy who was choking on a fishbone. In any case, St. Blaise, since the sixth century in the East, has been the patron saint of people who suffer from throat afflictions, and celebrations on this day in the Roman Catholic Church often include the blessing of throats by the priest. In Paraguay, the religious services are followed by a holiday festival.

Among the many tortures suffered by this saint was having his body torn by iron combs similar to those used at one time by wool-combers in England. St. Blaise thus became the patron saint of wool-combers as well, and his feast day has traditionally been celebrated in English towns where the woolen industry is important.

In Spain they bake small loaves, called *tortas de San Blas* 'San Blas's loaves,' or *panecillos del santo* 'little breads of the saint'. They are blessed during Mass and each child eats a bit to prevent him or her from choking during the year.

St. Bridget's Day

February 1

St. Bridget (or **Brig(h)id, Bride**) is the female patron saint of Ireland. Her feast day, February 1, was traditionally the first day of spring and of the new year in rural Ireland because it marked the start of the agricultural season. Bridget herself had a great love for the land and took part in tending the crops and caring for the cattle. She also established the first Irish convent, around which the city of Kildare eventually grew. She is credited with an almost endless number of miracles and was buried in 523 in the same church at Downpatrick where the bodies of St. Patrick and St. Columba lie. (See ST. PATRICK'S DAY, ST. COLUMBA'S DAY.)

Many old customs and folk beliefs are associated with St. Bridget's feast day. For example, people would not perform any work on this day that involved turning or twisting, or that required the use of a wheel. It was also customary on the eve of the saint's day for the oldest daughter of the family to bring a bundle of rushes to the door. Playing the role of St. Bridget, she would distribute the rushes among the family members, who would make crosses from them and, after the crosses were sprinkled with holy water, hang them throughout the house. Because St. Bridget is said to have woven the first cloth in Ireland, a cloth known as the *Brat Bhride* 'Bridget's cloak' was left outside on the steps, and during the night it was believed to acquire special healing powers.

The custom of having women propose marriage to men during Leap Year (see LEAP YEAR DAY) can also be traced to St. Bridget, who complained to St. Patrick about the fact that men always took the initiative and persuaded him to grant women the right to do so during one year out of every four. Then Bridget proposed to Patrick, who turned her down but softened his refusal by giving her a kiss and a silk gown.

St. Catherine's Day

November 25, suppressed in 1969 in the Roman Catholic Church

According to apocryphal writings, St. Catherine of Alexandria was sentenced to death by Emperor Maxentius for her extraordinary success in converting people to Christianity in the fourth century. He placed her in a torture machine that consisted of wheels armed with sharp spikes so that she would be torn to pieces as the wheels revolved. She was saved from this grim fate by divine intervention, but then the Emperor had her beheaded. The "Catherine Wheel" in England to-day is a type of firework that revolves in pinwheel fashion. In the United States, the "cartwheels" performed regularly by aspiring gymnasts repeat the motion of St. Catherine on the wheel of torture.

In eighteenth century England, young women in the textile districts engaged in merry-making or "catherning" on this day, which is sometimes referred to as **Cathern Day**. As the patron saint of old maids, St. Catherine is still celebrated in France by unmarried women under twenty-five, especially those employed in the millinery and dressmaking industries. They wear "Catherine bonnets" on November 25—homemade creations of paper and ribbon. The French expression *coiffer Sainte Catherine*, 'to don St. Catherine's bonnet' is used to warn girls that they are likely to become spinsters.

St. Cecilia's Day

November 22

According to her apocryphal acts, which date from the fifth century, St. Cecilia was a Roman from a noble family who was put to death in the second or third century for her Christian beliefs. How she became the patron saint of music and musicians is not exactly known, but according to legend she played the harp so beautifully that an angel left heaven to come down and listen to her. In any case, the Academy of Music in Rome accepted her as its patron when it was established in 1584.

In 1683, a musical society was formed in London especially for the celebration of St. Cecilia's Day. It held festival each year at which a special ode was sung. The poet John Dryden composed his "Ode for St. Cecilia's Day" in 1687 for this purpose. By the end of the seventeenth century it was customary to hold concerts on November 22 in St. Cecilia's honor—a practice which has faded over the years, but there are still many choirs and musical societies that bear her name.

St. Charles' Day

January 30

Charles I, crowned king of England in 1625, was illegally executed on Jan 30, 1649 primarily for defending the Anglican Church. His body was secretly buried in Windsor Castle. He was widely acclaimed as a martyr. A royal decree ordered a special service on this day to be in the Book of Common Prayer from 1662 to 1859. It also ordered it to be a day of national fasting. The anniversary of this event is commemorated by the Society of Charles the Martyr with an annual service at the site of his execution. Commemorative services are also held at the Church of St. Martin-in-the-Fields and in Trafalgar Square in London on or near February 2. St. Charles is the only post-Reformation figure to be honored in this way by the Church of England.

See also SAINTS, DOCTORS, MISSIONARIES AND MARTYRS DAY.

St. Christopher's Day
May 9 or May 22 in the East; July 25 in the West

The lack of reliable information about St. Christopher's life led the Roman Catholic church to remove his name from its universal calendar in 1969. But he is still widely venerated—especially by travelers, of whom he is the patron saint. According to the most popular legend, after his conversion to Christianity, St. Christopher became a ferryman, carrying people across a river on his strong shoulders while using his staff for balance. One day he carried a small child across, but the weight was so overwhelming that he almost didn't make it to the other side. When he did, the child revealed himself as Christ, explaining his great weight by saying, "With me thou hast borne the sins of the world." The name Christopher means 'Christ-bearer.'

St. Christopher's Day is observed by members of the Christopher movement in the United States, whose mission is to encourage individual responsibility and positive action. Founded by a member of the Roman Catholic Maryknoll order , the movement has its headquarters in New York City and embraces people of other denominations as well.

In Nesquehoning, Pennsylvania, St. Christopher's Day is the occasion for the **Blessing of the Cars**. The custom began in 1933, when the pastor of Our Lady of Mount Carmel Church started blessing automobiles on the feast day of the patron saint of travelers because he himself had been involved in three serious car accidents. Sometimes it takes an entire week to bless all the cars that arrive in Nesquehoning from Pennsylvania and other nearby states. In recent years other Catholic churches in the area have taken up the custom and perform their own blessing ceremonies. (See also ST. FRANCES OF ROME.)

St. Columba's Day
June 9

Along with St. Brigid and St. Patrick, St. Columba, also known as **Colm Cille**, **Columeille**, or **Columcille**, is the patron saint of Ireland. Although he led an exemplary life, traveling all over Ireland to set up churches, schools, and monasteries, he is chiefly remembered for his self-imposed exile to the island of Iona off the Scottish coast. According to legend, Columba felt that he was responsible for the battle of Cuildremne, where three thousand men were killed, and resolved to atone for his actions by winning three thousand souls for Christ. He landed at Iona on the eve of PENTECOST, and proceeded to found a monastery and school from which he and his disciples preached the Gospel throughout Scotland. Although he had been forbidden to see his native country again, he returned several years later, blindfolded, to save the poets of Ireland, who were about to be expelled because they had grown so arrogant and overbearing.

St. Columba is also associated with the story of how the robin got its red breast. When Columba asked the robin who landed on his window sill to sing him a song, the robin sang the story of the crucifixion and how he had pulled the thorns out of Christ's forehead and, in doing so, had been covered with his blood.

See also ST. BRIDGET'S DAY; ST. PATRICK'S DAY.

St. Crispin's Day
October 25

According to legend, Crispin and his brother Crispinian traveled from Rome to the French town of Soissons, where they preached and earned a living as shoemakers, offering shoes to the poor at a very low price and using leather provided by angels. The people of Soissons built a church in their honor in the 6th century, and since that time they have been known as the patron saints of shoemakers and other workers in leather. People who wore shoes that were too tight were said to be "in St. Crispin's prison."

This is also the day on which the French and English armies fought the battle of Agincourt in the middle period of the Hundred Years War (1415). The association between the feast day and the battle is so strong that writers sometimes use "St. Crispin's Day" as an expression meaning "a time of battle" or "a time to fight." Also called the **Feast of Crispian**, **St. Crispian**, **Crispin's Day**, **Crispin Crispian**, and the **Day of Crispin Crispianus**.

St. David's Day
March 1

The patron saint of Wales, St. David was a sixth

century priest who founded an austere religious order and many monasteries and churches, and eventually became primate of South Wales. His day is observed not only by the people of Wales but by Welsh groups all over the world. There are large communities of Welsh throughout the United States-particularly in Pennsylvania, Ohio, Wisconsin, and Florida—who celebrate St. David's Day with performances of choral singing, for which the Welsh are noted. The St. David's Society of New York holds an annual banquet on March 1, and the Welsh Society of Philadelphia, which was established in 1802, celebrates with eating, drinking, and songs.

The leek, Wales' national symbol, is often worn on St. David's Day. According to legend, when St. David was leading his people to victory against the Saxons, he commanded them to wear leeks in their hats to avoid being confused with the enemy. In the United States, the daffodil has replaced the leek.

St. Demetrius' Day
October 26 in the East; October 8 in the West

St. Demetrius is the patron saint of Salonika (Thessalonike) in northeastern Greece, where he was martyred in 306. His feast day marks the beginning of winter for farmers, and a spell of warm weather after October 26 is often called "the little summer" or "the summer of St. Demetrius." It is a day for opening and tasting the season's new wines. St. Demetrius is also the patron saint of soldiers.

October 26 is also the anniversary of the liberation of Salonika from the Turks in 1912.

St. Dismas' Day
March 25

According to the Bible, two thieves were crucified with Jesus. The one on his right, traditionally called Dismas, repented and was promised, "Today thou shalt be with me in Paradise" (Luke 23:43). He is therefore the patron saint of persons condemned to death. In the United States, the National Catholic Prison Chaplains' Association, by special permission from Rome, observes the second Sunday in October as **Good Thief Sunday** and holds Masses in American prisons in honor of St. Dismas. March 25 is also the FEAST OF THE ANNUNCIATION.

St. Dominique's Day
January 22

In Macedonia, St. Dominique's Day is known as **Midwife Day**, and only women of child-bearing

age participate in the celebrations, which honor the midwife and not the saint. They bring their local midwife food, wine, and gifts useful in her work. Each woman must kiss the *schema*—a phallic-shaped object usually made from a large leek or sausage. While the visiting women kiss and weep over the schema, the midwife sits on a makeshift throne wearing flowers, necklaces made out of currants, dried figs, and carob-beans, and a single large onion in place of a watch. A banquet follows, at which it is considered acceptable for the women to get drunk. Afterward, the midwife is drawn on a carriage through the village streets to the public fountain, where she is sprinkled with water. The songs and jokes of the women who accompany her are often lewd, and most men try to spend the day indoors.

St. Dymphna's Day
May 15

According to legend St. Dymphna was the daughter of a seventh century Irish king. She fled to Geel, Belgium to escape her pagan father's demand for an incestuous marriage. There she was found by the king and beheaded.

St. Dymphna came to be known as the patron saint of the insane, and for centuries mental patients were brought to her tomb in Geel, where the townsfolk looked after them. An infirmary was eventually built next to the Church of St. Dymphna, and by 1852 Geel was placed under state medical supervision. Today there is a large, well-equipped sanatorium for the mentally ill in Geel, known throughout the world for its "boarding out" system, which allows harmless mental patients to be cared for as paying guests in the homes of local citizens. On May 15 special church services are held and a religious procession moves through the streets carrying a stone from St. Dymphna's tomb—a relic that at one time was applied to patients as part of their therapy.

St. Elizabeth Ann Seton, Feast of
January 4

The first native-born American to be declared a saint, Elizabeth Ann Seton (1774–1821) was canonized in 1975. She was the founder of the first native religious community for women in the United States, the Sisters of Charity, and she was responsible for laying the foundations of the American Catholic school system. She also established orphan asylums, the forerunners of the modern foundling homes and child-care centers run today by the Sisters of Charity.

Special services commemorating Elizabeth Ann

Seton's death on January 4, 1821 are held on major anniversaries at the Chapel of St. Joseph's Provincial House of the Daughters of Charity in Emmitsburg, Maryland, the headquarters for her order of nuns, and at Trinity Episcopal Church in New York City, of which she was a member before her conversion to Roman Catholicism in 1805. Over one hundred thousand people attended her canonization ceremony at St. Peter's Basilica in Rome. On that same day, over 35,000 pilgrims flocked to Emmitsburg, where six Masses were said in honor of the new saint.

St. Elizabeth, Feast of
July 8

The **Fiesta de Santa Isabel** in Huaylas, Peru takes place on July 8 rather than July 2, St. Elizabeth's traditional feast day. This is because at one time the fights that broke out between the whites and the *indios* were so vicious that the *indios* were ordered to hold their own celebration on July 8. Eventually the whites' celebration died out because the Indians' fiesta was so much more lively. Most of the festivities center around musical contests and dancing in the streets. Bullwhip fights were a popular part of the festival until the 1930s.

St. Elizabeth was the mother of John the Baptist (see ST. JOHN THE BAPTIST'S DAY) and a cousin of the Virgin Mary. The Fiesta de Santa Isabel in Huaylas celebrates Mary's visit to her cousin after finding out that she was to become the mother of Jesus (see VISITATION, FEAST OF THE).

Saintes Maries, Fête des (Festival of the Holy Maries)
May 24–25

St. Sarah, patron saint of gypsies, was the Egyptian handmaid of Saints Mary Jacoby and Mary Salome, who were shipwrecked off the Provençal coast of France. According to legend, the three holy women died in the small Provençal village of Les Saintes Maries-de-la-Mer in Provence, where their remains are preserved in the fifteenth century church of Les Saintes-Maries. The relics of Saint Sarah are deeply venerated by the gypsies of southern France, who try to worship at her shrine at least once during their lifetime.

The highlight of the service held at the church during the Festival of the Holy Maries occurs when the flower-decked reliquary of the Maries is lowered slowly through a trap door in the ceiling. On the second day of the festival, there is a procession down to the sea for the blessing of the painted wooden vessel known as the "Bark of the Saints." The bark holds a silver urn which it is believed also contains some of the bones of the saints. Thousands of devout pilgrims make the journey to Les Saintes Maries-de-la-Mer each year.

St. Evermaire, Game of
May 1

The **Spel van Sint Evermarus** or Game of St. Evermaire is a dramatic reenactment of the slaying of eight pilgrims on their way to the Holy Land in 699. After spending the night at a farmhouse, the saint and his seven companions were murdered by their bandit host. This event is portrayed by the townspeople of Rutten, Belgium each year on the first day of May in the meadow near the Chapel of St. Evermaire. Following a procession around the casket believed to contain the saint's bones, costumed villagers representing St. Evermaire and his companions are attacked by fifty "brigands" riding heavy farm horses and led by Hacco, the legendary assailant. By the end of the drama, the saint and the seven pilgrims lie dead.

Although the event was not commemorated for two hundred years after its occurrence, the inhabitants of Rutten have faithfully presented their play for the past ten centuries.

St. Frances Cabrini, Feast of
November 13

The first American citizen to be proclaimed a saint of the Roman Catholic church, Francesca Xaviera Cabrini (1850–1917) was born in Italy. After serving as a nurse and a teacher in her native country, and seeing the miserable conditions under which so many orphans lived, she became a nun and was appointed superior of the orphanage at Codogno. Known thereafter as Mother Cabrini, she founded the Missionary Sisters of the Sacred Heart in 1880 and established a number of other schools and orphanages. Nine years later she and six of her nuns landed in New York, where they had been sent to help the Italian immigrants. She went on to establish orphanages, schools, and hospitals in many American cities; in North, Central, and South America; in Australia; in Europe; and in the Middle East. She was canonized on July 7, 1946.

St. Frances Cabrini's feast day is commemorated in many places, but particularly at Mother Cabrini High School in New York City, in whose chapel she is buried. November 13, the day on which she was beatified, is also observed at every establishment of the Missionary Sisters of the Sacred Heart.

St. Frances of Rome, Feast of
March 9

St. Frances of Rome (1384–1440), also known as **Francesca Romana** or **Frances the Roman**, was a model for housewives and widows. In her forty years of marriage to Lorenzo Ponziano, there was never the slightest dispute or misunderstanding between them. Despite the death of her children, her husband's banishment, and the confiscation of their estates, she continued to nurse the sick and to settle disputes wherever she went. Eventually she founded a society of women who pledged to offer themselves to God and to serve the poor. Known at first as the Oblates of Mary, they were afterwards called the Oblates of Tor de' Specchi, after the building in which they were housed. When she died, St. Frances' body was removed to Santa Maria Nuova in Rome, which is now known as the church of Santa Francesca Romana. She is the patron saint of widows

St. Frances' feast day is observed on March 9, the date on which she died. Because she is also the patron saint of motorists, although no clear reason was given, it is customary for Italian drivers to flock to the Colosseum in Rome for the blessing of their cars . Crowds also visit Tor de' Specchi and Casa degli Esercizi Pii (formerly the Palazzo Ponziano), whose rooms are opened to the public on this day.

See also ST. CHRISTOPHER'S DAY.

St. Francis of Assisi, feast of
October 3–4

The most important festival of the Franciscan calendar in Assisi, Italy, the feast of St. Francis commemorates the saint's transition from this life to the afterlife. For two days the entire town is illuminated by oil lamps burning consecrated oil brought from a different Italian town each year. A parchment in St. Francis' handwriting, believed to be the saint's deathbed blessing to his follower, Brother Leo, is taken to the top of the Santa Maria degli Angeli basilica—built in the sixteenth century around St. Francis' humble hermitage known as the *Porciúncula*—and the people are blessed by the Pope's representative (see FORGIVENESS, FEAST OF).

In the United States, it is not uncommon for children to bring their pets to the church to be blessed on St. Francis' feast day, because of his love for animals as expressed in his *Canticle of Creatures*.

See also ST. ANTHONY THE ABBOT.

St. Genevieve, Jour de Fête à (Days of Celebration)
Second weekend in August

Ste. Genevieve became the first permanent settlement in the state of Missouri when the French arrived in 1725. At one time it rivaled St. Louis in size and importance, and the town still prides itself on its authentic eighteenth- and nineteenth-century architecture. The annual Jour de Fête that has been held in mid-August each year since 1965 not only celebrates the area's French heritage but is a German and Spanish festival as well. Historic homes dating back to 1770 are opened to the public, schoolchildren parade in ethnic costumes, and there's an International Kitchen that serves Spanish, French and German dishes—among them the French *andouille*, a highly seasoned sausage of minced tripe; the Spanish *barbacoa* or barbecue in the form of peppery pork steaks; and the German *leberknaefle*, or liver dumpling.

St. George's Day
April 23; February 25

The patron saint of England, St. George is best known by the twelfth century legend for slaying a vicious dragon that was beseiging a town in Cappadocia. After demanding to be fed two sheep a day, the dragon started asking for people—beginning with the king's daughter. She was on her way to the dragon's den to be sacrificed when she met St. George, who insisted on fighting the dragon and, according to another legend, eventually stunned it with his spear. Making a leash out of the princess's sash, he let her lead the monster back to the city like a pet dog. When the people saw what had happened, they were converted to Christianity. To this day, the emblem of St. George is a dragon.

St. George's Day, sometimes referred to as **Georgemas**, has been observed as a religious feast as well as a holiday since the thirteenth century. In the United States, there are St. George's Societies in Philadelphia; New York City; Charleston, South Carolina; and Baltimore, Maryland dedicated to charitable causes who hold their annual dinner on this day. In former Soviet Union, St. George's Day is celebrated on February 25 as the national day of the Georgian Republic. A festival is held at the cathedral of Mtskheta, the old capital and religious center of Georgia.

See also ST. GEORGE'S DAY IN BULGARIA, PROCESSION OF THE GOLDEN CHARIOT.

St. George's Day in Bulgaria
February 25

ST. GEORGE'S DAY or **Georgiovden** is one of the most important celebrations in Bulgaria. It marks the start of the stock-breeding season. The sheep are turned out to graze on the eve of this day because the dew is believed to have curative powers. Special foods are served the following day, traditional songs are sung, and both livestock and their pens are decorated with blossoming willow twigs.

Bulgarian peasants believe that someone who is born on this day is blessed with wisdom and beauty. In some areas a lamb is slaughtered and the door sill is smeared with its blood to protect the house from witches, illness, and other forms of bad luck.

St. Grouse's Day *See* Glorious Twelfth, the

St. Gudula's Day
January 8

St. Gudula (or Gudule) is the patron saint of Brussels, Belgium. According to legend, Satan was so envious of her piety and influence among the people that he often tried to extinguish her lantern as she returned from midnight Mass. But as she prayed for help, an angel would re-light the candle.

She died in 712, and her relics were moved to Brussels in 978. Since 1047 they have remained in the church of St. Michael, thereafter named the Cathedral of St. Gudula. Her feast day is observed with great solemnity in Brussels, particularly at the cathedral that bears her name.

St. Hans Festival
June 24

Like other MIDSUMMER DAY celebrations, the St. Hans (St. John) Festival in Norway combines both pagan and Christian customs. This festival was originally held in honor of the sun-god, for the ancients believed that the sun's change of course at the solstice was an important event. The gates of the upper and lower worlds stood wide open at this time, and supernatural beings such as trolls and goblins roamed the earth.

After Christianity was introduced, the Norwegian midsummer festival was linked to the birth of John the Baptist (see ST. JOHN THE BAPTIST'S DAY), and it became known as **Sankt Hans Dag**, or **St. John's Day**. But some of the ancient customs and superstitions surrounding Midsummer Day have persisted. Only a century ago it was still common for Norwegians to hide their pokers and to carve a cross on their broomsticks as a way of warding off witches who might otherwise use these household items for transportation. The present-day custom of decorating with birch boughs also has its roots in ancient times, when the foliage was considered a symbol of the life force that awakens in Nature in the spring and early summer.

The festival of St. Hans is still celebrated in Norway much as it has been for hundreds of years. On *Jonsok*, or St. John's Eve, Norwegians who live near the fiords head out in their boats, which are decorated with green boughs and flowers, to get the best possible view of the St. John's bonfires on the mountains.

St. Hubert de Liège, feast of
November 3

Saint Hubert is the patron saint of hunters, of dogs, and of victims of hydrophobia (rabies). His feast day is especially honored at the church named for him in the little town of St. Hubert, Luxembourg. People who live in the Forest of Ardennes bring their dogs to the church to be blessed, and Saint Hubert's Mass marks the official opening of the hunting season. In some places special loaves of bread are brought to the Mass to be blessed, after which everyone eats a piece and feeds the rest to their dogs, horses, and other domestic animals to ward off rabies.

According to legend, Saint Hubert was more interested in hunting than he was in observing church festivals. But on GOOD FRIDAY one year, while he was hunting, he saw a young white stag with a crucifix between his antlers. The vision was so powerful that he changed his ways, became a monk, and was eventually made Bishop of Liège. The site of this event is marked by a chapel about five miles from St. Hubert.

Thousands of pilgrims visit Saint Hubert's shrine at the Church of Saint Hubert each year. Among the artifacts there are his hunting horn and mantle, supposedly given to him by the Virgin Mary—a thread of which, when placed on a small cut on the forehead, is supposed to cure people who suffer from rabies. His relics are enshrined at the cathedral in Liège.

St. Ignatius Loyola, Feast of
July 31

St. Ignatius Loyola (1491–1556) founded the Society of Jesus, the Roman Catholic religious order whose members are known as Jesuits. Now the largest single religious order in the world, the Jesuits are known for their work in education, which St. Ignatius believed was one of the best ways to help people. In the United States, which currently has more Jesuits than any other country, they train hundreds of thousands of high school, college, and university students every year. St. Ignatius is the patron saint of retreats and those who attend retreats.

The Feast of St. Ignatius is celebrated by Jesuits everywhere, but particularly in the Basque region of Spain where he was born. The largest Basque colony in North America, located in Boise, Idaho, holds its annual **St. Ignatius Loyola Picnic** on the Sunday nearest July 31—an event often referred to as the **Basque Festival**. The first Basques settled in America in 1865.

St. James's Day
July 25; April 30

The Apostle James the Great, also known as Santiago, is the patron saint of Spain. His feast day is celebrated in the Western church on July 25, the anniversary of the day on which, according to tradition, his body was miraculously discovered in Compostela, Spain, after being buried there for eight hundred years. A church was built on the site, which later became the town of Santiago de Compostela, once a place of pilgrimage second only to Jerusalem and Rome. St. James's Day is still celebrated in Compostela with a week-long festival that features a mock-burning of the twelfth century cathedral and an elaborate fireworks display.

In Loíza, Puerto Rico, the **Fiesta of St. James the Apostle** or **Fiesta de Santiago Apóstol** is the biggest celebration of the year. It focuses on three images of the saint—the *Santiago de los Muchachos* (St. James of the Children), the *Santiago de los Hombres* (St. James of the Men), and the *Santiago de las Mujeres* (St. James of the Women)—which are carried from the homes of the *mantenedoras* (keepers) who have kept guard over them all year to a place near the sea known as *Las Carreras* 'the racetracks'. Santiago de los Hombres begins the procession, stopping in front of the house where another Saint is kept. This second image joins the first and the procession continues until all three end up at Las Carreras, where the traditional ceremony of racing with the flags of the Saints takes place. Farm workers and fisherman dress in traditional costumes and perform music and dances of African origin. St.

James's Day is also a popular choice for baptisms and marriages.

His feast day in the Eastern church is April 30.

St. John's Day in Portugal
June 24

Both S T. J OHN THE B APTIST'S D AY and St. John's Eve (see M IDSUMMER E VE) are widely celebrated in Portugal with parades, pageants, bullfights, fireworks, and other popular amusements. Many of the traditional rites connected with fire, water, and love are still observed here as well. Young people dance around bonfires and couples often leap over these fires, holding hands. Mothers sometimes hold their children over the burning embers, and cattle and flocks are driven through the ashes—all to take advantage of the curative powers of St. John's fires. Similar traditions focus on water, which on St. John's Eve is supposed to possess great healing power.

One of the most interesting St. John's Day celebrations takes place in Braga and is known as the *Dança de Rei David* or Dance of King David. The role of King David is always performed by a member of a certain family living near Braga, and the dance itself probably dates back to medieval times. The King is dressed in a tall crown and voluminous cape. Ten shepherds or courtiers who accompany him wear velevet coats in brilliant colors and turban-style hats. Shepherds play ancient tunes on their fiddles, flutes, and triangles. As they parade through town this group stops frequently to perform the ritualistic Dance of King David.

St. John the Baptist, Martyrdom of
August 29

St. John the Baptist was beheaded by King Herod because he had denounced Herod's marriage to Herodias, the wife of his half-brother Philip (Luke 3:19,20), an illegal union according to Jewish law. Herodias' daughter by a former marriage, by legend called Salome, pleased Herod so much with her dancing that he swore to give her whatever she wanted. At her mother's urging she asked for the head of John the Baptist on a platter (Matthew 14:3-12). Herod, grief-stricken over having let himself be maneuvered into killing a good and innocent man, later had the head concealed within the palace walls to spare it any further indignities. It remained there until after the discovery of the holy cross by St. Helena, an event which drew many pilgrims to Jerusalem. Two of them found the head after St. John appeared to them in a vision.

The Martyrdom of St. John the Baptist—also known as the **feast of the Beheading** in the Eastern Orthodox Church—has been celebrated by Christians since the fourth century. The observance started at Sebaste (Samaria), where the Baptist was believed to have been buried. (See also ST. JOHN THE BAPTIST'S DAY, EXALTATION OF THE CROSS.)

St. John the Baptist's Day
June 24

It is unusual for a saint's day to commemorate his birth rather than his death, but John the Baptist and the Virgin Mary are the exceptions here. (See NATIVITY OF THE VIRGIN MARY, FEAST OF THE). Roman Catholics, Eastern Orthodox Christians, Anglicans, and Lutherans honor St. John on the anniversary of his birth; the Roman Catholic and Orthodox churches commemorate his death as well, on August 29 (see MARTYRDOM OF ST. JOHN THE BAPTIST).

John was the cousin of Jesus, born in their old age to Zachariah and Elizabeth, a kinswoman of the Virgin Mary. John was the one chosen to prepare the way for the Messiah. It is a pious belief of many that he was sanctified—that is, freed from original sin—in his mother's womb when she was visited by Mary. (See VISITATION, FEAST OF THE). He lived as a hermit in the wilderness on a diet of honey and locusts until it was time to begin his public ministry. He preached repentance of sins and baptized many, including Jesus. (See EPIPHANY.) He denounced King Herod and his second wife, Herodias, and it was she who vowed revenge for John's condemnation of her marriage, and who had her daughter, Salome, bring her the Baptist's head on a platter. (See MARTYRDOM OF ST. JOHN THE BAPTIST.)

Many St. John's Day customs date from pre-Christian times, when June 24 was celebrated as MIDSUMMER DAY. Celebrations in some areas still bear the hallmarks of the old pagan SUMMER SOLSTICE rites, such as bonfires, dancing, and decorating with flowers. For the French in Canada, the **Feast of the Nativity of St. John the Baptist** is one of the biggest celebrations of the year, especially in Quebec. The San Juan Fiesta in New York City takes place on the Sunday nearest June 24 and is the year's most important festival for Hispanic-Americans.

St. John's Day (el Día de San Juan) is a major holiday throughout Mexico. As the patron saint of waters, St. John is honored by decorating fountains and wells and by bathing in local streams and rivers. The bathing begins at midnight—often to the accompaniment of village bands—and it is customary for spectators to throw flowers among the bathers. In Mexico City and other urban centers, the celebration takes place in fashionable bath-houses rather than rivers, where there are diving and swimming contests as well. Street vendors sell small mules made out of cornhusks, decorated with flowers and filled with sugar cane and candy.

A family of yellow flowered plants, commonly called St.-John's-wort, is used by voodoo conjurors and folk medicine practitioners to ward off evil spirits and ensure good luck. In the southern United States, all species of the plant are called John the Conqueror root, or "John de Conker," and all parts of it are used: the root, leaves, petals, and stems. The plant's imagery is often mentioned in African-American folklore and blues.

The leaves, and often the petals, contain oil and pigment-filled glands that appear as reddish spots when held to the light. According to legend, these spots are John the Baptist's blood, and the plant is most potent if rituals are performed on his birthday.

See also ST. JOHN'S DAY IN PORTUGAL, ST. HANS FESTIVAL.

St. John the Evangelist's Day
December 27; formerly May 6

John the Evangelist, also called **St. John the Divine**, was not only the youngest of the Apostles but the longest-lived, dying peacefully of natural causes at the advanced age of ninety-four. Although he escaped actual martyrdom, St. John endured considerable persecution and suffering for his beliefs. He is said to have been forced to drink poison (so he is the patron saint of protection against poison), cast into a cauldron of boiling oil, and at one point banished to the lonely Greek island of Patmos, where he worked among the criminals in the mines. He remained healthy, vigorous, and miraculously unharmed throughout these trials and returned to Ephesus where it is believed he wrote the Gospel according to John. He is also believed to be the author of the New Testament Book of Revelation. See also ST. STEPHEN'S DAY.

St. Joseph's Day
March 12–19

The feast of the foster-father of Jesus, known as **Dia de San Giuseppe** is widely observed in Italy as a day of feasting and sharing with the poor, of whom he is the patron saint. Each village prepares a "table of St. Joseph" by contributing money, candles, flowers, or food. Then they invite three guests of honor—representing Jesus, Mary, and Joseph—to join in their feast, as well as others representing the twelve Apostles. They also invite the orphans, widows, beggars, and poor people of the village to eat with them. The food is blessed by the village priest and by the child chosen to represent Jesus; then it is passed from one person to the next. The **Feast of St. Joseph** is celebrated by Italians in the United States and in other countries as well.

It is a week-long festival in Valencia, Spain called **Fallas de San Jose (Bonfires of St. Joseph)**. It has its roots in medieval times, when on St. Joseph's Eve, the carpenters' guild made a huge bonfire out of the wood shavings that had accumulated over the winter—St. Joseph being their patron saint. This was considered the end of winter and the last night on which candles and lamps would have to be lighted. In fact, the carpenters often burned the *parot*, or wooden candalabrum, in front of their shops. One year the *parot* was dressed up as a local gossip and burned in effigy.

Nowadays the *parots* have become *fallas*, or huge floats of intricate scenes made of wood and papier-mâché, satirizing everything from the high cost of living to political personalities. On St. Joseph's Eve, March 18, the *fallas* parade through the streets. At midnight on March 19, the celebration ends with the spectacular ceremony known as the *crema*, when all the *fallas* are set on fire. One *Ninot* or 'doll' from each *falla* is chosen, and before the fire the best one is selected and preserved in a special museum. Another highlight is the *crida*, which consists of a series of public announcements made from the Torres de Serrano by the Queen of the Fallas and the city mayor. The festival is said to reflect the happy and satirical nature of the Valencians.

See also SWALLOWS OF SAN JUAN CAPISTRANO.

St. Joseph the Worker, Feast of
May 1

A public holiday in Malta, celebrated with festivities throughout the country. In Valletta, a highlight of the Mass conducted by the archbishop in St. John's Cathedral is the blessing of the tools and products of laborers and craftsmen.

St. Joseph, the husband of the Virgin Mary, was a carpenter who taught Jesus his craft. He is the patron saint of workers, laborers, carpenters, cabi-netmakers, and joiners. In 1955, Pope Pius XII established the Feast of St. Joseph the Worker on May 1 as a counter-celebration to the Communists' May Day celebrations honoring workers.

See also MAY DAY; DIA DE SAN GIUSEPPE.

St. Knut's Day
January 13

Tjugondag Knut or St. Knut's Day marks the end of the Yuletide season in Sweden. It was King Canute (or Knut), ruler of Denmark, England, and Norway in the eleventh century, who decreed that there should be no fasting between CHRISTMAS and the end of the Epiphany Octave (the eighth day after EPIPHANY). But rather than letting the holidays fade quietly, Swedish families throughout the country hold parties to celebrate the final lighting (and subsequent dismantling) of the Christmas tree. After letting the children eat the cookies and candies used to decorate the tree, and after packing the ornaments away in their boxes, it is customary to hurl the tree through an open window.

In Norway, January 13 is knowns as **Tyvendedagen**, or **Twentieth Day**, since it is the twentieth day after Christmas. It is observed in much the same way, with parties and the dismantling of the Christmas tree. But instead of throwing the tree out the window, it is chopped up and burned in the fireplace.

St. Lazarus's Day
Between March 27 and April 30; Saturday before Palm Sunday

In Bulgaria, St. Lazarus's Day (**Lazarouvane** or **Lazarovden**) is the great Slavic festival of youth and fertility and doesn't have much to do with Lazarus himself. The day takes its name from a series of ritual games and songs studied in advance by young girls during LENT. Although there are many versions of the ritual, they all have a common focus, which is the "coming out" of girls who are ready to be married. Particular attention is paid to dress, which usually involves colorful traditional costumes and heavy jewelry. In former times, the people of Bulgaria believed that the more elaborate the rituals devoted to marriage, the better the chances for happiness, long life, and a house full of children.

See also LAZARUS SATURDAY.

St. Leopold's Day
November 15

Saint Leopold, the patron saint of Austria, died

in 1136 and was buried in the abbey he had established in Klosterneuburg. His feast day is observed there with the ceremony known as **Fasselrutschen** or the **Slide of the Great Cask** in the abbey's wine cellar. Participants climb the narrow staircase that leads to the top of the cask, which was sculpted by a famous Viennese woodcarver and holds twelve thousand gallons of wine, and then slide down its smooth surface to a padded platform at its base. The faster the trip down, according to tradition, the better luck the person will have in the coming year.

St. Leopold's Day is also known as **Gaense Tag** or **Goose Day** because the traditional evening meal served on this day is roast goose. November 15 marks the beginning of the new wine season, and all over Austria there are wine-drinking picnics and parties on this day.

St. Lucy's Day
December 13

According to tradition, St. Lucy or Santa Lucia was born in Syracuse, Sicily in the third century. She was endowed with a fatal beauty that eventually attracted the unwanted attentions of a pagan nobleman, to whom she was betrothed against her will. She is the patron saint of the blind because in an attempt to end the affair, she cut out her eyes, which her suitor claimed "haunted him day and night." But God restored her eyes as a reward for her sacrifice. She was then killed by a sword thrust through her throat. Because of this she is the patron saint for protection from throat infections.

St. Lucy supposedly blinded herself on the shortest, darkest day of the year (see WINTER SOLSTICE), and she later became a symbol of the preciousness of light. Her day is widely celebrated in Sweden as **Luciadagen**, which marks the official beginning of the CHRISTMAS season. Lucy means "light," and to the sun-starved inhabitants of Scandinavia, she always appears in a shining white robe crowned by a radiant halo. It is traditional to observe Luciadagen by dressing the oldest daughter in the family in a white robe tied with a crimson sash. Candles are set into her metal crown, which is covered with lingonberry leaves. The younger girls are also dressed in white and given haloes of glittering tinsel. The boys—called *Starngossar* or Star Boys—wear white robes and tall cone-shaped hats made of silver paper, and carry star-topped scepters. The "Lucia Bride" with her crown of burning candles, followed by the Star Boys, younger girls, and dancing children, called *tomten* 'gnomes', wakens each member of

the household on the morning of December 13 with a tray of coffee and special saffron buns or ginger cookies.

Although this is a family celebration, the Lucia tradition nowadays is observed in schools, offices, and hotels as well. Specially chosen Lucias and their attendants visit hospitals to cheer up the sick and elderly. The largest public celebration in Sweden takes place in Stockholm , where hundreds of girls compete for the title of "Stockholm Lucia."

From Sweden the Lucy celebrations spread to Finland, Norway, and Denmark. Swedish immigrants brought St. Lucy's Day or Luciadagen to the United States, and the Swedish customs survive in Swedish-American communities throughout the country. The Central Swedish Committee of the Chicago Area holds a major citywide festival at the downtown Chicago Civic Center on the afternoon of December 13 each year. Nearly every Swedish club and organization in the city chooses its own Lucia bride, and one is chosen by lot to be crowned at this festival with a golden crown made by hand in Sweden. A similar celebration takes place at the American Swedish Historical Museum in Philadelphia, with Swedish Christmas songs, folk dances, and a Lucia procession. In Rockford, Illinois, the St. Lucy's Day program is staged by the Swedish Historical Society at the Erlander Home Museum. The young woman chosen as Lucia on this day has to meet certain criteria, such as participation in Swedish classes, contributions to Swedish culture, or membership in one of Rockford's many Swedish societies.

At Bethany College in Lindsborg, Kansas, freshmen in the women's dormitories are awakened at three o'clock in the morning by a white-clad Lucia bearing the traditional refreshments of coffee and baked goods. St. Lucy's Day is also observed by Swedish-Americans in Minneapolis-St. Paul, Seattle, and San Diego.

St. Marinus Day
September 3

This is the official foundation day of the Republic of San Marino, a landlocked area of less than thirty square miles on the Adriatic side of central Italy. The oldest independent country in Europe, San Marino takes its name from St. Marinus, a fourth century deacon and stonemason. According to legend, he was working on an aqueduct one day when a woman wrongly identified him as the husband who had deserted her. She pursued him into the mountains, where he barricaded himself in a cave until she eventually gave up. He spent the rest of his life on Monte Titano as a hermit. The present-day city of San Marino was built on the site of his original hermitage.

St. Mark's Day
April 25

In Hungary, St. Mark's Day is also known as **Buza-Szentelo** or the **Blessing of the Wheat.** The people follow their priest or minister in a procession to the wheat fields where the crop is blessed. They return to the village carrying spears of the blessed wheat which some believe has healing powers. The fields are again blessed when harvesting begins on June 29, SS. PETER AND PAUL'S DAY.

St. Mark the Evangelist is also associated with Venice, Italy, where the church bearing his name was built over the place where his relics were taken in 815.

St. Martin's Day *See Martinmas*

St. Mary's County Maryland Oyster Festival
Second weekend in October

Oyster festivals are common in areas where the oyster industry has survived. But the festival that has been held at the start of the oyster season in Leonardtown, Maryland since 1967 has a special significance for those skilled in the fine art of oyster shucking. The highlight of the October festival is the National Oyster Shucking Championship to see who can open the most oysters as quickly and neatly as possible. The winner of this contest goes on to compete in the Galway Oyster Festival in Ireland the following year.

The season's new oysters are served in every imaginable way: raw on the half-shell with sauce, steamed, fried, and stewed in a broth. The two-day festival also offers exhibits of oyster-opening knife collections, oyster shell collections, and films on the history, geography, and culture of southern Maryland.

St. Médardus' Day
June 8

St. Médardus, who lived from about 456 to 545, was the Bishop of Noyon and Tournai in France. Because he was the patron saint of farmers and good weather, he has come to play a role in weather lore similar to that of the English St. Swithin (see ST. SWITHIN'S DAY). In Belgium he is known as the rain saint, and there is an old folk rhyme that says, "If it rains on St. Médard's Day, it will rain for forty days."

St. Michael's Day
September 29 in the West; November 8 in the East; first Sunday in October in Finland

Coming at the end of the harvest season, St. Michael's Day has traditionally been a day for giving thanks and for celebrating the end of the season of hard work in the fields. In Finland, **Mikkelin Paiva** is observed on the first Sunday in October. In the countryside, servants are hired and next year's labor contracts signed. The harvesters celebrate the end of their labors on Saturday night by holding candle-light dances. The observation of Mikkelin Paiva replaced an earlier festival known as **Kekri**, which was celebrated by each landowner as soon as his crops were safely in the barns. The "Kekri" or spirits of the dead were rewarded with a feast for their help with the farm work. The Kekri festival was probably a remnant of some form of pagan ancestor worship.

In Ethiopia, where St. Michael's Day is observed on November 8, the people attend services at any churches consecrated to *Mika'el*. The celebrations include chanting and dancing by the clergy, and a procession carrying the holy ark or *tabot* out of the church and then, later in the day, returning it. The services are followed by singing and dancing, an occasion for young men to possibly find a bride.

See also TIMQAT; MICHAELMAS.

St. Modesto's Day
December 18

St. Modesto is the patron saint of farmers in Greece. His feast day is celebrated with various rituals in honor of farm animals. Sometimes a special Mass is said for the cattle. In Lemnos, *kollyva* (cooked wheat berries) and holy water are mixed with their fodder, while in Lesbos, the holy water is sprinkled on the fields to ward off locusts and disease. For horses and oxen, December 18 is a day of rest.

The Eastern Orthodox church reserves this day to commemorate St. Modestus who was patriarch of Jerusalem, 631–634. He had been abbot of St. Theodosius' Monastery in the desert of Judah, and was administrator of Jerusalem during the captivity of St. Zacharias in Persia. Modestus is known for a sermon he preached on the bodily assumption of the Virgin Mary into heaven.

St. Nicholas' Day
December 6

Very little is known about St. Nicholas' life, except that in the fourth century he was the bishop of Myra in what is now Turkey. One of the legends surrounding him is that he saved three sisters from being forced into prostitution by their poverty-stricken father by throwing three bags of gold into their room, thus providing each of them with a dowry. This may be the source of St. Nicholas' association with gift-giving. On December 6 in the Netherlands, St. Nicholas still rides into town on a white horse, dressed in his red bishop's robes and preceded by "Black Peter," a Satanic figure in Moorish costume who switches the bad children while the good are rewarded with candy and gifts. (See CHRISTMAS EVE) He is the patron saint of sailors, and churches dedicated to him are often built so they can be seen off the coast as landmarks.

The American Santa Claus, a corruption of 'St. Nicholas,' is a cross between the original St. Nicholas and the British "Father Christmas." The political cartoonist Thomas Nast created a Santa Claus dressed in furs and looking more like King Cole—an image that grew fatter and merrier over the years, until he became the uniquely American figure that adorns thousands of cards, decorations, and homes throughout the CHRISTMAS season. Although Americans open their gifts on CHRISTMAS or CHRISTMAS EVE, in the Netherlands, Switzerland, Germany, and some other European countries, gifts are still exchanged on December 5, St. Nicholas' Eve, or December 6, St. Nicholas' Day.

St. Nicholas' Day in Italy
May 7–8

The **Festa di San Nicola** is celebrated in Italy on May 7 and 8, the anniversary of the transfer of the saint's relics by a group of eleventh century sailors from Bari, who risked their lives to rescue St. Nicholas' body from the infidels who threatened to desecrate his tomb at Myra in Asia Minor. This is the St. Nicholas who is associated with Christmas and the giving of gifts to children. Therefore he is the patron saint of children.

Thousands of pilgrims come to the Romanesque Church of San Nicola in Bari to worship at the saint's tomb and to ask for his help. Nicholas is also the patron saint of sailors. There is a procession on this day in which a group of Barese sailors take the saint's image down to the water, where it is placed on a flower-decked boat and taken out to sea. Hundreds of small craft carrying pilgrims and fishermen accompany the vessel, and at night the statue is returned to its place of honor on the altar of San Nicola's crypt.

St. Olav's Day
July 29

The feast day of St. Olav, also known as Olsok, was at one time observed throughout Norway, although today the primary celebration takes place in Trondheim. It commemorates the death of Olav Haraldsson—the second King Olav—at the Battle of Stiklestad in the year 1030. By 1070, work had begun on Nidaros Cathedral, which was erected over King Olav's grave and drew crowds of pilgrims during the annual Olsok days throughout the Middle Ages. Although it is said that King Olav did not display many saintly qualities during his reign (1015–1028), he was responsible for introducing Christianity, and legend has embellished his reputation over the years, so that today he is also considered the champion of national independence.

St. Olav is the patron saint of Norway, and his name is identified with the highest Norwegian civilian decoration. The anniversary of his death is still marked by religious services, fireworks, and public merry-making. Every year the battle in which he died is reenacted by a large and colorful cast, occasionally drawing a well-known actor such as Liv Ullman, during the **St. Olav Festival** in Trondheim.

In the Faeroe Islands, this is known as **Olavsoka** 'St. Olaf's Wake,' their national holiday. Parliament opens on the twenty-ninth, but the festivities—that include dancing, rock concerts, sports events, speeches, drinking, a parade of members of *Logting* (parliament) to the church for a sermon then back for the opening session—begin the night before and continue into the early hours of the thirtieth.

St. Patrick's Day
March 17

St. Patrick was born about 390 in Roman Britain—scholars disagree as to exactly where—and named Magonus Sucatus. His grandfather was a Christian priest, and his father a deacon and an official of the Roman Empire in Britain. Although he was kidnapped at the age of sixteen by Irish raiders and sold into slavery in Ireland, he ended up as the country's patron saint. He escaped after six years, and received his religious training in continental monasteries. After being consecrated a bishop, he returned to Ireland about 432 as a missionary to the pagans. The association of St. Patrick with the shamrock stems from his supposed use of its three-part leaf to explain the concept of the Holy Trinity to his largely uneducated listeners (see TRINITY SUNDAY).

St. Patrick's Purgatory has been a famed site of pilgrimage since the early thirteenth century. It is on Station Island in Lough Derg in County Donegal where St. Patrick had a vision promising that all who came to the sanctuary in penitence and faith would receive an indulgence for their sins. Additionally, if their faith remained strong, they would be allowed a glimpse of the tortures of the damned and the joys of the redeemed.

The **Feast of St. Patrick** is celebrated by Roman Catholics, the Anglican Communion, and Lutherans on March 17. The day is also popularly celebrated by "the wearing of the green," with many people of Irish and other extractions wearing some item of green clothing. Parties featuring corned beef and cabbage, and even the drinking of beer dyed green with food coloring are also part of this celebration of Irish heritage. The St. Patrick's Day Parade in New York City, which dates back to 1762, is the largest in the United States, and a major event for Irish-Americans. As many as 125,000 marchers participate, stopping at St. Patrick's Cathedral on Fifth Avenue for the blessing of the archbishop of New York. In Boston the St. Patrick's Day Parade goes back even farther, to 1737. In fact, during the seige of Boston which forced the British evacuation on March 17, 1776, General George Washington used "Boston" as the day's secret password and "St. Patrick" as the appropriate response (see EVACUATION DAY).

See also ST. PATRICK'S DAY PARADE IN SAVANNAH.

St. Patrick's Day Encampment
Weekend nearest March 17

The winter of 1779–1780 was a time of discouragement and despair for the Continental Army. General George Washington set up camp in Morristown, New Jersey that year so he could rest and reassemble his men. The soldiers' winter routine was bleak and monotonous. There was so much work to be done that they did not even celebrate CHRISTMAS. General Washington did, however, grant his men a holiday on March 17, ST. PATRICK'S DAY. A good portion of the American army was Irish, and political changes taking place in Ireland at the time found a sympathetic following among the American revolutionaries.

The St. Patrick's Day Encampment of 1780 is reenacted each year at the Jockey Hollow Encampment Area in Morristown. Thirty to forty men and their camp followers set up camp for the weekend and perform more or less the same chores and activities that Washington's men per-

formed in the winter of 1779–1780, although the trend toward milder winters has robbed the event of some of its authenticity. The original March 17 encampment was not the first St. Patrick's Day celebration in America; the first celebration took place in Boston in 1737.

St. Patrick's Day Parade in Savannnah
March 17

One of the oldest and biggest parades in the country, held since 1824 in Savannah, Ga., a city with a long Irish history. The oldest Irish society in the United States, the Hibernian Society, was formed in Savannah in 1812 by thirteen Irish Protestants. The next year they held a private procession which was a forerunner to the present St. Paddy's parade. The first public procession is recorded in 1824, and public parades have been held ever since. There have been only six lapses of this parade: for wars, sympathy for the Irish Revolution, and for an unrecorded reason. The first floats appeared in 1875; according to reports of the time, one carried two women representing Ireland and America, and another had thirty-two women for the thirty-two counties of Ireland.

Today the parade, which follows a route through the city's historic district, comprises between 200 and 300 separate units, including family groups, commercial floats, Georgia and out-of-state high school bands, and military bands and marching units. The day begins with Mass at the Cathedral of St. John the Baptist. Members of the Fenian Society of Savannah, formed in 1973, start things off with a members' breakfast of green grits before they form a marching unit. The other main activity is eating. The fare is predominately green—grits, beer, doughnuts, etc. Crowds are estimated at anywhere from 300,000 to 500,000.

See also ST. PATRICK'S DAY.

St. Paul's Shipwreck, Feast of
February 10

A commemoration in Malta of the shipwreck of St. Paul there in 60 A.D., an event told about in the New Testament. Paul, the story says, was being taken as a prisoner aboard ship to Rome where he was to stand trial. When storms drove the ship aground, Paul escaped and was welcomed by the "barbarous people" (meaning they were not Greco-Romans). He got their attention when a snake bit him on the hand but did him no harm, and he then healed people of diseases. Paul stayed for three months in Malta, converting the people to Christianity (Acts 27:1–28:11). Paul is the patron saint of Malta and snakebite victims.

The day is a public holiday, and is observed with family gatherings and religious ceremonies and processions.

St. Paul Winter Carnival
Last week of January–first week of February

This ten-day winter festival was established in 1886 in response to a newspaper story from the East that described St. Paul, Minnesota as "another Siberia, unfit for human habitation." A group of local businessmen set out to publicize the area's winter attractions, and the first winter carnival featured an Ice Palace in St. Paul's Central Park constructed by a Montreal contractor. Since that time, an entire legend has developed about the founding of St. Paul. This legend is reenacted each year. The main players are Boreas, King of the Winds, the Queen of the Snows, and the fire-god Vulcanus, who storms the Ice Palace but is persuaded by the Queen to submit to Boreas and let the people enjoy their carnival celebration.

A highlight of the carnival is the five hundred mile snowmobile race from Winnipeg, Canada to St. Paul. There are also ice skating and ice fishing contests, ski and sled dog races, softball on ice, and a parade featuring antique sleighs and cutters. On Harriet Island in the Mississippi River there is a display of snow sculptures by master craftsmen from Hokkaido, Japan—home of the SAPPORO SNOW FESTIVAL.

St. Peter's Fiesta
Weekend nearest June 29

As the patron saint of fishermen, **St. Peter's Day** is celebrated in fishing villages and ports all over the world. Perhaps the largest American celebration takes place in Gloucester, Massachusetts, where St. Peter's Fiesta has been celebrated by the Italian-American fishing community for several decades. The life-sized statue of St. Peter donated by an Italian-American fishing captain in 1926 provided a focal point for the celebration, and the Sunday morning procession carrying this statue from the St. Peter's Club to an outdoor altar erected on the waterfront is still the highlight of the two-day festival. The Mass that follows is usually celebrated by the Roman Catholic archbishop of Boston, who also officiates at the Blessing of the Fleet that afternoon.

Other festival events include fishing boat races, concerts, fireworks, and a "greasy-pole" contest in which competitors try to retrieve a red flag from the end of a well-greased spar suspended over the water.

St. Rose of Lima's Day
August 30

St. Rose was the first canonized saint of the New World, born in Lima, Peru in 1586. She is the patron saint of Central and South America. When her parents tried to persuade her to marry, she began a self-imposed exile in the summerhouse of the family garden, where she lived as a Dominican nun and wore a thin silver circle on her head, studded with prickles like a crown of thorns.

On her feast day the people of Lima take the statue from her shrine in the Church of Santo Domingoand carry it, covered with roses, to the city's cathedral. The children wear white robes and sing hymns, while the adults wear purple robes and carry lit candles. St. Rose's Day is a public holiday throughout Peru.

St. Sarkis's Day
January 21

In Armenia St. Sarkis is associated with predictions about love and romance. Young lovers put out crumbs for birds and watch to see which way the birds fly off, for it is believed that their future spouse will come from the same direction. It is also customary to leave some *pokhint*—a dish made of flour, butter, and honey—outside the door on St. Sarkis' Day. According to legend, when St. Sarkis was battling the Georgians, the roasted wheat in his pocket miraculously turned into pokhint.

St. Sava's Day
January 14 in the West; December 5 in the East

St. Sava (1174–1237) was a Serbian noble of the Nemanja dynasty who renounced his right to the throne and chose instead to become a monk. When his brother was crowned king, Sava became archbishop of Serbia and the cultural and spiritual leader of his people. He was the founder of the Serbian Orthodox church and played a central role in education and the beginnings of medieval Serbian literature.

As the patron saint of the former Yugoslavia, St. Sava or *Sveti Sava* is commemorated on the anniversary of his death with special church services, speeches, and choral singing. School children sing, dance, and recite poems in his honor.

Saints, Doctors, Missionaries, and Martyrs Day
November 8

Since the Reformation the Church of England has not added saints to its calendar. Although there have certainly been many candidates for sainthood over the past 450 years, and many martyrs who have given their lives as foreign missionaries, the Church of England has not canonized them, although a few are commemorated on special days. Instead, since 1928 it has set aside November 8, exactly one week after ALL SAINTS DAY, to commemorate "the unnamed saints of the nation."

See also ST. CHARLES DAY.

SS. Peter and Paul's Day
June 29

It is said that St. Peter and St. Paul were both martyred on June 29, and for this reason their names have been linked in various observances around the world. In Malta, the feast of St. Peter and St. Paul is a harvest festival known as MNARJA. In Peru, the **Día de San Pedro y San Pablo** is celebrated in fishing villages beause St. Peter is the patron saint of fishermen. Processions of decorated boats carrying an image of the saint are common, and sometimes a special floating altar is set up, with decorations made out of shells and seaweed. In Valparaiso, Chile this sort of procession has been going on since 1682. In Trinidad the fishermen first go out to catch fish to give to the poor and as they return, the Anglican priest blesses them and the sea. Then the partying begins. After the priest leaves, bongo and bele dances are done to honor St. Peter.

St. Spyridon (Spiridon) Day
December 12 in the East; December 14 in the West

St. Spyridon is the patron saint of Corfu, Zakynthos, and Kephalonia; these are among the Ionian Islands located off the western coast of Greece. Although he was born a shepherd in Cyprus, he became bishop of Tremithus and was renowned for his rustic simplicity. At the Nicene Council (325) he defended the Apostolic faith against the Arians with earnestness and simplicity. After his death in the fourth century, his relics were brought from Cyprus to Constantinople and then to Corfu in 1456. Every year a sacred relic of the saint, dressed in costly vestments, is taken from the Church of St. Spiridon and carried through the streets on his feast day. Colorful folk festivities complete the day-long celebration. This day is celebrated on December 14 in the Roman Catholic church.

St. Stephen's Day
December 26

On this day in about the year 35, St. Stephen became the first Christian martyr. The New Testament book of Acts records that Stephen was chosen by the Apostles as one of the first seven deacons of the church in Jerusalem. He was later denounced as a blasphemer by the Sanhedrin, the Jewish council in ancient Palestine, and stoned to death. St. Stephen is the patron saint of bricklayers.

December 26, 27, and 28, otherwise known as St. Stephen's Day, ST. JOHN THE EVANGELIST'S DAY, and HOLY INNOCENTS' DAY, are considered examples of the three different degrees of martyrdom. St. Stephen's death is an example of the highest class of martyrdom—that is to say, both in will and in deed. St. John the Evangelist, who showed that he was ready to die for Christ but was prevented from actually doing so, exemplifies martyrdom in will, but not in deed. And the children who lost their lives in the slaughter of the Innocents provide an example of the martyrdom in deed but not in will.

In many countries, St. Stephen's Day is celebrated as an extra Christmas holiday. In England, it is known as BOXING DAY. In Austria the priests bless the horses because St. Stephen is their patron. In Poland tossing rice at each other symbolizes blessings and recalls Stephen's stoning. And in Ireland, boys with blackened faces carrying a paper wren, go about begging and "hunting the wren." The hunting of the wren is most likely a carryover from an ancient belief that the robin, symbolizing the New Year, killed the wren, symbolizing the Old, at the turning of the year.

St. Swithin's Day
July 15

When Swithin, the bishop of Winchester, England, died in 862, he was buried according to his wish, outside the cathedral in the churchyard, in a place where the rain from the eaves poured down. Whether this request was prompted by humility on his part or a wish to feel "the sweet rain of heaven" on his grave, it was reversed after his canonization, when clerical authorities tried to move his remains to a site within the church. According to legend, the heavens opened and there was a heavy rainfall that lasted for forty days—a show of the saint's displeasure that made it impossible to remove his body. This led to the popular belief that if it rains on St. Swithin's Day it will rain for forty days; but if it is fair, it will be dry for forty days. Swithin is the patron saint of rain, both for and against it.

Contrary to the legend, St. Swithin's body was

indeed moved to Winchester cathedral on July 15, 971—and the weather was clear.

St. Sylvester's Day
December 31

St. Sylvester was pope in the year 325, when the Emperor Constantine declared that the pagan religion of Rome was abolished and that Christianity would henceforth be the official religion of the Empire. Although it is unclear exactly what role, if any, St. Sylvester played in this important event, he is always given at least some of the credit for stamping out paganism.

Because St. Sylvester's Day is also NEW YEAR'S EVE, it is celebrated in Switzerland by lighting bonfires in the mountains and ringing church bells to signal the passing of the old year and the beginning of the new. It is a day for rising early, and the last to get out of bed or to reach school are greeted with shouts of "Sylvester!" In some Swiss villages, grain is threshed on specially constructed platforms to ensure a plentiful harvest in the coming year.

St. Sylvester's Eve is celebrated in Austria, Hungary, and Germany. It is not uncommon in restaurants and cafés for the owner to set a pig loose at midnight. Everyone tries to touch the pig because it is considered a symbol of good luck. In private homes, a marzipan pig may be hung from the ceiling and touched at midnight.

St. Tammany's Day
May 12

During the Revolutionary War, the American troops were amused by the fact that the "Redcoats" (i.e., the British) had a patron saint: St. George, who had a reputation for protecting English soldiers (see ST. GEORGE'S DAY). So they decided to adopt a patron saint of their own, and chose for the purpose a disreputable seventeenth century Delaware Indian chief named Tammanend. They dubbed him "St. Tammany," chose May 12 for his festival, and celebrated the day with pompous and ridiculous ceremonies.

After the revolution Tammany Societies were eventually formed in many cities and towns, representing middle-class opposition to the power of the aristocratic Federalist Party. In the early nineteenth century the Society of Tammany became identified with the Democratic Party. But the society's tendency to dole out gifts to the poor and to bribe political leaders—among them the notorious "Boss" Tweed of New York City—made the name "Tammany Hall" (the building in which the organization had its headquarters in New York City) synonymous with urban political corruption.

St. Thomas's Day
December 21 by Malabar Christians; July 3 in the West; October 6 in the East

St. Thomas the Apostle was dubbed "Doubting Thomas" because, after the Resurrection, the other Apostles told him that they had seen Jesus, and he wouldn't believe them until he had touched Jesus' wounds for himself. When the Apostles left Jerusalem to preach to the people of other nations, as Jesus had instructed them to do, tradition says Thomas traveled eastward toward India. In Kerala, the smallest state in India, the Malabar Christians (or Christians of St. Thomas) claim St. Thomas as the founder of their church. For them his feast day is a major celebration. Thomas is the patron saint of India and Pakistan.

In Guatemala on this day, the Mayan Indians honor the ancient sun god they worshipped long before they became Christians with a dangerous ritual known as the *palo voladore* 'flying pole dance.' Three men climb to the top of a fifty-foot pole. As one of them beats a drum and plays a flute, the other two wind a long rope attached to the pole around one foot and jump. If they land on their feet, it is believed that the sun god will be pleased and that the days will start getting longer—a safe bet in view of the fact that St. Thomas's Day coincides with the WINTER SOLSTICE. The Roman Catholic Church celebrates St. Thomas's Day on July 3; the Orthodox Church on October 6.

St. Thorlak's Day
December 23

Thorlak Thorhalli (1133–93) was born in Iceland and, after being educated abroad, returned there to become Bishop of Skalholt in 1177. He was canonized by the Icelandic parliament five years after his death, and his day traditionally marks the climax of CHRISTMAS preparations for Icelanders, even though the Roman Catholic church has never officially confirmed the cult. It is associated with house-cleaning and clothes-washing, as well as the preparation of special foods. The *hangiket* or smoked mutton for CHRISTMAS was usually cooked on this day, and in the western fjords, the ammonia-like smell of skate hash cooked on St. Thorlak's Day is still considered a harbinger of the holiday season.

St. Urho's Day
March 16

St. Urho, whose name in Finnish means 'hero,' is credited with banishing a plague of grasshoppers who were threatening Finland's grape arbors. His legend in the United States was popularized in the 1950s, largely through the efforts of Professor Sulo Havumaki of Bemidji State University in Minnesota. After being celebrated as a "joke holiday" for several years in the Menagha-Sebeka area, the idea spread to other states with large Finnish populations, and now the governors of all fifty states have issued official proclamations stating that March 16 (or the nearest Saturday) is St. Urho's Day.

The actual celebrations, which are largely confined to Finnish communities, include wearing St. Urho's official colors—Nile green and royal purple—drinking grape juice, and chanting St. Urho's famous words, "Grasshopper, grasshopper, go away," in Finnish. In some areas there is a ceremonial "changing of the guard"—in this case, two makeshift guards carrying pitchforks or chainsaws (to cut down the giant grasshoppers) who meet and exchange clothing, including humorous or unusual undergarments.

The similarities between this day and ST. PATRICK'S DAY, observed on March 17, can hardly be overlooked. St. Patrick, who is believed to have driven the snakes out of Ireland, is widely regarded as a rival to St. Urho and his grasshoppers. There is some evidence that native Finns who have visited friends and relatives in the U.S. are taking the St. Urho's celebration back to Finland with them.

St. Vaclav's Day
September 28

Also known as **St. Wenceslas,** St. Vaclav was a tenth-century Bohemian prince who became the patron saint of the former Czechoslovakia. He was raised a Christian and eventually took over the government, encouraging the work of German missionaries who were trying to Christianize Bohemia. His zeal antagonized his non-Christian opponents, however, and he was eventually murdered by his brother just as he approached the church door on his way to Mass. In 932 his remains were transferred to the Church of St. Vitus in Prague, which became a popular pilgrimage site in the medieval period.

St. Vaclav's Day is a national holiday in the Czech Republic. The virtues of "Good King Wenceslas" have been memorialized by the popular nineteenth-century Christmas carol of that name.

St. Vincent's Day
January 22

São Vicente is the patron saint of Lisbon, Portugal. He was murdered by Saracens (Islamic Arabs) from the Algarve region of Spain in 1173. According to legend, the boat carrying the saint's coffin was guided up the river Tagus to Lisbon by two ravens, an event which is depicted in Lisbon's coat of arms.

St. Vincent's Day is celebrated with processions and prayers in Lisbon, but there are a number of folk traditions associated with this day in the surrounding rural areas. Farmers believe that by carrying a resin torch to the top of a high hill on January 22, they can predict what the coming harvest will be like. If the wind extinguishes the flame, the crops will be abundant; if it continues to burn, a poor growing season lies ahead.

Sallah (Salah) Festival
10th Dhu-l-Hijjah

An occasion of much pomp and ceremony in Nigeria, celebrating the culmination of the Muslim pilgrimage to Mecca and a day of communal prayer. People throng together in their best regalia. Processions of nobles on horseback are led by the Emir to the prayer grounds. After a prayer service, the Emir, dressed in white and carrying the historic Sword of Katsina, is seated in state on a platform. Groups of men take turns galloping up, reining in so their horses rear up at the last moment, and salute the Emir. He raises the sword in response. Later, there is entertainment by musicians, acrobats, jesters, and dancers. Niger and some other African countries also celebrate the day with elaborate festivities.

Salzburg Festival
July–August

Although the city of Salzburg, Austria did little to honor its most famous native son during his lifetime, it has been making up for the oversight ever since. The Salzburg Festival is so closely identified with Wolfgang Amadeus Mozart that it is often referred to simply as the **Mozart Festival**. Although it features musical events by a wide variety of composers and performances by internationally-celebrated musicians, conductors, singers, and instrumentalists, the festival has always paid special homage to Mozart—especially so in 1991 during the Mozart bicentennial celebration.

The festival takes place at the end of July and

through most of August at different venues throughout the city. Most of the operatic and large orchestral pieces are performed in the Festspielhaus, while other performances take place in the Landestheater. Some concerts and sacred music, such as Masses, are presented in the Salzburg Cathedral, which boasts a 4,000-pipe organ, or in the Abbey of St. Peter's. The finest church music can be heard at the Franziskanerkirche, where Masses are performed on Sundays with orchestra and choir. Chamber music concerts are usually given in the hall of the Mozarteum, and the Residenz is the scene for serenade concerts held by candlelight. Visits to Mozart's birthplace at Getreidegasse 9 are especially popular during the festival.

Samhain (Samain)
November 1

The word *Samhain* means literally 'summer's end'. This ancient Celtic harvest festival honored Saman, the lord of the dead, at the beginning of winter. According to Celtic folklore, this was the day when the souls of all those who had died in the previous year would gather—thus giving rise to the fears about ghosts and goblins that we now associate with HALLOWEEN, or Samhain Eve. On this day the entrances to burial caves were left open to allow the spirits to come out for an airing. In Celtic mythology, this is the day in which winter giants expelled the fertility gods.

Samil-jol (Independence Movement Day)
March 1

A national holiday in Korea to celebrate the anniversary of the independence demonstrations in 1919 protesting the Japanese occupation. (*Samil* means 'three-one,' signifying third month, first day.) Japan had taken over Korea in 1910, depriving Koreans of many of their freedoms. The March 1 movement was a turning point; an estimated 2 million people took to the streets in peaceful demonstrations and a Declaration of Independence was read at a rally in Seoul. The demonstrations were met with thousands of arrests, and close to 23,000 Koreans were killed or wounded. Independence leaders formed a provisional government abroad, and there were major anti-Japanese rallies in the 1920s, but independence didn't come until 1945 with Japan's surrender and the end of World War II. The day is marked with the reading of the 1919 Declaration of Independence at Pagoda Park in Seoul.

See also LIBERATION DAY.

San Antonio, Fiesta
Ten days that include April 21

An extravaganza of events held since 1901 in San Antonio, Tex., at the time of San Jacinto Day on April 21. The fiesta celebrates the 1836 Battle of San Jacinto that won Texas's independence from Mexico, and is much more than a simple independence celebration. The distinctive highlight of the fiesta is the Battle of Flowers Parade alongside the Alamo. Merrymakers originally pelted each other with flowers, but now people crush *cascarones*, decorated eggshells filled with confetti, on each others' heads. Another focal event is "A Night in Old San Antonio," which brings thousands into La Villita, 'the little town,' the restored earliest residential area of the city, for block dancing and more than 200 booths selling all kinds of ethnic foods. Some 150 other events include concerts, flower and fashion shows, art fairs, a *charreada* (Mexican rodeo), dances and pageants with people in lavish costume, torchlit floats in the Fiesta Flambeau Parade, and decorated barges in the San Antonio River Parade.

See also SAN JACINTO DAY.

Sandcastle Days
Usually July

A cash-prize arts competition in the most ephemeral of media, sand and water, held since 1981 in Imperial Beach, Calif. Close to 250,000 spectators come for the parade, the food booths, the fireworks, the band concert—and the sandcastle building. This is no child's play; about 400 amateur and professional contestants compete for cash prizes totaling $19,000. Professionals make money building huge sand castles in malls and hotels.

There are specific rules regarding the construction of the castles: no adhesives can be used, but water spray rigs are allowed to keep the art works from drying out and blowing away; teams can number up to ten, but no substitutions are permitted.

In the past, the sand sculptures have represented assorted animals from the nearby San Diego Zoo, including hippos, lions, elephants, and creatures of the sea. One "castle" was a sand sofa with a sand man seated on it, a sand dog by his side, a sand television set, and a sand beer can. The sculpting is always scheduled for a Sunday, and by Sunday night the elaborate works of art, some fourteen feet long, are lost to high tide.

The date of the festival is set through checking oceanographic tide tables to make sure the sculpting day comes on a day when the tide is lower than normal. Events preceding the Sunday sand sculpturing are a casual-dress Sandcastle Ball on Friday night, a community breakfast, parade, children's sand-sculpting contest, art exhibits, and fireworks. On Sunday, there's nothing but sculpting and live music.

Sandhill Crane Migration *See* **Crane Watch**

San Estevan, Feast of
September 2

A harvest dance and annual feast day in the Indian pueblo of Acoma in New Mexico. Acoma is a cluster of adobes atop a barren mesa 367 feet above a valley. It was established in the twelfth century and is the oldest continuously inhabited community in America. Only about fifty people now live there year-round, but the Acoma people from nearby villages return for feast days and celebrations.

The mesa is dominated by the mission church of San Estevan del Rey, which was completed in 1640 under the direction of Friar Juan Ramirez. All the building materials, including massive logs for the roof, had to be carried from the valley below. Supposedly Friar Juan had gained both the confidence of the Acoma people and access to the mesa by saving an infant from a fall off the mesa's edge. His delivery of the child back to the mother was considered a miracle.

A Mass and procession begin the feast day. The statue of the patron saint is taken from the church to the plaza where the dances are performed from 9:00 A.M. to 5:00 P.M. There are fifteen or so different dances—Bear, Butterfly, and Rainbow are some of them.

Acoma also has two rooster pulls, one in June and one in July. These are religious sacrificial ceremonies, during which prayers are offered for rain, for persons who need help, and for the country. Animal rights activists have protested the sacrificial aspect of these rites.

Also see SAN JUAN PUEBLO FEAST DAY.

San Fermin Festival
July 6–14

The festivities surrounding this well-known festival in Pamplona, Spain honoring the city's bishop, begin with a rocket fired from the balcony of the town hall. Bands of *txistularis* (a Basque word pronounced chees-too-LAH-rees), a band with dancers, drummers, and *txistu* players (a mu-

sical instrument like a flute), and bagpipers march through the town and its suburbs playing songs announcing the "running of the bulls," an event that has taken place here for four hundred years. Each morning, young men, dressed in typical Basque costumes, risk their lives running through the streets of Pamplona ahead of the bulls being run to the bullring where the bullfights will be held. Perhaps the best-known portrayal of this scene occurs in Ernest Hemingway's novel, *The Sun Also Rises*.

San Gennaro, Feast of
September 19

San Gennaro or St. Januarius, bishop of Benevento, is the patron saint of Naples. According to legend, he survived being thrown into a fiery furnace and then a den of wild beasts, but was eventually beheaded during the reign of Diocletian. His body was brought to Naples, along with a vial containing some of his blood. The congealed blood, preserved since that time in the Cathedral of San Gennaro, liquefies on the anniversary of his death each year—an event that has drawn crowds to Naples since 1389. Scientists have recently come up with a possible explanation for the phenomenon: certain substances, including some types of mayonnaise, are normally thick gels that can be liquefied instantly by shaking or stirring. Left standing, such liquids soon revert to gels. The answer will probably never be known because the Roman Catholic Church forbids opening the vial and analyzing its chemical nature.

The Society of San Gennaro in New York City's "Little Italy" section has been holding its own San Gennaro festival on Mulberry Street since 1925. The eleven-day event attracts up to three million spectators. It includes a procession carrying a bust of St. Januarius from the society's storefront headquarters to a shrine on the corner of Hester and Mulberry streets as well as a street fair. One of the goals of the event is to find a mate for the festival queen, who more often than not has married within two years after her festival reign.

See also PROCESSION OF THE HOLY BLOOD.

San Geronimo Feast Day
September 29–30

The feast day for Saint Verome, the patron saint of Taos Pueblo, probably the best known of the nineteen Indian pueblos (villages) in New Mexico. For 1,000 years, the Tiwa-speaking Taos Indians have lived at or near the present pueblo. In the 1540s, Spanish soldiers arrived, thinking they had discovered one of the lost cities of gold. The gold-brown adobe, multistory structures are the largest existing pueblo structures of their kind in the U.S., unchanged from the way they looked to the Spaniards, and are still the home of about 1,500 residents.

The feast day commences on the evening of Sept. 29 with a sundown dance, followed by vespers in the San Geronimo Mission. On the following day, there are foot races in the morning, and in the afternoon, frightening looking "clowns" with black-and-white body paint and wearing black-and-white costumes climb a pole; the act has secret religious significance to the Taos. An Indian trade fair offers Indian crafts and foods for sale.

The Taos pueblo is also known for its CHRISTMAS celebrations, lasting from Christmas Eve through Dec. 29. On CHRISTMAS EVE, there is a pine torch procession from the church through the plaza, and on Christmas Day, the Deer Dance is often performed.

Sanghamita Day
May–June; full moon of Jyaistha
Observed by Buddhists in Sri Lanka (Ceylon), this day celebrates the arrival of Sanghamita, daughter of Emperor Asoka of India, in 288 B.C. According to legend, Buddhism was first brought to Sri Lanka by a group of missionaries led by Mahinda, Asoka's son. Mahinda later sent for his sister, Sanghamita, who arrived with a branch from the Bodhi tree at Gaya, sacred to Buddhists as the tree under which the Buddha was sitting when he attained Enlightenment. The sapling was planted in the royal city of Anuradhapura, where Sanghamita founded an order of nuns. Buddhists still make pilgrimages to the city on this day to see what is believed to be the oldest documented tree in the world.

See also POSON.

Sango Festival
Early November
Sango is one of the most powerful cults among the Oyo people of Nigeria. Because Sango, a former Oyo ruler, is identified with thunder and lightning, the festival held in his honor takes place toward the end of the rainy season in early November and features various ceremonies connected with rain magic.

On the first day of the seven-day festival, women form a procession to the river, where they sink a hollow calabash gourd filled with special medicines to mark the beginning of the dry season. The *Timi* or king meets the worshipers at a

place near the river, accompanied by drummers, trumpeters, and a huge crowd of onlookers. The women of the palace put on a special musical performance praising all the tribe's rulers throughout its history. The remainder of the week is devoted to similar performances of music and dance before the Timi, although their real purpose is to please and entertain the god Sango. The principal performer each day dances in a self-induced trance-like state, during which it is believed that he speaks with the voice of Sango and is impervious to pain. The festival concludes on the seventh day with a procession of fire in which a worshiper carries a large pot containing a sacred flame that brings blessing to all parts of the village.

San Isidro of Seville, Feast of
April 4
St. Isidore (c. 560–636) was born in Cartagena, Spain, and eventually succeeded his brother, St. Leander, as bishop of Seville. Among his accomplishments were the founding of schools throughout the country and the compilation of a twenty-volume encyclopedia of all the knowledge available at that time in Europe. His feast day is celebrated not only in Spain, but in many Latin American countries as well.

In Río Frío, Colombia, the beginning of April is usually the end of the dry season. On San Isidro's feast day, April 4, the saint's image is carried through town with all the townspeople following and singing his praises, in the hope that he will produce a much-needed rainfall, or at least a shower, before the procession is over. To give the saint as much time as possible to work his miracle, those participating in the procession take two steps forward and one backward. If, after several trips around the town, it has still not started to rain, the people who were chanting his praises begin to reproach him. The procession continues, and eventually the reproaches turn to loud complaints and often profanity. If the entire day passes without rain, San Isidro is returned to his niche for another year.

See also SAN ISIDRO THE FARMER.

San Isidro the Farmer, Feast of
May 15
The feast of Saint Isidore the Ploughman is celebrated in Madrid, Spain, with eight days of bullfighting at the Plaza de Toros, colorful parades, and many artistic, cultural, and sporting events. Street vendors sell pictures of the saint, small glass or pottery bells believed to ward off harm from thunder and lightning, and whistle-stemmed

glass roses, which provide a noisy accompaniment to the feasting and dancing that go on.

San Isidro is the patron saint of Madrid and also of farmers. According to legend, he worked on a farm outside Madrid. One day, as his master was spying on him to see how hard he was working, an angel and a yoke of white oxen appeared at Isidro's side. He was canonized in 1622, and local farmers still attend a special Mass on his feast day, May 15. The Festival of San Isidro is celebrated in other Spanish towns as well, particularly Leon and Alicante.

San Isidro is also the patron saint of Saipan, capital of the Northern Mariana Islands in the western Pacific Ocean near Guam. While dance groups practice, men form hunting and fishing parties to provide food, and youth organizations clean and prepare the festival site. The fiesta begins at the end of a novena (nine days of prayers and special religious services). It features games of skill and traditional dances with prizes for the winners, and a great variety of foods.

Philippine towns and villages also commemorate St. Isidro. They bathe and scrub their water buffalo (*carabaos*), manicure the animals' hooves, braid their tails with ribbons, and decorate their bodies with bunting and more ribbons. The water buffalo are brought to the plaza in front of the church and kneel (having been taught by their owners) for the priest's blessing. Then everyone goes to the fiesta site for *carabao* races and tricks, and lots of food and fun. In Quezon Province ornaments made from rice meal dyed in bright colors, called *kiping*, are attached to the front of the house. All the townspeople and the priest parade through town and when that's over, the *kiping* are eaten.

See also SAN ISIDRO OF SEVILLE

San Jacinto Day
April 21

Fresh from his March 1836 victory at the Battle of the Alamo (see ALAMO DAY), General Antonio López de Santa Anna (1795?–1876) of Mexico proceeded eastward until he encountered the Texan army general, Samuel Houston (1793–1863) at a place called San Jacinto, about twenty-two miles east of the present-day city of Houston. Raising the now familiar cry of "Remember the Alamo!" Houston's 900 soldiers defeated the Mexican force of nearly 1600 in a battle that lasted only eighteen minutes. Santa Anna was taken prisoner and forced to sign a treaty pledging

his help in securing independence for Texas, which was annexed by the United States in 1845.

A legal holiday in Texas, San Jacinto Day is celebrated throughout the state but particularly in San Antonio, where the highpoint of the ten-day FIESTA SAN ANTONIO is the huge Battle of Flowers parade winding through miles of the city's downtown streets.

Sanja Matsuri (Three Shrines Festival)
Second weekend in May

One of the most spectacular festivals in Tokyo, Japan, honoring Kannon, the goddess of mercy (known as Kuan Yin in Chinese), and three fishermen brothers who founded the Asakusa Kannon Temple in the fourteenth century. *Sanja* means 'three shrines,' and, according to legend, after the brothers discovered a statue of Kannon in the Sumida River, their spirits were enshrined in three places. The festival has been held each year since the late 1800s on a weekend near May 18. Activities are focused on the Asakusa Temple and Tokyo's "Shitamachi," or downtown area.

More than 100 portable shrines called *mikoshi*, which weigh up to two tons and are surmounted by gold phoenixes, are paraded through the streets to the gates of the temple. Carrying them are men in *happi* coats—the traditional short laborers' jackets that are worn by teams of men to advertise their districts. There are also priests on horseback, musicians playing "sanja-bayashi" festival music, and dancers in traditional costume. On Sunday, various dances are performed.

See also Birthday of the Goddess of Mercy.

San Juan and San Pedro Festivals
June 24; June 29

The celebrations of ST. JOHN'S DAY (June 24) and ST. PETER'S DAY (June 29) in Paraguay have much in common. The religious part of both celebrations involves a Mass (and, in the case of San Pedro, a formal procession), but it is the games that are played on these two days that set them apart from other religious festivals in Paraguay. There is a simulated bullfight in which the *toro candil* (a man wearing a hide-covered frame with a bull's skull attached to the front) chases the *cambá*, people with drums and flutes who taunt the bull and play their instruments. His horns are covered in kerosene-soaked rags and set on fire, so that when darkness falls and he chases spectators through the streets, the flaming horns make the game more exciting.

Two other costumed figures that play a part in

the game include a *ñandú guazú* (a rhea, which is similar to an ostrich) and a Guaycurú Indian dressed in rags with a blackened face. The *ñandú*-actually a child inside a small cage covered with leaves to represent feathers and a long stick for a neck-follows the bull around, bobbing its neck up and down and pecking at the *toro* from behind. The Guaycurú chases the women around and pretends to kidnap them. Other participants in the festival chase women with blazing torches—a remnant, perhaps, of the ancient festivals observed on June 24 with bonfires and the practice of walking barefoot over live coals (see MIDSUMMER DAY).

San Juan Bautista Festival
June 24

In Puerto Rico, ST. JOHN THE BAPTIST'S DAY is observed by gathering at the beaches to eat, dance, and drink. At midnight, the revelers take a swim in the ocean, a tradition based on the biblical scene in which John, the cousin of Jesus, baptizes him. Over the years, the religious significance of the event has been overshadowed, and today bathing in the water is believed to bring good luck in the coming year.

In Hartford, Connecticut, a San Juan Bautista Festival has been held on the Saturday nearest June 24 since 1979. Sponsored by the San Juan Center, Inc., it includes Puerto Rican food and entertainment, particularly bands that play Puerto Rican music and use traditional Puerto Rican instruments. Although the Hartford festival is designed to give the area's Puerto Rican population an opportunity to celebrate their heritage, it draws many other people as well. Attendance at the most recent festival was more than 15,000.

San Juan Day
June 24

The festival in honor of St. John the Baptist (see ST. JOHN THE BAPTIST'S DAY) is known as San Juan Day in Puerto Rico. The celebration begins at midnight on June 23, when people go down to the beaches and walk out of the water backwards seven times, throwing themselves on the sand for good luck and then jumping in for a swim. The beach parties, concerts, and street dances continue throughout the night, and the celebration ends with a church service at dawn the next morning.

San Juan Day is celebrated with similar customs in New York City, in California, and in other parts of the United States with large Hispanic-American populations. (See also SAN JUAN AND SAN PEDRO FESTIVALS.)

San Juan Pueblo Feast Day
June 24

A day to honor St. John the Baptist, the patron saint of the San Juan Indian pueblo, near Espanola, New Mexico. The pueblo, where the first New Mexican capital founded by the Spaniards in 1598, is headquarters today for the Eight Northern Indian Pueblos Council.

The San Juan feast day observations, like those of other New Mexican pueblos, combines Roman Catholic ritual with ancient Indian ceremonies.

The celebration begins in the evening of June 23 with Vespers and Mass in the Church of St. John the Baptist. After the services, St. John's statue is carried to a shrine prepared for it in the pueblo's plaza. This procession is followed by a one-mile run in which anyone can participate; a "sing" by the pueblo war chiefs, or officers; a procession of singers and runners; and two Buffalo dances, each presented by two men and one woman wearing buffalo costumes.

The actual feast day begins with a Mass, and is followed by an assortment of dances, which usually include Buffalo, Comanche, and Green Corn (harvest) dances. Men beat drums and chant as the dancers, arrayed in long lines and wearing body paint and elaborate costumes with feathers and beads, move slowly and rhythmically to the beat. Vendors sell jewelry, crafts, and assorted souvenirs, and a carnival with a ferris wheel and carousel is also part of the celebration.

Santacruzan *See* Exaltation of the Cross

Santa Fe Chamber Music Festival
Early June to late August for seven weeks

A festival in Santa Fe, N.M., that started in 1973 and has since produced a range of musical programs from the baroque to the modern. The festival began impressively: the acclaimed cellist Pablo Casals was the first honorary president, and artist Georgia O'Keeffe produced the first of her now-famous posters and program covers. Fourteen artists presented six Sunday concerts that first year; now about seventy musicians of international acclaim take part. Youth concerts, open rehearsals, in-state tours to Indian reservations and small communities, out-of-state tours, and National Public Radio broadcasts have expanded the audiences.

Santa Fe, with its ancient tri-ethnic culture, has a great roster of historic buildings, and from time to time they serve as concert halls. For instance, chamber music concerts have been presented in the Romanesque Cathedral of St. Francis, built in 1869; the Palace of the Governors, in continuous use since 1610; and the eighteenth-century Santuario de Nuestra Señora de Guadalupe, where altar bells rather than dimming lights signal the end of intermissions.

Santa Fe, Fiesta de
Weekend after Labor Day

A religious and secular festival said (without much argument) to be the oldest such event in the country. It dates to 1712 and recalls the early history of Santa Fe, New Mexico.

The Spanish *conquistadores* were ousted from Santa Fe in 1680 in a revolt by the Pueblo Indians. Led by Don Diego de Vargas, the Spanish peacefully regained control in 1693. Vargas had promised to honor *La Conquistadora*, the small statue of the Virgin Mary that is now enshrined in St. Francis Cathedral, if she granted them success. The first procession was held in 1712 to fulfill that promise.

The festivities start with a Mass early on the Friday morning after Labor Day. Then comes the grand procession: Vargas and the fiesta queen, *la reina*, lead the way on horseback to the town plaza, escorted by the *Caballeros de Vargas*.

Friday night brings the burning of Zozobra, or Old Man Gloom, a 44-foot-high fabric and wood effigy whose yearly immolation began in 1926. Thousands watch and shout "Burn him!" when the effigy groans and asks for mercy. Fireworks announce the end of Gloom, and then spectators make their way to the plaza for the start of two days of dancing, street fairs, a grand ball, and a parade with floats satirizing local politicians. The fiesta ends Sunday night with a Mass of thanksgiving and a candlelight procession to the Cross of Martyrs overlooking Santa Fe.

Santa Fe Opera Festival
End of June through August

An internationally acclaimed opera festival that began in 1957, survived the burning of the opera house in 1967, and is now staged in an open-air opera "house" atop a mesa outside Santa Fe, New Mexico. The stage is seven miles from Santa Fe, and the city lights are so distinct in the clear mountain air that they sometimes become part of the operatic scenery. Old classics, rarely performed old operas, and premieres are all presented.

The Gala Opening Celebration includes an Opera Ball to benefit apprentice programs for young artists, and, on opening night, a festive reception, tailgate parties (with tablecloths and caviar and people in formal dress) and, after the performance, waltzing for the entire audience.

Sant' Efisio, Festival of
Early May

Although nearly every town and village in Sardinia has its own festival, one of the most important is the **Sagra di Sant' Efisio** at Cagliari, which commemorates the martyrdom of a third century Roman general who was converted to Christianity. In early May a procession accompanies a statue of Saint Efisio, Sardinia's patron saint, through the streets of Cagliari to the church of Pula, the town where he suffered martyrdom. Three days later the statue returns to Cagliari. Several thousand pilgrims on foot, in carts, or on horseback, wearing costumes that date from the seventeenth century and earlier, take part in the procession, which culminates in a parade down Cagliari's main avenue that is said to rival the parade on SAINT PATRICK'S DAY in New York City.

Sapporo Snow Festival (Yuki Matsuri)
February 5–11 (or February 6–12 if February 11 falls on a Saturday or Sunday)

An exuberant celebration of snow and ice held since 1950 in Sapporo, the capital city of the Japanese island of Hokkaido. In 1974 the first international Snow Statue Contest was held. The week's activities feature a colorful parade and competitive events in winter sports. What particularly draws more than two million tourists, though, is the display of colossal ice sculptures along the main street and snow statues in Odori Park.

Because of the shortage of snow in the festival area, thousands of tons of snow are trucked in from the suburbs. The sculptures are spectacular—intricately carved and often several stories high. About three weeks before the festival the work begins: a wooden frame is built and packed with snow; after the snow has hardened the frame is removed and the carving begins. A different theme is chosen each year for the sculptures.

Sarasota Circus Festival and Parade
First week in January

Colossal! Spectacular! non-stop circus for the first days of the year in the capital of the circus

307

world, Sarasota, Fla. The festival begins on New Year's Day at the Sarasota County Fairgrounds and continues for several days, the highlight being a parade in downtown Sarasota usually held on the first Sunday in January.

During the week, events include hourly shows of magic, juggling, clowning, dog stunts, knife throwing, and various other acts all day long. In addition, there are outdoor "thrill shows"—performers on high sway poles, on high high wires, and on motorcycles on high wires. And there are displays of miniature circuses, arts and crafts, a circus art and photography show. On two days, there are circus performances under the big top, in which performers compete against one another for cash prizes.

Sarasota was put on the circus map in 1927 when John Ringling, one of the founding Ringling brothers, decided to make Sarasota the winter headquarters for the Ringling Bros. and Barnum & Bailey Circus. Winter headquarters was moved in 1960 to nearby Venice, but Sarasota was by then established as a circus mecca, and many circus people now make their year-round homes there. Furthermore, the city is home to the Circus Hall of Fame and the Ringling Museum of the Circus. John Ringling's palatial home, Ca' d'Zan, completed in 1925, can be seen there, along with the John and Mabel Ringling Museum of Art, which has a fine collection of Peter Paul Rubens.

Saratoga Festival
June–September

The Saratoga Performing Arts Center in Saratoga Springs, New York is the summer home of the New York City Ballet, the Philadelphia Orchestra, and the Spa Summer Theater. The festival held there every summer includes not only performances by these groups but a four-week summer school program for talented high school students interested in dance, orchestra studies, and theater. Ballet and orchestral performances take place in a partially enclosed amphitheater, and visitors often arrive a few hours early to picnic on the grass and enjoy the spacious grounds of the Saratoga Spa State Park, where the center is located.

The Saratoga Festival has seen a number of world premieres, among them the 1976 premiere of Gian Carlo Menotti's first symphony (see SPOLETO USA) and the 1974 world premiere of the ballet *Coppelia*. The summer theater performs both classical and contemporary plays in the center's 500-seat theater.

Sarbatoarea Blajinilor *See* Blajini, Feast of the

Saturnalia
December 17–23

This ancient Roman WINTER SOLSTICE festival began on December 17 and lasted for seven days. It was held in honor of Saturn, the father of the gods, and was characterized by the suspension of discipline and reversal of the usual order. Grudges and quarrels were forgotten; businesses, courts, and schools closed down; wars were interrupted or postponed; slaves were served by their masters; and masquerading or change of dress between the sexes often occurred. It was traditional to offer gifts of imitation fruit (a symbol of fertility), dolls (symbolic of the custom of human sacrifice), and candles (reminiscent of the bonfires traditionally associated with pagan solstice celebrations). A mock king was chosen, usually from among a group of slaves or criminals, and although he was permitted to behave in an unrestrained manner for the seven days of the festival, he was usually killed at the end. Not surprisingly, the Saturnalia eventually degenerated into a week-long spree of debauchery and crime-giving rise to the modern use of the term *saturnalia* meaning 'a period of unrestrained license and revelry.'

Sausage Fair *See* Bad Durkheim Wurstmarkt

Sausage Festival *See* Wurstfest

Savitri-Vrata (Savitri Vow)
May–June; (Jyaistha)

This day is observed by Hindu women in honor of the legendary princess Savitri, who loved her husband Satyavan so much that she refused to leave him when he died, eventually persuading Yama, King of Death, to give him back. Women whose husbands are alive spend the day fasting and praying, anointing their husbands' foreheads with sandalwood paste, and showering them with gifts of food and flowers. Women whose husbands have died beg to be delivered from the miseries of widowhood in a future existence. The *vrata* or vow is a ritual practice observed by Hindu women for a period of fourteen years to obtain their wish.

Savonlinna Opera Festival
July

A month-long music festival in Savonlinna, Finland. Considered one of Europe's most important musical events, it began in 1967 with a performance of Beethoven's *Fidelio*. In 1992, for its twenty-fifth anniversary, *Fidelio* was presented again, as well as George and Ira Gershwin's *Porgy and Bess*, produced by Opera Ebony of New York, and conducted by Estonian maestro Eri Klas.

The main site of the festivals is the Olavinlinna Castle the best preserved medieval fortress in Finland. It was built in 1475 and named by Swedes and Finns on the lookout for raiding Russian armies.

Scaling the Walls *See* **Escalade**

Schäferlauf
August 24
St. Bartholomew's Day is celebrated in Markgröningen and other towns in the Swabia district of Germany with a barefoot race among the shepherds and shepherdesses of the Black Forest. The competition originally began as a demonstration that they could run faster than any sheep who might go astray. Today the boys and girls still race barefoot, and the winning shepherd and shepherdess are given a sheep or a large mutton roast. After the race there are other pastoral activities, such as a shepherds' dance and a water-carriers' race in which contestants must balance a pail of water on their heads and pour it into a tub at the finish line.

Schemenlauf
Between January 26 and March 3; week preceding Ash Wednesday
The Schemenlauf or **Running of the Spectres** takes place during the Carnival season at Imst in the Tyrolean Alps. The roots of this traditional Austrian celebration can be traced back to the Middle Ages, when people believed that the densely wooded mountain slopes were populated by good and evil spirits with the power to prevent or promote the growth of seeds in the ground. To ward off the evil spirits, they resorted to mummery and wore frightening masks (see Perchtenlauf) as they danced through the village making as much noise as they could. Originally the festival may have been a way of welcoming spring.

Only men are allowed to participate in the Shemenlauf at Imst. About four hundred *Schemen* 'spectres' join the procession, often stopping to invite spectators to join them in the traditional circular dance. Visitors come from all over the world to see this colorful festival, which is followed by a night of revelry reminiscent of Mardi Gras celebrations elsewhere.

Schutzenfest (Marksmen's Festival)
Summer
This event in Germany is a tradition going back 400 years. There are a number of marksmen's festivals held during the summer months. The biggest of these, in Hanover is held for ten days at the beginning of July and attracts about 200,000 spectators. It features merry-go-rounds, other carnival rides, and food booths, many serving sausage. The fair is highlighted by Europe's longest festival procession. There are marksmen's brass-and-pipe bands, paraders in folk costumes, floats, and horse-drawn carriages. Other notable marksmen's festivals are in Dusseldorf in July and in Biberach in Upper Swabia in June or July. The Biberach festival has been celebrated every year since 1649 and features a procession of more than a thousand costumed children.

Schutzengelfest (Festival of the Guardian Angel)
Second Sunday in July
A religious and social occasion in northern Switzerland observed since the seventeenth century. Its setting is *Wildkirchli* 'chapel in the wild', a cave in the Alpstein mountain range in the Appenzell Innerrhoden Canton. A Capuchin monk decided in 1621 that the cave, which is now renowned for prehistoric finds, was an ideal place for a mountain worship service. In 1679, Paulus Ulmann, a priest in nearby Appenzell, set up a foundation to ensure that services would continue.

The festival starts at 10 A.M. when a priest or monk from Appenzell conducts the worship service. Then, a yodelers' choir gives a festive concert, and participants start walking to the villages of Ebenalp or Aescher for feasting and dancing.

Schwenkfelder Thanksgiving
September 24
The Schwenkfelders who now live in the Pennsylvania Dutch country are the descendants of a small Protestant sect that sprang up in Germany around the time of the Reformation. They were followers of Kaspar Schwenkfeld (1490–1561), a Silesian Reformation theologian, who founded the movement called "Reformation by the Middle Way." He and his followers separated themselves from orthodox Protestant circles and formed the small societies and brotherhoods that still survive in the United States as the Schwenkfelder Church, or 'Confessors of the Glory of Christ.'

In 1733 a handful of Schwenkfelder's followers arrived in Philadelphia, and a second group emigrated from Germany on September 22, 1734. On

September 24, two days after their arrival, they went to the state house as a group, swore their allegiance to the British king, and spent the rest of the day expressing their gratitude to God for having delivered them from persecution. In the Pennsylvania Dutch counties where the Schwenkfelders still live, this day is observed as a special THANKSGIVING DAY.

Sealing the Frost
Early May

The Cuchumatan Indians of Santa Eulalia in Guatemala believe that the frost "lives" in a rocky cliff outside of town. Once a year the Indian prayer makers lead a procession of villagers up to the cliff, where one of them is lowered over the edge with a rope around his waist. He seals a crack in the rock with cement so the frost can't get out and ruin the young corn plants. Afterward he is pulled up again, and the procession returns to the village.

Seaman's Day
First Sunday in June

A national holiday in Iceland, Seaman's or **Fishermen's Day** honors the role that fishing and fishermen have played in Icelandic history. Although each village has developed its own version of the celebration, most begin with a church service and a trip to the local cemetery to honor sailors lost at sea. Afterward there are children's parades, dances, outdoor cookouts, and bonfires in the evening. There are also a number of water events, including rowing, swimming, lifesaving, and rescue sailing competitions. The proceeds from the day's events throughout the country go to the national fund that supports old seamen's homes.

Sea Music Festival
First weekend in June

The only event of its kind in the western hemisphere, the annual Sea Music Festival takes place during the first week in June at Mystic Seaport Museum in Mystic, Connecticut. Since 1980 the ships and exhibits representing a nineteenth century maritime village along the Mystic River have been the backdrop for more than forty musicians and chantey (pronounced SHANTee) singers from around the world. The festival attracts about ten thousand visitors, a tribute to the music that has been an integral part of shipboard life since the sixteenth century.

The festival offers performances of chanteys or sailors' work songs as well as "forebitters"—songs sung for entertainment. Most of the lyrics and melodies are of British or Irish origin, although many incorporate American fiddle tunes, African-American minstrel ditties, older ballads, and the popular music of the time. Chanteys helped the sailor maintain the rhythm of a tedious job. In fact, it was considered **bad** luck to sing a chantey when no work was being done.

The event features daytime and evening concerts Thursday through Saturday, symposia, workshops, and a dance. There is also a special preview concert for museum members that highlights a well-known performer each year.

Sechselauten
Third Monday of April and preceding Sunday

A colorful springtime festival in Zurich, Switzerland, that ushers in spring by exploding the *Böögg* 'snowman,' the symbol of winter. *Sechselauten* means the 'six-o'clock ringing,' and the present custom stems from the fourteenth-century practice of ringing the bells at six in the evening (instead of wintertime seven) to proclaim the earlier end of the spring and summer work day. The first ringing of the six o'clock bell was a good excuse for a celebration.

Festivities begin with a children's parade on Sunday, with the children in historical costumes and accompanied by the *Böögg*, which is stuffed with cotton wadding and firecrackers. On Monday, members of the guilds (formerly associations of craftsmen, but now social groups) parade through the flag-festooned city in medieval costumes, accompanied by bands. Everyone converges at Sechselautenplatz on the shore of Lake Zurich at six that evening, the bells ring, groups on horseback gallop around the *Böögg* to the music of a hunting march, and then the *Böögg* explodes and burns. Torchlight parades go on into the night, and feasts are held at guildhalls.

Seged
November; Day 29 of the eighth lunar month

This is a religious festival of unclear origin observed only by the Falasha or Ethiopian Jews. It begins with a procession up the hill to the place where the ritual will be held. The participants wear clean, preferably white clothes with colored fringe, symbolic of the state of purity in which they have kept themselves by avoiding sexual intercourse and bodily contact with non-Falashas for seven days. The priests, who lead the procession, sing prayers and carry the *Orit* (the Jewish scriptures in Geez, written on parchment) and other holy books wrapped in colored cloth. Everyone who climbs the hill carries a stone, which is placed on an already existing circular wall marking the holy area where the *Orit* will be placed.

The ceremony itself includes a commemoration of the dead, where those who wish to honor their deceased relatives place a seed of grain on the stone wall for each relative and say a special prayer. There are also readings from the *Orit* and donations of money to the priests. After the service is over, the procession moves back down the hill to the prayerhouse, where food for the communal meal—usually *indjära* (bread), *kay wot* (meat stew), and *t'alla* (beer)—is distributed. The remainder of the day is spent in non-religious festivities, especially singing and dancing to the music of *masänqos* (one-stringed bowed lutes).

Seijin-no-hi (Adults Day; Coming-of-Age Day)
January 15

A national holiday in Japan honoring those who reached their twentieth birthday (voting age) in the previous year. Gatherings, usually with speakers, are held in community centers where the honorees show off their new adult finery. A traditional archery contest is held on this day at Sanjusangendo Temple in Kyoto, with people from throughout Japan participating.

Semana Santa, Guatemala
Between March 15 and April 18; Palm Sunday to Easter

Semana Santa or HOLY WEEK is without doubt the biggest occasion of the year in Antigua, the old colonial capital of Guatemala, and one of the largest EASTER celebrations in the New World. Thousands of tourists and believers come to the city to witness this massive display of religious theater. The entire Passion Play, beginning with Christ's entry into Jerusalem on PALM SUNDAY and ending with his Resurrection on Easter, is reenacted in the streets of Antigua—complete with armor-clad Roman soliders on horseback, who charge through the town early on GOOD FRIDAY looking for Jesus. Men in purple robes and accompanied by Roman soldiers take turns carrying *andas* 'floats' through the streets.

Semik
May–June; seventh Thursday after Easter

In pre-revolutionary Russia, Semik-from *semy*, meaning 'the seventh'-took place on the seventh Thursday after EASTER and was observed primarily by young girls. They would go to the woods and pick birch branches, decorating them with ribbons and wreaths. Then they would throw the wreaths into the nearest brook or river. If the wreath stayed on the surface, it meant that they would be married in a year, but if it sank, it meant that they would remain single-or, if married, would soon be widowed. In some areas the wreaths were hung on trees, and as long as they remained there, the girls would have good fortune. Another custom associated with the Semik was the performance of traditional songs and dances by young girls and boys in the forest, often around a decorated birch tree.

In pagan times, the Semik was the feast of a wood-god, celebrated at the time of year when the new leaves first appeared on the trees. Since it was the young girls who spent most of their time in the forest picking berries and mushrooms while the women worked in the fields, it is likely that the wreaths hung on the trees were at one time an offering to the wood-god.

See also WIANKI FESTIVAL OF WREATHS.

Sending the Winter Dress
Day 1 of tenth lunar month

This is the day on which the Chinese send winter garments to the dead. They are not real items of clothing but paper replicas packed in parcels bearing the names of the recipients. The gift packages are first exhibited in the home; the actual sending of the garments takes place in a courtyard or near the tomb, where they are burned.

This is the third occasion of the year for visiting ancestral tombs. The other two are CHUNG YEUNG (October) and CH'ING MING (April).

Septuagesima Sunday *See* Quadragesima Sunday.

Serreta, Festa da
September 8–15

The Festa da Serreta that has been held annually since 1932 in Gustine, California, is based on a similar festival held on the island of Terceira in the Azores, from which many of Gustine's residents emigrated. It is held in honor of *Nossa Senhora dos Milagres* 'Our Lady of Miracles', for whom a sixteenth century priest built a small chapel in the Azorean village of Serreta.

The week-long festival attracts thousands of visitors. Highlights include the *Bodo do Leite* 'Banquet of Milk', fresh-drawn from the cows as is the practice in the Azores. There are also *cantorías ao desafio* (extemporaneous song contests), which draw contestants from all over California and even some Azoreans. The image of

Nossa Senhora is carried in a procession from the church to a portable chapel or *capela* that is brought out specifically for use on this occasion. A group of women sit in the chapel and watch over the donations of money that are left there. Another festival event is the traditional bullfight, which takes place in a rectangular arena. The bull is held by a long rope, his horns are padded, and the men do not so much fight him as play with him.

Setsubun (Bean-Throwing Festival)
February 3 or 4

A ceremony observed in all major temples throughout Japan to mark the last day of winter according to the lunar calendar. People throng temple grounds where the priests or stars such as actors and sumo wrestlers throw dried beans to the crowd who shout, "Fortune in, Devils out!" Some people also decorate their doorways with sardine heads, because devils don't like their smell. Beans caught at the temple are brought home to drive out devils there.

Seven-Five-Three Festival See Shichi-Go-San

Seven Herbs or Grasses Festival See Nanakusa Matsuri

Seven Sisters Festival
Seventh day of seventh moon (usually August)

A celebration for would-be lovers, observed in China, Korea, Taiwan, and Hong Kong. It is based on an ancient Chinese legend and is also known as the **Maiden's Festival**, **Double Seventh**, **Chhit Sek**, and **Chilsuk**. In the legend, an orphaned cowherd is forced from his home by his elder brother and sister-in-law, who give him only a broken-down cart, an ox, and a tiny piece of land. The ox, called Elder Brother the Ox, takes pity on the cowherd, and tells him that on a certain day seven girls will visit earth from heaven to bathe in a nearby river. If the young man steals the clothes of any one of the girls, she will marry him.

The cowherd steals the clothes of the Seventh Maiden. They fall in love, marry, and live happily for three years, when she is ordered back to heaven by the gods. When the cowherd dies, he becomes immortal, but the Queen Mother of the Western Heaven keeps the two apart by drawing a line across the sky—the Silver River or Milky Way. They can cross this only once a year, on the seventh day of the seventh month, on a bridge formed by thousands of magpies.

On the sixth day of the seventh moon, unmarried men pay homage to the cowherd, and on the seventh day, young unmarried women make offerings to the Seventh Maiden of combs, mirrors, paper flowers, and powder puffs. The festival is celebrated chiefly at home, but in Hong Kong young women also visit Lover's Rock on Bowen Road on Hong Kong Island to burn *joss* 'incense' sticks, lay offerings at the rock, and consult soothsayers.

See also TANABATA.

Seville Fair
Six days in April

Over the past century, the Seville Fair (or **April Fair**) has developed into one of Spain's major spectacles. Originally a market for livestock, the fair with its multi-colored tents, wreaths, and paper lanterns now transforms the city of Seville . The singing, dancing, and drinking go on for six days, and a sense of joyousness pervades the city. The week's activities include a parade of riders and a number of bullfights held in the Plaza de la Maestranza (equestrian parade ground)—now considered the "cathedral" of bullfighting.

Seward's Day
Last Monday in March

When William Henry Seward, Secretary of State for President Andrew Johnson, signed the treaty authorizing the purchase of Alaska from Czarist Russia for $7 million on March 30, 1867, most Americans thought he was crazy. They called it "Seward's folly," "Seward's icebox," and "Johnson's polar bear garden." But public opinion quickly changed when gold was discovered in the region.

Since that time, Alaska's natural resources have paid back the initial investment many times over. Its natural gas, coal, and oil reserves, in addition to its seafood and lumber industries, have proved to be far more valuable than its gold. Unfortunately, Seward did not live to see his foresight commemorated as a legal holiday in the state of Alaska. The purchase of Alaska is now widely regarded as the crowning achievement of both William Seward and President Johnson. (See ALASKA DAY)

Sexagesima Sunday See Quadragesima Sunday.

Shab-Barat

Night of the 15th Sha'ban

Shab-Barat (or **Shab-i-Barat, Shaaban**) is a time when Muslims—particularly those in India and Pakistan—ask Allah to forgive the people they know who have died. They often spend the night in mosques praying and reading the Koran, and they visit graveyards to pray for the souls of their friends and ancestors. They also celebrate Allah's mercy by setting off fireworks, illuminating the outsides of their mosques, and giving food to the poor.

Also known as **Laylat al-Bara'ah** or the **Night of Forgiveness**, Shab-Barat is a time of intense prayer in preparing for RAMADAN, for it is believed that this is the night on which God fixes the destinies of humans for the coming year, and sins are absolved.

Shah Abdul Latif Death Festival

14–16 Safar

A celebration of the death of poet-musician Shah Abdul Latif (1689–1752) at Bhit Shah, Sind, Pakistan. He was one of the most beloved of Pakistan's mystic Sufi poet-musicians who founded a music tradition based on popular themes and using folk melodies. He was the author of the *Risalo*, the best-known collection of romantic poetry in the Sindhi language; its heroes and heroines have become symbols of the oppression of Sind by foreign occupiers.

At Latif's *urs* 'death festival', a huge fair takes place outside the poet's shrine. There are wrestling matches (a popular entertainment in Sind), transvestite dancing, a circus, theater, and numerous food and souvenir booths. Inside the shrine the atmosphere is quiet, and there is devotional singing by well-known Sind groups. The main event of the *urs* is a concert at which the annual Latif Award is presented to the best performers.

Shaker Festival

Starts second Thursday in July

A ten-day event staged by the Shaker Museum in South Union, Ky., to tell the story of this last western Shaker community, which survived from 1807 to 1922. A nightly outdoor drama, *Shakertown Revisited*, combines Shaker songs, dances, and the relating of history. Meals are served using Shaker recipes, and there are demonstrations of Shaker crafts. The festival was first held in 1962.

Shakers are members of the United Society of Believers in Christ's Second Appearing, a celibate sect founded in 1772 in England by Ann Lee; it is a Quaker offshoot. They adopted ritual practices of shaking, shouting, dancing, whirling, and singing in tongues. Communal settlements were established in the United States by Ann Lee, known as Mother Ann and believed to be the reincarnation of Jesus, who came to America in 1774 and founded the first church in what is now Watervliet, N.Y. The movement later spread through New England, Kentucky, Ohio, and Indiana. The simplicity of Shaker craftsmanship had a significant impact on American furniture design. They also invented the screw propeller, rotary harrow, and common clothespin, among other items. The Shaker movement reached its peak in the 1840s, when there were about 6,000 members; by 1905, there were only some 1,000. The few remaining Shakers live in Sabbathday Lake, Me.

Shakespeare Festival

April–December

In what has been called the longest festival in the world, the Royal Shakespeare Company offers the plays of William Shakespeare in repertory performed by some of the best actors in Great Britain from April through December every year. The eighteenth century actor, producer, and co-manager of the Drury Lane Theatre, David Garrick, was the first to try to establish a Shakespeare festival, but the idea apparently died with him in 1779. Another festival was started in 1864 by Charles Edward Flower, who raised the necessary funds and contributed the riverside site for the original theater in Stratford-upon-Avon, Shakespeare's birthplace. The first Shakespeare Memorial Theatre opened there in 1879, but it burned down in 1926. A new theater opened in 1932, and it became the home of the first permanent Royal Shakespeare Company in Stratford. Now there are two companies—one that is resident in Stratford and one that tours. In 1960 the Aldwych Theatre became the company's London home, and in 1970 it moved into its own London theater.

See also STRATFORD FESTIVAL.

Shakespeare's Birthday

April 23

No one really knows the exact date of William Shakespeare's birth, although he was baptized on April 26, 1564 and died on April 23, 1616. April 23 is also ST. GEORGE'S DAY, and this may be why it was decided to observe the birth of England's greatest poet and dramatist on the feast day of England's patron saint. Special pageants are held at Stratford-upon-Avon in Warwickshire, where

Shakespeare was born and where thousands of tourists go each year to see his plays performed. The bells of Holy Trinity Church ring out, and the Mayor of Stratford leads a procession there to lay flowers on Shakespeare's grave.

Shalako Ceremonial

Late November or early December

One of the most impressive of the Pueblo Indian dances, held at the Zuni Pueblo in southwestern New Mexico. In this ceremony of all-night dancing and chants, houses are blessed, the dead are commemorated, and prayers are offered for good health and good weather in the coming year. The dance features towering masked figures with beaks who represent messengers from the rainmakers. They make clacking noises as they approach designated houses, and once inside the houses, they remove their masks, chant, and share food. Other figures taking part in the ceremonial are rain gods, warriors carrying whips, and the fire god, who is depicted by a young boy. The dancing goes on all through the cold night. The following morning, there are foot races.

Sham al-Nassim (Cham al-Nessim; Fragrance of the Breeze)

Between April 5 and May 9; Monday after Coptic Easter

A folk festival in Egypt, observed for thousands of years as a day to smell the breezes and celebrate spring. *Nassim* means 'zephyr,' the spring breeze, and *sham* means 'to breathe in.' While the date is set by the Coptic calendar, the holiday is now a non-religious national holiday observed by everyone as a family affair. Traditionally, people pack picnics to have outings along the Nile River or in parks. Certain food is specified for the occasion: the main dish is *fessikh*, a kind of salted fish, and it's also traditional to have *mouloukhiya* (stuffed vine leaves) and eggs with decorated, colored shells. The foods are believed to prevent disease, and the eggs symbolize life. Vast numbers of fish are eaten in Cairo on Sham al-Nassim. Other traditions call for placing freshly cut flowers at doors and windows, and putting a clove of garlic at the head of each bed to prevent boredom and fatigue for those who lie there.

At the time of the pharaohs, spring was celebrated with gifts of lotus flowers to wives or loved ones, and families enjoyed river outings on flower-decorated barges and feluccas (small sailing vessels).

Shampoo Day

Day 15 of the sixth lunar month

In Korea, **Cold Water Shampoo Day** or **Yoodoonal** is a day spent near a stream or waterfall, where people bathe and wash their hair to ward off fever and other heat-related ills during the coming year. Macaroni, flour cakes, melons, and other fruits are offered at family shrines. For scholars, Shampoo Day is an opportunity to go on picnics, drink wine, and compose poems.

Shavuot (Shabuoth)

Between May 16 and June 13; 6 Sivan

Shavuot 'weeks' is the second of the three pilgrim festivals (see also PASSOVER and SUKKOT). It follows Passover by fifty days and is also known in English as **Pentecost** from the Greek word meaning "fiftieth," (like the Christian PENTECOST, which comes fifty days after EASTER). It is also called the **Feast of Weeks** or **Feast of the Harvest,** because it originally marked the end of the seven weeks of the Passover barley harvest and the beginning of the wheat harvest. At one time all adult male Jews were expected to bring their first *omer* 'sheaf' of barley to the Temple in Jerusalem as a thanksgiving offering. Today dairy dishes are associated with Shavuot, particularly cheese blintzes.

After the periof of Jewish slavery in Egypt, Shavuot took on a new meaning: it celebrated Moses' return from the top of Mt. Sinai with the two stone tablets containing the Ten Commandments, the most fundamental laws of the Jewish faith, and is therefore also known as the **Festival of the Giving of the Law.** Orthodox and Conservative Jews in the Diaspora celebrate two days of Shavuot as full holidays, while Reform Jews and those living in Israel observe only the first day.

See also LAG BA-OMER.

Sheboygan Bratwurst Days

First weekend in August

A celebration in Sheboygan, Wis., that is scented with the smoke from 3,000 to 4,000 bratwursts being grilled. Sheboygan, billing itself the "Bratwurst Capitol of the World," or alternatively, the "Wurst City of the World," is the home of several large sausage factories that ship bratwurst around the country and of numerous smaller markets that make tons of brat. *Brat*, incidentally, rhymes with *cot*, not *cat*.

The celebration's main event is a parade led by a thirteen-foot-tall balloon Bavarian figure in lederhosen who is known as the *Bratmeister* 'sausage master.' In 1991, a highlight of the parade was a float carrying giant twin-brats—two 130-pound brats on a hard roll made from forty pounds of dough.

The point of the festival is to eat brats, and the smell of them cooking on outdoor grills permeates the city. There are a brat-and-pancake breakfast and a brat-eating contest. (The record-holder is Roger Theobald who ate nine double-brats in fifteen minutes in 1953). Other events include band concerts, a magic show, wrestling matches, competitions for children, and a stumpf-fiddle contest. The stumpf fiddle is an instrument combining bells, springs, BB-filled pie plates, wood blocks, and taxi horns on a wooden pole with a rubber ball at the bottom.

Germans settled in Sheboygan in the 1830s and 1840s and immediately began making sausage. In 1953, to celebrate the city's 100th birthday, a Bratwurst Day was held in August. The mayor's proclamation noted that the city "has achieved national fame and recognition for the exclusive manufacture of a special kind of roasting sausage . . . "

The celebration was canceled in 1966 because it had become too rowdy. In 1978 Bratwurst Days came back for the city's 125th anniversary. Today the festival attracts about 50,000 people.

Sheelah's Day
March 18

Even the Irish aren't exactly sure who Sheelah was. Some say she was St. Patrick's wife; some say his mother. But one thing that they all seem to agree on is how this day should be celebrated: by drinking whiskey. The shamrock worn on St. Patrick's Day is supposed to be worn on the following day as well, until it is "drowned" in the last glass of the evening. If someone should drop his shamrock into his glass and drink it before the "drowning ceremony" takes place, he has no choice but to get a fresh shamrock and another glass.

Shem al Nessim
On or around March 21

The Vernal Equinox in Egypt is celebrated not only by Muslims but by people of all religions. Families usually go on picnics to the Mediterranean or the Red Sea, or sometimes take an excursion up the Nile River. Foods traditionally associated with the spring picnic include dried fish and kidney beans.

Shemini Atzeret
Between September 27 and October 25; 22 Tishri

Shemini Atzeret 'eighth day of solemn assembly' is actually the eighth day of the festival of Sukkot, but it is celebrated as a separate holiday dedicated to the love of God. The second day of Shemini Atzeret is known as Simhat Torah and is also celebrated separately by Orthodox and Conservative Jews. Most Reform Jews celebrate Shemini Atzeret concurrently with Simhat Torah.

In ancient times, prayers for rain were recited on this day—a practice that is still part of Orthodox services. It is also one of four Jewish holidays on which the *Yizkor* or memorial rite for the dead is observed. The other three are Yom Kippur, the second day of Shavuot, and the last day of Passover.

Shenandoah Apple Blossom Festival
Early May

A four-day celebration of the apple orchards of Virginia's Shenandoah Valley, held in Winchester, the state's apple center. The festival was inaugurated in 1924 to publicize the area's historic, scenic, and industrial assets. Its motto was, "The bounties of nature are the gift of God." Winchester was settled in 1732, and George Washington, an early landlord in the area, required each tenant to plant four acres of apples.

The festival comes when the orchards are in bloom. About 250,000 people visit to enjoy the pink and white blossoms and the special events, including the coronation of Queen Shenandoah, a title once held by Luci Baines Johnson, President Lyndon B. Johnson's youngest daughter. Other attractions are a parade, concerts, an apple-pie baking contest, fireworks, and square- and folk-dancing.

Shichi-Go-San (Seven-Five-Three Festival)
November 15

An ancient Japanese celebration that marks the special ages of seven, five, and three. It has long been traditional for families to take girls aged seven, boys of five, and all three-year olds, dressed in their finest, to the neighborhood Shinto shrine where their birth is recorded. There they are purified and the priest prays to the tutelary deity for their healthy growth. At the end the priest gives each child two little packages: one containing cakes in the form of Shinto emblems (mirror, sword, and jewel), and the other with sacred rice to be mixed with the evening meal. Afterwards, there are often parties for the children, and customarily they are given a special pink hard candy, called "thousand-year candy," to symbolize hopes for a long life. Because Nov. 15 is not a legal holiday, families now observe the ceremony on the Sunday nearest that date.

Legend says that the custom started because parents believed their children's mischievousness was caused by little worms that somehow entered their bodies. The visits to the shrines were to pray that the mischief-making worms would depart. A more likely story is that the festival began in the days when children often died young, and parents gave thanks for those who survived.

Shick-Shack Day (Shik-Shak Day, Shicsack Day, Shitsack Day, Shig-Shag Day)
May 29

The *Oxford English Dictionary* suggests that this day takes its name from a corruption of *shit-sack*, a derogatory term for the Nonconformists, Protestants who did not follow the doctrines and practices of the established Church of England. It was later applied to those who did not wear the traditional sprig of oak on May 29 or **Royal Oak Day**—the birthday of Charles II and the day in 1660 on which he made his triumphal entry into London as king after a twelve-year interregnum.

The association of Charles II and the oak tree dates back to 1651 when, after being defeated in battle, he took refuge from his pursuers in an oak tree behind a house known as Boscobel. *Shick-shack* has since become synonymous with the oak-apple or sprig of oak itself, and May 29 is celebrated-particularly in rural areas of England-in memory of the restoration of King Charles and his preservation in the Royal Oak. Also called **Oak Apple Day, Oak Ball Day, Bobby Ack Day, Yack Bob Day, Restoration Day,** or **Nettle Day.**

Shilla (Silla) Cultural Festival
October, every other year (October 8–10 in 1992)

An exuberant three-day festival, one of Korea's biggest and most impressive, to celebrate the country's ancient Shilla Kingdom. The celebrations are held in Kyongju, the capital of the Shilla Kingdom, and throughout the Kyongju Valley, where there is a great treasure of historic buildings: the Sokkuram Grotto, one of Asia's finest Buddhist shrines with a granite dome; Ch'omsongdae, a seventh-century bottle-shaped stone structure that is the world's earliest known extant observatory; royal tombs; palaces; and

pleasure pavilions. The Shilla Kingdom in the southeastern portion of what is now Korea flourished from 57 B.C. to 935 A.D., and defeated two rival kingdoms, unifying all three in 676. The Unified Shilla Period is considered a golden age of Buddhist arts and especially of granite Buddhist sculpture.

The festival features concerts, wrestling matches, Buddhist pagoda dancing, games and contests, and lavish processions with elaborate floats.

Shiprock Navajo Nation Fair
Usually first weekend of October

Also known as the **Northern Navajo Fair,** this fair began in 1924 and is considered the oldest and most traditional of Navajo fairs. It is a harvest fair held in Shiprock, New Mexico, the largest populated community of the Navajo Nation.

The fair coincides with the conclusion of an ancient Navajo healing ceremony, the Night Chant. This is a nine-day chant known as the *Yei Bei Chei,* and is a complex ritual usually conducted after the first frost. Parts of the ceremony may be witnessed by the public. Among the more colorful public rituals are *Two Yei's Come,* a Saturday-afternoon dance, and the grand finale in which sacred masked dancers begin a dance late Saturday night and continue into the pre-dawn.

After watching the healing ceremony, spectators go on to other events of the fair such as an all-Indian rodeo, an inter-tribal powwow, a livestock show, a carnival, the Miss Northern Navajo Pageant, Indian arts and crafts exhibits, and a Saturday morning parade.

See also NAVAJO NATION FAIR AT WINDOW ROCK.

Shivah Asar be-Tammuz *See* Tammuz, Fast of the 17th of

Shivaratri
February–March; Thirteenth day of dark half of Phalguna

A Hindu holiday observed throughout India and Nepal. Legend says that on this night Lord Shiva, the great god of destruction (who is also the restorer), danced the Tandav, his celestial dance of Creation, Preservation, and Destruction. Hindu devotees of Shiva eat only once on the day before this "Night of Shiva," and then fast and tell stories about him. In India, pilgrims throng the Shiva shrines in Chidambaram (Tamil Nadu), Kalahasti (Andhra Pradesh), and Varanasi (Uttar Pradesh), where special celebrations are held. Mandi in

316

Himachal Pradesh becomes one big party. Devotees carry deities on temple chariots, and there are folk dances and folk music. Hundreds of thousands make the pilgrimage to Pashupatinath Temple in Katmandu, Nepal, for worship, feasting, and ritual bathing in the holy Bagmati River. In Port Lovis, Mauritius, wooden arches covered with flowers are carried to Grand Bassin, to get water from the holy lake to wash the symbols of Shiva.

Shrimp Festival, National

Early October

A waterside festival held for four days in Gulf Shores, Ala., drawing crowds estimated at 200,000. This festival began in this shrimping and resort area in 1971 as a one-day event to liven things up after Labor Day. The big event was a shrimp-cooking contest, and shrimp dishes have been in the forefront since. About 30 percent of the food vendors' fare includes shrimp. This means lots of jambalaya and kabobs. Also on the menu are such dishes as shark and Greek foods including seafood gyros (pronounced YEER-ohs). Events of the festival include a parade, a sailboat regatta, musical entertainment, sky-diving exhibitions, a Miss Sunny beauty contest, and arts and crafts displays.

Shrove Monday

Between February 2 and March 8; Monday before Ash Wednesday

Many countries celebrate Shrove Monday as well as SHROVE TUESDAY, both days marking a time of preparation for LENT. It is often a day for eating pastry, as the butter and eggs in the house must all be used up before Lent. In Greece it is known as **Clean Monday** and is observed by holding picnics at which Lenten foods are served. In Iceland, the Monday before Lent is known as **Bun Day**. The significance of the name is twofold: It is a day for striking people on the buttocks with a stick before they get out of bed as well as a day for eating sweet buns with whipped cream. The latter custom is believed to have been introduced by Danish and Norwegian bakers who emigrated to Iceland during the late nineteenth century.

Shrove Tuesday

Between February 3 and March 9; day before Ash Wednesday

There are a number of names in the West for the last day before the long fast of LENT. The French call it MARDI GRAS (meaning 'Fat Tuesday') because it was traditionally a time to use up all the milk, butter, and eggs left in the kitchen. These ingredients often went into pancakes, which is why the English call it PANCAKE DAY and still celebrate it with games and races that involve tossing pancakes in the air. Other names include **Shuttlecock** (or **Football**) **Day**, after sports associated with this day; **Doughnut Day**; **Bannock** (or **Bannocky**) **Day** (a bannock being the Scottish equivalent of a pancake), and **Fastingong** (meaning 'approaching a time of fast'). The name "Shrove Tuesday" is derived from the Christian custom of confessing sins and being "shriven" (i.e., absolved) just before Lent.

In northern Sweden, people eat a meat stew. In the south, they eat "Shrove Tuesday buns" called *semlor*, made with cardamom, filled with almond paste, and topped with whipped cream.

No matter what its name, the day before ASH WEDNESDAY has long been a time for excessive eating and merrymaking. The Mardi Gras parade in New Orleans is typical of the masquerades and dancing in the streets that take place in many countries on this day as people prepare for the long Lenten fast.

See also CARNIVAL, FASTENS-EEN, FASCHING, MARDI GRAS IN NEW ORLEANS, MEAT FARE SUNDAY, DAIRY SUNDAY, and PANCAKE DAY.

Silent Days

Beginning between March 19 and April 22; Thursday, Friday, and Saturday before Easter

The last three days of HOLY WEEK-MAUNDY THURSDAY, GOOD FRIDAY, and HOLY SATURDAY-were at one time referred to as **the Swidages**, from an Old English word meaning 'to be silent.' From this came Silent Days or **Still Days**—three days during which the church bells in England remained silent. The bells were rung again at the Easter Vigil Mass.

Simbang Gabi *See* Misa de Gallo

Simhat Torah

Between September 28 and October 26; 23 Tishri

This Jewish holiday, which follows SUKKOT, celebrates the annual completion of the public reading of the Torah, or the first five books of the Bible, and the beginning of a new reading cycle. The hand-lettered scrolls of the Torah are removed from the Ark (a box-like container) and paraded around the synagogue—and sometimes through the streets—amidst singing and dancing. Simhat Torah means "rejoicing in the law," which is as good a description as any of what takes place on this day. To be chosen as the Bridegroom of the

Law, to read the final verses of the last book, Deuteronomy, or the Bridegroom of the Beginning, to read the opening verses of the first book, Genesis, is considered a great honor.

In Israel and among Reform Jews, this festival is observed on the twenty-second day of Tishri, concurrently with SHEMINI ATZERET; all other Jews celebrate it separately on the twenty-third day. Israelis also hold a second *hakkafot* 'procession around the synagogue' on the night after Simhat Torah, frequently accompanied by bands and choirs.

Simhat Torah customs have varied from country to country: in Afghanistan all the scrolls are taken out of their Arks and heaped in a pyramid almost to the synagogue's roof. In Cochin, China, a carpet was laid on the courtyard flagstones, coconut oil lamps were heaped in a pyramid in front of the synagogue entrance, and the Scrolls of the Law carried around the outside of the synagogue. One synagogue in Calcutta, India has fifty Scrolls, and the women go from scroll to scroll, kissing them. At the end of the holiday a Simhat Torah ball is held and a beauty queen chosen. Young Yemeni children are taken to the synagogue for the first time on this holiday.

In southern France, two mourners stand on either side of the reader, crying bitterly as the death of Moses is related. The Bridegrooms of the Law in Holland are escorted home in a torchlight parade accompanied by music. A crown from one of the Torah Scrolls was placed on the head of every reader in medieval Spain, and in some places in Eastern Europe, the reader wore a large paper hat decorated with bells and feathers.

Simnel Sunday *See* Mothering Sunday

Sinhala Avurudu (Sinhalese New Year)
April

The solar new year celebrated in Sri Lanka (formerly Ceylon) as a non-religious festival by both Sinhalese and Tamils. The exact hour of the new year is determined by astrologers, and often the new year does not begin when the old year ends. The few hours between the new and old year are known as the *nona gathe* 'neutral period' and all activities including eating and drinking, must stop in that time.

In the villages the new year begins with lighting a fire in the kitchen and wearing new clothes. The color of these clothes is determined by an almanac. The ceremonies reach a climax with an anointing ceremony. Oil is mixed with an herbal paste and a family elder rubs this oil on the head of all the family members as they sit with a white cloth under their feet. The holiday is also a day of sports, games, dancing, and special dinners.

Sinjska Alka
First weekend in August

A day of jousting on horseback in the small town of Sinj, near Split, in Croatia, former Yugoslavia. The festival commemorates a victory of a peasant army over the Turks in 1715, even though the 60,000 Turks outnumbered the Sinj warriors by three to one. The annual tournament was supposedly instituted soon after the 1715 victory.

On this day, young men who have trained throughout the year ride horses headlong down the steep 140-yard run and try to spear an iron ring—or *alka*—suspended from a rope about nine feet off the ground. The ring has a diameter of six inches and within it is another two-inch ring. The jouster who most successfully spears the rings in three tries is the winner, and receives a sash and silver medal. The band plays a triumphal march and shots are fired for all top scorers.

Before the contest, there is a ceremonial procession through the streets. The contestants march through Sinj accompanied by their mace bearers and shield bearers wearing eighteenth-century costumes decorated with gold and silver.

Sinterklass *See* St. Nicholas' Day

Sinulog Festival
Third weekend in January

A festival on the island of Cebu in the Philippines, held at the same time as the frenzied ATI-ATIHAN FESTIVAL in Kalibo and the more sedate DINAGYANG in Iloilo City. The word *sinulog* is derived from the rootword *sulog*, 'river current', and the dancing of the festival is thought to flow like a river.

The festival celebrates both early Cebuano culture and the history of the Christianization of Cebu, combining the pageanty of early years with today's Christian ritual. An image of Cebu's patron saint, the Santo Niño ('the Holy Child' Jesus), is carried in a procession along the streets, while drums beat in the ritual for a bountiful harvest, and revelers dance in the streets.

Sithinakha
May–June; sixth day, waxing half of Jyaistha

This is the birthday of the Hindu god Kumara, also known as Skanda, the god of war and first-born son of Shiva. Kumara has six heads because he was nursed by the Karttikas—six women who as stars comprise the Pleiades. For this reason he is also called *Karttikeya* 'son of Karttikas.' The six heads also represent the six senses (including extrasensory perception). He also has a large following under the name *Subrahmanya*, 'dear to the Brahmanas.'

Most Hindus observe this day with a ritual purification bath followed by processions to the temples to honor Kumara. It is also considered a good opportunity to clean out wells and tanks, because the snake gods are off worshipping on this day and it's safe to enter their habitats. In Nepal, eight different kinds of cakes, made from eight different grains, are offered to Kumara on his birthday, and for this reason Sithinakha is sometimes referred to as the **Cake Festival**. Lotus-shaped windmills are often set on rooftops at this time, to symbolize the end of bad times and the onset of holier days.

Sitka Summer Music Festival
June

A series of concerts featuring internationally known musicians, held during three weeks in June in Sitka, Alaska. Chamber music concerts are held on Tuesdays and Fridays, and there are programs ranging from classical to pop. The concerts are given in the Centennial Building auditorium, which has a wall of glass behind the stage. Since the nights are light in June, the audience can look at mountains, eagles, water, and mist while listening to the music. Violin virtuoso Paul Rosenthal founded the festival in 1972, producing the first musical event with four other musicians, and going on to emphasize a repertoire of eighteenth- and nineteenth-century classics.

Sjomannadagurinn (Sailors' Day)
First week in June

A day dedicated to seafarers, celebrated in all the coastal towns and cities of Iceland. Sailors take the day off, and the Seaman's Union sponsors celebrations. These include competitions in rowing and swimming, tugs-of-war, and sea rescue competitions. On the more solemn side, medals are awarded for rescue operations of the past year.

Smithsonian Kite Festival
Late March–early April

The Kite Festival held on the Mall in Washington, D.C. every spring is co-sponsored by the Smithsonian Resident Associate Program and the National Air and Space Museum. First held in 1966, the festival was started by Dr. Paul Garber, a kite fancier and historian emeritus of the National Air and Space Museum. Now in his nineties, Dr. Garber continues to serve as master of ceremonies for the festivities.

A major focus of the annual festival is the competition for hand-made kites, which must be capable of flying at a minimum altitude of one hundred feet for at least one minute. Kites are judged on the basis of appearance (design, craftsmanship, beauty) as well as on performance (takeoff, climb, angle, recovery). Trophies are awarded in many categories-for example, airplane, bird figure, box-kite, spacecraft, and delta-and age groups. Participants come from all regions of the United States as well as several foreign countries. Immediately following the kite display program, a kite building workshop is held for members of the Smithsonian Resident Associate Program.

Snow Hut Festival *See* Kamakura Matsuri

Sol (New Year's Day)
First day of first lunar month (usually late January or early February)

One of the biggest holidays of the year in Korea. This lunar new year is celebrated largely by rural people and is a two-day national holiday. January 1 and 2, also national holidays, are celebrated more by residents of cities. On Sol, tradition calls for families to gather in their best clothes and for children to bow to parents and grandparents to reaffirm family ties. A soup made of rice dumplings called *duggook* is always served, and it is customary to play *yut*, a game played with wooden blocks and a game board. Young girls see-saw standing up. During early Confucianism, women were not allowed any outdoor exercises. See-sawing this way bounced them above their enclosing walls and they could see their boyfriends. This made see-sawing a love sport and not exercise. It is still very popular.

Songkran (Pi Mai)
April 13 (Sixth or seventh moon of Dai calendar)

The traditional NEW YEAR in Thailand and a public holiday. The celebration actually lasts for three days, from April 12–14, and takes the form of religious ceremonies as well as public festivities. Merit-making ceremonies are held at Buddhist temples, water is sprinkled on Buddhist images, and captive birds and fish are freed. Water-splashing on the streets is also a part of the festivities, especially among young people. The young do not splash older people, but instead sprinkle water on their hands or feet to honor them.

The celebration is held with special elan in Chiang Mai with beauty contests, parades, dancing, and, of course, water splashing.

The Dai people of the southwestern Xinan region of China, celebrate the birthday of Buddha and the new year with the **Water-Splashing Festival**. In tropical Xishuangbanna, a land of elephants and golden-haired monkeys, the celebration begins with dragon-boat races and fireworks displays. On the second day, people visit Buddhist temples. The third day, which is NEW YEAR'S DAY, is the high point. Dressed in colorful national costumes, people carry buckets and pans of water to the temple to bathe the Buddha, and they then splash water at each other. The water symbolizes happiness and good health. It washes away the demons of the past year and welcomes in a new year of good harvests, better livestock, and increased prosperity.

Song of Hiawatha Pageant
Friday–Sunday, last two weeks of July, first week in August

Pipestone, Minnesota was named for the soft red stone used by the Native-American Dakota tribe to make their ceremonial pipes. The Dakotas believe that their tribe originated here, and that the stone was colored by the blood of their ancestors. On weekends in late July and early August each year, the story of Hiawatha—the chief of the Onondaga tribe immortalized in Henry Wadsworth Longfellow's poem, *Song of Hiawatha*—is told in symbolic pantomime with traditional Indian music and dances. The audience watches the performance from the opposite side of a quiet reflecting pool that lies at the bottom of the pipestone quarry where the pageant is held.

The Great Spirit appears at the top of the cliff, where he shows his children the pink stone and makes a calumet or peace pipe. With the last whiff on his pipe, the Great Spirit disappears in a cloud of smoke. The Three Maidens, who once guarded the place where the Great Spirit lived, can be seen in the form of three huge boulders. The pageant ends with the death of Hiawatha and his departure on a "long and distant journey."

South Carolina Peach Festival
Mid–July (July 12–21 in 1991)

A ten-day festival in Gaffney, S.C., to salute the state's peach industry. Events of the festival include a parade, truck and tractor pulls, country-music concerts, and peach desserts. Gaffney's year around tribute to the peach is the eye-catching *peachoid*, a one-million-gallon water tank in the shape and color of a peach with a great metal leaf hanging over it.

Southern 500 (Heinz Southern 500)
Labor Day weekend

The oldest southern stock-car race, held in Darlington, S.C. since 1950. The race, which draws about 80,000 spectators, is one of the four so-called crown jewels in the NASCAR (National Association for Stock Car Auto Racing) Winston Cup circuit and is considered the forerunner of those races. The others are the Daytona 500 (in Florida), the Winston 500 (Talladega, Ala.), and the Coca-Cola 600 (Charlotte, N.C.).

The first of the southern super speedways, the Darlington track was promoted and built by Harold Brasington, a sometime racing driver, and a group of Darlington citizens. The track was built on land owned by Sherman J. Ramsey, a farmer, and he insisted that his minnow pond not be disturbed. So the track had to skirt around it. Sports writers dubbed the oddly configured raceway the "Lady in Black" supposedly because it was fickle with drivers, like a mysterious woman. The winner of the first race in 1950 was Johnny Mantz. The all-time winner of the most Southern 500s is Cale Yarborough, who zipped past everybody else in 1968, 1973, 1974, 1978, and 1982.

Southern Ute Tribal Sun Dance
First weekend after July 4

A ritual ceremony of ancient origin held by the Southern Utes in Ignacio, Colo., usually on the Sunday and Monday after July Fourth. The dancers who perform the ceremony are chosen from those who dream dreams and see visions, and they fast for four days before the dancing. While the public is allowed to attend, dress must be circumspect, and women are not allowed who are "on their moon," that is, having their menstrual period.

One aspect of the ceremony involves chopping down a tree, which represents an enemy chief, stripping its bark and then dancing around it. The Sun Dance was at one time performed by most Plains tribes, and usually involved self-torture. The Utes, however, did not practice this.

Southwestern Exposition & Livestock Show & Rodeo

Last two weeks of January

The oldest continuously running livestock show in the United States, held since 1896 in Fort Worth, Tex. The exposition calls to mind Fort Worth's past when it was considered the capital of the southwestern cattle empire, and stockyards ringed the city. The world's first indoor rodeo was featured here in 1918.

Events of the exposition include a parade, horse shows, a midway, big-name entertainers, and $600,000 in show premiums and rodeo purses. The more than 17,000 head of livestock include beef and dairy cattle, sheep, swine, goats, horses, donkeys, mules, pigeons, poultry, sheepdogs, and llamas. The latter have been found to be more effective against coyotes than guns, dogs, electric fences, or chemical repellants. About 500 of them are now guarding sheep in the Rocky Mountain region.

Spartakiade

Once every five years in June

Czechoslovakia has had mass physical culture performances for more than a hundred years, although Spartakiade is a far more highly organized event than some of its predecessors. This is an eight-day national exercise competition, held in Prague once every five years. This allows the competitors—more than seventy thousand of whom are selected in elimination contests—time to train. Millions of spectators come to watch the various gymnastic contests, army drills, and dance performances. Held since 1955, the purpose behind Spartakiade is to promote physical fitness for Czechoslovakians.

Spearing the Dragon *See* Drachenstich

Spoleto Festival USA

May–June

Pulitzer Prize-winning composer Gian Carlo Menotti founded the Festival of Two Worlds in Spoleto, Italy in 1958, and brought it to Charleston, South Carolina in 1977 under the name of **Spoleto USA**. The annual seventeen-day international arts festival focuses on new works and productions, and routinely offers more than 100 events in opera, chamber music, symphonic concerts, theater, dance, and art.

There has been some controversy recently over whether or not the Spoleto festival should feature more contemporary art forms, such as jazz. Menotti, who turned eighty in 1991, prefers to keep the festival more traditional and convinced the Board of Directors to keep it so. The festival and the composer have been associated for so long that "Menotti" and "Spoleto" have become nearly synonymous.

Spring Break

Spring (March–April)

An annual celebration of spring—and of school vacations—by an estimated two million college students who whoop it up, sunbathe, party, drink, dance, and listen to loud music. From the early 1950s until 1985, Fort Lauderdale, Fla. was a prime destination. In 1960, the movie, *Where the Boys Are,* (based on the Glendon Swarthout novel of the same name), featuring Connie Francis, George Hamilton, and Yvette Mimieux, was all about spring break. It gave Fort Lauderdale great national exposure. But the hordes of students got to be too much; by 1985 350,000 people took over the city for six weeks and tied up not just traffic but the legal system. Fort Lauderdale started clamping down, and now only about 20,000 students visit. The popular destinations today are Panama City Beach, Fla., which drew about 500,000 young revelers in 1992; Daytona Beach, Fla.; South Padre Island, Tex.; Palm Springs, Calif.; the Bahamas; Jamaica, and Mexico. To lure the spring breakers, the various towns and resorts spend millions of dollars and offer an abundance of free activities, including beach sports, concerts, movie premieres, and contests.

Spring Festival *See* Lunar New Year

Springtime Festival

Beginning between March 11 and April 15; four successive Thursdays before Orthodox Easter

Celebrated by peasants of all religious faiths the Springtime Festival is a regional celebration throughout the Bekáa Valley, which extends from Syria through Lebanon into former Palestine. It takes place on four successive Thursdays preceding the Eastern Orthodox EASTER.

The first Thursday, known as Thursday-of-the-Animals, is a day of rest for domestic working animals. Henna, symbolic of blood and life, is dabbed on their foreheads. On the following Thursday, known as Thursday-of-the-Plants, young children and unmarried girls wash themselves in water scented with crushed flowers. Next is Thursday-of-the-Dead, a day for visiting the graves of family and friends. Last is Thursday-of-the-Jumping or Day of the Jumping, when peasants living in the mountains come down by the thousands to the plains to join in the festival activites. They visit the tomb of Noah and then the shrine of the Wali Zaur, a legendary Muslim saint. There they receive the blessings of health and well-being. Eventually everyone returns to the village, where there is dancing in the streets and even in the outdoor court of the mosque.

Spy Wednesday
Beginning between March 19 and April 22;
*   Wednesday before Easter*

The Wednesday before EASTER Sunday is the day on which the disciple Judas Iscariot betrayed Jesus . In order to arrest Jesus without exciting the populace, Judas led the Jewish priests to the Garden of Gethsemane, near Jerusalem, where Jesus had gone at night to pray with the other eleven disciples after the Last Supper. Judas identified Jesus by kissing him and addressing him as "Master." For this he was paid thirty pieces of silver, the price of a slave in the Old Testament.

The name "Spy Wednesday" is said to be of Irish origin, although the Bible never refers to Judas as a spy. His surname, Iscariot, is believed to be a corruption of the Larin *sicarius* meaning 'murderer' or 'assassin.'

Stamp Act Repealed *See* Repudiation Day

Star Festival *See* Tanabata

State Fair of Texas
Late September, beginning of October (September 25–October 18 in 1992)

Not surprisingly, one of the nation's biggest state fairs, claiming more than three million visitors to the 200-acre Fair Park in Dallas. The fair began in 1887, and in 1952 Big Tex, its symbol of bigness, arrived. Big Tex is a fifty-two-foot-tall cowboy with a thirty-foot chest and 7'-8" biceps, wearing a five-foot-high, seventy-five-gallon cowboy hat. The cowboy stands in the middle of the fairgrounds booming out welcomes and announcements. The skeleton of the cowboy was built in 1949 to be the world's tallest Santa Claus for a Christmas celebration in Kerens, Tex. It was sold to the State Fair, and Dallas artist Jack Bridges took baling wire and papier-mâché to create the cowboy that debuted in 1952. The following year, a motor was installed to move the cowboy's jaw in sync with a voice mechanism, and Big Tex has been booming ever since. Among fair events are a rodeo, college football game, and parades.

State Opening of Parliament
Early November

This colorful British ritual is observed at the beginning of November when the members of Parliament return after the long summer recess. Crowds assemble in the streets of Westminster, an inner borough of Greater London, in hopes to catching a glimpse of the Queen as she arrives in her horse-drawn coach, dressed in royal robes of state and escorted by the Household Cavalry. The Queen is not allowed to enter the House of Commons because she is not a commoner, so after being met by the Lord Chancellor she is led straight to the House of Lords. Seated on a magnificent throne and surrounded by various church and state officials in their robes, she reads aloud the speech that has been written for her by members of the government outlining their plans for the coming session.

An interesting tradition that accompanies the opening of Parliament is the searching of the cellars of both Houses. This goes back to 1605, when Guy Fawkes (see GUY FAWKES DAY) and his accomplices tried to blow them up.

Stephen Foster Memorial Day
January 13

Stephen Collins Foster (1826–1864) was a composer whose popular minstrel songs and sentimental ballads have found a lasting place in American music. When he died at the age of thirty-seven, suffering from poverty and alcoholism, he left behind more than two hundred compositions-among them "Camptown Races," "Beautiful Dreamer," "My Old Kentucky Home," "Oh! Susanna," "Swanee River," and "Jeanie with the Light Brown Hair."

January 13, the anniversary of Foster's death, was proclaimed as Stephen Foster Memorial Day in 1951. In Florida, this day is part of Stephen Foster Memorial Week, established by the state legislature in 1935. One of the most widely known observances of this week takes place at the Stephen Foster Center in White Springs, Florida, beginning on January 13. The events commemorating Foster's contributions to American music include performances by musical groups from schools and universities throughout the state and daily concerts from the 97-bell carillon tower. During the preceding October, the so-called "Jeanie auditions" (named for Foster's wife, the subject of "Jeanie with the Light Brown Hair") are held to determine the winner of a music scholarship for 18-to-21-year-old Florida women. The winner often appears at the Memorial Week festivities and performs some of Foster's songs.

Stewardship Sunday
Second Sunday in November

This is the day on which many churches in the United States and Canada begin their campaign for financial support in the coming year. The term "stewardship" refers to the Christian and Jewish teaching that all creation belongs to God and that each man and woman is an agent or steward to whom God's property is entrusted for a while. On this Sunday each year, the churches appeal to their members' sense of responsibility as stewards of the money God has entrusted to them.

In the United States, Stewardship Sunday is sponsored by the National Council of Churches' Joint Department of Stewardship and Benevolence.

Stickdance
Spring

A week of ceremonies to grieve for the dead, held by the Athapaskan Indians of Alaska. The ancient ceremony, usually held long after the deaths of those memorialized, is now observed only in two villages on the Yukon River—Kaltag and Nulato.

Each evening of the ceremony, people go to the community hall with traditional foods—moose, salmon, beaver, rabbit, ptarmigan—for a meal called a *potlatch*. After the meal, the women stand in a circle, swaying and chanting traditional songs for the dead. The hall becomes more crowded each night. On Friday night, as the women dance in a circle, the men carry in a tall spruce tree stripped of branches and wrapped in ribbons. The tree is erected in the center of the room and wolf and fox furs are draped on it. The people then dance around it and chant continuously through the night. In the morning, the men tear the furs and ribbons from the stick and carry it away to the Yukon River, where they break it into pieces and throw the pieces on the river ice.

On Saturday night, people representing the dead are ritually dressed in special clothes. Somberly, they leave the hall and go to the river where they shake the spirits from their clothing. On their return to the hall, the mood becomes festive; gifts are exchanged and a night of celebration begins. The following morning the people who have represented the dead walk through the village shaking hands with people, sharing food and drink, and saying farewell.

Stickdance is held at irregular intervals, since it takes months or longer to prepare for it. People must choose those who will represent the dead being honored and make their clothes, and they must also save up to buy gifts.

The Athapaskans, who may have descended from bands who crossed from Asia, have lived in Alaska longer than the Eskimos, and speak a language that is in the same family as that spoken by Navajos and Apaches.

Stiftungsfest
Last weekend in August

Appropriately enough, Minnesota's oldest continuous festival is held in the town of Young America. Loosely translated as 'founders' day,' Stiftungsfest was created in 1861 by the Young America Maennerchor (men's choir) as a way of bringing the music of old Germany to the new world. Well-known bands and singing groups from Germany as well as local groups perform during the three-day event, which includes a traditional German beer garden, a flower show, and a Grand Parade, which is held every fifth year.

Stir-Up Sunday
November–December; Sunday before Advent

The collect for the Sunday preceding ADVENT in the Church of England begins, "Stir up, we beseech Thee, O Lord, the wills of thy faithful people." But the real "stirring up" that takes place on this day is more literal: the stirring of the batter for the traditional Christmas pudding, which must be prepared weeks in advance. It is customary for each member of the family to take turns stirring the pudding with a wooden spoon (symbolic of Jesus' crib), which is thought to bring good luck. The stirring is done clockwise, with eyes closed, and the stirrer makes a wish.

Stockton Asparagus Festival
Last weekend in April

A two-day celebration in Stockton, Calif., the heart of the region that claims to be the "Asparagus Capital of the Nation". In fact, California accounts for about 90 percent of the fresh-market asparagus production in the country, and most of that asparagus comes from Stockton's San Joaquin Delta region.

The festival began in 1986 to promote the asparagus and it now draws 85,000 spectators to the varied events. These include more than fifty food booths in Asparagus Alley, a wine-tasting booth, a fun run (some runners wear asparagus spears in their headbands), a car show of some 200 antique and classic cars, arts and crafts, live entertainment (bands, jugglers, mimes, magicians, etc.), and children's activities. There's also a recipe contest; among the past winning entries have been enchiladas and lasagna made, of course, with asparagus. Other popular asparagus dishes served include asparaberry shortcake (it is said the asparagus gives a nutmeg flavor to the strawberries), asparagus-and-beef sandwiches, and asparagus bisque. The festival is also a time to promulgate information about the asparagus, and fair-goers learn that asparagus is a source of vitamins A and C; the first trainload of asparagus was sent east from California in 1900; the Greeks and Romans used asparagus as a medicine for bee stings, dropsy, and toothache, and also as an aphrodisiac.

Store Bededag *See* Common Prayer Day

Storytelling Festival, National
First weekend in October

A three-day festival in Jonesborough, Tenn., that was started in 1973 to revive the ancient folk art of storytelling. The popularity of storytelling seemed to be dying, replaced by radio, television, and movies. The first festival was the idea of Jimmy Neil Smith, a Jonesborough schoolteacher who became executive director of the festival's sponsor, the National Association for the Preservation and Perpetuation of Storytelling (NAPPS), which was formed in 1975 and is headquartered in Jonesborough. That first event drew about sixty people. At first, people sat on bales of hay, then the festival moved to kitchens and parlors and porches, and finally into the large tents now used. The festival has inspired scores of similar events around the country as well as college courses in storytelling.

About 6,000 people now attend to listen to storytellers relating ghost stories, sacred stories, ballads, tall tales, myths, legends, and fairy tales. Restaurants set up food booths, and a resource tent provides tapes and other material. The twentieth Anniversary Celebration in 1992 brought together more than eighty storytellers who had all appeared at previous festivals. A highlight was a special ghost-story concert by tellers of supernatural tales.

See also TELLEBRATION.

Stratford Festival
June–October

What started in Stratford, Ontario in 1953 as a six-week Shakespearean drama festival under the artistic leadership of Alec Guinness and Irene Worth has since expanded into a twenty-three week event drawing an audience of half a million people. All of Shakespeare's plays have been performed here over the years, as well as works by Sophocles, Ibsen, Molière, Chekhov, Sheridan, Beckett, and a number of Canadian playwrights. The festival's repertory company, known as the Stratford Company, goes on tour during the months when the festival is not in session.

See also SHAKESPEARE FESTIVAL.

Strawberry Festival
Strawberry time–usually June

One of several annual festivals held by the Iroquois Indians. At Tonawanda, N.Y., the people congregate in their longhouse to hear a lengthy recitation of the words of Handsome Lake. In 1799 this Seneca prophet delivered a message calling for abstention from hard drink, abandonment of witchcraft and magic, the prohibition of abortion, and other instructions. This is the basis of today's Longhouse religion.

Following the recitations and speeches are ceremonial dances accompanied by chants and the pounding of turtle-shell rattles. Lunch follows, with a strawberry drink and winding up with strawberry shortcake.

The Iroquois say "you will eat strawberries when you die," because strawberries line the road to heaven.

Other traditional Iroquois celebrations are a New Year festival, a Maple Dance held at the time of making maple syrup and sugar, a Planting Festival, and the Green Corn Dance, at which the principal dish is succotash, made not just with corn and lima beans but also with squash and venison or beef.

Sugar Ball Show
Sixteenth day of first lunar month

This temple festival is held at the Haiyun Buddhist Convent in Qingdao, Shandong Province, China. Set for the day of the first spring tide, this festival has been held since the convent was built in the seventeenth century near the end of the Ming Dynasty. Originally fishermen observed this time to pray for safety and a good harvest. Now sugar balls—yams, oranges, and dates dipped in hot syrup and then cooled until crisp—colorfully displayed on long skewers, are specialties of the fair. About 200,000 people attend the show.

Sugar Bowl Classic
January 1

New Orleans, Louisiana has been host to football and lots of hoopla since the Sugar Bowl originated there in 1935. The Southeastern Conference champion is always awarded a berth in this yearly event. Alabama has won the most games. Nineteen ninety-three was their eighth victory when they rolled over Miami of Florida 34–13. That game ended Miami's twenty-nine game winning streak and gave the Alabama Crimson Tide its first national collegiate football championship since 1979. The game is the grand finale in Sugar Bowl Week, a round of events that begins with a sailing regatta on Lake Pontchartrain and includes contests in basketball, tennis, and track.

Sukkot (Sukkoth, Succoth)
Begins between September 20 and October 18; 15–21 Tishri

After their escape from slavery in Egypt, the Jews wandered in the desert for forty years under the leadership of Moses. For much of the time they lived in huts or *sukkot* made of wooden frames covered with branches or hay. The festival of Sukkot, also known as the **Feast of Tabernacles** or the **Feast of Booths,** commemorates this period in Jewish history. It is also one of the pilgrim festivals (see also Passover and Shavuot).

The traditional way of observing Sukkot was to build a small booth or tabernacle and live in it during the seven-day festival. Nowadays Orthodox congregations build a *sukkah* in the synagogue, while Reform Jews make miniature models of the ancient huts and use them as centerpieces on the family table. Although linked to the Exodus from Egypt, Sukkot also celebrates the fall harvest and is sometimes referred to as the **Feast of the Ingathering.**

A major part of the festival is the four species: a palm branch, citron, three myrtle twigs, and two willow branches. These are tied together and waved at different points in the service, to "rejoice before the Lord."

Like other Jewish holidays, Sukkot begins at sundown on the preceding evening, in this case the fourteenth day of Tishri. The seventh day of Sukkot is known as Hoshana Rabbah and is the last possible day on which one can seek and obtain forgiveness for the sins of the previous year—an extension of the Day of Atonement. The eighth day of Sukkot is known as Shemini Atzeret, and the day after that is called Simhat Torah, which is now celebrated as a separate holiday by Orthodox and Conservative Jews.

Summer Festival
July 4

Something for everybody on the Fourth of July in Owensboro, Ky. A highlight is the "Anything That Goes and Floats Race," in which contestants must have a vehicle that gets them to the Ohio River and then floats them for a decent distance on the river. Vehicles that have made it into the water include bicycles attached to a canoe, a skateboard tied to a plastic raft, and large pontoons powered by bicycles on land and paddlewheels in the water.

Other events of the day include a pops concert, a gospel music show, a lighted boat parade, and, of course, fireworks.

Summer Solstice
June 21–22 (Northern hemisphere); December 21–22 (Southern hemisphere)

There are times during the year respectively in each hemisphere, when the sun is at its furthest point from the equator. It reaches its northernmost point around June 21, which is the longest day of the year for those living north of the equator, and its southernmost point around December 22, which is the longest day for those living in the southern hemisphere. The summer solstice marks the first day of the summer season—the word *solstice* is from the Latin *solstitium* 'sun-stopping,' since the point at which sun appears to rise and set stops and reverses direction after this day.

Although it was common to celebrate the Summer Solstice in ancient times, modern American observations are rare. The solstice celebration sponsored by the Institute of Advanced Thinking—the world's oldest, largest "think tank"—in Belfast, Maine attempts to recreate the ancient rituals. People from five countries and up to twenty different states arrive in Belfast the night before the solstice equipped with tents and sleeping bags. They get up at dawn to greet and worship the sun with prayers and ritual chants. The celebration continues for three hours. There are also a number of solstice observances held by New Age groups throughout the United States.

See also Midsummer Day; Winter Solstice.

Sunday School Day
First Sunday in May

In the Polynesian kingdom of Tonga, a group of islands whose inhabitants are primarily Methodist, the first Sunday in May is known as **Faka Me** or Sunday School Day. The children rise early and bathe in the sea, after which they put on the new clothes that their mothers have made: *valas* or kilts for the boys and new dresses for the girls. Then they all go to church, where the youngest children sing a hymn or recite a verse of scripture in front of the congregation and the older children present Biblical dramas. At the feast that always follows a church service, the children sit on mats spread on the ground. A variety of Polynesian specialties-including roast pig, lobster, chicken and fish steamed in coconut milk, and potato-like vegetables called *ufi*-are served to the children by the adults on long trays made of woven coconut fronds known as *volas*. The parents stand behind their children and fan them to keep them cool as they eat.

Sunday School Day is observed in various ways by Protestant children in other countries as well.

See also WHITE SUNDAY.

Sun Fun Festival
First week in June

A beach festival at Myrtle Beach, S.C., to celebrate the state's Grand Strand, a sixty-mile stretch of white-sand ocean beach. Myrtle Beach is the central city on the strand and so the fitting place for this five-day celebration that includes fireworks, beauty pageants, beach games, music and dance performances, and a sandcastle-building contest. The record for the world's longest sand castle was set here in 1990—the castle measured ten and a half miles long. As many as 200,000 attend.

Sun Pageant Day
January–March

It is not uncommon for towns in the northern part of Norway to observe **Solday** or **Sun Day** when the sun reappears at the end of January or in early February. In Narvik, for example, Sun Pageant Day is celebrated on February 8.

The sun's reappearance is particularly welcome for the people of Rjukan, which is nestled so deeply in a narrow valley that the sun doesn't shine there from October 5 to March 12.

Although the date of the Sun Pageant in Rjukan varies from year to year, it always entails weeks of preparation. The town square is decorated with tall ice columns topped by flaming torches. At one end there is a throne on a raised wooden platform for the "Prince of the Sun," who leads a procession of costumed figures into the square and offi-

cially begins the celebration. The eating, singing, folk dancing, and fireworks continue for most of the day and night.

Sun Yat-sen, Birthday of
November 12

Sun Yat-sen (1866–1925) was the leader of the Chinese Nationalist Party (Kuomintang). He served as the first provisional president of the Republic of (1911–1912) and later as its de facto ruler (1923–1925). Because he possessed an exceptionally broad knowledge of the West and developed a grand plan for China's industrialization, he is known as "the father of modern China."

Sun Yat-sen's birthday is a holiday in Taiwan. The anniversary of his death, March 12, is observed as Arbor Day in Taiwan.

Super Bowl Sunday
Often last Sunday in January

The day of the championship game of the National Football League, which marks the culmination of the American professional football season. The game is played at a preselected site, always either a warm-weather city or one with a covered stadium. The contestants are the winners from each of the league's two divisions, the American Football Conference and the National Football Conference.

The first game was played on Jan. 15, 1967, in the Los Angeles Coliseum; the Green Bay Packers beat the Kansas City Chiefs by a score of 35-10. Since then, the games have been identified by Roman numerals (e.g., Super Bowl XXVII in 1993), and, in keeping with this pretension, are surrounded by hoopla reminiscent of Roman imperial excess. Fans vie for Super Bowl tickets, and corporations woo clients with lavish Super Bowl trips. Nationwide, the day is celebrated with at-home parties to watch the game on televison, and many, many people watch: in 1993, an estimated 133.4 million viewers in the U.S. tuned to the Super Bowl—that's 45.1 percent of all U.S. households owning television sets. Millions more watch the game in other countries. At sports bars, fans gather to watch wall-sized television screens, drink beer, and cheer.

Susan B. Anthony Day
February 15; August 26

Susan Brownell Anthony (1820–1906) devoted her life to the temperance, anti-slavery, and women's suffrage movements. After the Civil War ended in 1865, she focused all of her energies on getting women the right to vote. That goal was achieved in 1920 with the passage of the Nineteenth Amendment to the Constitution of the United States, sometimes called "the Anthony Amendment." She was elected to the Hall of Fame for Great Americans in 1950, and was honored in 1979 when she became the first American woman to have her likeness on a coin: the Susan B. Anthony dollar.

Tributes to Anthony take place on her birthday, February 15, in various parts of the country. Sometimes a memorial service is held in the crypt of the Capitol in Washington, D.C., where there is a statue of the pioneers in the women's suffrage movement: Anthony, Elizabeth Cady Stanton, and Lucretia Mott. Ceremonies honoring Anthony are often held at her grave in Rochester, New York, near the home where for more than forty years she lived and frequently met with other influential reformers. Women's organizations, such as the National Organization for Women (NOW), usually play a major role in sponsoring memorial observances.

Some states observe Susan B. Anthony Day on August 26, the day on which the Nineteenth Amendment was ratified.

Svenskarnas Dag
Fourth Sunday in June

One of the largest festivals in the United States celebrating the traditions of a specific ethnic group, Svenskarnas Dag honors the Swedish heritage of the people of Minneapolis, Minnesota, and the longest day of the year. When the festival first started in 1934 it was observed in August, but in 1941 the day was changed to the fourth Sunday in June so that it would coincide with midsummer observances in Sweden (see MIDSUMMER DAY).

Held in Minnehaha Park in Minneapolis, the festival includes a band concert, Swedish folk dancing, choral group performances, and the crowning of a Midsummer Queen. A national celebrity of Swedish descent is often asked to officiate at this one-day event, which attracts more than 100,000 visitors each year.

Swallows of San Juan Capistrano (Fiesta de las Golondrinas)
October 23

San Juan Capistrano was the name of a mission built on the Pacific Coast by Father Junipero Serra in 1777. Even after the buildings collapsed in an earthquake thirty-five years later, thousands of swallows continued to nest in the ruins of the church. Local people noticed that the swallows tended to fly south on October 23, the death anniversary of St. John of Capistrano, and returned on March 19, St. JOSEPH'S DAY.

Beginning in 1940, the sentimental love song "When the Swallows Come Back to Capistrano" (words and music by Leon René) was recorded by a variety of artists. This brought attention to the event and media attention further made it known. A Swallow Festival is held each year around the time of the birds' return. Also known as the Fiesta de las Golondrinas it features the largest non-automotive parade in the country.

Swan-Upping
Monday-Thursday of the third full week in July

The tradition of marking newborn swans goes back six centuries, to a time when most of the swans on England's public waters were owned by the queen. Later the members of two livery companies (trade guilds), the Company of Dyers and the Company of Vintners, were given the right to keep swans on the Thames River between London and Henley. Every year since 1363, the Queen's swan master and the swan wardens of the two livery companies row up the Thames, starting at Blackfriars in the center of London and continuing forty miles west to Henley-on-Thames, and "up" all the swan families into the boats, where they pinion their wings so they can't fly away. Then they cut marks on the beaks of the cygnets-one nick for the Dyers, two for the Vintners, and none at all to indicate that they are owned by the Crown. There are very specific rules governing how ownership is decided, and the six boats, each flying a large silk flag as they row up the river, form a procession that has changed little over the centuries.

Swedish Homage Festival
Held during October in odd-numbered years

Svensk Hyllningsfest, or the Swedish Homage Festival, is a biennial event held for three days during the second week in October in Lindsborg, Kansas. It honors the Swedish pioneers who first settled the area and celebrates the heritage of Lindsborg's Swedish-American population. More than 50,000 people attend the festival, which started in 1941 and is now held only in odd-numbered years.

Events include Swedish folk dancing, singing, and band music; Swedish arts and crafts displays; and a huge *smörgasbord*, or hot and cold buffet, at Bethany College. Other highlights include an American-Swedish parade and the crowning of the Hyllningsfest Queen, who is traditionally a senior citizen of Swedish descent.

Sweetest Day
Third Saturday in October

More than forty years ago, a man from Cleveland came up with the idea of showing the city's orphans and shut-ins that they hadn't been forgotten by distributing small gifts to them on a Saturday in October. Over the years, other Clevelanders took up the idea of spreading cheer not only to the underprivileged but to everyone. The celebration of what came to be called Sweetest Day soon spread to Detroit and other American cities.

This holiday is unusual in that it is not based on any one group's religious beliefs or on a family relationship. Because it falls mid-way between FATHER'S DAY and CHRISTMAS, however, it has come to be regarded as a merchandising opportunity. Although it is still supposed to be an occasion to remember others with a kind act, a word of encouragement, or a long-overdue letter, local merchants in cities where Sweetest Day is observed usually get together and promote the day as a time to purchase gifts.

Sweetwater Rattlesnake Roundup
Second weekend in March

The World's Largest Rattlesnake Roundup, and one of several rattlesnake roundups in Texas. It was started in 1958 by ranchers in Sweetwater to thin out the snakes plaguing them and their livestock, and now the average annual catch is 12,000 pounds of Western Diamondback Rattlesnake. Some 30,000 spectators watch the goings-on.

The roundup is sponsored by the Sweetwater Jaycees, who stress the focus on safety (hunters are governed by state hunting laws) and the benefits of the roundup. The venom milked from the snakes is used in medical research and as an antidote for bite victims, and the skins are used for such items as belts and boots. The roundup supports various Jaycee charitable causes.

The weekend events include snake handling demonstations, snake milking (to extract the venom), and the awarding of prizes for the most pounds and the biggest snake. (The record for the Sweetwater Roundup is seventy-four inches, while the longest on record anywhere is eighty-four inches.) There are also a Miss Snake Charmer Queen Contest, a parade, rattlesnake dances with country bands, and a rattlesnake meat-eating con-

test. A cook shack fries and serves more than 4,000 pounds of rattlesnake meat each year.

Other Texas rattlesnake roundups are held from February through April in Cleburne, Breckenridge, Brownwood, Big Spring, San Angelo, Jacksboro, Gainesville, and Freer. A number of other southern states also have rattlesnake roundups.

Swing Day *See* Tano Festival

Swiss National Day
August 1

A nationwide celebration of the Swiss Confederation, observed with torchlight processions, fireworks, shooting contests, and folkloric events. The day commemorates the occasion in 1291 when representatives of the three original cantons of Schwyz, Uri, and Unterwalden met on the Rutli meadow and swore an oath of alliance and mutual defense to lay the foundations of the Confederation.

In 1991, year-long 700th anniversary festivities set different themes for the different language areas. A celebration of the Federal Pact of 1291 was the theme for the German-speaking region; a Four Cultures Festival, demonstrating cultural diversity, for the French-speaking region; and a Festival of Solidarity, illustrating Switzerland's role in the international community, in the Romansh- and Italian-speaking areas.

Syttende Mai Fest
May 17

Norwegian Constitution Day (see CONSTITUTION DAY IN NORWAY) is celebrated each year by the descendants of the Norwegian immigrants who first settled in Spring Grove, Minnesota. The town, incorporated in 1889, was the first Norse settlement in Minnesota, and the Norwegian language can still be heard in the town's streets and cafes. The Syttende Mai Fest offers ethnic foods, folk music and costumes, a show of traditional Norwegian arts and crafts, and a grand parade led by the "King of Trolls." Young children dressed as *Nisse* roam the streets during the festival, wearing green caps and playing tricks on people. Unlike the trolls, who thrive on darkness and are known for making things go wrong, the Nisse bring luck and help out with household tasks. During the festival, the store windows often feature displays with trolls or Nisse peeking out.

Syttende Mai is celebrated by Norwegian communities in other states as well. The celebration in

Stoughton, Wisconsin takes place on the weekend nearest May 17 and features folk dancing, a Norwegian smorgasbord, and demonstrations of rosemaling (painted or carved floral designs) and hardanger (a form of pulled thread embroidery).

Szüret
Late October

Since wine is the national drink of the Hungarian people, the Szüret or **Grape Gathering** is a time for great celebration. In fact, many peasant marriages take place after this yearly festival. As they have done since ancient times, the grape gatherers make an enormous "bouquet" out of grapes and two men carry it on a pole in procession to the vineyard owner's home, accompanied by gypsy musicians, clowns, and young girls dressed in white wearing flower wreaths on their heads. When they reach their destination, they hang the cluster of grapes from the ceiling and accept the vineyard owner's invitation to join in the feasting and dancing.

A traditional game known as robber is often played during the festival, either as the grapes are being gathered or during the dancing that takes place later. While several men guard the bouquet of grapes, the others try to steal the fruit off the vines. Anyone who gets caught is dragged before a mock judge and forced to pay a penalty—usually by performing a song, a solo dance, or a pantomime while his companions make fun of him.

T

Ta'anit Esther (Fast of Esther)
Between February 13 and March 13; 13 Adar

The **Fast of Esther** commemorates the three days that Queen Esther fasted before petitioning her husband, King Ahasuerus (Xerxes I) of Persia, to spare the Jews of her country from destruction by Haman, the Persian prime minister, in the sixth century B.C. (See PURIM).

Ordinarily observed on the thirteenth day of the month of Adar, Ta'anit Esther is observed on the preceding Thursday (Adar 11) when Adar 13 falls on the Sabbath.

This date was originally a minor festival commemorating Judah Maccabee's defeat of the Syrian general Nicanor, known as the "Day of Nicanor." In time it gave way to the present Fast of Esther.

Tabernacles, Feast of *See* **Sukkot**

Tabuleiros Festival (Festa dos Tabuleiros)
Four days in mid-July every third year

The town of Tomar in Portugal has been celebrating the Tabuleiros (headdresses) Festival for six hundred years as a way of expressing gratitude for the harvest and charity for the poor. The highlight of the festival is the the procession through town of 600 girls in traditional headdresses selected from Tomar and the surrounding communities.

The foundation of the headdress, which weighs about thirty-three pounds and must be at least as tall as the girl who carries it, is a round basket covered with a linen cloth. An elaborate framework of bamboo sticks and wires holds up thirty small loaves of bread arranged in five rows. Flowers made of colored paper disguise the wires and the entire structure is topped with a white dove or Maltese cross. The priest blesses the bread, and the girls keep their *tabuleiros* for the entire year to ward off sickness. This is also a time for making donations to the poor and the afflicted.

Tako-Age (Kite Flying)
April, May, June

Kite-flying battles are a favorite sport in Japan, and numerous kite festivals take place in the spring. In the battles, the object is to cut down other kites by means of skillful maneuvering; broken glass embedded in the kite lines also helps.

The kite festivals of Nagasaki are held on April 29 and May 3, with teams of as many as twenty people controlling colossal kites up to twenty-five by thirty feet.

In Hamamatsu in Shizuoka Prefecture, a kite festival is held on the beach on May 3–5. It is thought to have originated in the mid-sixteenth century when the lord of one of the fiefdoms celebrated the birth of a son by flying a giant kite. It is the biggest event now in the western region of the prefecture, with more than a thousand kites sparring in the sky. Other festival events include parades of fifty floats in the evenings.

In Shirone in Niigata Prefecture, two teams on opposite banks of the Nakanokuchi River wage kite battles on June 5–12. This festival supposedly dates back some 300 years when the people of one village accidentally crashed a huge kite onto a neighboring village.

Tam Kung Festival
Eighth day of the fourth moon (May)

A celebration of the birthday of the god Tam Kung, held at the Tam Kung Temple in Shau Kei Wan on Hong Kong Island. Like Tin Hau, Tam Kung is a popular deity among fisherfolk. He is a Taoist child-god, whose powers were apparent when he was only twelve years old. His greatest gift was controlling the weather, but he could also heal the sick and predict the future. Residents of the Shau Kei Wan area believe he saved many lives during an outbreak of cholera in 1967. His birthday is marked with a grand procession, Cantonese opera, and lion and dragon dances.

Tammuz, Fast of the 17th of (Shivah Asar be-Tammuz)
Between June 17 and July 24; 17 Tammuz

The **Fast of Tammuz** commemorates the breaching of the walls of Jerusalem in 586 B.C., when the Babylonians conquered Judah, destroyed the Temple, and carried most of the Jewish population off into slavery. But this destruction had a happy ending: after seventy years the people returned and re-built the Temple. Then the Roman army breached the walls of Jerusalem in the year 70 A.D., dooming both the city and its Temple for the second time. This time the destruction and the scattering of the people—known as the Diaspora—had a far more tragic finality. The Jews remain scattered over the face of the earth to this day. Other sad events associated with this day are the shattering of the first Tablets of the Law by Moses, and the collapse of the sacrificial system caused by the Roman invasion in 70 A.D.

The Fast of Tammuz begins three weeks of mourning lasting until TISHA BE-AV.

See also ASARAH BE-TEVET.

Tanabata (Star Festival)
July 7, August 6–8

A Japanese festival based on a Chinese legend of parted lovers who are identified with two of the brightest stars in the night sky. In the legend, Vega, representing a weaver-princess, is permitted by the king to marry the simple cowherd, Altair. But after they marry, the princess neglects her weaving, and the herdsman forgets his cows, so the king separates them, making them live on opposite sides of the River of Heaven, as the Milky Way is known in Japan. On the seventh day of the seventh month, the lovers are able to meet when a flock of magpies makes a bridge across the river. If it's rainy, the lovers have to wait another year.

The festival is observed throughout Japan, with people hanging colorful strips of paper on bamboo branches outside their homes. It is an especially colorful occasion in Sendai (Miyagi Prefecture), where it occurs a month later, on Aug. 6–8. The whole city is decked out with paper streamers and works of origami, the Japanese art of paper folding.

Tano Festival (Dano-nal; Swing Day)
May–June; fifth day of the fifth lunar month

An ancient spring agricultural festival in Korea that started as a planting ritual and a time to pray for a good harvest. It falls in the farming season between the planting of rice seedlings and their transplanting to the paddy fields. With the lunar SOL or New Year's Day and MID-AUTUMN FESTIVAL, it is one of the country's three great festivals on the lunar calendar, and a national holiday. Festivities in the countryside include swinging contests for girls: swings are suspended from tall poles or bridges, and the girls, sometimes in pairs, try to ring a bell with their feet as they swing. Boys and men sometimes compete in this, but usually they take part in *ssirum*, native Korean wrestling, a sport that can be dated to 400 A.D. Today *ssirum* matches are nationally televised.

In the usually sleepy east coast town of Kangnung, the festival goes on for a week, from the third through the eighth day of the month. Activities include a mask dance-drama of ancient tradition and shaman *kut*, ritualistic ceremonies combining theatrics with music and dance.

The ceremonies are performed by a shaman, or *mudang*, a priestess who is able to appease spirits to prevent natural disasters. The *mudang* is also a talented performer with supernatural powers when in a trance. Shamanism, a long-lived indigenous Korean faith of uncertain origin, involves the worship of spirits and demons who reside in natural objects—rocks, mountains, trees, and so on. Shamanists also believe the dead have souls, and that the *mudangs* can mediate between those still living and departed souls.

Korea is nominally more than 70 percent Buddhist and more than 15 percent Christian, but it actively remains about 90 percent shamanist.

Tater Day
Weekend and first Monday in April

Considered the oldest trade day in the U.S., and now a celebration of the sweet potato in Benton, Ky. The event started in 1843 when sweet potatoes were a staple crop of the area. Today the "tater" is honored with a parade, flea market, quilt show, road races, rodeo, gospel music, arts and crafts exhibits, a gun, coin, and knife show, horse and mule pulls, and a Miss Tater Day contest. Most of the food served is some kind of sweet potato concoction.

Ta'u Fo'ou
January 1

New Year's Day in Tonga, a Polynesian island kingdom in the South Pacific, is reminiscent of

CHRISTMAS EVE celebrations in the United States and Western Europe, when carolers go from house to house singing Christmas songs. But because the new year arrives in the middle of the southern hemisphere's summer, when schoolchildren are on holiday and the weather is warm, the caroling custom has a cultural twist. Boys and girls go from house to house singing hymns, rounds, and other songs that they have created specifically for the occasion. Instead of offering them hot chocolate or coffee, their friends and neighbors show their appreciation by offering fruit or cool drinks. Sometimes the children will be given a piece of *tapa*, Polyesian bark cloth.

Tazaungdaing

October–November; Tazaungmone full moon

The Tazaungdaing festival was observed in Burma (now called Myanmar) even before the spread of Buddhism. It was held in honor of the God of Lights, and it marked the awakening of the Hindu god Vishnu from his long sleep. Burmese Buddhists later attached their own religious significance to the festival, saying that this was the night that Siddhartha's mother, sensing that her son was about to discard the royal robes of his birth and put on the robes of the monkhood, spent the entire night weaving the traditional yellow robes for him. To commemorate her achievement, a weaving contest is held at the Shwe Dagon Pagoda in Rangoon. Another festival activity is the offering of *Kathin* robes to the Buddhist monks to replace the soiled robes they have worn throughout the rainy season. This offering ceremony begins on the first waning day of THADINGYUT and continues until the full moon night of Tazaungmone.

In Myanmar, the Tazaungdaing festival is celebrated by sending up fire balloons and lighting multi-colored lanterns, especially at the Sulamani Pagoda in Tavatimsa. Sometimes called the **Tawadeintha Festival**, this day commemorates the return of Gautama Buddha from his visit to heavenly Tawadeintha to visit his mother's reincarnated spirit. Holy men with lit candles illuminated his path back to earth.

Teacher's Day *See* Confucius's Birthday

Teej (Tij; Green Teej)

July–August; Third day of waxing Sravana

A welcome to the monsoon, the season when the wind from the Indian Ocean brings heavy rainfall. It is celebrated especially in the dry, desert-like state of Rajasthan in northwestern India. Because the monsoon augurs good crops and fertility, this is also a celebration for women and is dedicated to the Hindu goddess Parvati, consort of Lord Shiva, and patron goddess of women. On this day, she is supposed to have left the home of her father to go to Shiva.

On this day the women paint delicate designs on their hands and feet with henna. Specially decorated swings are hung from trees in every village, and women swing on them and sing songs in praise of Parvati. Married women go to their parents' home and receive gifts of clothes and jewelry. There are also local fairs and processions carrying the image of the goddess.

On this day in Katmandu, Nepal, Hindu women visit Pashupatinath Temple to worship Shiva and Parvati. Ritual bathing in the sacred Bagmati River is supposed to wash away the sins of the past year.

In Bundi and Jaipur, capital of Rajasthan, the day is called **Gangaur**. Women dressed in their finest go out to the main temple with flowers and brass vessels filled with water to worship the goddess, Gauri (another name for Parvati) and sing her praise. On the final day, a palanquin carrying an image of Parvati is carried through the streets in a procession of decorated elephants, camels, horses, chariots, dancers, and musicians.

Tellabration

Friday before Thanskgiving

A nationwide night of storytelling, started in 1988 by storyteller J. G. ("Paw-Paw") Pinkerton. The event began in 1988 with storytelling going on at six communities in Connecticut. The next year, Texas and Missouri also had Telleberations, and by 1991, storytelling on this night of storytelling was going on in seventy-two communities in twenty-seven states, and in locations in Bermuda and Canada. Proceeds of the event go toward developing the archives of the National Association for the Preservation and Perpetuation of Storytelling in Jonesborough, Tenn.

Pinkerton originated the event as a way to encourage storytelling for adults, feeling that storytelling keeps culture alive. He grew up in a small Texas town listening to family stories—especially those told by his grandfather who had herded cattle in the early days of Texas. Pinkerton became a mining executive and, after retiring in 1988, devoted his time to promoting storytelling from his Connecticut home.

See also NATIONAL STORYTELLING FESTIVAL.

Telluride Film Festival
Labor Day weekend

A three-day celebration of the silver screen in Telluride, Colo., featuring free outdoor showings in Elks Park with the audience bundled in blankets and sleeping bags. The festival attracts celebrity film makers, actors, and film scholars from all over the globe for national and international premieres and viewings of experimental filmmaking, retrospectives, and tributes.

Telluride Hang Gliding Festival
Second week in September

The largest hang gliding event in the country, held in Telluride, Colo., the small mountain resort that began life as a mining town and is known today as the "festival capital of the Rockies." Top hang gliders from throughout the world come here to soar and spin above Town Park. On the last day of the six-day event, in the competition for the world acrobatic championship, fliers skid, loop, somersault, and pirouette from the heights of the ski mountain, trailing colored smoke from their wingtips.

Telluride Jazz Festival
Mid-August

Three days of jazz in Telluride, Colo. Top artists produce jazz of all schools—traditional, Chicago, blues, big band, and Latin. On Fridays, the music happens at the historic Sherman Opera House and at various pubs, and on Saturdays and Sundays, the concerts are open-air in the Town Park. The festival began in 1977.

Telluride also boasts a three-day Bluegrass and Country Music Festival in late June, and a Chamber Music Festival held for two weekends in August. A special feature of that festival is the gourmet dessert concert, when fancy treats are served with the music, and the concert closes with a classical jam session.

Tennessee Walking Horse National Celebration
Ten days preceding the Saturday before Labor Day

Ten days and nights of pageantry and competition for about 2,100 Tennessee Walking Horses in Shelbyville, Tenn., the "Walking Horse Capitol of the World." The horses compete for more than $600,000 in prizes and the title of World Grand Champion, awarded on the final night of the show. The celebration is the nation's largest horse show in terms of spectators (close to 250,000 fans come to this town of 13,000) and the second largest in numbers of entered horses.

The blood lines of the Tennessee Walking Horse are traced back to the Thoroughbred, the Standardbred, the Morgan, and the American Saddle Horse. It was bred pure in the early days of Tennessee for the three-fold purpose of riding, driving, and general farm work. Today, it's a pleasure mount and a show horse with distinctive high-stepping gaits.

The three natural gaits of the Tennessee Walker are the flat-foot walk, the running walk, and the canter. The flat-foot walk, the slowest is a diagonally-opposed movement of the feet. The running walk starts like the flat-foot walk and, as speed increases, the hind foot overstrides the front track. It is the only gait of a horse where the fore foot strikes the ground a mere instant before the hind foot. The canter is a rhythmic motion known as the "rocking-chair" movement.

The Shelbyville celebration began in 1939, started by horse owner Henry Davis of Wartrace, Tenn. who thought his county should celebrate its most important asset. The celebration has been held ever since without interruption. From 1939 through 1991, forty-eight horses have been crowned World Grand Champion, some winning more than once. The 1991 champion was Flashy Pride, a thirteen-year-old sorrel stallion owned by Art and Frances Barnes of Shalimar, Fla., and Lewisburg, Tenn., and ridden by trainer Vicki Self of Lewisburg.

Besides the horse shows, the celebration features an equestrian trade fair, horse sales, an arts-and-crafts festival, and America's largest barn decoration competition. The barns and stalls are elegantly decorated with brass lanterns, chandeliers, fine art, rugs, and expensive furnishings.

Tenth of Tevet *See* **Asarah be-Tevet**

Terlingua Chili Cookoff
First full weekend in November

A contest of chili chefs held in Terlingua, Tex., an abandoned mining town near the Big Bend desert area in the southwestern part of the state. More than 200 cooks from as many as thirty states and occasionally from foreign countries show up to prepare the official state dish, and thousands of spectators drive or fly in. Humorists Wick Fowler and H. Allen Smith staged the first cookoff in 1967, deciding to locate it in the hot desert because it was a contest for a hot dish. It has become such an institution that the number of entrants has to be kept down by earning points at preliminary cookoffs, especially the CHILYMPIAD held in September in San Marcos and the State Ladies Chili Cookoff, held in early October in Luckenbach.

Terminalia
February 23

In ancient Rome, February 23 marked the end of the year and was therefore an appropriate time to honor Terminus, the god of boundaries and landmarks. The terminus or boundary stone marking the outer limits of Rome stood between the fifth and sixth milestones on the road to Laurentum. During the observance of the Terminalia, property owners would gather there—or at the boundary stones that marked their private lands—to place garlands around the stone and offer sacrifices. Afterward there would be singing and socializing among family members and servants.

Ceremonies that involve marking boundaries are common in England and Scotland as well. See COMMON RIDINGS DAY and BOUNDS THURSDAY.

Tet
First to seventh day of first lunar month (usually late January or early February)

The Vietnamese New Year, an abbreviation for **Tet Nguyen Dan**, 'first day.' This is the most important festival of the year, signifying both the beginning of the year and of spring. It's also seen as a precursor of everything that will happen in the coming year, and for that reason, efforts are made to start the year properly with family reunions, paying homage to ancestors, and wiping out debts. At the start of the festival, the Spirit of the Hearth goes to the abode of the Emperor of Jade to report on family members. The spirit should be in a good frame of mind, so a tree is built of bamboo and red paper to ward off evil spirits. At midnight the New Year and the return of the Spirit of the Hearth are welcomed with firecrackers, gongs, and drums. The festival then continues for a week, with special events on each day. A favorite food of the festival is *banh chung*, which is made of sticky rice, yellow beans, pig fat, and spices wrapped in leaves and boiled for half a day.

Tet became known worldwide in 1968 for the Tet Offensive of the Vietnam War. The lunar New Year truce was shattered on Jan. 31 with attacks by North Vietnam and the National Liberation Front against more than 100 South Vietnamese cities. The United States embassy in Saigon was attacked and parts of it held by the Viet Cong for six hours; the headquarters of U.S. Gen. William Westmoreland at Tan Son Nhut Airport outside Saigon was also attacked. The city of Hue was captured. The attacks were repulsed, and the U.S. and South Vietnam claimed victory. But television viewers had seen the ferocity of the attack and the flight of Saigon residents, and the offensive led to increased movements in America to end the war.

Texas Citrus Fiesta
Last week in January

An annual festival held in Mission, Tex., to salute the Texas citrus industry and especially the Texas Ruby Red Grapefruit. Mission, in the Rio Grande Valley, was founded by the Catholic Missionary Society of the Oblate Fathers, who built a mission here in 1824. They also are credited with being the first to plant citrus fruit in the region, which is now famous for the Ruby Red grapefruit.

Among the events of the fiesta are a style show featuring garments made of Rio Grande Valley agricultural products: dried orange peel, seeds, and onion skins are used in creating costumes that range from ballgowns to bikinis. Other events: parades, the coronation of a Citrus Queen, Mexican folklorico dance performances, and a Texas armadillo race.

Texas Independence Day
March 2

A legal holiday in Texas, March 2 commemorates both the convention at Washington-on-the-Brazos held on this day in 1836, when delegates prepared for the separation of Texas from Mexico, and the birthday of Sam Houston (1793–1863), who led the Texans to victory over the Mexicans in the battle of San Jacinto. The convention formed an interim government, drew up a constitution, and made Sam Houston commander-in-chief of the Texan military forces. But their work was interrupted by the invading Mexican army. It wasn't until the following month that the Republic of Texas forced the issue of independence at the battle of San Jacinto (see SAN JACINTO DAY). Texas is the only state to celebrate independence from a country other than England.

March 2 is also known as **Sam Houston Day** and **Texas Flag Day**, although these are "special observance days" rather than legal holidays. This period in Texas history-beginning with the Washington-on-the-Brazos convention and ending with

Sam Houston's decisive victory at San Jacinto, is celebrated each year during "Texas Week."

Texas Rose Festival
October

An annual tribute to roses in Tyler, Tex., center of the region that produces more than a third of the field-grown roses in the United States. Tyler's Municipal Rose Garden, one of the largest rose gardens in the country, covers twenty-two acres and has some 38,000 rose bushes, representing 500 varieties. They blossom among pines, fountains, gazebos, and archways, peaking in May but continuing through October. The five-day festival features the coronation of a Rose Queen, a rose show, a parade of floats decorated with roses, and tours of the rose gardens. There are also arts and crafts shows, a square-dance festival, and a symphony concert.

Thadingyut
September–October; full moon of Thadingyut

The period that begins with the full moon day of the eleventh month and continues until the full moon day of the twelfth month marks the end of the Buddhist Lent and the beginning of the *Kathin* or pilgrimage season. Also known as **Robe Offering Month**, this is a time when Buddhists make pilgrimages to various temples, bringing food and gifts—particularly new robes—to the monks. In Myanmar, Thadingyut is the day on which the Buddha completed his preaching of the *Abhidhamma* 'philosophy' and it is sometimes referred to as **Abhidhamma Day**. In Laos, it is called **Boun Ok Vatsa** or the **Festival of the Waters**, as it is a popular time for pirogue or canoe races. In Thailand, it is called **Tod Kathin**—the *kathin* being a wooden frame on which scraps of cloth were stretched before being sewn together to make into robes.

See also Tazaungdaing.

Thaipusam (Thai Poosam)
January–February; 3–12 days

A dramatic Hindu festival celebrated India, Malaysia, Sri Lanka, Singapore, South Africa, Mauritius, and elsewhere. The day marks the birthday and victory of the Hindu god Lord Subramaniam, also known as Lord Murugar, over the demons, and is a time of penance and consecration to the god, usually involving self-mortification in a test of mind over pain.

In Malaysia, the festival is a public holiday in the states of Perak, Penang, and Selangor. In Georgetown, Penang, a statue of Subramaniam, covered with gold, silver, diamonds, and emeralds, is taken from the Sri Mariamman temple and, with his consorts Valli and Theivanai, and placed in a silver chariot. Then begins a grand procession to his tomb in the Batu Caves, near the capital city of Kuala Lumpur, where the statue is carried up 272 steep steps, and placed beside the permanent statue kept there. The next day about 200,000 people begin to pay homage, while movies, carousels, and other entertainments are provided for their amusement.

The most intense form of penance and devotion is the carrying of *kavadee*, which the Tamil people of Mauritius practice in a unique way—much more elaborately and solemnly than in other countries.

Devotees, both male and female, abstain from all meat and sex during the sacred ten days before the festival. Each day they go to the temple (*kovil*) to make offerings, and in Port Louis, at Arulmigu Sockalingam Meenaatchee Amman Kovil, Murugar and his two consorts are decorated differently each day to depict episodes in the deity's life.

On the eve of the celebration, devotees prepare their *kavadees*, a wooden arch on a wooden platform, and decorate them with flowers, paper, and peacock feathers. They may be built in other shapes, such as a peacock or temple, but the arch is most common. The next morning, priests pour cow milk into two brass pots and tie them to the sides of each kavadee. Fruits or *jagger* (a coarse, brown sugar made from the East Indian palm tree) may also be placed on the platform. Then religious ceremonies are performed at the shrines to put the bearers in a trance. When ready, penitents have their upper bodies pierced symmetrically with *vels*, the sacred lance given to Lord Subramaniam by his mother, Parvati; some also have skewers driven through their cheeks, foreheads, or tongues.

The procession then begins, with the devotees carrying the kavadees on their shoulders. Some penitents draw a small chariot by means of chains fixed to hooks dug into their sides; some walk to the temple on sandals studded with nails. Groups of young men and women follow, singing rhythmic songs. Each region has 40 to 100 kavadees, but in places like Port Louis there may be 600 to 800. At the temple, the kavadee is dismounted, the needles and skewers removed by the priest, and the milk in the pots—which has stayed pure—is poured over the deity from head to foot. The penitents then go out and join the crowds.

Some believe carrying the kavadee washes away sins through self-inflicted suffering; others say the kavadee symbolizes the triumph of good over evil.

In Durban, South Africa, these rites last twelve days and are also performed during Chitray Massum in April–May.

Thanh-Minh
Moon 3, Day 5

Like MEMORIAL DAY in the United States, Thanh-Minh (which means 'pure and bright') in Vietnam is a day to commemorate the dead. Families brings flowers, food, incense, and other offerings to the graves of deceased relatives. Sometimes they visit the graves a few days in advance to prepare for Thanh-Minh by raking or sweeping the surrounding area and painting the tombs.

Thanksgiving
Fourth Thursday in November (USA); second Monday in October (Canada)

The Pilgrim settlers of New England were not the first to set aside a day for expressing their gratitude to God for the harvest. The Greeks and the Romans paid tribute to their agricultural goddesses, the Anglo-Saxons celebrated LAMMAS and HARVEST HOME, and the Jews have their eight-day SUKKOT or Feast of Tabernacles. The first American Thanksgiving was entirely religious, and took place on December 4, 1619, when a group of thirty-eight English settlers arrived at Berkeley Plantation on the James River. Their charter decreed that their day of arrival be celebrated yearly as a day of thanksgiving to God.

But most Americans think of the first "official" Thanksgiving as being the one that took place at Plymouth Colony in October 1621, a year after the Pilgrims first landed on the New England coast. They were joined in their three-day feast by Massasoit, the chief of the Wampanoag tribe, and about ninety of his fellow tribesmen. The Episcopal Church and many states declared Thanksgiving holidays, but it wasn't until 1863 that President Abraham Lincoln proclaimed the last Thursday in November as a day to give thanks. Each year thereafter, for seventy-five years, the President proclaimed the same day to be celebrated. In 1939, however, President Franklin D. Roosevelt moved it one week earlier to allow more time for Christmas shopping. Finally, Congress ruled that the fourth Thursday of November would be the legal federal holiday of Thanksgiving after 1941. Canadians celebrate their Thanksgiving on the second Monday in October.

Today Thanksgiving is a time for family reunions and traditions, most of which center around the preparation of an elaborate meal featuring turkey and a dozen or so accompanying dishes. Although some people go to special church services on Thanksgiving day, far more line the streets of Philadelphia and New York City, where huge toy parades are held. In many places Santa Claus arrives in town on this day, and the widespread sales that begin in department stores the next day mark the start of the CHRISTMAS shopping season.

See also PILGRIM THANKSGIVING DAY, SCHWENKENFELDER THANKSGIVING.

Thargelia
May–June

This ancient Greek festival was celebrated in Athens on the sixth and seventh of Thargelion (May–June) to honor Apollo. In addition to offerings of first fruits, or the first bread from the new wheat, it was customary to select two condemned criminals (either two men or a man and a woman) to act as scapegoats for community guilt. First they were led through the city and then driven out and banished. If circumstances warranted a greater sacrifice, they were killed—either thrown into the sea or burned on a pyre. On the second day of the festival there was an offering of thanksgiving, a procession, and the official registration ceremony for individuals who had been adopted.

Thesmophoria
October 24–26

An ancient Greek festival held in honor of Demeter Thesmophoros, the goddess of fertility and the protectress of marriage; it is unclear whether this festival was named after the goddess or vice versa. It was celebrated by women, perhaps only married women, and lasted three days, normally the twelfth through fourteenth days of the month of Pyanopsion (October). The rites performed on the first day were associated with fertility. Young pigs had earlier been ceremoniously cast into a chasm or underground chamber called the *megaron* and left to rot. The women who had observed chastity for nine preceding days prepared a sacrifice to Demeter that included the entrails from these pigs mixed with seed. This was sown into the ground to ensure the fertility of both the earth and of humanity. This sacrifice symbolized the annual decay and rebirth of nature. The women fasted on the second day, and on the third they celebrated the magic of fertility in the animal as well as the plant kingdom.

Thingyan
April 9–12; Tagu

The three-day feast of the NEW YEAR in Myanmar (formerly Burma) is also known as the **Water Festival** because of the custom of throwing or squirting water on others. The festival has been traditional for centuries; King Narathihapate (1254–1287), built enclosed corridors running from his palace to the banks of the Irrawaddy River; inside them he and his courtiers reveled in water throwing.

During the celebration, pots of clear cold water are offered to monks at monasteries to wash or sprinkle images of Buddha. Everyone else gets drenched; young men and women roam the streets dousing everybody with buckets of water or turning hoses on them. On the final day, the traditional Burmese New Year, birds and fish are set free, and young people wash the hair of their elders. The water-splashing custom originated with the idea that by this the bad luck and sins of the old year were washed away. Now splashing people is more a frolicsome thing to do and also a way of cooling off. This is the hottest time of year in Myanmar, and temperatures can sizzle above 100 degrees.

See also SONGKRAN; LUNAR NEW YEAR.

Third Prince, Birthday of the
Early May; eighth and ninth days of fourth moon

A Chinese Taoist festival to honor the Third Prince, a miracle-working child-god who rides on the wheels of wind and fire. In Singapore, Chinese mediums in trances dance, slash themselves with spiked maces and swords, and write charms on yellow paper with blood from their tongues. There is also a street procession of stilt-walkers, dragon dancers, and Chinese musicians.

Thomas Edison's Birthday
February 11

Although Thomas Alva Edison (1847–1931) is best known as the inventor of the incandescent electric light, his real achievement was to produce the first incandescent lamp of any practical value- one that could be produced inexpensively and distributed widely. In 1882 Edison lost a patent infringement case to Joseph Wilson Swan, who was developing an incandescent light at the same time in England. As a compromise the two men combined their resources and formed the Edison and Swan Electric Lamp Company.

Edison's genius is credited with a number of other important inventions, among them the carbon transmitter (which brought Alexander Graham Bell's newly invented telephone into general use and led to the development of the microphone), the dictating machine, a method for transmitting telegraphic signals from ship to ship (or ship to shore), the Kinetoscope (which made the motion picture a reality), and the phonograph. He is often quoted as saying, "Genius is one percent inspiration and ninety-nine percent perspiration."

Edison's birthday on February 11 is commemorated across the nation either as **Edison Day** or as **Edison Science and Engineering Youth Day**. The latter, sponsored by the Thomas Alva Edison Foundation in Southfield, Michigan, is an extensive program of cooperation between industry and education carried out not only in the United States but in twenty-two other nations. Most of the special programs honoring Edison and his achievements are held on or near February 11, but some last as long as a month and include essay contests, industrial and laboratory tours, scientific demonstrations, science project competitions, and other activities aimed at encouraging young people to pursue careers in technical, engineering, and scientific fields.

Each year the **International Edison Birthday Celebration** is held on February 10, 11, and 12 in one of the world's major cities. (See also EDISON PAGEANT OF LIGHT.)

Thomas Jefferson's Birthday
April 13

Unique among American presidents, Thomas Jefferson (1743–1826) was not only a statesman but a scholar, linguist, writer, philosopher, political theorist, architect, engineer, and farmer. In Europe, he was praised as the foremost American thinker of his time. In the United States, he is remembered primarily as the author in 1776 of the Declaration of Independence. After retiring from government service, Jefferson founded the University of Virginia, which opened in 1825. He died on July 4, 1826, the fiftieth anniversary of the signing of the Declaration of Independence.

Jefferson's birthday is a legal holiday in Alabama, Missouri, Nebraska, Oklahoma, and his native Virginia. As one of the founders of the Democratic party, along with Andrew Jackson, he has been honored since 1936 by the Democratic National Committee, which sponsors official dinners in various locations across the country known as "Jefferson-Jackson Day Dinners." Sometimes these dinners are held on January 8, the anniversary of the BATTLE OF NEW ORLEANS.

At the University of Virginia at Charlottesville, April 13 was observed for many years as **Founder's Day**, but in 1975 the date was shifted to early fall. There is a formal academic procession, after which an address is given by a nationally known figure. This is also the day on which the Thomas Jefferson Award is give to a leading member of the university community.

Thomas Wolfe Festival
October 3
A celebration of writer Thomas Wolfe's birthday in 1900 in Asheville, N.C.. The celebrations usually extend several days beyond the actual birthday and include dramatizations of Wolfe's works, the performance of musical compositions based on his writings, workshops conducted by Wolfe scholars, and a walking tour of "Wolfe's Asheville." This includes a visit to Riverside Cemetery, where Wolfe, members of his family, as well as some of the people he fictionalized in his novels are buried.

The center of the celebration is the Thomas Wolfe Memorial State Historic Site, the boarding house run by his mother, where Thomas Wolfe grew up. It still has the sign of his mother's time hanging over the porch, "Old Kentucky Home." In his famous first novel, *Look Homeward, Angel*, published in 1929, Wolfe fictionalized Asheville as Altamont and called the boarding house "Dixieland."

Other works by Wolfe include *Of Time and the River*, published in 1935, and *The Web and the Rock* and *You Can't Go Home Again*, both published after his death in 1938.

Three Choirs Festival
August
One of Europe's oldest continuing music festivals, the Three Choirs Festival alternates among the three English cathedral cities of Gloucester, Worcester, and Hereford. The festival opens with a performance by a choir of three hundred voices, accompanied by a symphony orchestra, at the host cathedral. Concerts during the rest of the week-long event take place either in the cathedral or in local theaters and historic homes.

Records show that the festival was founded before 1719, and that it was held, as it is now, in succession at the three cathedrals. In the early days of the festival, it was customary for two or more wealthy patrons—called stewards—to underwrite the cost of the event. Today, subscribers to the festivals are still referred to as stewards, and money collected at the doors of the cathedral following a performance still benefits the Charity for the Relief of Widows and Orphans of Clergy, which has been affiliated with the festival since 1724.

Three Kings' Day *See* **Epiphany; Dia de los Tres Reyes**

Three Kings Day (Epiphany) in Indian Pueblos
January 6
A day for the installation of new officers and governors at most of the nineteen Indian Pueblos in New Mexico. The inaugural day begins with a church ceremony during which four walking canes, the symbols of authority, are passed on to the new governor. The governor is honored with a dance, which starts in mid-morning and is usually some form of an animal dance—often the Eagle, Elk, Buffalo, and Deer dances. Spirited and animated, they are considered a form of prayer. Each dance is very different from the others, and the same dance differs from pueblo to pueblo, although certain aspects are similar. In the Deer Dance, for example, dancers "walk" holding two sticks that represent their forelegs. They wear elaborate costumes and antler headdresses.

New Mexico's nineteen pueblos are: Acoma, Cochiti, Isleta, Jemez, Laguna, Nambe, Picuris, Pojoaque, Sandia, San Felipe, San Ildefonso, San Juan, Santa Ana, Santa Clara, Santo Domingo, Taos, Tesuque, Zia, and Zuni. Each of them celebrates its saint's feast day as well as other occasions with dances and ceremonies that are an expression of thanksgiving, prayer, renewal, and harmony with nature. Many dances tell stories, legends, or history. Besides the feast days and Three Kings Day (EPIPHANY), most pueblos observe these other major holidays: NEW YEAR'S DAY, EASTER, and CHRISTMAS, which is often celebrated for two to five days.

Three Shrines Festival *See* **Sanja Matsuri**

Three Weeks
Begins between June 17 and July 24, ends between July 17 and August 14; 17th Tammuz until the 9th Av
The seventeenth of Tammuz, also known as Shivah Asar be-Tammuz, marks the day on which

the walls of Jerusalem were breached by the Babylonians under Nebuchadnezzar (see also ASARAH BE-TEVET). The three-week period between this day and the Ninth of Av (see TISHA B'AV) is known in Hebrew as the period *bén ha-metsarim* in reference to Lamentations 1:3, which describes the city of Jerusalem as having been overtaken by her persecutors 'between the straits.'

Because this period is associated with the destruction of the Temple, it is a time of mourning for the Jewish people. As the days draw closer to the ninth of Av, the signs of mourning increase in severity. Although there are differences between Ashkenazi and Sephardic customs, the restrictions include not shaving or cutting one's hair, not wearing new clothes, nor eating fruit for the first time in season. Beginning with the first day of Av, the Ashkenazi custom is not to eat any meat nor drink any wine until after Tisha b'Av, while Sephardim refrain from meat and wine beginning with the Sunday preceding the Ninth of Av. On Tisha b'Av itself, it is not permitted to eat or drink, to wear leather shoes, to anoint with oil, to wash (except where required), or to engage in sexual relations. On each of the three Sabbaths during the Three Weeks, a special prophetic passage of the Old Testament known as a *haftarah* is read.

Tichborne Dole
March 25

The custom of handing out a dole or allotment of flour to the village poor in Tichbourne, England dates back to 1150. Lady Mabella Tichbourne, who was on her deathbed at the time, begged her husband to grant her enough land to provide an annual bounty of bread to the poor, who were suffering from a recent failure of the wheat crop. Her husband, in a less charitable frame of mind, snatched a blazing log from the fire and said that his wife could have as much land as she was able to crawl across before the flames died out. Although she had been bedridden for years, Lady Mabella had her servants carry her to the fields bordering the Tichbourne estate and miraculously managed to crawl across twenty-three acres. With her dying breath, she proclaimed that if her heirs should ever fail to honor the bequest, the family name would die out.

On March 25 or LADY DAY each year, villagers in need of assistance gather at the porch of Tichbourne House to claim their portion of the gift: a gallon of flour for adults, half as much for children. The fields across which Lady Mabella dragged herself are still known as "The Crawls."

Tihar
October–November; waning Karttika

A five-day Hindu festival in Nepal which honors different animals on successive days. The third day of the festival, Laksmi Puja, dedicated to the goddess of wealth, is known throughout India as Dewali.

On the first day of the festival, offerings of rice are made to crows, thought to be sent by Yama, the god of death, as his "messengers of death." The second day honors dogs, since in the afterworld dogs will guide departed souls across the river of the dead. Dogs are fed special food and adorned with flowers. Cows are honored on the morning of the third day; they, too, receive garlands and often their horns are painted gold and silver.

The third day is the most important day of the festival, when Laksmi will come to visit every home that is suitably lit for her. Consequently, as evening falls, tiny candles and butter lamps flicker in homes throughout the country.

The fourth day is a day for honoring oxen and bullocks, and it also marks the start of the new year for the Newari people of the Katmandu Valley. On the fifth day, known as Bhai Tika, brothers and sisters meet and place *tikas* (dots of red sandalwood paste, considered emblems of good luck) on each other's foreheads. The brothers give their sisters gifts, and the sisters give sweets and delicacies to their brothers and pray to Yama for their brothers' long life. This custom celebrates the legendary occasion when a girl pleaded so eloquently with Yama to spare her young brother from an early death that he relented, and the boy lived.

Tij *See* Teej

Timqat (Timkat)
January 19–20

Because the Ethiopian CHRISTMAS, called Genna, falls on January 7, EPIPHANY (Timqat) is celebrated on January 19. Timqat celebrates the baptism of Jesus in the Jordan River. It begins at sunset on EPIPHANY EVE, when the people dress in white and go to their local church. From the church they form a procession with the *tabot* or holy ark, in which the ancient Israelites put the Tablets of the Law or *Torah*, the first five books of the Old Testament. Ethiopians do not believe it was lost, but that it is now preserved in the Cathedral of Axum in Ethiopia. Each Ethiopian Orthodox church has a blessed replica of it. They accompany it to a lake, stream, or pond. It is placed in a tent, where it is guarded all night while the clergy and villagers sing, dance, and eat until the baptismal service the following morning. At dawn the clergy bless the water and sprinkle it on the heads of those who wish to renew their Christian vows. Then the procession, again bearing the tabot, returns to the church. The festivities continue until the following day, January 20 or the feast of St. Michael.

Ethiopian religious processions are characterized by the priests' richly colored ceremonial robes, fringed, embroidered umbrellas, and elaborately decorated crosses. The national sport of *guks* is often played at Timqat. Warriors with shields of hippopotamus hide, wearing lion-mane capes and headdresses ride on caparisoned horses and try to strike each other with thrown bamboo lances.

Tin Hau Festival
Twenty-third day of the third moon (May 7 in 1991)

A birthday celebration in Hong Kong for Tin Hau, Queen of Heaven and Goddess of the Sea. She is one of the most popular deities in Hong Kong; there are about twenty-four Tin Hau temples throughout the territory, and fishermen always have shrines to her on their boats. Her story dates back many centuries when, it is said, a young girl, born with mystical powers in a fishing village in Fukien Province, saved her two brothers from drowning during a storm. Today she is revered for her ability to calm the waves and to guarantee bountiful catches, and for her protection from shipwrecks and sickness.

The festivities include parades, performances of Chinese opera, and the sailing of hundreds of junks and sampans, decked out with colorful streamers, through Hong Kong's waterways to the temples. The temple in Joss House Bay is especially known for its festival, with thousands of fisherfolk arriving. The original temple was built southwest of the present temple in 1012 by two brothers who said their lives were saved by the statue of Tin Hau that they clutched when they were shipwrecked. A typhoon destroyed that temple, and descendants of the brothers built another one on the present site in 1266.

See also TAM KUNG; MATSU, BIRTHDAY OF.

Tirgul de fete de pe muntele Gaina (Maidens' Fair on Mount Gaina)
Third Sunday in July

A major folk festival held at Mount Gaina in Transylvania, Romania. It was originally a marriage fair, where young men came to choose their future wives, but is now an opportunity for people to display their talents in handicrafts, costume making, singing, and dancing. Thousands of people gather for the events of the fair, which include dance competitions and concerts by folk bands and singers. Other aspects of the festival are feasts and bonfires, and the chanting of satirical verses during certain folk dances.

Tishah be-Av
Between July 17 and August 14; 9 Av

The Jewish **Fast of Av (or Ab)** is a twenty-four-hour period of fasting, lamentation, and prayer in memory of the destruction of both the First and Second Temples in Jerusalem. When the Babylonians under Nebuchadnezzar destroyed the First Temple in 586 B.C., the Jews rebuilt it, but continued the fast day. Then the Second Temple was destroyed by the Romans under Titus, who burned it down in 70 A.D., and a long period of exile began for the Jews.

The Fast of Av begins at sunset the previous day and lasts for more than twenty-four hours. The nine days from the beginning of the month of Av through Tisha B'Av mark a period of intense mourning for the various disasters and tragedies that have befallen the Jewish people throughout history.

See also ASARAH BE-TEVET and THREE WEEKS.

Tok Race of Champions Dog Sled Race
Late March

The last race of the Alaska dog-mushing season, held since 1954 in Tok, which claims to be the Dog Capital of Alaska. Mushers from Alaska, Canada, and the Lower 48 participate in six-dog, eight-dog and open-class events for cash prizes.

Tok, a trade center for nearby Athabascan villages, is also a center for dog breeding, training, and mushing. It's not quite certain where the name of the town came from; some say it derives from a native word meaning 'peace crossing,' and others believe the village was originally called Tokyo and shorted to Tok in World War II.

Tolling the Devil's Knell
December 24

To celebrate the birth of Christ and the death of

the Devil, the Church of All Saints in Dewsbury, Yorkshire rings its bell the same number of times as the number of the year (for example, 1,990 times in 1990) on CHRISTMAS EVE. The tolling starts at 11:00 P.M., stops during the church service from midnight to 12:45, and is then resumed until the years have been tolled away. The custom has been going on for almost seven hundred years, although there was an interruption in the early nineteenth century and again during World War II, when all bell-ringing was banned except to signal enemy invasion.

Although no one seems to remember exactly how the custom got started, there is a legend that says Sir Thomas Soothill donated the tenor bell to the Dunster parish church as a penance for murdering a young boy servant and then trying to conceal his body. The bell has been called "Black Tom of Soothill" since the thirteenth century, and **Tolling Black Tom** is supposed to keep the parish safe from the Devil for another twelve months.

Tom Mix Roundup
July

Tom Mix (1880–1940) was the first of the "rhinestone cowboys." He made more than 370 movies, most of them silent, and at the peak of his career in the Depression years he was earning $17,000 a week. He performed all of his own stunts, used real bullets when filming his movies, and was an expert knife thrower. When silent movies were replaced by "talkies," Mix's popularity declined somewhat because he had a speech impediment as a result of being shot in the neck during the Boer War.

In 1986 the site of Tom Mix's birthplace, a small house overlooking the Bennett Branch of the Sinnemahoning Creek about six miles from the village of Driftwood, Pennsylvania, was purchased by Ray Flaugh. Flaugh and his wife are restoring the house to its original state and have established a Tom Mix Park by selling one-inch-square plots of the Tom Mix Homestead to the public . One of the first purchasers was President Ronald Reagan.

The Tom Mix Roundup is a three-day event that has been held in the towns of Sinnemahoning , Driftwood, and Mix Run since 1986. The events include a wagon train, live country music, appearances by the national Tom Mix lookalike, and various sharpshooting competitions.

Tom Sawyer Days, National
Week of July 4

Sponsored by the Hannibal, Missouri Jaycees, the National Tom Sawyer Days celebration began in 1956 with a Tom Sawyer Fence Painting Contest and a Tom and Becky competition. Three years later, all of the events relating to the fictional character originally created by Mark Twain in his 1876 novel were combined with the traditional FOURTH OF JULY celebration in Hannibal, and Independence Day was officially proclaimed "Tom Sawyer Day." In 1961 it became a national event, and today the festival spans five days and includes a number of unique competitions.

Contestants for the fence-painting competition, who must be ten to thirteen years old, come primarily from the ten states bordering the Mississippi River. They are judged on the authenticity of their costumes (which must be based on details from Mark Twain's book), the speed with which they can whitewash a four-by-five-foot section of fence, and the quality of their work.

The Frog Jump Competition is another of the festival's highlights, drawing up to 350 children and their pet frogs, each of whom is allowed three jumps. Competitors for the Tom and Becky competition must be seventh graders living in Hannibal, and the winners serve as goodwill ambassadors for the year.

Torch Festival
July; 24–26th day of sixth month of Chinese lunar calendar

A traditional holiday of many of the minority national people in Yunnan and Sichuan provinces in China. Holiday-makers dress in fine clothes, and the girls are especially colorful in embroidered gowns and headdresses of all colors. Celebrations begin with the sound of firecrackers, followed by folk dancing, athletic contests in such sports as pole-climbing and wrestling, and a bullfight. At night, huge bonfires are lit, dancers whirl around them, and a parade of people carrying torches brightens the night.

Tori-no-ichi
November

The **Bird Fair** or **Eagle Market** in Japan takes its name not only from the sacred crow that guided the first Mikado out of the wilderness by the light from its shining wings, but also from a play on the Japanese words signifying financial gain. This may be because most of the members of the Shinto sect that observe this festival are wealthy merchants and speculators, and the bamboo rakes that can be seen everywhere at this time are supposed to resemble the *kumade* or bear-paw, which is the symbol of the Eagle market. People carry these rakes, usually decorated with good-luck emblems and the smiling face of the laughing goddess Okame, because they represent the power to pull toward them anything they desire. Some of the rakes are small enough to be worn in a woman's hair, while others are so large and heavily decorated that it takes several men to carry them through the streets. Sometimes signs advertising restaurants or shops are hung from them and used throughout the year.

Toro Nagashi *See* Floating Lantern Ceremony

Torta dei Fieschi
August 14

When Count Fieschi of Lavagna in Genoa was married in 1240, he invited his guests—and everyone else in town—to share a cake that was more than thirty feet high. The citizens of Lavagna haven't forgotten his generosity, and each year they celebrate the event on August 14. Dressed in costumes, they parade to the town square, where they pin to their clothes a piece of paper (blue for men, white for women) on which a word is written. When they find someone wearing the same word, the couple is given a piece of "Fieschi's cake."

Toshogu Haru-No-Taisai (Great Spring Festival of the Toshogu Shrine)
May 17–18

A festival, also known as the **Sennin Gyoretsu**, or **Procession of 1000 People**, that provides the most spectacular display of ancient samurai costumes and weaponry in Japan. The Toshogu Shrine, in Nikko, Tochigi Prefecture, was built in 1617 to house the mausoleum of Tokugawa Ieyasu, the first of the Tokugawa shoguns. The festival originated in honor of the reburial of Ieyasu in the new mausoleum.

On the first day of the festival, dignitaries and members of the Tokugawa family make offerings to the deities of the shrine. Also on this day, warriors on horseback shoot at targets with bows and arrows. On the morning of May 18 more than 1,000 people take part in the procession from Toshogu to Futaarasan Shrine, including hundreds of samurai warriors, with armor, helmets and weaponry. Also marching are priests with flags; men with stuffed hawks representing huntsmen; men in fox masks to honor the fox spirits that protect the shrine; and musicians with drums and bells.

Tour de France
July

The world's greatest bicycle race and also the annual sports event with the most viewers—an estimated one billion who watch television coverage beamed around the world, and 14.6 million who stand by the roadside. The tour, started in 1903, takes place mostly in France and Belgium, but also visits Spain, Italy, Germany, and Switzerland. It is divided into twenty-one timed stages, or legs, over three weeks, and has become a French national obsession. The newspaper sports columnist Red Smith once wrote that "an army from Mars could invade France, the government could fall, and even the recipe for sauce Béarnaise be lost, but if it happened during the Tour de France nobody would notice."

The route and distance of the tour is different each year, averaging 3,500 kilometers (about 2,100 miles, or the distance from Chicago to Los Angeles). It always includes strenuous mountain passes and a finale in Paris. The number of riders is limited to 200, and the rider with the lowest cumulative time for all stages is the winner. There have been three five-time winners: Jacques Anquetil (1957, 1961–1964), Eddy Merckx (1969–1972, 1974), and Bernard Hinault (1978, 1979, 1981, 1982, 1985). Merckx, a Belgian who seemed almost immune to pain, is considered the all-time greatest cycler. He competed in 1,800 races and won 525 of them. In 1986, Greg LeMond was the first American to win the tour. He was nearly killed in a 1987 hunting accident, and endured accidents and operations during the next two years, but came back to win the tour in 1989 and again in 1990.

The first tour in 1903 was organized as a publicity stunt by Henri Desgranges, bicyclist and publisher of the cycling magazine *L'Auto*. On July 1, 1903, 60 bikers started from the Alarm Clock Café on the outskirts of Paris, and three weeks later Maurice Garin was the winner, and the tour was born. In 1984, the Tour Feminin, a special women's race, was added to the tour, and is now a stage race of about 1,000 kilometers, run concurrently with the final two weeks of the men's tour. The first winner was an American, Marianne Martin.

Tournament of Roses (Rose Parade)
January 1

One of the world's most elaborate and most

photographed parades, held every New Year's Day in Pasadena, Calif. The parade is made up of about sixty floats elaborately decorated—and completely covered—with roses, orchids, chrysanthemums, and other blossoms that portray the year's theme. Additionally there are more than twenty bands, more than 200 horses and costumed riders, a grand marshal, a Rose queen, and the queen's princesses. The parade is 5 1/2 miles long, and attracts about 1.5 million spectators along the route, and is televised nationally.

The first festival, called the BATTLE OF FLOWERS, was held on Jan. 1, 1890, under the auspices of the Valley Hunt Club. The man responsible was Charles Frederick Holder, a naturalist and teacher of zoology. He had seen the Battle of Flowers on the French Riviera, and figured California could do something similar; his suggestion resulted in a parade of decorated carriages and buggies followed by amateur athletic events. The parade evolved gradually. Floral floats were introduced, and in 1902 the morning parade was capped by a football game, which was replaced in following years by chariot races. In 1916, football came back, and the Rose Bowl Game is now traditionally associated with the parade.

In 1992, the theme of the tournament was "Voyages of Discovery," and it kicked off the Columbus Quincentennial. Co-grand marshals were Cristobal Colon, a descendant of Christopher Columbus and Colorado Rep. Ben Nighthorse Campbell, a Cheyenne chief.

Town Meeting Day
First Tuesday of March

An official state holiday in Vermont, this is the day on which nearly every town elects its officers, approves budgets, and deals with other civic issues in a day-long public meeting of the voters. It more or less coincides with the anniversary of Vermont's admission to the Union on March 4, 1791 (see ADMISSION DAY). Vermonters pride themselves on their active participation in these meetings, which often include heated debates on issues of local importance.

Transfiguration, Feast of the
August 6

As described in the first three Gospels, when Jesus' ministry was coming to an end, he took his three closest disciples—Peter, James, and John—to a mountaintop to pray. While he was praying, his face shone like the sun and his garments became glistening white. Moses (symbolizing the Law) and Elijah (symbolizing the prophets) ap-

peared and began talking with him, testifying to his Messiahship. Then a bright cloud came over them, and a voice from within the cloud said, "This is my beloved Son, with whom I am well pleased; listen to him." The disciples were awestruck and fell to the ground. When they raised their heads, they saw only Jesus (Matthew 17).

Observance of this feast began in the Eastern church as early as the fourth century, but it was not introduced in the Western church until 1457. It is observed by Roman Catholics, Orthodox Christians, Lutherans, and Anglicans; most Protestants stopped observing it at the time of the Reformation. The mountaintop on which the Transfiguration took place is traditionally believed to be Mount Tabor, a few miles east of Nazareth in Galilee. However, many scholars believe it was Mount Hermon, or even the Mount of Olives.

Transpac Race
July, biennially in odd-numbered years

It was in 1906, the year of the great San Francisco earthquake, that the first yacht race across the Pacific was held. Because of the earthquake, only three yachts participated, ranging in length from 48 to 115 feet overall. The course was from Los Angeles to Honolulu.

The Transpac Race was originally held in even-numbered years, with a long break between 1912 and 1923, and another interruption, after the Japanese attack on Pearl Harbor, between 1941 and 1947. It is currently held in odd-numbered years, beginning on the FOURTH OF JULY, and is sponsored by the Transpacific Yacht Racing Association.

The finish can be close: in the 1965 race, with fifty-five yachts participating, there was less than a hundred yards between the first two finishers as they struggled up the Molokai Channel. One had lost her main boom and the other's boom was badly damaged.

Treaty of Paris Day *See* Ratification Day

Trinidad and Tobago Carnival
Between February 2 and March 8; Monday and Tuesday before Ash Wednesday

One of the most spectacular and frenzied CARNIVAL celebrations of the pre-Lenten season, the Trinidad and Tobago Carnival is a non-stop forty-eight-hour festival in which almost everyone on the island participates. It started out in the late nineteenth century as a high-spirited but relatively sedate celebration involving a torchlight procession in blackface called *canboulay*—from *cannes brulées* or 'burned cane'—patterned after the procession of slaves on their way to fight fires in the cane fields. There was also music in the streets and masked dancing, although slaves were not permitted to wear masks. With the emancipation of the slaves, Carnival became a free-for-all with raucous music and displays of near-nudity. The government tried to crack down on the celebrations, but in 1881 there were *canboulay* riots in which thirty-eight policemen were injured. After that, a law was passed that forbade parading before six o'clock in the morning on Carnival Monday. That moment is still known as *jouvé* (possibly from *jour ouvert* or 'daybreak').

Today the main events are the two carnival day parades, which involve twenty-five to thirty costumed bands, each with about 2500 marchers and its own king and queen. There is a calypso competition in which steel bands and calypso composers vie for the title of "Calypso Monarch." No one sleeps during the two-day celebration, and the event ends with the "las lap," which is a wild, uninhibited dance in the streets.

Trinity Sunday
Between May 17 and June 20; first Sunday after Pentecost in the West; Monday after Pentecost in the East

Trinity Sunday differs from other days in the Christian calendar in that it is not associated with a particular saint or historic event. Instead, it is a day that celebrates the central dogma of Christian theology: that the One God exists as Three Persons with One Substance—as the Father, the Son, and the Holy Spirit. The idea of a festival in honor of the Trinity was first introduced by Stephen, Bishop of Liège, Belgium, in the tenth century. But it took several more centuries for a feast in honor of so abstract a concept to find its way into the church calendar. It became popular in England perhaps because of the consecration of Thomas à Becket on that day in 1162, but it wasn't until 1334 that it became a universal observance decreed by Pope John XXII. The day after Trinity is sometimes referred to as Trinity Monday.

Tradition has it that St. Patrick of Ireland used a shamrock as a symbol of the "three-in-one," triune God.

Triple Crown Pack Burro Races
July–August

Three races of pack burros and human runners in the Colorado Rocky Mountains. The first leg of the triple crown starts in Fairplay and is held the last weekend in July. The second leg, the first weekend in August, starts in Leadville. The final race is two weeks later in Buena Vista. The first organized pack burro races were held in 1949 along a route over Mosquito Pass between Leadville and Fairplay; in 1979, the Buena Vista race became the final leg of the triple crown. The races cover from fifteen to thirty miles over 13,500-foot mountain passes, sometimes in snow, and generally take the twenty to twenty-five entrants three to four hours. Women run a different shorter course than men. Contestants can't ride their burros, but must run alongside them. (They can and frequently do push the animals.) Winners of individual races get cash prizes; the total purse at Buena Vista is $5,020. The men's winner at Leadville gets $1200.

The word *burro* is Spanish and means 'donkey'. The history of these animals in the West goes back to the Gold Rush days of the 1800s when pack burros carried great loads of machinery and supplies to mining camps. Pack burro racing is thought to have started in those times.

The race days are surrounded by a variety of activities and are now major events in the small Colorado towns. In Buena Vista, for example, there are bed races, toilet-seat races, simulated hangings, a horseshoe tournament, and a chili cookoff. Leadville holds contests in mine drilling events. There's also a triple crown outhouse race; each town in the burro triple crown also stages an outhouse race, with definite rules (e.g., one member of the outhouse team must sit in the outhouse during the race wearing colored underwear and/or a bathrobe).

Trois Glorieuses
Third Saturday-Monday in November

The **Three Glorious Days** to which the name of this French wine festival refers occur in mid-November on the Côte d'Or in eastern France, and are observed in three different wine-producing centers. On the first day, at Nuits-Saint-Georges, the Confrerie des Chevaliers du Tastevin put on their red robes and square toques to receive their new members—the *tastevin* is a small silver cup used to taste wines. This event is followed by a pig dinner during which a thousand bottles of wine are uncorked. The second day of the festival takes place at Beaune, where a wine auction is held at the Hospice de Beaune, whose cellars are open to the public. On the third and final day in Meursault, everyone who has taken part in the work of the wine harvest is invited to a huge banquet. There is folk dancing and merry-making as the festival draws to a close.

The Confrerie des Chevaliers du Tastevin was formed in 1934 to put the French wine industry back on its feet after a number of disastrous vintage failures. They hold a series of winetasters' banquets throughout Burgundy, but the most elaborate ones are part of this three-day festival.

Trout Festival, National *See* Michigan Brown Trout Festival

Tsom Gedalyah *See* Gedaliah, Fast of

Tuan Yang Chieh *See* Dragon Boat Festival

Tu Bishvat *See* Bi-Shevat

Tucson Meet Yourself Festival
Second weekend in October

The annual folk and ethnic festival known as Tucson Meet Yourself has been held in Tucson, Arizona since 1974. Designed to promote southern Arizona's wide mix of cultures—which includes Mexican-, Czechoslovakian-, Italian-, German-, and Indian-American groups—the festival features formal presentations of traditional music and dance, demonstrations by folk artists and crafts-people, and workshops in which various experts on ethnic customs and traditions hold informal discussions, give lessons, and organize games.

Food, however, is the festival's primary attraction. Dozens of food booths, each operated by a non-profit organization identified with a specific cultural heritage and elaborately decorated to represent elements of "the old country," are set up throughout the park in which the event is held. Although American Indian and Mexican-American specialties predominate, the booths have featured Irish, Finnish, Hungarian, Ukrainian, Greek, Armenian, Vietnamese, Japanese, Sri Lankan, and many other ethnic dishes, giving the festival the well-earned name of "Tucson Eat Yourself."

Tulip Time
Second weekend in May

When a group of high school students in Pella, Iowa staged an operetta called *Tulip Time in Pella* in 1935, the only tulips growing in the town were in wooden pots. But the musical performance gave the local chamber of commerce an idea for promoting the town's Dutch heritage. They hired tulip specialists from the Netherlands to teach them how to plant and care for tulips. Then they planted thousands of bulbs and got the local historical society started preserving the town's Dutch buildings and heirlooms. Today Pella (named 'city of refuge' by the first Dutch immigrants, who were fleeing religious intolerance in their homeland) has been renovated to resemble a typical village in the Netherlands. During the festival the townspeople dress in Dutch provincial costumes and engage in such activities as street-scrubbing, authentic Dutch dancing and folk music, and tours of the formal tulip gardens. One of these gardens features a Dutch windmill and a pond shaped like a wooden shoe.

Unlike most local festivals, Tulip Time is not a commercial event. There are no souvenir stands or food booths, although the local shops, museums, and restaurants offer a wide variety of Dutch specialties. Many of the events take place at the Tulip Torne, a tower with twin pylons more than sixty-five feet high that was built as a memorial to the early Dutch settlers.

Turon
December; the week after Christmas

A Polish peasant's festival observed in the week following CHRISTMAS, Turon is a remnant of an ancient festival in honor of the winter god Radegast. The *turon* is a legendary beast with a huge wooden head and jaws that open and close. This is one of several animal disguises that the peasants wear as they go from house to house singing carols and receiving food and drink from their neighbors in return. Other traditional costumes worn in the celebration represent a wolf, a bear, and a goat. The original *turon* symbolized frost, consuming vegetation with its huge mouth.

Tutti Day *See* Hocktide

Twelfth Night
January 5

The evening before EPIPHANY is called **Epiphany Eve** or Twelfth Night, and it traditionally marks the end of the Christmas season, also called **Twelfthtide** in England. Since **Twelfth Day** is January 6, there is some confusion over exactly when Twelfth Night occurs, and it is often observed on the night of Epiphany rather than the night before.

Twelfth Night is an occasion for merrymaking, as reflected in Shakespeare's comedy, *Twelfth Night*. Celebrations reflect ancient WINTER SOLSTICE rites encouraging the rebirth of the New Year and also the Magis' visit to the Christ child.

Pageants held on this night typically include fantastic masked figures, costumed musicians, and traditional dances, such as the Abbots Bromley Antler Dance in England. Customarily the Twelfth Night cake is sliced and served and the man who gets the hidden bean and the woman the pea are the king ("King of the Bean" or "Lord of Misrule") and queen for the festivities.

U

Uhola Festival

Various

Observed by the Dakkarkari in Nigeria, the Uhola Festival is preceded by a housecleaning period during which the villages, the shrines, and the surrounding hills are cleaned up and put in order. This time is dominated by the drinking of local beer, called *m'kya*. The *Yadato*—boys and girls from wealthy families—go into seclusion for a four-week period prior to the Uhola, where they are properly fed and fattened, and encouraged to rest up for the celebration.

On the first day of the festival, the Yadato must dance in front of the chiefs' palace and present the chiefs with Uhola gifts. The celebration then moves to the village square, where they continue to dance and sing songs satirizing prostitutes, unmarried pregnant girls, irresponsible men-even political figures. The highlight of the second day of the festival is the wrestling contest, which also takes place in the village square. Sometimes the Dakkarkari wrestle against other tribes, and the victor in each match receives a prize from the chief. The wrestling, prize-giving, and speeches continue for about four more days, until the priest declares that the festival is over.

Only girls who are engaged to be married are allowed to participate in the Uhola. Their future husbands must have completed their *golmo*—a period of farm labor in lieu of paying for their brides. After the Uhola, the girls move into their prospective husbands' homes, while new boys go into *golmo*.

Ullr Fest

Third week in January

A winter festival in Breckenridge, Colo., to recognize Ullr, the Norse god of winter and a stepson of Thor. Highlights are a broomball tournament, town skiing championship races, skiing along lantern-lit trails, ice sculpture, fireworks, wine tasting, Norwegian dancing, and a Grand Ullr Ball.

United Nations Day

October 24

The international peace-keeping organization known as the United Nations was formally established on October 24, 1945, in the wake of World War II. Representatives from the United States, Great Britain, the Soviet Union, and Nationalist China first met in August and September of 1944 at the Dumbarton Oaks estate in Washington, D.C. to discuss the problems involved in creating such an agency, and the results of their talks became the basis for the United Nations Charter that was ratified the following year. Although it has not always been successful in maintaining world peace, the UN has served as an important international forum for the handling of conflicts in the Middle East, Korea, Somalia, the former Yugoslavia, and other troubled areas.

Each member nation observes October 24, and in some places the entire week is known as **United Nations Week**. In the United States, events taking place on this day include parades, international fairs, and dinners featuring foods from different countries. It is also common to hold debates and discussions designed to acquaint the public with the U.N.'s functions. Schools frequently observe United Nation's Day by holding folk festivals that teach students the music, songs, and dances of different countries, or by organizing special programs focusing on their geography, products, government, and culture.

United States Air and Trade Show

Biennially in June

Dayton, Ohio has been a center for aeronautical research and development ever since two of its local residents, Orville and Wilbur Wright, created the first successful flying machine in their bicycle shop and tested their invention just a few miles outside of town (see WRIGHT BROTHERS' DAY). Dayton began celebrating its heritage as "the birthplace of aviation" by staging informal air shows shortly after the turn of the century, and by the early 1970s, the **Dayton Air Fair** was a regular annual event consisting of flying demonstrations and aircraft displays. By 1988 it was called the **Dayton Air and Trade Show**, reflecting a growing emphasis on the commercial aspects of the aviation and aerospace industry. It was renamed the United States Air and Trade Show in 1990, when it became an international exposition, and since that time it has been held biennially for six days in June. Two of those days are devoted to the air show, which features bi-planes, gliders, helicopters, and jets flown by some of the most famous names in the field of aviation.

Held at the Dayton International Airport, the show hosts over 250 exhibitors from the United States and other countries. Conferences and seminars, flight demonstrations, and tours of the latest makes and models of aircraft draw an international and largely professional crowd. Visitors and participants can also visit the United States Air Force Museum, the National Aviation Hall of Fame, the restored Wright Brothers Cycle Shop, and Wright-Patterson Air Force Base, which continues to play a major role in the development of aerospace technology.

United States Grand Prix
First Sunday of October

Formerly part of the international racing series that includes the MONACO GRAND PRIX, the first U. S. Grand Prix was held in 1959 at Sebring, Florida. After 1961 it was held at Watkins Glen, Detroit, and then Phoenix. In 1991, however, the racing committee rejected the Phoenix site so there will be no United States Grand Prix until a new location is approved. Points won in this race count toward the World Championship of Drivers. More than fifteen Grand Prix races are held yearly in countries around the world.

Like other Grand Prix races, the race at Watkins Glen was for Formula One race cars, which are generally smaller and more maneuverable than the cars used in speedway racing. Engine size, fuel, and other specifications are strictly controlled by the Féderation Internationale de L'Automobile (FIA).

United States Open
September

The final tournament in the four events that make up the Grand Slam of tennis. (The others are the AUSTRALIAN and FRENCH OPENS and WIMBLEDON.) Also known as the **U.S. Championships**, the games are played on hard courts at Flushing Meadows Park in Queens, N.Y. They had

been played from 1915 to 1978 in Forest Hills, also in Queens. Separate amateur and professional open championships were held in 1968 and 1969, and the tournament became exclusively an open in 1970.

The U. S. National Lawn Tennis Association was established in 1881, and the first official U.S. National Championship was played under its auspices that year in Newport, R.I. The first women's championship was played in 1887. The golden age at Forest Hills is considered to have been the 1920s when William T. "Big Bill" Tilden 2d dominated the game. He was U.S. Open champion seven times, from 1920–25 and in 1929. Other seven-time winners were Richard Sears (1881–87) and William Larned (1901, 1902, 1907–11). Jimmy Connors took the title five times (1974, 1976, 1978, 1982, 1983). In the women's championships, Molla Bjurstedt Mallory is the all-time champ; she won eight times (1915–18, 1920–22, 1926). Helen Wills Moody won seven times (1923–25, 1927–29, 1931). "Little Poker Face," as she was called, also won eight Wimbledons and four French Opens.

Ranking near the top of the excitement scale were the wins in the U.S. Championships that sewed up the Grand Slam championship. In 1938, Don Budge was the first to win all four Grand Slam titles. The feat wasn't equaled until 1962 when Rod Laver won all four. Then he did it again in 1969. In 1953, Californian Maureen Connolly became the first woman to sweep the Grand Slam titles. Known as "Little Mo," she had won her first U.S. Championship at the age of sixteen in 1951. A horse-riding accident in 1954 cut her career short, and she died in 1969. Women who have won all Grand Slam titles since then are Margaret Smith Court in 1970 and Steffi Graf in 1988.

United States Open Championship in Golf
Four days ending the third Sunday in June

The **U.S. Open**, conducted by the United States Golf Association, is the oldest golf tournament in North America, and was first held in 1895. More than six thousand professional and amateur golfers vie for only 156 available places. Unlike THE MASTERS, which is an invitational tournament, the U. S. Open is for anyone good enough to survive the qualifying rounds. Rather than being played on the same course each year, its location changes. It is traditionally played on the nation's best courses, such as Merion in Philadelphia, Oakland Hills in Detroit, Baltusrol in Union County, New Jersey, and Winged Foot in

Mamaroneck, New York, and Pebble Beach on the Monterey Peninsula of California. Since the 1930s, it has been the U.S.G.A.'s practice every ten to fifteen years to take the Open back to certain courses that have demonstrated they can produce a rigorous test for the world's top golfers. The tournament itself takes four days. There is a qualifying round followed by three days of eighteen holes each, for a total of seventy-two holes.

The U. S. Open is one of the most difficult golf championships to win. Its list of champions includes Bobby Jones, Walter Hagen, Gene Sarazen, Ben Hogan, Arnold Palmer, Jack Nicklaus, Lee Trevino, and Tom Watson. The 1913 tournament, which was won by an unknown twenty-year-old store clerk named Francis Ouimet, is considered to have marked the transformation of golf in America from an elite game to a public pastime.

Universal Prayer Day (Dzam Ling Chi Sang)
Usually June or July; fourteenth to sixteenth day of fifth Tibetan lunar month
A Tibetan Buddhist festival and a time for spiritual cleansing. At this time, people hang prayer flags on tree tops, burn juniper twigs, and build bonfires to worship the Buddha and local gods. Fire in the Tibetan culture is symbolic of cleansing. Family picnics are also common during the festival.

This is also the time of the once-a-year display of the famous giant *thangkas* 'scroll paintings', at Tashilhunpo (which means Heap of Glory) Monastery in Shigatse, Tibet. Tashilhunpo, the seat of the Panchen Lamas, once had more than 4,000 monks, but the monastery was disbanded by the Chinese in 1960, and only about 600 monks remain.

At this time, three huge *thangkas* with images of the Buddha are displayed for three days on a nine-story wall on the monastery grounds. *Thangkas,* which are made in all sizes, were first known in Tibet in the tenth century, and were used in monastery schools as teaching devices. Before being hung, they were always consecrated.

Panchen Lamas came into being in the 17th century when the fifth Dalai Lama gave the title *panchen,* meaning 'great scholar,' to his beloved tutor. The tutor was then found to be the reincarnation of Amitabha, the Buddha of infinite light, and subsequent Panchen Lamas are new incarnations. As with Dalai Lamas, when a Panchen Lama dies, a search is made for an infant boy who is the new incarnation.

See also DALAI LAMA, BIRTHDAY OF THE.

University of Pennsylvania Relay Carnival
Seven days, beginning on the Sunday before the last weekend in April
The **Penn Relays** is the oldest and largest track and field event in the United States. The first relay meet held on the campus of the University of Pennsylvania in Philadelphia was on April 21, 1895—but even back then the tents and the festival atmosphere contributed to its reputation as a "carnival" rather than just a series of races. Since that time, the Penn Relays have served as a springboard for athletes who later went on to win Olympic medals—such as Carl Lewis, Joan Benoit, Edwin Moses, and Frank Shorter. It is also a breeding ground for rising track and field stars, with over seven hundred high school teams and one hundred eighty college teams participating.

The event begins on the Sunday before the last weekend in April (unless that day is EASTER, in which case the Relays would begin a week earlier) with a twenty-kilometer road race. There is a heptathlon and a decathlon on Tuesday and Wednesday, and the rest of the week is filled with walk, sprint, distance, and field events for athletes of all ages and abilities—including Special Olympians. More than seventy thousand spectators are drawn to the event, which receives wide press coverage.

Up-Helly-Aa
Last Tuesday in January
This ancient fire festival is observed by the people of Lerwick in the Shetland Islands. In pre-Christian times their Norse ancestors welcomed the return of the sun god with YULE, a twenty-four-day period of feasting, storytelling, and bonfires. The last night of the festival was called Up-Helly-Aa or 'End of the Holy Days.'

Today a group known as the Guizers builds a thirty-one-foot model of a Viking longship, complete with a dragon's head and many oars, in honor of those Viking invaders who decided to remain in Scotland. On the night of Up-Helly-Aa, the Guizers dress in Norse costumes and helmets and carry the boat to a large open field. There they throw lit torches into the ship and burn it.

Uphaliday originally referred to EPIPHANY, or January 6—the day when the Yuletide holidays came to an end. The shifting of the date to the end of January probably reflects the change from the Julian to the Gregorian calendar in 1752. This day is also referred to as **Uphelya, Up-Helly-Day, Uphalie Day**, or **Uphalimass**.

Urini Nal (Children's Day)
May 5

A national holiday in South Korea since 1975. Schools are closed and parks are packed with children. Events of the day may include wrestling and martial arts exhibitions, dancing, and the presentation of puppet shows and plays. Cake shops give away rice cake favors. The holiday is intended to forge the bonds of family life.

Utah Arts Festival
Late June

The only state-sponsored arts festival in the country, bringing together more than 100 performing groups. The festival was founded in 1977 in Salt Lake City and is now a five-day event held on stages and in the streets, plazas, and galleries. Hundreds of booths are set up for native foods and for exhibits of sculpture, painting, pottery, folk arts, and photography. In a Children's Art Yard, stories are told of Utah mining days and natural history. Live performances of contemporary, jazz, bluegrass, folk, and salsa music are presented from two outdoor stages, and in the evening, there are dance, theater, symphony, and opera performances in the Utah Symphony Hall and restored 19th-century Capitol Theatre.

Ute Bear Dance
Memorial Day weekend

An ancient ceremony of the Southern Ute Indians held now on the Sunday and Monday of Memorial Day weekend in Ignacio, Colo. Originally the ritual was held in late February or early March, at the time of the bears awakening from their hibernation. It stemmed from the belief that the Utes were descended from bears, and the dance was given both to help the bears coming out of hibernation and to gain power from them, since bears were believed to cure sickness and to communicate with people in the Spirit World.

Today the dance is largely a social occasion, and is what is called a women's dance, since the women ask the men to dance. This practice is rooted in the habits of bears: supposedly the female bear wakes first and then chases the male bear. In earlier days, two bears—a man and woman wearing bearskins, with red paint around their mouths to suggest the bloody ferocity of the bears—romped around a corral, the female chasing the male, and both responding ferociously toward anyone who might laugh. In the present-day dance, lines of women and men advance toward each other, gradually dancing in pairs. The dancing goes on until sunset, when there is a feast.

V

Vaisakh (Baisak(hi))

April–May; 1 Vaisakha

The Hindu solar NEW YEAR and a harvest festival, celebrated primarily in northern India and Bangladesh with temple worship, ritual bathing in rivers, and a New Year's fair. For Sikhs, it is their most important holy day.

In Malaysia and India, especially in the Indian state of Punjab, where the gospel of the Sikhs began, **Baisakh** is particularly significant because on this day in 1689 Guru Gobind Singh chose the five leaders (called the *Panch Pyare* 'Beloved Five') who formed the Khalsa, the militant fraternity of the Sikhs. There the holiday is celebrated in the temples, with a forty-eight hour reading of the Granth Sahib (the Sikh Bible), prayers, hymns, and sermons. Castelessness, an important Sikh principle, is emphasized by everyone eating and sitting together. Afterwards, there is feasting and dancing of the *bhangra*, a popular and athletic folk dance for men, depicting the entire farming year.

In the Indian state of Kerala, the festival is known as **Vishu**. Activities include fireworks and what is called Vishu Kani, a display of grain, fruits, flowers, gold, new cloth, and money, which are supposed to ensure a prosperous year.

The festival is called **Bohag Bihu** in Assam, and there it is celebrated for a week with music, folk dances, and community feasting. Traditions include decorating cattle, smearing them with turmeric, and giving them brown sugar and eggplant to eat. Also during this time, there is a day on which young people look for marriage partners. The girls wear beautiful scarves, and the boys look for the most lovely orchids; they present these to each other and then dance.

See also KUMBH MELA, VESAK.

Valentine's Day

February 14

St. Valentine is believed to have been a Roman priest who was clubbed and beheaded on this day in the year 270. How he became the patron saint of lovers remains a mystery, but one theory is that the Church used the day of St. Valentine's martyrdom in an attempt to Christianize the old Roman LUPERCALIA, a pagan festival held around the middle of February. Part of the ancient ceremony entailed putting girls' names in a box and letting the boys draw them out. Couples would thus be paired off until the following year. The Church substituted saints' names for girls' names, in the hope that the participant would model his life after the saint whose name he drew. But by the sixteenth century, it was once again girls' names that ended up in the box. Eventually the custom of sending anonymous cards or messages to those one admired became the accepted way of celebrating **St. Valentine's Day**.

Valley of the Moon Vintage Festival

Last full weekend in September

California's oldest wine festival, held since the late 1890s in Sonoma, the cradle of the state's wine industry. Located in Sonoma Valley, which Jack London made famous as the "Valley of the Moon," the city was founded in 1835 by Gen. Mariano Guadalupe Vallejo. In 1846, the Northwest became part of the United States, and, on June 14 of that year, American settlers invaded Sonoma, captured Vallejo and his Mexican garrison, and raised an improvised Bear Flag to proclaim California a republic. On July 9, the flag was replaced by the Stars and Stripes. In the 1850s, Hungarian nobleman Count Agoston Haraszthy planted thousands of cuttings from European grape vines to establish the Buena Vista Winery, now the state's oldest premium winery, becoming the father of California's wine industry. In 1863, a double wedding united the two promi-

353

nent wine-making families—the Vallejos and the Harszthys.

The two-day festival focuses on this history, presenting reenactments of the 1846 Bear Flag Revolt and of the double wedding. There are also wine tastings, parades, live music, cooking-with-wine demonstrations, a firemen's water fight, and grape stomps.

Vandalia Gathering
Memorial Day weekend

A folk festival held on the state capitol grounds in Charleston, W. Va., to exhibit the best of the state's traditional arts, music, dance, crafts, and food. Events include music by fiddle players, banjo players, and lap-dulcimer players, clogging, craft demonstrations, liars' contests, storytelling, and an exhibition of quilts made by West Virginia's top quilters. Held since 1976, the festival attracts about 35,000 people.

See also WEST VIRGINIA DAY.

Vappu (May Day)
May 1

A national holiday and celebration of the coming of spring in Finland. The holiday, once a pagan festival to rejoice at the end of the long northern winter, is also LABOR DAY, and country factories that are said to "never close" do close on May 1 and CHRISTMAS DAY.

For students (and even gray-bearded former students), the "anything goes" celebration begins at midnight on the eve of MAY DAY, called Vapunaatto, when they wear white student caps and indulge in anything not indecent or criminal. It's traditional in Helsinki for students to wade across the moat that surrounds the statue of Havis Amanda, a mermaid, to place their caps on her head. There are balloons, streamers, horns, and masks everywhere. No one does much sleeping. On May Day itself, the students lead processions through the streets of Helsinki, and then enjoy carnivals and concerts. Workers in most provincial towns generally gather in more solemn fashion to celebrate with speeches and parades.

See also PREMIER MAY.

Vaqueros, Fiesta de los
February, the four days starting the last Thursday

A four-day event in Tucson, Ariz., featuring the world's longest non-motorized parade and the largest outdoor midwinter rodeo in the United States. The fiesta starts with the parade—a two-

mile-long procession of some 300 entries, including such old horse-drawn vehicles as buckboards, surreys (with or without the fringe on top), western stagecoaches, and Conestoga wagons. The first parade was in 1925; now about 200,000 people line the parade route.

The three days of rodeo include the standard events as well as daily Mutton Bustin' contests. In these, four-to six-year-olds test their riding skills on sheep. There are also demonstrations by Appaloosa trick stallions and by the Quadrille de Mujeres, a women's precision-riding team.

Vasalopp, The
First Sunday in March

The biggest cross-country ski race in the world takes place in Sweden on the first Sunday in March each year. The course begins on the border between Norway and Sweden, in a huge frozen field outside the village of Sälen, and ends fifty-four miles away in the Swedish town of Mora. The race was named for a young Swedish nobelman, Gustav Vasa, who persuaded the people of Mora to help him drive out the Danes in 1520. He later ruled the country for almost forty years as King Gustavus I.

More than eight thousand men compete in the annual race, which for even the strongest skier takes over five hours to complete. Because they consider this to be a test of their manhood, many Swedish men celebrate their fiftieth birthdays by entering the race. More than seventy thousand have officially completed the Vasalopp since the race became a national ski festival in 1922.

Vasant Panchami (Basant Panchami)
January–February

A Hindu festival of spring, celebrated throughout India at the end of January or in early February. People wear bright yellow clothes, the color of the mustard flower that heralds the onset of spring, and mark the day with music, dancing, and kite-flying. In Shantiniketan, West Bengal, the festival is celebrated with special lavishness in honor of Saraswati, the goddess of learning and the arts. Her images are taken in procession to rivers to be bathed, and books and pens are placed at her shrine.

Vata Savitri
May–June; Jyaistha

Hindu married women traditionally prefer to die before their husbands rather than be left as widows. In this festival they bathe early in the morning, dress in their best clothes, then go out in groups to worship the banyan tree (*vata*). A type of fig tree which sends roots directly from the branches down to the ground, the banyan has special significance for Hindu women because Savitri, a deified woman in Hindu scriptures, was able to rescue her husband from Yama, the god of death, after she had worshiped the *Vata* tree.

During the worship ceremony, the tree is sprinkled with vermilion and its trunk is wrapped in raw cotton threads. The women walk around the tree seven times and place various articles of worship near it. Those who are unable to find a banyan tree on this day pay their respects to a twig of it in their homes. They fast until their worship is done.

See also KARWACHOTH.

Vegetarian Festival

First nine days of ninth lunar month of Chinese calendar (usually late September or October)

An annual nine-day affair observed on the island of Phuket off southwestern Thailand by residents of Chinese ancestry. During the nine days, observers eat only vegetarian foods. The festival begins with a parade in which devotees wear white, and continues with ceremonies at temples, performances of special feats by ascetics, and acts of self-mortification—walking on hot coals, piercing the skin, and so on. The festival celebrates the beginning of the month called "Taoist Lent," when devout Chinese abstain from meat. It is thought, however, that the self-mortification acts are derived from the Hindu festival of THAIPUSAM.

Vendimia, Fiesta de la

Second week in September

Spain is famous for its sherry, and some of the best sherry comes from the southwestern part of the country, in a district known as *Jerez de la Frontera*. This is said to be one of the few remaining places where the juice of the grapes is extracted by trampling them in huge wooden vats or *lagares*. Although most people think this is done with bare feet, the participants actually wear specially designed hobnail boots.

In mid-September Jerez de la Frontera holds its **Grape Harvest Festival** or Fiesta de la Vendimia, which includes flamenco dancing, *cante jondo* singing (a distinctive and deeply moving variety of Spanish gypsy song), and bullfighting. There is also an official "blessing of the grapes" and the season's first wine before the statue of San Ginés de la Jara, the patron saint of the region's wine growers. The blessing is part of a col-orful pageant held at the Collegiate Church of Santa Maria. All of the events that take place during the festival pay tribute in one way or another to wine sherry, the area's most famous product.

Vermont Maple Festival

Last weekend in April

Vermont is the official maple capital of the world, the maple festival held there each spring is really a statewide celebration. Maple sugaring—the process of tapping maple trees, gathering the sap, and boiling it in the sugarhouse to produce syrup—was a main source of income for the early settlers in Vermont as well as their main source of sweets. The sugaring industry flourished until World War II, when the number of producers dropped sharply. In the 1940s, '50s and '60s the growing emphasis on dairy farming resulted in the suspension of many sugaring operations. Although there has been a resurgence of interest in recent years, mild winters have taken their toll on the maple sugar crop because cold nights are needed to make the sap flow.

Since 1968 the three-day festival has promoted Vermont maple products through educational exhibits, sugaring equipment displays, essay contests, syrup competitions, and maple cooking contests. In addition to maple syrup, the festival gives visitors an opportunity to sample maple cream, maple candy, and maple sugar on snow.

Vernal Equinox

March 21 or 22

The vernal equinox, Latin for 'of spring' and 'equal night,' is one of the two occasions during the year when the sun crosses the equator, and the days and nights everywhere are nearly of equal length. It marks the beginning of spring in the northern hemisphere and the beginning of autumn in the southern hemisphere. (See also AUTUMNAL EQUINOX.)

In Japan, the **Festival of the Vernal Equinox** or **Shunki Korei-Sai** is a day on which schools and places of business are closed and people worship their imperial ancestors.

Verrazano Day

April 17

Observed in New York state, Verrazano Day commemorates the discovery of New York harbor by the Italian navigator Giovanni da Verrazano on April 17, 1524. With the backing of King Francis I of France, Verrazano sailed his ship *La Dauphine* to the New World, reaching the Carolina coast in March 1524 and then sailing northward, exploring the eastern coast of North America. In addition to discovering the present-day site of New York City's harbor, he also discovered Block Island and Narragansett Bay in what is now Rhode Island, plus thirty-two islands off the coast of Maine, including Monhegan. Verrazano was the first European explorer to name newly discovered sites in North America after persons and places in the Old World.

In naming the Verrazano-Narrows Bridge, New York gave Verrazano official recognition. Spanning New York harbor from Brooklyn to Staten Island, the 4,260-foot suspension bridge, built between 1959 and 1964, succeeded the Golden Gate Bridge in San Francisco as the world's longest suspension bridge until the Humber Bridge was completed in 1981 in Kingston upon Hull, England.

Vesak (Wesak; Buddha's Birthday)
April–May; full moon of Vaisakha

This is the holiest of Buddhist holy days, celebrating the Buddha's birth, enlightenment, and death, or attaining of Nirvana. While these anniversaries are observed in all Buddhist countries, they are not always celebrated on the same day. In Theravada Buddhist countries, all three anniversaries are marked on the full moon of the sixth month. In Japan and other Mahayana Buddhist countries, the three anniversaries are usually observed on separate days—the birth on April 8, the enlightenment on December 8, and the death on February 15.

Vesak is a public holiday in many countries, including Thailand, Indonesia, Korea, and Singapore.

This celebration differs from country to country, but generally activities are centered on the Buddhist temples, where people gather to listen to sermons by the monks. In the evening, there are candle-lit processions around the temples. Homes are also decorated with paper lanterns and oil lamps. Because it's considered important to practice the virtues of kindness to all living things, it's traditional in some countries to free caged birds on this day. In some areas, booths are set up along streets to dispense food. In Myanmar they water the Bodhi tree with blessed water and chant prayers around it.

The Buddha was born at Lumbini, Nepal, an isolated spot near the border with India, and Lumbini is one of the most sacred pilgrimage destinations for Buddhists, especially on Vesak. A stone pillar erected in 250 B.C. by the Indian emperor Ashoka designates the birthplace, and a brick temple contains carvings depicting the birth. Another center of celebrations in Nepal is the Swayambhunath temple, built about 2,000 years ago. On this day it is constantly circled by a procession of pilgrims. The lamas in colorful silk robes dance around the stupa (temple) while musicians play. On this day each year, the stupa's collection of rare thangkas (embroidered religious scrolls) and mandalas (geometrical and astrological representations of the world) are shown on the southern wall of the stupa courtyard.

Sarnath, India, is the place where the Buddha preached his first sermon, and a big fair and a procession of relics of the Buddha highlight the day there. Bodh Gaya (or Buddh Gaya) in the state of Bihar is also the site of special celebrations. It was here that the prince Siddhartha Gautama sat under the Bodhi tree, attained enlightenment, and became known as the Buddha, meaning the 'Enlightened One.'

Gautama was born about 563 B.C. into a regal family and was brought up in great luxury. At the age of twenty-nine, distressed by the misery of mankind, he renounced his princely life and his wife and infant son to become a wandering ascetic and to search for a path that would give relief from suffering. For six years he practiced severe austerities, eating little. But he realized that self-mortification wasn't leading him to what he sought. One morning, sitting in deep meditation, under a ficus tree now called the Bodhi tree, he achieved enlightenment, or awakening. This was at Bodh Gaya in about 528 B.C., Gautama was thirty-five years old. In the years that followed, he laid down rules of ethics (see MAGHA PUJA) and condemned the caste system. He taught that the aim of religion is to free oneself of worldly fetters in order to attain enlightenment or Nirvana, a condition of freedom from sorrow and selfish desire. The Buddha trained large numbers of disciples to continue his work. He died in about 483 B.C.

From its start in northern India, Buddhism spread throughout Asia. The religion grew especially after Ashoka, the first great emperor of India, adopted it as his religion in the third century B.C. and traveled about preaching and building hospitals and monasteries. He also sent his son, Mahinda, to preach the tenets of Buddhism in Sri Lanka (See PONSON). The Buddhism practiced in Southeast Asia is the oldest form of the religion, known as Theravada Buddhism, or 'The Way of the Elders.' As Buddhism went north, into Nepal, Bhutan, Tibet, China, Korea, and then Japan, it took a different form called Mahayanna Buddhism, or 'The Great Vehicle.'

Vesak or Wesak is also known as **Waicak**, **Vesakha Puja** (Thailand), **Buddha Jayanti** (Nepal, India), **Phat Dan Day** (Vietnam), **Buddha Purnima** (India), **Full Moon of Waso** or **Kason** (Myanmar), **Vixakha Bouxa** (Laos) and sometimes the **Feast of the Lanterns**.

See also BUN BANG FAI, HANA MATSURI, and SONGKRAN (PI MAI).

Veterans Day
November 11; second Sunday in November in Great Britain
On November 11, 1918, the armistice between the Allied and Central Powers that halted the fighting in World War I was signed in Marshal Ferdinand Foch's railroad car in the Forest of Compiègne, France. In the United States, the name **Armistice Day** was changed to Veterans Day in 1954 to honor those who have served their country in other wars as well. In Great Britain, Canada, and France, it is dedicated primarily to those who died in both World Wars. The British call it **Remembrance Day**, or **Poppy Day**, for the red paper flowers sold by the British Legion to benefit veterans. The association of poppies with World War I was popularized by the poet John McCrae, who wrote the lines "In Flanders fields the poppies blow/ Between the crosses, row on row." Flanders was the site of heavy fighting during the war, and for many who wrote about it later, the poppy came to symbolize both the beauty of the landscape and the blood that was shed there. Poppies are sold by veterans' organizations in most countries. An attempt in 1971 to make Veterans Day conform to the "Monday Holiday Law" by observing it on the fourth Monday in October triggered widespread resistance, and seven years later it was moved back to the traditional November 11 date. In many places the eleventh day of the eleventh month is celebrated by observing a two-minute silence at 11:00 in the morning, the hour at which the hostilities ceased.

Victoria Day *See* Commonwealth Day

Victory Day (Our Lady of Victories Day)
September 8
A national holiday in Malta in celebration of the lifting of two sieges:

In 1565, the Hospitallers, or the Knights of the Order of St. John of Jerusalem, with 6,000-9,000

men, held Malta against a four-month siege by the some 29,000 Ottoman Turks. The onslaught left half the knights dead, but the Turks didn't fare well either—the knights used the heads of Turkish captives as cannonballs, and the defeat of the Turks humbled the Ottoman Empire. (Malta was under the control of the knights, a religious and military order of the Roman Catholic Church dedicated to tending the sick and poor, and warring against Muslims, from 1530 until June 1798, when Napoleon took possession of the island.)

During World War II, the island fought off Axis powers (Germany and Italy) despite three years of severe air bombardment. In April 1942, air-raid alerts averaged about ten a day; the ruins included the Royal Opera House in Valletta , destroyed by a German bomb. British Prime Minister Winston Churchill called Malta "our only unsinkable aircraft carrier." On April 15, 1942, England's King George VI awarded the island of Malta the George Cross, Britain's highest decoration for civilian gallantry, to "honour her brave people . . . to bear witness to a heroism and devotion which will long be famous in history." This was the first time a medal was conferred on any part of the commonwealth. At this time, Britain also declared that self-government would be restored at the end of hostilities.

The holiday is celebrated with parades, fireworks, and a colorful regatta and boat races in the Grand Harbour at Valletta. A highlight of the boat races is that of the *dgnajsas*, oared taxi boats with painted designs. They are thought to date back to Phoenician times (800 BC).

See also INDEPENDENCE DAY, MALTA.

Victory over Japan Day *See* V-J Day

Vidalia Onion Festival
Third weekend in May
No tears here: a tribute to Georgia's state vegetable, the sweet Vidalia onion, said to be burp-free, good for the digestion, *and* tearless. The festival is held in Vidalia (nearby Glenville has a rival onion festival, usually a week earlier) at the height of the harvest season, which extends from mid-April to early June.

This onion is an interesting vegetable, officially the F-1 hybrid yellow granex, a round white onion with a yellow skin. Local folks hail it as the "world's sweetest onion," and, in fact, it has a sugar content of 12.5 percent, making it as sweet as a Valencia orange. If the seed is planted anywhere but Georgia, however, it becomes a normal sharp-tasting onion probably due to the soil. Therefore, the name Vidalia may be given only to onions grown in thirteen Georgia counties and parts of seven more (by act of the state legislature and federal directive).

According to a local story, Vidalia onions have been known since 1931, when a farmer discovered the onions didn't make him cry and so got a premium price for them even in the Depression. But they didn't get widely known until Delbert Bland, of Bland Farms, a big onion producer, started a marketing campaign and mail-order onion business in 1984. In 1990, the sweet-onion business in Georgia amounted to about $35 million.

The celebration of the onion includes standard festival fare—music, a street dance, a rodeo, and sports tournaments. It also has a Vidalia Onion Masquerade Contest, and a competition for Miss Vidalia Onion (a beautiful high school or college woman). In 1991, other beauty pageant winners were Miss Vidalia Onion Seed (age 4), Miss Vidalia Onion Sprout (age 9), and Junior Miss Vidalia Onion (age 12). Finally, there are onion eating contests, and a Vidalia Onion Cook-Off, which produces cakes, breads, and muffins made with onions.

Vienna Festival
May–June

This six-week festival, founded in 1951, regularly attracts more than a million people to the city of Vienna, Austria. There are over one thousand performances of music, opera, ballet, and drama by some of the best known Austrian and foreign companies in the world-including the Royal Shakespeare Company, the Merce Cunningham Dance Company, the Martha Graham Dance Company, the Noh Theater of Japan, and the Malegot Ballet of St. Petersburg.

Like the EDINBURGH FESTIVAL, the Vienna Festival also includes many "fringe" events offered by independent theater, dance, and musical groups.

Vinegrower's Day
First half of February

This pre-harvest vineyard festival in Bulgaria is the day on which the vines are pruned and sprinkled with wine. Ritual songs and dances are performed in hopes of a plentiful grape harvest. In some areas, a "Vine King" is crowned with a wreath of twigs from the vineyards. Everyone treats him with great respect, for it is believed that fertility depends on the King's happiness.

Participation in the **Trifon Zarezan** festivities

is something that both locals and foreign tourists look forward to. Visits to well-known Bulgarian vineyards are organized, the vines are pruned, and guests are given an opportunity to sample the local wine and foods.

Virginia Scottish Games
Fourth weekend in July

Alexandria, Virginia was founded by Scotsmen in 1749 and named for Scottish merchant John Alexander. The city celebrates its Scottish heritage with a two-day Celtic country fair featuring bagpipe bands, world-class athletes, Celtic dancers, a national fiddling championship, and an international harp competition.

One of the most colorful attractions is the Highland dancing, which involves hundreds of competitors ranging in age from pre-schoolers to adults. The highlight of the athletic contests is the caber toss (see HIGHLAND GAMES), which is part of a seven-event competition known as the Highland Heptathlon. These contests trace their origins to the ancient Highland games of Northern Scotland, where military chiefs demonstrated their strength at annual clan gatherings.

Virgin Islands Carnival
April

Unlike CARNIVAL in New Orleans, Brazil, and elsewhere in the world, where it is a pre-Lenten celebration, the Virgin Islands Carnival is held after EASTER, usually near the end of April. It dates back to the days when Danish plantation owners gave their slaves time off to celebrate the end of the sugar cane harvest. Although the first Carnival in 1912 was a great success, it wasn't held again for four decades. Since 1952 it has been an annual event in the capital city of Charlotte Amalie on the island of St. Thomas.

Preliminary events begin a week or more beforehand, and the official Carnival period runs from Sunday until midnight the following Saturday. The celebrations include calypso competitions, steel bands, and dancing in the streets. The climax comes on Saturday with the grand carnival parade, featuring limbo dancers, masked figures, and mock stick-fights between Carib Indians and "Zulus."

Virgin of the Pillar, Feast of the
October 12

According to an ancient legend, the Virgin Mary appeared to Santiago, or St. James the Apostle, when he was in Saragossa, Spain. She spoke to him from the top of a pillar, which he interpreted as a sign that he should build a chapel where the column stood. *Nuestra Señora del Pilar* has since become a major pilgrimage center.

The ten-day feast of the Virgin of the Pillar is observed with special Masses and processions in honor of *La Virgen*. The *Gigantes*—giant cardboard and canvas figures concealing the men who dance behind them—are brought out especially for the occasion. Often representing Spanish kings and queens or famous literary and historical figures, they can be twenty to thirty feet tall. The *cabezudos* or 'big heads', on the other hand, are grotesque puppets with huge heads which are meant to poke fun at certain professions or personalities. Also characteristic of the festival are *jota* contests in which Aragon's regional folk dance is performed to the accompaniment of guitars, mandolins, and lutes. (See also ST. JAMES'S DAY.)

Visitation, Feast of the

May 31, Roman Catholic, Protestant; July 2, Church of England

On this day churches in the West commemorate the Virgin Mary's visit to her cousin Elizabeth. After learning that she was to be the mother of Jesus, Mary went into the mountains of Judea to see her cousin, the barren wife of Zechariah, who had conceived a son who would come to be known as John the Baptist. According to the Gospel of Luke, Elizabeth's baby "leaped in her womb" (1:41) at the sound of Mary's voice. It was at this moment, according to the pious belief of some Roman Catholics, that John the Baptist was cleansed from original sin and filled with heavenly grace. Mary stayed with Elizabeth for three months and returned home just before John was born.

See also ST. ELIZABETH, FEAST OF

Visvakarma Puja

End of Bhadrapada, the sixth Hindu month

Dedicated to Visvakarma, the patron god of all Hindu artisans, the **Festival of Tools** is a workers' holiday dedicated to each individual's most important tool or instrument. A pitcher representing the god is set in a place of honor in every home and shop, and before it the people lay their most important tool. Students might place one of their schoolbooks there, musicians would place the instrument they play, artists would put their favorite brushes before the pitcher, tailors their scissors, gardeners their rakes, fishermen their nets, etc. A candle is lit in front of the pitcher, and sometimes incense is burned or scented water is sprinkled over the tool. Workers give thanks for their tools and implore Visvakarma's help in plying their trade.

After this ceremony is over, people gather in parks or public places and spend the rest of the day in games and feasting.

V-J Day (Victory over Japan Day)
August 14

The anniversary of Japan's surrender to the Allies in 1945, ending World War II. The atomic bombs dropped on Hiroshima on Aug. 6 and Nagasaki on Aug. 9, and the Soviet Union's invasion of Manchuria in the previous week made the surrender inevitable. The announcement of the surrender by President Harry S Truman set off street celebrations from coast to coast in the United States. In New York City, Times Square was jammed with people embracing and dancing. In Naples, Italy, the Andrews Sisters had just finished singing "Don't Sit Under the Apple Tree" to U.S. troops when Maxine Andrews was given a slip of paper and read the news; joyous bedlam ensued. The official end of the war didn't come until Sept. 2, when Gen. Douglas MacArthur accepted the Japanese surrender from Gen. Yoshijiro Umezu aboard the U.S.S. Missouri in Tokyo Bay. He said, "Today the guns are silent. A great tragedy has ended . . . The holy mission has been completed." President Truman declared Sep. 2 as official V-J Day.

V-J Day is a legal holiday only in the state of Rhode Island, where it is called Victory Day. In Connecticut, the tiny village of Moosup (a section of the town of Plainfield) claims to have the only V-J Day parade in the country. Sponsored by the local American Legion post, it began small in 1961 and now features more than 200 units— marching bands, floats, civic groups, color guards, and Gold Star Mothers (women who lost a son or daughter in war)—and attracts some 10,000 spectators.

Vlöggelen

Between March 22 and April 25; Easter Sunday and Monday

As practiced in the eastern Netherlands village of Ootmarsum, the Vlöggelen or **Winging Ceremony** is believed to be the remnant of an ancient spring fertility rite. It is a ritualistic dance through the narrow cobbled streets performed by the villagers, linked to form a human chain that advances slowly, "like birds on the wing." The dancers enter the front doors of shops, inns, farmhouses, and barns, emerging through the back doors to the melody of an old EASTER hymn with so many verses that the dancers must read the words pinned to the back of the person in front of them.

Von Steuben Day
September 17; fourth Sunday in September

Baron Friedrich Wilhelm Ludolf Gerhard Augustus von Steuben (1730–1794) was an experienced Prussian soldier who came to America in 1777 and volunteered to serve in the Continental army without rank or pay. He was sent to join General George Washington at Valley Forge, where he trained Washington's men in the intricacies of military drill, earning himself the sobriquet "Drill Master of the American Revolution." Steuben led one of Washington's divisions at the Battle of Yorktown (see YORKTOWN DAY), and his experience in siege warfare helped the American troops achieve the victory that soon brought the Revolutionary War to an end. In gratitude for his contributions, he was granted American citizenship and given a large piece of land in the Mohawk Valley and a yearly pension.

Steuben's birthday, September 17, was first celebrated by members of the Steuben Society of America, an organization founded in 1919 by U. S. citizens of German descent. The Society now has branches in many states, who observe the anniversary with patriotic exercises. At Valley Forge State Park in Pennsylvania, there is a von Steuben birthday celebration featuring German music and speeches at the monument to him erected in 1915. There is also a Steuben Day parade in New York City on the Saturday following September 17; in Philadelphia on the fourth Sunday in September; and in Chicago on or near the Prussian hero's birthday. These parades are usually large and colorful, with boys in lederhosen (leather shorts with suspenders) and girls in dirndls (skirts gathered at the waistband, with a bib top) marching to the sounds of polka-playing bands and martial music.

Vossa *See* **Waso**

W

Waitangi Day
February 6

A national public holiday in New Zealand, February 6 commemorates the signing of the 1840 Treaty of Waitangi, in which the Maori natives agreed to co-exist peacefully with the European settlers. Although it was first declared a national day of commemoration in 1960, Waitangi Day was not observed as a public holiday outside the North Island until it became **New Zealand Day** in 1973. It was observed as such until 1976, when it again became known as Waitangi Day.

The town of Waitangi is located on the Bay of Islands at the northern end of the North Island, and the day on which the treaty was signed is observed there by the Royal New Zealand Navy and the Maoris each year.

Walpurgis Night (Walpurgisnacht)
April 30

People who lived in the Harz Mountains of Germany believed for many centuries that witches rode across the sky on the eve of St. Walpurga's Day to hold a coven on Brocken Mountain. To frighten them off, they rang church bells, banged pots and pans, and lit torches topped with hemlock, rosemary, and juniper. The legend of Walpurgis Night is still celebrated in Germany, Austria, and Scandinavia with bonfires and other festivities designed to welcome spring by warding off demons, disaster, and darkness.

St. Walpurga (or Walburga) was an eighth century English nun who later became a German abbess. She is the patron saint against dog bites and hydrophobia (rabies). On the eve of May 1 her remains were moved from Heidenheim to Eichstätt, Germany, where her shrine became a popular place of pilgrimage. Legend has it that the rocks at Eichstätt give off a miraculous oil possessing curative powers. She is the saint who protects against magic.

Wangala (Hundred Drums Festival)
Late fall, after harvest

A festival that lasts several days and celebrates the harvest, held in the Garo Hills of the state of Meghalaya in northeastern India. It involves a ceremony led by the village priest, climaxing in a dance to the sound of 100 drums and the music of gongs, flutes, and trumpets.

Waratambar
August 24

Waratambar, or THANKSGIVING Day, is observed by the Christian population of Papua New Guinea, which is about half of its two million people. It is a day for giving thanks to the Lord for what Christianity has done for people throughout the world. Farmers and their families take time off work to participate in the celebration, which focuses on singing and dancing. The songs express an appreciation of and closeness to nature and all creatures; the dances dramatize tribal wars. Costumes worn by the dancers are usually hand made of ferns, moss, leaves, flowers, and other natural materials.

Waratambar is observed on different days in August in different provinces. In New Ireland, the date is August 24.

Washington's Birthday
February 22 or third Monday in February

George Washington's birthday was not always celebrated in the United States as widely as it is today. The date itself was in question for a while, since the Gregorian calendar was adopted in England during Washington's lifetime and this shifted his birthday from February 11 to February 22 (see OLD CHRISTMAS DAY). Then there was a period when Washington's association with the Federalist party made the Antifederalists (or Jeffersonian Republicans) uncomfortable, and they put a damper on any official celebrations. It wasn't until Washington's death in 1799 that such feelings disappeared and he was regarded as a national hero.

Washington's Birthday Celebration in Los Dos Laredos

As commander-in-chief of the Continental Army during the American Revolution and as the first president of the United States, George Washington looms large in American literature and legend. By the centennial of his birth in 1832, celebrations were firmly established, and his name had been given not only to the nation's capital, but to a state and more than twenty cities and towns. While the third Monday in February is observed as Washington's Birthday by the federal government and in most states, some combine it with the February birthday of another famous American president, Abraham Lincoln, and call it **Washington-Lincoln Day** or PRESIDENTS' DAY.

At his death Washington was a lieutenant general, then the highest military rank in the United States. In 1799 Congress had established the nation's highest military title: General of the Armies of the United States, intending it for him, but he never received it. Subsequently, he was outranked by many U.S. Army officers, so in 1976 Congress finally granted it to him. He is now the senior general officer on Army rolls; General John J. Pershing is the only other officer to have been so honored—he received it in September 1919 for his work during World War I.

See also GEORGE WASHINGTON'S BIRTHDAY IN ALEXANDRIA and WASHINGTON'S BIRTHDAY CELEBRATION IN LOS DOS LAREDOS.

Washington's Birthday Celebration in Los Dos Laredos
Mid–February (February 14–23 in 1992)

A ten day celebration in honor of George Washington, held since 1898 by Laredo, Tex., and its sister city on the other side of the Mexican border, Nuevo Laredo. The two Laredos (*los dos Laredos*) are linked by history and by three bridges across the Rio Grande. Founded by the Spanish in 1755, Laredo has been under seven different national flags. Both cities also celebrate Mexican Independence Day during Expomex in September.

Washington's birthday events include dances, fireworks, mariachi music, an international bike race, a five-kilometer race, a waiters' race, a jalapeño-eating contest, and parades with lavishly decorated floats.

Washington State Apple Blossom Festival
May

The oldest blossom festival in the United States, this event has been held annually in Wenatchee, Washington since 1920 (with the exception of the World War II years). It began with a suggestion from Mrs. E. Wagner, a Wenatchee resident who wanted to see something similar to the celebration held in her native New Zealand when the apple orchards were in bloom. Originally called **Blossom Days**, the event grew in size and popularity until it reached its current status as an eleven-day festival drawing up to 100,000 spectators.

In 1947 the name of the festival was officially changed from the **Wenatchee Apple Blossom Festival** to its present name, although it continues to be held in Wenatchee, the "Apple Capital of the World." In addition to seeing the Wenatchee Valley orchards in full bloom, the events include apple relay races, a horse show, a foodfest, and a marching band competition. In 1967 the Aomori Apple Blossom Festival in Japan became Wenatchee's "sister festival," and the two towns have exchanged visitors a number of times.

Waso (Buddhist Rains Retreat)
June/July–September/October; Full moon of Asadha (or Waso) to full moon of Asvina (or Thadingyut)

A three-month period when monks remain in monasteries to study and meditate. At other times of the year, monks wander the countryside, but this is the time of monsoons in Southeast Asia, and the Buddha chose this period for retreat and prayer so they wouldn't walk across fields and damage young rice plants. However, even in China, Japan, and Korea, countries that don't have monsoons, the Waso is observed. It is also known as the **Buddhist Lent**. In Cambodia and India it is called **Vassa** or **Vossa**. In Burma and Thailand it is called **Phansa**, **Waso**, **Wasa**, or **Wazo Full Moon Day**; and in Laos, **Vatsa**.

The months are considered a time of restraint and abstinence. Weddings are not celebrated, and people try to avoid moving to new homes. Many young men enter the priesthood just for the retreat period, and therefore many ordinations take place. The new young monks have their heads shaved and washed with saffron, and they are given yellow robes. Many lay people attend the monasteries for instruction.

The day just prior to the retreat commemorates the Buddha's first sermon to his five disciples, forty-nine days after his enlightenment.

In Thailand, the start of the retreat, called Khao Phansa, is observed in the northeastern city of Ubon Ratchathani with the Candle Festival, in which elaborately carved beeswax candles in the shapes of birds and other figures, several yards high, are paraded and then presented to the temples. In many places, a beeswax candle is lit at the beginning of Waso and kept burning throughout the period. In Saraburi, people offer flowers and incense to monks who walk to the hilltop Shrine of the Holy Footprint where they present the offerings as tribute. It is traditional everywhere for people to bring food and other necessities to the monasteries.

The end of this period called **Ok-Barnsa** or **Full Moon Day of Thadingyut,** is a time of thanksgiving to the monks, and also, according to legend, the time when the Buddha returned to earth after visiting his mother in heaven and preaching to her for three months. During the month of celebration (known as Kathin), lay people present monks with new robes and other items for the coming year.

Boat races are held on the rivers in Laos at Vientiane, Luang Phabang and Savannakhet, and in Thailand at numerous places. A special ceremony takes place in Bangkok when elaborate golden royal barges, rowed by oarsmen in scarlet, proceed to Wat Arun (the Temple of Dawn), where the king presents robes to the monks.

At Sakon Nakhon in northeastern Thailand, people build temples and shrines from beeswax and parade them through the streets to present them at temples. After the presentations, there are regattas and general festivities.

In Myanmar (formerly Burma), a Festival of Lights called the **Tassaung Daing Festival** is held at this time, when the moon is full. Homes are lit with paper lanterns, and all-night performances are staged by dancers, comedians, and musicians. A major event of the festival is an all-night weaving contest at the Shwe Dagon pagoda in Yangon (Rangoon); young unmarried women spend the night weaving robes, and at dawn they are offered to images of the Buddha at the pagoda. Similar weaving competitions are held throughout the country.

Water-Drawing Festival
Beginning between September 20 and October 18; night following the first day of Sukkot and each night of the festival thereafter
The name of this ancient Jewish festival comes from Isaiah 12:3, which says, "Therefore with joy shall ye draw water out of the wells of salvation." The water-drawing ceremony, also known as **Simhat bet Ha-sho'evah**, was a matter of dispute between Pharisees, who regarded it as an oral tradition handed down from Sinai, and the

Sadducees, who saw no basis for it and often showed outright contempt for the entire ritual. The more the Sadducees opposed it, the more emphasis the Pharisees placed on the water libation, which was considered a particularly joyful occasion and was performed in the temple on the night following the first day of SUKKOT and then on each remaining night of the festival. Huge bonfires were lit throughout Jerusalem and the people stayed up dancing and singing for most of the night, often dozing off on each other's shoulders.

There have been attempts to revive the water-drawing festival in a more modern form, primarily among Israel's contemporary *kibbutzim* or agricultural communities.

See also OMIZUTORI MATSURI.

Watermelon Eating and Seed Spitting Contest
Second Sunday in September
The only event of its kind sanctioned by the United States Bureau of Agriculture, the Watermelon Eating and Seed Spitting Contest held since 1965 in Pardeeville, Wisconsin is attended by up to nine thousand people—eaters, spitters, and spectators. It takes eight people an entire day to cut up the 4500-5000 watermelons used in the contest. This festival also includes a watermelon volleyball competition, watermelon carving and growing contests, a parade, and a T-shirt design contest. But it is the eating and spitting contests that most people come to see. To date, the watermelon eating record is 3.6 seconds for a two-pound slice. The spitting record is forty-eight feet.

Tongue-in-cheek rules for the spitting contest are strictly enforced: professional tobacco spitters are not eligible; denture wearers must abide by the judge's decision if their teeth go further than the seed; and no one is allowed to propel their seeds through a pipe, tube, or other hollow object. There is a team spitting competition, a couples' spitting competition, and separate competitions for men and women.

Watermelon Thump
Last weekend in June
A celebration of the watermelon harvest in Luling, Tex. The chief watermelon-related events are watermelon judging, a watermelon auction, watermelon-eating competitions, and watermelon seed-spitting contests leading to a Championship Seed Spit-Off. Among other activities are a parade, the coronation of the Watermelon Thump Queen, a

fiddlers' contest, a carnival, and golf, baseball, and bowling tournaments.

Water-Splashing Festival *See* **Songkran**

Wayne Chicken Show
Second Saturday in July

This lighthearted one-day event takes place in Wayne, Nebraska, a town that is known primarily as a pork capital. But, as one of the festival's organizers admits, "We didn't want to make fun of pigs," and since there were some egg processing plants and chicken farms in the area who were willing to contribute to the cause, the Wayne Chicken Show was "hatched" in 1981. Billed as an "eggszotic eggstravaganza," up to 10,000 people witness competitions in rooster crowing, chicken flying, egg dropping and catching, and a national cluck-off whose winner has appeared on the Tonight Show with Johnny Carson. There are prizes for the oddest egg, the most beautiful beak, and the best chicken legs on a human. The eggs and chefs for the free "omelette feed" are donated by egg producers in the area.

W. C. Handy Music Festival
First full week of August

A festival honoring the "Father of the Blues" in the Alabama Quad-Cities of Florence, Muscle Shoals, Sheffield, and Tuscumbia in the northwestern part of the state known as Muscle Shoals. William Christopher Handy, the son and grandson of ministers, was born in 1873 in Florence, took an early interest in music and went on to become a prolific composer, performer, orchestra leader, and music publisher despite his father's ministerial influence. In 1911, he wrote an election campaign song for Mayor Edward H. "Boss" Crump of Memphis, Tenn., that became known as the *Memphis Blues* and was one of the works that made him famous. Others included the classic *St. Louis Blues, Beale Street Blues*, and *Careless Love*.

Handy, working in the period of transition from ragtime to jazz, fused elements of black folk music with ragtime to create distinctive blues pieces. He also organized a publishing firm, issued anthologies of black spirituals and blues and studies of American black musicians, and wrote his autobiography, *Father of the Blues*, published in 1941. He expressed his philosophy with these words: "Life is like this old trumpet of mine. If you don't put something into it, you don't get nothing out." When Handy died in 1958, a Harlem minister said, "Gabriel now has an understudy."

The festival celebrates not only Handy's musi-

cal heritage but also the musical roots of spirituals and jazz. Opening ceremonies are at the W. C. Handy Home & Museum, a log cabin housing Handy's collected papers and memorabilia. His piano and trumpet are on display.

Throughout the festival there is music by nationally known musicians night and day, street dancing, a foot race, folk art exhibits, and music workshops. Events are held in such nontraditional locations as ball fields, parks, and nursing homes, and concerts are performed in the church where Handy's father and grandfather served as pastor, and in restaurants and clubs. The small community of Muscle Shoals, where several events are held, is known in music circles for having given birth to the "Muscle Shoals Sound" through a recording studio that was set up in 1965. Artists as varied as Aretha Franklin, Peggy Lee, Liza Minelli, Bob Seger, and the Rolling Stones have recorded here.

Wedding Festivities in Galicnik, Macedonia
July 12

It was common practice at one time in the former Yugoslavia for the men to leave their villages or even to emigrate in search of higher-paying work. On a specific day they would all return to their villages and mass wedding celebrations would be held. Galicnik is one of the last strongholds of this ancient custom, and on **St. Peter's Day** each year a multiple wedding feast is held. It begins on St. Peter's Eve with a torchlight procession of brides to three fountains where water is drawn for a purification ceremony. The most interesting feature of the wedding ceremony itself is that brides, bridegrooms, and guests knock their heads together. The first night of the marriage is spent in a complicated hide-and-seek game and the newlyweds do not sleep together. There is a great feast on the second day and that night the marriages are consummated.

Because the village of Galicnik is cut off from the rest of the world by snow for much of the winter, the village is transformed during the summer, when many former residents and tourists come for the July 12 wedding festivities. Similar village wedding ceremonies are held in Ljubljana at the end of July and in Bled in mid-August.

Weeks, Feast of *See* **Shavuot**

Wesak *See* **Vesak**

West Virginia Day
June 20

A state holiday in West Virginia to celebrate its joining the Union in 1863 as the thirty-fifth state. The creation of the state was a result of the Civil War. The settlers of western Virginia defied the state's vote to secede from the Union, and President Lincoln justified the "secession" of West Virginia from Virginia as a war act. He proclaimed its statehood in April of 1863 and on June 20 West Virginia formally entered the Union as an anti-slave state. The western Virginians' movement for independence from Virginia had actually started long before the Civil War; as early as 1776, western Virginians had the idea of establishing a separate colony called Vandalia, named for Queen Charlotte, wife of British King George III, who believed herself to be a descendant of the Vandals of early Europe.

The day is marked with ceremonies at the state capitol in Charleston and at the West Virginia Independence Hall in Wheeling. It was there that the conventions were held to declare West Virginia's independence from Virginia.

West Virginia Italian Heritage Festival
Labor Day weekend

A three-day street festival in Clarksburg, W. Va., celebrating Italian culture. The festival began in 1979 and attracts from 175,000 to 200,000 visitors for tastes of food, music, dance, crafts, and sports. A queen, known as Regina Maria, reigns over the festivities. Distinctively Italian events are a bocci tournament, a homemade wine contest, a pasta cookoff (prizes for the best red sauce and best white sauce) for both professional and amateur cooks, and Italian religious observances. There are also strolling musicians, organ grinders, and puppeteers.

About 40 percent of Clarskburg's population is of Italian descent. Italians came here around the turn of the century for plentiful coal-mining jobs and because the mountains reminded them of their homes in northern Italy.

West Virginia Strawberry Festival
Usually late May or early June

A long-standing, good-tasting tradition in Buckhannon, W. Va., the center of a strawberry-growing region. The festival began in 1936, was suspended during World War II, and celebrated its 50th anniversary in 1991 with a block-long strawberry shortcake. Visitors, who numbered about 100,000, got free samples.

The festival focuses on what can be done culinarily to the strawberry: there are pancake breakfasts with strawberry jam, strawberry syrup, and fresh strawberries. There's a strawberry recipe contest, with recipes for such delights as strawberry cakes, pies, and cookies, kiwi-and-strawberry pizza, chicken glazed with strawberries, and strawberry stirring sticks (take drinking straws and fill with strawberries). The festival begins with a blessing of the berries, and moves on to the coronation of a king and queen, a Strawberry Party Gras (a street festival of music and dancing), strawberry auctions, the sweetest strawberry tasting contest, an antique-car show, and contests and parades.

Whale Festival
March

In Mendocino, Fort Bragg, and Gualala, on the northern coast of California, festivals to watch migrating whales are held on varying weekends.

At Mendocino, local vintners host a wine tasting, and there are also marine art exhibits, music, and lighthouse tours.

Fort Bragg offers tasting of brews from state-wide micro-breweries. Local restaurants compete in a chowder contest, and there is live music. Fort Bragg is also the home of what it calls the WORLD'S LARGEST SALMON BARBECUE.

Gualala has wine tastings, food buffets, an art show, photo contest, children's activities, and music.

Wheat Harvest
Late summer

In Transylvania, a region of Romania that was at one time part of Hungary, the gathering of the wheat harvest in late summer reflects traditional customs that have been largely supplanted by modern agricultural methods elsewhere. Here the owner of a farm must still rely on his friends and neighbors to gather his crops. When the last sheaf is harvested, a wreath made of wheat and wild flowers is taken to the farmer's house by young girls in traditional dress. The other farm laborers lie in wait for the procession, and ambush them by drenching everyone in water. When the landowner first appears in the harvest field, the harvesters tie him up and demand a ransom for his release.

When the procession arrives at the landowner's house, poems in his honor are recited. The wreath is hung in a special place where it will remain until the next harvest. There is a feast for everyone, followed by dancing to the music of a gypsy band. A special delicacy associated with the harvest feast is gingerbread cookies. In fact, elaborately shaped and decorated gingerbread cookies are considered a part of the region's folk art tradition.

Wheat Harvest Festival in Provins, France
Last weekend of August

Like most harvest festivals, which date back to ancient Roman times, the Wheat Harvest Festival in Provins, a small village in central France honors Ceres, the ancient goddess of wheat and mother of the earth. On the last Saturday and Sunday of August, the villagers celebrate a plentiful harvest by decorating their homes and shops with wheat and wildflowers. There are also exhibits of antique farming tools and parades featuring harvest floats pulled by tractors. The villagers reenact ancient rituals involving wheat and perform demonstrations of how the grain is separated, ground, and baked to make bread.

Whe'wahchee (Dance of Thanksgiving)
First full moon of August

The annual dance and celebration of the Omaha Indian tribe of Nebraska, held on the Omaha Reservation in northeastern Nebraska. The 188th dance was held in 1991, making this the oldest powwow in the United States. Lewis and Clark encountered the Omahas in 1803 and mentioned the **Omaha Dance of Thanksgiving** in their journal. The time of the festival is set for the first full moon in August, because a full moon traditionally guarantees no rain.

Whistlers Convention, National
Second or third weekend in April

A convocation of whistlers in Louisburg, N.C., highlighted by whistlers' contests for children, teenagers, and adults. Held since 1974, it grew out of a folk festival.

The convention features a school for whistlers, a concert in which the performer is usually someone who can both sing and whistle, and a processional march—a very short affair led by a man dressed as Benjamin Franklin (because the county is named for him). The town serves an annual salt herring breakfast on the day of the contest; the menu is salt herring, hush puppies, and sweet potatoes, all cooked in boiling pork fat. On the Sunday after the contest, whistlers whistle at church services and on Monday give demonstrations in schools.

The grand champion in 1992 was Sean Lomax

of Murrieta, Calif., who whistled the First Movement of Beethoven's Fifth Symphony and a selection from Bizet's *Carmen*. This is serious whistling.

This convention isn't a big event, but it is the only one in the United States, and in 1992 it attracted people from ten states and three Canadian provinces. In addition, Masaaki Moku, a whistler from Osaka, Japan, was there; he whistled the Japanese national anthem for the contest audience.

White Nights
June 21–29

The time of year in St. Petersburg (formerly Leningrad), Russia, when the nights are so short that the sky appears white, or light grey, and twilight lasts only thirty or forty minutes. The city, with its many buildings painted in pastel shades of lavender, green, pink, and yellow, has a particularly beautiful charm in the white nights. The time is celebrated with a fine-arts festival that focuses on ballet and folk dancing but also includes opera and musical theater. The Kirov Opera and Ballet Theatre presents its best productions of classical and Soviet ballets, and traditionally there are also performances by students of St. Petersburg's famous Vaganova School of Choreography. Concerts are given by the Symphony Orchestra of the Leningrad Philharmonic. About 250,000 attend each year.

White Sunday
Second Sunday in October

This is a special day celebrated in the Christian churches of Samoa to honor children. Every child dresses in white and wears a crown of white frangipani blossoms. The children line up and walk to church, carrying banners and singing hymns, while their parents wait for them inside. Instead of the usual sermon, the children present short dramatizations of Bible stories such as "the good Samaritan," "Noah's ark," and "the prodigal son." After the performance is over, the children return to their homes, where their parents serve them a feast that includes roast pig, bananas, taro, coconuts, and cakes. They are allowed to eat all they want, and in a reversal of the usual custom, **Lotu-A-Tamaiti** is the one day of the year when the adults don't sit down to eat first. (See also SUNDAY SCHOOL DAY)

Whitewater Wednesday
third Wednesday in June

A day of whitewater rafting on the New River

Gorge National River in West Virginia, as well as food and musical entertainment in Oak Hill. The New River is said to rival the Colorado when it comes to whitewater thrills. On Whitewater Wednesday, thousands of people raft down the river through the breathtaking New River Gorge and under the engineering marvel, the New River Gorge Bridge.

See also Bridge Day.

Whit-Monday (Whitmonday)
Between May 11 and June 14; Monday after Whitsunday

The day after Whitsunday (PENTECOST) is known as Whit-Monday, and in Britain it is also known as the **Late May Bank Holiday**. The week that includes these two holidays, beginning on Whitsunday and ending the following Saturday, is called Whitsuntide.

Until fairly recently, Whit-Monday was one of the major holidays of the year in the Pennslvania Dutch country. In the period from 1835 to just after the Civil War, Whit-Monday was referred to as the "Dutch Fourth of July" in Lancaster, Pennsylvania, where rural people came to eat, drink, and be entertained. In Lenhartsville, another Pennsylvania Dutch town, Whit-Monday was known as **Battalion Day**, and it was characterized by music, dancing, and military musters. So much carousing went on that one Pennsylvania newspaper suggested that the name "Whitsuntide" be changed to "Whiskeytide."

Whitsunday *See* Pentecost

Whole Enchilada Fiesta
First full weekend in October

Lots of red chili, lots of corn meal, lots of cheese, and lots of people. This festival in Las Cruces, New Mexico, draws about 100,000 people who scramble to get a taste of the world's biggest enchilada. It's ten feet long and is made of 185 pounds of corn dough, sixty gallons of red chili sauce, and 175 pounds of cheese. The enchilada is prepared as the climactic Sunday afternoon event: while thousands watch and cheer, giant tortillas are lifted from seventy-five gallons of bubbling vegetable oil and smothered with the chili sauce and cheese and served. Before this grand moment, there will have been a parade, street dances, arts and crafts exhibits, and a horseshoe-pitching contest. Las Cruces is the largest business center in southern New Mexico, but its eco-

nomic foundation is agriculture, and chilis are a big crop.

See also HATCH CHILE FESTIVAL.

Wianki Festival of Wreaths
June 23

On St. John's Eve in Poland, young girls perform a ritual that can be traced back to pagan times. They weave garlands out of wild flowers, put a lit candle in the center, and set them afloat in the nearest stream. If the wreath drifts to shore, it means that the girl will never marry, but if it floats downstream, she will find a husband. If the wreath should sink, it means that the girl will die before the year is out. Since the boy who finds a wreath, according to the superstition, is destined to marry the girl who made it, boys hide in boats along the river banks and try to catch their girlfriends' wreaths as they float by.

A variation on this custom, known as the Wianki Festival of Wreaths (*wianki* means 'wreath' in Polish), is observed by Polish-Americans in Washington, D.C. on this same day every year. The wreaths are made out of fresh greens, the candles are lit at twilight, and they're set afloat in the reflecting pool in front of the Lincoln Memorial. Because there is no current, the wreaths don't drift much at all. But young men gather around the pool anyway, in the hope that the wind will blow their girlfriends' wreaths toward them.

See also SEMIK, MIDSUMMER EVE.

Wigilia
December 24

Christians in Poland, like Christians around the world, regard the entire period from CHRISTMAS EVE (December 24) to EPIPHANY (January 6) as part of the CHRISTMAS season. Although their customs and the timing of their specific Christmas celebrations may differ from village to village, it all occurs during these two weeks. The Wigilia-from the Latin *vigilare* 'to watch or keep vigil' takes place on Christmas Eve and commemorates the vigil that the shepherds kept on the night of Christ's birth. But it's very possible that the celebration goes back to pre-Christian times. Showing forgiveness and sharing food were part of the Poles' ancient WINTER SOLSTICE observance, a tradition that can still be seen in what is known as the *Gody*—the days of harmony and good will that start with the Wigilia and last until Epiphany or Three Kings Day.

Because some people still cling to the ancient belief that wandering spirits roam the land during the darkest days of the year, it is not uncommon for Poles to make an extra effort to be hospitable at Christmas time, leaving out a pan of warm water and a bowl of nuts and fruits for any unexpected visitors.

William Tell Pageant
Labor Day weekend

New Glarus, Wisconsin was settled by a group of Swiss immigrants in 1845 and is still referred to as "Little Switzerland." It is the location of several annual events designed to draw attention to the area's Swiss heritage. These include the Heidi Festival in June and the Volksfest in August. But one of the most popular is the William Tell Pageant that has been performed each year on LABOR DAY weekend since 1938.

The highlight of the William Tell story, of course, is the famous "apple scene" where the imprisoned patriot is given a chance at freedom if he can shoot an apple off his son's head. The play includes performances by the famous New Glarus yodelers and the costumed usherettes, who perform Swiss folk dances. The play is given in Swiss-German on Sunday afternoon and in English on Monday. The pageant weekend includes dancing on the green, Swiss singing, and other traditional Swiss forms of entertainment.

Will Rogers Day
November 4

The birthday of America's "cowboy philosopher" is observed as a legal holiday in Oklahoma, where he was born on November 4, 1879 when it was still the Indian Territory (see OKLAHOMA DAY). After his first appearance as a vaudeville entertainer in 1905 at Madison Square Garden, he developed a widespread reputation as a humorist. He went on to become a writer, a radio performer, and a motion picture star, best loved for his gum-chewing, homespun image.

Will Rogers died in a plane crash on August 15, 1935 while flying with the well-known aviator, Wiley Post. A monument to the two men was erected at the site of the crash near Point Barrow, Alaska. Rogers' birthday was first observed in 1947, with a celebration at the Will Rogers Memorial near the town of Claremore where he was born. Beneath the statue of Rogers at the memorial is the phrase for which he is best remembered: "I never met a man I didn't like."

Wimbledon
Late June–early July; six weeks before first Monday in August

The oldest and most prestigious tennis tournament in the world, the **Lawn Tennis Championships** at Wimbledon are held for thirteen days each summer, beginning six weeks before the first Monday in August, on the manicured courts of The All England Lawn Tennis and Croquet Club. The first competition in 1877 was supposedly an attempt to raise money to purchase a new roller for the croquet lawns, and it featured only the men's singles event. Today the world's best tennis players compete for both singles and doubles titles that are the most coveted in tennis. The event is watched on television by tennis fans all over the world, many of whom get up at dawn or conduct all-night vigils around their television sets so as not to miss a single match. Members of the English royal family often watch the finals from the Royal Box.

The Centre Court at Wimbledon, where the championships are held, is off-limits to members and everyone except the grounds staff. On the Saturday before the competition begins, four women members of the club play two or three sets to "bruise" the grass and make sure the courts are in good shape.

Wind Festival
Moon 2, Day 1

In the rural districts of Korea's Kyongsang-namdo and Kyongsang-pukto provinces, a grandmother known as *Yungdeung Mama* comes down from heaven every year on the first day of the Second Moon and returns on the twentieth day. If she brings her daughter with her, there is no trouble; but if she brings her daughter-in-law, who is an epileptic, it means that a stormy wind known as *Yungdeung Baram* will wreck ships and ruin the crops. To prevent such devastation, farmers, fishermen, and sailors offer special prayers and sacrifices to Yungdeung Mama and her daughter-in-law. Tempting foods and boiled rice are set out in the kitchen or garden, and little pieces of white paper containing the birthdates of family members are burned for good luck: the higher the ashes fly, the better the luck. Sometimes altars are made out of bamboo branches with pieces of cloth or paper tied to them. Sacrifices are laid under the altars, which remain standing until the twentieth day of the moon.

Windjammer Days
Last Wednesday—Friday in June

The annual Windjammer Days Festival in Boothbay Harbor, Maine celebrates the U.S. Coast Guard's two hundred years of service to coastal Maine. The three-day festival is also a salute to the large sailing merchant ships that once carried trade along the New England coast. The locals claim that this festival, which has been going on since 1963, was the original gathering of "tall ships," although they are for the most part sailing schooners rather than the full-rigged clipper ships and barks that have gathered in New York, Boston, and other port cities for more recent celebrations.

The festival begins with a boat parade in which the owners compete for prizes in various classes. That afternoon the coastal schooners sail into Boothbay Harbor and are met by a flotilla of local vessels with flags flying. There is a competition for Miss Windjammer and Captain Windjammer, and band concerts, lobster suppers, and street dances add to the merrymaking. The ships leave Boothbay the last morning of the festival—again watched by thousands on the water and from the shore.

In the nineteenth century the Boothbay region played an active role in the shipping trade, carrying lumber to South America and the West Indies. There was a time when more than a hundred of these coastal vessels might have been seen in Boothbay Harbor, waiting out a spell of bad weather.

Winegrowers' Festival *See Vinegrowers' Day*

Wings 'n Water Festival
Third weekend in September

This two-day event celebrates the coastal environment of southern New Jersey. It is sponsored by The Wetlands Institute, an organization dedicated to conserving coastal salt marshes and educating the public about marshland ecology. Since 1983 the Institute has held the Wings 'n Water Festival in September every year to raise funds for its various educational and research projects as well as to raise public awareness of the salt marsh by offering activities that relate to its unique environment. Salt marsh safaris and boat cruises, a decoy and decorative bird carving show, exhibits of naturalist and maritime art, and a wildlife craft market are among the events. There is also a Black Lab retriever demonstration, musical entertainment featuring traditional American instruments, and various booths serving oysters, clams on the half shell, "shrimpwiches," chowders, Maryland hard-shelled crabs, and Maine lobster. Festival events are held along a fifteen-mile stretch of

the South Jersey coast that includes Avalon, Stone Harbor, and Cape May Court House.

Winston 500
First Sunday in May

This 500-mile stock-car race is Alabama's biggest sporting event. It's held at the Talladega Superspeedway, known as the "World's Fastest Speedway." The Winston 500 is one of the Big Four NASCAR (National Association for Stock Car Auto Racing) Winston Cup events, the others being the Daytona 500, the Coca-Cola 600, and the Southern 500. The Winston is considered the fastest of the four. The winner in Talladega in 1991 was fifty-one-year-old Harry Gant, who had never won two races in a row in his eleven years on the circuit and was the surprise of the season. He won four straight in 1991, beginning with the Southern 500 at Darlington International Raceway in South Carolina. "Age don't have nothing to do with it," Gant said about the streak. His day's work at Talledega driving an average speed of 165.62 miles an hour entitled him to $81,950.

Talladega, which opened in 1969, has 83,200 permanent grandstand seats and each year attracts more than 350,000 spectators.

Winter Festival of Lights
Early November through late January

A premier light show in Wheeling, W.Va., started in 1985 and now considered a rival of the light show at Niagara Falls. More than a million people visit each year to see half a million lights on the downtown Victorian buildings, dozens of giant displays, 200 lighted trees, and about ten miles of drive-by light displays with architectural and landscape lighting designed by world-famous lighting designers. Some 300 acres of the city's Oglebay Park (a former private estate that was left to the city) are covered with animated light displays that depict symbols of Hanukkah and Christmas and general winter scenes. There are also nighttime parades and storefront animations.

Winterlude
Ten days in February

A midwinter civic festival held in Ottawa, Canada, Winterlude is primarily a celebration of winter sports. The Rideau Canal, which has been referred to as "the world's longest skating rink," is eight kilometers long and provides an excellent outdoor skating facility. There is also snowshoeing, skiing, curling (a game in which thick heavy stone and iron disks are slid across the ice toward a target), speedskating, dogsled racing, barrel jumping, and tobogganing. For those who prefer not to participate in the many sporting events, there is an elaborate snow sculpture exhibit known as Ice Dream. Nearly half a million people attend the ten-day festival each year.

Winter Solstice
June 21–22 (Southern hemisphere); December 21–22 (Northern hemisphere)

This is the shortest day of the year, respectively in each hemisphere, when the sun has reached its furthest point from the equator. It also marks the first day of winter.

The winter solstice has played an important role in art, literature, mythology, and religion. There were many pre-Christian seasonal traditions marking the winter solstice, and huge bonfires were an integral part of these ancient solar rites. Although winter was regarded as the season of dormancy, darkness, and cold, the gradual lengthening of the days after the winter solstice brought on a more festive mood. To primitive peoples this return of the light was cause for celebration that the cycle of nature was continuing.

See also SUMMER SOLSTICE, MIDSUMMER DAY.

Wolf Trap Summer Festival Season
Late May–early September

Located just thirty minutes from downtown Washington, D. C. in Vienna, Virginia, Wolf Trap Farm Park for the Performing Arts hosts musical performances on a year-round basis. But Wolf Trap is best known for the Summer Festival Season. Recent seasons have featured productions by the New York City Opera, the National Symphony Orchestra, the Kirov Ballet from Leningrad (now St. Petersburg), the Bolshoi Ballet, and the Joffrey Ballet as well as performances by Ray Charles, Johnny Cash, John Denver, Willie Nelson, Emmylou Harris, and jazz trumpeter Wynton Marsalis.

Concerts are held in the 6,900-seat Filene Center II, about half of which is exposed to the open sky. Many concertgoers bring a picnic supper and dine on the grass. Smaller concerts are held during the off-season in the pre-Revolutionary, 350-seat German Barn.

Women's Day, International
March 8

Not only is this day commemorating working women one of the most widely observed holidays of recent origin, but it is unusual in that it began in the United States and was adopted by many other countries, including the former USSR and the People's Republic of China. This holiday has its roots in the March 8, 1857 revolt of American women in New York City, protesting conditions in the textile and garment industries, although it wasn't proclaimed as a holiday until 1910.

In Great Britain and the United States, International Women's Day is marked by special exhibitions, films, etc. in praise of the working woman. In the former USSR, women received honors for distinguished service in industry, aviation, agriculture, military service, and other fields of endeavor.

World Championship Crab Races
Sunday before third Monday of February

A sporting event in Crescent City, Calif. featuring races of the nine-to eleven-inch Dungeness crabs that are caught off this Northern California coastal city. The crabs are urged down a four-foot raceway, prizes are awarded, and the winning crab gets a trip back to the harbor for a ceremonious liberation. This is also an eating event: throughout the day about 3,000 pounds of fresh cracked crab are served.

The event began in 1976, but its origins are older. Traditionally, local fisherman returned to port after a day of crabbing and celebrated the catch by racing their liveliest crabs in a chalked circle.

World Cup
June–July, every four years

The world series of soccer. Since 1930 (except during World War II), the international championship games have been played every four years, sandwiched between the Olympic Games. The series was started under the auspices of the Fédération Internationale de Football Association (FIFA) and is now the best attended sporting event in the world. It's claimed that, including television viewers, more than 500 million people watch it.

Soccer is also called football or association football; the word soccer comes from assoc., an abbreviation for association. It originated in England in the public (private) schools, and spread to universities and then into local clubs, attracting more and more working-class players. British sailors took the game to Brazil in the 1870s, and businessmen carried it to Prague and Vienna in the 1880s and 1890s. Belgium and France began an annual series of games in 1903. In 1904, international competition was such that FIFA was formed, and by 1982, it claimed 146 member nations. In 1946, the trophy was named the Jules Rimet Cup for the president of FIFA from 1921 to 1954.

The World Cup is played on a rotating basis in six different regions—Africa, North and Central America and the Caribbean, South America, Europe, Asia, and Oceana. In 1994, the United States will host the games.

In 1991, the first women's World Cup Tournament was held and was won by the U.S. It was the first cup ever taken by America.

The first World Cup was played in Montevideo, Uruguay, and Uruguay won. Since then, in fourteen championships played through 1990, three countries have been three-time winners: Italy, Brazil, and West Germany. Brazil's wins came in 1958, 1962, and 1970 under the leadership of Edson Arantes do Nascimento, better known as Pelé and sometimes as the *Pérola Negra*, or 'Black Pearl.' A Brazilian national hero, and at the time one of the best known athletes in the world, the five-foot-eight-inch Pelé combined kicking strength and accuracy with the knack of anticipating other players' moves. He announced his retirement in 1974 but in 1975 signed a three-year $7 million contract with the New York Cosmos; after leading them to the North American Soccer League championship in 1977, he retired for good.

World Eskimo-Indian Olympics
Middle or late July

A gathering in Fairbanks, Alaska, of native people from throughout the state and Canada to participate in games of strength and endurance. Events include the popular blanket toss, which originated in whaling communities as a method of tossing a hunter high enough to sight far-off whales. The tossees are sometimes bounced as high as twenty-eight feet in the air. Also on the program are a sewing competition, a seal-skinning contest, native dancing, and such events as the knuckle-hop contest, in which contestants get on all fours and hop on their knuckles. The winner is the one who goes the farthest.

World Religion Day
Third Sunday in January

A day initiated in 1950 by the National Spiritual Assembly of the Baha'i faith in the United States. The purpose was to call attention to the harmony of the world's religions and emphasize that the aims of religion are to create unity among people, to ease suffering, and to bring about peace. The

day is observed with gatherings in homes, public meetings and panel discussions, and proclamations by government officials.

World's Biggest Fish Fry
Last full week in April

A four-day spring festival in Paris, Tenn. that makes use of the catfish in nearby Kentucky Lake. The fish fry began in 1954, and by the next year more than 1,600 pounds of catfish were served. Now, some 13,000 pounds of catfish are cooked from Wednesday through Saturday, and about 100,000 people show up in this town of 10,000 to eat, fish, and look around. Events include a car show, arts and crafts exhibits, a two-hour parade and a smaller Small Fry Parade, and the coronation of a Queen of the Tennessee Valley and a Junior King and Queen. In the Fishing Rodeo, prizes are awarded for the biggest bass and biggest crappie, which must be caught in Kentucky Lake on legal sport equipment. Besides fried fish to eat, there are hush puppies, small deep-fat fried corn meal balls, originally made and tossed to puppies to keep them from begging while meals were being prepared.

World's Championship Duck Calling Contest and Wings Over the Prairie Festival
Tuesday through Saturday of Thanksgiving Week

An annual sporting event in Stuttgart, Ark., the "Rice and Duck Capital of the World." The first duck-calling contest was held in 1937 and attracted seventeen contestants. The winner that year was Thomas E. Walsh of Mississippi who was awarded a hunting coat valued at $6.60. Today, there are hundreds of participants in the various calling events (including the women's, intermediate, and junior world's championships). The main World's Championship contest is limited to between fifty and eighty callers who have qualified in sanctioned state and regional calling events. These elite duck callers vie for a top cash prize of $5,000. This celebration of the waterfowl hunting season is held when the rice fields around Stuttgart have been harvested and the ducks have ample opportunity for feeding. The duck hunting here is billed as the finest in the world.

Ducks are called by blowing a "duck call," a device about the size of a cigar. Originally the callers had to demonstrate four calls—the open-water call, the woods call, the mating call, and the scare call. Now contestants are judged on the hail, or long-distance call; the mating, or lonesome-duck, call; the feed, or chatter, call; and the comeback call. Judges sit behind a screen so they can't see the contestants.

Since 1955, a "Champion of Champions" contest for former World Champions has been staged every five years. Johnny "Boo" Mahfouz of Stuttgart was the 1990 Champion of Champions.

The related events that have sprung up around the contest have been formalized as the Wings Over the Prairie Festival. Included are fun shoots, an arts-and-crafts fair, the sportsmen's dinner and dance, a retriever demonstration, children's duck-call clinics, and a duck-gumbo cookoff. In 1957 the Grand Prairie Beauty Pageant debuted in which a Queen Mallard is crowned.

World Series
October

Also known as the **Fall Classic**, this best-of-seven-games play-off is between the championship baseball teams of the American and National Leagues. Games are played in the home parks of the participating teams, but the Series is truly a national event. For many it marks the spiritual end of summer and is a uniquely American occasion—like the Fourth of July. At work places, Series betting pools are common; in the days before night telecasts, radios droned the play-by-play broadcasts.

The first World Series was played in 1903 between the Boston Red Sox and the Pittsburgh Pirates. There was a lapse in 1904, but the Series resumed in 1905 and has been played annually ever since. The seven-game format was adopted in 1922.

Highlights of the Series mirror the symbolism of life that some see in the game itself; they include moments of athletic perfection and of human error, of drama and of scandal.

The scandal came when eight team members of the Chicago White Sox (ever afterwards to be known as the Black Sox) were accused of conspiring with gamblers to lose the 1919 World Series. Star left fielder "Shoeless" Joe Jackson admitted his part in the scandal, and on leaving court one day, heard the plea of a tearful young fan, "Say it ain't so, Joe."

Brooklyn Dodgers catcher Mickey Owen brought groans from fans with an error that has resounded in Series history. He let a ball get away from him—in 1941, in the ninth inning, on the third strike, with the Dodgers ahead of the New York Yankees by one run. The Yankee team revived and went on to win. Fifteen years later, in 1956, Yankee pitcher Don Larsen gave fans a rare thrill when he pitched a perfect game (no hits, no walks, no runners allowed on base) against the Dodgers, beating them 2-0. It remains the only perfect game pitched in a Series. Both these World Series were called Subway Series, because New York City fans could commute by subway from the Dodgers' Ebbets Field in Brooklyn to Yankee Stadium in the Bronx.

Another dramatic moment came in the 1989 Series. On Oct. 17, at 5:04 P.M., while 60,000 fans were waiting for the introduction of the players at San Francisco's Candlestick Park, an earthquake struck, and the ballpark swayed. Players and fans were safely evacuated (although sixty-seven people in other parts of the city died in the quake), and ten days later the Series resumed in the same park. The Oakland Athletics mowed down the San Francisco Giants in four straight games.

World's Largest Salmon Barbecue
Late June or early July

Some 5,000 pounds of salmon are barbecued for close to 5,000 visitors in the city of Fort Bragg on the northern coast of California. Besides salmon freshly caught in local waters and freshly barbecued, the menu offers corn on the cob, salad, hot bread and ice cream. The feasting is followed by fireworks and dancing. The event is sponsored by the Salmon Restoration Association of California, and proceeds from it help restore the once abundant salmon runs on the rivers of the area.

World Wristwrestling Championships
Second Saturday of October

The original world championship matches in wrist-wrestling, which is similar to but slightly different from arm-wrestling. The one-day competitions, held in Petaluma, Calif. since 1962, originated in Mike Gilardi's Saloon, in 1957. A bank building has now replaced Gilardi's. The excitement generated by the first backroom bar contests led Bill Soberanes, a columnist for the *Petaluma Argus-Courier*, to transform the bar sport into an international championship.

Fifty men entered the first world championship in 1962. The final pairings that year pitted David-and-Goliath contestants Earl Hagerman, at five feet eight, and Duane Benedix, six feet four. In four seconds, Hagerman won. There was only one division at that time; now there are five men's divisions and three women's. Contestants number from 250 to 300 with wrestlers coming from as far away as Australia, Germany, and Russia. The event has been viewed by a TV audience of 200 million. Sometimes there are cash prizes, sometimes not. In the past a purse of $7,500 has been split among the winning contestants. But there are always medals and trophies awarded.

Wright Brothers Day
December 17

It was on the morning of December 17, 1903 that Wilbur and Orville Wright became the first men to fly and control a powered heavier-than-air machine. Orville Wright took his turn at piloting on this particular day and his historic twelve-second flight (120 feet) near Kitty Hawk, North Carolina was witnessed by only a handful of observers. It wasn't until the brothers went on to set additional flight records that they received widespread acclaim for their achievements. Their original plane (patented in 1906) can be seen today at the National Air and Space Museum in Washington, D.C.

Although Wright Brothers Day has been observed in one way or another and under various names throughout the United States almost since the flight took place, the more notable observations include the annual Wright Brothers Dinner held in Washington, D.C. by the National Aeronautic Association, and the awarding of the Kitty Hawk Trophy at an annual dinner on this day on Los Angeles. In North Carolina, celebrations are held at Kitty Hawk and in Dayton, Ohio, where the brothers were born and where they opened their first bicycle shop in 1892. Events on December 17 traditionally include a "flyover" by military aircraft and a special ceremony held at the Wright Brothers National Memorial, a 425-acre area that features a sixty-foot granite pylon on top of Kill Devil Hill, where the Wright Brothers' camp was located. The flyover takes place at precisely 10:35 a.m., the time of the original flight in 1903.

Wurstfest (Sausage Festival)
End of October through first week in November (October 30–November 8 in 1992)

A festival billed as "The Best of the Wurst," held in the town of New Braunfels, Tex. to celebrate the sausage-making season and recall the town's German heritage. New Braunfels was settled in 1845 by German immigrants led by Prince Carl of Solms-Braunfels, a cousin of Queen Victoria. The prince chose lands along the Comal and Guadalupe rivers, envisioning a castle on the riverbanks. But the rigors of the wilderness proved too much, and he abandoned his castle plans and went home, while those who had followed him were left behind. They were decimated by starvation and disease, but the survivors eventually prospered, finding abundant water and rich soil.

The eight-day festival features polka music, German singing and dancing, arts and crafts, sporting events, a biergarten, and German food—especially sausage.

Wuwuchim
Eve of the new moon in November

The new year for the Hopi Indians, observed in Hopiland in northeastern Arizona. This is thought to be the time when *Kachina* spirits emerge from Shipap, the underworld, to stay a short time on earth. It is the most important of Hopi rituals because it establishes the rhythms for the year to come. For four days, prayers, songs, and dances for a prosperous and safe new year are led by the priests in the *kivas*, or ceremonial chambers. The men of the tribe dance, wearing embroidered kilts, and priests from the Bear Clan chant about the time of creation.

Y

Yale-Harvard Regatta
First Sunday in June

This famous college crew race has been held since 1865 between arch-rivals Yale and Harvard on the Thames River (pronounced THAYMZ) in New London, Connecticut. The event, which claims to be the oldest crew competition in the country, is timed to coincide with the movement of the tide upriver. It begins with a two-mile freshman race, followed by a two-mile combination race featuring the best rowers from all classes. Then there is a three-mile junior varsity race. But the highlight is the four-mile varsity race.

Prior to World War II, crowds of up to sixty thousand used to line the banks of the Thames to watch the race, but nowadays only a third as many come to watch-many of them by boat.

Yellow Daisy Festival
Second weekend in September

A tribute to a rare flower, the Yellow Daisy or *Viguiera porteri*, that blooms on Stone Mountain near Atlanta, Ga. The flowers, 2 1/2 feet tall, grow in granite crevices, sprouting in April, and not blooming until September, when they give the mountain a golden blanket. They wilt if they are picked, and seem to thrive only in the crevices. They were first discovered in 1846 by the Pennsylvania missionary, Thomas Porter, who sent a specimen to the noted botanist Asa Gray for identification. Gray decided it was the *Viguiera* genus, comprising about sixty other species that grow largely in Central America and Mexico. The only other place in the United States the "yellow daisy" has been identified is California, but there the plant is larger and woodier.

The festival, held since 1969 at Georgia's Stone Mountain Park, offers tours to view the daisy and much more: one of the South's largest arts and crafts shows, bluegrass music, and puppet shows. A Yellow Daisy Princess reigns over it all.

Yodeling Festivals *See* Jodlerfests

Yom Hashoah *See* Holocaust Day

Yom ha-Zikkaron
Between April 15 and May 13; 4 Iyyar

In Israel, the **Day of Remembrance** honors those who died fighting for the establishment of the Israeli state. It is observed on the day preceding Yom ha-Atzma'ut, or ISRAELI INDEPENDENCE DAY. During Shahavit (the morning service), a candle is lit in memory of fallen soldiers, the ark is opened, and Psalm 9, "Over the death of the son," is recited. This is followed by a prayer for the war dead and other prayers for lost relatives. The service concludes with a reading of Psalm 114.

At the end of the day, sirens are sounded and a few minutes of silence are observed throughout Israel. At sundown, Yom ha-Atzma'ut begins and the mood shifts to one of celebration.

Yom Kippur
Between September 15 and October 13; 10 Tishri

Also known as the **Day of Atonement** or **Yom ha-Din**, the **Day of Judgment**, Yom Kippur is the holiest and most solemn day in the Jewish calendar, and the last of the ten High Holy Days or Days of Penitence that begin with ROSH HA-SHANAH, the Jewish New Year. It is on this day that Jews acknowledge transgressions, repent through confession, then make atonement to God to obtain his forgivenesss, with the hope of being inscribed in the Book of Life. It is not uncommon for Jews to spend the entire twenty-four hours at the synagogue, where five services are held.

Yom Kippur is a strict day of fast; not even water may be taken from sundown to sundown. It is also a day of reconciliation for those who have done each other harm during the past year and a day of charity toward the less fortunate. It is the only fast day never postponed if it falls on the Sabbath.

Yom Yerushalayim
Between May 9 and June 6; 28 Iyyar

Jerusalem Day commemorates the capture and reunification of Jerusalem during the Six-Day War (on 28 Iyyar 5727 on the Jewish calendar; June 7, 1967), after which Israel gained possession of the Old City of Jerusalem, which had been under Jordanian rule, and other Arab lands. It is the most recent addition to the Jewish calendar and is observed primarily in Israel.

Although there are no specific rituals connected with this relatively new holiday, it is common to recite the Hallel (Psalms 115–118), Psalm 107, and the Aleinu or concluding prayer. Because this day falls during the LAG B'OMER period-which begins on the second night of PASSOVER and continues through SHAVUOT—the mourning customs traditionally observed during this time are suspended for the day.

York Festival and Mystery Plays
Mid-June–early July; every three years

From 1350 until 1570, a series of "mystery plays"—dramas recounting the story of mankind from the Creation to the Last Judgment-were produced in the city of York, England on CORPUS CHRISTI Day by the medieval craft guilds. The event was revived in 1951 and has been held on a triennial basis since then, beginning in mid-June and extending through early July. Modern adaptations of the original plays are performed in the garden of the Abbey of St. Mary—with the exception of one that is given in medieval style on a wagon in the street.

In addition to the mystery plays, there is a festival of music and the arts, with piano and violin recitals, orchestral performances, opera, and art exhibitions.

Yorktown Day
October 19

On October 19, 1781, Lord Cornwallis surrendered his British and German troops to General George Washington's Allied American and French troops at Yorktown, Virginia. Although the peace treaty recognizing American independence was not ratified until January 14, 1784, the fighting was only sporadic in the intervening two years, and the Battle of Yorktown is widely considered to mark the end of the Revolutionary War.

There has been some sort of patriotic observance of this day since its first anniversary in 1782. But since 1949, Yorktown Day activities have been planned and sponsored by the Yorktown Day Association, composed of representatives from thirteen different patriotic and government organizations. Events held at the Colonial National Historical Park in Yorktown include a commemorative ceremony at the French Cemetery and the placing of a wreath at both the French Monument and the Monument to Alliance and Victory. There are other patriotic exercises, eighteenth-century tactical demonstrations, a parade of military and civilian units, and musical presentations by fife and drum units from all over the eastern United States. The events are often attended by visiting French dignitaries.

Young Woman of the Year Finals
Late June

The final competitions and awards for the title of Young Woman of the Year has been held since 1958 in Mobile, Ala. The winner, a high school senior chosen on the basis of scholarship, fitness, creativity, and human relations, receives a $30,000 college scholarship. More than 26,000 participants in fifty states take part in local programs that lead to the Mobile finals.

The program traces its start to the late 1920s when the Mobile Junior Chamber of Commerce organized an annual azalea program. After World War II, to make this program more attractive, the Jaycees invited high school senior girls from the area to compete for modest awards, and a court of Azalea Trail Maids was selected. By 1957, girls from Florida and Mississippi were joining the Alabama girls, and the Jaycees decided to set up a national program. It got under way in 1958 as the America's Junior Miss Pageant with eighteen states represented; the winner that year was Phyllis Whitnack of West Virginia. The name of the pageant was changed to its present one in 1989. Probably the best known one-time Junior Miss is Diane Sawyer of Kentucky, who took the title in 1963 and went on to become a star television journalist for ABC.

Ysyakh
On or near December 21

This is a celebration of the midnight sun, in the Jatutsk region in the northeastern part of Russia. The festivities include foot races, horse races, and often sled dog and reindeer races. Folk dancing and feasting—primarily on boiled beef and *kumiss* or fermented mare's milk—complete the celebration, which often goes on all night.

376

Yuan Hsiao Chieh *See* **Lantern Festival**

Yuki Matsuri *See* **Sapporo Snow Festival**

Yukon Discovery Day *See* **Klondike Gold Discovery Day**

Yule
December 22; December 25

Also known as **Alban Arthan**, Yule was one of the 'Lesser Sabbats' of the Wiccan year, a time when ancient believers celebrated the re-birth of the Sun God and the lengthening of the days. This took place annually around the time of the WINTER SOLSTICE and lasted for twelve days.

The Sabbats are the eight holy days generally observed in modern witchcraft (Wicca) and neo-Paganism. They revolve around the changing of the seasons and agricultural events, and were generally celebrated outdoors with feasting, dancing, and performances of poetry, drama, and music. There are four 'Greater Sabbats,' falling on February 2 (see IMBOLC), April 30, July 31, and October 31 (see SAMHAIN). The Lesser Sabbats fall on the solstices and equinoxes.

Yule or **Yule Day** is also an old Scottish expression for CHRISTMAS DAY, 'Yule' deriving from the old Norse word *jól*, referring to the pre-Christian winter solstice festival. CHRISTMAS EVE is sometimes referred to as 'Yule-Even.'

Z

Zarthastno Diso
April 30; May 29; June 1

This is the day on which the followers of Zoroaster (or Zarathushtra), the sixth century Persian prophet and religious reformer, commemorate their founder's death in 551 B.C. Zoroaster was a legendary figure associated with occult knowledge and the practice of magic on the one hand, and on the other, with the monotheistic concept of God familiar in modern-day Christianity and Judaism. The largest group of his followers are the Parsis of India, although they can also be found in isolated areas of Iran.

Zoroaster's death is observed on April 30 by the Fasli sect of the Parsis, on May 29 by the Kadmi sect, and on June 1 by the Shahenshai sect.

Zibelemarit (Onion Market)
Fourth Monday in November

A great celebration of onions and the principal festival of Bern, the capital of Switzerland known for its bear pit and mechanical clock that displays a parade of wonderful mechanical figures every hour. The onion market is said to date back to the great fire of 1405, after which farmers of the lake region of Canton Fribourg were given the right to sell their products in Bern because they helped rebuild the city. This story is probably a made-up story, since the first documented mention of onions came in the middle of the nineteenth century.

Farmers at hundreds of stalls offer for sale more than 100 tons of strings of onions, as well as other winter vegetables and nuts. There is a carnival spirit, with confetti battles, people dressed in disguises, and jesters doing satires of the year's events.

Zulu Festival
First day in July to the last Sunday

The Zulu Festival, also known as the **Shembe Festival**, for Isaiah Shembe, the sect's founder, is one of three annual festivals observed by the Nazareth Baptist Church (Church of the Ama Nazaretha) at the Ematabetulu village near Inanda, South Africa. The other two are the October festival, observed at Judia near Ginginglovu, and the January festival observed on Inhlangakazi Mountain. All aspects of worship, ritual, dress, and festivals were established by Shembe in 1911. The church's beliefs are a mixture of pagan, Old Testament, and Christian.

The **July Festival** is the most popular of the three, and church members come from all over South Africa to attend it. Some live in temporary encampments for the three to four week festival, which begins on the first day of July and ends on the last Sunday. Throughout this period there are alternate days of dancing and rest. The sacred dancing that takes place on the final Sunday usually draws large numbers of spectators. Other activities during the festival include sermons by a variety of preachers, testimonies by church members, and prayer for the sick.

The men and women dance separately, and their costumes vary considerably. The two male groups of dancers, for example, are the Njobo and the Iscotch. The Njobo, who are mostly older men, wear traditional Zulu dress, as do the female groups. But the younger male dancers of the Iscotch group wear a long white smock with a tasseled hem over a black pleated kilt, a white pith helmet, black army boots with black-and-white football socks, and a light green tie bearing icons of the prophet Shembe and other church leaders.

The dances, which can last an entire day, involve rows of fifty or more dancers, each of which takes its turn at the front and then gradually works its way to the back, allowing those who tire to leave the group without being noticed.

Special Indexes

Several different Special Indexes provide reference to entries (as appropriate) for each of the following categories.

Chronological Indexes

Fixed Days and Events—Indexes events that are celebrated on a specific date.

Movable Days—Indexes events whose date of celebration is not fixed, particularly those that are observed according to non-Gregorian calendars and those that depend on the date of Easter.

Major Religious Groups Index

Indexes events with a significant religious element.

Special Subject Indexes

Ancient/Pagan—Indexes holidays rooted in ancient times.

Calendar—Indexes festivals that deal specifically with the calendar.

Folkloric—Indexes events rooted in folklore and tradition.

Historic—Indexes festivals commemorating specific events from history.

Promotional—Indexes festivals that promote something, be it a location or activity.

Sporting—Indexes festivals that are based on or revolve around sporting events.

Chronological Indexes

Fixed Days and Events

Entries in **HFCWD** are indexed below according to the month or specific date(s) on which they are observed. For each month, those holidays within the month are given first, followed by holidays celebrated on specific date(s), then those observed at the same time every year, although not on a fixed date (e.g., the first Monday, the last week, etc.).

January

January
Australian Open (tennis)
Bonfim Festival (Festa do Bonfim)
Cowboy Poetry Gathering

January 1
Bom Jesus dos Navegantes
Circumcision, Feast of the
Cotton Bowl Game
Emancipation Day
First-Foot Day
Kissing Day
New Year's Day
New Year's Day in the Former Soviet Union
Orange Bowl Game
Oshogatsu (New Year's Day)
Polar Bear Swim Day
Rose Bowl Game
St. Basil, Feast of
Sugar Bowl Classic
Ta'u Fo'ou
Tournament of Roses (Rose Parade)

January 1; June 24
Ladouvane

January 1–9
Black Nazarene Fiesta

January 1–10
Minstrels' Carnival

January 2
Berchtold's Day

January 4
St. Elizabeth Ann Seton, Feast of

January 5
Befana Festival
Epiphany Eve in France
Twelfth Night

January 5–February 5
Harbin Ice and Snow Festival

January 6
Día de los Tres Reyes
Epiphany, Feast of the
Haxey Hood Game
Maroon Festival
Orthodox Epiphany
Perchtenlauf
Three Kings Day (Epiphany) in Indian Pueblos

January 6 or 7
Old Christmas Day

January 7
Distaff Day
Ganna (Genna)
Nanakusa Matsuri (Seven Herbs or Grasses Festival)
Russian Orthodox Christmas

January 8
Battle of New Orleans Day
Gynaecocratia
St. Gudula's Day

January 13
Old Silvester
St. Knut's Day
Stephen Foster Memorial Day

January 14
Ass, Feast of the
Ratification Day

January 14 in the West; December 5 in the East
St. Sava's Day

January 15
Seijin-no-hi (Adults Day; Coming-of-Age Day)

January 17
Benjamin Franklin's Birthday
St. Anthony the Abbott, Feast of

January 18
Four an' Twenty Day

January 19–20
Timqat (Timkat)

January 20
Babin Den
Inauguration Day
St. Agnes' Eve

January 21
St. Sarkis's Day

January 22
St. Dominique's Day
St. Vincent's Day

January 23
Hobart Cup Day

January 24
Alacitas Fair

January 25
Burns Night

January 26
Republic Day in India

January 26 or following Monday
Australia Day

January 29
Conversion of St. Paul, Feast of the

Chronological Indexes

January 30
Day of the Three Archbishops
St. Charles' Day

January, first Monday of the year; January 12, first Monday after
Handsel Monday

January, first week
Sarasota Circus Festival and Parade

January; Sunday after Epiphany
Holy Family, Feast of the

January, third Monday
Robert E. Lee Day

January, third Monday; January 21
Martin Luther King's Birthday

January, third Sunday
World Religion Day

January, third week
Ullr Fest

January, third weekend
All American Championships Sled Dog Races
Ati-Atihan Festival
Sinulog Festival

Jan, mid
National Western Stock Show

January, last three weeks
Hong Kong Arts Festival

January, last Tuesday
Up-Helly-Aa

January, last Thursday
Dicing for the Maid's Money Day

January, last two weeks
Southwestern Exposition & Livestock Show & Rodeo

January, last week
Texas Citrus Fiesta

January, last week–February, first week
St. Paul Winter Carnival

January, last weekend
Dinagyang

January, usually last Sunday
Mt. Cameroon Race
Super Bowl Sunday

February

February
Argungu Fishing Festival
Black History Month
Buffalo's Big Board Surfing Classic
Dartmouth Winter Carnival
Daytona 500
Finnish Sliding Festival
Great Lapp Winter Fair
Hobart Regatta Day
Iemanjá Festival
Powamû Festival

February 1
St. Bridget's Day

February 1, Saturday nearest to
Clark Gable Birthday Celebration

February 2
Candlemas (Candelaria)
Groundhog Day
Imbolc (Imbolg)

February 3
St. Blaise's Day

February 3 or 4
Setsubun (Bean-Throwing Festival)

February 3, Sunday nearest or Monday after
Hurling the Silver Ball

February 3–5
St. Agatha Festival

February 3 and March 9, between; Shrove Tuesday
Pancake Day

February 5
Mihr, Festival of
Roger Williams Day

February 5, Sunday nearest
Igbi

February 5–11 or February 6–12
Sapporo Snow Festival (Yuki Matsuri)

February 6
Waitangi Day

February 8
Boy Scouts' Day
Hari-Kuyo

February 10
St. Paul's Shipwreck, Feast of

February 11
Thomas Edison's Birthday

February 12
Georgia Day
Lincoln's Birthday

February 12, Sunday nearest
Race Relations Sunday

February 12, 13, 14
Borrowed Days

February 13
Parentalia

February 14
Valentine's Day

February 14 in the West; May 11 in the East
Holy Day of Letters

February 15
Lupercalia

February 15; August 26
Susan B. Anthony Day

February 15–17
Kamakura Matsuri (Snow Hut Festival)

February 17
Quirinalia

February 17; September 12
Monkey God, Birthday of the

February 22; February, third Monday
Washington's Birthday

February 22; October 22
Abu Simbel Festival

February 22, Sunday nearest to
Brotherhood Sunday

February 23
Terminalia

February 25
Fiesta sa EDSA (People Power Anniversary)
St. George's Day in Bulgaria

February 25–March 1
Ayyam-i-Ha

February 27
Dominican Republic Independence Day

February 29
Leap Year Day

February–March in even-numbered years
Adelaide Festival of the Arts

February, early
Québec Winter Carnival

February, first half
Vinegrower's Day

February, first Thursday
Carnaval de Quebec

384

February, Monday following first Tuesday
Gasparilla Pirate Festival

February, weekend after first Friday
Ice Worm Festival

February, second Wednesday through third Saturday in
Edison Pageant of Light

February, Sunday before third Monday
World Championship Crab Races

February, third Monday
Presidents' Day

February, third Monday, and preceding weekend
George Washington Birthday Celebration in Alexandria, Virginia

February, mid
Anchorage Fur Rendezvous
Washington's Birthday Celebration in Los Dos Laredos

February, four days beginning last Thurs
Vaqueros, Fiesta de los

February, last two weeks
Houston Livestock Show & Rodeo

February, last Saturday in
Buena Vista Logging Days

February, three days at end of
American Birkebeiner

February, late and early spring
Nenana Ice Classic

February, ten days
Winterlude

March

March
Hanami
Natchez Spring Pilgrimage
Phra Buddha Bat Fair
Whale Festival

March 1
Martenitza
St. David's Day
Samil-jol (Independence Movement Day)

March 1–3
Drymiais

March 1–14
Omizutori Matsuri (Water Drawing Festival)

March 1 and April 4, between; Laetare Sunday (three weeks before Easter)
Groppenfasnacht (Fish Carnival)

March 2
Texas Independence Day

March 3
Hina Matsuri (Doll Festival)

March 5
Boston Massacre Day

March 6
Alamo Day
Magellan Day

March 8
Women's Day, International

March 9
St. Frances of Rome, Feast of

March 10
Forty Martyrs' Day
Jousting the Bear

March 11–20
Farvardegan Days

March 12
Girl Scout Day
Moshoeshoe (Moshoeshoe's) Day

March 12–19
St. Joseph's Day

March 15
Andrew Jackson's Birthday
Buzzard Day
Hilaria

March 16
St. Urho's Day

March 17
Camp Fire Founders' Day
St. Patrick's Day
St. Patrick's Day Parade in Savannah

March 17
Evacuation Day

March 17, weekend nearest
St. Patrick's Day Encampment

March 18
Sheelah's Day

March 20, about
Ibu Afo Festival

March 20 or 21
Shem al Nessim

March 20 or 21; September 23 or 24
Higan

March 21
Jamshedi Naoroze (Jamshed Navroz)

March 21
Khordad Sal

March 21 or 22
Vernal Equinox

March 21, Saturday or Sunday nearest to
Marzenna Day

March 25
Annunciation of the Blessed Virgin Mary, Feast of the
Greek Independence Day (Greece)
Lady Day
Maryland Day
Tichborne Dole

March 25
St. Dismas' Day

March 26
Prince Kuhio Day

March 29, 30, 31; February 12, 13, 14
Borrowed Days

March–April
Bermuda College Weeks
Boat Race Day
Cherry Blossom Festival
Houses and Gardens, Festival of
Spring Break

March, early
Iditarod Trail Sled Dog Race
North Pole Winter Carnival

March, first Sunday
Vasalopp, The

March, first Tuesday
Town Meeting Day

March, first week
Motorcycle Week (Camel Motorcycle Week; Bike Week)

March, first two weeks
Carnaval Miami

March, second Sunday
Holmenkollen Day

March, second Sunday; May 24
Commonwealth Day

Chronological Indexes

April

April, first weekend after last Wednesday
Butter and Egg Days

April, week before last weekend
University of Pennsylvania Relay Carnival

April, last Friday; April 22 in Nebraska
Arbor Day

April, last Saturday
Cynonfardd Eisteddfod
Maryland Hunt Cup

April, last Sunday
Landsgemeinden

April, last weekend
Landing of d'Iberville
Stockton Asparagus Festival
Vermont Maple Festival
World's Biggest Fish Fry

April, last weekend, through first weekend in May
Buccaneer Days

April, late, or early May
Cheung Chau Bun Festival
New Orleans Jazz and Heritage Festival

May

May
Alpaufzug
Cannes Film Festival
Divine Holy Spirit, Festival of the
Mayfest, International
Mayoring Day
Monaco Grand Prix
Tako-Age
Washington State Apple Blossom Festival

May 1
Lei Day
Loyalty Day
May Day
Premier Mai
St. Evermaire, Game of
St. Joseph the Worker, Feast of
Vappu (May Day)

May 1; 25
Moving Day

May 3
Día de la Santa Cruz (Day of the Holy Cross)
Polish Constitution Day

May 3–4
Hakata Dontaku

May 4
Kent State Memorial Day
Rhode Island Independence Day

May 5
Cinco de Mayo
Dutch Liberation Day
Kodomo-no-Hi (Children's Day)
Napoleon's Day
Urini Nal (Children's Day)

May 7
Rabindranath Tagore, Birthday of

May 7–8
St. Nicholas' Day in Italy

May 8
Furry Day

May 9, 11, 15
Lemuralia

May 10
Golden Spike Anniversary

May 11
Our Lady Aparecida, Festival of
Holy Day of Letters

May 11–13
Frost Saints' Days

May 12
Hospital Day, National
St. Tammany's Day

May 12; 29
Garland Day

May 12 and June 15, between ; Whit Tuesday
Dancing Procession

May 15
Aoi Matsuri (Hollyhock Festival)
St. Dymphna's Day
San Isidro the Farmer, Feast of

May 16–17
Black Ships Festival

May 17
Constitution Day in Norway
Mut l-ard
Syttende Mai Fest

May 17–18
Toshogu Haru-No-Taisai (Great Spring Festival of the Toshogu Shrine)

May 18, near
Sanja Matsuri (Three Shrines Festival)

May 20
Mecklenburg Independence Day

May 20–24
Ch'un-hyang Festival

May 21–23
Anastenaria

May 22
Maritime Day, National

May 23
Bab, Declaration of the

May 24–25
Saintes Maries, Fête des (Festival of the Holy Maries)

May 25
Argentine Independence Day

May 29
Baha'u'llah, Ascension of
Shick-Shack Day

May 29; April 6
Founder's Day

May 30; May 9
Joan of Arc, Feast day of

May 30–31
Padi Harvest Festival

May 31
Flores de Mayo
Republic Day in South Africa

May 31; July 2
Visitation, Feast of the

May–June
Bergen International Festival
French Open (tennis)
National Pike Festival
Spoleto Festival USA
Vienna Festival

May–September
Jodlerfests (Yodeling Festivals)
Oberammergau Passion Play
Wolf Trap Summer Festival Season

May, begins first Sunday
Family Week

May, early
Emmett Kelly Clown Festival
Mille Miglia
Sant' Efisio, Festival of
Sealing the Frost
Shenandoah Apple Blossom Festival

May, first Saturday
Kentucky Derby

May, first Sunday
Chongmyo Taeje (Royal Shrine Rite)
Cosby Ramp Festival
Sunday School Day
Winston 500

May, first weekend
Crawfish Festival
Irrigation Festival
Mushroom Festival

May, second Sunday
Mother's Day

May, second Sunday; every three years
Kattestoet (Festival of the Cats)

May, second weekend
Tulip Time

May, third Saturday
Preakness Stakes

May, third Sunday
Malcolm X Day

May, third week
Carabao Festival

May, mid
Bar-B-Q Festival, International

May, third weekend
Calaveras County Fair and Frog
Jumping Jubilee
Chestertown Tea Party Festival
Dulcimer Days
Kingsburg Swedish Festival
Vidalia Onion Festival

May, last Monday
Memorial Day

May, last Sunday
Cavalcata Sarda

May, late
Barbados/Caribbean Jazz Festival
Hay-on-Wye Festival of Literature

Italian Festival

May, end of; Memorial Day weekend
Alma Highland Festival and Games
Coca-Cola 600
Dakota Cowboy Poetry Gathering
General Clinton Canoe Regatta
Great Monterey Squid Festival
Indianapolis 500
I Madonnari Italian Street Painting
Festival
Mule Days
Northwest Folklife Festival
Ole Time Fiddlers' and Bluegrass Festival
Ute Bear Dance

May, late–June, early
Cotton Carnival
Derby Day
Humor and Satire Festival, National
Queen's Birthday
West Virginia Strawberry Festival

June

June
Alaska Festival of Music
Alexandra Rose Day
Alpaufzug
Common Ridings Day
Egungun Festival
Encaenia Day
Holland Festival
Juvenalia
Le Mans (motor race)
Portland Rose Festival
Sitka Summer Music Festival
Tako-Age

June, biennially
Newport to Bermuda Race
United States Air and Trade Show

June 6
D-Day
Flag Day in Sweden

June 8
St. Médardus' Day

June 9
St. Columba's Day

June 11
King Kamehameha Celebration
St. Barnabas' Day

June 13
St. Anthony of Padua, Feast of

June 13–29
Bumba-meu-Boi Folk Drama

June 14
Flag Day

June 15
Flag Day in Denmark
Magna Charta (Carta) Day

June 17
Bunker Hill Day

June 17
Iceland Independence Day

June 19
Juneteenth
New Church Day

June 19, Saturday nearest
Departure of the Continental Army

June 20
West Virginia Day

June 21
Midnight Sun Festival

June 21–22
Summer Solstice

June 21–29
White Nights

June 23
Wianki Festival of Wreaths

June 24
Human Towers of Valls
Inti Raymi Fiesta
Ladouvane
Midsummer Day
St. Hans Festival
St. John's Day in Portugal
St. John the Baptist's Day

San Juan Bautista Festival
San Juan Day
San Juan Pueblo Feast Day

June 24, 29
Kupalo Festival
San Juan and San Pedro Festivals

June 24, Saturday nearest
Juhannus (Midsummer Day)

June 25
Plow, Festival of the

June 25, weekend nearest
Little Big Horn Days

June 28–29
Palio of the Goose and River Festival

June 29
Mnarja (Imnarja; Feast of St. Peter
and St. Paul)

June 29, weekend nearest
St. Peter's Fiesta

June–July
Crop Over
Montreal Jazz Festival
Music and Dance Festival (Granada,
Spain), International

June–July, every four years
World Cup

June–August
Black Hills Passion Play
Jacob's Pillow Dance Festival
Santa Fe Chamber Music Festival

June–September
Pied Piper Open Air Theater
Ravinia Festival
Saratoga Festival

June–October
Midumu Ceremony
Stratford Festival

June of every fifth year
Spartakiade

June, early
Casals Festival
Country Music Fan Fair, International
Elfreth's Alley Fete Day

June, first Sunday
Regatta of the Great Maritime Republics
Seaman's Day
Yale-Harvard Regatta

June, first Monday
Jefferson Davis's Birthday

June, second Sunday
Children's Day
Grant Wood Art Festival
Race Unity Day

June, second week
Agriculture Fair at Santarém, National
Field Days, National

June, second weekend
Morris Rattlesnake Roundup

June, second weekend and third week
Frankenmuth Bavarian Festival

June, 3rd Sunday
Father's Day

June, mid
Great American Brass Band Festival
Royal Ascot

June, Sunday after the 22nd
Lily Festival (Festa del Giglio)

June, third week
NEBRASKAland DAYS
Old-Time Fiddlers' Contest, National

June, third Wednesday
Whitewater Wednesday

June, third Saturday
Alabama Blueberry Festival
Jousting Tournament

June, third weekend
Kiamichi Owa-Chito (Festival of the Forest)
Okmulgee Pecan Festival

June, four days ending third Sunday
United States Open Championship in Golf

June, fourth Sunday
Svenskarnas Dag

June, last week
Kiel Week

June, last Saturday
Possum Festival

June, last weekend
Blessing of the Shrimp Fleet

Helen Keller Festival
Idaho Regatta
Kingdom Days
Water-Splashing Festival *See* **Songkran**

June, late
Jackalope Days
Marbles Tournament, National
Utah Arts Festival
Young Woman of the Year Finals

June, end of
Acadian Festival
Harbor Festival

June, last Wednesday—Friday
Windjammer Days

June, end – July, beginning
Gettysburg Civil War Heritage Days

June, last weekend–July, first weekend
American Folklife, Festival of

June, late—July 5
Barnum Festival

June, late or early July
World's Largest Salmon Barbecue

June, late–July, early; 6 wks before first Monday in August
Wimbledon

June, late, and early July, every three years
Landshut Wedding

June in odd-numbered years
Paris Air and Space Show

July

July
Bologna Festival
British Open
Calgary Exhibition and Stampede
Camel Market
Choctaw Indian Fair
Dairy Festival
Dramatic Arts Festival at Avignon
Flagstaff Festival of the Arts
Fur Trade Days
Hortobágy Bridge Fair and International Equestrian Festival
Niman Festival
Oath Monday
Savonlinna Opera Festival
Tom Mix Roundup
Tour de France
Zulu Festival

July 1
Canada Day

July 1, formerly
Most Precious Blood, Feast of the

July 2
Bahia Independence Day
Visitation, Feast of

July 2; August 16
Palio, Festival of the

July 4
Apache Maidens' Puberty Rites
Calvin Coolidge Birthday Celebration
Caricom Day
Fourth of July in Denmark
Independence Day (Fourth of July)
Summer Festival

July 4, Friday after
Great Schooner Race
Souther Ute Tribal Sun Dance

July 4 in odd-numbered years
Transpac Race

July 4 weekend
Deep Sea Fishing Rodeo
Kutztown Fair

July 4, week of
Tom Sawyer Days, National

July 5, Sunday after
Giants, Festival of the (Fête des Géants)

July 6
Dalai Lama, Birthday of the

July 6–14
San Fermin Festival

July 7
Saba Saba Day

July 7; August 6–8
Tanabata (Star Festival)

August

September

West Virginia Italian Heritage Festival

September, weekend after Labor Day
Camel Races, International
Santa Fe, Fiesta de

September, first Sunday after Labor Day
Grandparents' Day

September, weekend before Labor Day
Connecticut River Powwow

September; week after Labor Day
Miss America Pageant

September, second Sunday
Watermelon Eating and Seed Spitting Contest

September, second week
Pendleton Round-Up and Happy Canyon
Telluride Hang Gliding Festival
Vendimia, Fiesta de la

September, second weekend
Knabenschiessen (Boys' Rifle Match)
Yellow Daisy Festival

September, second weekend in even numbered years
Living Chess Game (La Partita a Scácchi Viventi)

September, mid
Banana Festival, International
Corn Palace Festival

September, third Tuesday
Day of Peace, International
Prinsjesdag

September, third week
Bluegrass Fan Fest
Idaho Spud Day
Nuestra Senora de Peñafrancia, Feast of

September, third weekend
Acadiens, Festivals
Castroville Artichoke Festival
Chilympiad (Republic of Texas Chili Cookoff)
Clearwater County Fair and Lumberjack Days
Johnny Appleseed Festival
Monterey Jazz Festival
Wings 'n Water Festival

September, weekend after fourth Friday
Miwok Acorn Festival

September, last full weekend
Annual Patriots' Weekend
Louisiana Sugar Cane Festival
Valley of the Moon Vintage Festival

September, late
Jordbruksdagarna
Marion County Ham Days

September, end—October, early
Hunters' Moon, Feast of the
Mountain State Forest Festival
State Fair of Texas

September–October
Aloha Week Festivals
Middfest International
Oktoberfest

September–December, every odd year
Europalia

September, four days ending with second weekend after Labor Day
Air Races, National Championship

October

October
Barcelona Festival
Boomerang Festival
Dahlonega Gold Rush Days
Horse, Festival of the
Norsk Høstfest
Potato Days
Texas Rose Festival

October 2
Gandhi Jayanti (Mahatma Gandhi's Birthday)

October 3
Leyden Day
National Foundation Day
Thomas Wolfe Festival

October 3–4
St. Francis of Assisi, feast of

October 5
Han'gul Day

October 6
Armed Forces Day (Egypt)
Ivy Day
October War of Liberation Anniversary

October 8
St. Demetrius' Day

October 9
Leif Erikson (Ericson) Day

October 10
Double Tenth Day
Oklahoma Historical Day

October 10–20
Nagoya City Festival

October 11
Pulaski Day

October 12
Columbus Day
Virgin of the Pillar, Feast of the

October 17
Black Poetry Day
Romería of Our Lady of Valme

October 18
Alaska Day

October 19
Martyrs of North America, Feast of the
Yorktown Day

October 20
Bab, Birth of the

October 21
Black Christ, Festival of the

October 22
Abu Simbel Festival
Jidai Matsuri (Festival of the Ages)

October 23
Chulalongkorn Day
Swallows of San Juan Capistrano (Fiesta de las Golondrinas)

October 24
Pennsylvania Day
United Nations Day

October 25
St. Crispin's Day

October 26 in the East; October 8 in the West
St. Demetrius' Day

October 28
Czechoslovak Independence Day
Oxi Day

October 29
Republic Day in Turkey

October 30
Angelitos, Los

October 31
Apple and Candle Night
Halloween
Halloween in New Orleans
Reformation Day

October, early
Albuquerque International Balloon Fiesta
James Whitcomb Riley Festival

London Bridge Days
Shrimp Festival, National

October, alternate years
Shilla (Silla) Cultural Festival

October, first full weekend
Bridge Day
Great Locomotive Chase Festival
Paul Bunyan Show
Storytelling Festival, National
Whole Enchilada Fiesta

October, first Saturday
Battle of Germantown, Reenactment of
Black Cowboys Parade
Daniel Boone Festival

October, first Sunday
Agua, La Fiesta de
Rosary, Festival of the
United States Grand Prix

October, second Sunday
Círio de Nazaré
White Sunday

October, second Saturday
Eldon Turkey Festival
World Wristwrestling Championships

October, second week
Frankfurt Book Fair (Buchmesse)

October, second weekend
Billy Moore Days
Cactus Jack Festival
St. Mary's County Maryland Oyster Festival
Tucson Meet Yourself Festival

October, first weekend after Columbus Day
Half Moon Bay Art and Pumpkin Festival

October, mid
Heritage Holidays
Open Marathon, International
Peanut Festival, National

October, mid, in odd-numbered years
Swedish Homage Festival

October, third Saturday
Bridge Day
Sweetest Day

October, ten days ending third weekend
Georgia Peanut Festival

October, third full weekend
Boggy Bayou Mullet Festival

October, fourth Sunday
Mother-in-Law Day

October, last Thursday
Punky (Punkie) Night

October, last Saturday
Guavaween

October, last Sunday
Christ the King, Feast of
Saffron Rose Festival

October, last week
Pirates Week

October, last weekend
Chesapeake Appreciation Days

October, late
Impruneta, Festa del
Szüret

October, late or early November
Basket Dances
Reversing Current, Festival of the (Water Festival)

November

November
American Royal Livestock, Horse Show and Rodeo
Tori-no-ichi

November 1
Day of the Awakeners (Den na Buditelite)
Samhain (Samain)

November 2
All Souls' Day
Balfour Declaration Day

November 3
Bunka-no-hi (Culture Day)
St. Hubert de Liège, feast of

November 4
Mischief Night
Will Rogers Day

November 5
Día del Puno
Guy Fawkes Day

November 6
Gustavus Adolphus Day (Gustaf Adolfsdagen)

November 6 or nearest weekend
Leonhardiritt (Leonard's Ride)

November 7
Revolution Day

November 8
Saints, Doctors, Missionaries, and Martyrs Day
Michaelmas

November 9–10
Kristallnacht (Crystal Night)

November 11
Concordia Day
Gansabhauet
Martinmas
Martinsfest

November 11; 2nd Sunday in November (Great Britain)
Veterans Day

November 12
Baha'u'llah, Birth of
Sun Yat-sen, Birthday of

November 13
St. Frances Cabrini, Feast of

November 15
St. Leopold's Day

November 15, about
Haile Selassie's Coronation Day

November 15 or nearest Sunday
Shichi-Go-San (Seven-Five-Three Festival)

November 17
Queen's Day

November 19
Equal Opportunity Day

November 21
Presentation of the Blessed Virgin Mary, Feast of the

November 22
St. Cecilia's Day

November 23
Repudiation Day

November 25, formerly
St. Catherine's Day

November 26
Day of the Covenant

November 28
'Abdu'l-Baha, Ascension of

November 29
St. Andrew's Eve (Noc Swietego Andreja)

November 30
St. Andrew's Day

November, early
Sango Festival
State Opening of Parliament

November, first Sunday
New York City Marathon

November, first Tuesday
Melbourne Cup Day

November, Tues after first Monday
Election Day

November, Thursday after Election Day
Return Day

November, first week
Ozark Folk Festival
Wurstfest (Sausage Festival)

November, first full weekend
Terlingua Chili Cookoff

November, second Sunday
Quintaine, La
Stewardship Sunday

November, second Saturday
Lord Mayor's Show

November, mid
Grey Cup Day

November, third Thursday
Great American Smokeout

November, third weekend
Elephant Round-Up
Trois Glorieuses

November, Friday before Thanksgiving
Tellabration

November, fourth Monday
Zibelemarit (Onion Market)

November, Thanksgiving week
World's Championship Duck Calling Contest and Wings Over the Prairie Festival

November, fourth Thursday
Thanksgiving

November, Friday and Saturday after Thanksgiving Day
Chitlin' Strut

November, last Thursday in
Pilgrim Thanksgiving Day in Plymouth

November, last week
River Kwai Bridge Week

November–December
Davis Cup
Dom Fair
Stir-Up Sunday

November–January
Lights, Festival of

December

December 1
National Day, Romania

December 4
St. Barbara's Day

December 5
King's Birthday
St. Sava's Day

December 6
Independence Day, Finland
St. Nicholas' Day

December 7
Burning the Devil
Pearl Harbor Day

December 7–8
Itul

December 8
Immaculate Conception, Feast of the

December 8; February 8
Hari-Kuyo (Festival of Broken Needles)

December 9
Independence Day, Tanzania

December 11
Escalade (Scaling the Walls)

December 12
Jamhuri (Kenya Independence Day)
Our Lady of Guadalupe, Fiesta of

December 12, 14
St. Spyridon (Spiridon) Day

December 13
St. Lucy's Day

December 15
Bill of Rights Day
Dukang Festival

December 16
Day of the Covenant

December 16–24
Misa de Gallo (Cock's Mass; Simbang Gabi)
Posadas

December 17
Wright Brothers Day

December 17–23
Newport Harbor Christmas Boat Parade
Saturnalia

December 18
St. Modesto's Day

December 21
Doleing Day

December 21, 22
Forefathers' Day
Winter Solstice

December 21
Chaomos
St. Thomas's Day

Ysyakh

December 22, 25
Yule

December 23
Night of the Radishes
St. Thorlak's Day

December 23–24
Giant Lantern Festival

December 24
Christmas Eve
Tolling the Devil's Knell
Wigilia

December 24–25
Koledouvane

December 24, 30
Christmas Shooting

December 25
Christmas
Crossing of the Delaware

December 25–Jan 5
Russian Winter Festival

December 25–January 6
Christmas Pastorellas in Mexico

December 26
Boxing Day
St. Stephen's Day

December 26
Jonkonnu Festival (John Canoe)

Movable Days

The index below lists entries in *HFCWD* that are observed according to the dates of non-Gregorian calendars, including the Jewish calendar, Islamic calendar, and the Buddhist lunar calendar, or movable Christian holidays that depend on the date of Easter.

The listings for each month are followed by listings of miscellaneous dates and dates according to the Islamic calendar.

January

February

March

March 26 and April 23, begins between; 14–20 Nisan	Hagodol
March 27 and April 24, begins between; 15–21 (22) Nisan	Passover
March 27 and April 30, between	Lazarus Saturday St. Lazarus's Day
March 28 and April 25, between; day after Passover	Maimona (Maimuna)
March 29 and May 2, between	Low Sunday
March–April	Dipri Festival Easter Fires Mothering Sunday

March–April; 13th of waxing Chaitra	Mahavir Jayanti
March–April; Chaitra	Hanuman Jayanti
March–April; Chaitra, 9, waxing half of	Ramanavami (Ram Navami)
March–April; Easter holiday	Royal Easter Show
March–April, nineteenth day of the third moon	Goddess of Mercy, Birthday of the
March, full moon	Phagwa
March or April; second day of second month of Chinese lunar calendar	Bok Kai Festival

April

April	Sinhala Avurudu (Sinhalese New Year)
April, early	Chinhae Cherry Blossom Festival
April 4 and May 8, between, in East	Easter
April 5 and May 9, between; Monday after Coptic Easter	Sham al-Nassim (Fragrance of the Breeze)
April 5 and May 9, between; second Monday and Tuesday after Easter	Blajini, Feast of the (Sarbatoarea Blajinilor) Hocktide
April 7 and May 18, between; third Tuesday after Easter	Ropotine (Repotini)
April 8 and May 6, between ; Nisan 27	Holocaust Day (Yom Hashoah)
April 9 and 12, between	Thingyan
April, mid—May, mid; 23rd day of third lunar month	Matsu, Birthday of
April, mid to May; Kasone full moon	Kasone Festival of Watering the Banyan Tree

April 13; Sixth or seventh month of Dai calendar (mid Apr)	Songkran (Pi Mai)
April 15 and May 13, between; Iyyar 4	Yom ha-Zikkaron
April 16 and May 14, between; Iyyar 5	Israeli Independence Day
April 18 and May 21, between; fourth Friday after Easter	Common Prayer Day (Store Bededag)
April 29 and June 2, between; 25 days after Easter	Rousa, Feast of
April 30 and June 3, between; 40 days after Easter	Ascension Day Banntag Dew Treading Grillo, Festa del Holy Thursday Meenakshi Kalyanam
April; full moon of Phalguna	
April–May	Pooram
April–May; 1 Vaisakha	Rato (Red) Machhendranath Vaisakh (Baisak(hi))
April–May; full moon dat of Vaisakh	Bun Bang Fai Vesak (Wesak; Buddha's Birthday)

May

May, early	Royal Ploughing Ceremony
May, early; 8th and 9th days of 4th moon	Third Prince, Birthday of the
May 8 and June 11, between	Meistertruck Pageant Pilgrimage of the Dew
May 9 and June 6, between; Iyyar 28	Yom Yerushalayim
May 9 and June 12, between; Saturday before Pentecost	Divino, Festa do Luilak
May 10 and June 13, between	Pinkster Day
May 10 and June 13, between; coincides with Pentecost	Kataklysmos, Feast of (Festival of the Flood)

May 10 and June 13, between in West; between May 24 and June 27 in East	Pentecost
May 11 and June 14, between	Whit-Monday (Whitmonday)
May 16 and June 13, between; Sivan 6	Shavuot (Shabuoth)
May 17–June 20; beginning between	Rousalii
May 17 and June 20, between; Monday after Pentecost in East, Sunday after in West	Golden Chariot and Battle of the Lumecon, Procession of the Trinity Sunday
May 21 and June 24, between; Thursday after Trinity Sunday	Corpus Christi Decorated Horse, Procession of the Lajkonik

May 22 and June 25, between	Sacred Heart of Jesus, Feast of the	May–June; Jyaistha, 6, waxing half	Sithinakha
May 24 and June 27, between, in East	Pentecost	May–June; Jyaistha, full moon of	Poson Sanghamita Day
May; Eighth day of the fourth moon	Tam Kung Festival	May–June; seventh Thursday after Easter	Semik
May; twenty-third day of the third moon	Tin Hau Festival	May through October, four successive full-moon nights	Ramayana Ballet
May–June; Jyaistha	Ganga Dussehra Gawai Dayak Savitri-Vrata (Savitri Vow) Thargelia Vata Savitri		

June

June	Bach Festival, International	June, mid- to mid-July; full moon of Asadha	Esala (Asadha) Perahera (Arrival of the Tooth Relic)
June 17 and July 24, between; Tammuz 17	Tammuz, Fast of the 17th of (Shivah Asar be-Tammuz)	June, late	Bawming the Thorn Day
		June or July, usually	Hemis Festival

July

July 17 and August 14, between ; Av 9	Tishah be-Av	July–August; waxing Shravana	Naag Panchami
July 23 and August 21, between; Av, 15	Fifteenth of Av (Hamishah Asar be-Av)	July–August; Sravana, 14th of waning half of	Ghanta Karna
July; 24th-26th day of sixth month of Chinese lunar calendar	Torch Festival	July–August; Sravana, third day of waning half of	Marya
July–August	Dog Days Panathenaea Raksha Bandhan (Janai Purnima; Brother and Sister Day)	July–October; full moon of eighth lunar month to full moon of tenth lunar month	Waso (Buddhist Rains Retreat)
July–August; full moon of Sravana	Amarnath Yatra Rath Yatra	July, thirteenth day of the sixth moon	Lu Pan, Birthday of
July–August; third day of waxing Sravana	Teej (Tij; Green Teej)		

August

August, early	Pjodhatid	August and September, between	Homowo (Hunger-Hooting Festival)
August, first full moon	Whe'wahchee (Dance of Thanksgiving)	August–September; Photrobot, waning half of	Kan-Ben
August; full moon or 15th day of 7th lunar month	Hungry Ghosts, Festival of	August–September; waxing Bhadrapada	Ganesh Chathurthi
August–Sept	Onam Paryushana	August, seventh day of seventh moon	Seven Sisters Festival
August–September; new moon of Bhadrapada	Janmashtami (Krishnastami; Krishna's Birthday)		

September

September	Geraldine R. Dodge Poetry Festival Pffiferdaj Rosh ha-Shanah	September 8 and October 6, between; 3 Tishri	Gedaliah, Fast of (Tsom Gedalyah, Tzom Gedaliahu)
September 6 and October 4, begins between; 1–2 Tishri		September 15 and October 13, between; 10 Tishri	Yom Kippur

October

November

December

Miscellaneous Dates

After the fifth day of the fifth moon	Dragon Boat International Races	Late fall	Wangala (Hundred Drums Festival)
Fifth day of fifth month of Chinese Lunar calendar	Dragon Boat Festival (Tuan Yang Chieh)	Every 12 years (February in 1989)	Kumbh Mela (Pitcher Fair)
14th to 16th day of 5th lunar month (June, Jul)	Universal Prayer Day (Dzam Ling Chi Sang)	every 28 years; Nisan, first Wednesday	Blessing the Sun (Birchat Hahamah)
Bhadrapada, end of; sixth Hindu month	Visvakarma Puja	Moon 1, day 15	Burning the Moon House
25th day of 10th lunar month	Lights, Festival of (Ganden Ngamcho)	Moon 1, Day 15	Butter Sculpture Festival
		Moon 1, Day 19	Great Fifteenth, the
Full moon in February	Magha Puja (Maka Buja, Full Moon Day)	Moon 1, Day 9	Rat's Wedding Day
		Moon 2, Day 1	Making Happiness Festival
Phalguna, full moon day of	Dol Purnima	Moon 3, Day 5	Wind Festival
of Bhadra, first day, Nepalese month, (August–Sep)	Gai Jatra	Moon 3, Day 23	Thanh-Minh
		Moon 5, day 14	Matsu Festival
		Moon 6, day 6	Boat Race Day in Okinawa
		Moon 6, Day 15	Airing the Classics
		Moon 6, day 24	Shampoo Day
Friday 13th	Carberry Day	Moon 9, first nine days	Lotus, Birthday of the
Spring, first month of	Isthmian Games	Moon 10, Day 1	Nine Imperial Gods, Festival of the
Good Friday	Pleureuses, Ceremony of	Moon 12, Day 8	Sending the Winter Dress
			Mochi No Matsuri

Islamic Calendar Dates

Muharram 1–10	Ashura (Husain Day)	Ramadan, one of the last 10 days	Laylat al-Qadr
Safar	Mandi Safar		
Safar 14, 15, and 16	Shah Abdul Latif Death Festival	Ramadan 30	Lanterns Festival
Safar 18 and 19	Data Ganj Baksh Death Festival	Shawwal, first day of	'Id (Eid) al-Fitr
Rabi al-Awwal, 12	Mawlid al-Nabi (Maulid al-Nabi; Prophet's Birthday)	Dhu-l-Hijjah 8–13	Pilgrimage to Mecca (Hajj)
		10th Dhu-l-Hijjah	Sallah (Salah) Festival
Rajab 27	Laylat al Miraj	Dhul-Hijjah	'Id (Eid) al-Adha (Feast of Sacrifice)
Sha'ban 15	Shab-Barat		
Ramadan	Boys' Dodo Masquerade		

Major Religious Groups Index

Indexed below are those festivals and holidays appearing in *HFCWD* that have a significant religious element and that are celebrated by one or more of the world's major religions.

Anglican *See* **Christian (Church of England)**

Animist
Dipri Festival

Baha'i
Ascension of 'Abdu'l-Baha
Ascension of Baha'u'llah
Ayyam-i-Ha
Birth of Baha'u'llah
Birth of the Bab
Day of the Covenant
Declaration of the Bab
Feast of Ridvan
Martyrdom of the Bab
Race Unity Day
World Religion Day

Buddhist
Airing the Classics
Birthday of the Goddess of Mercy
Boun Phan Vet
Esala (Asadha) Perahera (Arrival of the Tooth Relic)
Festival of Lights (Ganden Ngamcho)
Floating Lantern Ceremony (Toro Nagashi)
Hana Matsuri (Flower Festival)
Hemis Festival
Higan
Kasone Festival of Watering the Banyan Tree
Lotus, Birthday of the
Magha Puja/Maka Buja (Full Moon Day)
Marya
Monlam (Prayer Festival)
Neri-Kuyo
Obon Festival
Omizutori Matsuri (Water Drawing Festival)
Oshogatsu (New Year's Day)
Phra Buddha Bat Fair
Poson
Sanghamita Day
Songkran (Pi Mai)
Sugar Ball Show
Thadingyut
Thingyan
Universal Prayer Day (Dzam Ling Chi Sang)
Vegetarian Festival

Vesak or Wesak, (Buddha's Birthday)
Waso (Buddhist Rains Retreat)

Buddhism (Tibetan)
Birthday of the Dalai Lama
Butter Sculpture Festival
Dosmoche
Losar
Mid-autumn Festival
Panchadaan
Paro Tshechu

Christian
Advent
All Saints' Day
All Souls' Day
Annunciation of the Blessed Virgin Mary, Feast of the
Ascension Day
Ash Wednesday
Assumption of the Blessed Virgin Mary, Feast of the
Ati-Atihan Festival
Awoojoh
Baptism of the Lord, Feast of the
Black Hills Passion Play
Blessing of the Grapes (Haghoghy Ortnootyoon)
Blowing the Midwinter Horn
Bom Jesus dos Navegantes
Candlemas (Candelaria)
Carabao Festival
Carling Sunday
Carnaval de Binche
Carnival
Carnival in Malta
Carnival in the U. S. Virgin Islands
Carnival in Venice
Carnival of Binche
Christ the King, Feast of
Christkindlesmarkt (Christmas Market) in Nuremberg
Christmas
Christmas Eve
Christmas Pastorellas in Mexico
Circumcision, Feast of the
Collop Monday
Conversion of St. Paul, Feast of the
Día de la Santa Cruz (Day of the Holy Cross)
Día de los Tres Reyes
Día de San Lorenzo
Dancing Procession

Easter
Ember Days
Epiphany Eve in France
Epiphany, Feast of the
Evamelunga
Exaltation of the Cross, Feast of the
Fasching
Fasinada
Fastens-een
Feast of St. Anthony the Abbott
Feast of St. Paul's Shipwreck
Festas Gualterianas
Festival of Sant' Efisio
Fig Sunday
Flores de Mayo
Footwashing Day
Fritter Thursday
Game of St. Evermaire
Giant Lantern Festival
Good Friday
Grotto Day
Halloween in New Orleans
Holy Innocents' Day
Holy Saturday
Holy Thursday
Holy Week
Hurling the Silver Ball
Hurricane Supplication Day
Juhannus (Midsummer Day)
Karneval in Cologne
Keaw Yed Wakes Festival
Kiddies' Carnival
Koledouvane
Lady Day
Lent
Lily Festival (Festa del Giglio)
Low Sunday
Marriage of Goliath
Martinsfest
Martyrdom of St. John the Baptist
Maundy Thursday
Mi-Carême
Michaelmas
Midsummer Day
Misa de Gallo (Cock's Mass), or Simbang Gabi
Moors and Christians Fiesta
Moriones Festival
Mothering Sunday
Nativity of the Blessed Virgin Mary, Feast of the
Palm Sunday
Oberammergau Passion Play

Church of Jesus Christ of the Latter-Day Saints (Mormon)
Latter-Day Saints, founding of the Church of
Hill Cumorah Pagent
Morman Pioneer Day

Confucian
Chongmyo Taeje (Royal Shrine Rite)
Confucius's Birthday (Teacher's Day)
Qing Ming Festival (Ching Ming Festival)

Hindu
Amarnath Yatra
Dewali (Divali, Deepavali, Festival of Lights)
Dol Purnima
Durga Puja
Float Festival
Galungan
Ganesh Chathurthi
Ganga Dussehra
Ghanta Karna
Hanuman Jayanti
Holi
Indra Jatra
Janmashtami, or Krishnastami (Krishna's Birthday)
Kan-Ben
Karwachoth
Kumbh Mela ('Pitcher Fair')
Lord Krishna's Birthday
Meenakshi Kalyanam
Naag Panchami
Phagwa
Pitra Visarjana Amavasya
Pongal
Pooram
Pushkar Mela
Ramanavami (Ram Navami)
Ramayana Ballet
Rath Yatra
Savitri-Vrata (Savitri Vow)
Shivaratri
Sithinakha
Tazaungdaing
Teej/Tij, Green Teej
Thaipusam or Thai Poosam
Tihar
Vaisakh, Baisak(hi)
Vasant Panchami (Basant Panchami)
Vata Savitri
Visvakarma Puja

Hindu; Buddhist
Raksha Bandhan (Janai Purnima, Brother and Sister Day)
Rato (or Red) Machhendranath
Royal Ploughing Ceremony

Islamic
Ashura
'Id (Eid) al-Adha (Feast of Sacrifice)
'Id (Eid) al-Fitr
Hosay Festival
Khamis al-Amwat
Lanterns Festival
Laylat al Miraj
Laylat al-Qadr
Mandi Safar
Mawlid al-Nabi (Maulid al-Nabi, Prophet's birthday)
Pilgrimage to Mecca (Hajj)
Ramadan
Sallah (or Salah) Festival
Shab-Barat

Islamic (Sufi)
Data Ganj Baksh Death Festival
Shah Abdul Latif Death Festival

Jain
Mahavir Jayanti
Paryushana

Jewish
Asarah be-Tevet (Tenth of Tevet)
Bi-Shevat (B'Shevat, Tu Bishvat, Hamishah Assar Bi-Shevat)
Blessing the Sun (Birchat Hahamah)
Fast of Gedaliah (Tsom Gedalyah, Tzom Gedaliahu)
Fast of the 17th of Tammuz (Shivah Asar be-Tammuz)
Fast of the First-born
Fifteenth of Av (Hamishah Asar be-Av)
Hagodol
Hanukkah (Chanukah)
Holocaust Day (Yom Hashoah)
Hoshana Rabbah
Maimona, Maimuna
Passover
Pilgrim festivals
Purim (Ta'anit Esther, the fast of Esther)
Purims, Special
Rosh ha-Shanah

Seged
Shavuot (Shabuoth)
Shemini Atzeret
Simhat Torah
Sukkot (Sukkoth, Succoth)
Ta'anit Esther (Taanith Esther)
Three Weeks
Tishah be-Av (Tisha be-Av, Tisha B'Ab)
Water-Drawing Festival
Yom Ha-Zikkaron
Yom Kippur
Yom Yerushalayim

Mormon See **Church of Jesus Christ of the Latter-Day Saints**

Rastafarian
Haile Selassie's Coronation Day

Shinto
Hari-Kuyo (Festival of Broken Needles)
Shichi-Go-San (Seven-Five-Three Festival)
Tori-no-ichi

Sikh
Hola Mohalla

Taoist
Birthday of Lu Pan
Matsu Festival
Tam Kung Festival
Tin Hau Festival

Taoist (Buddhist)
Festival of Hungry Ghosts
Nine Imperial Gods, Festival of the

Taoist (Chinese)
Birthday of the Monkey God
Birthday of the Third Prince

Voodoo
Iemanjá Festival
Rara (Ra-Ra)

Zoroastrian
Farvardegan Days
Jamshedi Naoroze (Jamshed Navroz)
Khordad Sal
Zarthastno Diso

Special Subject Indexes

Entries appearing in *HFCWD* are indexed into one of the six categories below, as appropriate.

Ancient/Pagan

Holidays rooted in ancient Greece, ancient Rome, or in Europe before the spread of Christianity.

Agwunsi Festival
Anthesteria
Awoojoh
Bawming the Thorn Day
Bear Festival
Beltane
Bonfire Night
Burgsonndeg
Carnea (Karneia, Karnea, Carneia)
Cataclysmos Day
Cromm Dub's Sunday
Día del Puno
Dædala
Dionysia (or Bacchanalia)
Dog Days
Egungun Festival
Ember Days
Festival of Mihr
Galungan
Garland Day
Halloween
Hilaria
Hogmanay
Horn Dance, the
Ides
Imbolc (Imbolg)

Isthmian Games
Juhannus (Midsummer Day)
Kupalo Festival
Lammas
Lemuralia
Ludi
Lupercalia
Martenitza
Marzenna Day
May Day
Midsummer Day
Minehead Hobby Horse Parade
Mount Ceahlau Feast
Nemean Games
Nice Carnival
Odo Festival
Okpesi Festival
Onwasato Festival
Panathenaea
Parentalia
Perchtenlauf
Plough Monday
Pythian Games
Quirinalia
Robigalia

Ropotine (Repotini)
Samhain (Samain)
San Juan and San Pedro Festivals
Sango Festival
Saturnalia
Semik
Shampoo Day
St. Hans Festival
St. John the Baptist's Day
St. John's Day in Portugal
St. Stephen's Day
St. Thomas's Day
Summer Solstice
Terminalia
Thargelia
Thesmophoria
Turon
Twelfth Night
Up-Helly-Aa (Up-Helly-A)
Vlöggelen
Wheat Harvest Festival in Provins, France
Wigilia
Winter Solstice
Yule

Calendar

Festivals that deal specifically with the calendar or that are held in celebration of the time of the year (solstices and equinoxes), the beginning and end of seasons, etc.

Abu Simbel Festival
Almabtrieb
Argungu Fishing Festival
Autumnal Equinox
Ayyam-i-Ha
Beltane
Borrowed Days
Buzzard Day
Carnival in Venice
Chinese New Year (Spring Festival)

Coptic New Year
Cure Salée
Dewali (Divali, Deepavali, Festival of Lights)
Doan Ngu, or Summer Solstice Day
Enkutatash
Excited Insects, Feast of
Festa del Impruneta
Festival of the Reversing Current or Water Festival

First Day of Summer in Iceland
First Night in Boston
Groppenfasnacht (Fish Carnival)
Hanami
Harvest Moon Days
Higan
Holi
Homowo (Hunger-Hooting Festival)
Ibu Afo Festival
Ides

Folkloric

Festivals deeply rooted in folklore and tradition, as well as those celebrating specific folk tales.

St. Anthony of Padua, Feast of
St. Barbara's Day
St. Bridget's Day
St. Christopher's Day
St. Columba's Day
St. Dominique's Day
St. George's Day in Bulgaria
St. Hans Festival
St. John's Day in Portugal
St. Lazarus's Day
St. Leopold's Day

St. Médardus' Day
St. Marinus Day
St. Sarkis's Day
St. Swithin's Day
St. Sylvester's Day
St. Urho's Day
St. Vincent's Day
Stir-Up Sunday
Swallows of San Juan Capistrano (Fiesta de las Golondrinas)
Tanabata (Star Festival)

Tolling the Devil's Knell
Trinidad and Tobago Carnival
Ute Bear Dance
Valentine's Day
Vinegrower's Day
Walpurgis Night (Walpurgisnacht)
Wedding Festivities in Galicnik, Macedonia
Wianki Festival of Wreaths
Wigilia
William Tell Pageant

Historic

Festivals commemorating specific events from history, such as battles, the birth dates of famous people, national independence, etc.

Airing the Classics
Alamo Day
Alaska Day
Alexandra Rose Day
Andorra National Day
Andrew Jackson's Birthday
Annie Oakley Festival
Annual Patriots' Weekend
Anzac Day
Aoi Matsuri (Hollyhock Festival)
Appomattox Day
Argentine Independence Day
Armed Forces Day
Armenian Martyrs' Day
Ati-Atihan Festival
Australia Day
Aviation Day
Bahia Independence Day
Balfour Declaration Day
Barnum Festival
Bartholomew Fair
Bastille Day (Fête Nationale)
Bataan Day (Araw ng Kagitingan)
Battle of Britain Day
Battle of Germantown, reenactment of
Battle of New Orleans Day
Benjamin Franklin's Birthday
Bennington Battle Day
Bill of Rights Day
Billy Bowlegs Festival
Billy Moore Days
Birthday of Rabindranath Tagore
Black Friday
Black History Month
Black Poetry Day
Black Ships Festival
Boat Race Day
Bok Kai Festival
Bonfire Night
Boston Massacre Day
Boun Phan Vet
Brauteln
Buccaneer Days
Buena Vista Logging Days
Bunker Hill Day
Burns Night
Cabrillo Day
Cactus Jack Festival
Calvin Coolidge Birthday Celebration
Canada Day
Canberra Day

Captain Brady Day
Cavalcata Sarda
Chakri Day
Cherokee Strip Day
Chester Greenwood Day
Chestertown Tea Party Festival
Chief Seattle Days
Chinhae Cherry Blossom Festival
Chongmyo Taeje (Royal Shrine Rite)
Chulalongkorn Day
Cinco de Mayo
Citizenship Day
Clark Gable Birthday Celebration
Columbus Day
Common Ridings Day
Concordia Day
Confederate Memorial Day
Confucius's Birthday (Teacher's Day)
Constitution Day in Norway
Cromwell's Day
Crossing of the Delaware
Czechoslovak Independence Day
Dahlonega Gold Rush Days
Daniel Boone Festival
Day of the Covenant
Days of '76
De Soto Celebration
Defenders' Day
Departure of the Continental Army
Dicing for the Maid's Money Day
Discovery Day
Doggett's Coat and Badge Race
Dominican Republic Independence Day
Double Tenth Day
Dragon Boat Festival (Tuan Yang Chieh)
Dutch Liberation Day
Edison Pageant of Light
Elfreth's Alley Fete Day
Elvis International Tribute Week
Emancipation Day
Emancipation Day in Trinidad and Tobago
Emmett Kelly Clown Festival
Equal Opportunity Day
Escalade (Scaling the Walls)
Evacuation Day
Fast of Gedaliah (Tsom Gedalyah, Tzom Gedaliahu)

Fast of the 17th of Tammuz (Shivah Asar be-Tammuz)
Fast of the First-born
Feast of the Hunters' Moon
Festa del Redentore
Festa do Divino
Festival de la Bastille
Festival of Independence
Festival of the Giants
Fiesta San Antonio
Fiesta de Santa Fe
Fiesta sa EDSA (People Power Anniversary)
Fifteenth of Av (Hamishah Asar be-Av)
Flag Day
Flag Day in Sweden
Float Festival
Floating Lantern Ceremony (Toro Nagashi)
Forefathers' Day
Founder's Day
Four an' Twenty Day
Fourth of July in Denmark
Fox Hill Day
Frankenmuth Bavarian Festival
Game of St. Evermaire
Gandhi Jayanti (Mahatma Gandhi's Birthday)
Gansabhauet
Gasparilla Pirate Festival
General Clinton Canoe Regatta
George Washington Birthday Celebration in Alexandria, Virginia
Georgia Day
Gettysburg Civil War Heritage Days
Gion Matsuri (Gion Festival)
Glorious Twelfth, the
Gold Discovery Days
Golden Spike Anniversary
Great American Brass Band Festival
Great Locomotive Chase Festival
Greek Independence Day(Greece)
Green River Rendezvous
Gustavus Adolphus Day (Gustaf Adolfsdagen)
Gutzon Borglum Day
Guy Fawkes Day
Haile Selassie's Coronation Day
Hakata Dontaku
Halifax Day
Han'gul Day

Harbor Festival
Haxey Hood Game
Helen Keller Festival
Heritage Holidays
Hippokrateia Festival
Hiroshima Peace Ceremony
Holocaust Day (Yom Hashoah)
Holy Thursday
Hosay Festival
Iceland Independence Day
Iditarod Trail Sled Dog Race
Inconfidência Week
Independence Day (Finland)
Independence Day (Fourth of July)
Independence Day (Liberia)
Independence Day (Malta)
Independence Day (Tanzania)
Independence Day (Zimbabwe)
International Banana Festival
International Camel Races
International Children's Book Day
International Open Marathon
Irrigation Festival
Israeli Independence Day
Ivy Day
Jamaica Independence Day
James Whitcomb Riley Festival
Jamhuri (Kenya Independence Day)
Jefferson Davis's Birthday
Jeshn (Afghan Independence Day)
Jidai Matsuri (Festival of the Ages)
Joan of Arc, Feast day of
Johnny Appleseed Festival
Jordbruksdagarna
Juneteenth
Kartini Day
Kent State Memorial Day
Kinderzeche (Children's Party)
King Kamehameha Celebration
Kingdom Days
Klondike Gold Discovery Day
Kristallnacht (Crystal Night)
Landing of d'Iberville
Landshut Wedding
Latter-Day Saints, founding of the
    Church of
Leiden Day
Leif Erikson (Ericson) Day
Leyden Day
Liberation Day
Lincoln's Birthday
Little Big Horn Days
Living Chess Game (La Partita a
    Scácchi Viventi)
Loi Krathong
Looking Glass Powwow
Lord Mayor's Show
Lou Bunch Day
Louisana Shrimp and Petroleum Festi-
    val
Lucy Stone Day
Magellan Day
Magha Puja/Maka Buja (Full Moon
    Day)
Magna Charta (Carta) Day
Maimona, Maimuna
Malcolm X Day
Mallard Ceremony

Mardi Gras
Maroon Festival
Martinsfest
Martyrs of North America, Feast of the
Maryland Day
Mecklenburg Independence Day
Medora Musical
Meistertrunk Pageant (Master Draught
    Pageant)
Merdeka Day
Mollyockett Day
Moon Day
Moors and Christians Fiesta
Moreska Sword Dance
Mormon Pioneer Day
Moshoeshoe (Moshoeshoe's) Day
NEBRASKAland DAYS
Napoleon's Day
National Day (Romania)
National Day (Singapore)
National Hospital Day
National Maritime Day
National Pike Festival
National Quilt Festival
National Tom Sawyer Days
Nebuta Matsuri
Night Watch, the
Oath Monday
October War of Liberation Anniversary
Odwira
Ohio River Sternwheel Festival
Oklahoma Day
Oklahoma Historical Day
Ommegang
Orange Day (Orangemen's Day)
Oxi Day
Palio of the Goose and River Festival
Pan American Day
Pascua Florida Day
Patriots' Day
Payment of Quit Rent
Pearl Harbor Day
Pennsylvania Day
Peppercorn Ceremony
Pig's Face Feast
Pilgrim Thanksgiving Day in Plymouth
Pirates Week
Pjodhatid
Plague Sunday
Plow, Festival of the
Polish Constitution Day
Polish Liberation Day
Polish Solidarity Day
Pony Express Ride
Primrose Day
Procession of the Penitents
Prudence Crandall Day
Pulaski Day
Purims, Special
Queen Juliana's Birthday
Queen's Day
Race Relations Sunday
Ratification Day
Red Waistcoat Festival
Reformation Day
Regatta of the Great Maritime Repub-
    lics

Republic Day (India)
Republic Day in South Africa
Republic Day in Turkey
Repudiation Day
Return Day
Revolution Day
Rhode Island Independence Day
River Kwai Bridge Week
Rizal Day
Robert E. Lee Day
Roger Williams Day
Rose of Tralee Beauty Contest
Roy Rogers Festival
Rushbearing Festival
Saba Saba Day
Samil-jol (Independence Movement
    Day)
San Jacinto Day
Schwenkfelder Thanksgiving
Seward's Day (Seward Day)
Shakespeare's Birthday
Shick-Shack Day
Shilla (Silla) Cultural Festival
Sinjska Alka
St. Charles' Day
St. Crispin's Day
St. Demetrius' Day
St. Olav's Day
St. Patrick's Day Encampment
St. Tammany's Day
St. Thorlak's Day
State Opening of Parliament
Stephen Foster Memorial Day
Sun Yat-sen, birthday of
Susan B. Anthony Day
Swan-Upping
Swiss National Day
Texas Independence Day
Thanksgiving
Thomas Edison's Birthday
Thomas Jefferson's Birthday
Thomas Wolfe Festival
Tichborne Dole
Tom Mix Roundup
Torta dei Fieschi
Toshogu Haru-No-Taisai (Great Spring
    Festival of the Toshogu Shrine)
United Nations Day
V-J Day (Victory over Japan Day)
Valley of the Moon Vintage Festival
Verrazano Day
Veterans Day
Victory Day, or Our Lady of Victories
    Day
Von Steuben Day
Waitangi Day
Washington's Birthday
Washington's Birthday Celebration in
    Los Dos Laredos
West Virginia Day
Will Rogers Day
William Tell Pageant
Wright Brothers Day
Yom Yerushalayim
Yorktown Day

Promotional

Festivals that promote everything from city, state, and national pride to agricultural products; from activities (film, quilting, rodeo) to social values (conservation, harmony among peoples).

Ak-Sar-Ben Livestock Exposition and Rodeo
Alabama Blueberry Festival
Aloha Week Festivals
Alpenfest
American Royal Livestock, Horse Show and Rodeo
Annie Oakley Festival
Antique and Classic Boat Rendezvous
Aviation Day
Baby Parade
Bad Durkheim Wurstmarkt (Sausage Fair)
Barnum Festival
Bat Flight Breakfast
Battle of Flowers, Vienna
Bermuda Rendezvous Time
Big Iron Farm Show and Exhibition
Boggy Bayou Mullet Festival
Bologna Festival
Boy Scouts' Day
Buena Vista Logging Days
Butter and Egg Days
Calico Pitchin', Cookin', and Spittin' Hullabaloo
Camp Fire Founders' Day
Canadian National Exhibition
Cannes Film Festival
Carnaval de Quebec
Castroville Artichoke Festival
Central Maine Egg Festival
Chesapeake Apprecation Days
Chester Greenwood Day
Chilympiad (Republic of Texas Chili Cookoff)
Chitlin' Strut
Christkindlesmarkt (Christmas Market) in Nuremberg
Chrysanthemum Festival
Clark Gable Birthday Celebration
Corn Palace Festival
Cotton Carnival
Cowboy Poetry Gathering
Craftsmen's Fair
Cranberry Harvest Festival
Crop Day (Cotton Row on Parade)
Czech Festival, National
Dairy Festival
Dinosaur Days
Dodge City Days
Dogwood Festival
Dukang Festival
Earth Day
Eastern States Exposition
Eldon Turkey Festival
Father's Day
Festival of American Folklife
Festival of Lights
Fiesta de la Vendimia
Flemington Fair

Floriade, the
Frankenmuth Bavarian Festival
Fur Trade Days
Galway Oyster Festival
Georgia Peanut Festival
Geraldine R. Dodge Poetry Festival
Geranium Day
Gilroy Garlic Festival
Ginseng Festival
Grandparents' Day
Grape Festival
Great American Smokeout
Great Monterey Squid Festival
Half Moon Bay Art and Pumpkin Festival
Harbor Festival
Hatch Chile Festival
Hill Cumorah Pageant
Hope Watermelon Festival
Idaho Spud Day
International Banana Festival
International Children's Book Day
International Country Music Fan Fair
International Literacy Day
Iowa State Fair
Jackalope Days
Keiro-no-ki (Respect-for-the-Aged Day)
Keukenhof Flower Show
Kewpiesta
Kingdom Days
Kutztown Fair
Limassol Wine Festival
Lindenfest
London Bridge Days
Lou Bunch Day
Macon Cherry Blossom Festival
Maine Lobster Festival
Marion County Ham Days
Miss America Pageant
Mother's Day
Mother-in-Law Day
Mountain State Forest Festival
Moxie Festival
Mule Days
Mushroom Festival
NEBRASKAland DAYS
Natchez Spring Pilgrimage
National Cherry Festival
National Dump Week
National Fair of Agriculture at Santarém
National Fieldays
National Hard Crab Derby
National Hospital Day
National Humor and Satire Festival
National Peanut Festival
National Quilt Festival
National Shrimp Festival
National Tom Sawyer Days
National Western Stock Show

Nisei Week
Norsk Høstfest
Northern Games
Ohio River Sternwheel Festival
Okmulgee Pecan Festival
Paris Air and Space Show
Paul Bunyan Show
Pickle Festival
Pirates Week
Portland Rose Festival
Possum Festival
Professional Secretaries' Day
Québec Winter Carnival
Race Relations Sunday
Ragbrai
Reggae Sunsplash
Roy Rogers Festival
Royal Easter Show
Saffron Rose Festival
Saint Paul Winter Carnival
San Juan Bautista Festival
Sarasota Circus Festival and Parade
Sheboygan Bratwurst Days
Shenandoah Apple Blossom Festival
South Carolina Peach Festival
St. Mary's County Maryland Oyster Festival
State Fair of Texas
Stockton Asparagus Festival
Sun Fun Festival
Tater Day
Tellabration
Terlingua Chili Cookoff
Texas Citrus Fiesta
Texas Rose Festival
Tom Mix Roundup
Trois Glorieuses
Tucson Meet Yourself Festival
Tulip Time
Ullr Fest
United Nations Day
United States Air and Trade Show
Vermont Maple Festival
Vidalia Onion Festival
Vinegrower's Day
Washington State Apple Blossom Festival
Watermelon Eating and Seed Spitting Contest
Wayne Chicken Show
West Virginia Strawberry Festival
Whitewater Wednesday
Whole Enchilada Fiesta
Windjammer Days
Wings 'n Water Festival
World Championship Crab Races
World's Largest Salmon Barbecue
Wurstfest (Sausage Festival)
Zibelemarit (Onion Market)

Special Subject Indexes

Sporting

Important sporting events (golf tournaments, horse races) often have festivals grow up around them; this index includes entries that are based on or revolve around sporting events. It does not include the many fairs and festivals in which games and contests form only a part, although these games, etc. can be found in the General Index.

Ak-Sar-Ben Livestock Exposition and Rodeo
Albuquerque International Balloon Fiesta
All-American Soap Box Derby
America's Cup, The
American Birkebeiner
American Royal Livestock, Horse Show and Rodeo
Anchorage Fur Rendezvous
Annie Oakley Festival
Annual Bottle Kicking and Hare Pie Scramble
Argungu Fishing Festival
Australian Open (tennis)
Belgian-American Days
Belmont Stakes
Bering Sea Ice Golf Classic
Bermuda College Weeks
Black Hills Motor Classic
Boat Race Day
Boat Race Day in Okinawa
Bonneville Speed Week
Boomerang Festival
Boston Marathon
Braemar Highland Gathering
Bridge Day
British Open
Buffalo's Big Board Surfing Classic
Calaveras County Fair and Frog Jumping Jubilee
Calgary Exhibition and Stampede
Carnaval de Quebec
Caruaru Roundup
Charleston Sternwheel Regatta
Chesapeake Appreciation Days
Clearwater County Fair and Lumberjack Days
Coca-Cola 600
Cotton Bowl Game
Cow Fights
Dartmouth Winter Carnival
Davis Cup
Daytona 500
Deep Sea Fishing Rodeo
Derby Day
Doggett's Coat and Badge Race
Dragon Boat International Races
Elfstedentocht
Ellensburg Rodeo
Festival of the Horse
Finnish Sliding Festival
French Open (tennis)
General Clinton Canoe Regatta
Glorious Twelfth, the
Grand National
Grandfather Mountain Highland Games and Gathering of Scottish Clans
Grasmere Sports

Great Fifteenth, the
Great Schooner Race
Grey Cup Day
Hambletonian Harness Racing Classic
Haxey Hood Game
Highland games
Hobart Cup Day
Hobart Regatta Day
Holmenkollen Day
Hortobágy Bridge Fair and International Equestrian Festival
Houston Livestock Show & Rodeo
Human Towers of Valls
Hurling the Silver Ball
Idaho Regatta
Iditarod Trail Sled Dog Race
Indianapolis 500
International Open Marathon
Ironman Triathlon Championships
Jousting Tournament
Jousting the Bear
Kentucky Derby
Kiel Week
Klondike International Outhouse Race
Knabenschiessen (Boys' Rifle Match)
La Fiesta de los Vaqueros
Le Mans (motor race)
Little League World Series
Ludi
Lumberjack World Championships
Maryland Hunt Cup
Master's Golf Tournament, the
Melbourne Cup Day
Michigan Brown Trout Festival
Mille Miglia
Monaco Grand Prix (motor race)
Morris Rattlesnake Roundup
Motorcycle Week, or Camel Motorcycle Week, or Bike Week
Mt. Cameroon Race
NEBRASKAland DAYS
Nadam
National Championship Air Races
National Circuit Finals Rodeo (or Dodge National Circuit Finals Rodeo)
National Finals Rodeo
National Frisbee Festival
National Hard Crab Derby
National Hot Air Balloon Championships
National Marbles Tournament
National Western Stock Show
National Whistlers Convention
Navajo Nation Fair at Window Rock
New Jersey Offshore Grand Prix
New York City Marathon
Newport to Bermuda Race
Ohio River Sternwheel Festival
Olympic Games

Omak Stampede and Suicide Race
Orange Bowl Game
Palio of the Goose and River Festival
Palio, Festival of the
Partridge Day
Payson Rodeo
Pendleton Round-Up and Happy Canyon
Plow, Festival of the
Polar Bear Swim Day
Preakness Stakes
Québec Winter Carnival
Ragbrai
Regatta of the Great Maritime Republics
Rose Bowl Game
Royal Ascot
Safari Rally
Saint Paul Winter Carnival
San Fermin Festival
Schäferlauf
Schutzenfest (Marksmen's Festival)
Sinjska Alka
Smithsonian Kite Festival
Southern 500 (or Heinz Southern 500)
Spartakiade
Sugar Bowl Classic
Super Bowl Sunday
Sweetwater Rattlesnake Roundup
Tako-Age (Kite Flying)
Telluride Hang Gliding Festival
Tennessee Walking Horse National Celebration
Tok Race of Champions Dog Sled Race
Tour de France
Transpac Race
Triple Crown Pack Burro Races
United States Grand Prix (motor race)
United States Open (tennis)
United States Open Championship in Golf
University of Pennsylvania Relay Carnival
Vasalopp, the
Virginia Scottish Games
Watermelon Eating and Seed Spitting Contest
Wimbledon
Winston 500
Winterlude
World Championship Crab Races
World Cup
World Eskimo-Indian Olympics
World Wristwrestling Championships
World's Biggest Fish Fry
World's Championship Duck Calling Contest and Wings Over the Prairie Festival
Yale-Harvard Regatta
Ysyakh

General and Key-Word Index

The General and Key-Word Index lists all people, places, institutions, and other items of significance appearing within the text of the entries. Many events are listed under both their official titles and further cross-referenced under more general terms. Entries given in **boldface** type within the index show the main headings and page numbers where those events can be found in the text.

Cromwell's Day   73
Father's Day   105
Klo Dance   171
Kwanzaa   174
Misisi Beer Feast   208
Padi Harvest Festival   243
Ramadan   268
Rosh ha-Shanah   277
Safari Rally   281
Tom Sawyer Days, National   342
Yom Kippur   375

More general terms are given in light type, followed by one or more cross references to the main headings and page numbers.

Cromwell, Oliver   **Cromwell's Day,** 73
Five Pillars   **Ramadan,** 268
Frog Jump Competition   **Tom Sawyer Days, National,** 342
High Holy Days
    Rosh ha-Shanah, 277
    Yom Kippur, 375
peanuts   **Klo Dance,** 171
Uganda
    Misisi Beer Feast, 208
    Safari Rally, 281

General and Key-Word Index

415

General and Key-Word Index

431

435

Immaculate Conception, Feast of the 152

Imnarja **Mnarja (Imnarja; Feast of St. Peter and St. Paul), 209**

Imperial Beach, Calif **Sandcastle Days, 302**

Imperial Castle **Christkindlesmarkt (Christmas Market) in Nuremberg, 61**

Imperial Palace **Jidai Matsuri (Festival of the Ages), 161**

Impérios **Holy Ghost, Feast of the, 142**

Impruneta, Festa del 152

Impruneta, Italy **Impruneta, Festa del, 152**

Imst, Austria
Perchtenlauf, 251
Schemenlauf, 309

In a Mist **Bix Beiderbecke Memorial Jazz Festival, 33**

Inanda, South Africa **Zulu Festival, 379**

Inari, Finland **Reindeer Driving Competition, 271**

Inaugural Address **Inauguration Day, 152**

inaugural ball **Inauguration Day, 152**

Inauguration Day 152

Inauguration Parade **Inauguration Day, 152**

incandescent light **Thomas Edison's Birthday, 338**

Incas
Carnival of Binche, 54
Carnival of Oruro, 54
Día del Puno, 83
Inti Raymi Fiesta, 155

incense **Hungry Ghosts, Festival of, 148**

incense-burning **Dalai Lama, Birthday of the, 78**

Inconfidência Week 153

Incwala 153

Independence Day
Republic Day in India, 272
Tom Sawyer Days, National, 342

Independence Day, Argentina
Argentine Independence Day, 14

Independence Day, Finland 153

Independence Day (Fourth of July) 153

Independence Day, Jamaica 153

Independence Day, Liberia 153

Independence Day, Malta 154

Independence Day, Tanzania 154

Independence Day, Zimbabwe 154

independence for Texas **San Jacinto Day, 305**

independence from England **Rhode Island Independence Day, 273**

Independence, Mexico, Festival of 154

independence movement **Alamo Day, 4**

Independence Movement Day **Samiljol (Independence Movement Day), 302**

Independence Park **Dominican Republic Independence Day, 87**

India
Airing the Classics, 4
Amarnath Yatra, 8
Ashura (Husain Day), 16
Dewali (Divali, Deepavali, Festival of Lights), 83
Dol Purnima, 87
Durga Puja, 90
Farvardegan Days, 103
Gandhi Jayanti (Mahatma Gandhi's Birthday), 114
Ganesh Chathurthi, 114
Ganga Dussehra, 114
Hemis Festival, 136
Holi, 140
Jamshedi Naoroze (Jamshed Navroz), 160
Janmashtami (Krishnastami; Krishna's Birthday), 160
Khordad Sal, 169
Kumbh Mela (Pitcher Fair), 173
Magha Puja (Maka Buja, Full Moon Day), 191
Mahavir Jayanti, 192
Middfest International, 205
Naag Panchami, 217
Nawruz (Naw roz; No Ruz; New Year), 221
Onam, 238
Paro Tshechu, 246
Paryushana, 246
Pitra Visarjana Amavasya, 254
Pongal, 256
Pooram, 257
Poson, 258
Pushkar Mela, 262
Raksha Bandhan (Janai Purnima; Brother and Sister Day), 268
Republic Day in India, 271
St. Thomas's Day, 300
Sanghamita Day, 304
Shab-Barat, 313
Shivaratri, 316
Teej (Tij; Green Teej), 333
Thaipusam (Thai Poosam), 336
Tihar, 340
Vaisakh (Baisak(hi)), 353
Vasant Panchami (Basant Panchami), 354
Vesak (Wesak; Buddha's Birthday), 356
Wangala (Hundred Drums Festival), 361
Waso (Buddhist Rains Retreat), 362
Zarthastno Diso, 379

India, Empress of **Republic Day in India, 272**

India Independence Act **Republic Day in India, 272**

Indiana
Lincoln's Birthday, 182
Pulaski Day, 261
Shaker Festival, 313

Indianapolis 500 154

Indianapolis, Indiana **Indianapolis 500, 155**

Indianapolis Motor Speedway **Indianapolis 500, 154**

Indian art **Indian Market, 155**

Indian, Canadian **Northern Games, 229**

Indian ceremonies **Omak Stampede and Suicide Race, 237**

Indian crafts **San Geronimo Feast Day, 304**

Indian food **Nations, Festival of (Minnesota), 220**

Indian fry-bread **Navajo Nation Fair at Window Rock, 220**

Indian Grinding Rock State Historic Park, California **Miwok Acorn Festival, 208**

Indian Market 155

Indian nationalism **Gandhi Jayanti (Mahatma Gandhi's Birthday), 114**

Indian Ocean **Teej (Tij; Green Teej), 333**

Indianola, Iowa **Hot Air Balloon Championships, National, 146**

Indian pudding **Pilgrim Thanksgiving Day in Plymouth, 254**

Indian pueblo **San Estevan, Feast of, 303**

Indian rodeo associations **Navajo Nation Fair at Window Rock, 220**

Indians
Cosby Ramp Festival, 70
Frankenmuth Bavarian Festival, 110
Green River Rendezvous, 126
Oklahoma Historical Day, 233
Pennsylvania Day, 249
Pony Express Ride, 257

Indian story-telling **Connecticut River Powwow, 69**

Indian summer **Martinmas, 197**

Indian Territory
Oklahoma Day, 233
Will Rogers Day, 368

Indian tribal dances **Mountain Man Rendezvous, 213**

India's biggest yearly religious bathing festival **Kumbh Mela (Pitcher Fair), 173**

Indigenous Peoples Day **Columbus Day, 67**

indjära **Seged, 311**

Indonesia
American Folklife, Festival of, 8
Children's Day, 59
Galungan, 113
'Id (Eid) al-Fitr, 150
Kartini Day, 166
Mawlid al-Nabi (Maulid al-Nabi; Prophet's Birthday), 201
Nyepí, 230
Vesak (Wesak; Buddha's Birthday), 356

Indonesian mask carving **American Folklife, Festival of, 8**

Indra
Indra Jatra, 155
Meenakshi Kalyanam, 202

Indra Jatra 155

industrial exhibits **Royal Show Days, 278**

industrial fair **Eastern States Exposition, 94**

industrial tours **Thomas Edison's Birthday, 338**

Indy-class car races **Portland Rose Festival, 257**

lentils **Magh Sankranti,** 192

Leominster, Massachusetts **Johnny Appleseed Festival,** 162

Leonardtown, Maryland **St. Mary's County Maryland Oyster Festival,** 295

Leonhardiritt (Leonard's Ride) 180

Leonowens, Anna **Chulalongkorn Day,** 65

Leon, Spain **San Isidro the Farmer, Feast of,** 305

le part à Dieu **Epiphany, Feast of the,** 99

Le Petit Caporal **Napoleon's Day,** 218

leprechaun **Christmas Eve,** 63

Le Pretre House **Halloween in New Orleans,** 132

Lerwick, Scotland **Up-Helly-Aa,** 351

Les **Saintes Maries, Fête des (Festival of the Holy Maries),** 288

Lesbos, Greece **St. Modesto's Day,** 295

Lesotho **Moshoeshoe (Moshoeshoe's) Day,** 212

Les Saintes-Maries church, France **Saintes Maries, Fête des (Festival of the Holy Maries),** 288

Les Saintes-Maries-de-la-Mer, France **Madeleine, Fête de la,** 191

Lesser Sabbats **Yule,** 377

Lessing, Doris **Hay-on-Wye Festival of Literature,** 136

Let's remember Pearl Harbor, and go on to victory **Pearl Harbor Day,** 248

Let's remember Pearl Harbor, as we did the Alamo **Pearl Harbor Day,** 248

Let's remember Pearl Harbor, as we go to meet the foe **Pearl Harbor Day,** 248

lettuce **Maimona (Maimuna),** 193

lettuce leaf **Maimona (Maimuna),** 193

Leutze, Emanual **Crossing of the Delaware,** 74

lewd jokes **St. Dominique's Day,** 287

Lewis and Clark **Whe'wahchee (Dance of Thanksgiving),** 366

Lewisburg, Tenn. **Tennessee Walking Horse National Celebration,** 334

Lewis, Carl **University of Pennsylvania Relay Carnival,** 351

Lexington and Concord, battle of **Patriots' Day,** 247

Lexington, Massachusetts **Patriots' Day,** 247

Leyden Day 180

Leyden, Netherlands **Leyden Day,** 180

Lhabuleng Monastery, China **Lantern Festival (Yuan Hsiao Chieh),** 177

Lhasa, Tibet
  Butter Sculpture Festival, 46
  Dalai Lama, Birthday of the, 78
  Lantern Festival (Yuan Hsiao Chieh), 177
  Monlam (Prayer Festival), 210

liars' contests **Vandalia Gathering,** 354

libation gourd **Misisi Beer Feast,** 208

Liberal, Kansas **Pancake Day,** 244

Liberation Day 181

Liberia **Independence Day, Liberia,** 153

Liberty Bell **Fourth of July in Denmark,** 110

Libya
  Cure Salée, 74
  Maimona (Maimuna), 192
  Mawlid al-Nabi (Maulid al-Nabi; Prophet's Birthday), 201

Licinius, Emperor **Forty Martyrs' Day,** 109

Lido, the **Redentore, Festa del,** 270

Liechtenstein, Johann Adam von **Prince's Birthday,** 260

lifesaving **Seaman's Day,** 310

lifting **Easter Monday,** 94

lighted boat parade **Summer Festival,** 325

lighthouse tours **Whale Festival,** 365

Lighting of the National Christmas Tree 181

lightning **Sango Festival,** 304

lightning, god of **Nyambinyambi,** 230

Lights, Festival of (Ganden Ngamcho) 181

Lights, God of **Tazaungdaing,** 333

lignum vitae sticks **Jonkonnu Festival (John Canoe),** 162

L'il Abner **Sadie Hawkins Day,** 281

lilies-of-the-valley **Premier Mai,** 259

Lille, France **Giants, Festival of the (Fête des Géants),** 119

Lillehammer, Norway **American Birkebeiner,** 8

Lily Festival (Festa del Giglio) 181

lima beans **Strawberry Festival,** 324

Lima, Peru
  Argentine Independence Day, 13
  St. Rose of Lima's Day, 298

Limassol, Cyprus **Kataklysmos, Feast of (Festival of the Flood),** 167

Limassol Wine Festival 181

limbo dancers
  Carnaval Miami, 52
  Virgin Islands Carnival, 358

lime **Peppercorn Ceremony,** 250

Limulunga, Zambia **Ku-omboko,** 173

Lincoln, Abraham
  Black History Month, 34
  Camel Races, International, 49
  Chulalongkorn Day, 65
  Emancipation Day, 98
  Equal Opportunity Day, 100
  Fourth of July in Denmark, 110
  Gutzon Borglum Day, 128
  Juneteenth, 164
  Lincoln's Birthday, 182
  Marbles Tournament, National, 194
  Thanksgiving, 337
  Washington's Birthday, 362
  West Virginia Day, 365

Lincoln Fellowship of Pennsylvania **Equal Opportunity Day,** 100

Lincoln Memorial
  Lincoln's Birthday, 182
  Loi Krathong, 184
  Wianki Festival of Wreaths, 367

Lincoln's Birthday 182

Lindbergh, Charles
  Iowa State Fair, 156
  Paris Air and Space Show, 245

Lindenfest 182

linden tree **Lindenfest,** 182

Lind, Jenny **Barnum Festival,** 25

Lindsborg, Kansas
  St. Lucy's Day, 294
  Swedish Homage Festival, 327

lingam
  Amarnath Yatra, 8
  Bisket Jatra, 33
  Indra Jatra, 155

Lin Moniang **Matsu, Birthday of,** 200

Linville, N.C. **Grandfather Mountain Highland Games and Gathering of Scottish Clans,** 122

Linwood, Michigan **Pickle Festival,** 251

Linz, Austria **Battle of Flowers, Vienna,** 27

Lion **Nadam,** 217

lion **Ommegang,** 238

lion dance
  Cheung Chau Bun Festival, 58
  Ginseng Festival, 119
  Lunar New Year, 188
  Tam Kung Festival, 332

Lionora **Living Chess Game (La Partita a Scácchi Viventi),** 183

Lions Club **Bering Sea Ice Golf Classic,** 30

Lipizzaner horses **Hortobágy Bridge Fair and International Equestrian Festival,** 145

liquor **Dukang Festival,** 89

Lisbon, Maine **Moxie Festival,** 214

Lisbon, Portugal
  Red Waistcoat Festival, 270
  St. Anthony of Padua, Feast of, 283
  St. Vincent's Day, 301

Lisse, Holland **Keukenhof Flower Show,** 169

Litchfield Park, Ariz. **Billy Moore Days,** 32

Literacy Day, International 182

litham **Camel Market,** 48

Lithuania
  Baltic Song Festivals, 23
  Obzinky, 232

little angels **Angelitos, Los,** 10

Little Big Horn, Battle of **Little Big Horn Days,** 182

Little Big Horn Days 182

Little Boy **Hiroshima Peace Ceremony,** 139

little breads of the saint **St. Blaise's Day,** 284

Little Claus and Big Claus **Hans Christian Andersen Festival,** 133

Little Italy, New York City
  St. Anthony of Padua, Feast of, 283
  San Gennaro, Feast of, 303

Little League Museum **Little League World Series,** 183

Little League World Series 182

Little, Malcom **Malcolm X Day,** 193

Little Match Girl, The **Children's Book Day, International,** 59

General and Key-Word Index

517

General and Key-Word Index